AI Game
Programming
Wisdom 2

AI Game Programming Wisdom 2

Edited by Steve Rabin

CHARLES RIVER MEDIA, INC.

Hingham, Massachusetts

Publisher: Jenifer Niles
Production: Publishers' Design and Production Services, Inc.
Cover Design: The Printed Image
Cover Images: Monolith Productions, Inc., Vivendi Universal, Activision Publishing, Inc.

CHARLES RIVER MEDIA, INC.
10 Downer Avenue
Hingham, Massachusetts 02043
781-740-0400
781-740-8816 (FAX)
info@charlesriver.com
www.charlesriver.com

This book is printed on acid-free paper.

Steve Rabin. *AI Game Programming Wisdom 2.*
ISBN: 1-58450-289-4

All brand names and product names mentioned in this book are trademarks or service marks of their respective companies. Any omission or misuse (of any kind) of service marks or trademarks should not be regarded as intent to infringe on the property of others. The publisher recognizes and respects all marks used by companies, manufacturers, and developers as a means to distinguish their products.

Library of Congress Cataloging-in-Publication Data
AI game programming wisdom 2 / edited by Steve Rabin.
      p.   cm.
   ISBN 1-58450-289-4 (Hardcover with CD : alk. paper)
   1. Computer games—Design. 2. Computer games—Programming.
3. Computer graphics. I. Rabin, Steve.
   QA76.76.C672 A426 2003
   794.8'1536—dc22
                    2003019939
Printed in the United States of America
03 7 6 5 4 3 2 First Edition

Contents

Preface

Steve Rabin

Welcome to the second, all-new volume of *AI Game Programming Wisdom*! Within this book, you'll find nearly 70 articles that will inundate you with tricks, techniques, algorithms, architectures, and philosophies on game artificial intelligence (AI). The wealth of knowledge and expertise in this book is overwhelming, and is completely at your disposal. This book is designed primarily to provide practical advice on building state-of-the-art game AI for shipping commercial games; however, it also strives to be forward-looking with insight toward leading-edge techniques. Use it as both a weapon for your pressing needs and as a mentor for future explorations.

As the second volume in the *AI Game Programming Wisdom* series, this book has much to live up to. The first volume was widely acclaimed and has become required reading for AI courses at game universities, such as the DigiPen Institute of Technology and the Full Sail School of Game Design & Development. While this new volume stands on its own (and in many ways exceeds the first volume), together these books create a formidable collection that no respectable game AI programmer can be without. These are the advances, discoveries, and triumphs that will influence and drive game AI for the next decade. All of the authors sincerely hope that you will learn from their work and use it in your own creations. They also hope that you'll return the favor someday and teach them a trick or two.

Diversity and Breadth

What is remarkable about this book is the diversity of its over 50 contributing authors. They represent not only an industry-wide cross-section of experience, but also a worldwide influence, spanning the globe from Australia, Canada, England, Finland, France, the Netherlands, Switzerland, and the United States. They also have very different industry backgrounds. Many authors come from large, key publishers such as Sony, Nintendo, Microsoft, Electronic Arts, Activision, Acclaim, Eidos, and LucasArts, while others come from smaller, yet influential, developers like Lionhead Studios, Monolith Productions, Ion Storm Austin, Firaxis Games, Gas Powered Games, Surreal Software, Stainless Steel Studios, and Red Storm Entertainment. Also contributing are authors from AI middleware companies like MASA Group and Stottler Henke Associates. There are even contributions from the AI experts who run the top game AI Web sites, such as GameAI.com, AI-Depot.com, AI-Junkie.com, and Generation5.org. Lastly, authors from game universities such as DigiPen and Full Sail contributed, as well as authors from universities around the world, such as the University of Zürich (Switzerland), University of Turku (Finland), and the University of Queensland (Australia).

The authors of this book are truly leaders in their field. They have worked on such groundbreaking current and future titles as *Civilization III, Black & White II, Thief 3, Deus Ex 2, Quake IV, Everquest II, Age of Mythology, Age of Empires II, Empire Earth, No One Lives Forever 2, Unreal 2, Munch's Oddysee, Master of Orion 3, Mech-Warrior 4, Soldier of Fortune 2, Dungeon Siege, Need for Speed: Underground, Conflict: Desert Storm, Independence War 2, Amped 1 & 2, Worms 2, Worms Armageddon, The Thing, NBA Inside Drive, All-Star Baseball, Drakan: Order of the Flame,* and *Lord of the Rings: The Fellowship of the Ring.* While this is nowhere near an exhaustive list, it surely demonstrates that the authors of this book have a wide range of expertise and are the ones paving the way for the next generation of game AI.

The Need to Know

Many people have asked why I work so hard to put the *AI Game Programming Wisdom* series together. In many respects, it is a purely selfish endeavor. When I first started attending the Game Developers Conference and started writing for the *Game Programming Gems* series, I was amazed at the goodwill and sharing that both ordinary developers and legendary developers freely offered to others. However, the couple of articles and talks offered every year on game AI were not enough to quench my thirst. I knew that if I personally drove a new series on game AI, I would be able to read about cutting-edge techniques from games I loved and developers I admired. I wanted to find out what everybody was doing and learn the most I could, and this series was my own small way of accomplishing that. When I look at the table of contents, I get giddy at having access to so much wisdom that once was impossible to obtain. Between the *AI Game Programming Wisdom* series, the *Game Programming Gems* series, and the *Game Developers Conference*, over 150 articles on game AI techniques were written in just the last two years (with nearly 90 percent of them appearing in this particular series). I can finally say that I'm a well-fed man and that I have plenty of inside tricks and information to keep me busy (at least for another year).

Learning: Still the Next Big Thing

In the first volume of *AI Game Programming Wisdom*, I made the prediction that learning within the field of game AI would be the next big thing. I still believe this, but I am a little more conservative in how I think the gaming public will witness it. Learning is a refinement that generally shouldn't be waved in the player's face. When used correctly, it will help make games more robust and resilient to player exploits. It will adapt to the players, giving them a more enjoyable experience. These are all subtle advances and it might never be impressive to brag about such achievements on the back of a game box. Yet, as time marches on, AIs that learn and adapt will become commonplace and required for most game genres. While it might never be fully appreciated by players, the players will clearly benefit.

Game AI: The Last Frontier

AI is truly the last frontier of game development. Progress in graphics and sound has slowed in recent years to the point where the mass-market player has either become oblivious or indifferent to the incremental improvements. For this audience, the 3D environments have become complex enough that subtle bump mapping or better lighting is not noticeable at a conscious level. Now, more than ever, good gameplay is at the forefront and AI is one of the most critical components. With the advent of mass-market online gaming, pressure is even greater for AI to be just as good as online human opponents. With the challenge set before us, there is great reason to be excited about the future of game AI.

Bonus Material on the CD-ROM

As you might know, many of the articles in this book feature demos and source code on the accompanying CD-ROM. In addition to this great resource, be sure to check out the *bonus* articles, demos, and source code also on the CD-ROM. Since many of the articles in this book reference other works, we have decided to include some of them on the CD-ROM to make sure that you have access to them. As material on the Internet comes and goes, the material on the CD-ROM is permanently yours to reference. We've included such resources as the Free Fuzzy Logic Library, the AI Roundtable Moderator reports from the 2003 Game Developers Conference, additional introductory articles on neural networks and genetic algorithms, an in-depth tutorial on A* used at the Full Sail School of Game Design & Development, and seminal papers such as "Steering Behaviors for Autonomous Characters" by Craig Reynolds. The "About the CD-ROM" appendix at the end of this book details the full list of bonus material.

www.AIWisdom.com

As announced in the first volume, the home page for this book is *www.AIWisdom.com*. This Web site also serves a key purpose in that it tracks and catalogues game AI articles from a variety of sources, including the annual *Game Developers Conference*, *Game Developer* magazine, the *Game Programming Gems* series, the *AI Game Programming Wisdom* series, and the Internet. As of the year 2003, there are more than 250 game AI articles listed. Articles can be searched by topic (such as A* pathfinding or influence mapping), by genre (such as real-time strategy or first-person shooter), or by publication date. Remember to use this Web site as one of your tools in tracking down relevant information on game AI topics. In addition, please check *www.AIWisdom.com* for corrections to this book and announcements for opportunities to write for future volumes.

Acknowledgments

As I look over the articles in this book, I am overwhelmed by the breadth and depth of experience that sits before me. I want to personally thank all of the authors for their kindness and generosity in sharing their knowledge, wisdom, and source code. These are the people who make the game industry hum, and their willingness to share their personal experience is greatly appreciated.

I would like to thank Jenifer Niles and Dave Pallai at Charles River Media for being so supportive of this series. Their hard work and professionalism make it all turn out so perfect.

This series is indebted to the vision and perseverance of Mark DeLoura who pioneered the *Game Programming Gems* series, which has spun off many other successful books. Little did he know he had created so many monsters.

All of the authors helped review articles to ensure quality, but some of them went beyond the call of duty. In particular, I would like to thank Greg Alt, Dan Fu, Ryan Houlette, John Manslow, Jeff Orkin, and Alex Sramek. I would also like to thank the following people for helping review articles: Stéphane Assadourian, Jim Boer, Mark Brockington, Shekhar Dhupelia, Mike Ducker, Dan Higgins, Ismo Horppu, Syrus Mesdaghi, and Marco Tombesi.

Above all, I would like to thank my family—my wife Leslie for her tireless support, and my two beautiful children, Aaron and Allison. They, more than anything, fill my life with joy. I'd also like to thank my parents, Barry and Diane, who have always motivated me to do my best in life.

—Steve Rabin

About the Cover Images

The four images on the cover represent several game AI achievements by the authors of this book. While the images are not meant to imply that the games exist on the CD-ROM that accompanies this book, they stand as a tribute to the hard work of the respective authors.

Top Images: *No One Lives Forever 2*

Monolith Production's *No One Lives Forever 2* introduced game characters with unprecedented realism in both combat and noncombat situations. In his articles "Simple Techniques for Coordinated Behavior" and "Constraining Autonomous Character Behavior with Human Concepts," Jeff Orkin from Monolith Productions describes techniques used to achieve group coordination, and interaction with the environment, all without scripting. The top-left cover image depicts Indian H.A.R.M. Guards coordinating an attack on the player. The top-right image shows the boss ninja Isako engaging the player in katana combat in the confines of an Ohio trailer swept up in a tornado.

Bottom-Left Image: *The Thing*

Based on John Carpenter's classic movie of the same name, *The Thing* (Computer Artworks/Black Label Games) introduced advanced AI to the survival horror genre. This screenshot shows the game's hero, Blake, in combat with a humanoid form of the movie's shape-shifting alien organism. The organism is vulnerable to damage from fire, and so, in the game, needed to intelligently avoid it while attacking. In his article "Avoiding Dynamic Obstacles and Hazards," Geraint Johnson explains how this was achieved.

Bottom-Right Image: *Soldier of Fortune 2*

While a terrorist attempts to get to cover by vaulting over an airport bench, his compatriot provides some suppressing cover fire. This heated battle scene is taken from the recent tactical shooter *Soldier of Fortune 2* (Raven Software/Activision), where an enhanced navigation system embeds behaviors directly in the nodes and edges, making scenes like this possible anywhere in the game without explicit scripting or state programming. For a detailed account on how the terrorist was able to vault in the middle of a firefight, see Christopher Reed and Benjamin Geisler's article "Jumping, Climbing, and Tactical Reasoning: How to Get More Out of a Navigation System."

Author Bios

Greg Alt—Surreal Software

galt@eskimo.com

Greg Alt (*www.eskimo.com/~galt*) got started with games in the fifth grade by writing *Mars Mission* for the TRS-80 Model I, which led eventually to earning an M.S. in computer science from the University of Utah. More recently, he has been in the games industry for the past seven years, developing for the PC and PlayStation 2. He has worked on four published game titles, *Drakan: Order of the Flame, Drakan: The Ancients' Gates*, and *Fellowship of the Ring* by Surreal Software; and *StixWorld* by PsychoHazard Software. He is currently working for Surreal Software as an AI programmer, where he designed and implemented the AI system for *The Fellowship of the Ring* and two upcoming titles.

Mat Buckland—www.ai-junkie.com

fup@ai-junkie.com

Mat Buckland is a freelance programmer and writer. He has been coding since the day his school bought a Research Machine 380Z way back in the late 1970s. He became interested in AI a few years later when he coded Waddington's *Monopoly* for the ZX Spectrum, and over the years his passion for making computers think has never faded. He is the author of the book *AI Techniques for Game Programming* and the founder of *ai-junkie.com*, a popular Web site that specializes in AI tutorials. He has received much acclaim for his ability to present difficult AI theory in a fun and down-to-earth manner. Mat lives in Sheffield, England.

Phil Carlisle—Team17 Software Ltd.

pc@team17.com

Phil has been game programming for more than 20 years after getting access to a friend's Atari home computer. He spent many years in pursuit of a career as an architect, but later decided to switch from architecture to game programming. After completing a BSc Hons degree in network and distributed systems at Leeds Metropolitan University, he began working for Team 17 Software, where has spent the last seven years working on various games, including *Worms 2* and *Worms Armageddon*. He has been involved with all types of game programming from graphics to networking, and everything between, but is now focusing on gameplay and character interaction.

Upon completion of *Worms 3D*, Phil moved to The Bolton Institute (a local university) where he teaches various aspects of game development as a senior lecturer. He also runs his own small development studio.

Alex J. Champandard—AI Depot

alex@ai-depot.com

Alex J. Champandard is the author of the book *AI Game Development*, focusing on learning and reactive behaviors to create intelligent NPCs. As the lead engineer of FEAR (an open-source game AI project), he consults with professional programmers to integrate state-of-the-art prototypes into commercial games. Founder of *AI-Depot.com*, a popular community AI site, he brings tutorials to an audience of AI enthusiasts. He has a strong academic background in AI with degrees from York and Edinburgh, often speaking about his AI research—notably at GDC 2003. Alex is also part of the AI Interface Standards Committee, intending to define a common specification for game AI techniques.

Dr. Emmanuel Chiva—MASA Group

emmanuel.chiva@masagroup.net

Emmanuel Chiva has a post-graduate degree from the Ecole Normale Superieure, in Paris, and an English degree from Harvard University. A biologist, he received his Ph.D. in biocomputing in the field of dynamic complex systems modeling, focusing on complex proteins network dynamics.

He joined MASA Group at its inception, helped develop the Biomethodes subsidiary, and became director of industrial services. He is now vice president, in charge of technology and corporate business development.

Alex Darby—FreeStyleGames Ltd.

alex.darby@freestylegames.com

Alex graduated from the University of Nottingham in 1996 with a joint honors degree in computer science, artificial intelligence, and psychology. Following graduation, he took a design/R&D programmer job at Codemasters in their then embryonic design department. During the following four and a half years, Alex became one of the most senior members of the Codemasters design team, and worked on the majority of their games, including the *Micromachines*, *ToCA Touring Cars*, and *Colin McRae Rally* series.

Over this time, Codemasters grew from a development staff of 25 to over 250, and fed up of spending more time in meetings than doing work, Alex took a job with the small developer Smartdog working on the AI for the PS2 racing title *Downforce*. Once *Downforce* was finished, Alex took on the additional responsibility of managing a small design team for Smartdog's next title. Unfortunately, Smartdog's parent company Titus closed Smartdog down.

Luckily, at this point FreeStyleGames was born; and Alex took a job with them. Comprised of both ex-Codemasters and ex-Rare staff, FreeStyleGames is working on a multiplatform trans-genre racing title, due for release Q3 2003.

Julien Devade—MASA Group

julien.devade@masagroup.net

Julien graduated from both the Ecole Polytechnique and the ENSTA (Advanced Techniques National School) where he acquired an expertise in computer science and artificial intelligence.

He joined MASA Group's video game unit in 1999 where he was in charge of the AI development and participated in projects such as *Conflict Zone*. After having managed the development of the *DirectIA SDK 2.0*, Julien is now the operation manager in the MASA simulation department.

Mike Dickheiser—Red Storm Entertainment

mike.dickheiser@redstorm.com

Mike is a seven-year veteran of the computer game industry currently working at Red Storm Entertainment. His primary areas of professional interest are constructing efficient AI systems for games, and coding the fun and sophisticated behaviors afforded by them. Mike's current work centers on AI control of highly realistic vehicles, as well as first-person and vehicular combat tactics. He has a degree in computer science from North Carolina State University.

Kevin Dill—Quicksilver Software, Inc.

lanorolen@yahoo.com

After completing his B.A. in computer science at Carleton College, Kevin went into the Army for four years, where he worked his way up to the rank of sergeant. He served with an infantry platoon in the 101st Airborne, and then in battalion and division headquarters in the 25th Infantry Division. Upon receiving his honorable discharge, he decided to apply his training to something truly important: computer games. To prepare himself for this challenge, he decided to pursue a graduate degree in computer science. He first attended the University of Pittsburgh, where he studied simulations, real-time systems, and parallel programming. Next, he transferred to Northwestern University, where he studied AI. After completing his M.S. at Northwestern, he took a job with Quicksilver Software, Inc., to work on the military AI for *Master of Orion 3*. He is currently employed with TimeGate Studios, Inc., working on the AI for an as-yet-unannounced title.

Dr. Jean-Yves Donnart—MASA Group

jean-yves.donnart@masagroup.net

Jean-Yves has a Ph.D. in biocomputing from University of Paris 6. He worked as a research engineer at InfoDyne and then was a researcher at the Ecole Normale Superieure biocomputing laboratory. He's an expert in machine learning, adaptive planning, and behavior modeling. After joining MASA Group at its inception, Jean-Yves contributed to the creation of the *DirectIA* kernel. He is now in charge of research and business development in the MASA simulation department.

Penny Drennan—School of ITEE, University of Queensland

pennyd@itee.uq.edu.au

Penny Drennan received a bachelor of engineering degree in software with honors from the University of Queensland in 2001. She is currently undertaking Ph.D. studies in the School of Information Technology and Electrical Engineering at the University of Queensland. The focus of her Ph.D. is getting nonplayer characters able to interact with human players in a more flexible way than we have seen in most computer games. This means that she spends far too much time playing computer games "for research purposes."

Eric Dybsand—Glacier Edge Technology

edybs@ix.netcom.com

Eric Dybsand's last project was the design/development of the AI for a tactical combat simulator now used by the U.S. Army during training. He has consulted on an extensive list of computer games, including designing the strategic AI for the *Master of Orion* sequel *MOO3*; and for the AI for racing, baseball, and wrestling games; and he developed the AI opponents for the RTS game *Enemy Nations*, for the FPS games *Rebel Moon Revolution* and the *War in Heaven*, and a number of turn-based wargames. Eric has been involved with computer game AI since 1987, doing game design, programming, and testing, and is a contributing author on AI to the *Game Programming Gems* and now the *AI Game Programming Wisdom* series.

Euan Forrester—Electronic Arts Black Box

euan@ea.com, euan_forrester@pobox.com

Euan Forrester has worked at EA Black Box since 2001. During that time, he has worked on the racecar and traffic AI for *Need for Speed: Underground*, and the PlayStation 2 version of *Need for Speed: Hot Pursuit 2*. He also worked briefly on *Nascar Thunder 2002* for the PlayStation. Prior to that, he graduated with a degree in computer science from the University of Calgary.

James Freeman-Hargis

paradox@this-statement-is-false.net

James thinks it is odd to be writing of himself in the third person. He graduated from the University of Chicago in June 2002 with a degree in computer science. At the time of this writing, he makes his living as a Web programmer. He has a passion for games, both playing and creating, and aspires to design or program for a company in the industry. He assists in the building of Lensmoor, an online MUD, although he has neglected it as of late to focus on his article included here. Much of his idle time is spent contemplating puzzles, paradoxes, and strange conceptions of the universe as a whole. Video games and cartoons fill his vision, and heavy metal fills his ears. His days are fueled by Hot Pockets and Mac&Cheese along with the occasional home-cooked meal. He dabbles in Zen, martial arts, and card tricks. He also needs a ride home. You can have a peek at his hodgepodge of insanity and accomplishments at *www.this-statement-is-false.net.*

Dan Fu—Stottler Henke Associates, Inc.

fu@stottlerhenke.com

Dan Fu has been programming for over 20 years, starting on a TRS-80 in high school. He went on to study for a B.S. in computer science at Cornell where he implemented his first machine learning algorithm. Later, Dan received a Ph.D. in computer science from the University of Chicago where he focused on AI planning, machine vision, and robotics. Since then, Dan has worked at Stottler Henke, an AI consulting company in the Bay Area of California. He manages development of an AI middleware tool called *SimBionic.*

Benjamin Geisler—Raven Software/Activision

bgeisler@ravensoft.com

Benjamin Geisler is a graduate of the University of Wisconsin—Madison Computer Science Department, where he received a master of science degree with an emphasis in AI. His thesis paper, *An Empirical Study of Machine Learning Algorithms Applied to Modeling Player Behavior in a "First Person Shooter" Video Game,* was published by the University of Wisconsin Press, and he was a contributing author for the paper *Modeling Agent Preferences via Theory Refinement* for the Intelligent User Interfaces Conference 2001. He is currently working for Raven Software, where he is credited in *Soldier of Fortune II: Double Helix, X-Men: Legends,* and *Quake IV.* He is a member of the American Association for Artificial Intelligence, and the International Game Developer's Association: AI Standards Committee.

Mario Grimani—Sony Online Entertainment

mgrimani@soe.sony.com,
mariogrimani@yahoo.com

Mario Grimani is an industry veteran who joined the gaming industry almost two decades ago. After publishing his first game in 1987, he poured all of his development effort into the Amiga platform. The early demise of the Amiga platform marked his departure from the gaming industry, expecting never to come back. Since re-emerging in the mid 1990s, he has joined big name studios such as Ion Storm, Ensemble Studios, Verant Interactive, and Sony Online Entertainment. While at Ensemble Studios, he was a dedicated AI specialist in charge of improving the computer player competitiveness. He has developed a scripting system and a computer player AI for the *Age of Empires II: The Age of Kings* and *Age of Empires II: The Conquerors*. During the early stages of *Age of Mythology* development, Mario served as AI lead in charge of AI architecture. After joining Verant Interactive, in an attempt to help create a new MMO RTS genre, he took over as lead programmer on *Sovereign*. Currently, he is working for Sony Online Entertainment and implementing various game systems for *Everquest II*. Mario has a bachelor's degree in electrical engineering from the University of Zagreb, Croatia, and a master's degree in computer science from Southwest Texas State University.

Sebastian Grinke—Pivotal Games

seb.grinke@pivotalgames.com,
sebgrinke@hotmail.com

Sebastian has been working as a video game programmer, designer, and freelance reviewer for over eight years. Titles he has worked on include *Conflict Desert Storm*, *Warzone 2100*, *Star Trek: New Worlds*, *Zeewolf*, and *Zeewolf 2*. He is currently writing AI, scripts, and game code for *Conflict Desert Storm 2*.

Harri Hakonen—Department of Information Technology, University of Turku, Finland

harri.hakonen@it.utu.fi

Harri Hakonen's innate nerd was awakened by a C compiler on the C64. Since then, he has been interested in various aspects of problem solving with computers, ranging from bit fiddling to software construction processes. He does not believe in time but has still spent lots of it on string algorithmics, object orientation, and high-response concurrent systems. In real life, he baldly goes with the often-tried law of nature: The sum of the probabilities is far less than the sum of the improbabilities.

Chris Hargrove—Gas Powered Games

chargrove@gaspowered.com

Chris is currently working as a senior engineer at Gas Powered Games. Prior to joining Gas Powered Games, Chris was at Legend Entertainment, where his work experience included engine technology for *Unreal II*, including the design and implementation of its character animation and rendering system, various scripting language improvements, and related content authoring tools. Before coming to Legend to work on *Unreal II*, Chris shipped two other titles at Raven Software and worked on a third at 3D Realms Entertainment. In his seven years of industry experience, he has written a number of programming articles for various Web sites, in addition to the articles appearing in this book.

Alexander Herz—Lionhead Studios Ltd.

aherz@lionhead.com

Alex was introduced to programming by his father using QBasic at the age of 10. Soon hitting the limits of this language, Alex moved on to Pascal 7.0 to create more impressive games on his Intel 386. After getting his hands on a Voodoo 1 3D accelerator, Alex moved on to C/C++ to explore the world of 3D using Glide under Win32. Having created his first large-scale 3D engine, Alex started to explore the world of scripting to create a complete game. Within the next two years, Alex created a fully featured C/C++ and VertexShader compatible compiler, along with a Virtual Machine and an IDE to debug scripts and execute them fast enough to incorporate them into real-time rendering (similar to Cg/Render Monkey tools, which were unavailable at this time). Sadly, the Glide API disappeared along with 3DFX, so Alex started his odyssey through Direct3D and OpenGL, while working part-time for Carl Zeiss Vision GMBH to aid in the development of microscopy and digi-cam software and SDKs. Finally, having finished gymnasium (German high school) at age 19, Alex attempted to start his position as a 3D programmer at Vulpine GMBH developing cutting-edge 3D middleware, but he was drafted by the German army right from school. During his nine months of army service, he worked part-time for MaxX GMBH to develop a DBase database interface application that manages bicycle component and construction databases. Shortly after Alex finished his duty, he joined Lionhead Studios Ltd. to work on the core 3D technology for *Black & White II*, where he still enjoys making improvements to the original *Black & White*.

Ryan Houlette—Stottler Henke Associates, Inc.

houlette@stottlerhenke.com

Ryan Houlette is a lead software engineer at Stottler Henke, an artificial intelligence software consulting firm, where he has worked for the past five years on a variety of government and commercial AI applications. He is the architect of the runtime engine for Stottler Henke's *SimBionic* game AI middleware product. His primary research interests are in game/simulation AI engines, visual AI authoring environments, and interactive narrative systems. Ryan holds a master's degree in AI from Stanford University, and when he's not thinking about AI he's usually performing as a singer/songwriter or playing a CRPG with his wife.

Geraint Johnson—Computer Artworks Ltd.

geraintjohnson@hotmail.com

Geraint Johnson first started writing games and AI about 20 years ago, when his parents bought him a BBC Micro. In 1994, he graduated from the University of Edinburgh with a joint honors degree in artificial intelligence and computer science, his dissertation being on a logic-based approach to resolving ambiguity in natural language. He later received a Ph.D. in neural networks from Oxford Brookes University. After a brief stint working on the genetic programming for a Darwinian sound-to-light package at Notting Hill Publishing, Geraint decided to enter the games industry and joined Computer Artworks. He worked on the AI for their first two games, the third-person shooter *Evolva* and the squad-based horror license *The Thing*. He is currently lead game programmer on one of their forthcoming titles. Outside of games, Geraint is a fan of British cult TV, Russian literature, and American cinema.

Soren Johnson—Firaxis Games

sjohnson@firaxis.com

Soren Johnson has a B.A. in history and an M.S. in computer science from Stanford University. After working as an intern at Electronic Arts (Redwood Shores), he moved to Baltimore in 2000 to join Firaxis Games. While working as co-designer and lead programmer on *Civilization III*, he authored the game's AI. Soren is currently the lead designer on one of Firaxis' unannounced projects.

Timo Kaukoranta—Department of Information Technology, University of Turku, Finland

Timo Kaukoranta passed away shortly before Christmas 2002. He received his MSc and Ph.D. degrees in computer science from the University of Turku, Finland, in 1994 and 2000, respectively. He was a researcher with the University of Turku from 1994 to 2000, and a post-doctoral researcher with Turku Centre for Computer Science (TUCS) since 2001. His primary research interests were in distributed interactive simulations, multiplayer computer games, and vector quantization.

Tom Kent—Atomic Games, Inc.

tick@houston.rr.com

Tom received his bachelor's degrees in computer science and physics, and a master's degree in physics from Penn State University. After a brief foray into the Dilbert-esque world of programming for a cellular telecommunications firm, he returned to his first love: computer gaming. In his seven-year career in game development, he worked on four of the five *Close Combat* titles by Atomic Games, mostly developing strategic and computer player AI systems. Additionally, he developed the computer player AI system for TimeGate Studios' *Kohan: Immortal Sovereigns* and much of the AI for Freedom Games' *GI Combat* and *Eric Young's Squad Assault* titles. Tom has recently been lured back to Atomic Games to lead the development of a new project.

Sandeep Kharkar—Microsoft Corporation

eltoro_the_deep@hotmail.com

Sandeep Kharkar has a bachelor's degree in computer engineering from India and a master's degree in computer science from Utah State University. Throughout his education he scoffed at AI, calling it "fool's gold," and stuck with parallel processing as his line of interest. However, he has realized the folly of his ways and is a hardcore AI follower now. He has published papers in various fields, including parallel processing, software engineering, and game architecture. He has been programming professionally for seven years and has programmed mostly games, but also compilers, video phones, and agricultural data analysis tools. His AI credits include three hunting simulations for Sierra, the golfer/creature AI for *Links 2001*, and the camera AI for *Amped*. He is currently sneaking AI techniques into *Amped 2*, an upcoming Xbox title.

Kristin King

kaking@eskimo.com

Kristin King (*www.eskimo.com/~kaking*) has worked as a technical writer for seven years. She's been published in several Microsoft Windows Resource Kits and the magazine *NetWare Connection*, and her work has won awards from the Society for Technical Communication. She wrote the story for *StixWorld*, a game by PsychoHazard Software. She is also a published fiction writer, with an M.F.A. from the University of Washington, and the recipient of a Pushcart Prize. She is currently teaching technical communications at Seattle Central Community College, and in her spare time, she likes to juggle.

Neil Kirby—Lucent Technologies' Bell Laboratories

nak@lucent.com

Neil Kirby is a member of the technical staff at Lucent Technologies' Bell Labs. His recent work there is mentioned in the April 2003, *Bell Labs Technical Journal*. He was also a contributor to the first *AI Game Programming Wisdom*. He is a regular speaker at the Game Developers Conference and co-hosts the AI Roundtables at the conference. He has published works in the computer game industry beginning in 1991 and has been writing multiplayer, tactical combat games since 1986. He lives in central Ohio with his spouse and son.

Dr. Brett Laming—Argonaut Sheffield

brett@argonaut-sheffield.com

Dr. Brett Laming is a senior programmer for Argonaut Sheffield and AI programmer on two simulation titles. Having completed a BSc in cognitive science and a Ph.D. in computational neuroscience at the University of Sheffield, England, he joined the industry in 1998 and spent five years designing and implementing the AI for the award-winning *Independence War 2—The Edge of Chaos* and the forthcoming revision of the futuristic racing game *Powerdrome*.

He has first-hand experience of the pitfalls, problems, and stresses associated with AI programming, has faced the daunting task of architectural design without prior knowledge, and has successfully survived the "baptism by fire" that is the transition from university graduate to AI programmer. He has a Web site, *brettlaming.com*, which will probably still be under construction.

François Dominic Laramée

francoislaramee@videotron.ca

Since 1991, François Dominic Laramée has designed, produced, programmed, and/or written over 20 games for half a dozen platforms. He is the editor and principal author of *Secrets of the Game Business* and *Game Design Perspectives*, and a contributor to *Game Programming Gems 2* and *AI Game Programming Wisdom*. His published writings include over 50 articles in mass-market and trade magazines, several short stories, content for a television game show, and a considerable amount of comedy material.

Lars Lidén

larsliden@yahoo.com

Lars has had a long-time interest in computational intelligence and computer games. After receiving a Ph.D. in cognitive and neural systems from Boston University, he found the perfect merge of the two by joining the games industry as an artificial intelligence specialist. His introduction to the games industry was at Presto studios, where he designed their AI engine from the ground up. After Presto, he moved on to developing synthetic characters and working on the second-generation AI engine for Valve.

John Manslow

john@jmanslow.fsnet.co.uk

John Manslow has an honors degree in microelectronic engineering and a doctorate in AI from the University of Southampton in the UK. After a brief period of contractual work developing embedded software, John moved to Neural Computer Sciences, then to Neural Technologies, finally arriving at UK-based games developer and publisher Codemasters. John worked as Codemasters' dedicated game AI researcher, investigating the technologies that will lie at the heart of next-generation game AI. John currently operates as a freelance AI consultant, helping developers access the technologies they need to create the future of game AI.

Stéphane Maruéjouls—MASA Group

stephane.maruejouls@masagroup.net

Involved in the gaming industry since 1995, Stéphane has a master's degree in computer science. As the lead programmer for three years at Cryo Interactive, he contributed to projects such as *Ubik*, *Treasure Hunter*, and *LA Blaster* (all games were released). He then joined MASA where he contributed to the development of *Direct-IA* and then became the lead programmer for *Conflict Zone*. Stéphane is now the lead developer of the *DirectIA Software Development Kit*.

James Matthews—Generation5

jmatthews@generation5.org

James Matthews has five years experience being the chief-editor of Generation5 (*www.generation5.org*), one of the Internet's largest AI/robotics Web sites. He is currently studying artificial intelligence and Japanese at the University of Leeds, UK. Outside of AI, James loves playing his Ibanez guitars, visiting Japan, and is an avid gamer.

Alex McLean—Pivotal Games Ltd.

alex@pivotalgames.com

Alex started out programming with assembly language on 8-bit computers such as the Sinclair ZX81 and Commodore C64. Initially a hobby and later commercially came the move to 16-bit systems and a strong involvement in the European demo-coding scene. In 1990, he began four years at Edinburgh University studying artificial intelligence and computer science. A role as a software engineer at MicroProse UK followed, and later a position as head of software engineering at Eidos' Pumpkin Studios. Here, Alex was lead programmer on the real-time strategy title, *Warzone 2100*. Now, as co-founder and technical director of Pivotal Games, Alex is presently working on the sequel to Pivotal's multiplatform million-selling first title, *Conflict: Desert Storm* and *The Great Escape*.

Syrus Mesdaghi—Full Sail, Inc.

syrusm@fullsail.com

Syrus teaches the AI course that is part of Full Sail's Game Design & Development curriculum. He has been researching and developing AI techniques for many years. Besides his immeasurable passion for AI, he has put forth many efforts in improving, demonstrating, and promoting the Java technology. He has developed cutting-edge game technology demos for Full Sail and Sun Microsystems displayed at various conferences such as GDC, SIGGRAPH, and QuakeCon. The projects include genres such as FPS, RTS, and racing games. He also presented at GDC2003 and is currently working on a game-programming book. He holds a degree in computer science and hopes to pursue his Ph.D. as soon as days become longer than 24 hours.

Jeff Orkin—Monolith Productions

jorkin@blarg.net

Jeff Orkin has been developing AI and animation systems for games since 1996. His work on *No One Lives Forever 2: A Spy in H.A.R.M.'s Way* at Monolith Productions contributed to the game earning *Computer Games Magazine*'s 2002 Best A.I., and GameSpy's 2002 PC Game of the Year awards. Jeff was a contributing author for *AI Game Programming Wisdom*, and gained previous game industry experience on two titles at Sierra. Jeff holds a master's degree in computer science from the University of Washington. His undergraduate computer science studies include a minor in studio art through joint programs between Tufts University and the School of the Museum of Fine Arts, Boston. His personal Web site is *www.jorkin.com*.

Nick Porcino—LucasArts

nporcino@lucasarts.com

Nick currently develops high-performance engines and libraries at LucasArts. He has been involved in artificial intelligence work for many years, getting his start designing controllers for autonomous submersibles in the early 1990s, and publishing a few papers on neural net applications to robotics. He spent a year working with Bandai's R&D group in Tokyo on the applications of microprocessors, robotic technologies, and AI to toys, long before such things were commonplace or even successful commercially! Nick entered the games industry in 1982 with the release of *Race to Space* for the Apple][, and created *Aquattack* for Colecovision in 1984, a pixel-smooth side scrolling isometric shooter. Between then and now, besides shipping dozens of products, he has worked stints as an artist, modeler, game designer, writer, teacher, and producer, because he's a strong believer in walking a mile in another's shoes. Currently, he's helping to craft tools and technologies to help smooth the transition to the next-generation platforms that will follow the current consoles and PCs.

Steve Rabin—Nintendo of America, Inc.

steve@aiwisdom.com, steve_rabin@hotmail.com

Steve Rabin has been in the game industry for more than a decade and currently works at Nintendo of America. He has written AI for three published games and was a contributor to *Game Programming Gems 1, 2, 3,* and *4.* He served as the AI section editor for *Game Programming Gems 2* and is the founder and chief editor of the *AI Game Programming Wisdom* series. He has spoken on AI at the Game Developers Conference and holds a degree in computer engineering from the University of Washington, where he specialized in robotics. In addition to working full-time, Steve is currently pursuing a master's in computer science at the University of Washington.

Michael Ramsey—2015, Inc.

miker@masterempire.com

Mike has been writing games for fun and profit since he was in high school; having written games for platforms ranging from DOS, OS/2, Windows, to the PS2. Mike has been the lead 3D client engineer on *Lost Continents* at VR1, worked on *Hired Guns,* wrote the 3D engine for *Mike Piazza's Strikezone, Master of the Empire,* as well as a slew of RPGs in the early 1990s. His passions include AI research, 3D programming, and parallel ray tracing; which includes a cluster in his basement that occasionally works, along with some ray tracing software, that also occasionally works. He has a degree in computer science from MSCD. Mike has written articles for a number of magazines and online sites over the years. His current science experiment is his three-year-old daughter—and with the assistance of his wife, it's going great!

Christopher Reed—Raven Software/Activision

creed@ravensoft.com

Christopher Reed is a graduate of the University of Wisconsin—Madison Computer Science department, and is currently working for Raven Software (a division of Activision). His credits include such games as *Star Trek: Voyager—Elite Force, Soldier of Fortune II: Double Helix, X-Men: Legends,* and *Star Wars: Jedi Knight 3.* He is a member of the American Association for Artificial Intelligence, and the International Game Developer's Association: AI Standards Committee.

John Reynolds—Creative Asylum Ltd.

john@creative-asylum.com

John has been programming computer games since 1983, taking time out to earn a degree in applied computing from Manchester Metropolitan University. He now works for Creative Asylum, in the UK, and recent projects include *Rally Championship*, *Pac-man: Adventures in Time*, and *BattleBots*. John is also a columnist for the game industry magazine *Develop*.

Gilberto Rosado—DigiPen Institute of Technology

grosado@digipen.edu, grosado716@hotmail.com

Gilberto Rosado is a student at DigiPen Institute of Technology, where he will graduate in the spring of 2004 with a bachelor's degree in real-time interactive simulations. Along with some of his classmates, Gilberto has worked on the 2D side-scrolling game *Moebius* and the first-person shooter *Fight Zone*, both available for download at *digipen.edu*. When not working on the latest homework assignment or the next feature for his current game project, Gil tries to find some time to relax and spend some precious video game playing time.

Shawn Shoemaker—Stainless Steel Studios, Inc.

shansolox@yahoo.com

Shawn Shoemaker is in his sixth year in the game industry. At Stainless Steel Studios, his credits include unit AI, combat, graphic effects, and random maps for *Empire Earth* and *Empires: Dawn of the Modern World*. Shawn has earned a B.S. and M.S. both in computer engineering from Virginia Tech. Prior to working at Stainless, Shawn worked for Intel and in a CAVE virtual reality environment. Shawn is quick to point out that he never wanted to do this for a living—he always wanted to be a lumberjack.

Jouni Smed—Department of Information Technology, University of Turku, Finland

jouni.smed@it.utu.fi

Ever since he got his first computer at the age of 13, Jouni has been keen in programming and playing computer games. However, there is more to computers than just games, and so he got serious for a while and took MSc and Ph.D. degrees in computer science. As a post-doctoral researcher with Turku Centre for Computer Science (TUCS) he is currently trying to raise awareness inside academia of the algorithmic problems present in computer games. His research interests range from code tweaking to object-oriented programming, and from simple puzzles to interactive story generation. He lectures, he supervises students, and yes, he still likes to program and play computer games.

P.J. Snavely—Sony Computer Entertainment America

pj_snavely@playstation.sony.com

P.J. Snavely is one of the game industry's premier experts on sports game development and artificial intelligence in sports games. He received a computer engineering bachelor of science degree from the University of South Carolina, and completed some post-graduate work involving chess and game theory. P.J. spent four years at Stormfront Studios working on the *Madden*, *Tony La Russa Baseball*, and *NASCAR* game franchises. He then spent four years at Acclaim Studios Austin as the producer for the *All-Star Baseball* series. Currently, he is working for Sony Computer Entertainment America as the producer on *NBA Shootout*. He enjoys basketball, baseball, golf, bowling, chess, and fantasy sports.

Alex Sramek—Quicksilver Software, Inc.

alex_ai@bluepineapple.com

Alex is studying computer science and music composition at California State University, Long Beach. His first experience with game programming involved copying Commodore 64 games out of a book at age 10; his first taste of AI was pathfinding for the *MicroMouse* robotics project. In 2001, he joined the team at Quicksilver Software, Inc., where he implemented user interfaces and pathfinding AI for *Master of Orion 3*. Alex greatly enjoys coding, composing, and playing the clarinet, and always has an eye out for ways to combine his interests. He is currently working on a project to apply Conway's *Game of Life* to music composition and sound synthesis.

Penny Sweetser—School of ITEE, University of Queensland

penny@itee.uq.edu.au

Penny Sweetser is a Ph.D. student at the University of Queensland, Australia. Her research interests include enhancing the gaming experience through improved AI and user-centered game design. She has presented papers on research in games in Japan, Australia, and the United States, and is a founder of the Centre for Recreational and Affective Computing (*www.itee.uq.edu.au/~crac*) at the University of Queensland. She is particularly fond of playing RTS and RPGs and is currently in remission from *Elder Scrolls III: Morrowind*.

Dale Thomas—AILab, University of Zürich

dale_thomas@hotmail.com

Dale Thomas received a B.Sc. in cybernetics and control engineering from the University of Reading, UK. He worked in Japan for a while in Tokyo and Osaka, and is currently working toward his Ph.D. in the area of artificial life and robotics at the University of Zürich, Switzerland, where he also teaches artificial life and artificial intelligence. Apart from robotics, AL, and AI, he also has a deep interest in computer graphics, particularly raytracing and physical simulation techniques. His brief dip into the computer games industry involved working in the research and development section of Cyberlife Technology Ltd.

Paul Tozour—Retro Studios

gehn29@yahoo.com

Paul Tozour most recently developed a shared AI architecture for *Thief 3* and *Deus Ex 2: Invisible War* at Ion Storm Austin. Prior to that, he developed the combat AI systems for Microsoft's *MechWarrior 4: Vengeance*. Paul was also a founding member of Gas Powered Games and was the design and programming lead for a real-time strategy game called *WarBreeds* for Broderbund/Red Orb Entertainment. Paul has authored numerous AI articles for the *Game Programming Gems* and *AI Game Programming Wisdom* series.

William van der Sterren—CGF-AI, the Netherlands

william@cgf-ai.com

William van der Sterren develops tactical AI for computer games and simulations. He is a developer/consultant and founder at CGF-AI. William has spoken at the Game Developer Conference and contributed to the *AI Game Programming Wisdom* book and the *Game Programming Gems* series.

William worked as a research scientist in the fields of embedded systems and defense simulations.

Neil Wallace—Black & White Studios/Lionhead Studios

nwallace@lionhead.com

Neil Wallace completed a degree in computer science and AI at the University of Edinburgh in 2001. Since then, he has worked as an AI programmer at Black & White Studios and is currently working on creature and army AI for *Black & White II*.

Terry Wellmann—High Voltage Software, Inc.

terry.wellmann@high-voltage.com

Terry Wellmann has been programming computers since 1983 and has been developing games professionally for over six years at High Voltage Software. He has been responsible for architecting and writing the AI for Microsoft's *NBA Inside Drive* franchise on the PC and Xbox and has been the lead programmer on the last three versions, the most recent being 2004. In addition to his work on basketball, Terry was the lead programmer on *All-Star Baseball 2001* for the N64. He holds a computer science degree from Purdue University. In the summer, you can find him playing baseball in a Chicago adult league and working in his garden; in the fall, you'll find him lurking around the marshes of Minnesota hunting ducks.

Steven Woodcock—GameAI.com

ferretman@gameai.com

Steven Woodcock's background in game AI comes from nearly 20 years of ballistic missile defense work building massive real-time wargames and simulators. He did a stint in the consumer arena with arcade and console games, and then returned to the defense world to apply his AI knowledge to that realm. He maintains a Web page dedicated to game AI at *www.gameai.com*, and is the author of a number of papers and publications on the subject. He now pursues game AI through a variety of contract work, helps moderate the Game AI Roundtables at the Game Developer's Conference, and has had the honor of serving as contributor to and technical editor for several books and magazines in the field, including the prestigious *Game Programming Gems* and *AI Game Programming Wisdom* series. Steve lives in gorgeous Colorado Springs at the foot of Pikes Peak with his lovely wife Colleen, an indeterminate number of pet ferrets, and one wild basenji pup. Hobbies include shooting, writing, playing games, and working on old GMC trucks (go figure). He can be reached at *ferretman@gameai.com*.

Eric Yiskis—Sammy Studios

erk1024@hotmail.com

Eric Yiskis entered the gaming business in 1991 by co-founding Alexandria, a development studio that created Genesis and SNES games: *Demolition Man* and *Sylvester and Tweety Cagey Capers*. He then went on to create the AI systems and was the lead programmer on several development efforts at Oddworld Inhabitants, including *Abe's Oddysee*, *Abe's Exoddus*, and *Munch's Oddysee*. He felt that AI was often overlooked in the quest for higher polygon counts; when in fact, the compelling gameplay occurs when the player interacts with the characters. Active in the development community, he has given lectures at San Diego IGDA events. An evangelist for subsumption architectures and actor component systems, he is now building a new AI engine at Sammy Studios.

GENERAL WISDOM

1.1

Common Game AI Techniques

Steve Rabin—Nintendo of America Inc.

steve@aiwisdom.com

The emerging field of game artificial intelligence (AI) has made significant progress over the last decade. From the flurry of information shared through conferences, magazines, Web sites, and books, there has evolved a loose consensus on game AI techniques that are commonly used in practice, and AI techniques that look promising for the future. This article and the following article ("Promising Game AI Techniques") attempt to survey these algorithms and architectures so that you can easily see where the field stands and where it is going.

A main goal of these two articles is to boil down each technique into a couple of descriptive paragraphs. By forcing each topic into such a confined space, the crust is scraped off and you can clearly see what these techniques are all about. Each explanation is followed by references so that you can further explore the details.

A* Pathfinding

A* pathfinding (pronounced A-star) is an algorithm for finding the cheapest path through an environment. Specifically, it is a directed search algorithm that exploits knowledge about the destination to intelligently guide the search. By doing so, the processing required to find a solution is minimized. Compared to other search algorithms, A* is the fastest at finding the absolute cheapest path. Note that if all movement has the same traversal cost, the cheapest path is also the shortest path.

Game Example

The environment must first be represented by a data structure that defines where movement is allowed [Tozour03a]. A path is requested by defining a start position and a goal position within that search space. When A* is run, it returns a list of points, like a trail of breadcrumbs, that defines the path. A character or vehicle can then use the points as guidelines to find its way to the goal.

A* can be optimized for speed [Cain02, Higgins02b, Rabin00a], for aesthetics [Rabin00b], and for general applicability to other tasks [Higgins02a]. Variations like D* attempt to make path re-planning cheaper [Stentz94].

ON THE CD

As a bonus, an A* tutorial used at the Full Sail School of Game Design & Development is included on the accompanying CD-ROM [Mesdaghi04]. The tutorial walks you through different algorithms such as Breadth-First, Dijkstra, Best-First, and finally A* in order to give you a deep understanding of how A* works, and why it is better than the other planning algorithms.

Further Information

Google Search: <"A*" path finding pathfinding>
Game Programming Gems: [Rabin00a, Rabin00b, Stout00]
AI Game Programming Wisdom: [Cain02, Higgins02, Matthews02]
AI Game Programming Wisdom 2 CD-ROM: [Mesdaghi04]

Command Hierarchy

A *command hierarchy* is a strategy for dealing with AI decisions at different levels, from the general down to the foot soldier. Modeled after military hierarchies, the general directs the high-level strategy on the battlefield, while the foot soldier concentrates on individual combat. The levels in between deal with cooperation between various platoons and squads. The benefit of a command hierarchy is that decisions are separated at each level, thus making each decision more straightforward and abstracted from other levels.

Game Example

A command hierarchy is often used in real-time strategy or turn-based strategy games where there are typically three easily identifiable levels of decisions: overall strategy, squad tactics, and individual combat. A command hierarchy is also useful when a large number of agents must have an overall coherency.

Further Information

Google Search: <AI command hierarchy -class>
AI Game Programming Wisdom: [Reynolds02]
AI Game Programming Wisdom 2: [Kent04]

Dead Reckoning

Dead reckoning is a method for predicting a player's future position based on that player's current position, velocity, and acceleration. This simple form of prediction works well since the movement of most objects resembles a straight line over short periods of time. More advanced forms of dead reckoning can also provide guidance for how far an object *could have moved* since it was last seen.

Game Example

In a first-person shooter (FPS) game, an effective method of controlling the difficulty level is to vary how accurate the computer is at "leading the target" when shooting projectiles. Since most weapons don't travel instantaneously, the computer must predict the future position of targets and aim the weapon at these predicted positions. Similarly, in a sports game, the computer player must anticipate the future positions of other players to effectively pass the ball or intercept a player.

Further Information

AI Game Programming Wisdom: [Stein02]
AI Game Programming Wisdom 2: [Laramée04]

Emergent Behavior

Emergent behavior is behavior that wasn't explicitly programmed but instead emerges from the interaction of several simpler behaviors. Many life forms use rather basic behavior that, when viewed as a whole, can be perceived as being much more sophisticated. In games, emergent behavior generally manifests itself as low-level simple rules that interact to create interesting and complex behaviors. Some examples of rules are seek food, seek similar creatures, avoid walls, and move toward the light. While any one rule isn't interesting by itself, unanticipated individual or group behavior can emerge from the interaction of these rules.

Game Example

Flocking is a classical example of emergent behavior in games [Reynolds87, Reynolds01]. Another example is insect-like behavior described in this book by Alex Darby for racecar applications [Darby04] and Nick Porcino for general-purpose creatures [Porcino04].

Further Information

Google Search: <emergent behavior alife>
Internet: [Alife03, Reynolds87, Reynolds01]
AI Game Programming Wisdom 2: [Darby04, Porcino04]

Flocking

Flocking is a technique for moving groups of creatures in a natural and organic manner. It works well at simulating flocks of birds, schools of fish, and swarms of insects. Each creature follows three simple movement rules that result in complex group behavior. It is said that this group behavior *emerges* from the individual rules (emergent behavior). Flocking is a form of artificial life that was popularized by Craig Reynolds' work [Reynolds87, Reynolds01].

The three classic flocking rules devised by Reynolds are:

- **Separation:** Steer to avoid crowding local flockmates.
- **Alignment:** Steer toward the average heading of local flockmates.
- **Cohesion:** Steer toward the average position of local flockmates.

Game Example

Games typically use flocking to control background creatures such as schools of fish or swarms of insects. Since the path of any one creature is highly arbitrary, flocking is typically used for simple creatures that tend to wander with no particular destination. The result is that flocking techniques, as embodied by the three core rules, rarely get used for key enemies or creatures. However, the flocking rules have inspired several other movement algorithms, such as formations and swarming [Scutt02].

Further Information

Google Search: <flocking boids>
Internet: [Reynolds87, Reynolds01]
Game Programming Gems: [Woodcock00]
AI Game Programming Wisdom: [Scutt02]

Formations

Formations are a group movement technique used to mimic military formations. Although it shares similarities to flocking, it is quite distinct in that each unit is guided toward a specific goal location and heading, based on its position in the formation.

Game Example

Formations can be used to organize the movement of ground troops, vehicles, or aircraft. Often, the formations must split or distort themselves to facilitate movement through tight areas [Pottinger99a, Pottinger99b].

Further Information

Google Search: <military formations>
Internet: [Pottinger99a, Pottinger99b]
AI Game Programming Wisdom: [Dawson02]

Influence Mapping

An *influence map* is a method for viewing the distribution of power within a game world. Typically, it's a two-dimensional (2D) grid that is superimposed onto the landscape. Within each grid cell, units that lie in the cell are summed into a single number representing the combined influence of the units. It is assumed that each unit also has an influence into neighboring cells that falls off either linearly or exponentially with distance. The result is a 2D grid of numbers that gives insight into the location and influence of differing forces.

Game Example

Influence maps can be used offensively to plan attacks; for example, by finding neutral routes to flank the enemy. They can also be used defensively to identify areas or positions that need to be strengthened. If one faction is represented by positive values and the other faction is represented by negative values within the same influence map, then any grid cells near zero are either unowned territory or the "front" of the battle (where the influence of each side cancels each other out) [Tozour01].

There are also nonviolent uses for influence maps. For example, the *Sim City* series offers real-time maps that show the influence of police and fire departments placed around the city. The player can then use this information to place future buildings to fill in the gaps in coverage. The game also uses the same information to help simulate the world.

Further Information

Google Search: <"influence mapping" code>
Game Programming Gems 2: [Tozour01]
AI Game Programming Wisdom: [Woodcock02]
AI Game Programming Wisdom 2: [Tozour04b, Sweetser04]

Level-of-Detail AI

Level-of-detail (LOD) is a common optimization technique in 3D graphics where polygonal detail is only used when it can be noticed and appreciated by the human viewer. Close-up models use large numbers of polygons, while faraway models use fewer polygons. This results in faster graphics processing since fewer polygons are rendered, yet there is no noticeable degradation in visual quality. The same concept can be applied to AI where computations are performed only if the player will notice or appreciate the result.

Game Example

One approach is to vary an agent's update frequency based on its proximity to the player. Another technique is to calculate paths only for agents that the player can see; otherwise, use straight-line path approximations and estimate off-screen movement. This technique becomes important when there are more than several dozen agents in a game and collectively they use too much processing power. This often occurs with RPG, RTS, strategy, and simulation games.

Further Information

Google Search: <"level of detail" AI>
AI Game Programming Wisdom: [Brockington02a]
AI Game Programming Wisdom 2: [Fu04]

Manager Task Assignment

When a group of agents tries to independently choose tasks to accomplish, like selecting a target in battle, the performance of the group can be rather dismal. Interestingly,
the problem can be turned around so that instead of the individuals choosing tasks, a
manager has a list of required tasks and assigns agents based on who is the best suited
for the job. Note that this is very different from having the manager run through the
list of individuals and assign tasks. Task assignment considers the tasks themselves
first and uses them as the basis for prioritizing. This avoids duplication of tasks, and
the best candidate for a task is always chosen. This type of tactical planning is more
deliberate than the emergent coordination that can be achieved with a blackboard
architecture. However, the resulting plan might not be as optimal as performing an
exhaustive planning search [Orkin04a].

Game Example

In a baseball game with no runners on base, it might be determined that the first priority is to field the ball, the second priority is to cover first base, the third priority is to
back up the person fielding the ball, and the fourth priority is to cover second base.
The manager can organize who covers each priority by examining the best person for
the job for a given situation. On a soft hit between first and second base, the manager
might assign the first baseman to field the ball, the pitcher to cover first base, the second baseman to back up the first baseman fielding the ball, and the shortstop to cover
second base. Without a manager to organize the task assignment, it can be significantly harder to get coherent cooperation out of the players using other methods.

Further Information

AI Game Programming Wisdom 2 **CD-ROM:** [Rabin98]

Obstacle Avoidance

A* pathfinding algorithms are good at getting a character from point to point through
static terrain. However, often the character must avoid players, other characters, and
vehicles that are moving rapidly through the environment. Characters must not get
stuck on each other at choke points, and they must maintain enough spacing to
maneuver when traveling in groups. *Obstacle avoidance* attempts to prevent these
problems using trajectory prediction and layered steering behaviors [Reynolds99].

Game Example

In an FPS game, a group of four skeletons wants to attack the player, but must first
cross a narrow bridge over a river. Each skeleton has received a route to the player
through the navigation system. The skeleton closest to the bridge has a clear path
across. The second skeleton predicts a collision with the first, but sees space to the
right, which is still within the boundaries of the path across the bridge. The last two

skeletons predict collisions with the first two, so they slow their rate of travel to correctly queue up behind the first two.

Further Information

Internet: [Saffiotti98]
AI Game Programming Wisdom 2 **CD-ROM:** [Reynolds99]

Scripting

Scripting is the technique of specifying a game's data or logic outside of the game's source language. Often, the scripting language is designed from scratch, but there is a growing movement toward using Python and Lua as alternatives. There is a complete spectrum for how far you can take the scripting concept.

Scripting influence spectrum:

Level 0: Hard code everything in the source language (C/C++).
Level 1: Data in files specify stats and locations of characters/objects.
Level 2: Scripted cutscene sequences (noninteractive).
Level 3: Lightweight logic specified by tools or scripts, as in a trigger system.
Level 4: Heavy logic in scripts that rely on core functions written in C/C++.
Level 5: Everything coded in scripts—full alternative language to C/C++.

Commercial games have been developed at all levels of this spectrum, with the oldest video games at level 0 and games such as *Jak and Daxter* at level 5 (with their GOAL language based on LISP). However, the middle levels are where most games have settled, since the two extremes represent increased risk, time commitment, and cost.

Game Example

Programmers must first integrate a scripting language into the game and determine the extent of its influence. The users of the scripting language will typically be artists and level designers. The written script will either be compiled into byte code before actual gameplay or interpreted on the fly during gameplay.

Advantages of scripting:

• Game logic can be changed in scripts and tested without recompiling the code.
• Designers can be empowered without consuming programmer resources.
• Scripts can be exposed to the players to tinker with and expand (extensible AI).

Disadvantages of scripting:

• More difficult to debug.
• Nonprogrammers are required to program.
• Time commitment to create and support scripting language and complementary debugging tools.

Further Information

Google Search: <"scripting language" games AI>
AI Game Programming Wisdom: [Barnes02, Brockington02b, Berger02, Poiker02, Tozour02]
AI Game Programming Wisdom 2: [Herz04a, Herz04b, Kharkar04, Orkin04b, Snavely04]

State Machine

A *state machine* or *finite-state machine* (FSM) is a widely used software design pattern that has become a cornerstone of game AI. An FSM is defined by a finite set of states and transitions, with only one state active at any one time. In common practice, each state represents a behavior, such as PatrolRoute, within which an agent will perform a specific task. The state either polls or listens for events that will cause it to transition into other states. For example, a PatrolRoute state might check periodically if it sees an enemy. When this event happens, it transitions into the AttackEnemy state. An exhaustive explanation of FSMs for games, along with common enhancements, can be found in this book [Fu04].

Further Information

Google Search: <finite state machines AI>
AI Game Programming Wisdom 2: [Fu04]

Stack-Based State Machine

A *stack-based state machine* is a technique and design pattern that often appears in game architectures. Also sometimes referred to as *push-down automata*, the stack-based state machine can remember past actions by storing them on a stack. In a traditional state machine, past states are not remembered, since control flows from state to state with no recorded history. However, it can be useful in game AI to be able to transition back to a previous state, regardless of which state it was. This stack concept can be used to capture previous states, or even entire state machines.

Game Example

In a game, this technique is important when a character is performing an action, becomes interrupted for a moment, but then wants to resume the original action. For example, in a real-time strategy game, a unit might be repairing a building when it gets attacked. The unit will transition into an attack behavior and might destroy the enemy. In this case, the conflict is over and the unit should resume its previous activity. If past behaviors are stored on a stack, then the current attack behavior is simply popped from the stack and the unit will resume the repair behavior.

Further Information

AI Game Programming Wisdom 2: [Fu04, Tozour04c, Yiskis04a]

Subsumption Architecture

A *subsumption architecture* cleanly separates the behavior of a single character into concurrently running layers of FSMs. The lower layers take care of rudimentary behavior such as obstacle avoidance, and the higher layers take care of more elaborate behaviors such as goal determination and goal seeking. Because the lower layers have priority, the system remains robust and ensures that lower layer requirements are met before allowing higher level behaviors to influence them. The subsumption architecture was popularized by the work of Rodney Brooks [Brooks89].

Game Example

Subsumption architectures have been used in many games, including the *Oddworld* series of games, *Jedi Knight: Dark Forces 2*, and *Halo: Combat Evolved*. The architecture is ideally suited for character-based games where movement and sensing must coexist with decisions and high-level goals.

Further Information

Google Search: <subsumption brooks>
AI Game Programming Wisdom 2: [Yiskis04b]

Terrain Analysis

Terrain analysis is the broad term given to analyzing the terrain of a game world in order to identify strategic locations such as resources, choke points, or ambush points [Higgins02c]. These locations can then be used by the strategic-level AI to help plan maneuvers and attacks. Other uses for terrain analysis in a real-time strategy game include knowing where to build walls [Grimani04] or where to place the starting factions. In a first-person shooter (FPS) game, terrain analysis can assist the AI in discovering sniper points, cover points, or where to throw grenades from [Lidén02, Reed03, Tozour03b, van der Sterren00]. Terrain analysis can be viewed as the alternative approach to "hard-coding" regions of interest in a level.

Further Information

Google Search: <"terrain analysis" AI>
Internet: [van der Sterren00]
Game Programming Gems 3: [Higgins02c]
AI Game Programming Wisdom: [Lidén02]
AI Game Programming Wisdom 2: [Kent04, Reed04, Tozour04b]

Trigger System

A *trigger system* is a highly specialized scripting system that allows simple if/then rules to be encapsulated within game objects or the world itself. It is a useful tool for level designers since the concept is extremely simple and robust. Often, it is exposed through a level design tool or a scripting language.

Game Example

A designer might put a floor trigger in the middle of a room. When the player steps on the floor trigger (the condition), the designer might specify that a scary sound effect is played and that a dozen snakes drop from the ceiling (the response). In this way, a trigger system is a simple way to specify scripted events without designing a complex scripting language. As an example, the level editor for *StarCraft* allowed users to define their own missions with a Windows-based trigger system tool.

Further Information

Google Search: <"trigger system" scripting>
Game Programming Gems 3: [Rabin02]
AI Game Programming Wisdom: [Orkin02]

Acknowledgments

Several people helped contribute to the ideas and knowledge within this article. In particular, Mark Brockington, Daniel Higgins, Lars Lidén, John Manslow, Syrus Mesdaghi, Jeff Orkin, Steven Woodcock, and Eric Yiskis helped a great deal.

References

[Alife03] International Society of Artificial Life, *www.alife.org*.
[Barnes02] Barnes, Jonty, and Hutchens, Jason, "Scripting for Undefined Circumstances," *AI Game Programming Wisdom*, Charles River Media, 2002.
[Berger02] Berger, Lee, "Scripting: Overview and Code Generation," *AI Game Programming Wisdom*, Charles River Media, 2002.
[Brockington02a] Brockington, Mark, "Level-of-Detail AI for a Large Role-Playing Game," *AI Game Programming Wisdom*, Charles River Media, 2002.
[Brockington02b] Brockington, Mark, and Darrah, Mark, "How *Not* to Implement a Basic Scripting Language," *AI Game Programming Wisdom*, Charles River Media, 2002.
[Brooks89] Brooks, Rodney, "How to Build Complete Creatures Rather than Isolated Cognitive Simulators," *Architectures for Intelligence*, Lawrence Erlbaum Associates, Fall 1989, available online at *www.ai.mit.edu/people/brooks/papers/how-to-build.pdf*
[Cain02] Cain, Timothy, "Practical Optimizations for A* Path Generation," *AI Game Programming Wisdom*, Charles River Media, 2002.
[Darby04] Darby, Alex, "Vehicle Racing Control Using Insect Intelligence," *AI Game Programming Wisdom 2*, Charles River Media, 2004.

[Dawson02] Dawson, Chad, "Formations," *AI Game Programming Wisdom*, Charles River Media, 2002.

[Fu04] Fu, Dan, and Houlette, Ryan, "The Ultimate Guide to FSMs in Games," *AI Game Programming Wisdom 2*, Charles River Media, 2004.

[Grimani04] Grimani, Mario, "Wall Building for RTS Games," *AI Game Programming Wisdom 2*, Charles River Media, 2004.

[Herz04a] Herz, Alex, "Optimized Script Execution," *AI Game Programming Wisdom 2*, Charles River Media, 2004.

[Herz04b] Herz, Alex, "Advanced Script Debugging," *AI Game Programming Wisdom 2*, Charles River Media, 2004.

[Higgins02a] Higgins, Dan, "Generic A* Pathfinding," *AI Game Programming Wisdom*, Charles River Media, 2002.

[Higgins02b] Higgins, Dan, "How to Achieve Lightning-Fast A*," *AI Game Programming Wisdom*, Charles River Media, 2002.

[Higgins02c] Higgins, Dan, "Terrain Analysis in an RTS—The Hidden Giant," *Game Programming Gems 3*, Charles River Media, 2002.

[Kent04] Kent, Tom, "Multi-Tiered AI Layers and Terrain Analysis for RTS Games," *AI Game Programming Wisdom 2*, Charles River Media, 2004.

[Kharkar04] Kharkar, Sandeep, "A Modular Camera Architecture for Intelligent Control," *AI Game Programming Wisdom 2*, Charles River Media, 2004.

[Laramée04] Laramée, François Dominic, "Dead Reckoning in Sports and Strategy Games," *AI Game Programming Wisdom 2*, Charles River Media, 2004.

[Lidén02] Lidén, Lars, "Strategic and Tactical Reasoning with Waypoints," *AI Game Programming Wisdom*, Charles River Media, 2002.

[Matthews02] Matthews, James, "Basic A* Pathfinding Made Simple," *AI Game Programming Wisdom*, Charles River Media, 2002.

[Mesdaghi04] Mesdaghi, Syrus, "Path Planning Tutorial," *AI Game Programming Wisdom 2* CD-ROM, Charles River Media, 2004.

[Orkin02] Orkin, Jeff, "A General-Purpose Trigger System," *AI Game Programming Wisdom*, Charles River Media, 2002.

[Orkin04a] Orkin, Jeff, "Applying Goal-Oriented Action Planning to Games," *AI Game Programming Wisdom 2*, Charles River Media, 2004.

[Orkin04b] Orkin, Jeff, "Adding Error Reporting to Scripting Languages," *AI Game Programming Wisdom 2*, Charles River Media, 2004.

[Poiker02] Poiker, Falko, "Creating Scripting Languages for Nonprogrammers," *AI Game Programming Wisdom*, Charles River Media, 2002.

[Porcino04] Porcino, Nick, "An Architecture for A-Life," *AI Game Programming Wisdom 2*, Charles Rivers Media, 2004.

[Pottinger99a] Pottinger, Dave, "Coordinated Unit Movement," *Game Developer Magazine*, January 1999, available online at *www.gamasutra.com/features/19990122/movement_01.htm*

[Pottinger99b] Pottinger, Dave, "Implementing Coordinated Movement," *Game Developer Magazine*, February 1999, available online at *www.gamasutra.com/features/19990129/implementing_01.htm*

[Rabin98] Rabin, Steve, "Making the Play: Team Cooperation in Microsoft Baseball 3D," Computer Game Developers Conference Proceedings, 1998, available on the *AI Game Programming Wisdom 2* CD-ROM.

[Rabin00a] Rabin, Steve, "A* Speed Optimizations," *Game Programming Gems*, Charles River Media, 2000.

[Rabin00b] Rabin, Steve, "A* Aesthetic Optimizations," *Game Programming Gems*, Charles River Media, 2000.

[Rabin02] Rabin, Steve, "An Extensible Trigger System for AI Agents, Objects, and Quests," *Game Programming Gems 3*, Charles River Media, 2002.

[Reed03] Reed, Christopher, and Geisler, Benjamin, "Jumping, Climbing, and Tactical Reasoning: How to Get More out of a Navigation System," *AI Game Programming Wisdom 2*, Charles River Media, 2003.

[Reynolds87] Reynolds, Craig, "Flocks, Herds, and Schools: A Distributed Behavioral Model," *Computer Graphics, 21(4) (SIGGRAPH '87 Conference Proceedings)*, pp. 25–34, 1987, available online at *www.red3d.com/cwr/papers/1987/boids.html*

[Reynolds99] Reynolds, Craig, "Steering Behaviors for Autonomous Characters," Game Developers Conference Proceedings, 1999, available on the *AI Game Programming Wisdom 2* CD-ROM.

[Reynolds01] Reynolds, Craig, "Boids," available online at *www.red3d.com/cwr/boids/*

[Reynolds02] Reynolds, John, "Tactical Team AI Using a Command Hierarchy," *AI Game Programming Wisdom*, Charles River Media, 2002.

[Saffiotti98] Saffiotti, Alessandro, "Autonomous Robot Navigation," Handbook of Fuzzy Computation, Oxford Univ. Press and IOP Press, 1998, available online at *aass.oru.se/Agora/FLAR/HFC/home.html*

[Scutt02] Scutt, Tom, "Simple Swarms as an Alternative to Flocking," *AI Game Programming Wisdom*, Charles River Media, 2002.

[Snavely04] Snavely, P.J., "Empowering Designers: Defining Fuzzy Logic Behavior through Excel-Based Spreadsheets," *AI Game Programming Wisdom 2*, Charles River Media, 2004.

[Stein02] Stein, Noah, "Intercepting a Ball," *AI Game Programming Wisdom*, Charles River Media, 2002.

[Stentz94] Stentz, Tony, "Original D*," *ICRA 94*, 1994, available online at *www.frc.ri.cmu.edu/~axs/doc/icra94.pdf*

[Stout00] Stout, Bryan, "The Basics of A* for Path Planning," *Game Programming Gems*, Charles River Media, 2000.

[Sweetser04] Sweetser, Penny, "Strategic Decision-Making with Neural Nets and Influence Maps," *AI Game Programming Wisdom 2*, Charles River Media, 2004.

[Tozour01] Tozour, Paul, "Influence Mapping," *Game Programming Gems 2*, Charles River Media, 2001.

[Tozour02] Tozour, Paul, "The Perils of AI Scripting," *AI Game Programming Wisdom*, Charles River Media, 2002.

[Tozour04a] Tozour, Paul, "Search Space Representations," *AI Game Programming Wisdom 2*, Charles River Media, 2004.

[Tozour04b] Tozour, Paul, "Using a Spatial Database for Runtime Spatial Analysis," *AI Game Programming Wisdom 2*, Charles River Media, 2004.

[Tozour04c] Tozour, Paul, "Stack-Based Finite-State Machines," *AI Game Programming Wisdom 2*, Charles River Media, 2004.

[van der Sterren00] van der Sterren, William, "AI for Tactical Grenade Handling," *CGF-AI*, 2000, available online at *www.cgf-ai.com/docs/grenadehandling.pdf*

[Woodcock00] Woodcock, Steven, "Flocking: A Simple Technique for Simulating Group Behavior," *Game Programming Gems*, Charles River Media, 2000.

[Woodcock02] Woodcock, Steven, "Recognizing Strategic Dispositions: Engaging the Enemy," *AI Game Programming Wisdom*, Charles River Media, 2002.

[Yiskis04a] Yiskis, Eric, "Finite-State Machine Scripting Language for Designers," *AI Game Programming Wisdom 2*, Charles River Media, 2004.

[Yiskis04b] Yiskis, Eric, "A Subsumption Architecture for Character-Based Games," *AI Game Programming Wisdom 2*, Charles River Media, 2004.

1.2

Promising Game AI Techniques

Steve Rabin—Nintendo of America, Inc.

steve@aiwisdom.com

Some of the most promising game AI techniques have been lurking in the shadows for years. Many have been used in games, but most are still on the fringe of mainstream game development. What these techniques lack is not usefulness, but rather the impetus for game developers to take them seriously. Too often we become lazy and overly complacent with simpler techniques, failing to realize the potential that lies beyond our own comfortable knowledge. Current trends suggest that it is mostly academics who transfer into the game industry who push these newer techniques, but this needn't be the case. This article attempts to get the word out in the hope that you'll take up the challenge and personally push the limits of mainstream game AI.

Bayesian Networks

Bayesian networks allow an AI to perform complex humanlike reasoning when faced with uncertainty. In a Bayesian network, variables relating to particular states, features, or events in the game world are represented as nodes in a graph, and the causal relationships between them as arcs. Probabilistic inference can then be performed on the graph to infer the values of unknown variables, or conduct other forms of reasoning.

Game Example

One particularly important application for Bayesian networks in games lies in modeling what an AI should believe about the human player based on the information it has available. For example, in a real-time strategy game, the AI can attempt to infer the existence or nonexistence of certain player-built units, like fighter planes or warships, based on what it has seen produced by the player so far. This keeps the AI from cheating and actually allows the human to deceive the AI by presenting misleading information, offering new gameplay possibilities and strategies for the player.

Further Information

Google Search: <"bayesian networks" nets>
Internet: [IDIS99]
AI Game Programming Wisdom: [Tozour02]

Blackboard Architecture

A *blackboard architecture* is designed to solve a single complex problem by posting it on a shared communication space, called the *blackboard*. Expert objects then look at the blackboard and propose solutions. The solutions are given a relevance score, and the highest scoring solution (or partial solution) is applied. This continues until the problem is "solved."

Game Example

In games, the blackboard architecture can be expanded to facilitate cooperation among multiple agents. A problem, such as attacking a castle, can be posted, and individual units can propose their role in the attack. The volunteers are then scored and the most appropriate ones are selected [Isla02].

Alternatively, the blackboard concept can be relaxed by using it strictly as a shared communication space, letting the individual agents regulate any cooperation. In this scheme, agents post their current activities and other agents can consult the blackboard to avoid beginning redundant work. For example, if an alarm is sounded in a building and enemies start rushing the player, it might be desirable for them to approach from different doors. Each enemy can post the door through which it will eventually enter, thus encouraging other enemies to choose alternate routes. Within this book, Jeff Orkin describes many cooperation problems within FPSs that can be solved using this approach [Orkin04].

Further Information

Google Search: <blackboard architecture architectures>
AI Game Programming Wisdom: [Isla02]
AI Game Programming Wisdom 2: [Orkin04]

Decision Tree Learning

A *decision tree* is a way of relating a series of inputs (usually measurements from the game world) to an output (usually representing something you want to predict) using a series of rules arranged in a tree structure. For example, inputs representing the health and ammunition of a bot could be used to predict the probability of the bot surviving an engagement with the player. At the root node, the decision tree might test to see whether the bot's health is low, indicating that the bot will not survive if that is the case. If the bot's health is not low, the decision tree might then test to see how much ammunition the bot has, perhaps indicating that the bot will not survive if its ammunition is low, and will survive otherwise. Decision trees are particularly important for applications like in-game learning because (in contrast to competing technologies like neural networks) extremely efficient algorithms exist for creating decision trees in near real-time.

Game Example

The best known game-specific use of decision trees is in the game *Black & White* where they are used to allow the creature to learn and form "opinions" [Evans02]. In *Black & White*, a creature will learn what objects in the world are likely to satisfy his desire to eat, based on feedback it gets from the player or world. For example, the player can provide positive or negative feedback by stroking or slapping the creature. A decision tree is then created that reflects what the creature has learned from its experiences. The creature can then use the decision tree to decide whether certain objects can be used to satisfy its hunger. While *Black & White* has demonstrated the power of decision trees to learn within games, they remain largely untapped by the rest of the game industry.

Further Information

Google Search: <decision tree learning>
Google Search: <decision tree ID3 ID4>
AI Game Programming Wisdom: [Evans02]
AI Game Programming Wisdom 2: [Fu04]

Filtered Randomness

Filtered randomness attempts to ensure that random decisions or events in a game appear random to the players. This can be achieved by filtering the results of a random number generator such that non-random looking sequences are eliminated, yet statistical randomness is maintained. For example, if a coin is flipped eight times in a row and turns up heads every time, a person might wonder if there was something wrong with the coin. The odds of such an event occurring are only 0.4 percent, but in a sequence of 100 flips it is extremely likely that either eight heads or eight tails in a row will be observed. When designing a game for entertainment purposes, random elements should always appear random to the players.

Game Example

Simple randomness filtering is actually very common in games. For example, if a character plays a random idle animation, often the game will ensure that the same idle animation won't be played twice in a row. However, filtering can be devised to remove all peculiar sequences. For example, if an enemy can randomly spawn from five different points, it would be extremely undesirable for the enemy to spawn from the same point five times in a row. It would also be undesirable for the enemy to randomly spawn in the counting sequence 12345 or favor one or two particular spawn points in the short term, like 12112121. Although these sequences can arise by chance, they are neither intended nor anticipated when the programmer wrote the code to randomly choose a spawn point. In this book, Steve Rabin describes how to effectively filter random number sequences and provides an assortment of classes on the accompanying CD-ROM [Rabin04].

ON THE CD

Further Information

AI Game Programming Wisdom 2: [Rabin04]

Fuzzy Logic

Fuzzy logic is an extension of classical logic that is based on the idea of a fuzzy set. In classical crisp set theory, an object either does or does not belong to a set. For example, a creature is a member of the set of hungry creatures or is not a member of that set (it is either hungry or not hungry). With fuzzy set theory, an object can have continuously varying degrees of membership in fuzzy sets. For example, a creature could be hungry with degree of membership 0.1, representing slightly hungry, or 0.9, representing very hungry, or any value in between.

Further Information

Google Search: <"fuzzy logic">
Game Programming Gems: [McCuskey 00]
AI Game Programming Wisdom: [Zarozinsky02]
AI Game Programming Wisdom 2: [Snavely04]
AI Game Programming Wisdom 2 **CD-ROM:** [Zarozinsky04]

Genetic Algorithms

A *genetic algorithm* (GA) is a technique for search and optimization that is based on evolutionary principles. GAs represent a point within a search space using a chromosome that is based on a handcrafted genetic code. Each chromosome consists of a string of genes that together encode its location in the search space. For example, the parameters of an AI agent can be the genes, and a particular combination of parameters a chromosome. All combinations of parameters will represent the search space.

By maintaining a population of chromosomes, which are continually mated and mutated, a GA is able to explore search spaces by testing different combinations of genes that seem to work well. A GA is usually left to evolve until it discovers a chromosome that represents a point in the search space that is good enough. GAs outperform many other techniques in search spaces that contain many optima, and are controlled by only a small number of parameters, which must be set by trial and error.

Game Example

Genetic algorithms are very good at finding a solution in complex or poorly understood search spaces. For example, your game might have a series of settings for the AI, but because of interactions between the settings, it is unclear what the best combination would be. In this case, a GA can be used to explore the search space consisting of all combinations of settings to come up with a near-optimal combination. This is typically done offline since the optimization process can be slow and because a near-optimal solution is not guaranteed, meaning that the results might not improve gameplay.

Further Information

Google Search: <"genetic algorithms" games>
AI Game Programming Wisdom: [Laramée02a]
AI Game Programming Wisdom 2: [Buckland04a, Laramée04, Sweetser04a,
Thomas04]
AI Game Programming Wisdom 2 **CD-ROM:** [Buckland04b]

N-Gram Statistical Prediction

An *n-gram* is a statistical technique that can predict the next value in a sequence. For
example, in the sequence 18181810181, the next value will probably be an 8. When
a prediction is required, the sequence is searched backward for all sequences matching
the most recent *n*-1 values, where *n* is usually 2 or 3 (a *bigram* or *trigram*). Since the
sequence might contain many repetitions of the n-gram, the value that most commonly follows is the one that is predicted. If the sequence is built up over time, representing the history of a variable (like the last player's move), then a future event can be
predicted. The accuracy of the predictions made by an n-gram tends to improve as the
amount of historical data increases.

Game Example

For example, in a street fighting game, the player's actions (various punches and kicks)
can be accumulated into a move history. Using the trigram model, the last two player
moves are noted; for example, a Low Kick followed by a Low Punch. The move history is then searched for all examples where the player preformed those two moves in
sequence. For each example found, the move following the Low Punch and Low Kick
is tallied. The statistics gathered might resemble Table 1.2.1.

Table 1.2.1 Statistics Gathered from Past Player Moves

Player Sequence	Occurrences	Frequency
Low Kick, Low Punch, Uppercut	10 times	50%
Low Kick, Low Punch, Low Punch	7 times	35%
Low Kick, Low Punch, Sideswipe	3 times	15%

From Table 1.2.1, the computer would predict that the player's next move will be
an Uppercut (with a 50-percent likelihood based on past moves). These statistics are
quickly calculated on the fly when a prediction is requested. A moving window into
the past can be used so as not to consider moves that occurred too long ago.

A very similar technique is to analyze the move history for the longest pattern
match to the current situation [Mommersteeg02]. The assumption is that the longest
match in the history is the best predictor of the future. Whether this is true depends
on your application.

Further Information

AI Game Programming Wisdom: [Laramée02b, Mommersteeg02]

Neural Networks

Neural networks are complex nonlinear functions that relate one or more input variables to an output variable. They are called neural networks because internally they consist of a series of identical nonlinear processing elements (analogous to neurons) connected together in a network by weights (analogous to synapses). The form of the function that a particular neural network represents is controlled by values associated with the network's weights. Neural networks can be trained to produce a particular function by showing them examples of inputs and the outputs they should produce in response. This training process consists of optimizing the network's weight values, and several standard training algorithms are available for this purpose. Training most types of neural networks is computationally intensive, however, making neural networks generally unsuitable for in-game learning. Despite this, neural networks are extremely powerful and have found applications in the games industry.

Game Example

In games, neural networks have been used for gesture recognition in *Black & White*, steering racecars in *Colin McRae Rally 2.0*, and for control and learning in the *Creatures* series. Unfortunately, there are still relatively few applications of neural networks in games, as very few game developers are actively experimenting with them.

Further Information

Google Search: <neural networks games>
AI Game Programming Wisdom: [Champandard02]
AI Game Programming Wisdom 2: [Sweetser04b, Sweetser04c]
AI Game Programming Wisdom 2 **CD-ROM**: [Buckland04c, Fahey04]

Perceptrons

A *perceptron network* is a single-layer neural network, which is simpler and easier to work with than a multilayer neural network. A perceptron network is composed of multiple *perceptrons*, each of which can either have a "yes" or "no" output. In other words, each perceptron either gets stimulated enough to trigger or it does not. Since a perceptron can classify things as "yes" or "no," it can be used to learn simple Boolean decisions such as attack or don't attack. They take up very little memory and are easier to train than a multilayer neural network or a decision tree. It is important to note, however, that perceptrons and perceptron networks have some limitations and can only learn simple (linearly separable) functions.

Game Example

In the game *Black & White*, every desire of a creature was represented by a different perceptron [Evans02]. For example, a single perceptron was used to represent the desire to eat (or hunger). Using three inputs (low energy, tasty food, and unhappiness), a perceptron would determine whether a creature was hungry. If the creature ate and received either positive or negative reinforcement, the weight associated with the perceptron would be adjusted, thus facilitating learning.

Further Information

Google Search: <perceptron learning>
AI Game Programming Wisdom: [Evans02]

Planning

The aim of *planning* is to find a series of actions for the AI that can change the current configuration of the game world into a target configuration. By specifying preconditions under which certain actions can be taken by the AI, and what the effects of those actions are likely to be, planning becomes a problem of searching for a sequence of actions that produces the required changes in the game world. Effective planning relies on choosing a good planning algorithm to search for the best sequence of actions, choosing an appropriate representation for the game world, and choosing an appropriate set of actions that the AI will be allowed to perform and specifying their effects.

Game Example

When the domain of a planning problem is sufficiently simple, formulating small plans is a reasonable and tractable problem that can be performed in real-time. For example, in a game, a guard might run out of ammo during in a gunfight with the player. The AI can then try to formulate a plan that will result in the player's demise given the guard's current situation. A planning module might come back with the solution of running to the light switch, turning it off to provide safety, running into the next room to gather ammo, and waiting in an ambush position. As game environments become more interactive and rich with possibilities, planning systems can help agents cope with the complexity by formulating reasonable and workable plans.

Further Information

Google Search: <AI planning>
AI Game Programming Wisdom 2: [Orkin04, Wallace04]

Player Modeling

Player modeling is the technique of building a profile of a player's behavior, with the intent of adapting the game. During play, the player's profile is continuously refined by accumulating statistics related to the player's behavior. As the profile emerges, the game can adapt the AI to the particular idiosyncrasies of the player by exploiting the information stored in his or her profile.

Game Example

In an FPS, the AI might observe that the player is poor at using a certain weapon or isn't good at jumping from platform to platform. Information like this can then be used to regulate the difficulty of the game, either by exploiting any weaknesses or by shying away from those same weaknesses.

Further Information

Internet: [Beal02]
AI Game Programming Wisdom 2: [Houlette04]

Production Systems

A *production system* (also known as a *rule-based system* or *expert system*) is an architecture for capturing expert knowledge in the form of rules. The system consists of a database of rules, facts, and an inference engine that determines which rules should trigger, resolving any conflicts between simultaneously triggered rules. The intelligence of a production system is embodied by the rules and conflict resolution.

Game Example

The academic community has had some success in creating bot AI for *Quake II* using the *Soar* production system [van Lent99], although the system requires upwards of 800 rules in order to play as a fairly competent opponent [Laird00]. Another applicable area is sports games where each AI player must contain a great deal of expert knowledge to play the sport correctly.

Further Information

Google Search: <"production systems" AI>
Internet: [AIISC03, Laird00, van Lent99]

Reinforcement Learning

Reinforcement learning (RL) is an extremely powerful machine learning technique that allows a computer to discover its own solutions to complex problems by trial and error. RL is particularly useful when the effects of the AI's actions in the game world are uncertain or delayed. For example, when controlling physical models like steering an airplane or racing a car, how should the controls be adjusted so that the airplane or car follows a particular path? What sequences of actions should a real-time strategy AI perform to maximize its chances of winning? By providing rewards and punishments at the appropriate times, an RL-based AI can learn to solve a variety of difficult and complex problems.

Further Information

AI Game Programming Wisdom 2: [Manslow04]

Reputation System

A *reputation system* is a way of modeling how the player's reputation in the game world develops and changes based on his or her actions. Rather than a single reputation model, each character in the game knows particular facts about the player [Alt02]. Characters learn new facts by witnessing player actions or by hearing information from others. Based on what the characters know about the player, they might act friendly toward the player or they might act hostile.

Game Example

In a cowboy gunfighter game, the player's reputation might be very important. If the player goes around killing people indiscriminately, others might witness the killings and relay the information to whomever they meet. This would give the player motivation to either play nice or to make sure there are no witnesses.

Further Information

Massively Multiplayer Game Development: [Brockington03]
AI Game Programming Wisdom: [Alt02]

Smart Terrain

Smart terrain is the technique of putting intelligence into inanimate objects. The result is that an agent can ask the object what it does and how to use it. For example, a smart microwave oven knows what it can accomplish (cook food) and how it should be used (open door, place food inside, close door, set cooking time, wait for beep, open door, take food out, close door). The advantage of such a system is that agents can use objects with which they were never explicitly programmed to interact.

The use of smart terrain is enlightened by *affordance theory*, which claims that objects by their very design allow for (or afford) a very specific type of interaction [Gibson87]. For example, a door on hinges that has no handles only permits opening by pushing on the non-hinged side. This is similar to letting the objects themselves dictate how they should be used.

Game Example

The term *smart terrain* was popularized by the very successful game *The Sims*.

In *The Sims*, the objects in the game world contain most of the game's intelligence. Each object broadcasts to agents what it has to offer and how it can be used. For example, an agent might be hungry, and food on the table will broadcast "I satisfy hunger." If the agent decides to use the food, the food instructs the agent how to interact with it and what the consequences are. By using this smart terrain model, agents are able to use any new object that is added into the game either through expansion packs or from Internet sites.

Further Information

Google Search: <"smart terrain" sims>
AI Game Programming Wisdom 2 **CD-ROM:** [Woodcock03]

Speech Recognition and Text-to-Speech

The technology of *speech recognition* enables a game player to speak into a microphone and have a game respond accordingly. In the games industry, there have been a few attempts to add speech recognition to games. The most notable are Sega's *Seaman* for the Sega Dreamcast and Nintendo's *Hey You, Pikachu!* for the Nintendo 64. While these first attempts were somewhat gimmicky, they serve an important role by feeling out the territory for viable speech recognition in games, both in terms of the current state of the technology and the possibilities for enhancing gameplay. Currently, any game developer can incorporate speech recognition into their PC game through Microsoft's Speech API [Matthews04a].

Text-to-speech is the technique of turning ordinary text into synthesized speech. This allows for endless amounts of speech without having to record a human actor. Unfortunately, at this point in time, virtually no games use text-to-speech technology, perhaps because it sounds rather robot-like. In practice, it's more effective to record a human voice, especially since most games have access to enough disk space to store high-quality audio samples. The quality of voice acting in games has also risen in recent years, which makes text-to-speech less appealing. However, for some games, it can be quite entertaining for the player to enter his or her name and have the game speak it. For the right game, text-to-speech can be a novel technology that can set the game apart. As with speech recognition, PC game developers can use Microsoft's Speech API to incorporate text-to-speech into their games.

Further Information

AI Game Programming Wisdom 2: [Matthews04a, Matthews04b]

Weakness Modification Learning

Weakness modification learning helps prevent an AI from losing repeatedly to a human player in the same way each time. The idea is to record a key gameplay state that precedes an AI failure. When that same state is recognized in the future, the AI's behavior is modified slightly so that "history does not repeat itself." By subtly disrupting the sequence of events, the AI might not win more often or act more intelligently, but at least the same failure won't happen repeatedly. An important advantage of weakness modification learning is that potentially only one example is required in order to learn [van Rijswijck03].

Game Example

Within a soccer game, if the human scores a goal against the computer, the position of the ball can be recorded at some key moment when it was on the ground before the goal was scored. Given this ball position, the game can create a gravity well vector field that will subtly draw the closest computer players toward that position. This particular vector field is then phased in whenever the ball appears near the recorded position in a similar situation (and phased out when the ball moves away). This example lends itself well to many team sports games such as soccer, basketball, hockey, and perhaps football. However, the general concept is very simple and can be applied to almost any genre.

Further Information

AI Game Programming Wisdom **CD-ROM:** [van Rijswijck03]

Acknowledgments

Several people helped contribute to the ideas and knowledge within this article. In particular, John Manslow was a huge resource and influence. In addition, Jim Boer, Mark Brockington, Lars Lidén, Syrus Mesdaghi, Jeff Orkin, Steven Woodcock, and Eric Yiskis helped a great deal.

References

[AIISC03] "Working Group on Rule-Based Systems Report," *The 2003 AIISC Report*, AIISC, 2003, available online at *www.igda.org/ai/report-2003/aiisc_rule_based_systems_report_2003.html*

[Alt02] Alt, Greg, and King, Kristin, "A Dynamic Reputation System Based on Event Knowledge," *AI Game Programming Wisdom*, Charles River Media, 2002.

[Beal02] Beal, C., Beck, J., Westbrook, D., Atkin, M., Cohen, P., "Intelligent Modeling of the User in Interactive Entertainment," *AAAI Stanford Spring Symposium*, 2002, available online at *www-unix.oit.umass.edu/~cbeal/papers/AAAISS02Slides.pdf and www-unix.oit.umass.edu/~cbeal/papers/AAAISS02.pdf*

[Brockington03] Brockington, Mark, "Building a Reputation System: Hatred, Forgiveness and Surrender in Neverwinter Nights," *Massively Multiplayer Game Development*, Charles River Media, 2003.

[Buckland04a] Buckland, Mat, "Building Better Genetic Algorithms," *AI Game Programming Wisdom 2*, Charles River Media, 2004.

[Buckland04b] Buckland, Mat, "Genetic Algorithms in Plain English," *AI Game Programming Wisdom 2* CD-ROM, Charles River Media, 2004.

[Buckland04c] Buckland, Mat, "Neural Networks in Plain English," *AI Game Programming Wisdom 2* CD-ROM, Charles River Media, 2004.

[Champandard02] Champandard, Alex, "The Dark Art of Neural Networks," *AI Game Programming Wisdom*, Charles River Media, 2002.

[Evans02] Evans, Richard, "Varieties of Learning," *AI Game Programming Wisdom*, Charles River Media, 2002.

[Fahey04] Fahey, Colin, "Artificial Neural Networks," *AI Game Programming Wisdom 2* CD-ROM, Charles River Media, 2004.

[Fu04] Fu, Dan, and Houlette, Ryan, "Constructing a Decision Tree Based on Past Experience," *AI Game Programming Wisdom 2*, Charles River Media, 2004.

[Gibson87] Gibson, James, *The Ecological Approach to Visual Perception*, Lawrence Erlbaum Assoc., 1987.

[Houlette04] Houlette, Ryan, "Player Modeling for Adaptive Games," *AI Game Programming Wisdom 2*, Charles River Media, 2004.

[IDIS99] "Bayesian Networks," *IDIS Lab*, 1999, available online at *excalibur.brc .uconn.edu/~baynet/*

[Isla02] Isla, Damian, and Blumberg, Bruce, "Blackboard Architecture," *AI Game Programming Wisdom*, Charles River Media, 2002.

[Laird00] Laird, John, and van Lent, Michael, "Human-level AI's Killer Application: Interactive Computer Games," AAAI, 2000, available online at *ai.eecs.umich.edu/ people/laird/papers/AAAI-00.pdf*

[Laramée02a] Laramée, François Dominic, "Genetic Algorithms: Evolving the Perfect Troll," *AI Game Programming Wisdom*, Charles River Media, 2002.

[Laramée02b] Laramée, François Dominic, "Using N-Gram Statistical Models to Predict Player Behavior," *AI Game Programming Wisdom*, Charles River Media, 2002.

[Laramée04] Laramée, François Dominic, "Advanced Genetic Programming: New Lessons from Biology," *AI Game Programming Wisdom 2*, Charles River Media, 2004.

[Manslow04] Manslow, John, "Using Reinforcement Learning to Solve AI Control Problems," *AI Game Programming Wisdom 2*, Charles River Media, 2004.

[Matthews04a] Matthews, James, "SAPI: An Introduction to Speech Recognition," *AI Game Programming Wisdom 2*, Charles River Media, 2004.

[Matthews04b] Matthews, James, "SAPI: Extending the Basics," *AI Game Programming Wisdom 2*, Charles River Media, 2004.

[McCuskey00] McCuskey, Mason, "Fuzzy Logic for Video Games," *Game Programming Gems*, Charles River Media, 2000.

[Mommersteeg02] Mommersteeg, Fri, "Pattern Recognition with Sequential Prediction," *AI Game Programming Wisdom*, Charles River Media, 2002.

[Orkin04] Orkin, Jeff, "Applying Goal-Oriented Action Planning to Games," *AI Game Programming Wisdom 2*, Charles River Media, 2004.

[Rabin04] Rabin, Steve, "Filtered Randomness for AI Decisions and Game Logic," *AI Game Programming Wisdom 2*, Charles River Media, 2004.

[Snavely04] Snavely, P.J., "Empowering Designers: Defining Fuzzy Logic Behavior through Excel-Based Spreadsheets," *AI Game Programming Wisdom 2*, Charles River Media, 2004.

[Sweetser04a] Sweetser, Penny, "How to Build Evolutionary Algorithms for Games," *AI Game Programming Wisdom 2*, Charles River Media, 2004.

[Sweetser04b] Sweetser, Penny, "How to Build Neural Networks for Games," *AI Game Programming Wisdom 2*, Charles River Media, 2004.

[Sweetser04c] Sweetser Penny, "Strategic Decision-Making with Neural Networks and Influence Maps," *AI Game Programming Wisdom 2*, Charles River Media, 2004.

[Thomas04] Dale, Thomas, "The Importance of Growth in Genetic Algorithms," *AI Game Programming Wisdom 2*, Charles River Media, 2004.

[Tozour02] Tozour, Paul, "Introduction to Bayesian Networks and Reasoning Under Uncertainty," *AI Game Programming Wisdom*, Charles River Media, 2002.

[van Lent99] van Lent, M., Laird, J., Buckman, J., Harford, J., Houchard, S., Steinkraus, K., Tedrake, R., "Intelligent Agents in Computer Games," *AAAI*, 1999, available online at *hebb.mit.edu/people/russt/publications/Intelligent_Agents_in_Computer_Games(AAAI99).pdf*

[van Rijswijck03] van Rijswijck, Jack, "Learning Goals in Sports Games," *Game Developers Conference Proceedings*, 2003, included on the *AI Game Programming Wisdom 2* CD-ROM.

[Wallace04] Wallace, Neil, "Hierarchical Planning in Dynamic Worlds," *AI Game Programming Wisdom 2*, Charles River Media, 2004.

[Woodcock03] Woodcock, Steven, "AI Roundtable Moderator's Report," *Game Developers Conference*, 2003, included on the *AI Game Programming Wisdom 2* CD-ROM.

[Zarozinsky02] Zarozinsky, Michael, "An Open-Source Fuzzy Logic Library," *AI Game Programming Wisdom*, Charles River Media, 2002.

[Zarozinsky04] Zarozinsky, Michael, "Free Fuzzy Logic Library," *www.loudert-hanabomb.com*, included on the *AI Game Programming Wisdom 2* CD-ROM.

New Paradigms in Artificial Intelligence

Dale Thomas—AILab, University of Zürich

dale_thomas@hotmail.com

Nature is full of examples of many different types of intelligence, but most of them are unrecognized by *old school* AI. This good old-fashioned AI (GOFAI) focuses on reproducing high-level human cognitive abilities in a highly abstract way. There are, however, many problems with this approach. First, high-level human intelligence is only one type of intelligence, and GOFAI has not even come close to duplicating it anyway. The main problem with GOFAI was the assumption that if you can get all the high-level stuff, then the low-level stuff would be easy. That was a very big mistake. This article offers a different approach to defining what intelligence is, and how this New AI can offer many advantages when designing AI agents.

Central concepts will be discussed such as morpho-functional, embodiment, sensory-motor coordination, the symbol-grounding problem, ecological balance, and many more. Some of these ideas might have direct gaming applications, while others are simply a different way of looking at AI. As games and computer technology evolve, gamers are expecting much more from computer games, especially from their AI. *Believability* is the buzzword, and with increased computing power comes an increase in potential complexity. By being inspired by nature, agents can be made to appear much more natural. A respect for various types of intelligence and the methods being invented to implement them will offer great advantages for AI programmers and the games they make.

Natural Intelligence

Before beginning any discussion about AI, it is pertinent to say a few words about natural intelligence. Just what exactly is intelligence? Is it measurable, and if so, what type of units does it have? Is it a Boolean quality, there or not, or is it a continuous property, available in small, large, and larger amounts? Is it unambiguously definable? If we want to discuss something, a solid definition is very useful. The problem is that intelligence (like life) seems to have evaded a concrete definition since time immemorial.

Intelligence has always been a controversial topic and it still is, generating many intense arguments, which seem mainly to be definition problems. Attempts to measure it quantitatively have been tenuous at best. Some methods of measurement try to reduce it to a single number (like IQ), while others recognize that there are, in fact, different types of intelligence.

One aspect of intelligence, which is apparent in the NewAI philosophy, is the idea of looking at complete systems; that is, the study of intelligence cannot be limited to the brain. To understand an intelligent system, one needs to look at the entire system, which includes the brain, the sensors (and their placement), the body configuration (and its physical properties), and the environment with which the system interacts. Only by looking at the overall system can we begin to understand how and why intelligence arises.

The goal of this article is to introduce the main concepts of NewAI and how they can add to our understanding of intelligence. Some of these concepts are familiar techniques, while others are more like useful design principles. As regards to computer games, these techniques can add much needed adaptivity, unexpected behavior, and life-like attributes to agents. In the next section, we discuss GOFAI in more detail and discover some of its limitations. Following that is an introduction to some central NewAI concepts and, finally, a small discussion and some conclusions.

Old School Artificial Intelligence

We will not go into a deep historical account of AI, but if we are to talk about NewAI, we also need to know what GOFAI is. About 50 years ago, when computers were still new and huge, people began work on trying to automate many tasks. What soon became apparent was that the things that are easy for humans are very difficult for a computer, and vice versa. Finding the roots of a tenth order polynomial takes even a gifted mathematician some time, whereas a computer does it amazingly fast, while deciding if a piece of fruit is an apple or a pear is not trivial for a robot.

A pioneer of AI, Alan Turing proposed a test for AI: the Turing Test. If a computer can fool a human into thinking it is another human just by the answers it gives on the screen, the holy grail of AI will have been found. This seems now to be a fairly naïve, biased, and limited view of intelligence. First, human intelligence is admittedly spectacular, but why should it be the upper limit? There are many things we are unable to do and plenty of things computers and animals can do much better than we. Second, why should mastery of the English language alone be considered a huge intellectual achievement? A five-year-old child has a good grasp of language, not to mention many other types of intelligence: emotional, spatial, numerical, visual, and so forth. Therefore, if we are designing agents to be intelligent, we need a much wider view of intelligence. In an RPG, it might be nice to converse intelligently with a character on the works of Oscar Wilde, but in a shoot-em-up, witty retorts will not save a bot from your rocket launcher.

A nice example of GOFAI is chess. Fifty years ago, chess was considered a very intellectual pursuit. People said a machine could never play chess. Then it was done. Then they said that computers could never play amateur chess. Done. Play chess well. Done. Beat a master. Done, yawn. Beat a grandmaster. DONE. Finally, in 1997, IBM's Deep Blue computer beat the world champion [IBM97]. This is considered by many to be an amazing achievement, but now chess is considered just another formal domain rather than a real test of intelligence. No one would say that Deep Blue is more intelligent than Gary Kasparov. Deep Blue cannot tie shoelaces, speak Russian, or play poker. This just goes to show how transient and socially dependent our definitions of intelligence are.

Expert systems are GOFAI—a clunky system of thousands of "IF . . . THEN . . . " rules. Any new situation calls for a programmer to append many new rules, thereby making it clunkier. Semantic networks are GOFAI also. These are huge databases of objects and relationships. A DOG(object) HAS(relationship) a TAIL(object). The problem is: what *is* a tail? What properties does it have? People hoped that by making the database extremely complex and large, there might be some critical mass whereby intelligence would spontaneously burst into existence. No such luck. This is a critical flaw and is called the symbol-grounding problem—more on that later.

The philosophy of GOFAI seems to be to try to solve problems using mathematics, heuristics, and algorithms. GOFAI believes that we are better than nature because we can think in abstract terms; therefore, we can solve problems more efficiently. This works well in finite, formal domains (like chess), but completely fails in the most important domain: the *real world*. The real world has two main properties, which are the bane of all GOFAI approaches: it is continuous (in space and time), and it is noisy. Nature has solved many problems in this problematic domain. Therefore, more recently, researchers have humbly looked at nature for inspiration. This is NewAI.

New School Artificial Intelligence

NewAI is interested in the foundations of intelligence from the bottom up. Concepts like *emergence* are important when looking at natural intelligence: cells, brains, social insects, and so forth. In addition, complete systems are thought about and how they interact with and relate to the environment. Instead of putting human intelligence on a pedestal and trying to imitate high-level cognitive functions, NewAI researchers respect that all types of intelligence have an important part to play. Understanding how these intelligences are derived from organic mechanisms can lead to the development of more sophisticated techniques for AI.

Neural Networks and Genetic Algorithms

Most people reading this are probably somewhat familiar with some NewAI concepts such as neural networks (NNs) and genetic algorithms. These are two methods, inspired by nature, which can make a system adaptive; in other words, capable of learning.

Neural networks are abstract representations of the functioning of organic brains. They are called sub-symbolic because a piece of data flowing through an artificial neuron might not be a total symbol; for example, *DOG*. It might be a small piece of a symbol, which comes together later with many other such data elements into something meaningful. This makes the system much more tolerant of noise. Learning is accomplished by changing the way these sub-symbols are modified en route. Neural networks can be considered extremely good pattern recognition filters even in the presence of a noisy input signal. If that is what your system needs, there are many different types of NNs from which to choose.

The genetic algorithm (along with its sibling methods: genetic programming, evolution strategies, and simulated annealing) is a method inspired by the process of natural selection. Evolution seems to be a good designer and solver-of-problems; it is robust and adaptive. The idea is to have a population of solutions (perhaps enemy agents) and determine how good they are at the defined task (perhaps the task of blowing the player away with a shotgun while not being blown away). Then, the better solutions breed, in that they produce new child solutions, which contain a mixture of attributes from the two parents, just like the mixture of DNA you received from your parents. Repeat the process over many generations and the population becomes better at the task. Again, it is tolerant of noise because any solution that succumbs to the confusion that noise brings will eventually be eliminated (bred out of the population).

Both of these methods offer huge adaptivity and robustness; they are highly tolerant of change and noise. The main difference between them is the timescale at which they perform. NN learning occurs over the lifetime of an individual, but GAs progress over generations of individuals.

Frame of Reference Problem

Imagine you are sitting in a café, looking out the window at a woman walking down the street. She stops. Why? It is a mystery. You can make assumptions. Maybe she senses danger around the corner, maybe she is wondering if she left the gas on, maybe she heard someone call her name, or maybe she recognizes someone coming. Who knows? Well, only *she* knows. It becomes even worse if the subject is not human.

A biologist observing a mouse might say that a mouse stops because it detects cheese, or is frightened or tired, but how can we ever know? If we watch an ant scurrying around in a complicated path to its nest, we do not believe the ant remembers the complicated path [Simon69]. The path is a complicated emergent phenomenon. It is the result of the interaction of *simple* rules with a *complicated* environment. The ant's brain is quite simple, but the behavioral complexity is related to environmental complexity. An ant in an empty white room will have a very different path. In addition, if the ant is blind in one eye, or has only five legs, it will behave differently again. Therefore, we can say that sensors and bodies are also important in determining behavior. This is also true of artificial agents, simple or not. The AI designer *cannot* foresee the behavior of the agent, even if it is extremely simple. Therefore, the underlying point is that behavior is an emergent property resulting in the interactions of the agent with the environment. Read the next sentence carefully: *Behavior cannot be reduced to an internal mechanism.* This is the crux of the frame of reference problem [Pfeifer99, Clancy91].

Adaptivity

In the last section, we saw that an AI designer cannot predict how an agent will react in a particular circumstance and cannot predict all circumstances that an agent will come across. How, then, shall we design good agents? Well, nature's solution is to make them adaptive. We can consider three types of adaptivity: neurological, ontogenetic, and phylogenetic (brains, growth, and evolution). Let us look at examples of these three methods of adaptivity.

Neurological: Neural networks were introduced earlier as a method of system adaptation. These are simple abstractions of biological brains, which can exhibit learning and generalization. These have been used successfully in a variety of games, and there is a large community (academic and otherwise) continually improving and discussing these systems.

Ontogenetic: When we exercise, our muscles grow in response to repetitive use so we can perform the repeated task better. In addition, plants are continuously growing toward the light. This is a physiological response to the environment. Perhaps the flora on an alien world could grow in response to a player, better linking the player to the environment for more realism. Paths through a jungle could be a response to a playing style, not a path defined by level designers.

Phylogenetic: This means evolutionary adaptivity. Organisms are constantly evolving to compete with other species and survive. Genetic algorithms have also been used in a number of games, and have been proven to be a useful method.

Researchers have tried to include learning and adaptivity in GOFAI systems without much success. However, these biologically inspired methods perform very well at finding good solutions, and can make gaming systems adapt to the style or competence of the gamer. In the future, these techniques will possibly become more common in games, simply because they allow each game to be different, to adapt, and surprise.

Environment—Embodiment

The thing to remember about behavior (as we saw earlier) is that it is not something that is contained within an agent's brain. It is a complex phenomenon emerging from the interaction between the environment and the agent expressing itself through its body. What would happen if you suddenly made a large change to the agent's body, without changing the brain (or vice versa)? Well, it would behave differently. Perhaps the agent is sophisticated enough to detect the difference and compensate. Maybe it learns to adapt due to a neural network. What if you put the agent on ice, or soft snow, or sand? How would its behavior change?

The environment is an integral part of the intelligence feedback loop and cannot be ignored. An agent senses the world, decides what to do, and then performs the action. All the while, the environment is responding accordingly, by providing forces on the feet and changing its structure (perhaps a rock topples underfoot or sand gives a little). The environment is an adaptive system, too. Then, the agent senses the new situation and makes a new action decision (perhaps shifting its weight or lifting a foot higher). This is a continuous feedback loop. The point is that you cannot expect a system to be intelligent if it is just a brain-in-a-box with no interaction with the environment. This is what is meant by the term *embodiment* [Brooks90, Pfeifer99]. An agent needs to be inside the environment and interacting with it to be, or become, intelligent.

Morphofunctional

Human technology seems to focus on how hard, accurate, and complex we can build something, whereas nature seems to be the opposite [Vogel98]. Nature's design principle seems to be about how simple an organism can get away with being. Nature can certainly build hard materials, but it seems to go more for the soft stuff. This, of course, does have its advantages. If our fingertips were made from hard, rigid materials, gripping an object would be a great deal more difficult and require much more processing to apply enough pressure in precisely the right places for the object not to fall, but not too much that we damage it. As it is, our soft fingertips conform nicely to the surface. It is almost as if the materials themselves were doing much of the processing [Arimoto01]. This is a serious and valid way of looking at things.

Look at our arms. Our arms have more degrees of freedom than are necessary. For example, touch your nose with your index finger. Now, move your elbow all around without taking your finger from your nose. You will see that there is an infinite set of arm joint angles, which will allow you to touch the same point in space. The problem is, how can we calculate the most efficient set? This is a complicated mathematical problem called *inverse kinematics*. However, the nice thing about our arms is that they are bones with muscles, tendons, ligaments, skin, and other messy stuff wrapped around them. All of the materials have their own properties and rest states, so they will relax into an efficient configuration without needing complicated control.

The position of limbs and sensors is also something that nature uses intelligently, whereas we do not seem to acknowledge it very much. Some research is being done into the evolution of sensor placement [Lichtensteiger99], but it is still an underdeveloped research area.

These are the central concepts of the term *morphofunctional* [Hara00, Pfeifer99]. That is, if you give a little thought to the materials an agent is made of, its body configuration and sensor placement, you can eliminate a great deal of unnecessary control, and that has to be a good thing!

Passive Dynamics

Have you ever thought about how difficult walking is? It is very difficult, but we take it for granted every day. Our bodies are like inverted pendulums. The pivot is where our feet touch the ground, and our center of mass is somewhere around our lower abdomen. If you have ever tried to balance a pole from the bottom, you know it is quite difficult and needs constant control. How about walking? Walking has been described as controlled falling, which is somewhat true. When we walk, we have something called *dynamic stability*. This means that we do not fall over because we keep walking. If you suddenly locked your body halfway through a step, your frozen body would topple over because it is not statically stable in that configuration. It takes tremendous control to keep walking (as many robotics researchers will tell you), but we do it without even thinking about it.

Interestingly, although walking takes a tremendous amount of control, and although we have many muscles in our legs, we do not use those muscles permanently. We pull on those muscles in a very complex, closed loop sequence, which allows us to have very robust and efficient walking. In each step, we pull a leg forward, and then balance on this leg while the other swings forward with little control; that is, we reuse some of the potential energy we gave the now passive leg in the last half-step. Not only that, our tendons act a little bit like springs, storing energy from the last step in its tension and releasing it for the next step. Nature has found ways to exploit the material and physical properties of creatures to make locomotion more efficient. We could learn something here. In addition, we swing our arms to create a counter-rotation to the rotational forces created by our legs. This gives us smooth walking and is very important.

There have been many great walking robots built recently; one of the most famous being the Honda Asimo [Honda00]. It is indeed a marvelous feat of robotic engineering, but there are a few problems. First, the robot has incredibly heavy batteries that only last 40 minutes. This is due in part to the limitations of electrical batteries, but also due to inefficient use of power. Almost all motors are straining constantly, which also means that the gearboxes in the joints need to be replaced often. Second, the computational power needed to control the legs alone is incredible. If only some of the processing could be done by the materials of the legs (as we saw in the last section), much of the processing could be used elsewhere. Actually, a biped *robot* was built that can walk down a slight incline with absolutely no power or control, purely passive dynamics [Collins01].

Therefore, if we take a leaf from nature's book, and give some thought to the structure, materials, and intrinsic dynamics of a robot, we can build better robots. This is also true for agents. It is fair to say that locomotion efficiency is not an issue in a computer game, but something to think about is that a great deal of control for the

Honda robot goes into making smooth motion. For systems that exploit passive dynamics, the motion is automatically very smooth and life-like, and is achieved with much less control.

As more and more game developers begin to use physics engines, rather than techniques like motion capture, natural-looking motion generation techniques will become an increasingly important topic!

Symbol-Grounding Problem (Searle's Chinese Room)

Suppose you have a GOFAI system, which can understand natural language to a certain extent. Now, somebody says to it, "The cat sat on the mat." The system might be able to respond intelligently by breaking down the sentence grammatically (the subject noun verbed on the object noun), and linking the "cat" string to "mammal" and the "mat" string to "floor." The problem is that such a system does not *know* what a cat or mat is, it is just processing symbols. Such systems do have their uses and can become very complex, but they will never actually understand anything, which will lead to big mistakes because there is no common sense. A classic example is "Time flies like an arrow. Fruit flies like a banana." The two sentences are grammatically identical, but have very different meanings.

The renowned philosopher John Searle [Searle80] proposed the following thought experiment: Imagine somebody in a room, which has a huge library of Chinese character manipulation rules. Now, a piece of paper is passed into the room with some Chinese characters, meaningless to him. He follows the symbol manipulation rules in the books, writing down the result in different characters, and passes the piece of paper out of the room. To the Chinese person outside who fed in a question, and got an intelligent answer, the room is intelligent. However, to the man in the room, it was all without meaning; he just processed abstract squiggles. The point is, with this type of GOFAI system, all we can ever hope to achieve is cheap, fragile imitations of intelligence.

Some people believe that neural networks can solve this problem, because we have real biological neural networks in our heads, and symbols are grounded for us. That might be true, but we do not yet know how to connect a neural network up to achieve it. Creating a huge NN system and hoping for some critical mass whereby intelligence spontaneously bursts into existence is nothing more than wishful thinking.

The main problem is that we want to perform high-level operations on symbols, but the symbols being manipulated must have meaning. Harnad [Harnad90] proposed a hybrid system involving the high-level processing of symbols, but the symbols are grounded (they have meaning) by using neural networks to relate sensory stimulation patterns into symbols. Symbols must be related to sensory experiences somehow. Work continues and we are still far from a solution, but one day, we could have a game with non-player characters (NPCs) whose conversation skills and behaviors are intelligent and robust.

Sensory-Motor Coordination

Some mobile robots have very sophisticated mechanisms for performing navigation. These robots can wander around a building, without hitting the walls. The GOFAI approach was to take a snapshot of the scene with a camera, perform many image processing operations on the image (extracting lines, recognizing faces/walls/doors), decide what do, move blindly for two seconds, and then repeat the process. This is called a *sense-think-act cycle*. Eventually, the robot finds its way around. Nature does not do things this way. Animals are constantly moving and observing the environment in a completely closed-loop way. A bee knows that flapping its wings in a certain way will have a certain effect on its visual field. Sensory patterns are related to motor patterns *over time*. It is by learning these patterns that animals learn how to act in the world. The advantage of this is that a system becomes more robust to noisy sensors. In addition, the system has some control over what sensory patterns it experiences. This means that the agent can structure the inputs into something it can process easily, and therefore aids learning [Brooks90, Pfeifer99].

Ecological Balance

An important and extremely simple concept that seems obvious in hindsight but is surprisingly new is the concept of *ecological balance* [Pfeifer99]. This states that there exists a need for balance between the complexity of the brain, the complexity of the body, and the complexity of the environment. It is no good having an agent with an extremely large number of neurons if it has only two wheels and lives in a cardboard box. People always forget about an agent's environment and its interactions with it, but it is the most important consideration.

Self-Organization

Self-organization is about order arising from chaos. It all depends on the level at which you view something. An animal is a wonderful, intelligent machine made up of many different components (organs). The animal as a whole works very well, but cannot be explained just by looking at the individual components in isolation. Muscle, heart, brain, eyes, skin, bone, immune system, and many other components are all specialized subsystems that are all needed if the entire system is to function. Then, if you look at an organ—for example, the heart—you cannot explain its function simply by studying a single cell. Then, if you look at a cell, it is made of little proteins, and if you look at a protein, it is made of molecules, and so on. Moreover, going the other way, you cannot explain a school of fish just by understanding a single fish, and you cannot understand a biosphere by looking at a single species.

Therefore, the point of self-organization is that if you have a system with many *simple* agents interacting in a very *simple* way, its global behavior can be surprisingly *complex* [Steels95]. Look at the brain. An individual neuron is a relatively simple processing unit, but when billions of them work together, we get Einstein, da Vinci, and

Turing. A complex system's behavior is *more than the sum of its parts*. This is called *synergy*.

A famous example of self-organized behavior is Boids [Reynolds87, Reynolds01]. These are incredibly simple agents, which fly around in a flock, interacting with each other using three very simple rules:

- Move toward the center of the close neighbors (cohesion).
- Try to match velocity with neighbors (alignment).
- Do not get too close to any other boid (separation).

These are very simple rules and very simple to implement, but the resulting flocking behavior is surprisingly life-like and robust. If the flock encounters an obstacle, some boids might bump into it (they are really stupid), but the flock is relatively undisturbed and automatically sorts itself out. In fact, the flock will split into two, with half the boids going one way around the obstacle and the others going the other way and then reforming the large flock once past the object. If your game needs flocking or any other group behavior, the chances are that simple rules can achieve it.

Conclusion

In this article, we looked at traditional AI with a slightly critical eye. We praised nature and discussed how its inspiration can help in the design of agents. How can these concepts be implemented in computer games? Some perhaps can be included quite easily, while others might be irrelevant for games in the near future but become more applicable as the sophistication of game AI increases by orders of magnitude. Time will tell. We discussed the role of the observer in determining whether something is intelligent. Some people say, "If it seems intelligent, that's okay with me." For games, that is certainly good enough; in fact, that is the point.

Some people are very much of the opinion that nature has solved most of the problems we will ever have to face, so all we need do is copy natural systems. Others totally disagree, saying that nature is messy and noisy and that mathematics and logics can solve everything far more accurately and efficiently. The obvious area to research is the area in between. Both arguments are correct; nature has had billions of years and an entire planet on which to try out, test, and refine its solutions. However, nature is very much limited by the materials it has available (nature does not or cannot use metal), by the backward compatibility, and the fact that during evolution and the organism's lifetime, every animal needs to be viable. Human design has no such engineering limitations. This is also true for the design of intelligent agents. Nature created neural networks, which work very well, but that does not mean it is the best or only way to produce intelligence. Evolution can optimize and introduce adaptivity, but other optimization methods might be more effective for different problems.

So, by knowing of the different approaches, game AI programmers can choose the best technique available for a particular situation, be it an A* pathfinding system or a reactive neural network. A better understanding of the principles of intelligence and the standard techniques of AI will hopefully add an entire new dimension to game AI.

References

[Arimoto01] Arimoto, Suguru, et al., "Sensory Feedback for Secure Grasping by a Pair of Robot Fingers with Soft Tips," *Proceedings of the International Workshop on Morpho-functional Machines*, 2001, pp. 183–193.

[Brooks90] Brooks, Rodney, "Elephants Don't Play Chess," *Robotics and Autonomous Systems 6*, 1990, pp. 3–15.

[Clancey91] Clancey, William, "The Frame-of-Reference Problem in the Design of Intelligent Machines," *Architectures for Intelligence*, 1991, pp. 357–423.

[Collins01] Collins, Steve, Wisse, Martijn, and Ruina, Andy, "A 3-D Passive Dynamic Walking Robot with Two Legs and Knees," *The International Journal of Robotics Research 20(7)*, 2001, pp. 607–615.

[Hara00] Hara, Fumio, and Pfeifer, Rolf, "On the Relation among Morphology, Material, and Control in Morpho-Functional Machines," *From Animals to Animats 6*, 2000.

[Harnad90] Harnad, Stevan, "The Symbol Grounding Problem," *Physica D 42*, 1990.

[Honda00] Asimo, *www.world.honda.com/ASIMO/*

[IBM97] Deep Blue, *www.research.ibm.com/deepblue/home/html/b.html*

[Lichtensteiger99] Lichtensteiger, Lukas, and Eggenberger, Peter, "Evolving the Morphology of a Compound Eye on a Robot," *Third European Workshop on Advanced Mobile Robots*, 1999, pp. 127–34.

[Pfeifer99] Pfeifer, Rolf, and Scheier, Christian, *Understanding Intelligence*, MIT Press, 1999.

[Reynolds87] Reynolds, Craig, "Flocks, Herds, and Schools: A Distributed Behavioral Model," *SIGGRAPH Conference Proceedings*, 1987, pp. 25–34.

[Reynolds01] Reynolds, Craig, "Boids (Flocks, Herds, and Schools: a Distributed Behavioral Model)," available online *www.red3d.com/cwr/boids/*, 2001.

[Searle80] Searle, John, "Minds, Brains and Programs," *Behavioral and Brain Sciences 3*, 1980, pp. 417–424.

[Simon69] Simon, Herbert, *The Sciences of the Artificial*, MIT Press, 1969.

[Steels95] Steels, Luc, and Brooks, Rodney, *The Artificial Life Route to Artificial Intelligence: Building Embodied, Situated Agents*, Lawrence Erlbaum Associates, 1995.

[Vogel98] Vogel, Steven, *Cats' Paws and Catapults: Mechanical Worlds of Nature and People*, W. W. Norton & Co, 1998.

1.4

Artificial Stupidity: The Art of Intentional Mistakes

Lars Lidén
larsliden@yahoo.com

Everything should be made as simple as possible, but no simpler.

—Albert Einstein

What makes a game entertaining and fun does not necessarily correspond to making its computer-controlled opponents smarter. The player is, after all, supposed to win. However, letting a player win because the artificial intelligence (AI) controlling the opponents is badly designed is also unacceptable. Fun can be maximized when mistakes made by computer opponents are intentional. By finely tuning opponents' mistakes to be intentional but plausible, programmers can prevent computer opponents from looking unintelligent, while ensuring that the player is still capable of winning. Additionally, by catching, identifying, and appropriately handling genuine problems with an AI system, one can turn situations in which computer opponents would otherwise look dumb into entertainment assets.

A common mistake in designing and implementing computer game AI systems is that they are often over-designed. As an AI programmer, it is easy to get caught up in the excitement of making an intelligent game character and to lose sight of the ultimate goal; namely, making an entertaining game. As long as the player has the illusion that a computer-controlled character is doing something intelligent, it doesn't matter what AI (if any) was actually implemented to achieve that illusion. The hallmark of a good AI programmer is the ability to resist the temptation of adding intelligence where none is needed and to recognize when a cheaper, less complex solution will suffice.

AI programming is often more of an art than a science. Knowing when one can apply cheap tricks and when to apply more sophisticated AI is not always straightforward. For example, as a programmer with full access to game data structures, one can easily cheat by making non-player characters (NPCs) omniscient. NPCs can know where their enemies are, or know where to find weapons or ammunition, without seeing them. Players, however, often eventually detect cheap tricks of this type. Even if they can't determine the exact nature of the cheating, they might report feeling that NPC's behavior seems somehow unnatural.

A Few Tricks

Creating an NPC that can beat a human player is relatively easy. Creating one that can lose to the player in a challenging manner is difficult. The challenge lies in demonstrating the NPC's skills to the player, while still allowing the player to win. The following are a few tricks that allow a game to show off NPC intelligence and help to ensure that a game is fun. The tricks are primarily for the first-person shooter (FPS) genre, but some can be applied in other arenas.

Move Before Firing

Nothing is more disturbing than walking into a new room or arena and being immediately shot by a computer opponent. A player entering a novel location is likely to be overwhelmed with new textures, new objects, and new geometry. Trying to recognize the unique textures associated with an enemy in the morass of background textures is not inherently a pleasurable experience. This is particularly true as polygon and texture budgets have grown enormously. Any NPC attacks that take place during this time are aggravating. Such cheap shots should be avoided at all costs. In such situations, the player has no warning of the impending danger and often no way of knowing where the shot came from.

One of the simplest concepts for decreasing the frustration factor is that opponent NPCs should move the first time they see the player rather than shoot at them. Making an NPC run from a vulnerable open position into a location that is covered before attacking cues the player that a combat situation is about to begin. In situations with multiple opponents, it is usually sufficient to have only one of the opponents move as long as the remaining NPCs wait before attacking the player.

Cueing the player that combat is about to commence is particularly important in action-adventure and FPS games as they typically consist of two primary modes of play. The player is usually either in an exploratory/puzzle-solving mode, during which little or no combat takes place, or they are actively engaged in a combat situation. Warning players that they are about to enter combat mode is vital for game pacing as the player switches from a slow, deliberate form of game play to a fast-paced one.

Be Visible

Although in real-life combat situations, opponents do their best to remain invisible, in the game world great camouflage makes for bad gameplay. Pixel scrubbing while searching for opponents is not an enjoyable experience. Making opponent NPC textures high-contrast with the background allows the player to more readily spot enemies and start the real game experience. Opponents can still have camouflage-like patterns on their uniforms, but their color or brightness should contrast strongly with those of the environment.

Have Horrible Aim

Abundant gunfire is desirable, as it keeps players on the move and the tension high, thus increasing the pace of the game. However, abundant gunfire is undesirable if the player dies too quickly. One of the simplest tricks for dumbing-down NPCs and to amplify the pace of the game is to give computer opponents horrible aim. By doing so, one can have abundant gunfire without making the game prohibitively difficult for the player. FPSs often use a bullet spread as wide as 40 degrees.

Alternatively, one can reduce the player's difficulty by making opponent bullets do very small amounts of damage. However, in doing so, one loses some of the secondary benefits of bad aim. One of the fortuitous by-products of bad aim is the tension created by bullet tracers flying past the player's head or puffs of concrete dust or sparks exploding from projectiles impacting walls next to the player. Additionally, there is a feeling of reward imparted by having just been missed by a bullet. Players will often attribute near misses as an affirmation of their clever movement skills.

Miss the First Time

For weapons that do more damage, such as those that kill with one or two shots, something more than bad aim is required. In general, it is not fun to suddenly and unexpectedly take large amounts of damage. Players often feel cheated in such situations. One can alleviate this frustration by intentionally missing the player the first time. Doing so gives the player a second to react and maintains a high level of tension.

In addition, intentional first misses can be strategically placed. One of the irritating aspects of being shot from behind in an FPS is that the player has no idea where the shot came from. Several FPSs have attempted to alleviate this problem by adding screen cues (such as flashing red icons) that indicate the direction of attack. Such cues (usually justified as being part of a heads-up display) tend to break the illusion of reality and are surprisingly not as salient to players as one might expect.

Intentional misses, particularly those coming from behind the player, can alleviate this problem by indicating the direction of attack without breaking the illusion of reality. A laser beam or projectile with a tracer that is strategically placed to hit the floor or a wall just in front of a fleeing player conveys the direction from which the attack commenced. Additionally, the directional information conveyed by lasers or tracers is more informative than simple flashing screen cues, allowing the player to respond to the attack in a more appropriate manner.

Another valuable way to employ intentional misses is to hit particular environmental targets. For example, as the player nears a water barrel, porcelain statue, or glass vase, rather than aim for the player, the NPC aims for the nearest breakable object, preferably one that shatters as dramatically as possible. Remember, the goal of a good AI programmer is not to kill the player, but to create tension.

One final and more advanced use of intentional misses is that they give the game designer a method for herding the player. Carefully placed rounds of projectiles shooting next to the player can compel the player to move in a direction determined by game design.

Warn the Player

Another effective method to increase game enjoyment is to warn the player before attacking. This can be done visually, by playing a short "about-to-attack" animation, or aurally by playing a sound (a beep, click, etc.), or having a human opponent announce "Gotcha!" or "Take this!" before attacking. Aural cues are particularly important when the player is being attacked from behind. They give the player a chance to react to the attack without feeling cheated.

As humans in real combat situations would never pause to warn their enemies, one might think this would make the computer opponents appear to be less intelligent. To the contrary, such warnings can actually be used to draw attention to other more remarkable aspects of the AI. For example, an intelligent NPC can be programmed to discover routes to flank an enemy or locations to set up an ambush [Lidén02]. If the players are immediately killed as they fall into the ambush, they won't have time to comprehend their opponent's crafty tactics. The intelligent behavior will be more salient if the NPC makes a warning sound so the player has time to turn and see the NPC hunkering down in the clever ambush location before the player is attacked. If the ambushing NPC consistently kills the player, the game will no longer be enjoyable. Warning players gives them time to see the clever AI, yet have to time to react to it without being killed.

Another advantage with aural cues is that players readily become conditioned to react to specific sounds as long as they are consistent [Madhyastha95]. For example, if a particular phrase ("Gotcha!") precedes an attack, after enough occurrences, the sound will elicit a physical reaction in the player. Such conditioning can dramatically increase tension in a game. Furthermore, if the phrase "Gotcha!" is only used when an enemy employs a particular AI combat strategy (such as figuring out how to flank the player), after witnessing the flanking maneuver/"Gotcha!" pairing several times, the player will eventually infer that a sophisticated flanking maneuver has occurred even if it wasn't witnessed.

Attack "Kung-Fu" Style

In many games, the player is in the role of "Rambo" (in other words, one man taking on an army). Although for some genres, mowing down large number of enemies with single shots might be appropriate, opponents in such games are like lambs to the slaughter with little in the way of artificial intelligence. If our opponents are intelligent, however, then taking on more than a few at a time will prove to be too much of a challenge to the player. On the other hand, having many enemies makes for a more exciting, dynamic, and fast-paced game.

A solution is to design combat to occur "Kung-Fu" style. In other words, although many NPCs might be in a position to attack the player, only a couple should do so at a time. Others should occupy themselves reloading weapons, finding cover, or changing their position. No opponent should stay in a particular location for too long, even when the current location provides a good attacking position. By swapping who is attacking and keeping the opponents moving, a fast-paced combat situation is created in which the player is confronted by many enemies but only attacked by a few. Surprisingly, players confronted with this scenario usually don't realize that only two opponents are actively attacking them at a time, even when confronted with a large number of enemies.

Tell the Player What You Are Doing

When a player witnesses an NPC's actions, it can be difficult for the player to interpret what the NPC is actually doing. Is a running opponent going for cover, getting reinforcements, doing a flanking maneuver, or just running aimlessly trying not to get shot? Complex NPC behavior is often missed by the player. When this happens, an AI developer has done of lot of work for nothing. One effective way to overcome this difficulty is to literally tell the player what the AI is doing. For example, an opponent might yell "Flanking!" or "Cover me!" or "Retreat!" to his compatriots when performing an action. Such cues can be highly effective and often have the beneficial side effect that players assume intelligence where none exists.

React to Mistakes

Even the most sophisticated AI system makes mistakes; they are inevitable. If not handled correctly, they make NPCs appear to be dumb. By recognizing when a mistake has occurred and reacting to it intelligently, not only can the illusion of intelligence be preserved, but the mistakes can be turned into features.

Consider the computations required to accurately throw a projectile at a target. In a rich 3D world with moving objects (including other NPCs and the player), it's unavoidable that occasionally a mistake will be made despite sophisticated physics calculations. A grenade will bounce off another object or another NPC and land back at the feet of the NPC that threw the grenade. (Note that players occasionally make this mistake too!)

If we simply let the NPC stand there and blow himself up, the AI will appear to be pretty pathetic. However, if we recognize the mistake we can react to it appropriately. If the NPC that threw the misguided grenade covers his head with his arms, shows an expression of surprise and/or fear, and yells "Oh no!" it no longer looks like a failure of the AI. Instead, the mistake has now been turned into a feature, adding personality to the NPC, as well as humor and some interesting variety to the game.

Pull Back at the Last Minute

The goal of an AI system is to create excitement and tension for the player. The ideal is to have the player feel challenged, pushed to the edge, but still win the game. One trick is to directly architect the pushed-to-the-edge scenario into the AI. In this model, NPCs will attack vigorously until the player is near death. The performance of the player is monitored carefully so that the player's health or resources are pushed to the limit, but not beyond. Once the player has reached the edge, the AI will pull back, attack less effectively, and become easier to kill. After winning, a player experiencing this scenario really feels like he or she accomplished something. A caveat to using this technique is that the developer must be very careful that the players are not aware that they are being manipulated in this way. If the trick is perceptible, it unequivocally ruins the game-playing experience.

Intentional Vulnerabilities

Players learn to capitalize on opponent's weaknesses even when they are unintentional. Rather than allowing a player to discover such vulnerabilities, it is often better to design them into an NPC's behavior. For example, a running NPC might have to pause and prepare its weapon, taking longer to attack than a stationary one. An opponent attacked from behind might act surprised and be slow to react. Adding imperfection into NPCs' behavior can also make them seem more realistic and give them more personality. Occasionally, an NPC might fumble when loading a gun. One that knows how to avoid trip mines might occasionally run into one. Planned vulnerabilities make computer-controlled characters seem more realistic. Unintentional mistakes break the realism. Extensive play-testing is required to get the balance right.

Play-Testing

An AI programmer's most important tool is play-testing. Even for a developer with years of experience developing AI, play-testing is the only sure way to determine when one can use cheap solutions and when one must apply more sophisticated artificial intelligence techniques. One can't overemphasize the importance of testing naïve players' reactions to the artificial intelligence. Even expert AI developers are often surprised by the results of play-testing and the interpretation made by players.

The choice of play-testers is crucial. Play-testers should certainly not be members of the game development team and preferably not in the game development industry. Any knowledge of artificial intelligence techniques and tricks will influence the play-tester's interpretation of events. Second, the pool of play-testers must be large. There are two reasons for this. First, as adjustments are made to the AI, a fresh pool of naïve players is required. Play-testers who are used repeatedly will be biased by their previous exposure to the AI. Their interpretation of NPC behaviors and their playing techniques will be different than those of a naïve user. Second, as players vary widely in their skill set, it is important to use a large number of play-testers. Only one player out of 30 might find that fatal flaw in the AI that makes the NPC look dumb or easy to kill. The AI might look flawless when tested with only a handful of players, but get trashed when the game hits the larger market.

Play-testing should be done throughout the game development process, not just at the end of production. Determining what will be fun and challenging is a difficult and time-consuming process. Plan on throwing out ideas and starting from scratch multiple times. Additionally, it is important to allow some of the play-testers to play-test throughout the entire development process. Game players get better with time and are more likely to find loopholes in the AI over time. They are also more likely to see through AI tricks after playing the game for a prolonged period.

Multiple observers should be present at each play-test. During the session, observers should take notes about the in-game actions of the player as well as their physical reactions such as posture and facial expression. Notes should also be taken for questions to ask the play-tester, but questions should only be asked after gameplaying is complete. It is important that observers say nothing during the course of the play-test, even when the player runs into difficulty.

After gameplay is complete, the play-testers should be interviewed for their reaction to the game. What is important is to determine what the players think happened, not what AI was actually implemented. There is a tendency for players to assume that complex behaviors are happening when they are not. Conversely, players also fail to notice complexities in the AI. Ask the play-tester about the actions and intentions of the NPCs. Be careful not to ask leading questions. More sophisticated game engines will include a recording mode where one can play back the entire play-test session to the player and ask questions about his or her actions.

A Few Examples

A common mistake of AI developers is that of over-design. Often, a much simpler solution will suffice, and cheaper, more creative solutions turn out to be considerably better. As a first example, one area in which programmers often over-design is in developing squad tactics. Complex communication and relationships between combat units is often lost on the player and not necessary. Valve's *Half-Life* [Valve98] offers an impressive example of how simple behaviors can produce rich gameplay that capitalizes on players' impulse to assume intelligent behavior.

The marines in *Half-Life* used the "Kung-Fu" style of fighting, meaning that regardless of the number of marines that the player is fighting, only two are actually allowed to shoot at the player at any given time. No actual communication exists between the marines. Instead, each squad of marines is given two attack slots; if a marine wants to attack and both slots are filled, he finds something else to do (such as reloading his weapon or moving to a new attack position). When one of the attacking marines runs out of ammo, he releases the attack slot and goes into his find-cover-and-reload behavior. Then, one of the non-attacking marines, finding an empty slot, grabs the attack slot and starts shooting at the player.

A simple rule was added that whenever an attack slot opens up and there is more than one marine present, the marine vacating the attack slot should yell "Cover Me!"

Although there is no communication between the marines, the perceived effect is one of a marine asking for cover and another opening fire to cover him. In reality, an attack slot opened up and was filled by another marine who knows nothing about the one reloading.

During play-testing, it was discovered that occasionally when a player threw a grenade at a group of NPCs, *Half-Life*'s pathfinding algorithm was unable to find a path for all of the NPCs to escape. The behavior of remaining NPCs looked exceptionally dumb as they shuffled around trying to find a way out. Rather than redesigning the pathfinding system (a huge undertaking), Valve's solution was to detect when the problem occurred and play specialty animations of the trapped marines crouching down and putting their hands over their heads. This was very well received by play-testers, as it added to the character of the game.

Conclusion

This article discussed several important concepts. Developers' efforts in the arena of artificial intelligence are often so focused on making their computer opponents smart that they neglect to adequately address how the AI makes a game fun. The goal of a sophisticated AI is not to kill the player but to add tension, to control the pace of the game, and to add personality to nonplayer characters. Simple solutions are often better and more entertaining than complex artificial intelligence. By adding intentional vulnerabilities to NPCs, we can ensure that players capitalize on planned weaknesses in AI rather than discover unintentional weaknesses.

This article also introduced several tricks for creating AI systems that maximize the entertainment factor. However, it can't be overemphasized that even years of expertise developing AI systems will never be a replacement for extensive play-testing.

References

[Lidén02] Lidén, Lars, "Strategic and Tactical Reasoning with Waypoints," *AI Game Programming Wisdom*, Charles River Media, 2002.

[Madhyastha95] Madhyastha, Tara and Reed, Daniel, "Data Sonification: Do You See What I Hear?" *IEEE Software*, Vol. 12, No. 2, 1995.

[Valve98] Valve LLC, "Half-Life," 1998. See *www.valvesoftware.com*

1.5

Arcade AI Doesn't *Have* to Be Dumb!

Steven Woodcock—GameAI.Com

ferretman@gameai.com

As all AI developers know, it can be a challenge to write a PC game AI that manages to avoid looking dumb. There are unique challenges posed by writing an AI for an arcade- or handheld-based game with very limited RAM constraints (512K is fairly standard) on CPUs that are slow by PC standards. Many developers just want to throw in the towel and just do something quick and dirty—preferably something that builds off an existing code base and won't need much tweaking! As a result, we see games for these platforms that are sequels of sequels of sequels, or have more in common with the free *Java* games found on the Web portals than any PC- or console-based game.

Arcade games in particular usually address their flair for flashy graphics combined with limited memory and CPU by focusing on games that are, to be honest, generally pretty simple. A huge majority are simply shooters of one kind or another and feature enemies that simply "pop up" to engage the player according to a predefined script. Many take this approach one step further by placing the players on a "rail," in effect "dragging" them through the database to shoot at the bad guys as they scroll by. Difficulty levels are usually handled by increasing the player's speed through the database, increasing the strength of the enemy, and/or throwing more enemies at the player. There's not much room for giving players the feeling that they are controlling the experience, and not much need for AI of any significance.

This article covers three of the techniques we used at Real3D to try to solve these problems during our development of an arcade game for Sega named *Behind Enemy Lines* (*BEL*). *BEL* was a rail-based shooter rather similar to Sega's *Gunblade* in which the players are gunners riding on the back of a Hum-Vee being driven by a computer-controlled friendly AI. In general, we took three basic approaches to the game's AI: we made it *look* smarter, we made it *act* smarter, and we made it *be* smarter. Interestingly enough, most of our leverage came from the first two techniques.

Technique #1: Make It *Look* Smarter

A major advantage of rail-based games such as Sega's *House of the Dead* is that developers can push the graphics throughput of the hardware. By carefully scripting the player's move through the game database, developers can put every polygon possible on the screen at one time. Environmental elements and enemies can be turned off the instant they are out of the player's view, allowing designers to push the hardware to its maximum and giving the player a rich visual experience.

Unfortunately, this runs the risk of making the game a bit repetitive and rather predictable by PC game standards. Knowing that a given level will always begin with enemies leaping out from behind the barrels on the right, players can get their light guns ready and aimed at that part of the screen. It might not be fun, but it's what gets the score pumped up. And when it comes to the enemy AIs, they just plain *seem* dumb, since they generally don't need to know more than how to aim and shoot. After all, they're only expected to live about five seconds . . . how smart should they be?

We were faced with this problem during our development of *BEL*. While our customer was keen on the game being very repeatable (as *Gunblade* generally is), we knew that a North American audience would expect some surprises and variation from game to game. We elected to expand on the players' options by providing them with multiple paths through the database.

Solving the Problem

Fundamentally, our design for player paths through the *BEL* world was relatively straightforward. We constructed the game's database to allow for two alternate paths to follow any given path (our original design had three alternates, but memory and artwork constraints forced us to reduce this). Each individual path was stored in a simple PATHDATA structure that contained some basic data about the path in question. In turn, data on all of the paths was accumulated into a basic Path structure that mostly contained pointers to information relating to each path. It all ended up looking something like this:

```
/* Pre-defined Path Data */
typedef struct _pathdata {

    short   x_offset;    /* offset to x position */
    short   y_offset;    /* offset to y position */
    short   z_offset;    /* offset to z position */

    short   y_ang;       /* y orientation along next segment */

    short   delta;       /* amount of time (in frames) to reach
                            this point from the last point */

} PATHDATA;
```

```
/* Path Information */
typedef struct _paths {

    char        *name[20];      /* name of this path */

    short       num_points;     /* number of points in this path */

    short       startxang;      /* initial X orientation */
    short       startyang;      /* initial Y orientation */
    short       startzang       /* initial Z orientation */

    int         startx;         /* starting X position */
    int         starty;         /* starting Y position */
    int         startz          /* starting Z position */

    PATHDATA *ptr;              /* pointer to path data */
    PATHDATA *pNextPath;        /* pointer to next path */
    PATHDATA *pAltPath1;        /* pointer to alternate path #1 */
    PATHDATA *pAltPath2;        /* pointer to alternate path #2 */

} Paths;
```

Implementation was relatively simple, since the *BEL* world was (by design) full of things to blow up. For example, at the end of Level 1 we might place a machine gun tower covering the road with a squad of enemy soldiers at the base. The player's Hum-Vee roars down the road toward the tower. If the players ignored the tower and engaged the soldiers, they would use the default path pointed to by pAltPath1 to transition out of the level and proceed to their next path. If the players instead destroyed the tower, its destruction handler routine would set the pNextPath pointer to the alternate path indicated by pAltPath2. To make this appear seamless to the player, the tower would fall across the road and the player's Hum-Vee would veer onto the second path as if that were perfectly normal.

Positives and Negatives

It was amazing how replayable this one simple enhancement made the game. By providing the players with multiple paths through the *BEL* world, they gained the sense of actually traversing a larger, more interactive world rather than being simply dragged along a predefined path. It also gave the players a feeling of control over their environment, since they directly saw their actions alter the course of the game. Finally, and of most importance to this technique, the AI of the game was enhanced simply because the enemies seemed more reactive—they responded to the player's actions and received the benefit of the player giving them credit for being smarter than they actually were (always a bonus).

This all came at some cost, however. There was considerable strain on the artists to provide models for the alternate paths, and these paths had to be populated with additional enemies. There was additional play-testing and more opportunities for bugs to be found. On a memory-limited game, these were significant costs, and as a result we didn't implement alternate paths as much as we had originally wanted.

Technique #2: Make It *Act* Smarter

Another problem usually faced by arcade games is that they face a bit of a dilemma. If they provide the player with a single "boss" enemy to fight, he generally has to be ridiculously tough or the player will kill him too easily. If, on the other hand, there are several enemies on the screen, each one has to essentially amount to a paper tiger or their sheer mass will overwhelm the player. Some games even make certain enemies in the background invulnerable to the player's fire so they can't be killed too quickly.

Needless to say, when faced with this problem during our design of *BEL*, we wanted to find better solutions than these. After some discussion we found inspiration in the 1970s *Kung Fu* movies. If you've ever seen one of those flicks, you've no doubt noted that despite the fact that our heroes are surrounded by literally dozens of enemies, the bad guys obligingly line up and attack our heroes one at a time. We decided to take a similar approach in our game.

Solving the Problem

Implementation of a "*Kung Fu*" AI capability was tricky, given that our enemies were on predefined rails just as the players were. We needed to find a way to have every enemy be a plausible threat while drawing the player's attention and focus to a specific enemy who was, as we called him, the "Kung Fu Leader."

The following code is what we ended up implementing:

```
/* Do we need to pick a Kung Fu Leader? */
if (pKungFu == NULL) {

    /* yep */

    pKungFu = FindNearestEnemy(fDistance);

}

/* Have our Leader charge the player's vehicle */
if (pKungFu) {

    /* Modify the Leader's speed based on
       how close he is to the player */

    iSpeed = (min(KungFuDist, fDistance)/KungFuDist)
             * KungFuSpeed;

}
```

Execution was relatively simple:

- If there was no current Kung Fu Leader, the code would select the nearest enemy to the players and designate him as the new Kung Fu Leader. For efficiency's sake (and not shown here), the function `FindNearestEnemy()` only checked enemies within a certain "Kung Fu Distance" of the player.

- The Kung Fu Leader would then have his speed increased in proportion to his distance from the player, increasing if far from the player and then gradually ramping down if he got close.

The overall effect of this very small block of code was very similar to what one might see in the movies. Suppose the players have just entered a level and are being chased by a hoard of enemy jeeps. One jeep breaks from the group and rushes toward the players, eventually slowing down and maintaining a certain distance from the player, as if the enemy driver is trying to give his gunners a stable platform. The other jeeps are in the background firing away, but the players' main attention is on the enemy directly in front of them.

Positives and Negatives

This "Kung Fu" code gave us precisely the behavior we wanted while providing something clearly different from similar games. It also had the nice side effect of having some natural randomness due to slight variations in timing and distance at a given point in the game when the current Kung Fu Leader was killed. Play-testers told us that they felt that the game was engaging them selectively, a nice bonus we hadn't really counted on. In effect, the AI *acted* more intelligent than it really was.

Downsides mostly lay in the processing and selection of a Kung Fu Leader. Since this particular enemy tended to run right up to the player, it was generally dispatched fairly quickly, resulting in the game being forced to run through the previous code literally dozens of times per level. Constantly checking distance is relatively expensive, so this became a problem if there were several enemies on-screen at once. We solved that problem by selectively designating certain enemies as "Kung Fu Capable" while allowing others to act normally.

The other main downside is that the enemies sometimes acted *too much* like their counterparts in the movies, foolishly charging the players one by one instead of simply concentrating their firepower and destroying them. Careful play-testing combined with difficulty level balancing mostly solved this problem, or at least minimized it.

Technique #3: Make It *Be* Smarter

Most rail-based games, which drag the player through the database, generally feature enemies that are also on predefined paths. They activate at a given time and promptly race along their path, eventually either running out of sight of the player (and thus being immediately deactivated) or dying in a hail of gunfire.

One of the problems we faced in *BEL* was discovered as we were implementing the Kung Fu technique. Often, we had a mixture of enemies (jeeps, Hum-Vees, and helicopters) chasing the players as in any good car chase scene, exchanging gunfire merrily. Unfortunately, since the enemies were running along predefined paths, it wasn't too difficult for players to figure this out and determine that an enemy jeep was going to proceed along its path regardless of the amount of damage it was taking.

This was terribly unrealistic, of course, since in reality enemies taking damage would try to dodge and hide behind protection. While we couldn't really have vehicles involved in a high-speed chase hide, we decided we could make them *veer away* from the player's gunfire.

Solving the Problem

Figure 1.5.1 is a debugging view of a piece of the *BEL* database showing various enemy paths through the section.

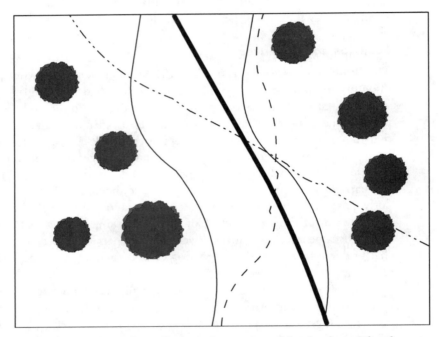

FIGURE 1.5.1   *Sample paths through a section of the database. The player moves on the thick path, while an enemy ATV moves on the dashed path and an enemy helicopter moves on the dash-dot path.*

In this example, Figure 1.5.1 shows a portion of the database in which the player runs down the thicker path in the center of the figure while an ATV moves along the dashed path and a helicopter flies along the dash-dot path crossing over the trees. Both the ATV and the helicopter have a Path structure as defined previously assigned to it, and they will follow those paths in time with the player in order to "chase" the player.

We decided that if we were to allow enemies to temporarily veer away from the player as if reacting to being wounded, they would appear more intelligent. This was relatively simple to implement:

```
/* Are we hurt? */
if (iDamage >= iVeerLevel) {

    /* Yes. Set our wounded timer. */

    iWounded = WOUNDED_FRAME_COUNTDOWN_TIMER;

    /* Compute Veer values and store for next frame's update */

    fXVeer = SIGN(x.position - player->x.position);
    fYVeer = SIGN(y.position - player->y.position);

}
```

Later, when processing a given enemy's movement, we simply apply the Veer values computed in the preceding code to its next position along the path to make it veer away from the player. We also check to see if it's time to cease this temporary reaction and move back toward our regular path:

```
/* Wounded timer still active? */
if (iWounded- <= 0) {

    /* We're done licking our wounds. */
    /* Compute Veer values to move back towards the player */

    fXVeer = SIGN(player->x.position - x.position);
    fYVeer = SIGN(player->y.position - y.position);
}
```

Figure 1.5.2 shows a zoomed-in portion of this path and illustrates what it looked like. At Frame 0 (most arcade games run at 60 frames per second), the enemy ATV takes sufficient damage to trigger the preceding Veer calculation code. This iWounded timer counts down until it reaches zero at Frame 360 (six seconds later), when the Veer calculations are reversed and the enemy ATV begins to move back towards its original path. It rejoins the path at Frame 720 (12 seconds after initially veering off in reaction to being hit).

Positives and Negatives

This enhancement really helped make the AI come alive. When an enemy took enough hits, he would suddenly veer off from the player and move away, as if temporarily stunned and licking his wounds. Since this could happen at nearly any point, there was a great deal of subsequent interaction with the player. It was easy to apply to any enemy we designated, not just ground vehicles—helicopters overhead could also move away if they took too many hits, and then rejoin the battle after a few moments.

There was an added bonus in that this feature, when combined with the previous Kung Fu code, automatically resulted in even more dynamic interactions with the player. If the enemy that was damaged happened to be the Kung Fu Leader, he would move off in apparent confusion. This would automatically move him farther away

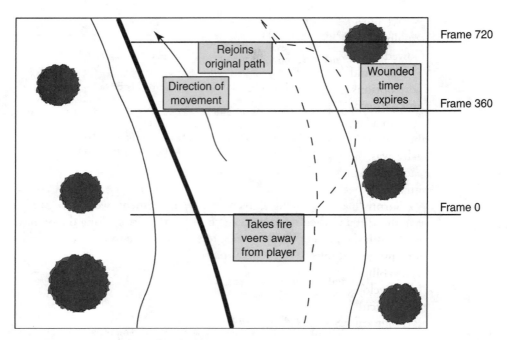

FIGURE 1.5.2 *Segment of path showing temporary veering.*

than some other enemy, and so a new Kung Fu Leader would be selected and subsequently rush up to engage the players. This made for a very natural and fluid combat situation, which was exactly what we were trying to achieve.

Of course there were some downsides limiting the utility of this approach, particularly on an arcade box with limited CPU. Enemy paths were carefully laid out during database design to avoid collision detection, which as game developers know is always an expensive proposition. By allowing vehicles to stray from their paths at an arbitrary moment, we automatically induced additional collision detection tests. These could be mitigated somewhat by reducing the amount of veer an enemy was allowed to induce, and by building the buffer zones around the paths large enough to accommodate most variations. Still, we were worried that we could easily find ourselves in situations where several vehicles were veering from their paths and (potentially) into each other. Fortunately, this rarely happened in practice.

Conclusion

During our development of *Behind Enemy Lines*, we found that the arcade world forced a number of restrictions on us that we'd never had to face before. We were desperate to avoid the pitfalls of similar games in which the AIs exist primarily to shoot the player for three seconds until they're destroyed; we wanted to provide enemies that acted more like real enemies would.

We found that we could use a variety of techniques to make our AIs *look*, *act*, and actually *be* smarter that didn't require too much memory or processing time and still allowed us to maximize graphics output (always a big concern in the arcade world).

AIs could *look* smarter by simply giving the player more choices, giving the player more options, and hence less opportunity to study the AIs on a given level. AIs could *act* smarter by forcing the player's attention to a specific enemy that would be giving chase in a fashion not unlike the real world, leveraging off of what the player expected and giving the AI just enough "smarts" to let the player assume it was brighter than it really was. Finally, AIs could actually *be* smarter by building in relatively low-cost reactions to the player's fire that were in line with what the player would do in similar situations.

Surprisingly, we saw most of our gains from the first two techniques, which shows that the difference between a good AI and a dumb-as-rocks AI doesn't have to be much. What mattered most was that the game's enemies ended up with smart, seemingly tough AIs that didn't act like they were pre-scripted, and that was a big boon to replayability overall.

Developers of arcade and hand-held platforms don't have to make their AIs simple, particularly in shooters. A few simple techniques and minor changes to the overall design can work wonders.

References

Since *Behind Enemy Lines* hit the market in 1997, it generally came and went long before there were many online references on game AI. As a result, most of our design came from either late-night brainstorming sessions or asking ourselves what other, similar games did.

Still, since the game came out there have been some articles about arcade AI and some of the techniques we used that might be of interest to the reader.

[Biasillo02a] Biasillo, Gari, "Representing a Racetrack for the AI," *AI Game Programming Wisdom*, Charles River Media, 2002.

[Biasillo02b] Biasillo, Gari, "Racing AI Logic," *AI Game Programming Wisdom*, Charles River Media, 2002.

[Snook00] Snook, Greg, "Simplified 3D Movement and Pathfinding Using Navigation Meshes," *Game Programming Gems*, Charles River Media, 2000.

[Woodcock00] Woodcock, Steve, "GameAI.Com," 2000, available online at *www.gameai.com*

1.6

The Statistics of Random Numbers

James Freeman-Hargis

paradox@this-statement-is-false.net

What happens to a predictable game? Patterns form in the gameplay, players learn to foresee outcomes, and their enjoyment of the game eventually lessens. Who wants to play a game when they know what happens at every step and they've seen it all dozens of times before? A logical solution to this is to introduce randomness into the game. Spice things up. Keep the players guessing. Let every time they play be a new adventure; keeping them engrossed playing it over and over to see what might happen the next time.

The use of random numbers, however, can be tricky. It's easy to fall into a few common traps, which can make unpredictability just as bad as regularity. With some insight into the nature of random numbers, their characteristics, how they're generated, and how to use them, these pitfalls can be avoided.

Probability Theory

Understanding randomness requires some basic probability theory. Assume we have a random variable; for example, the roll of a fair die. There is no certain way to predict what the result would be, thus it is a random event. An *experiment* is one roll of the die. Each such experiment has six potential *outcomes*. The *sample space*, S, is the set of all outcomes. In our experiment, the sample space can be written as:

$S = \{1, 2, 3, 4, 5, 6\}$.

Each number in the set corresponds to the count of the dots on a particular face of the die. Sample spaces can be represented by any appropriate information, but for the use of random variables, it is often easier to represent the sample space as numbers. The sample space for a coin flip, for example, can be written as:

$S = \{H, T\} = \{0, 1\}$.

Every outcome has associated with it a *probability*. The probability represents how likely an outcome is to occur. It is also the approximate proportion of times the outcome would occur if we were to repeat the experiment several times. There is an important distinction between empirical probability and mathematical probability. The former arises from observations of experimental data, while the latter arises from mathematical theory of what would happen in an infinitely long series of repetitions of the experiment.

In the case of the die and the coin, the mathematical probabilities are *uniform*. This means that each outcome in S is equally likely to occur. There are cases in which the outcomes have different probabilities, such as the normal ("bell-curve") distribution. Indeed, the uniform distribution is a special case, but, for our purposes, it is the most significant. If a sample space contains n outcomes, each equally likely to occur, then each outcome has a probability of $1/n$. In our die rolling experiment, S has six outcomes, each equally likely. The probability of each outcome is 1/6. This is the mathematical probability. An empirical probability would only arise from rolling the die repeatedly and tallying the results, and then calculating the proportion of occurrences of each outcome to the total number of rolls.

Outcomes and sets of outcomes form *events*. An event is usually denoted with a capital letter, such as A, and might be something as simple as "rolling a 1," thus encompassing only one outcome from the sample space. Alternatively, it can be more complex and contain a larger subset of S, such as "rolling an odd number." Each event has a probability associated with it, denoted $p(A)$. The probability of any event can be found by simply adding the probabilities of the outcomes comprising the event. For example, an event consisting of only one outcome, such as "roll a 1," has the same probability as that outcome (in this case, $p(A) = 1/6$). If the event contains more than one outcome, such as in the second example where $A = \{1, 3, 5\}$ and contains three outcomes, we see that

$$p(A) = p(1) + p(3) + p(5) = \frac{1}{6} + \frac{1}{6} + \frac{1}{6} = \frac{3}{6} = \frac{1}{2}$$

These, and all other probabilities, must conform to a pair of fairly simple rules:

- Any probability $p(A)$ must be a number between 0 and 1 (inclusive). An event with a probability of 1 will occur in every trial (in which the outcome is a possibility), while an event with a probability of 0 will never occur. An event with a probability closer to 1 occurs more frequently than one with a probability closer to 0.
- The sum of all probabilities of all outcomes in a trial must equal 1.

Discrete vs. Continuous

All probabilities discussed thus far have been "discrete": there have been finite possible outcomes. Continuous variables, on the other hand, have an infinite sample space containing all numbers in some interval, usually [0,1] (inclusive), although there are many distributions for which the interval is from negative to positive infinity. Because there are an infinite number of possible results, it becomes impossible to assign a probability to each outcome, as in the case of a discrete variable. Instead, we assign the probability in terms of area under the density curve, which defines the variable.

An event for a continuous random variable occurs when the variable falls within an interval of numbers rather than a single discrete number or set of discrete numbers. If X is the value taken by the random variable, then one possible example of an event could be:

$$p(0.2 \leq X \leq 0.5) = 0.3$$

The probability given, in this case, is for a continuous uniform distribution, between 0 and 1 (inclusive), in which all intervals of equal length have the same probability. Generally speaking, however, the probability of any continuous variable can be found by using the probability distribution function, which we'll call $f(x)$.

$$p(a \leq X \leq b) = \int_{a}^{b} f(x)dx$$

The probability distribution function has rules similar to those of discrete variables:

- $f(x)$ must be non-negative, greater than or equal to 0. $f(x)$ can go above 1, as long as the following rule still holds.
- The integral of the density $f(x)$ over the entire interval is equal to 1. This is directly analogous to the total sample space probability for discrete variables.

Generating Random Numbers

So, how does one actually generate random numbers on a computer? There are more methods than can be detailed here. Some of these methods are quite good, while others are horrid. Of course, the definition of a "good" random number generator (RNG) depends entirely on what you plan to use it for. Applications in cryptography have (and for good reason) far more stringent requirements for an RNG than video games.

First, it's important to note that computers do not, in fact, generate random numbers. The only source of true random numbers is a natural phenomenon (the classic example being radioactive decay). Most computer random numbers are the result of a deterministic algorithm. If the algorithm is a good one, the numbers can appear random. However, they aren't random at all since they're being calculated from previous numbers. Because of this, we call these "pseudo-random" number generators (PRNG).

There are ways to include true random numbers in your applications, but they are mostly impractical. There is hardware on the market that will generate thousands of random numbers each second. The problem with this is that not everyone has such hardware, so your program shouldn't rely on them. Another option might be to create a table of true random numbers by recording an external source. However, tables large enough to be satisfactory as a random number generator take up too much memory. Alternately, tables not loaded into memory would have to be stored in external files and could be too slow to load for your application.

One possibility for including true-ish random numbers is to use various aspects of user interaction. This requires only hardware that is already present, be it mouse, keyboard, or video game controller. It is possible to sample user input and use values (which key is pressed?), positional data (where is the mouse?), or timing data (how long has it been since the last interaction?) to generate random numbers [Isensee01]. They aren't *exactly* true random numbers, since people will likely have patterns in the way they interact with your program, but they will be more random than a deterministic algorithm. The downside to this is that sampling user input is slower than a PRNG and will probably have some bias, so getting usable values can be tricky [McGraw00].

True random numbers have another downside. With the exception of storing the random numbers in a table, the numbers are not reproducible. PRNGs, on the other hand, are reproducible. They start with a single number, called the *seed*. The PRNG uses the seed to generate every other number in the sequence. The desirable characteristics of a PRNG are as follows:

- **Reproducibility:** If we know the original seed, we can reproduce the entire stream of numbers [Lecky-Thompson00]. This can assist with debugging potential problems with our PRNG. One option is to seed the PRNG with a true-random number to make the entire sequence seem "more" random. A common practice is to seed the PRNG with the system time, as it is a perfectly acceptable arbitrary number.
- **Efficiency:** True random numbers are slow and can occupy too much memory. PRNGs are much faster and store relatively few variables.
- **Long Period:** PRNGs repeat after a number of steps, which varies depending on the generator used. A good PRNG will have a period long enough that you will never need more numbers than its period, so it will never need to repeat.
- **Statistical Acceptance:** PRNGs do not generate random numbers, but they can appear random. Statistical tests exist that test for uniformity and independence. Uniformity ensures that each possible value has the correct probability. Independence ensures that one value does not affect the probability of another value. Note that the latter condition is difficult for many PRNGs because each subsequent value is determined by the previous value.

Linear Congruential PRNG

Many algorithms out there claim to generate random numbers. By far the most common are variations of the Linear Congruential method. These are surprisingly simple formulae consisting only of basic arithmetic operations. However, enough theory and study has been invested in these generators that they are good for general use. The basic formula is:

$$x_{n+1} = (ax_n + c) \bmod M$$

The variables, a, c, and M are all constant and pre-chosen. All should be unsigned integers. Much theory has gone into making good choices for these constants. The longest possible period (the amount of numbers generated before repeating) cannot exceed M. The generator gives some permutation of the set $\{0, 1, \ldots, M-1\}$. The seed, x_0, is the starting point of the generator and determines which sequence of numbers is returned. Passing the same seed into the same generator will yield the same sequence. The term "mod M" in the equation means we divide the result $(ax_n + c)$ by M and take the remainder. Thus, every generated number is between 0 and $M-1$.

Not all generators of this form have the maximum period. The choices of constants determine the period, and some choices are much better than others. For convenience sake, many people choose M to be 2^b, where b is the number of bits in an unsigned integer. Modulus division is a relatively slow operation, but if the value of M is taken to be this convenient value, the modulus operation is trivial to implement and can be excluded. If the result is over M, the computer discards the overflow so that what remains is exactly b bits and the hardware has performed the mod operation for us without additional computational cost. There are arguments against the use of 2^b as a value for M [Knuth81], but for games, it should be good enough.

Assuming we have selected a value for M, which need not be 2^b but which should definitely be a large number, we must choose our values of a and c to achieve a maximum period. In general, for any M, a and c must meet the following criteria:

- c is relatively prime to M; the greatest common divisor of c and M must be 1.
- For all prime factors, p, of M, p must also be a factor of $a-1$.
- 4 must be a factor of $a-1$ if 4 is a factor of M.

If we take M to be 2^b, then this can be simplified to the following two conditions:

$$a = 4k + 1$$
$$c = odd$$

ON THE CD

where k is some positive integer. You can find a demo of this Linear Congruential PRNG on the accompanying CD-ROM.

Multiplicative Generator

There is a special case, when $c=0$, that should be mentioned. Linear Congruential generators of this form are called "multiplicative generators." They are slightly faster because there is no addition in the equation. They can be tricky to use, however. If any number in the sequence is a 0, every number after will also be 0. That's not very random. Thus, a multiplicative generator cannot have a maximum period of M. It can come close with good choices of a and x_0. If M is 2^b, the maximum period is $M/4$ = 2^{b-2}. This can be achieved if the seed (x_0) is an odd number and a constrains to the equation:

$$a = 8k \pm 3$$

Again, k is some integer. A demo of this Multiplicative Generator method is also included on the accompanying CD-ROM.

Additive Generator

Another method, similar but more complex than the Linear Congruential methods, is the combination or additive generator. A basic version of this generator, the Mitchell Moore algorithm, can be found on the accompanying CD-ROM. The equation is as follows:

$$x_n = (x_{n-24} + x_{n-55}) \bmod M$$

where n is some number greater than 55 [Knuth81]. The values x_0 through x_{55} are stored as an array. This is faster than the previous generators because it uses no multiplication. Moreover, it has a significantly longer period for similar M values. The only downside is that it requires the storage of an array of values, which can be a disadvantage.

Randomization by Shuffling

Some of the previously described methods might not be sufficiently random for some applications. To improve randomness, shuffling can be employed. This procedure puts a section of a random sequence into an array and then uses the outcome of the generator to select random elements of the array, which are then replaced. Although, like the additive generator discussed previously, it requires a table of values to shuffle, it has the potential to improve the randomness of a generator. A demonstration of shuffling can be found on the accompanying CD-ROM.

Randomization within Numbers

Let's suppose you've generated a sequence of numbers. If you used any of the previous generators, the resulting numbers are unsigned integers between 0 and $M-1$. What if you happen to need a number in another interval? Setting M to something lower is a mistake, since that would reduce the generator's period. Using the modulus operator (% in C/C++) to force it into a given interval is a common practice, but is also a mistake because it returns the least random bits of the number; thus, the outcome isn't very random.

There are alternatives. One method is to convert the integer into a real number (type float or double in C/C++). If you divide the random number, x, by the modulus

M–1, you get a number, call it y, in the interval [0,1] (inclusive). Multiplying this resulting real number by some constant K will return a real number in the range [0,K]. This provides more randomness in the desired interval than the use of the modulus operation (%K). Adding a constant, T, will return a number in the range [T, $K+T$].

Another option is to circular shift the bits of the number. What this means is that the bits are shifted off the left and back onto the right of the number. Then, the rightmost bits are no longer the least significant and the entire result has been mixed around. It is then safer to use the modulus operation. If a random number of bits are shifted around each time, this can greatly improve the randomness of your generator.

Another way to improve the randomness of a given number is to take bits from two numbers and mix them together. You might use the leftmost bits from one and the rightmost of another, or just use the most random (leftmost) of two numbers to generate one. The Mersenne Twister generator [Matsumoto96] makes use of bit-concatenation (in conjunction with several other methods). It is quite possibly the best generator available, since it is fast and has an astronomically large period while still generating numbers that fit into an unsigned integer. The Mersenne Twister is included on the accompanying CD-ROM.

ON THE CD

Statistical Methods

Now we have a PRNG, but how random are the numbers it generates? If it is to be a fair replacement for true random numbers, the resulting values should be both uniform and independent. There are a slew of tests out there, more than can be detailed here, but in general they are just different methods to test for one of these two characteristics.

Expectation

Expectation is significant in the study of random variables. While one might hear the term "expected value," it's misleading. If a random variable has an expected value of 0.5, as is the case with a uniform number, we don't expect the random variable to take on that value every time—that wouldn't be random. What it means is that, in the long run (after a very large number of experimental trials), the mean of the observed values will be very close to the expected value. After an infinite number of observations, the two would be equal. This is also called the "Law of Large Numbers." Formally, as the number of random observations increases, the sample mean (the mean of the observations) approaches the population (true) mean.

The expected value of a random variable X is denoted $E(X)$. For a discrete random variable, with n possible outcomes in the sample space; and for a continuous random variable, where [a,b] is the variable's interval, $E(X)$ is (respectively):

$$\mu = E(X) = \sum_{i=1}^{n} x_i p(x_i)$$

$$\mu = E(X) = \int_{a}^{b} xp(x)dx$$

In both cases, these equations can be summarized as the weighted mean of the variable X in which the probabilities, $p(x)$, of the outcomes are considered in the mean. As the number of random samples increases, the mean of these samples should converge on the expected value. How close it is can be determined by examining another value, the variance $Var(X)$, which can be calculated as follows:

$$Var(X) = \sum_{i=1}^{n} (x_i - \mu)^2 p_i$$

$$Var(X) = \int_{a}^{b} (x - \mu)^2 p(x)dx$$

ON THE CD

A formal test of these values using the t and f statistical tests can be found on the accompanying CD-ROM.

Chi-Square Frequency Test

The simplest test for uniformity is the frequency test, which there are two major methods for performing: the Chi-Square test and the Kolmogorov-Smirnov test. Of the two, the former has the benefit of simplicity. It divides the interval [0,1] into k equal-length subintervals (bins). A stream of N uniform random numbers (on [0,1]) is generated, and we count the values that fall into bin i (C_i). If the numbers are truly uniform, we would expect to see the same count for each bin: N/k. This is the expected count, E_i. We want N to be large, usually such that $N/k \geq 5$. Then, we calculate the chi-square statistic as follows:

$$\chi^2 = \sum_{i=1}^{k} \frac{(C_i - E_i)^2}{E_i}$$

We want this value to be fairly small. How small, exactly, is dependent on the chi-square value and our value of k. Then, we compare the chi-square value against the chi-square distribution (from a table, or by calculation) with $k-1$ degrees of freedom. If the computed chi-square value is less than or equal to the value in the table, the generator passes the test. It is important to note that if a PRNG passes this test, it doesn't mean the numbers are random; it must still be tested for independence.

Runs Test

Probably the simplest test for independence takes the form of the runs test. The runs test takes a sequence of numbers and partitions it into upward runs and downward runs.

An upward "run" is a series of numbers in which each number is greater than the last. A downward run is the reverse: a series in which each number is less than the previous.

To perform this test, one calculates the mean and variance of the total number of runs (up and down) and then calculates a Z statistic. The mean, variance, and Z-statistic are as follows:

$$\mu = \frac{2N - 1}{3}$$

$$\sigma^2 = \frac{16N - 29}{90}$$

$$Z = \frac{a - \mu}{\sigma}$$

N is the length of the number sequence and should be large; a is the total count of runs (up or down). We can then compare this Z-value to a *standard normal distribution* in a manner similar to the chi-square comparison shown previously.

PRNG Test Suites

In addition to the few tests described here and included on the CD-ROM, there are several programs available that run a variety of tests on a stream of random numbers. Two such programs, perhaps the best known and most widely used, are "ENT" [Walker98] and "Diehard" [Marsaglia96]. Both source code and executables are freely available for each of these packages and can be downloaded from their respective Web sites; a copy of ENT has also been included on the CD-ROM.

ON THE CD

How Good Is rand()?

The rand() function can be used with varying success. This is largely because rand() itself is inconsistent in implementation. Although it is expected to conform to the standard, there are only two minor requirements: it must produce an integer between 0 and RAND_MAX, and the latter value must be at least 32767. The standard does include an implementation of rand(). It is merely an example, however, allowing anyone to invent his or her own generator, as long as it conforms to the criteria.

As a result, its behavior might be inconsistent on different systems, which can cause trouble if your code is intended for multiple platforms. To make matters worse, not all varieties of rand() are actually good. For many implementations, the numbers generated seem less than random and fail many statistical tests. Other implementations, however, can perform fairly well. If you intend to use rand(), you should subject it to a barrage of statistical tests before assuming that it's a good random number generator.

One of the strengths of using a PRNG, the ability to reproduce a stream of numbers, is only marginally present in rand(). The function srand() is provided to allow the user to seed the PRNG, but this does not necessarily return the generator to the desired state. The function maintains an internal state of 32 bits, and the 15-bit return value (in the cases where RAND_MAX is defined to be 32767) is an insufficient representation of the generator's state. This means that rand() cannot be reliably re-seeded, thus eliminating one of the advantages of using a PRNG [Dawson01].

While rand() is convenient, it might not perform as well as you would like. As with any generator you intend to use, it should be tested thoroughly before it's put into use. Even if it does perform particularly well, you might consider using another generator; one that you know will behave the same on all platforms and you can reliably re-seed.

Getting Values You Want: Non-Uniform Numbers

Everything discussed so far has assumed the values are in a uniform distribution. The tests examined even try to ensure that the generated numbers conform to that distribution. There are cases, however, in which the uniform distribution just isn't appropriate for your needs. Consider, for example, a game entity in combat with the player: Do you want it to be equally likely to flee from combat as it is to fight, or would you rather it have a tendency toward one or the other? Perhaps you have a genetic algorithm in which certain characteristics should be more likely to mutate than others. These effects can be achieved using non-uniform numbers.

It is possible to generate variables from other distributions in which certain values are more probable than others. These distributions are usually obtained by some function on a uniform variable in the interval [0,1], so having a reliable uniform RNG is required.

Normal (Gaussian) Distribution

Probably the most significant distribution in statistics is the standard normal distribution with a mean of 0 and a standard deviation of 1, denoted N(0,1). Because of its significance, and because the normal distribution can be used to generate other distributions, it will provide our demonstration. By no means is the normal distribution the only one able to be generated. A random number can be generated from any distribution, with appropriate computation.

Several methods have been developed that generate random variables from an N(0,1) distribution, but we'll look at one in particular—the Box-Muller method. The following code snippet generates two normal random variables by use of the "polar method." Assume, in the following code [Carter01], that the function uniform() generates a uniform random variable on the interval [0,1].

```
double u1, u2, w, n1, n2;
do {
    u1 = 2.0 * uniform() - 1.0;
    u2 = 2.0 * uniform() - 1.0;
    w = u1 * u1 + u2 * u2;
} while ( w >= 1.0 );
```

```
w = sqrt( (-2.0 * ln( w ) ) / w );
n1 = u1 * w;
n2 = u2 * w;
```

We obtain two independent normal random numbers n1 and n2. This can be useful if you want a given value to occur more frequently than others. The most probable value, which occurs at the mean, can be used to trigger the entity's more likely action or mutate the more volatile traits. Likewise, the less probable values, which occur at the tails of the distribution, can be used to trigger the less likely actions or mutate the more stable traits of genetic code. As gameplay progresses, and perhaps the entity is wounded, it might become more likely to flee. By simply shifting the result of the random numbers, by adding a constant, the mean shifts with it and thus the actions as well (see Figure 1.6.1).

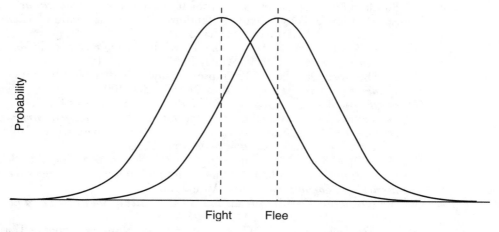

FIGURE 1.6.1 *Shifting the mean of the curve can change the likelihood of certain actions.*

Conclusion

It is essential to use random numbers in game AI. Before doing so, it helps to understand the method used to generate them and to ensure that the numbers are random enough. Although convenient, rand() should not be used. There are linear congruential generators with better choices of constants that can be employed instead. Beyond that, there are other methods that are even more effective, such as the Mersenne Twister. Regardless of what you choose, run statistical tests to ensure that the generator you're using appears random.

Don't forget to take advantage of the key benefit of using pseudorandom numbers instead of true-random numbers: reproducibility. The seed value of your chosen PRNG can be used to debug any potential problems in your PRNG, and to find potential bugs in your game engine or AI system. Once it has been tested extensively, you can seed the generator with truly random numbers obtained from random user interaction.

The methods described here, both for the generation and testing of random numbers, only scratch the surface. The Internet is a perfect place to look for more information on a given topic, or you can visit *www.this-statement-is-false.net* for additional resources and links to other pages about random number generation.

References

[Carter01] Carter, Dr. Everett, "Generating Gaussian Random Numbers," available online at *www.taygeta.com/random/gaussian.html*, 2001.

[Dawson01] Dawson, Bruce, "Game Input Recording and Playback," *Game Programming Gems 2*, Charles River Media, 2001.

[Hellekalek02] Hellekalek, Peter, et al., "pLab: A Server on the Theory and Practice of Random Number Generation," available online at *crypto.mat.sbg.ac.at/*, 2002.

[Isensee01] Isensee, Pete, "Genuine Random Number Generation," *Game Programming Gems 2*, Charles River Media, 2001.

[Knuth81] Knuth, Donald Ervin, *The Art of Computer Programming Vol. 2: Seminumerical Algorithms*, Addison-Wesley Publishing Co., 1981.

[Lecky-Thompson00] Lecky-Thompson, Guy, "Predictable Random Numbers," *Game Programming Gems*, Charles River Media, 2000.

[Marsaglia96] Marsaglia, George, "Diehard: A Battery of Tests for Random Number Generators," 1996, available online at *stat.fsu.edu/~geo/diehard.html*

[Matsumoto96] Matsumoto, Nishimura, "Mersenne Twister," available online at *www.math.keio.ac.jp/~matumoto/emt.html*, 1996.

[McGraw00] McGraw, Gary, and Viega, John, "Make Your Software Behave: Software Strategies," available online at *www-106.ibm.com/developerworks/security/library/s-randomsoft/index.html*, April 2000.

[Moore99] Moore, David, *Introduction to the Practice of Statistics*, Third Edition, W.H. Freeman and Company, 1999: pp. 289–359.

[Walker98] Walker, John, "ENT: A Pseudorandom Number Sequence Test Program," 1998, available online at *www.fourmilab.ch/random/*

1.7

Filtered Randomness for AI Decisions and Game Logic

Steve Rabin—Nintendo of America Inc.

steve@aiwisdom.com

Probability theory and random numbers are strange beasts. Take, for example, a woman who gives birth to eight boys in a row. As humans, we are amazed and bewildered when we see anomalies such as this, even though we know it's perfectly probable. The truth is that there is a big difference between what randomness can create and what humans will perceive as being random.

The problem is that over the short term, we somehow expect random numbers to randomly result in an average distribution. When we get cases like eight heads in a row from eight coin flips, we start to wonder if there is something wrong with the coin. In games, this might manifest itself as an enemy in a first-person shooter (FPS) picking the same spawn point five times in a row, or in an AI with a 10-percent chance of hitting the player scoring four direct hits one right after another. We don't want these outcomes, yet random numbers allow for these possibilities. Although rare, players notice these events and will wonder if the game is broken.

This article presents some algorithms for creating random numbers that seem more random over the short term to players. In reality, we are making the numbers slightly less random, but players will recognize the outcomes as more likely to have been produced by a random process—devoid of any bewildering or annoying anomalies.

The Coin Flip: The Problem with Random Numbers

The problem with random numbers is most obvious in the coin flip. The following are the results of a fair coin (a penny) flipped 300 times:

```
0111100010010010011101100101110101001011110011000011010001111111110100
0110111010011111110110111010110101111101100010110010001110111011110100
1111000111110111011011111110000001000001010110000001010011011111010100
1010100000000001011100100111101000010000111000111111111011100010011010
0110001100011000100011100
```

If you don't trust my coin flipping, then here are the first 300 results of `rand()%2` from a generation of 10,000 (which scored extremely high on randomness benchmarks):

01011000110100011110111100011101101101111111000101000010010000101101 0
01010001001001111011000010110100010001100000000010111101111110101101 1
00110111111000000110000011111111100111101110011011011011110111110100 11
01101101111010101001100011011100101011100000100011000100010001010000 0
1111011000001101001100 10

Now, stare at these lists of numbers and count the number of women who just gave birth to five girls in a row or eight boys in a row. When you focus on a small segment of the numbers, they don't seem very random—that's the problem with random numbers. Now examine the following filtered list of 300 random Boolean numbers:

01010100010100011011001010010010100101110010111010110100010001101010 11
10101110100110001010110110010101000110010010101110101011001000110110
10101100010110001101010101010001101101100101001000110110101011001110 01
10110101011011100111010110101001100010100110110101011000110111001010 1
001011100101110100101101

These numbers have been filtered to appear more random. Not only do they seem more random over the short term, they will produce better results in your game since there won't be a run of the same value 6, 8, or 10 times in a row. Further, annoying patterns that humans pick up on have also been eliminated, like the pattern 11001100 or the pattern 01010101.

The Appearance of Randomness

The field of psychology has studied this apparent disparity between true randomness and perceived randomness. In particular, Falk and Konold [Falk97] found that human subjects tended to score sequences as more random when the random head/tail sequence alternated between heads and tails at a higher rate than a true random result would give. On average, a sequence of 20 flips will produce 10 alternations between heads and tails. As shown in Figure 1.7.1, human subjects reported that, given a sequence of 20 flips, sequences that alternated 14 times between heads and tails appeared to be the most random.

This idea of alternations is important. It's obvious that for a sequence to appear random, it must not repeat a particular value for too long. For example, given a 50-percent chance of heads or tails, it seems very wrong to see a sequence of 10 heads in a row. However, the evidence from Falk and Konold suggests that there must also be more alternations than randomly occurs, or else it won't appear as random. Since random number generators don't create enough alternations naturally, part of the solution toward making sequences appear more random is to artificially increase the number of alternations.

Psychology researchers have also identified several other properties that make sequences appear less random [Falk97]. The following is a list of each property.

- A long run of a single outcome, like 00000000.
- Too few alternations between outcomes, like 11110000.

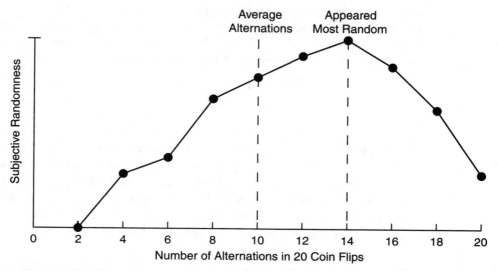

FIGURE 1.7.1 *Given sequences containing 20 coin flips each, test subjects rated the randomness of various sequences. Sequences that alternated 14 times between heads and tails appeared the most random. Data adapted from [Falk97].*

- The repetition of a motif, like 11001100 where the motif is 1100.
- Symmetry from a motif and its reflection, like 11100111 where the motif is 1110.

If we want random numbers that appear random to humans, we need to filter random number generation to eliminate these properties.

Required Forms of Randomness

When randomness is required in games, there are four forms that it comes in. The first is in the form of a Boolean output based on a specified chance, like "Score a direct hit on the player 10 percent of the time." In this case, a function is needed that returns TRUE given a particular chance in the range [0,1], as in:

```
bool genrand(float chance);
```

The second form of randomness consists of a range, like "Return a random spawn location, given eight spawn points." In this case, a function is needed that returns a random integer in the interval [0,range], given an upper limit range, as in:

```
int genrand(int range); //returns [0,range]
```

The third way to request randomness is in the form of a uniformly distributed floating-point number in the range of [0,1]. Sometimes, to make particles or objects unique, you need a random floating-point number to offset their attributes, like speed, rotation, or health. In this case, a function is needed that returns a random real number in the range [0,1]. The result can then be scaled to fit any floating-point range. The function that produces these numbers doesn't require any arguments and would resemble the following:

```
float genrand(void);     //returns [0,1]
```

The fourth way to request randomness is in the form of a Gaussian distributed floating-point number in the range of [−1,1]. This can be used for identical purposes as uniformly distributed floating-point numbers, except that the numbers will be biased toward a Gaussian distribution centered on 0.0 (also known as a Bell curve). This type of randomness is often ideal for aiming at targets or any other attribute in a population that follows a Bell curve distribution, such as height, size, or intelligence. The function that produces these numbers would resemble the following:

```
float genrand(void);     //returns [-1,1]
```

Generating Perceived Randomness

Normally, the four forms of randomness are easily created from a single random integer that ranges from 0 to RAND_MAX, in the case of the rand() function. However, perceived randomness will differ with each form. Therefore, we must cater to each form separately to ensure that the player perceives each as random.

Boolean Chance

The first form of randomness, Boolean chance, was shown at the beginning of this article with the coin toss example. However, with a coin, the chance is fixed at 50 percent. For this model to be generally applicable and useful, we must consider chances ranging from 0 to 100 percent.

Based on the psychological studies, there are three core ways a random Boolean sequence should be filtered to appear more random:

- Raise the number of alternations above the natural value.
- Restrict unreasonable runs of the same value.
- Eliminate recognizable patterns.

The following 300 Boolean values have been filtered using the previous three rules (applied in that order). This is the same filtered sequence as shown at the beginning of the article. There are symbols inserted where each of the rules has flipped the next value.

```
Key:
- Flipped next value to make it alternate
  between 12 to 14 times per 20 values.
```

```
' Flipped next value to prevent a run of more
  than three values.

. Flipped next value to eliminate a repeating
  motif of four values, like 00110011.

^ Flipped next value to eliminate the pattern
  000111 or 111000.

0101010.0010100011-011001-01001001-010010111001011101
.0110100-1000'11-0-10101.11'01.0111-01001100.0-1-0101
1-0-1100-1010100-0'11001.001010111-0-1-0101-1100^1000
1-.1-011-010-1-0110001-01100011-01-010-11-01000-11-01
1011001-0100100011-0-1101010110011-.100-110-1101-010-
1.1-0111'00^111-0-101101-0100-1100.01010011011-010101
1000'1101110.010-1010-.0-1-0111'00-101110100-1011-01
```

ON THE CD

On the accompanying CD-ROM, you can find the class `FilteredRandomChance` that produces the random Boolean chance shown previously. Due to the subjective nature of these random numbers, the constraint values for rules 1 and 2 had to be hand tuned for each percentage chance. For example, with a 50-percent chance, an arbitrary choice was made to restrict runs of more than three. For a 10-percent chance, runs of TRUE are completely restricted and runs of FALSE are restricted to 15 in a row. The constraints for each percentage were tuned to guarantee that the resulting percentage of TRUE/FALSE values was within 1 percent of the requested chance.

Integer Range

The second form of randomness, the integer range, requires more filtering than the Boolean chance. The filtering comes in the form of rules that have no precedence—the sequence must pass every rule. However, sometimes the rules over-constrain the sequence, in which case it must break an arbitrary rule if a solution can't be found.

The following are the filtering rules for an integer range:

1. Restrict repeating numbers (this can be relaxed to allow limited runs).
2. Restrict the number of times a given value can appear in the last 10 values.
3. Restrict the number of values in a row that form an increasing or decreasing counting sequence, like 2345 or 3210.
4. Restrict the number of values in a row that are at the bottom of the range or at the top of the range. For example, in the range of 0 to 9, the sequence 7968796 has too many values in a row at the top of the range.
5. Restrict two pairs of numbers in a row, like 5533 or 2288.
6. Restrict a motif of two numbers repeating immediately, like 4545 or 2929.
7. Restrict a motif of three numbers appearing in the last 10 values, like the motif 246 in the sequence 2461246.

8. Restrict a motif of three numbers and its mirror from appearing in the last 10 values, like the motif 246 in the sequence 2461642.

The following random sequence in the range [0,9] has been filtered with the previous rules. Each new number is first generated with rand()%range (where range is 10 in this case). This new number along with past values is then compared against each rule. If it violates any rule, the number is thrown away and a new number is generated with rand()%range. If for some reason the sequence is over constrained by the rules and a satisfactory number can't be generated within 50 tries, then an arbitrary rule is broken by simply accepting the fiftieth generated number.

In the following sequence, each time a rule throws out a number, the number is surrounded by a symbol indicating which rule it violated.

```
Key:
Rule 1: ()      Rule 2: []      Rule 3: {}      Rule 4: $$
Rule 5: ##      Rule 6: --      Rule 7: **      Rule 8: **

098(8)637410464-6-798526250758090-9-51[0]9743(3)17501
82095253608(8)67(7)18594281806586$5$025(5)059(9)27178
491972073780[7]5398137(7)61732(2)734186572856149(9)65
9290252809415808*2*-0-386[8]10595(5)-9-2(2)6085325350
[5]738186(6)2618(8)2[8]383(3)461(1)74312(2)8612976810
20$1$6(6)2595(5)60859808637274(4)7(7)1(1)[7]698925478
{9}381(1)350282-8-16908197581076{5}7-6-9[7]*1*(9)$8$0
130(0)$2$582(2)1673721*6*(1)95(5)365638703547(7)0(0)4
10(0)61039251(1)2(2)7436125710408(8)07398
```

ON THE CD

On the accompanying CD-ROM, you can find the class FilteredRandomRange that produces random integers in a specified range.

Uniformly Distributed Floating-Point

The third form of randomness, uniformly distributed floating-point in the range [0,1], can be generated by leveraging the FilteredRandomRange class. The key is to use the previous integer range results returned in the range [0,9] to become the tenths place of the generated floating-point number. This will guarantee that most patterns and oddities have been removed. For the fractional portion beyond the tenths place, a random number generated directly from rand() can be used.

The floating-point numbers generated at this point must still be filtered for three particular cases:

1. Ensure that each newly generated number differs by more than 0.02 from the previous number. For example, in the sequence 0.432359, 0.443987, the numbers are too close and the second number should be rejected.

2. Ensure that the last three consecutive numbers are more than 0.10 away from each other. For example, in the sequence 0.783421, 0.801928, 0.743248, the third number should be rejected.

3. Ensure that the last five consecutive numbers don't form an increasing or decreasing sequence. For example, in the sequence 0.398452, 0.599343, 0.633491, 0.823497, 0.987564, the last number should be rejected.

On the accompanying CD-ROM, you can find the class `FilteredRandomReal` that produces random uniformly distributed floating-point numbers in the range [0,1].

Gaussian Distributed Floating-Point

The fourth form of randomness, Gaussian distributed floating-point in the range [−1,1], can be filtered identically to the uniformly distributed floating-point except with a single additional rule:

4. Ensure that there are no more than three consecutive numbers above zero and no more than three consecutive numbers below zero. For example, in the sequence 0.297630, 0.834391, 0.373610, 0.104320, the last number should be rejected.

Figure 1.7.2 shows an unfiltered series of 50 random Gaussian numbers compared with the same sequence after it has been filtered by the four rules. Figure 1.7.3 shows an unfiltered set of 100 random Gaussian numbers that have been sorted to show their distribution compared with the same set after it has been filtered. Notice how the distribution remains extremely similar, demonstrating that the filtering process does not disturb the desired Gaussian distribution.

On the accompanying CD-ROM, you can find the class `FilteredRandomGauss-ian` that produces random Gaussian distributed floating-point numbers in the range [−1,1]. The Gaussian random number generator was adapted from [Carter02].

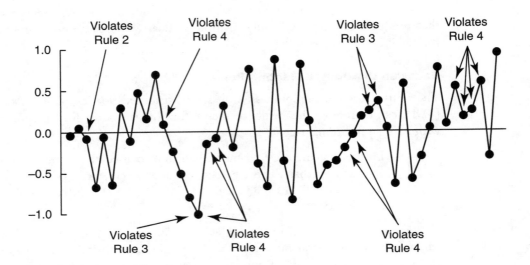

Unfiltered Random Gaussian Numbers

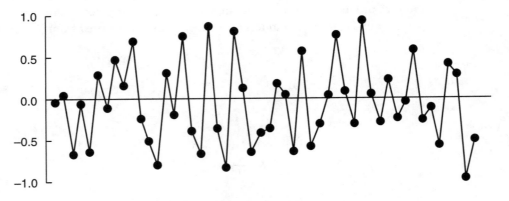

Filtered Random Gaussian Numbers

FIGURE 1.7.2 *An unfiltered series of 50 random Gaussian numbers compared with the same sequence after it has been filtered by the four rules.*

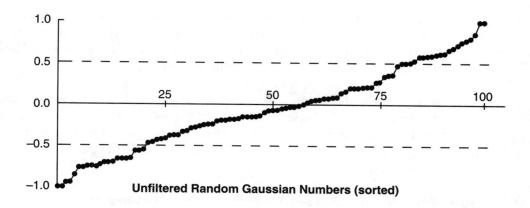

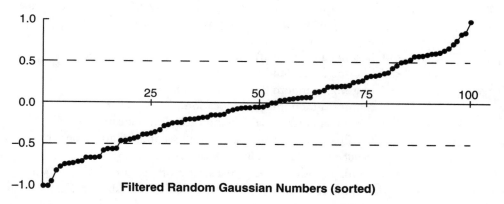

FIGURE 1.7.3 *An unfiltered set of 100 random Gaussian numbers sorted to show the distribution compared with the same set after it has been filtered. Notice how the distribution of values remains relatively undisturbed after the filtering.*

Using the Source Code

ON THE CD

As mentioned, the source code for generating these filtered random numbers is included on the accompanying CD-ROM. However, using the classes requires some diligence. For example, the whole point of this filtering is that a particular decision, like which spawn point to regenerate enemies, appears random. For this to work properly with the supplied code, each decision requires its own instance (for the duration of the game) of the filtered random number generating class (either `FilteredRandomChance`, `FilteredRandomRange`, `FilteredRandomReal`, or `FilteredRandomGaussian`). This is necessary so that it can track the past numbers for a given decision.

The overhead for each class is not significant, only several dozen bytes of allocated data per class instance, so it is not unreasonable to create a permanent instance for each random request in the code. However, it might be more complicated if the random requests come from an outside script that can't easily instantiate one of the random classes. In this case, the random classes can be modified to take in an ID that will uniquely identify the request and be able to track its past history.

Another concern with using the source code is being able to fix the random seed so that predictable random numbers can be generated, which can be useful when debugging a game [Lecky-Thompson00, Rabin04]. Within the filtered random classes, all randomness comes from rand() before being filtered, so setting the random seed to a fixed value with srand() will make all filtered random numbers from all four classes predictable.

Sample Uses for the Filtered Randomness Classes

FilteredRandomChance
- Choosing whether to score a direct hit given a 10-percent chance.
- Choosing whether to retreat given a 5-percent chance.

FilteredRandomRange
- Choosing a random attack move.
- Choosing a random idle animation.
- Choosing a random death animation.
- Choosing a random spawn location.
- Choosing a random pain sound each time a creature is hit.
- Choosing a random time interval in seconds to attack again.

FilteredRandomReal, FilteredRandomGaussian
- Assigning random speeds to a swarm of creatures.
- Assigning random variation to particle effects (size, acceleration, speed, and angular rotation).
- Assigning random variation when aiming at a target.
- Random placement of trees or bushes.

Quality of Randomness

ON THE CD

The demo on the accompanying CD-ROM shows how to use each class and generates a 100K file for each of the four forms of randomness. By running benchmarks on these files (such as the program ENT, which is included on the CD-ROM), the quality of the randomness can be examined. Table 1.7.1 compares some key results from a typical rand() function and the filtered random classes (using the ENT benchmarking package).

One problem with filtered randomness, in general, is that the filtering rules sometimes make it possible to predict the next random number, especially for the FilteredRandomChance class. This is why the FilteredRandomChance class performs worse on the ENT tests than the rand() function (as shown in Table 1.7.1). For example, if the series 00011 is seen, the filtering rules dictate that the next bit must

Table 1.7.1 Randomness benchmarks performed on 100K files containing output from `rand()` and the four filtered random classes. Each benchmark is explained in the ENT documentation on the CD-ROM. The key point is that the filtered random classes perform very close to `rand()` over a variety of benchmarks.

Randomness Benchmarks (ENT program)	Visual C++ 6.0 `rand()`	Filtered Random Chance	Filtered Random Range	Filtered Random Real	Filtered Random Gaussian
Entropy (bits per byte)	7.998415	6.927874	7.993484	7.988776	7.965304
Optimum Compression	0%	13%	0%	0%	0%
Mean (127.5 = random)	127.5380	127.7658	127.5403	120.4014	122.4576
Monte Carlo Pi Value	3.144967	3.430447	3.145435	3.365991	3.248096
Serial Correlation Coefficient (uncorrelated = 0.0)	0.000351	0.050102	−0.062553	−0.011140	0.016304

not be 1. For Boolean decisions by the AI, it is probably unlikely that the player will pick up on this, and more likely that the player would be disturbed by the sequence 000111, which doesn't seem very random. However, this tradeoff between mathematical randomness and perceived randomness is subjective and must be carefully considered for each decision.

Interestingly, the `FilteredRandomRange`, `FilteredRandomReal`, and `FilteredRandomGaussian` classes show surprisingly good mathematical randomness that rivals the `rand()` function (although `FilteredRandomGaussian` performs a little worse since it's purposely biasing its numbers toward zero). For these generators, the filtering doesn't over-constrain the sequence to the point where the next number can be occasionally predicted. This is the best of all situations: excellent randomness with all anomalies filtered out.

Conclusion

This article presented four random number generation classes that will make your random game logic and random AI decisions appear more random to the player. While the cost and complexity of generating a random number has increased, the result will clearly make your game more random in the way that you originally intended, and it will be devoid of anomalous and hurtful random sequences.

References

[Carter02] Carter, Everett, "Generating Gaussian Random Numbers," *Taygeta Scientific Inc. Web site*, 2002, available online at *www.taygeta.com/random/gaussian.html*

[Falk97] Falk, R., and Konold, C., "Making Sense of Randomness: Implicit Encoding as a Bias for Judgement," *Psychological Review*, 104:301–318, 1997.

[Griffiths01] Griffiths, Thomas, and Tenenbaum, Joshua, "Randomness and Coincidences: Reconciling Intuition and Probability Theory," *Proceedings of the 23rd*

Annual Conference of the Cognitive Science Society, 2001, available online at *www-psych.stanford.edu/~gruffydd/papers/random.pdf*

[Griffiths03] Griffiths, Thomas, and Tenenbaum, Joshua, "Probability, Algorithmic Complexity, and Subjective Randomness," submitted to *CogSci 2003*, 2003, available online at *www-psych.stanford.edu/~gruffydd/papers/complex.pdf*

[Lecky-Thompson00] Lecky-Thompson, Guy, "Predictable Random Numbers," *Game Programming Gems*, Charles River Media, 2000.

[Rabin04] Rabin, Steve, "The Science of Debugging Games," *Game Programming Gems 4*, Charles River Media, 2004.

PATHFINDING AND MOVEMENT

Search Space Representations

Paul Tozour—Retro Studios

gehn29@yahoo.com

A number of articles [Matthews02, Rabin00] have addressed the problem of using a search algorithm in game AI pathfinding. However, the actual search algorithm is only half the picture—the underlying data structure is also critical.

In the C++ Standard Template Library (STL), there are a number of algorithms (such as *sort()*, *find()*, and *copy()*) that work on a number of different types of container classes (such as lists, vectors, and deques). This architecture allows you to apply any algorithm to any container, so you can generally mix and match algorithms and containers—although a given algorithm will exhibit different performance characteristics from one container to another.

The pathfinding problem works the same way. You can use any number of different algorithms, such as breadth-first search, depth-first search [Luger98], Dijkstra's algorithm, or, more likely, A* [Rabin00]—but the algorithm is only half the picture. The representation of the underlying search space will have a dramatic impact on the performance and memory requirements of the pathfinding system and the quality of the paths the characters follow.

In this article, we discuss all the major approaches to representing a search space in games. You can use any of these approaches with any standard search algorithm. We will detail the advantages and disadvantages of each approach and some of the considerations to take into account when selecting a representation.

We will concern ourselves only with pathfinding for characters that walk on the ground or hover at a fixed height above it. Fully three-dimensional pathfinding for flying and swimming characters poses a different set of challenges, and such issues are beyond the scope of this article.

Search Space Considerations

Two of the considerations when selecting a search space representation are performance and memory overhead. We need a pathfinding representation that fits into a reasonable amount of memory and allows the fastest possible search.

Fundamentally, all search spaces are *graphs*: they all consist of some number of atomic units of navigation, or *nodes,* and some number of connections, or *edges,* between pairs of nodes. Larger graphs—that is, graphs with more nodes and more edges between those nodes—will most likely require more memory to store the nodes and edges. In addition, larger graphs will usually result in slower searches, as each search will have more nodes and more edges with which to contend.

Therefore, we can say that smaller, simpler graphs typically provide a smaller memory footprint and allow faster search performance. However, if we make things too simple, we can easily end up with a graph that doesn't represent the game world accurately.

This brings us to the issue of *path optimality*. Whenever we attempt to find a path from some point A in the game world to some other point B, we want to determine the *optimal* path—that is, the least expensive path from A to B.

Note that the optimal path is not always the shortest path. For example, it might be better for a character to follow a curved road around a swamp rather than walking directly through it. Although a straight line through the swamp would be a more direct route, the character can travel much more quickly on the road than he can through the swamp.

As we will see, many search space representations achieve simplicity at the expense of optimality—that is, they allow fast pathfinding but often generate low-quality paths.

Agent Movement Capabilities

Another key consideration is how well a given representation can handle the different capabilities of various AI agents. It's tempting to assume that all our AI agents will navigate through the game world in the same way, but this is quite often not the case.

Different AI agents have different movement capabilities, and a good search space representation must take these factors into account. Some AIs can open doors; others can't. Some can use elevators, teleporters, or jump pads. Some can swim, and some can climb ladders. If we assume that all AIs have cylindrical bounding volumes, then each character has a width and a height, and different characters might be taller and wider than others. Some AIs can jump over small chasms. Some can move safely through rooms full of poison gas or drive directly over fences and barbed wire that would stop other characters in their tracks. Some AIs are giant robots with very large feet that prevent them from walking up steps.

Figure 2.1.1a shows an example of why these differences are important. Three characters with different widths (say, a dragon, an ogre, and a rabbit) should follow different paths to the same destination point. In Figure 2.1.1b, we have two rooms, connected by a hallway and a crawl shaft. The six-inch-tall rabbit can navigate directly through the crawl shaft, while the eight-foot-tall ogre must use the hallway.

Search Space Generation

Another key consideration is how the search space representation is created in the first place. Some search space representations lend themselves to automated generation in the game editor—it's possible to derive them automatically from the game world's raw

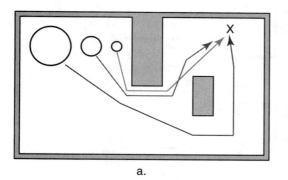 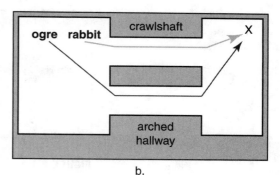

a. b.

FIGURE 2.1.1 *AI agents take different paths to a destination on account of different widths (a) or heights (b).*

geometry or from a physics collision mesh. Others require level designers to place the nodes in the pathfinding graph by hand for every level they create.

It's usually a bad idea to require designers to place pathfinding graph nodes by hand. Manual graph node placement allows designers to introduce bugs in the AI, and it can be very awkward for an AI developer to tell a level designer, "The AI is broken in your level because you put the path nodes in the wrong place."

With a large number of designers creating a large number of world pieces, a design team can end up wasting a lot of time adding path points just to allow the AI to navigate the game world properly. An automated solution also allows you to solve the problem just once, rather than having to address it in every part of the game world separately.

Scripted AI Paths

It's important to note that the AIs' search space representation is different from a patrol path creation tool. Designers quite often need to create scripted behavior sequences and patrol paths by manually constructing paths for AI characters to follow in the game.

However, these paths work well only for predefined scripted sequences. They generally cannot be used for highly interactive behaviors such as combat or area-searching behavior. Therefore, it's usually a bad idea to force the two systems to have the same representation—it's more effective to create a scripted sequence editing system that's entirely separate from the underlying search space.

The Sample Game World

We will use the game world shown in Figure 2.1.2 as our archetypical example of a game world, and show how each search space representation handles this environment.

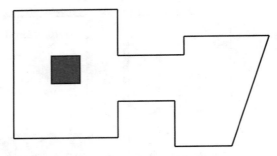

FIGURE 2.1.2   *The game world.*

Regular Grids

The simplest way to represent a search space is with a regular grid of squares, rectangles, hexagons, or triangles. Figure 2.1.3 shows examples of regular grids made from squares and hexagons.

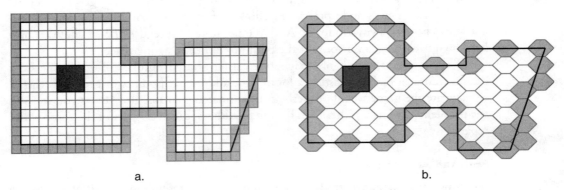

a.   b.

FIGURE 2.1.3   *Grid representations based on square and hexagonal cells.*

Grids are most useful in 2D environments and cannot be used in 3D game worlds without modification. Grid-based search spaces are the most popular in 2D games, especially strategy games with a top-down perspective.

Grids are limited in that they often require a large number of grid cells to adequately represent a game world. Larger game worlds and higher-resolution grids increase the total number of cells used in the grid, which increases the grid's memory footprint and can make pathfinding significantly slower.

On the plus side, grids support random-access lookup. In other words, it's possible to determine the tile that lies at any given world-space coordinate in constant (O(1)) time. None of the other search space representations described later in this article provide random-access lookup—they all require a graph search in order to determine the node closest to a given (X,Y) or (X,Y,Z) coordinate.

Grid-based systems can also suffer from path quality issues as a result of the underlying grid representation. If AI agents can only walk along the four cardinal directions between neighboring cells (assuming a square grid rather than a hexagonal grid), this will likely result in unattractive angular paths composed entirely of straight lines and 90-degree turns, as in Figure 2.1.4a. Allowing AIs to walk along diagonals improves the situation somewhat (Figure 2.1.4b), but the path is still clearly less than optimal.

At this point, we can introduce a technique called "string-pulling" (also known as "line-of-sight testing" [Snook00]). String-pulling works by deleting any point P_N from the path whenever it's possible to get from P_{N-1} to P_{N+1} directly. This gives us the simplified path shown in Figure 2.1.4c. As we will see, string-pulling can be useful with many other search space representations as well.

Finally, we can use Catmull-Rom splines [Rabin00] to create a smooth, curved path, as in Figure 2.1.4d. Splines will allow us to automatically convert a sequence of points into a smooth spline-based path.

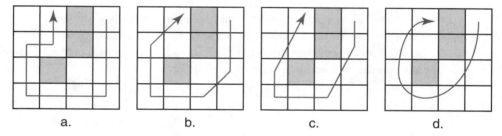

a.   b.   c.   d.

FIGURE 2.1.4 *Four paths on a square grid: (a) is constrained to north-south-east-west movement; (b) allows diagonals; (c) shows the same path with "string-pulling"; and (d) is optimized with a Catmull-Rom spline.*

All of the other representations we will discuss in this article are based on graphs, and it might seem as though a grid is an entirely different kind of data structure. However, a grid is fundamentally a graph at heart. In a square grid, for example, each cell in the grid is a graph node, and it shares implicit edges with its neighbors to the north, south, east, and west, as in Figure 2.1.5. If we allow a search to move along diagonals, then each cell has four additional neighbors (NW, SW, NE, SE) for a total of eight.

Note that it might be useful to handle the grid as a graph rather than an array. For example, imagine a small cliff that a character can jump down but cannot scale up again. Nodes A and B in Figure 2.1.5 are along the top of the cliff, and C and D are along the bottom. We could then change the A–C and B–D links to be unidirec-

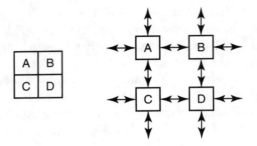

FIGURE 2.1.5   *The implicit "edges" between adjacent grid tiles.*

tional, such that AIs could get from A to C and from B to D, but not vice versa. A graph that has these unidirectional links is called a *directed graph*.

Corner Graphs

A *corner graph* consists of waypoints placed at the corners of the obstacles in a game world, with edges between them.

To generate a corner graph, simply identify all convex corners in the game world, and then determine whether it's possible for a character to walk in a straight line between any given pair of corner nodes. Add an edge wherever it's possible to walk between the two nodes, as shown in Figure 2.1.6.

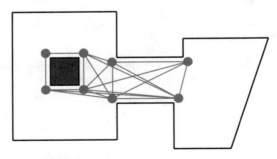

FIGURE 2.1.6   *A corner graph.*

The most obvious problem with this approach is that it often creates sub-optimal paths. Corner graphs limit AI agents to walking along the edges between corner nodes. As a result, AIs will often appear to be "on rails" as they navigate around in the world.

Figure 2.1.7 shows a sample path from a point X in the northwest corner of our game world to a point Y along the southern edge. This path is the optimal path—the shortest and simplest path we could possibly find.

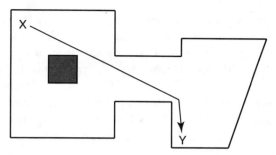

FIGURE 2.1.7 *The optimal path from X to Y.*

Unfortunately, it's difficult to obtain this path computationally with a corner graph. The diagram on the left side of Figure 2.1.8 shows the path we generate if we find the nearest node to each of X and Y and then apply a search algorithm to find a path between them. Clearly, this path is very different from the optimal path in Figure 2.1.7.

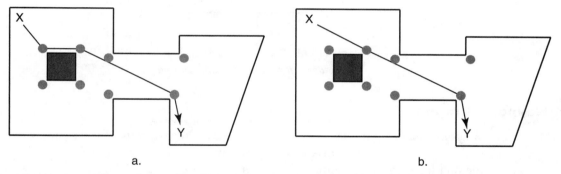

a.   b.

FIGURE 2.1.8 *The path from X to Y according to a corner graph (8a) and the same path after string-pulling (8b).*

We can optimize this a bit further by taking the resulting path and determining what nodes we might delete. In this example, we don't really need to start the path at the node closest to X; we can start at the second or third node along the path since it's possible to get there from X using a straight line. We then end up with the path shown on the right side of Figure 2.1.8, which is nearly identical to the optimal path.

Unfortunately, this optimization requires us to perform expensive line-testing in the world to determine when it's appropriate to skip path nodes. The corner graph itself has no way to tell us if any such line is unobstructed; it only knows about direct connections between graph nodes.

Even when we can obtain such near-optimal paths, the corner graph will often cause characters to walk very close to the walls when it would be more appropriate for them to move through the empty space farther from the walls. This also means that corner graphs present difficulties in handling characters of different widths. As we saw with the previous dragon/ogre/rabbit example, some characters have a wider girth than others, and they will often generate different paths between the same two points.

Perhaps the most compelling disadvantage is that generating a corner graph has $O(n^2)$ complexity. In other words, it's necessary to test every node in the graph against all the others ($n * n = n^2$) in order to determine whether it's possible to place an edge between them. In Figure 2.1.9, for example, a square room with 4 exits and 16 square pillars requires no less than 72 corners, requiring tests for 2556 (= 72 * 71 / 2) edges!

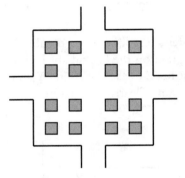

FIGURE 2.1.9   *A worst-case game world for a corner graph approach.*

Waypoint Graphs

Waypoint graphs are similar to corner graphs, except that they usually place the graph nodes in the middle of rooms and hallways, away from walls and corners. This avoids the wall-hugging issues exhibited by corner graphs (see Figure 2.1.10).

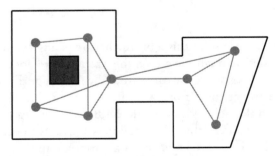

FIGURE 2.1.10   *A waypoint graph.*

Waypoint graphs tend to be very popular with 3D games, as they generally handle 3D game worlds quite easily. Because you can place a waypoint at any point in 3D space, you can use waypoint graphs very easily for navigating outdoor terrain or three-dimensional game worlds.

Unfortunately, waypoint graphs also suffer from the $O(n^2)$-complexity generation exhibited by corner graphs. Generating graph edges requires a test for each possible pair of nodes.

Additionally, waypoint graphs cannot easily provide optimal paths. The diagram on the left side of Figure 2.1.11 illustrates how a waypoint graph handles the problem of finding a path from X to Y. This path is clearly different from the optimal path of Figure 2.1.7.

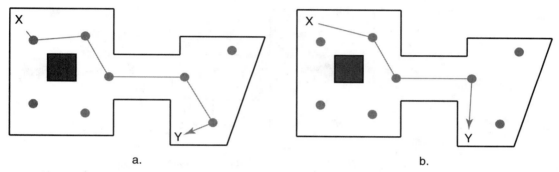

a.   b.

FIGURE 2.1.11 *A path from X to Y along a waypoint graph (a), and the same path after string-pulling (b).*

We can apply the same optimization we used with the corner graph, and remove nodes from the path if we can navigate to them directly in a straight line. This results in the path shown on the right side of Figure 2.1.11.

Waypoint-based search space representations work fairly well in human architecture, particularly in tight corridors and other areas where the environment constrains characters' movement to straight lines. However, they tend to work poorly in large rooms and open terrain, where they introduce artificial limitations that do not exist in the actual game world.

Another big problem with waypoint graphs is that they usually require hand-tuning by level designers. Although there are some systems that place waypoints automatically, most waypoint-based navigation systems require level designers to scatter waypoints all around their level, and an automated tool then attempts to place the edges between them automatically. As mentioned in the "Search Space Considerations" section at the beginning of this article, this can cause some severe workflow problems.

Waypoint graphs place path quality at odds with simplicity. The only way to achieve higher-quality paths in a given area is by adding more nodes. This increases the graph's memory footprint, makes searching more expensive, and slows the edge-detection process dramatically (since it is an $O(n^2)$ operation).

The pathological case for a waypoint graph is a very large, empty room. Such an environment will typically require you to add a very large number of graph nodes—with an exponentially greater number of edges between them—in order to achieve aesthetically pleasing character navigation.

Circle-Based Waypoint Graphs

Circle-based waypoint graphs are a variant of waypoint graphs that add a radius parameter to each waypoint to roughly indicate the amount of open space around the waypoint. Figure 2.1.12 shows an example.

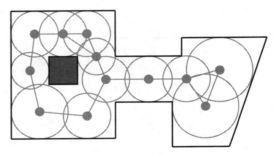

FIGURE 2.1.12   *A circle-based waypoint graph.*

A circle-based waypoint system only allows characters to navigate between overlapping circles. Therefore, unlike a standard waypoint graph, in which we generate all viable edges between node pairs, a circle-based waypoint graph will only attempt to create edges between two nodes if their circles actually overlap. This makes circle-based systems much simpler than waypoint graphs for many environments and avoids the problem of $O(n^2)$-complexity edge generation.

This approach generally allows paths that are more optimal than a point-based system can provide. It's easy to achieve the optimal path within any given circle, since the optimal path will always be a straight line if the origin and the global point both lie within the same circle. For navigating between multiple circles, it's sometimes possible to achieve the optimal path, depending on the degree to which the circles overlap.

Circle-based representations generally work well in open terrain, but are not ideally suited to angular environments (such as our sample game world) that do not lend themselves to circular representations. Naturally, it is possible to create hybrid systems that use points in indoor environments and circles in open terrain, and several games have used this approach.

Adding a height parameter to indicate the height of each circle in the graph results in a variant of the circle-based waypoint graph referred to as the *cylinder-based waypoint graph*.

Space-Filling Volumes

The *space-filling volume* approach is similar to the circle-based approach, except that it uses rectangles or 3D boxes instead of circles (see Figure 2.1.13).

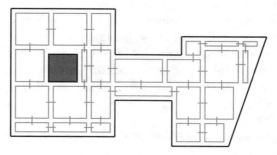

FIGURE 2.1.13 *Space-filling volumes.*

There are two ways to generate space-filling volumes. The simplest approach is to drop a number of small boxes or rectangles at regular intervals throughout the game world as "seeds," either by hand-placing them or inserting them with an automated tool. You can then incrementally "grow" each side of these boxes in the X and Y dimensions until they can grow no further—that is, any side of a box stops growing as soon as it hits an obstacle or another box.

Alternatively, you can start with a regular grid, and then attempt to merge neighboring cells into larger rectangles.

Space-filling volumes tend to work better than circle-based waypoint systems in angular environments. However, they aren't guaranteed to completely fill any given game world. As you can see on the right side of Figure 2.1.13, this can sometimes cause problems in places where axis-aligned boxes have difficulty representing curved or non-axis-aligned geometry in the game world, and this can make certain parts of the game world unreachable.

Navigation Meshes

A *navigation mesh* [Snook00, White02] is a representation that covers the walkable surfaces of the world with convex polygons.

The navigation mesh (or "NavMesh") representation has certain key advantages. NavMeshes allow you to reliably find the optimal paths for characters with various shapes and movement capabilities. They handle indoor environments and expansive outdoor terrain equally well.

The main disadvantage of a NavMesh is that it can require storage of a large number of polygons, particularly in expansive and geometrically complex environments.

The guarantee of convexity is essential. Convex polygons allow us to guarantee that a character can freely walk from any point within a polygon to any other point within that same polygon. Each polygon is therefore a node in the search graph, and the links between adjacent polygons are the edges of the graph.

It's possible—although not necessarily easy—to generate a navigation mesh using an automated tool to analyze and optimize the level geometry [Tozour02]. Note that it's generally not feasible to use the raw world geometry itself for pathfinding, as this will be unnecessarily complex. Moreover, a game world is usually not represented as a single unified polygon mesh—modern game worlds are typically composed of multiple separate intersecting geometric objects, and this representation is not amenable to AI pathfinding.

Triangle-Based and N-Sided-Poly-Based Navigation Meshes

There are two major types of navigation meshes. *Triangle-based* navigation meshes (Figure 2.1.14a) require that all of the NavMesh polygons be triangles. *N-sided-poly-based* navigation meshes [Tozour02] (Figure 2.1.14b) allow polygons with any number of sides, so long as they remain convex.

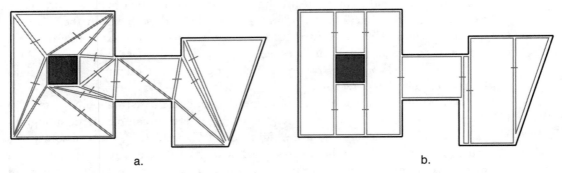

a.   b.

FIGURE 2.1.14 *Triangle-based (a) and N-sided-poly-based (b) navigation meshes.*

Navigation meshes based on N-sided polygons can usually represent a search space more simply than is possible with triangles. This allows faster pathfinding and a smaller memory footprint [Tozour02]. For example, this approach allows you to represent an octagonal room using a single eight-sided polygon, where a triangular mesh would require at least six triangles.

Wall-Avoidance Problems

However, N-sided polygons have another subtle disadvantage: they can sometimes lead to paths that hug the walls too tightly. Figure 2.1.15 shows an example of this.

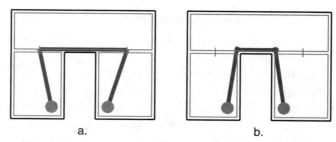

a.   b.

FIGURE 2.1.15 *An N-sided-poly-based navigation mesh, before and after string-pulling.*

Figure 2.1.15a shows our initial NavMesh path, before "string-pulling." The path runs through the center of the two links between the three successive NavMesh nodes. String-pulling (Figure 2.1.15b) simplifies the path somewhat; the path becomes tighter, but it still hugs the wall much too tightly along the topmost path segment.

Note that string-pulling works somewhat differently in a navigation mesh from the way it works in a grid environment. Besides eliminating unnecessary steps in the path, string-pulling in a NavMesh can also move the path points to any point along the *link* between two nodes—that is, the line segment between two adjacent NavMesh polygons. Therefore, we can tighten our path along these line segments, although we must be careful to avoid bringing the path too close to the walls.

It's certainly possible to address this problem by performing some post-processing on the navigation mesh path. Once you know the correct sequence of NavMesh nodes to traverse, you can analyze each NavMesh node and determine which parts of its various edges are immediately adjacent to walls, as in Figure 2.1.16. With this data, you can then perform an extra step after string-pulling to push the path away from the walls—although this will often require you to insert additional vertices into the NavMesh path.

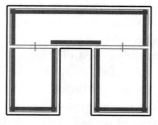

FIGURE 2.1.16 *The same navigation mesh with the segments of the edges next to walls highlighted.*

Triangle-Based Navigation Meshes

When used correctly, triangle-based navigation meshes solve this problem automatically.

We first build a triangular mesh such that each side of each triangle is either entirely against a wall or entirely adjacent to another mesh triangle. Because the string-pulling algorithm works by determining the appropriate position for the path along the link between a pair of adjacent NavMesh nodes, it automatically adjusts the path away from the walls as appropriate, as shown in Figure 2.1.17.

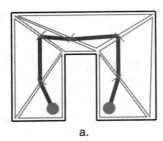 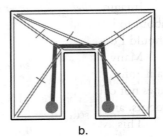

a.   b.

FIGURE 2.1.17   *A triangle-based navigation mesh, before (a) and after (b) string-pulling.*

Triangular meshes also have the key advantage that they lend themselves much more easily to vertex pooling. That is, it's possible to store all NavMesh vertices in a single shared data structure so that NavMesh polygons can refer to vertices via indexes into a data structure rather than requiring each polygon to store its vertices separately. Although a triangle-based navigation mesh will have many more polygons than one based on N-sided convex polygons, it will typically have a similar number of vertices; only the arrangement of the vertices into polygons differs.

Interacting with Local Pathfinding

Another key consideration with search space representations is how they will interact with an obstacle-avoidance system or a local pathfinding system.

As game designs grow increasingly complex and game worlds feature more and more physically modeled dynamic objects—crates and barrels that players can push, vehicles that can move in the game world, tables and chairs scattered about that players can kick or throw around the room—it becomes increasingly important to give AI characters the ability to navigate around dynamic objects.

Although simple obstacle avoidance systems can sometimes handle these obstacles (that is, swerving left or right around a single obstacle), this approach quickly breaks down in highly populated game worlds with many complex physical objects.

Unfortunately, an introduction to local pathfinding techniques is beyond the scope of this article, since we are primarily concerned solely with the question of pathfinding against the static, fixed geometry of the game world. The search space representations we discuss here are static by definition, and therefore they cannot hope to represent dynamic obstacles that can move around using the game's physics system.

However, it's critical that your underlying representation of the game world be robust enough to provide the local pathfinding system the information it needs to avoid obstacles properly. In particular, a search space often needs to be able to help the local pathfinding system avoid obstacles and answer queries about which parts of the game world are safe to walk through in order to avoid the obstacle.

Imagine that a game character is walking along a path and suddenly realizes it's about to bump into a barrel. At this point, it needs to be able to ask the search space: should I dodge left or right?

Many search space representations cannot answer this question. They only contain information about how characters would walk in an empty environment that does not contain enormous quantities of crates, barrels, tables, chairs, lamps, vehicles, robots, and other dynamic objects.

This is a particular problem with search space representations based on waypoints, such as corner graphs and waypoint graphs. These representations usually can provide little or no information to a local pathfinding or obstacle avoidance system when it needs to creatively avoid an unexpected obstacle.

Figure 2.1.18 shows an example of this problem. A character is walking from waypoint X to waypoint Y. Unfortunately, the player has moved a barrel directly into the AI agent's path (the outlined circle in Figure 2.1.18). Because our waypoint graph is entirely pregenerated and therefore static, there is no way we could have known about the barrel.

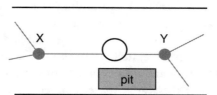

FIGURE 2.1.18 *A dynamic obstacle (the outlined circle) along an edge in a waypoint graph.*

Assume that our AI character is a small monster that has no hands and therefore cannot push the barrel out of the way. How can he avoid the barrel?

In this case, there's just not enough information to determine whether to go around the barrel to the left or the right. The waypoint graph doesn't have any data to warn us about the spike-filled pit on the south side of the path. It knows about a bunch of nodes and a number of edges between them, but it knows nothing about the game world outside of that set of points and lines.

We can try to compensate by using line-testing against the game world to see which direction is best, but this will still be problematic, since line-testing will have a hard time noticing the existence of the pit unless we use it very carefully.

In general, navigation mesh and grid-based representations tend to provide the most information about the walkable surfaces in the game world. Both of these types of representations are *complete*—that is, they can provide a comprehensive picture of *all* of the walkable surfaces in the game world, and they can thus allow a local pathfinder to make an informed decision when it needs to modify the original path.

Space-filling volumes and circle- and cylinder-based waypoint graphs also provide some information, although they usually do not cover all walkable surfaces, and as Figures 2.1.12 and 2.1.13 illustrate, they will often consider areas to be blocked that are actually open.

Hierarchical Representations

One final consideration in selecting a search space representation is how it can be used with *hierarchical pathfinding* [Rabin00].

Hierarchical pathfinding is nothing more than breaking the navigation problem down into levels, from the global to the local level. Imagine that someone needs to get from a library in New York to a diner in Seattle. At the topmost level is the plane ride from New York to Seattle. Beneath that are the problems of getting from the New York library to the airport, and on the other side, getting from Seattle's airport to the diner. Underneath each of these nodes is a third level—for example, navigating out of the library, walking down 5th Avenue, catching a cab to the airport, and navigating through the airport to the plane.

In games, hierarchical pathfinding is most useful for performing fast searches across large areas. Rather than performing a search from one end of a massive search graph to the other, you can break the problem down and perform much simpler searches at multiple hierarchical levels—for example, from region to region, from zone to zone within any region, and from room to room within any zone.

Nearly all of the search space representations described here lend themselves to some form of hierarchical pathfinding. For square grid representations, quadtrees can be an excellent way to simplify the pathfinding problem. It's also possible to automatically generate a rectangle-based navigation mesh from a square grid representation [Board02].

In general, the key to hierarchical pathfinding on a graph is to identify natural zones or regions—that is, clusters of nodes in the search graph. This essentially results in two different search graphs: a region-to-region search graph, along with a graph for pathfinding within any given region.

Figure 2.1.19 shows how we might be able to split the sample waypoint graph into two separate subgraphs, G_1 and G_2.

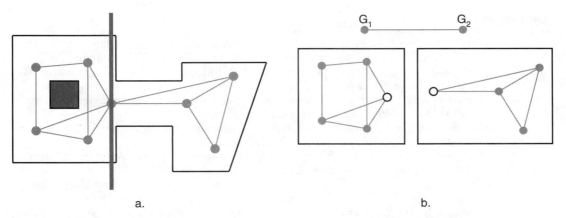

FIGURE 2.1.19 *Splitting a waypoint graph (a) into hierarchical pathfinding regions (b).*

We can do the same with other graph-based representations, such as navigation meshes and space-filling volumes, by identifying specific nodes or edges in the graph that naturally separate the graph into mutually exclusive regions.

Many modern 3D games use a portal system to subdivide the world—that is, they break up the game world into separate zones, with planar "portals" separating them. In many cases, it makes sense to take advantage of this data. We can use these portals to split our search space into regions such that there is a one-to-one mapping between a zone of the game world and a region of the search graph. This will give us an easy way to determine where to divide the graph into separate regions.

Conclusion

The design of the search space representation is just as important as the design of the search algorithm that will operate on it.

All of the search space representations described in this article have been used in shipped games, with varying degrees of success. Regular grid representations have been quite successful in 2D games, and waypoint graphs and navigation meshes have been the most popular approaches in 3D environments. However, as game worlds grow ever larger and more populated, it seems inevitable that the hand-placed-waypoint problem and the local-pathfinding-interaction problem will limit the viability of the waypoint graph approach.

Again, there is no single "correct" way to handle pathfinding and navigation for games. It's critical to understand the benefits and drawbacks of all of the available approaches when selecting a search space representation. The best representation will ultimately depend on the layout of the game world, the design of your game's AI systems, and the memory and performance characteristics of the target platform.

References

[Board02] Board, Ben, and Ducker, Mike, "Area Navigation: Expanding the Path-Finding Paradigm," *Game Programming Gems 3*, Charles River Media, 2002.

[Higgins02] Higgins, Dan, "Generic A* Pathfinding," *AI Game Programming Wisdom*, Charles River Media, 2002.

[Luger01] Luger, George F., *Artificial Intelligence: Structures and Strategies for Complex Problem Solving (4th Edition)*, Addison-Wesley, 2001.

[Matthews02] Matthews, James, "Basic A* Pathfinding Made Simple," *AI Game Programming Wisdom*, Charles River Media, 2002.

[Rabin00] Rabin, Steve, "A* Speed Optimizations" and "A* Aesthetic Optimizations," *Game Programming Gems*, Charles River Media, 2000.

[Snook00] Snook, Greg, "Simplified 3D Movement and Pathfinding Using Navigation Meshes," *Game Programming Gems*, Charles River Media, 2000.

[Stout99] Stout, W. Bryan, "Smart Moves: Intelligent Path-Finding," available online at *www.gamasutra.com/features/19990212/sm_01.htm*, February 12, 1999.

[Tozour02] Tozour, Paul, "Building a Near-Optimal Navigation Mesh," *AI Game Programming Wisdom*, Charles River Media, 2002.

[White02] White, Stephen, and Christensen, Christopher, "A Fast Approach to Navigation Meshes," *Game Programming Gems 3*, Charles River Media, 2002.

2.2

Inexpensive Precomputed Pathfinding Using a Navigation Set Hierarchy

Mike Dickheiser—Red Storm Entertainment

mike.dickheiser@redstorm.com

Precomputed solutions for pathfinding are rapidly gaining favor in modern game AI systems. As the sophistication of AI in the game industry grows, developers are spending an increasing amount of computer resources in the attempt to deliver interesting and complex AI behaviors. Unfortunately, basic functions like pathfinding often serve as CPU hogs that prevent or cripple the creation of the more exciting features. Dynamic pathfinding is expensive, and developers would very much like to find a way to spend more of the valuable CPU cycles on the bigger problems. Precomputing navigation information accomplishes this by almost completely eliminating the runtime cost of pathfinding.

Of course, any precomputed solution comes with a price: memory. Today's game levels are enormous, and even well optimized navigation maps can contain literally thousands of nodes. The sheer volume of information can render an otherwise very attractive preprocessed solution completely unfeasible, especially on console platforms where memory is at a premium. In this article we attack the problem directly using a method for dramatically reducing the amount of precomputed data necessary to represent a complete pathfinding solution for a game level. Specifically, we introduce the idea of a *Navigation Set Hierarchy*, a multitier extension of the basic preprocessed solution described by [Surasmith02] that offers comparable speed with considerably less memory overhead.

Precomputed Pathfinding Basics: The Transition Table

The basic component of the precomputed pathfinding scheme is a lookup table that effectively encodes the best paths between every pair of nodes in a level. This lookup table is called a *transition* (or *solution*) table, because each of the entries represents the next step in the path from some source node toward a specific goal node. In other words, for every pair of nodes S and G, the table entry [S][G] gives the index of the node that should be visited next when moving from S to G.

As an example, consider the simple navigation map in Figure 2.2.1, which shows a network of nodes including connectivity information and path costs.

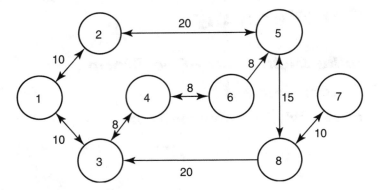

FIGURE 2.2.1　*A simple navigation map. Circles represent nodes, and arrows represent connecting edges. Each number along an edge is the cost to traverse the edge.*

For this simple navigation network, we can describe a complete best-path solution using a transition table, as shown in Figure 2.2.2.

Goal Node

	1	2	3	4	5	6	7	8
1	1	2	3	3	2	3	2	2
2	1	2	1	1	5	1	5	5
3	1	1	3	4	4	4	4	4
4	3	3	3	4	6	6	6	6
5	2	2	8	8	5	8	8	8
6	4	5	4	4	5	6	5	5
7	8	8	8	8	8	8	7	8
8	3	5	3	3	5	3	7	8

Source Node

FIGURE 2.2.2　*The transition table for the map in Figure 2.2.1.*

Putting the Transition Table to Good Use

To determine the best path from one node to another, we simply do a series of lookups into the table that gives us each of the steps (or transitions) from the source node to the goal node. For example, to determine the best path from node 3 to node 8, we first look at the [3][8] entry in the table, which is 4. This tells us that to get from node 3 to node 8, we must first move to node 4. Now we've reduced the problem to determining the best path from node 4 to node 8. The table entry for [4][8] gives us 6, which is the next node on the path. We continue in this fashion until the table returns the goal node, at which point we have the complete path solution. In this example, the final path solution is 3, 4, 6, 5, 8.

Using the transition table, the actual code for determining a best path is very simple indeed:

```
void buildBestPath(int source, int goal, list<int>& path)
{
    path.push_back(source);

    while (source != goal)
    {
        source = _transitionTable[source][goal];
        path.push_back(source);
    }
}
```

As indicated in the code sample, the process of building the path from source to goal is simply a series of table lookups. This is significantly faster than performing a full search at runtime whenever a path is needed.

The Bad News

While a transition table like that in Figure 2.2.2 gives us lightning-fast best path determination, a similar table for a large monolithic navigation map could be prohibitive in size. A game level today can easily contain a thousand navigation nodes or more. The corresponding table would require $n^2 = 1,000,000$ entries, potentially using several megabytes of precious memory. This brings us back to the problem of maintaining fast path determination while minimizing the amount of precomputed data needed to represent the complete path solution.

The Hierarchical Approach

Hierarchies are structures long known to be effective at reducing the search space in a variety of programming situations, and as [Rabin00] and [Tozour04] indicate, they are perfectly applicable to the problem of game AI navigation as well. The method we present here focuses primarily on reducing the number of transition table entries. We accomplish this by transforming the single monolithic navigation map into a hierarchy of several smaller sub-maps called *navigation sets*.

The Navigation Set

We define a *navigation set* to be a self-contained collection of nodes that requires no links to external nodes in order to complete a path from one internal node to another.

In other words, for any path between an arbitrary pair of nodes within the set, every node in the path is also contained in the set. An immediate consequence of this self-containment is that a complete precomputed transition table can be constructed for the set.

Obviously, by this definition, the small sample level shown in Figure 2.2.1 and the large monolithic level we seek to partition are themselves navigation sets. The point to be made, however, is that when we break up the large level we make certain that each partition is strictly a navigation set according to the definition. Thus, as a result of the partitioning process, we are left with several smaller collections of navigation data, each of which comes complete with its own best-path solution.

Note that the definition does not preclude nodes of one set being connected to nodes of another set. In fact, the partitioning process does not destroy any connectivity information between nodes in the original monolithic map. Instead, it simply regroups the nodes in a manner that facilitates localized pathfinding within distinct regions of the entire map.

Interface Nodes and the Interface Navigation Set

Once we have the individual navigation sets, we are still left with the problem of dealing with paths that extend across multiple sets. To solve this, we first identify all of the nodes within each navigation set that connect to nodes in other navigation sets. We call these nodes *interface nodes*, as they serve as the connective boundaries between navigation sets and gateways to the entire navigation map.

The interface nodes collectively form a navigation set of their own. This *interface set* essentially exists as a second tier of navigation data sitting on top of the other sets, and provides a means for finding paths that cross set boundaries. Because the interface set is a true navigation set itself, a transition table can be constructed for it yielding a precomputed best path solution for all pairs of nodes on the boundaries between navigation sets.

The Complete Hierarchy

The first-tier navigation sets along with the second-tier interface set provide all the information that is needed to quickly find a path from any node in the entire system to any other. The combination of the two tiers forms a hierarchy that allows a large pathfinding problem to be broken up into more tractable localized pathfinding problems that are then combined to give the complete solution. More importantly, this hierarchy provides significant memory savings over the original monolithic navigation map.

A simple but complete hierarchical navigation map is shown in Figure 2.2.3. The original underlying monolithic map has been partitioned into three distinct navigation sets: A, B, and C. Also shown are the resulting interface nodes: A6, A7, B1, B2, C3, and C5. The corresponding transition tables are shown in Figure 2.2.4.

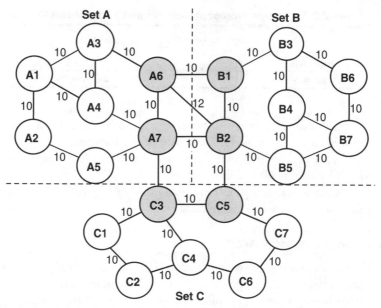

FIGURE 2.2.3 *A hierarchical navigation map, with the second-tier interface set shaded.*

Set A Transition Table

	A1	A2	A3	A4	A5	A6	A7
A1	A1	A2	A3	A4	A2	A3	A4
A2	A1	A2	A1	A1	A5	A1	A5
A3	A1	A1	A3	A4	A6	A6	A4
A4	A1	A1	A3	A4	A7	A7	A7
A5	A2	A2	A2	A7	A5	A7	A7
A6	A3	A7	A3	A3	A7	A6	A7
A7	A4	A5	A6	A4	A5	A6	A7

Set B Transition Table

	B1	B2	B3	B4	B5	B6	B7
B1	B1	B2	B3	B3	B2	B3	B2
B2	B1	B2	B1	B5	B5	B5	B5
B3	B1	B1	B3	B4	B4	B6	B4
B4	B3	B5	B3	B4	B5	B3	B7
B5	B2	B2	B4	B4	B5	B7	B7
B6	B3	B7	B3	B3	B7	B6	B7
B7	B6	B5	B6	B4	B5	B6	B7

Set C Transition Table

	C1	C2	C3	C4	C5	C6	C7
C1	C1	C2	C3	C2	C3	C2	C3
C2	C1	C2	C1	C4	C4	C4	C4
C3	C1	C1	C3	C4	C5	C4	C5
C4	C2	C2	C3	C4	C3	C6	C6
C5	C3	C3	C3	C3	C5	C7	C7
C6	C4	C4	C4	C4	C7	C6	C7
C7	C5	C6	C5	C6	C5	C6	C7

Interface Set Transition Table

	A6	A7	B1	B2	C3	C5
A6	A6	A7	B1	B2	A7	B2
A7	A6	A7	A6	B2	C3	C3
B1	A6	A6	B1	B2	B2	B2
B2	A6	A7	B1	B2	C5	C5
C3	A7	A7	C5	C5	C3	C5
C5	B2	C3	B2	B2	C3	C5

FIGURE 2.2.4 *The transition tables for three navigation sets and interface set associated with the hierarchical map in Figure 2.2.3.*

Table 2.2.1   Comparison of Monolithic and Hierarchical Transition Table Entries

	Total Nodes	Navigation Sets	Transition Table Entries
Monolithic Map	21	1	$441\ (21^2)$
Hierarchical Map	21	4 (including interface set)	$183\ (7^2 + 7^2 + 7^2 + 6^2)$

Table 2.2.1 shows the number of transition table entries required for both the monolithic and hierarchical versions of the navigation map in Figure 2.2.3. From the table, we can see that with only three partitions, we have reduced the memory overhead by almost 60 percent.

Before discussing how the hierarchy in Figure 2.2.3 is used for pathfinding, we first turn to how it is created.

Constructing the Hierarchy

The partitioning of the navigation data by automated means is a complex problem, and is beyond the scope of this article. We will instead briefly visit the key goals of the partitioning process and discuss how it is accomplished manually.

As previously shown, the objective of the hierarchical system is to reduce the number of transition table entries by breaking the single large transition table into a number of smaller ones. The two main issues to be addressed by this process are determining the number of smaller tables to create, and intelligently choosing where the partitioning should occur.

Selecting the Number of Navigation Sets

The actual number of navigation sets is determined quite easily by the resource needs of the project. In general, when a monolithic map is broken into n equal-sized partitions, the resulting amount of data will be approximately $1/n$ of the original size, plus the cost of the interface set. Fortunately, careful selection of partition boundaries will yield a relatively small number of interface nodes, which means that as the size of the navigation sets increases, the cost of the interface set becomes less and less of a factor.

In Table 2.2.2, we illustrate the savings that can be realized when partitioning a 1000-node navigation map into different numbers of navigation sets. In each case we assume that all the partitions contain roughly the same number of nodes. Furthermore, we deliberately choose the number of interface nodes per set to be five—a reasonable goal when partitioning a map. As the table reveals, increasing the number of navigation sets decreases the number of transition table entries, but increases the number of interface table entries. In each case, however, the total number of table entries is substantially less than that required by the original monolithic navigation map.

Table 2.2.2   Various Ways to Partition a 1000-Node Navigation Map

Partitions	Transition Table Entries	Interface Nodes	Interface Table Entries	Total Table Entries
1 (monolith)	$1000^2 = 1,000,000$	0 (none required)	0	1,000,000
2	$2 \times 500^2 = 500,000$	10	100	500,100
5	$5 \times 200^2 = 200,000$	25	625	200,625
10	$10 \times 100^2 = 100,000$	50	2500	102,500
50	$50 \times 20^2 = 20,000$	250	62,500	82,500

Selecting the Partition Boundaries

The harder issue when partitioning a map is usually the selection of partition boundaries. There is one very important goal during the selection process, which is to keep the number of interface nodes in any given navigation set as low as possible. There are two reasons for this: 1) fewer interface nodes results in a smaller interface table size, which saves memory, and, more importantly 2) the fewer interface nodes there are per set, the faster the hierarchical pathfinding process will be, as we will show later.

In general, the process of determining the partitions for a map centers on identifying natural "choke points" in the navigation data. We use the term "choke point" to refer to a small collection of nodes that single-handedly connects two larger collections of nodes. For example in Figure 2.2.3, the nodes C3 and C5 are navigation choke points because all paths entering or exiting set C must go through one of these two points. Likewise, A6 and A7 seem natural choke points for another set, as do B1 and B2.

When natural choke points do not present themselves in the navigation data, it is often necessary to modify the map slightly to create them. While this requires additional work in the design of the navigation layout, the investment is typically small and well worth the effort.

Adding It All Up

The final choice of navigation sets is a balancing act between the desired memory savings and the task of choosing good partitions. While it might be difficult to find the perfect number and arrangement of sets for a given level, it is usually very easy to create a reasonable partitioning that yields substantial memory savings without compromising performance.

A Complete Pathfinding Solution

We now turn to the method for finding the best path between a pair of nodes within the hierarchy. If the source and goal nodes are in the same navigation set, the solution is simply given by the transition table for that set as we have already seen. If the source and goal nodes are in different sets, however, a bit more work needs to be done to construct the best path.

Inter-Set Pathfinding

Solving the inter-set best path is a process that involves four distinct steps. First, we determine the best paths leading from the source node to the boundary of the source set. Second, we determine the best paths leading from the source set boundary to the goal set boundary. Third, we determine the best paths from the goal set boundary to the goal node. Finally, we create a list of complete paths assembled from the first three steps and choose the path with the least cost from source to goal.

This process is best illustrated with an example. Using the navigation system shown in Figures 2.2.3 and 2.2.4, we demonstrate finding the best path from A3 to C7:

1. Using the transition table for set A, we find the best paths leading from A3 to the boundary of set A, which consists of the nodes A6 and A7. The possible paths and their costs are shown in Table 2.2.3.

Table 2.2.3   Sub-Path Options from Source Node A3 to the Set A Boundary

Source	Goal	Sub-path	Cost
A3	A6	A3, A6	10
A3	A7	A3, A6, A7	20

2. Using the interface node transition table, we find the best paths leading from the boundary of set A to the boundary of set C. In other words, for each interface node in set A, we find the best path to every interface node in set C. The possible paths for the interface step are shown in Table 2.2.4.

Table 2.2.4   Sub-Path Options between the Boundaries of Sets A and C

Source	Goal	Sub-path	Cost
A6	C3	A6, A7, C3	20
A6	C5	A6, B2, C5	22
A7	C3	A7, C3	10
A7	C5	A7, C3, C5	20

3. Using the transition table for set C, we find the best paths from the boundary of set C to the goal node, C7, as shown in Table 2.2.5.

Table 2.2.5   Sub-Path Options from the Set C Boundary to Goal Node C7

Source	Goal	Sub-path	Cost
C3	C7	C3, C5, C7	20
C5	C7	C5, C7	10

4. The first three steps generate a collection of sub-paths that can be combined in various ways to form complete paths from source to goal. The final step involves determining the distinct paths that can be generated, and choosing the path with the least cost. In this case, when redundancies in the sub-paths are resolved, two distinct paths emerge, as shown in Table 2.2.6.

Table 2.2.6   Distinct Complete Paths from Source to Goal

Path	Cost
A3, A6, A7, C3, C5, C7	50
A3, A6, B2, C5, C7	42

From Table 2.2.6, we see that the path with the lowest cost is A3, A6, B2, C5, C7, and we are done.

Performance Issues?

At first glance, it might appear that the four-step process just described has returned us to the use of costly runtime searching. Certainly, there is a small amount of work to be done to consider the various path combinations. However, it is very important to note that the amount of searching required is determined entirely by the *number of interface nodes in the source and goal sets only*. In this example, we only need to consider the four interface nodes for sets A and C. Even if there were many other navigation sets between A and C, we would still only need to consider these four nodes because the interface transition table provides all of the intervening data.

Simply put, the cost of the inter-set path search *does not scale up with increases in navigation set size, number, or complexity.* In fact, a navigation system with 1000 navigation sets each containing 1000 nodes would require no more runtime searching than the previous example if each set has only a small number of interface nodes.

Applications of the Navigation Set Hierarchy (NSH)

The hierarchical method described in this article is very flexible in that it makes few assumptions about the underlying data structures used to represent the navigation map. In fact, the only significant assumption that is made is that the navigation map uses some form of a *node*, and that these nodes have some means of *connecting* to other nodes. With this simple requirement, the hierarchy can be applied to a variety of pathing schemes, including the traditional points-of-visibility approach as well as navigation meshes [Snook00].

Beyond the stated purpose of reducing data, the NSH lends itself to other creative uses as well. These include:

Interfacing heterogeneous navigation regions: Games that have different types of navigation regions often encounter difficulties in allowing AIs to move between those regions. For example, driving games that combine vehicle paths with off-road pedestrian paths often require a modest amount of extra programming to allow AIs to seamlessly find routes from one path type to another. The modular nature of the NSH facilitates such transitions because each region can have its own customized pathfinding solution. Furthermore, the interface set can be enhanced to provide additional information about the types of AIs can move between various regions.

Navigation data on demand: Another benefit of the partitioned nature of the NSH is that it lends itself directly to on-demand use within a dynamic level loading scheme. A single navigation set can often provide all the data that is needed at a particular time to operate on a large map for which only certain sections are in memory at a time.

Extension beyond two tiers: While in this article we focus entirely on a two-tier hierarchy, this is by no means a fixed limit. The structures and algorithms described easily extend into larger hierarchies should two tiers not be enough to accommodate a map with enormous navigational content. The self-contained nature of the pathfinding information within a navigation set allows it to function simultaneously as an interface set for lower tiers as well as a general set sitting under a higher tier.

Memory Optimizations

There are a number of improvements to the lookup tables described in the article that could be incorporated, but were left out of the discussion to facilitate the introduction of the material. The most important of these is simple to implement and immediately yields dramatic savings: using edge indices in the transition tables instead of node indices. In other words, rather than storing the index of the node to be visited, we store the index of the edge that leads to that node. Node indices can easily take up two bytes each in large maps, but the nodes themselves rarely have more than eight connections to other nodes, which means that edge indices can be stored using only 3 or 4 bits.

To take this optimization a step further, significant gains can also be made by storing transition information internally per node rather than in external tables. The reason for this is that the table information can be specifically optimized according to the number of connections the node has to other nodes. Nodes having only one link require no transition information at all, as it can be safely assumed that all movement from that node must pass through the same connection. Nodes with exactly two links can store transition information using a single bit per index, and so on. Of course, storing transition information this way requires a little extra coding, but it pays for itself rapidly in considerable memory savings.

Conclusion

With a Navigation Set Hierarchy, we attempt to give a game the "best of both worlds": extremely fast pathfinding at relatively low memory cost. For many types of projects, this method can be a very important and useful component of a navigation system that otherwise would have to rely on clunky dynamic computations. While the lookup tables still require a good bit of memory, often this overhead weighs in at well under 500K for even large navigation maps.

The method we present is fairly easy to implement, and generally requires very little invasion of a game's existing navigation system. This is because the navigation sets and tables sit on top of the underlying data structures, referencing the existing node and edge lists as needed. On the design side, a few touches to the navigation maps here and there might be required to facilitate the partitioning process, and typically a little interface work is required in the level editor to allow the selections of nodes into sets.

Beyond that, once the hierarchy is in place, all that remains to be done is to rip out that clunky A* pathfinding algorithm and start thinking of creative uses for all those extra CPU cycles!

References

[Rabin00] Rabin, Steve, "A* Speed Optimizations," *Game Programming Gems*, Charles River Media, 2000.

[Snook00] Snook, Greg, "Simplified 3D Movement and Pathfinding Using Navigation Meshes," *Game Programming Gems*, Charles River Media, 2000.

[Surasmith02] Surasmith, Smith, "Preprocessed Solution for Open Terrain Navigation," *AI Game Programming Wisdom*, Charles River Media, 2002.

[Tozour04] Tozour, Paul, "Search Space Representations," *AI Game Programming Wisdom 2*, Charles River Media, 2004.

2.3

Path Look-Up Tables— Small Is Beautiful

William van der Sterren—CGF-AI

william@cgf-ai.com

The fastest way to "find" a path from waypoint A to B is not to search. It is much faster to look up a path from a precomputed table. Being able to find paths 10 to 200 times faster than with A* can make a big difference. This frees up the CPU budget for other AI decisions and allows us to use paths and travel times in a much larger portion of the AI's reasoning.

However, path look-up tables are not without disadvantages. The amount of memory required for the tables often prohibits using them for anything other than small levels. Furthermore, path look-up tables have problems reflecting changes in the terrain, such as a door being unlocked or a passage being blocked. Path look-up tables do not easily represent different unit sizes and movement capabilities.

In this article, we discuss optimizations of path look-up tables, and look at two designs that offer the performance benefits at lower costs: a path look-up matrix using indices, and an area-based path look-up table. We briefly discuss how to modify these tables to handle runtime changes to the terrain.

Table 2.3.1   Memory consumption and performance relative to A* for a 1530 waypoint indoor level (higher performance numbers are better).

Pathfinding Approach	Memory Consumption	Short Paths (avg)	Short Paths (worst case)	Far Paths (avg)	Far Paths (worst case)	Far Travel Costs (avg)
Optimized A* (reference)	32KB	1	1	1	1	1
Path look-up matrix	4572KB	55	70	140	135	140
Path look-up matrix, indexed	1187KB	52	67	133	128	133
Area-based look-up table	274KB	13	13	80	90	160

Table 2.3.1 offers a preview of the results for a 1530 waypoint indoor level. The memory consumption numbers are absolute, whereas the performance is expressed rel-

ative to the performance of an optimized A* pathfinder [Rabin00]. For example, a path look-up matrix is, on average, 135 times faster than A* for far paths. In the remainder of this article, we give more insight into the performance and memory consumption.

ON THE CD

The CD-ROM accompanying this book contains source code for the path look-up algorithms discussed. The CD-ROM also contains a demonstrator, similar to James Matthew's A* Explorer [Matthews03], along with example levels.

Note that all performance numbers given in this article are for real game content, not for the more artificial examples created with the demonstrator.

Path Look-Up Matrix

The straightforward way to store paths for fast retrieval is a matrix [Surasmith02]. For N waypoints, this matrix has size $N \times N$. Each cell in the matrix contains, for the corresponding source and destination pair, the "next neighboring waypoint to visit" on the path, or a "no path available" marker otherwise.

We can retrieve the path from a to b by retrieving the next neighbor n_0 to visit at (a, b), followed by the next neighbor n_1 at (n_0, b), et cetera, until n_i equals b. If there is no path from a to b, this is detected in the first look-up because the n_0 value will indicate the absence of a path.

The path retrieval performance is not influenced by the terrain layout (unlike A* and the area-based path look-up tables): it deals as efficiently with deserted plains as with 3D mazes.

The big problem with the path look-up matrix is its memory consumption, which increases quadratically with the number of waypoints. Typically, the number of waypoints is between 256 and 65535, so the $N \times N$ table entries each consume two bytes. This corresponds to 2MB for 1,000 waypoints, and 8MB for 2,000 waypoints. In practice, that limits the use of these tables to smaller levels, especially for console games.

A path look-up matrix contains a static representation of the terrain. It can only reflect changes to the terrain via an update or patch. Updating the table is an $O(n^3)$ operation and typically too expensive. Patching is also problematic, because the consequences of a terrain change. For example, unlocking a door in the center of the level might spread across the whole table. To handle the central door being unlocked for a 1,000 waypoint level, we would have to replace the full 2MB table. You might want to experiment with the demonstrator to get a better feeling for this effect.

A Smaller Indexed Path Look-Up Matrix

For most kinds of terrain, we can reduce the path look-up matrix's memory consumption by a factor of four. We do this by replacing the 2 byte "next waypoint to visit" data by a 4-bit index in the waypoint's list of outgoing waypoints.

The use of a 4-bit index assumes that (for pathfinding purposes) we can reduce the waypoint graph to use a maximum of 15 outgoing waypoints per waypoint. We use 15 rather than 16 outgoing waypoints, since we need to reserve a sentinel value to indicate the "no path" case.

If necessary, we can automatically reduce the waypoint graph to 15 outgoing way-points per waypoint by iteratively trimming away those outgoing links that are best approximated by another link or by a short path via another waypoint.

The memory consumption for this 4-bit index path look-up matrix is N × N × 0.5 for the matrix plus N × 15 × 2.0 for a table containing 15 outgoing waypoints per each waypoint. This amounts to 542KB for 1,000 waypoints and 4MB for 2,000 waypoints. The reduction in footprint typically is better than we would achieve using run-length encoding on complete rows.

Obviously, this smaller path look-up matrix scales as badly as its larger brother, and is as hard to update for terrain changes.

However, we have successfully increased the range of the path look-up matrix solution: it can now deal with four times as much terrain for the same amount of memory, at a mere 5-percent reduction in performance.

Area-Based Path Look-Up Tables

Using 1MB for path look-up tables is not an option on many game platforms, no matter how much we appreciate the low and predictable costs of the path look-up.

The matrix look-up tables consume a lot of memory because they store for every waypoint detailed information how to arrive at every other waypoint, even for way-points that are far away. We can do better than that.

Area-Based Look-Up Algorithm—Concept

With the area-based approach, we do path look-up at two levels (see Figure 2.3.1). At the higher level, we think of the terrain as a set of portals, connected by clusters of waypoints (dubbed "areas"). To get from point *a* to *b* at this level, we determine the nearby portals for *a* and *b*. Then, we determine the shortest portal path between these nearby portals using a portal path look-up table.

At the lower level, we translate this portal path into a waypoint path. For each pair of portals on the portal path, we retrieve the waypoint path between them using

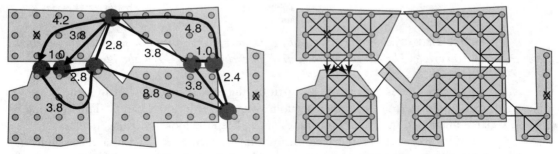

FIGURE 2.3.1 *Paths at two levels: paths between portals, connected by areas (left), and the paths within the areas (right).*

the look-up table of the area connecting this portal pair. This translation is possible because the "high-level" portals correspond to waypoints bridging two or more areas at the lower level.

This area-based approach uses many smaller look-up tables (one for the portal paths, and several for the paths within the areas) rather than one large table. This saves a lot of memory for larger numbers of waypoints, since the look-up tables are quadratic in size, and $a^2 + b^2 < (a + b)^2$.

Partitioning the Terrain

To benefit from this area-based approach, we first need to partition the terrain into areas and portals (see Figure 2.3.2). Areas should consist of co-located waypoints with good interconnectivity. Preferably, areas have small borders to neighboring areas. Portals follow from the waypoints that connect the areas.

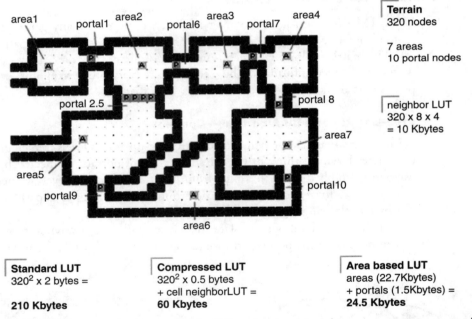

FIGURE 2.3.2　*Terrain, represented by 320 nodes, partitioned into seven areas connected by 10 portals. The memory consumption for each type of LUT is also illustrated.*

In many cases, it is trivial to partition the terrain in areas, but in some cases, we might need to split large open sections of terrain in multiple areas. This splitting of large open sections of terrain is necessary to keep the look-up tables small.

With respect to memory consumption, the theoretically optimal area size is $\sqrt{N}$, for terrain consisting of N waypoints and large N [Waveren01]. For 2,000 waypoints, the optimal area size would be 44.

In practice, the optimal size for an area also depends on the terrain at hand, and on the details of the underlying data structure. For the implementation provided on the accompanying CD-ROM, the optimal area size is closer to 100, since the memory consumption is as follows:

ON THE CD

N/M (areas) $\times M^2$ (matrix size) $\times$ per-area travel info, plus
P^2 (connections) $\times$ inter-area travel info.

For example, for terrain of $N = 2,000$ waypoints, areas of $M = 90$ waypoints, every fifteenth waypoint involved in inter-area connections ($P = 133$), per-area travel info consuming 1.75 bytes per entry, and inter-area travel info consuming 9 bytes per entry, the total memory consumption is 463KB. The costs per entry (1.75 and 9) are averages derived from some game content.

When partitioning the terrain, it is also important to keep the number of portals (area interconnections) per area low and preferably at 10 or less. This reduces the memory consumption and speeds up the look-up.

Note that the memory consumption of the area-based look-up table increases less aggressively compared to the plain and compressed look-up matrices. Look at the terrain shown in Figure 2.3.3, constructed by concatenating three times the terrain from Figure 2.3.2.

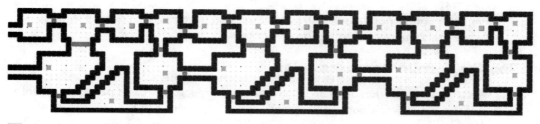

Terrain	neighbor LUT	**Standard LUT**	**Compressed LUT**	**Area based LUT**
964 nodes	964 x 8 x 4	964^2 X 2 bytes =	964^2 X 0.5 bytes	areas (69.6 Kbytes)
	= 30 Kbytes		+ cell neighborLUT =	+ portals (11.1Kbytes) =
21 areas		**1845 Kbytes**	**484 Kbytes**	**81 Kbytes**
34 portal nodes				

FIGURE 2.3.3   *A stretch of three times Figure 2.3.2, with 964 waypoints, 21 areas, and 34 portals.*

When we triple the number of areas, the memory consumption from the area-based matrices triples. Of course, the table storing the paths between the areas becomes nine times as big, but this table contains far fewer entries than N. The memory consumption for Figure 2.3.3 is just 3.3 times as large as that of Figure 2.3.2, as opposed to 3^2 as large for the other LUTs.

We now translate the concept of area-based path look-up tables into a design for the terrain representation and look-up algorithm.

Look-Up at Top Level

Once terrain is split-up into areas and their connections, we can look-up a path from a (in area A) to b (in area B) as follows:

- If $A = B$, we retrieve the local path from area A's own (and small) look-up matrix.

If $A \neq B$, we do the following:

- For source area A, retrieve the outgoing connections Ap.
- For destination area B, retrieve the incoming portals Bp.
- Pick the pair (outgoing connection Ap_o, incoming connection Bp_i) that yields the shortest path ($a - Ap_o - Bp_i - b$).
- For the pair Ap_o, Bp_i, retrieve a path consisting of inter-area connections ($Ap_o - Mp_x \ldots Np_y - Bp_i$).
- Finally, retrieve and construct the detailed waypoint path, by retrieving the in-area path for each area on the path ($A: a - A: Ap_o + M: Ap_o - M: p_x + \ldots + N: Mp_y - N: Bp_i + B: Bp_i - B: b$). Don't forget to remove the double entries at the area transitions; for example, Ap_o and Bp_i.

To use this look-up algorithm, we need the following information. For each area, we need to record how to travel from any waypoint in this area to another waypoint also in the area. We also need to record all connections from that area to other areas. For every connection between two areas, we need to record the cost and shortest path to any other inter-area connection.

Building the Terrain Representation

We need to prepare the AI terrain representation to support area-based path look-up tables. First, we need to partition the waypoints in areas. We can modify our level editor, so it allows us to mark (or paint) every waypoint with the color (ID) of the containing area.

Then, we can compute all links between the areas. For a map with some 1,500 waypoints and 20 areas, there might be some 300 waypoints lying on the border of two (or more) connected areas. However, instead of simply using all these 300 waypoints to represent the connections between areas, we can attempt to find a minimal set of waypoints that together still represent all inter-area connections. This minimum set is typically 60 to 75 percent smaller. For example, in Figure 2.3.4, there are 16 waypoints involved in the inter-area connections, but we can represent all connections with just seven waypoints. We call these waypoints "portals."

This reduction of inter-area connections to a smaller set of portal waypoints makes path look-up at the higher level more efficient. Far fewer portal-combinations need to be considered for paths between areas. Moreover, the reduction also leads to a smaller inter-area travel info matrix.

This reduction can easily be automated: iteratively pick the waypoint that represents the largest number of connections between areas, and then store the waypoint and remove all connections represented by the waypoint.

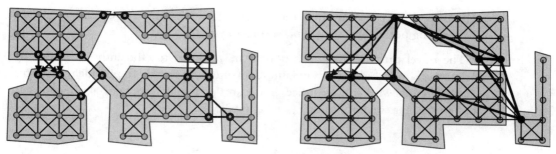

FIGURE 2.3.4 *Terrain with 16 waypoints on the borders between two areas. However, we need just seven waypoints to represent all inter-area connections.*

Once we have identified the areas and selected the portal waypoints, we can construct the look-up tables for areas and area interconnections. We start by computing all paths in a path look-up matrix, which serves as a consistent source also in those cases when two waypoints are connected by multiple paths of the same costs. Obviously, we use this solely for construction purposes and discard it afterwards.

With the cost information available, we can test whether the areas meet several restrictions. In particular, we would like the areas to contain fewer than 254 waypoints, including any connected external portal waypoints. We also would like every area waypoint to be within 254 units of travel cost from that area's incoming and outgoing portal connections. Both restrictions stem from the intention to represent waypoint indices and travel costs with just 1 byte per entry.

For your "asset pipeline" to remain robust, it is recommended to accompany these restrictions with a tool that automatically splits any area failing to meet these restrictions. Level designers will also be happier when we provide tools that automatically create areas from unassigned waypoints.

Design—Per Area Information

For each pathfinding area, we need to record the following information (as illustrated in Figure 2.3.5):

- Record the waypoints within the area, and the connected portals (2 bytes per waypoint).
- Record the incoming and outgoing waypoints in dedicated arrays (2 bytes per waypoint).
- Record all in-area paths, as a matrix containing the index to the next neighbor. The index is a 1-byte index into the array of area waypoints. We use two sentinel values: 0xFF for "no path available," and 0xFE for "this path moves out of the area" (an exceptional situation that we will get into in a moment).
- Record the travel time to the outgoing portal, for every combination (area waypoint, area outgoing portal), using 1 byte per entry.

- Record the travel time from the incoming portal, for every combination (area incoming portal, area waypoint), using 2 bytes per entry.

The travel times to and from portals are recorded to efficiently determine the shortest path from the source waypoint to an outgoing portal. To provide the external portal waypoints with unique indices in the area path matrix, the portal waypoints are added to the area waypoints array (see Figure 2.3.5).

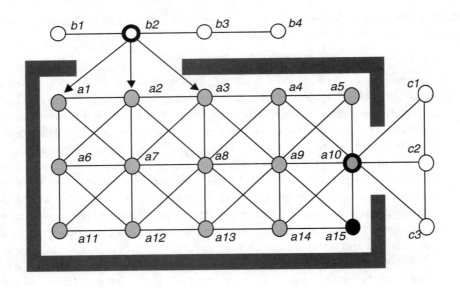

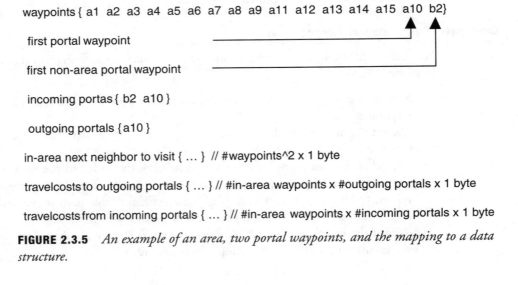

FIGURE 2.3.5   *An example of an area, two portal waypoints, and the mapping to a data structure.*

The total number of waypoints, including connected external portal waypoints, should be less than 254. This leaves room for the two sentinels values 0xFE (outside this area path) and 0xFF (no path available).

In addition, we use a global table that records for every waypoint the ID or pointer to the containing area.

In-Area Path Look-Up

In the majority of the cases, the in-area path look-up is a simple loop (in pseudocode):

```
wp = from
while ( wp != to ) {
        path[count++] = wp
        wp = lookup_table.GetNextToVisit(wp, to)
}
path[count++] = to
```

However, we are very likely to find areas where a shortest path between two waypoints in the same area runs through another area. Obviously, these "outside-area" area paths are likely to occur with U-shaped areas (see Figure 2.3.6). However, "outside-area" area paths can also arise when an area allowing fast movement is parallel to a slow movement area.

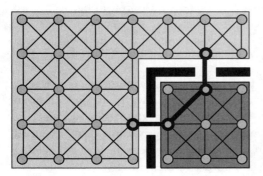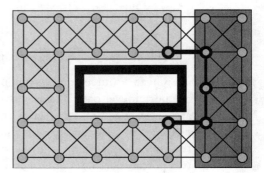

FIGURE 2.3.6 *Two examples of shortest paths moving through another area to connect two waypoints of one area.*

We can deal with "outside-area" area paths in two ways. First, we could break up the areas, to prevent "outside-area" area paths. We get rid of the "U"-shape and the corresponding outside-area shortcut by splitting the areas until they all are convex. However, this splitting will result in numerous small areas, which is inefficient with memory. Furthermore, control is taken away from the level designer who might want to use the areas for other AI purposes.

Alternatively, we can change the look-up algorithm to deal with "outside area" area paths. While expanding the path, we test for an "outside-area" marker value for the next waypoint's index. When we run into such a marker, the current waypoint must be one of the area's outgoing portals. From there, we can retrieve the remainder of the path, starting with a passage through some other area, by a recursive call to the area-based pathfinder.

```
wp = from
while ( wp != to ) {
        path[count++] = wp
        wp = lookup_table.GetNextToVisit(wp, to)
        if ( wp == OUTSIDE_AREA_PATH_MARKER ) {
        --count;
        return count + GetArea(path[count], to);
        }
}
path[count++] = wp
return count
```

Design—Portal Path Information

We design the portal path information as follows. We use a matrix that contains for every pair of portal waypoints (p_i, p_o):

- The travel time from p_i to p_o (or an "no path" value to indicate the absence of path), in two bytes.
- The next portal to visit to get to p_o, or p_o if there is no portal in between (two bytes).
- The next area to traverse to get from p_i to the next portal (two bytes for an area ID, or four bytes for an area pointer).

Given a source portal waypoint and a destination portal waypoint, we can retrieve the portal level path in a way that's similar to retrieving the waypoint path from an area. However, to fully describe the path, we need both the next portal to visit and the next area to visit. Because we selected a small set of portal waypoints to represent all the connections between areas, we end up with situations where the area connecting two portals does not contain either of the two portals (see Figure 2.3.7).

We compute the "next area to traverse" by first retrieving the shortest path from portal p_i to p_o. We then pick the first area that is different from the starting area before we hit p_o, or use the starting area otherwise. In the example in Figure 2.3.7, area D is the area to traverse for the portal pair (5, 7). For $p_i = p_o$, we store the area containing p_i as the next area to visit.

Now, to retrieve a path between two points in different areas, we do the following:

- For source area A, retrieve the outgoing portals Ap.
- For destination area B, retrieve the incoming portals Bp.
- Pick the pair (outgoing portal Ap_o, incoming portal Bp_i) that yields the shortest path $(a - Ap_o - Bp_i - b)$.
- Return the series of portals and corresponding series of areas to visit.

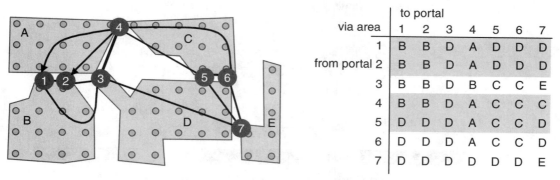

via area	to portal						
	1	2	3	4	5	6	7
1	B	B	D	A	D	D	D
from portal 2	B	B	D	A	D	D	D
3	B	B	D	B	C	C	E
4	B	B	D	A	C	C	C
5	D	D	D	A	C	C	D
6	D	D	D	A	C	C	D
7	D	D	D	D	D	D	E

FIGURE 2.3.7   *A path from* a *(a point in* A*) to* b *(a point in* B*), where the portals (5 and 7) are connected by an area (area D) not containing either of the portals.*

Note that for adjacent areas Ap_o might equal Bp_i. In that case, the portal path has zero costs, but still consists of a single step.

We should avoid such a single step portal path when we can also use a multistep portal path of equal costs. This is to prevent infinite recursion in the path look-up. We use an example to explain why recursion could occur, and why can we can avoid it (but feel free to skip the explanation if you just want to have an overall understanding of the algorithm).

Preventing Infinite Recursion

Picking a single-step portal path leads to infinite recursion in the following situation, which is illustrated in Figure 2.3.8 (for a path from $a9$ to $b1$). The path visits a portal $a9$, at the border of areas A and B. The portal $a9$ is part of area A. Areas A and B are also connected by additional portals ($b6$ in the example). There are multiple shortest paths from a to b, branching at a. The path matrix, from which we derived the area and portal paths, chooses to route the shortest path from a to b through A (via $a8$) rather than through B (via $b9$).

Because $a9$ and $b1$ are in different areas, we need to retrieve the portal path between areas A and B. The portal travel info table will provide three alternatives of equal costs. Entry ($a9$, $b6$) is a multistep answer and tells us to move through A to $b6$ and continue in B from there. Alternatively, there are two single-step answers ($a9$, $a9$) that suggest us to move through A to $a9$, and continue in B from there. Moreover ($b6$, $b6$), suggest us to move via B to $b6$, and continue in B from there on.

Although these single-step answers might seem weird, they are the correct (and necessary) answers for many paths, such as from $a4$ to $b9$ or $a6$ to $b1$. However, the single-step answers might lead to problems when there are multiple shortest path branching from $a9$. In this example, where the shortest path from $a9$ to $b1$ moves via $a8$, the single-step answers ($b6$, $b6$) in area B leads to infinite recursion.

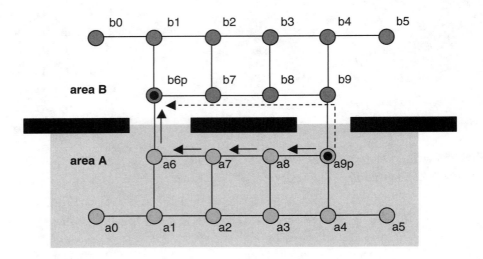

area B: { b0, b1, b2, b3, b4, b5, b7, b8, b9, *b6*, <u>*a9*</u> }
    incoming portals: b6 (internal), a9 (external)
    outgoing portals: b6 (internal), a9 (external)

area A: { a0, a1, a2, a3, a4, a5, a6, a7, a8, *a9*, <u>*b6*</u> }
    incoming portals: a9 (internal), b6 (external)
    outgoing portals: a9 (internal), b6 (external)

FIGURE 2.3.8   *Multiple equal length paths from portal* a9 *to waypoint* b1, *with 1 portal "hop" options.*

Following the (*b6*, *b6*) suggestion, we start using area *B*, and look up the next waypoint to visit from *a9* towards *b6*. Area *B* will inform us when we run into an outside area path, and we should perform a recursive call to get an outside area path from *a9* to *b6*. This call will detect that *a9* and *b6* are in different areas, retrieve a portal path, and go on and on to get from *a9* to *b6* via *B*.

We cannot run into infinite recursion using a multistep portal path, since the entry for that path (*a9*, *b6*) will refer to the correct area to pass through corresponding to the shortest path chosen in the source path matrix. The risk of infinite recursion solely occurs when there are multiple shortest paths branching from the starting portal to the destination. The only condition in which there can be multiple shortest paths from a portal between *A* and *B* to a destination in *B* is when there is at least another portal between *A* and *B*. In that case, we cannot go wrong picking the multistep portal path via those two portals.

Consequently, the revised and robust portal path look-up procedure is as follows:

- For source area A, retrieve the outgoing portals Ap.
- For destination area B, retrieve the incoming portals Bp.
- Pick the pair (outgoing portal Ap_o, incoming portal Bp_i) that yields the shortest path $(a - Ap_o - Bp_i - b)$. When costs are equal, prefer a solution where $Ap_o \neq Bp_i$.
- Return the series of portals and corresponding series of areas to visit.

Design—Performance

Table 2.3.1 already provided some example performance numbers for the path look-up algorithms. In this table, "short paths" refer to paths of up to 16 waypoints, and "long paths" refer to paths longer than 16 waypoints. The average costs refer to the average costs of all paths retrieved, whereas the worst-case cost refers to the cost level solely exceeded by 5 percent of the queries. The A* worst-case costs were typically two to three times the average costs. "Far travel costs" refers to the costs of paths longer than 16 waypoints. The AI typically compares travel costs when selecting the nearest item or power-up to fetch.

For raw performance or predictable and low CPU consumption, path look-up matrices offer 50 to 150 times better performance than A*, and two to five times better performance than area-based look-up tables. When we have several hundred KB available for faster pathfinding, an area-based look-up table provides a speed-up of 10 to 80 times. The area-based path look-up table outperforms the other look-up tables for travel cost look-ups, simply because it is the only one storing some travel cost information in its tables.

The memory consumption of the path look-up matrices solely depends on the number of waypoints. For the area-based look-up table, the consumption depends on the quality of the areas (manually or automatically created) and the size of the area-interconnections. Table 2.3.3 provides some examples from game content. Open areas lead to larger area interconnections, and consequently to more portals.

Table 2.3.3 Memory Consumption for Various Types of Levels

Style	Map			Memory		
	Waypoints	Areas	Portals	Matrix	Indexed Matrix	Area-Based Look-Up
Outdoor, trenches	1047	20	66	2164KB	535KB	183KB
Plain level, few obstacles	1117	14	135	2436KB	641KB	392KB
Indoor, multilevel	1530	20	87	4572KB	1187KB	274KB

Patching for Dynamic Terrain

In most games, the terrain is not completely static. Key cards and triggers serve to provide or prohibit access to certain regions.

The area-based path look-up table is slightly more suitable for patching to reflect these terrain changes, because of the partitioning of terrain in areas and portals. Changes to portals (for example, a portal being closed) can often be applied by patching or replacing the portal table. In case the portal is used for "outside-area" paths within an area, that area would also have to be patched. Alternatively, you might want to prevent "outside-area" paths near the portal being closed by breaking up non-convex areas near that portal.

When terrain changes are simply localized to an area and do not reduce the use of any of the area's portals (for example, part of a room catches fire, and should not be visited), the area's table can be patched on the fly.

In both cases, the patches consist of several tens of KB in the worst case. Typically, they can be "compressed" by solely recording the delta with the original table. We also have a lot of control over the patch size when we define the areas.

Patching becomes more complicated when several portals can be opened or closed in arbitrary order. In that case, we might have to compute various patches for all the possible sequences.

Conclusion

Path look-up tables "find" paths from waypoint A to B in the fastest and most predictable way. However, their memory consumption might rule out their use. In this article, we discussed two optimizations to reduce the tables' memory consumption significantly while retaining the performance benefits.

One simple optimization is to store indices to neighboring waypoints, at 4 bits per entry. This reduces a table for 500 waypoints to less than 250KB. However, the table size still increases quadratically with the number of waypoints.

Another optimization is area-based path look-up (also known as hierarchical pathfinding). This approach scales much better with large numbers of waypoints, provided the terrain can be partitioned in loosely connected areas. The table size scales linearly with the number of areas, and increases quadratically only with the number of area interconnections.

We can achieve a small area-based path look-up system by representing the area interconnections by a minimum set of waypoints, although this adds some complexity to the look-up algorithm.

Area-based path look-up tables are more easily modified to reflect changes in the terrain, since the effects of the change are better localized. That means that we can update the tables with relatively small patches.

Quake III Arena uses an approach similar to the area-based look-up tables, but for volume-based navigation data. [Waveren01] explains that approach, and the theory behind it extensively.

Path look-up tables are not a solution to every pathfinding problem. Often, we have a need for more than static predictable paths. However, even in those cases, we might benefit from path look-up tables to efficiently answer the bulk of navigation requests, leaving us more CPU to dynamically deal with more special requests.

References

[Matthews03] Matthews, James, "A* Explorer," *www.generation5.org/ase.shtml*, 2003.

[Rabin00] Rabin, Steve, "A* Speed Optimizations," *Game Programming Gems*, Charles River Media, 2000.

[Surasmith02] Surasmith, Smith, "Preprocessed Solution for Open Terrain Navigation," *AI Game Programming Wisdom*, Charles River Media, 2002.

[Waveren01] van Waveren, Jan Paul, *The Quake III Arena Bot Documentation*, pp. 24–47, *www.idsoftware.com/home/jan/q3abotai/*, 2001.

2.4

An Overview of Navigation Systems

Alex J. Champandard—AI Depot

alex@ai-depot.com

Movement is such an important part of modern games that it can be a limiting factor for the development in many ways—let alone the design. A competent navigation system can assist programmers and not restrict designers when synthesizing motion. Frankly, there is no ideal solution; navigation is a tradeoff between capabilities and resources used. There is a right balance to suit your needs. A flurry of research and experimentation has been done on the subject, spread across so many fields you'll need your toes to count them. This wealth of information can be somewhat confusing, as it is not always obvious how everything clicks into place. Understanding the big picture is essential to craft human-level movement, ease the development process, or simply to maximize the performance of the final system (more so than clever algorithms).

This article starts by defining the—somewhat elusive—concept of a navigation system, showing why it can be beneficial to AI developers. Then, the level of abstraction of navigation systems is discussed, in order to understand how much functionality it should contain. To allow the navigation system to interact with the rest of the AI architecture, an interface is needed. The next section emphasizes its importance, and investigates the different types of specifications possible. Looking at possible AI paradigms for the implementation, both reactive and deliberative approaches are analyzed. Specific techniques are proposed, notably suitable alternatives to A* search. Finally, hints to build the system are provided, as well as managing its development.

Definition

The precise definition of a navigation system differs from one AI developer to another, as they can be used for a myriad of different things. Fortunately, there are some common concepts:

A navigation system is a separate component responsible for synthesizing movement behaviors.

So, why do you need one? You will no doubt have come across the benefits of modularity in software development; AI is no different. By isolating the navigation system, it becomes straightforward to implement and debug as a unit—instead of functionality being divided within the AI. When navigation is encapsulated into a component, crafting behaviors is simpler and the entire system is easier to implement. However, the benefits are dependent on the design, as there are many different ways of splitting up the AI and navigation.

Levels of Abstraction

It's not always obvious what components are part of the navigation system. First, code to handle movement can be scattered throughout the implementation, and second, all the components can be tightly integrated with the rest of the AI architecture (e.g., as behaviors). If it's possible to separate the navigation system, you'll get the full benefits of the modular approach, such as encapsulation and abstract interfaces.

Various degrees of responsibility can be assigned to the navigation system, ranging from plain pathfinding to entire architectures storing the terrain model and all movement behaviors. Choosing this level of abstraction mostly depends on the complexity of the agent AI.

Planner: In this case, only the shortest path algorithm is abstracted out and implemented separately. The planner is often a common starting point for AI developers, due to the abundance of literature on the subject. In this case, the agent is responsible for making the path request and interpreting the result.

Pathfinder: Giving slightly more responsibility to the navigation system, the pathfinder would deal with the execution of the plans. The agent still has direct control of the paths, but the common post-processes (iterating through paths, smoothing trajectories) are factored out.

Sub-architecture: It's possible to use an AI architecture specifically for navigation. This will generally be composed of different movement behaviors and planning abilities, including the terrain model.

Once the level of abstraction is decided upon, there are guidelines to determine what falls within the navigation system, and what doesn't. Higher levels of abstraction lead to more flexibility for the implementation of the navigation system—which can be a great advantage. Indeed, the components of the navigation system can be designed as a consistent set and highly optimized together—regardless of the integration with the agent's AI.

Deciding the scope of the navigation system is a somewhat controversial issue. How much functionality should it include? Should other components be internal or external? Things such as low-level animation and locomotion, tactical decisions, and non-movement behaviors can undoubtedly benefit from interaction with the navigation system, but how should this be done?

To some extent, it's easy to get carried away with encapsulating too much functionality within the navigation system. To that end, it seems best to let the navigation system handle only movement and develop it initially for this purpose. Then, independent interfaces would allow collaborating components to use information from the navigation system (e.g., accessing terrain data). With regard to the overall functionality of the navigation system, this is defined by the main interface.

Navigation Interfaces

The agent's AI has a certain level of complexity in the desires and motivations (more or less explicit, depending on the design). Creating intelligent movement involves transmitting these motivations to the navigation system. To that extent, the interface is important since it allows information about these motivations to be expressed (e.g., as weighted rewards in space).

The interface is also useful to help define the level of abstraction of the navigation system and formalize its functionality. The design of such an interface isn't something that AI coders generally worry about; with good agile development practices, a suitable specification will generally arise from refactoring the source code itself. Whichever method you use to obtain your interface, you're on the right track if you've given consideration to its far-reaching consequences.

Expressiveness

Choosing—or designing—an interface involves making a compromise between focus and flexibility. A highly focused interface can be better tuned to a specific problem, while a more flexible interface can have the expressiveness to handle a wider variety of scenarios. Generally, a complex system will be more efficient with a flexible interface, while a simpler system will benefit from the focused models. There's no intrinsic computational cost in having a flexible interface instead of a focused one; it's essentially about the restrictions imposed upon the implementation.

Taking a look at existing paradigms, starting with the most focused:

Single pair: Two points are specified in the world (origin and destination), and the shortest path between them is returned.

Weighted destinations: Instead of limiting the requests to one destination, this can be extended to multiple goals, each with its own reward coefficient. An optimal path that maximizes the tradeoff between reward and cost.

Spatial desires: Abstracting out space, it's possible to specify the movement by passing the motivations from the agent to the navigation system (e.g., get armor or a weapon). This is an implicit way to specify the weighted destinations.

Converting a focused interface onto a more flexible one is a trivial matter. A single-pair request corresponds to a single weighted destination of value 1.0. Converting weighted requests to single pair requires much more effort, in the form of prioritization of goals and task planning. Generally, this involves simplifying the problem in a convenient fashion.

Specifying Movement

So, what does all this imply for expressing behaviors? If you have agents that only need to go to one point in space (e.g., directly following a click or order), then a single-pair interface is perfect. If agents have multiple goals, you'll need a destination selection function to decide where to go next, simplifying the problem slightly. This can be done with a small script that evaluates the goals and picks the most appropriate—using a distance tradeoff, for example. The process of ranking these goals requires extracting travel times from the terrain data (among other information). This can be quite costly computationally, so it's best kept to a minimum.

In some cases, using such a reactive selection of goals can be shortsighted and the choice of paths can shatter the illusion of intelligence. For example, an agent might decide to go for the larger object that's isolated at one extremity of the level. A better choice would have been to head toward three smaller objects, whose accumulated benefits are better. To decide on the optimal sequence of single-pair targets, a high-level plan needs to be formulated. At this stage, you've implemented a "task planner" simply to get around the limitations of the interface. This would not have been necessary if a more flexible interface was used instead, removing the single destination bottleneck. If you find yourself overwhelmed by this destination selection process—especially while creating believable agents with multiple spatial desires—perhaps you could consider a different interface and give the navigation system more responsibility.

AI Paradigms for Movement

Selecting the right implementation is a similar process to picking the interface or the level of abstraction; there is no universal solution, so you need to assess the requirements and build a system capable of satisfying them. It's a good idea to keep the solution minimal at the same time, as it will always lead to a more efficient system. To build the most appropriate system, you'll need to know about the options available.

Reactive Behaviors

A reactive behavior takes the sensory input and performs a direct mapping to determine the output. In the case of movement, the input is local information about obstacles and the output corresponds to motor commands. Possible behaviors include obstacle avoidance, seeking, or fleeing [Reynolds99].

The type of movement created by reactive steering is fundamentally limited. There are traps and complex layouts that these behaviors cannot handle efficiently. Although there are tricks to improve the handling of such situations, by adding randomness or a small sense of state, they do not perform realistically or reliably.

Simple situations, on the other hand, are perfect for reactive behaviors. They can cope realistically with simple obstacles and perform reliably too. The types of environments you should think of applying reactive behaviors to are uncluttered environments (e.g., a field), simple convex obstacles (e.g., a forest), or even sparse crowds.

You should prefer reactive behaviors for the following reasons:

- Highly localized spatial queries, predictable ray traces. Acquiring information can be efficiently batched, optimized for memory accesses.
- Instantaneous computation of the steering vector, and does not need to be computed often (every second or so in a static world).
- Fully reactive behaviors are intrinsically dynamic and can cope with moving obstacles reliably.

These benefits make them a very good choice, although be aware of their emergent nature and the implicit control (reactive behaviors are typically not goal directed).

Deliberative Planning

Reactive behaviors are not able to handle all situations—including complex layouts, intricate scenarios, and human-level movement generally. Planning can help solve all these problems by formulating a suitable path in the world before it is even used.

One fundamental aspect of deliberative solutions is that they generally perform computation on a terrain graph. This involves both computation time and memory resources, unlike the reactive behaviors that are practically instantaneous and by definition memory-less. So, you get what you pay for! Here are some of the advantages:

- Provably optimal paths, returned within known worst-time complexity.
- Higher-level of spatial intelligence; plans are made according to the terrain representation.
- Easier to control than emergence. You tell the planner what you want, and you'll most likely get the expected result.

It sounds like the feature list of a middleware library! However, it's not all that easy. There's a lot of work involved, specifically to acquire and prepare the terrain data [Tozour04].

Hybrid Systems

Many problems can be overcome by simply combining different reactive behaviors (e.g., to escape most reactive traps), or accumulating levels of planning (to optimize for speed or quality of movement). However, there are also some benefits in combining the two types of movement. Either approach has its disadvantages, although the hybrid approach seems to have a few more things going for it.

In many cases, it is not necessary to plan over a fine grid; this allows precise control, but it's often not necessary. Indeed, a lot of processing time is wasted on paths that could be handled straightforwardly—thanks to the common sense provided by the reactive behaviors. Therefore, in many cases the terrain data can be much higher-level, which considerably reduces computation and memory overheads [Champandard03].

On the other hand, the system will get into trouble where step-by-step planning is required. In the case where static and dynamic obstacles have accidentally become arranged in a mazelike configuration, a hybrid approach will not be realistic—if it works at all. You'll undeniably need a local planner for this, using similar planning algorithms on a finer grid.

It is quite likely you'll spend a similar amount of time developing either of these alternatives. In the hybrid case, the steering behaviors that execute plans need to be debugged; with levels of planning, the implementation needs to identify situations, and gather and represent dynamic obstacle data. From this point of view, the choice of the initial system is crucial since it will facilitate these tasks and leave room for other extensions,

Implementation

When deciding on implementation, make sure you are considering the proper tool for the job. An ill-selected tool can have lasting ramifications throughout the system's development. Deciding on the implementation is linked to the paradigm you choose.

Reactive Behaviors

Here, the most applicable techniques are steering behaviors. Based on highly explicit mathematical equations, it's possible to decide where to steer next. These work fine in most cases, although can struggle on two accounts: integration of multiple behaviors and realism. To get around the first problem, using a subsumption architecture [Brooks91] is an extremely simple way to select action (the behaviors are prioritized, and higher levels get to override the lower ones). This too can have trouble with realism (especially smoothness), so fuzzy logic can come to the rescue [Saffioti97]. In the context of game AI, using a fuzzy interpreter to blend the behaviors together works perfectly most of the time—although it can prove problematic when mutually exclusive steering forces are blended.

Deliberative Planning

Single-pair algorithms will be a wise choice if you have chosen a focused interface. If you're using weighted destinations instead, you might have to delve into network flow theory to find an implementation.

However, don't necessarily associate planning with a search. Other techniques can prove more efficient in many cases. Identifying your type of problem in static worlds will help you make a decision:

- In environments of manageable size, it is often possible to precompute everything [Surasmith02, van der Sterren04].

- For larger worlds, it can be possible to use reactive approximation techniques to build near optimal paths without a search.
- Hierarchical solutions can provide a solution in a lazy incremental fashion [Rabin00].

Things can get trickier for dynamic environments:

- If the problem can be simplified, use a threshold to trigger a replan when the conditions have changed sufficiently. Events in the game environment can also be used to alert the planner.
- If you decide to use a search, it is often possible to sacrifice some memory to prevent a complete new search. Indeed, D* reuses the search tree from A* [Stentz94], and [Gallo80] reuses the previous minimum spanning tree; both provide better time-complexity for most re-optimization problems. However, be aware that the implementation of such algorithms are not straightforward, and might cost you valuable development time.
- Finally, there are also "quality of service" algorithms available, which do not rely on searches at all. However, it can be tricky to cope with suboptimal paths or dynamically changing estimates of best paths [Champandard02].

There's a wide spectrum of techniques that can provide deliberative movement, ranging from static precomputed single-pair paths to dynamic quality of service processes that can deal with weighted destinations. One of these will suit your system best.

Building the System

There is more to game AI than just programming. Specific development methods and design patterns can enhance the process of developing a navigation system.

Development

Depending on the paradigm you opted for, the navigation system will be a kind of decomposition: *functional* (each of the components will perform a function for the entire system) or *behavioral* (components correspond to palpable abilities). Naturally, in a hybrid system, you might have a bit of both!

A functional decomposition is generally common in software development, so standard techniques apply to improve the development: separation of interface and implementation, unit tests, and so forth. For behavioral decompositions, you should turn to methodologies used by the AI and robotics communities. Specifically, building the system incrementally from a basic behavior, and testing the capabilities in a real game environment at each stage. This assures that the system is consistent throughout the iterations [Brooks91].

Management

Even starting with detailed design and thoughtful implementation, your navigation system can end up being very complex. It takes a surprising amount of work to synthesize realistic movement. For game AI projects where handling movement correctly is becoming essential, it's important to have a methodology to deal with all this code. How to handle this depends heavily on the level of abstraction.

With a small "navigation system," many lines of code will be written on the outside. To this extent, you'll benefit from designing the entire AI architecture first in order to maintain a coherent organization; the benefits of having the navigation as a separate component are not as pronounced. On the other hand, it's possible to keep the movement code entirely within larger navigation systems. This is great for the rest of the AI architecture, but it also means you'll need a good methodology to handle the internals of the navigation system.

There are many little tasks that you'll find yourself dealing with. These smaller components cause the code to increase somewhat unexpectedly. This glue code ties all the larger objects together, for example:

- Handling triggers from the environment that affect movement.
- Controlling the order of execution of the internal components and behaviors.
- Managing the flow of information between components.
- Identifying the situation and applying the appropriate motion behavior.
- Keeping track of states, requests, and state changes.

Managing the flow of code and information can be done nicely by a *finite-state machine* [Fu04]. This would make the navigation system a data-driven sub-architecture, taking into account requests from the agent, as well as data from the environment.

This is the kind of behavior that you might be familiar with on the agent level, rather than the navigation level. Either aspect can have its advantages from this point of view, although the divide and conquer approach seems applicable here too. Handling movement *could* be done mostly independently from the rest of the AI. Complex agents will greatly benefit from a strong navigation system that's abstracted out completely.

Conclusion

The development of a navigation system takes more than understanding a heuristic search algorithm. There are numerous issues involved in synthesizing realistic movement in games. Ignoring these can lead to a suboptimal solution, unnecessarily complex code, and visible problems with the behaviors.

In particular, if you're attempting to replicate human-level intelligence for path planning, you might want to consider a more flexible interface than single-pair. If you're trying to make your navigation handle huge worlds with simple obstacles, opt for reactive behaviors. Finally, if you're interested in dynamic solutions that do not oversimplify the problem, look at the quality-of-service solutions.

Having identified and explained the key decisions to be made during the development, you should now be capable of building a personalized navigation system—rather than blindly opting for the most popular solution. Choosing the right navigation architecture will improve the quality of the behaviors and increase performance too, so make sure you consider the design before you start implementing!

References

[Brooks91] Brooks, R. A., "Intelligence without Representation," *Artificial Intelligence 47*, pp. 139–159, 1991.

[Champandard02] Champandard, Alex J., Realistic Autonomous Navigation in Dynamic Environments, MSc Thesis, The University of Edinburgh, *www.base-sixteen.com/Navigation/*, 2002.

[Champandard03] Champandard, Alex J., "Pathematics: Routing for Autonomous Agents," *Game Developers Conference Proceedings*, 2003.

[Fu04] Fu, D., and Houlette, R., "The Ultimate Guide to FSMs in Games," *AI Game Programming Wisdom 2*, Charles River Media, 2004.

[Gallo80] Gallo, G., "Reoptimization Procedures in Shortest Path Problems," *Rivista di Mathematica per le Scienze Economiche e Sociali 3*, pp. 3–13, 1980.

[Rabin00] Rabin, S., "A* Speed Optimizations," *Game Programming Gems*, Charles River Media, 2000.

[Reynolds99] Reynolds, C.W., "Steering Behaviors for Autonomous Characters," *Game Developers Conference Proceedings*, 1999.

[Saffioti97] Saffioti, A., "The Uses of Fuzzy Logic in Autonomous Robot Navigation," *Soft Computing*, 1(4):180–197, 1997.

[Stentz94] Stentz, T., "Original D*," *ICRA 94*, 1994, available online at *www.frc.ri.cmu.edu/~axs/doc/icra94.pdf*

[Surasmith02] Surasmith, S., "Preprocessed Solution for Open Terrain Navigation," *AI Game Programming Wisdom*, Charles River Media, 2002.

[Tozour04] Tozour, P., "Search Space Representations," *AI Game Programming Wisdom 2*, Charles River Media, 2004.

[van der Sterren04] van der Sterren, William, "Path Look-up Tables—Small Is Beautiful," *AI Game Programming Wisdom 2*, Charles River Media, 2004.

2.5

Jumping, Climbing, and Tactical Reasoning: How to Get More Out of a Navigation System

Christopher Reed and Benjamin Geisler—Raven Software/Activision

creed@ravensoft.com, bgeisler@ravensoft.com

Many articles have been written about various technical approaches to A* and related pathfinding algorithms. This is not one of those articles. This is about using navigation to give AI more than just routes from one place to another.

Does your AI need to know when and how to throw a grenade over a wall at an enemy? Want your characters to automatically climb a ladder or jump over a gap? Or perhaps you would like to know what locations are useful for snipers to lean around a corner. These are just a few examples of behavior that can easily be embedded into the navigation data and automatically detected during a preprocessing step or encoded by hand.

We first introduce how embedded environment information may be used for both "high-level" tactical reasoning and "low-level" animation and steering. Then, we will explain in more detail some of the environment information that must be embedded to make the desired usages run. Having implemented these techniques in *Soldier of Fortune II: Double Helix* (*SOF2*), we offer some suggestions as to what works well and what does not.

An Example Navigation System

Pathfinding allows AI to navigate between locations, and is usually based on graph theory. Although other non-graph-based approaches have been presented, particularly for use in RTS games, we will assume a graph-based navigation system, and will use the term *point* to represent locations, and *edge* to represent safe routes between these locations. Points are usually placed near the ground, where connection tests can easily detect navigation problems. Connecting edges go through doorways and up stairs, down hallways, and across open areas—anywhere that AI might want to go to. Edges and points form a graph, which is then navigated using the A* search algorithm [Stout00].

There have been a few articles written about using a navigation graph for tactical [Lidén02] and behavioral [Hancock02] reasoning. This article expands on these ideas.

AI Architecture Considerations

In addition to selecting a path from one point to another, embodied game agents need to be able to actually follow the path they selected. We recommend the use of an AI layer, in addition to the typical decision maker, which specializes in movement, steering, animation, and other low-level movement details that the path planner is typically not designed for. Such an architecture follows two of Steve Rabin's strategies for optimizing AI [Rabin01]:

- Strategy #8—Do the Hard Work Offline
- Strategy #9—Use Emergent Behavior to Avoid Scripting

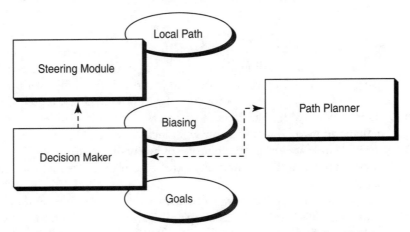

FIGURE 2.5.1   *An example of a layered architecture well suited for navigation behavior.*

High-Level Point Selection and Pathfinding

The higher levels of AI can benefit from an organized representation of the game world. Any data that AI can easily look at is potentially usable. Perhaps an agent is looking for somewhere to hide, looking for somewhere he can go to use an object, or just generally trying to avoid dangerous locations. All these problems can be solved with enriched navigation data.

Finding Cover and Combat Tactics

An enhanced path planner can be an important tool for portraying cooperation between agents, allowing coordinated movements [van der Sterren02]. Many action games depict enemy troops acting in tandem to secure a goal, including a common tactic of war called "Bounding Overwatch" [USArmy92]. Once a leader has advanced to a suitable spot, he provides cover fire for his partner. Then, the partner advances along the leader's path, moving toward the same eventual goal. Using embedded information in the points, the partner also selects a suitable cover spot a little farther down the path. The process repeats until the pair reaches their goal.

The key to this type of behavior lies in the ability to choose an appropriate location for providing cover fire. To aid in that selection, any number of factors can be embedded in the points, such as obstacle and visibility information. Later, we will discuss some examples of simple point attributes that can easily be detected and recorded.

Throwing Grenades

Throwing grenades can be tricky. An agent must either be completely scripted or must evaluate if a thrown grenade would make it to its destination. For the purposes of decision making, it is not practical to evaluate grenade trajectories during the game. Due to the multiple ways a grenade could be thrown, it is preferable to encode possible grenade throws into the navigation system. The trajectory must be evaluated from all points to all other points within a given radius during the processing of the navigational data. If the trajectory succeeds, label this edge as a "grenade throw edge." The agent queries the navigation system and locates the closest spot that allows him to throw the grenade. The decision-making code will instruct the agent how to get to the calculated spot and how to throw his grenade based on this embedded information. An example is shown in Figure 2.5.2.

For a more in-depth look at grenade handling and precomputing grenade trajectories, see [van der Sterren00].

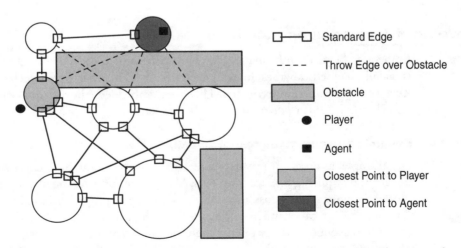

FIGURE 2.5.2 *Navigation graph augmented with information for throwing grenades. Dotted lines (Throw Edge lines) show what areas can be reached with grenades.*

Biasing Edge Cost

Normally, the "cost" of traversing an edge is simply the distance between the two points it connects; however, sometimes modifying that number can produce some very handy results. You can make an agent avoid a given edge simply by adding to its cost. For example, edges that lead off the main path or are narrow and tight can be slightly biased to help stop agents from "cutting corners."

It is also useful to bias edges requiring unique behavior. For example, consider the following portion of the path planner:

```
ParentPoint = OpenList.GetFromOpenList()
For each edge from ParentPoint
      Switch Edge.type()
            Case FLY_EDGE:
                  If ( actor.CanFly() )
                        Edge.cost = actor.FlyBiasCost()
                        OpenList.AddToOpenList(Edge)
```

Note that by using the function `FlyBiasCost()`, we can allow for agents to determine the likelihood that they will use a flying path.

We found that encoding temporal events into the navigation system was also useful. When an agent is killed in SOF2, his body temporarily biases all the edges near it for any agents on his team. In this way, agents will automatically avoid navigating through areas where their comrades have fallen, and attempt to find an alternate route.

Be careful when altering a cost for A*. Getting too far away from the standard distance function reduces the optimality of the algorithm. It's best to keep any biasing as a linear scale of the base distance.

Low-Level Animation and Steering

Embedded behavior information can be very helpful at the lower level as well. A path is usually handed down as an abstract series of points that were selected by a higher level and now must be navigated. However, embedded information will give AI the knowledge it needs to do a number of behaviors.

Dynamic Movement: Jumping, Opening a Door

For example, as an agent traverses his planned path, he might encounter a crevice in the ground requiring him to jump over. With jump information already embedded in the edge connecting across the crevice, selecting a proper animation and steering through the air can happen automatically. There is no need to script or plan the jumping behavior, it just happens when the agent needs to get across. We will discuss detecting jump and vault edges in more detail shortly.

The path planner and high-level decision-making code need not worry about doors either. Should a path edge lead through a door, the agent should be able to select an animation to open the door, wait, and then steer through it. This is possibly the best feature of embedded world information. Because high-level decision making can be decoupled from dynamic movement, new movement types (special doors, unique ladders, and so forth) can be added, and all existing combat behavior will automatically make use of it.

The Navigation Point

Now it is time to establish the particulars of how these enhanced points and edges are actually formatted, created, and detected. We'll begin a step-by-step analysis by returning to the basic concept of the navigation point. Whether placed by hand or automatically generated, these points form the core of most navigation systems, providing discrete locations in space where AI agents can move to and from.

Radius and Size

Navigation data exists to inform an agent how to safely get from one location to another (see Figure 2.5.3). Neither the beginning location nor the end one is usually exactly on one of the points of the graph, so it is helpful to use spatial volumes for testing reachability and "openness." Volume can be represented with any kind of geometric shape: box, triangle, sphere, and so forth. However, the sphere offers some additional information for area of influence and is easy to detect and store (see the following section *Obstacle Visibility—Side to Side*).

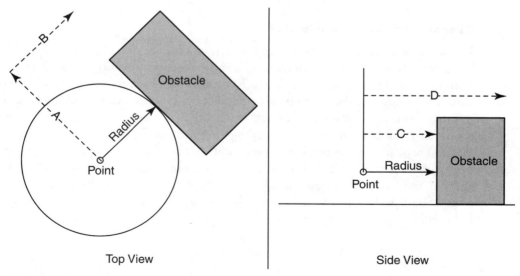

FIGURE 2.5.3 *The anatomy of a navigation point.*

Detecting the sphere of influence for a navigation point depends on what you are trying to represent; however, the most common use is to detect how far out the neighboring navigable area extends. For example, in a room a point sphere should not include any walls, holes in the floor, or other obstacles that could impede an agent's mobility. Finding these obstacles is as easy as running a series of collision tests radiating out from the center of the point. Run these tests with as much granularity as you want—the more tests you do, the more accurate your radius will be. The closest collision that you detect is the radius.

The radius of a navigation point alone can offer some useful information to a savvy agent: Points with small radii are close to walls and other obstacles, thus making them possible locations for protection, stealth, and ambush.

Obstacle Visibility—Vertical

Should the radius algorithm detect an obstacle near to a point, a great deal of information can be automatically discovered about visibility above and around that obstacle with just a few more collision tests.

First, you will want to know the height of your obstacle. Locations where an agent might safely crouch or stand behind and fire a projectile weapon are immensely useful. You can find out the height of your obstacle by running a number of collision tests in the same direction as the original test that detected the collision, with increasing heights (shown as collision tests C and D in Figure 2.5.3). As with the radius, the more tests you do the more accurate information you will have. If any tests report that they didn't hit anything, thus clearing the top of the obstacle, then you've found the height of the obstacle and probably a good place to hide.

Obstacle Visibility—Side to Side

If your vertical height test found that you have an obstacle that no agent can possibly see over the top of, your point might still be near a corner, providing an excellent location for shooting or setting an ambush. To detect a corner, you can run collision tests from the location of the obstacle in perpendicular directions to the direction of the test that detected the obstacle. This test can be whatever distance you deem appropriate for a corner, but is often determined by the size of the agent who will be using the point. Then, if your perpendicular test didn't hit anything, run another test—this time parallel to the original—to see if there is anything around the corner (shown as collision tests A and B in Figure 2.5.3). Knowing about corners can be a powerful tool to any agent, as shown in Figure 2.5.4, where an agent uses side-to-side visibility with lethal effect.

FIGURE 2.5.4   *A character in* SOF2 *leans around a corner.*

The Navigation Edge

Points provide a good deal of information, but alone are not sufficient for navigation. The points must be connected by edges to one another, telling an agent how to safely move through space without hitting anything.

The simplest edge only records that it is safe to go from one point to another; however, "safety" can mean many things. Characters might have features making the traversal possible for one agent and impossible for another. The following edge features have been found useful.

Size

In many games, agents have dramatically different sizes. A human might be able to walk through a hallway in a building easily enough, but an elephant would be too big. The maximum size of any character wanting to traverse an edge can be detected by running a series of collision tests, starting with the largest possible size and growing progressively smaller with each failure. Record the largest test that succeeds and anything of equal or smaller size can pass through.

If the points have size (see The Navigation Point—Radius and Size*), you can quickly narrow down or eliminate any edge size that is larger than the point size.*

Over a Crevice—Jump or Fly to the Other Side

If your game has characters that can jump or fly, you'll want to record places where they can use their abilities to get over a hole in the ground. For this type of edge, you will need to know the locations on either side of the crevice where the character needs to begin his maneuver (be it to jump or fly across). There are two ways to detect the sides of a crevice:

- Invisible "crevice" geometry. Placed as an invisible part of the game, this bit of geometry can be detected only by your navigation collision tests, and is the most efficient way to find holes in the ground.
- If no such invisible geometry is available, continually tracing down along the edge can detect a crevice. Should one be found, additional tests are needed "inside" the crevice in order to find its extents. This second process is much more complicated than the first and less reliable (shown as the edge between Point B and Point C in Figure 2.5.5).

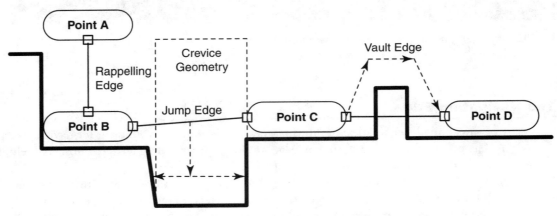

FIGURE 2.5.5 *A side view of embedded behavior for jumping and climbing.*

Into the Air—Fly

Although it is common for navigation points to be placed near the "ground," airborne points are sometimes needed for characters that fly. Any edge that connects a ground point to an air point needs to be specially flagged so ground-based characters do not attempt to use it. If a point is not already specially flagged as airborne, running a simple collision test straight down from each point is an easy way to detect them.

Over an Obstacle—Vault or Jump

So, your collision test has found an obstacle along the path from one point to another? That's not necessarily the end of the story. The connection might still be possible, if the agent is able to jump or vault. Detecting this is similar to detecting the vertical obstacle visibility in the previous *Navigation Point* section. However, in this case, jumping or vaulting is usually tied to animation, and requires a very strict set of requirements for it to work. The obstacle might need to be a certain height and width, and the space over the obstacle often needs to be a particular size too. At least two additional collision tests need to be run in order to detect an "over obstacle" vaulting edge (shown as the edge between Point C and Point D in Figure 2.5.5, and in the *SOF2* screenshot Figure 2.5.6).

FIGURE 2.5.6   *A character in* SOF2 *vaulting over an obstacle. Also shown in Color Plate 1.*

Through a Movable Obstacle—Open a Door or Move a Box

Perhaps your character cannot jump over an obstacle, but some obstacles can be moved out of the way or destroyed, allowing passage. Doors, breakable crates, and elevators are common obstacles of this type. If your collision test finds such an obstacle, retry your collision test after either removing it or relocating it to the place where it would go when moved. If the second test succeeds, the edge is still valid, given that an agent is able to either destroy or move the obstacle. That question is best answered by examining the properties of the obstacle.

In many cases, movement or destruction of the obstacle requires an agent to execute a complex sequence of behaviors (e.g., reach out, pull the door open, and step back) before continuing. Store the necessary behavior information in your navigation edge and you will never have to worry about it again.

Up and Down—Stairs, Slopes, Ladders, and Ropes

If the two points that are being connected exist at different heights in the world, you might need to check for special situations. If the slope of the connection is not vertical or nearly vertical, you have either stairs or a slope. Some slopes are too steep, so although a collision trace might not hit any obstacles, the edge should be discarded. Stairs can help, but are very difficult to detect automatically.

If your points are nearly on top of each other vertically (shown as the edge between Point A and Point B in Figure 2.5.5), chances are that any edge connection between them will require some type of climbing or rappelling (see Color Plate 2). Detecting which kind of climbing may require invisible geometry with special flags.

Conclusion

Few AI related systems are more common and pervasive in games than character navigation. Simply walking or running around becomes repetitive quickly, and as 3D game engines become increasingly complex, characters will look best if they too adapt with equally complex behavior. From opening a door, to hopping over an errant boulder and crouching behind it, keeping AI tied to the environment of your game is often one of the most difficult and important challenges. Your navigation system can save the day, automatically detect useful information about the environment, and bring your characters to life.

References

[Hancock02] Hancock, John, "Navigating Doors, Elevators, Ledges and Other Obstacles," *AI Game Programming Wisdom*, Charles River Media, 2002.

[Lidén02] Liden, Lars, "Strategic and Tactical Reasoning with Waypoints," *AI Game Programming Wisdom*, Charles River Media, 2002.

[Rabin01] Rabin, Steve, "Strategies for Optimizing AI," *Game Programming Gems 2*, Charles River Media, 2001.

[Stout00] Stout, Bryan, "The Basics of A* for Path Planning," *Game Programming Gems*, Charles River Media, 2000.

[USArmy92] Army Infantry School, "Infantry Rifle Platoon and Squad Field Manual," Department of the Army, 1992, *155.217.58.58/cgi-bin/atdl.dll/fm/7-8/toc.htm*

[van der Sterren00] van der Sterren, William, "AI for Tactical Grenade Handling," *CGF-AI*, 2000, available online at *www.cgf-ai.com/docs/grenadehandling.pdf*

[van der Sterren02] van der Sterren, William, "Squad Tactics: Planned Maneuvers," *AI Game Programming Wisdom*, Charles River Media, 2002.

Hunting Down the Player in a Convincing Manner

Alex McLean—Pivotal Games Ltd.

alex@pivotalgames.com

In many games we require non-player characters (NPCs) to convincingly chase and hunt down the player. A likely example of this behavior is when a guard has spotted the player and begins pursuit. Modern game players expect intelligent behavior from opponents, but sometimes it's all too easy to let the AI cheat a little too much. To bring about believable searching behavior, it is often not sufficient to simply route a game character directly toward its goal; the path will be too direct, too contrived, and will generally afford little in the way of gameplay possibilities. In such circumstances, the player will probably feel cheated since a chasing or hunting character that routes directly to them does not offer the player any opportunity to hide or retreat from the NPC. It is also not possible for the player to lure the NPC into regions or behind obstacles and then double back to escape.

To offer the potential for more interesting gameplay, we must ensure that the character *explores* and looks like it's trying to find its *nonvisible* target by a process of search rather than following direct, shortest-path routes. This might imply that the character occasionally goes past the player or even sometimes starts out on a path that takes the character away from the player. This article will show why this behavior can be desirable and goes on to demonstrate how to do this effectively and with low processing cost. The result is convincing searching and/or hunting behavior that will gradually home in on a static or moving target. The types of targets are game specific, but in most applications a target is likely to be a player moving about within the game environment.

Enabling a Range of Behaviors

For the most flexible control over any searching or hunting mechanism, we need to be sure that we have parameters available that allow us to control the scope or domain of the search. We will need to be able to vary these parameters in order to offer a range of behaviors that implement a varied set of search patterns. The resulting behaviors should include everything from a seemingly bumbling, wandering, accidental, discovery of the player all the way to a search path that is purposeful, efficient, and direct.

These controlling parameters therefore allow us to control how *quickly* discovery of the player occurs and how *direct* the resulting path is, with these two qualities being very closely related. The reason for allowing this variance and scalability is to offer the player a range of opponents, each exhibiting different gameplay potential. We will show the benefits and scope of *indirect* paths in terms of the opportunities offered for gameplay, perceived character intelligence, and believability.

The Approach

We require gameplay where the player is being chased or hunted down. The game entities that are engaged in chasing the player, and their intentions for doing so, can take many forms, but in simple terms they will share a common objective: to get themselves generally closer to the player over time. To do this, they will most likely make use of some form of pathfinding; however, this will require a *destination*. For the purposes of our hunting and searching behavior, the destination will *usually* place us closer to the player than when we started. The simplest possible method would be to simply travel directly to the player's present location in just one route, but this doesn't give us a very rich outcome in terms of gameplay.

A classic example of this failing is when the player decides to hide in a location, perhaps a room that the hunting character has not seen the player enter. Were we to route the character directly to the player and immediately into the room, the player would have every reason to feel that the AI was cheating and that there was no way to legitimately deceive it. It's acceptable that sometimes the hunting character gets lucky and straightaway "finds" the player even though the character did not see the player enter the room, but it shouldn't happen every time.

One of our goals is that we need to arrive at more interesting destinations. Destinations that, while random, give scope for rich gameplay and, ideally, scope for the player to seemingly evade and deceive the NPC. The method we will look at is relatively simple to implement and has few requirements in respect of the existing game engine. Along the way we will see how to extend the approach to take in all types of AI inputs and give us much more than just a simple run-directly-to-player approach. We will stay with the example of an NPC pursuing the player and assume the existence of a fully functional pathfinding system [Higgins02]. We further require that this pathfinding system is capable of establishing relatively quickly the accessibility of any specified world location.

Application

This method is iterative and therefore requires multiple calls to give the behavior we need. Before we look at the iterative process, we should first look at the high-level description of the controlling framework. This framework controls a general character hunting a player and comprises three distinct scenarios. We periodically review our present situation and decide which scenario is most applicable. Once this decision has been made, the logic for that scenario can then be applied.

We require that we know the absolute positions of the hunting character and the target player. We also require a facility to decide whether the character can presently see the player. The basic approach is that we will periodically generate a new search destination. It is important to appreciate that within the most complex scenario, these search destinations are *intermediate* locations—they are not necessarily near or at the player's location. It will require a number of calls to finally reach or "discover" the player assuming we do not catch sight of him or her along the way. This might happen because of the player moving around, the interval between reassessing our destination being too long, or because there is very little intervening scenery to block line of sight. These areas of implementation will require experimentation to get right and balance for any given game.

The frequency with which these intermediate destinations are generated will depend on the goals of the AI and the processing time available, but we will certainly generate a new search destination if we haven't yet found our target and we have arrived at our present search destination. It's worth pointing out that the generation of the search destinations is a relatively infrequent event in AI terms; it's extremely unlikely, for example, that we'd need to calculate a new character search destination more frequently than one character per frame [McLean02]. Intervals lasting several seconds will be perfectly acceptable for many types of game worlds. We will now state the three possible scenarios for the high-level control. At any given update, we decide which of the following three cases is most appropriate:

- The player is visible (by the NPC).
- The player was recently seen (by the NPC).
- The player has never been seen (by the NPC).

The relative frequencies under which the varying scenarios hold true within this system are entirely governed by the metrics of the game world and the details of the environment. Examples are how populated the world is and how complex its topology. These are our three scenarios and the flow of logic is as follows.

Scenario One: The Player Is Visible

The simplest case for the hunting behavior is when the NPC can actually see the player. At this point, the hunting behavior is over and we must transition into an appropriate attacking behavior. The attacking behavior might look for cover that is within weapon range, move to that spot, and begin attacking [Tozour02]; or it could be as simple as moving directly toward the player to engage in hand-to-hand combat.

Scenario Two: The Player Was Recently Seen

Things get more interesting if the NPC has recently seen the player, but does not currently have a line of sight with the player. In this scenario, the NPC will simply move toward the last seen player location, since it would be unreasonable to do anything else.

Interestingly, this scenario has the ability to create fun gameplay mechanics where the player can trick the NPC. An example is running behind an obstacle. Once out of sight, rather than staying stationary, the player can continue to circle the object in order to come around behind the NPC. This gameplay potential is a particular benefit of the system. It's worth pointing out that even this simple rule can degenerate into nothing more than a direct route to the player if we repeatedly follow this scenario. For now, however, we will assume it is performed only once our intermediate destination is reached or we catch sight of the player.

To facilitate recently seen locations, the game engine should automatically store the "last seen" location when it calculates the NPC's vision. Specifically, if the NPC sees the player, it should store away the time and location where the player is standing. This information is then readily available when this scenario comes into play.

In both of the preceding scenarios, it is important to clear the last-seen location of the player as soon as the NPC begins moving on its route. The stored location information must also be refreshed whenever the NPC receives a positive line-of-sight test to the player. Without taking these steps, the AI might fall into states that are inappropriate due to out-of-date information.

Scenario Three: The Player Has Never Been Seen

If we can neither see the player nor are aware of a last-seen location, then we must generate a search location. This is where we must actually *create* a location rather than extract one from the existing AI system. One method is to simply generate a random location somewhere close to the player, perhaps within a certain radius of the player. This is certainly cheap but it's not very purposeful or guided. Figure 2.6.1 shows a way of improving this random point selection with minimal additional processing cost, while offering more interesting paths.

We will generate two random parameters, with the first being a direction heading. For this we generate a *direction* vector to the true player's location. We then alter this vector randomly subject to a certain window of variance, this window being ϕ in Figure 2.6.1. The other value is S, a straight-line distance to travel, which lies within the interval $[S_{min}, S_{max}]$. This interval can be considered a multiplier for the actual distance to the player. *It is this dependency on the true distance to the player that makes this method useful.* It is also this dependency that allows us, over time, to home in on the player, subject to certain restrictions being adhered to. A value of 1.0 for S is the true distance to the player, 0.5 is half the distance to the player, and so forth. These two values will enable us to generate a routing destination that we might use for searching purposes. In Figure 2.6.1, this example destination is designated d.

Note that while we haven't headed directly toward the player, on arrival we will be closer. It's important to realize that since this destination is randomly generated, it might not be specifically accessible to the character. In this case, it's sufficient to route

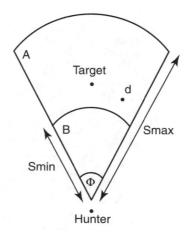

FIGURE 2.6.1 *How to choose a destination. The target is a player's present location.*

to the *nearest accessible location* to that destination. Since it's likely that the existing pathfinding system will already offer this functionality, this isn't too restrictive a request. However, should we be unable to quickly establish the nearest accessible location, then other approaches might have to be taken, with perhaps the nearest location being calculated over the next few frames. It's also necessary to appreciate that we will likely not proceed directly to d in a straight-line route, since there might be many intervening obstacles in the way; this is where the router comes in and our scope for indirect paths becomes evident. The diagram in Figure 2.6.1 implies nothing of scale; individual searching destinations along the route to the player might be large distances apart with complex intervening terrain or geometry.

So, now we have a new destination. We go to that destination and, assuming we do not catch sight of the player along the way, we then start again. We will need vision to be updated more frequently than the generation of search destinations to make sure that we can see the player during any stage of our journey. Should this occur, then scenario three is no longer valid and we revert to the simple direct routing of scenario one.

As long as scenario three remains in effect, each iteration of this search will take us closer to the player subject to the controlling parameters being within certain ranges. It's conceivable that we might sometimes not want to guarantee this requirement, and in this case we could use values for the search distance that exceed twice the distance to the player and/or ranges of ϕ that exceed 180 degrees. When we do this, our generated search destinations might end up being farther away from the target than when we started. Since this isn't often useful, we'll stay with values of ϕ being less than 180 degrees, and values for S being less than 2.0. Restricting the parameters to useful values, we then make multiple calls to generate these points and end up with our search path.

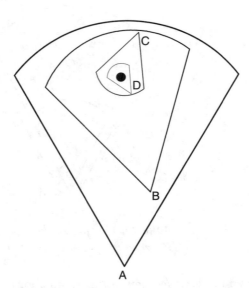

FIGURE 2.6.2   *Successive calls to the algorithm
show the path getting closer to the player.*

Figure 2.6.2 is an example of a generated path and shows four successive calls. Note that the actual route taken between points in the path [*ABCD*] is once again unlikely to be direct due to objects in the game world, and as such, these path points can be viewed simply as staging points along the way.

The area labeled *A* in Figure 2.6.1 shows the domain of our generated search destinations. By having a value of S_{min} greater than 0.0, it should be clear that we will narrow our search over time since area B will be chopped from our remaining search space each time we call this routine. Even with a value of 0.0 for S_{min}, we will still hone in on our target provided we have positive values for S_{max}. With each successive call to the routine, the new cone becomes smaller but always orientated toward the player's true location and originating from the starting or previous search destination. It should now be clear that by varying S_{min}, S_{max}, and ϕ we are able to control the domain of our search. We can also revert to simply routing directly to the player's present location when the following holds true:

$$S_{min} = S_{max} = \text{actual true distance to target, } \phi = 0$$

It is up to the specific implementation to specify the allowable domain for the parameters, but it should be clear that it is possible to control how quickly the search behavior finds the player.

The actual values for these variables can readily be incorporated into existing character "stat tables." Finally, note that due to working with cones, the area in which we search is non-linear with the variation of our parameters. Depending on whether our world is 2D or 3D, we will be working with a search space whose size is a function of the square or cube of the parameters of the cone.

With these parameters, we can now create a range of behaviors. Purposeful characters that appear to find the player relatively quickly can be given S_{min} and S_{max} values very close to 1.0 with small values for ϕ. "Bumbling," less informed characters that appear to wander around relatively aimlessly, and are slow to find the player, will require larger values for ϕ with S_{min} and S_{max} far from 1.0. Even with fairly large ranges in place for our variables, Figure 2.6.2 should illustrate that, subject to certain limits being in place, the character will eventually hone in on the player.

Consider Figure 2.6.2 again. Since S_{max} is less than twice the distance to the target and ϕ is relatively small, we are guaranteed to ultimately find the target through successive calls. The path $[ABCD]$ is much more indirect than $[AD]$, and it should be clear that this might take us around obstacles and even past the target since S_{max} is greater than 1.0. This allows for strategies such as hiding in a room and being able to watch the searching character go past the door outside rather than routing directly into the room. This is exactly what we want and leads to much more interesting AI.

Extending into 3D

It should be easy to see that we can readily extend this method into 3D. In this instance, a point will be generated inside a 3D cone. We ask the router to route to this destination with again the understanding that should it not be accessible, it will send us to the nearest location that is accessible. The cost of moving from 2D to 3D is not very significant and the approach works just as well. Again, the relative sizes of the regions that will be searched will vary non-linearly, and this must be taken into consideration when appreciating the dimensions of the search space. For example, halving the radius of the cone will more than halve the search space. This means that the character will find its target much more than twice as fast.

Reconsidering the Destination

Above this method sits the general AI. At points along the way to our destination, we must recall the routine and evaluate the most applicable scenario. This is to prevent situations whereby the player runs right in front of the character, unnoticed, while the character is on its way to a search destination.

So far, we have made little distinction between a static player and a moving player. With a static player, assuming we don't see the player along the way, it should be clear that it is only necessary to make another call to this hunting behavior to generate a new search destination when we have reached our present one. However, in the case of a moving player it might be necessary to make much more frequent calls. The reasons for making these calls will be game specific, but an obvious example would be that we should make another call when the player is more than a specific distance from our present destination. If we fail to do this, we might end up always going to where the player *was* and not where it is now.

Other AI inputs can readily cause us to generate another destination, such as hearing and witnessing the actions of others. The NPC might choose to stop going to its present destination as a result of a noise that it heard, or it might look for another destination as a result of seeing another teammate requiring assistance or obviously chasing something that it hasn't seen. At all times, it's necessary to appreciate that we fall out of this searching behavior the instant we see our target, and at that point we revert to scenario one.

As well as varying the controlling parameters for S and Φ, we can also vary the time between successive calls to the routine. There is also scope for altering the controlling parameters on the fly. We could widen the search domain to simulate the character becoming confused. We could also restrict the domain (and make the resultant search more direct) in the event of receiving some further AI stimulus, such as evidence of the player's present location obtained through sight, hearing, or information inheritance from another character.

Extensions

There are many ways to extend this searching and hunting behavior. In addition to routing to last-seen locations for the player, as in scenario two, we could route to locations where we last heard the player make a sound. In the *Conflict: Desert Storm* series of games, where we most recently employed these methods, we stored away the locations where sounds were heard. The stored location was shifted a little from its true location depending on the radius of the sound and the experience level of the searching character. Experienced characters worked with locations that were close to the true sound's origin, while less experienced characters used "fake" locations that were some way from the true origin. These positions are then considered evidence of the player's location and are used in the absence of a last-seen location as discussed in scenario two.

We can also decide to drop the character we're chasing should we catch sight of a more interesting search target such as a closer player or a player that has been assessed as being favorable over the one we are presently pursuing.

One final extension to this system is to move beyond having merely one hunting character and to look at multiple search paths for many characters. By integrating this into a formation system [Dawson02], we should be able to divide the search space among many characters in the formation. By looking at the overlap of the cones used for each character, we can see how dense the search is likely to be in certain areas. This allows us to concentrate the search around areas in the game world that might be designated as being particularly interesting or worthy of investigation.

Conclusion

In this article, we looked at how indirect paths make a searching character a great deal more interesting than simply routing the character directly to the player. This opens up opportunities to add new gameplay mechanics and strategies.

Overall, this discussion showed how to generate purposeful, informed-looking searching behavior at very low cost. It can be readily extended to suit the particular needs of most modern games since it is essentially an accommodating framework from which to hang a range of AI inputs. Since this basic framework is computationally cheap, it also frees up our much-valued processing time for further game-specific enhancements.

References

[Dawson02] Dawson, Chad, "Formations," *AI Game Programming Wisdom*, Charles River Media, 2002.

[Higgins02] Higgins, Dan, "Pathfinding Design Architecture," *AI Game Programming Wisdom*, Charles River Media, 2002.

[McLean02] McLean, Alex, "An Efficient AI Architecture Using Prioritized Task Categories," *AI Game Programming Wisdom*, Charles River Media, 2002.

[Pinter02] Pinter, Marco, "Realistic Turning Between Waypoints," *AI Game Programming Wisdom*, Charles River Media, 2002.

[Tozour02] Tozour, Paul, "The Basics of Ranged Weapon Combat," *AI Game Programming Wisdom*, Charles River Media, 2002.

2.7

Avoiding Dynamic Obstacles and Hazards

Geraint Johnson—Computer Artworks Ltd.

geraintjohnson@hotmail.com

Static obstacle avoidance is, barring efficiency considerations, a solved problem in games. The A* algorithm [Stout00, Matthews02] is generally used to search a graph data structure representing the navigable terrain in the level to find a route to a goal. However, many game agents still cope badly with dynamic obstacles encountered along the route, often relying entirely on collision code to get them out of trouble. Bumping into entities not only looks unintelligent, it can also have negative gameplay implications, especially if the entity is a hazard.

This article outlines a pragmatic approach to solving this problem at the level of short-range movement, used successfully in *The Thing* [Artworks02]. Inspired by obstacle avoidance in flocking algorithms [Reynolds87, Reynolds03, Woodcock00], the method involves taking an agent's desired velocity and adding "repulsion" vectors from nearby entities in the agent's memory. The resulting velocity will tend to send the agent around dynamic obstacles and hazards. A nice feature is that two agents on a collision course will intelligently sidestep in opposite directions in order to avoid each other. Moreover, the situation in which a short-range destination is completely blocked by an entity is detected early, so that a new long-range route can be found well before a collision has taken place. The approach is fast and produces very convincing avoidance behavior.

The Problem

Figure 2.7.1 illustrates a simple example of the problem we're trying to solve, and the behavior that we'd like see once we've solved it. It shows an intelligent agent aiming for a particular destination, and a dynamic obstacle. By dynamic, we mean that the obstacle is capable of movement, even if it isn't currently moving.

If the agent takes the straight-line path to its destination, it will bump into the obstacle, and won't look very clever. What we want is for the agent to take the curved path around it.

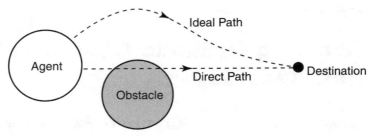

FIGURE 2.7.1   *Straight and curved paths to a destination.*

Repulsion Vectors

We can achieve this by adding a *repulsion vector* to the straight-line destination direction. The repulsion vector is in the direction of the agent from the obstacle. We then normalize the result to find a new adjusted move direction, which we can multiply by our desired speed to find a desired velocity. If we repeat this every time the agent's movement is updated, then the agent will take a curved path around the obstacle over time.

Figure 2.7.2 illustrates this for a single time step. It shows the agent from Figure 2.7.1 a little way through its journey, as well as the repulsion vector and destination direction used to calculate the agent's desired velocity at that particular moment. We can imagine that as the relative positions of the agent and obstacle change over time, we would see the agent move in a curved path like the one shown in Figure 2.7.1.

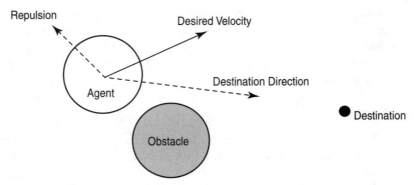

FIGURE 2.7.2   *Vectors used to calculate the desired velocity of an agent.*

For clarity, let's express this mathematically. Equation 1 shows how we calculate the repulsion vector on an agent *a* from an entity *e*, which might be an obstacle or a hazard:

$$R_{ae} = \frac{m_{ae}(P_a - P_e)}{|P_a - P_e|} \tag{1}$$

P_a is the position of the agent a, and P_e is the position of the entity e. To be precise, since we ought to represent incomplete knowledge, P_e should be the agent's *assumed* position for e, which might be inaccurate if e is not in sight. The magnitude of the repulsion vector is shown as m_{ae}, and we'll see how this is calculated later.

In general, we want to add a repulsion vector for every nearby dynamic obstacle or hazard that an agent is aware of. Therefore, we have this equation for finding the total repulsion R_a acting on an agent a:

$$R_a = \sum_{e=1}^{n_a} R_{ae} \tag{2}$$

Here, a is aware of n_a entities and R_{ae} is the (potentially zero) repulsion vector from a particular entity e. We can then use the total repulsion to calculate the agent's desired velocity V_a:

$$V_a = s_a \frac{D_a + R_a}{|D_a + R_a|} \tag{3}$$

In this equation, s_a is the agent's desired speed, and D_a is the normalized direction to its destination.

Repulsion Magnitude

Looking back at Equation 1, we know the *direction* of a particular repulsion vector R_{ae} between agent a and entity e. But what should its magnitude m_{ae} be? There is of course no "correct" answer to that question. Instead, we have to find a suitable heuristic that results in realistic-looking avoidance behavior.

Given that larger magnitudes will result in more pronounced movement away from the obstacle or hazard, we at least know that the following are desirable characteristics for our heuristic:

- If e is not an entity that a should bother avoiding, m_{ae} should be zero.
- If e is too far away from a, m_{ae} should be zero.
- Otherwise, the closer e is to a the larger m_{ae} should be.
- If a and e are on a collision course, m_{ae} should be larger.
- m_{ae} should be clamped so that it doesn't get too large.

The following code illustrates a fairly simple algorithm for repulsion vector calculation with those characteristics. Distances are in meters, and angles are in degrees.

```
3DVec GetRepulsion(const Agent&  Agent,
                   const Entity& Entity,
                   const 3DVec&  DestinationDir)
{
    const float MAX_DISTANCE              (5.f);
    const float MAX_ANGLE                 (10.f);
    const float COLLIDE_DISTANCE_FACTOR   (0.5f);
    const float MAGNITUDE_FACTOR          (0.22f);
    const float MAX_MAGNITUDE             (0.38f);

    // No repulsion if Entity isn't worth avoiding:
    if (!Agent.ShouldAvoid(Entity))
        return 3DVec::ZERO;

    // The direction part of the repulsion:
    3DVec RepulsionDir(Agent.GetPosition()
        - Agent.GetAssumedPosition(Entity));

    // The distance between Agent and Entity:
    const float Distance(RepulsionDir.Magnitude());

    // No repulsion if Entity is in the same place
    // as Agent, or is too far away:
    if (Distance < EPSILON || Distance > MAX_DISTANCE)
        return 3DVec::ZERO;

    // Normalize the direction:
    RepulsionDir /= Distance;

    // If the agent is heading toward the entity:
    if (Angle(DestinationDir,
            -RepulsionDir) <= MAX_ANGLE)
        // Decrease the distance:
        Distance *= COLLIDE_DISTANCE_FACTOR;

    // If the entity is heading toward the agent:
    if (Angle(Agent.GetAssumedVelocity(Entity),
            RepulsionDir) <= MAX_ANGLE)
        // Decrease the distance:
        Distance *= COLLIDE_DISTANCE_FACTOR;

    // Magnitude inversely proportional to distance:
    float Magnitude(1.f/Distance);

    // It should be zero at the maximum distance:
    Magnitude -= 1.f/MAX_DISTANCE;

    // Scale it by some factor that works well:
    Magnitude *= MAGNITUDE_FACTOR;

    // Make sure it doesn't get too large:
    Magnitude = MIN(Magnitude, MAX_MAGNITUDE);

    // Finally, the repulsion vector for Entity:
    return RepulsionDir * Magnitude;
}
```

One embellishment to this code is to take the size and shape of the agent and obstacle into account in the distance calculation; for example, by subtracting their respective radii from the center-to-center distance. This ensures that for a given center-to-center distance, a larger entity will produce a larger repulsion. For a hazardous entity, it's useful to have the concept of an *influence radius* that can be used here instead of the entity's physical radius. For example, the influence radius of a primed grenade is the range within which it will do damage when it eventually explodes.

Note that whenever an agent a shouldn't bother avoiding an entity e, the virtual function `Agent::ShouldAvoid()` can return false, producing an early exit and zero repulsion. It should certainly return false if a is actually trying to get close to e (perhaps to take part in combat), or if e is nonphysical and is not considered dangerous by a.

Sidestepping

We now know exactly how to calculate R_a, the total repulsion acting on an agent a from all the obstacles and hazards of which he's aware. Most of the time, this total can be added directly to the destination direction D_a as part of the velocity calculation in Equation 3. However, we encounter a problem when the direction of R_a is roughly opposite to D_a, as shown in Figure 2.7.3.

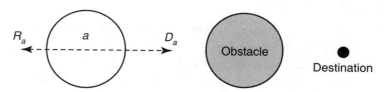

FIGURE 2.7.3   *A case where repulsion is opposite to the destination direction.*

The problem is that if the magnitude of the repulsion $|R_a|$ is larger than $|D_a|$, then the agent will move away from the destination rather than toward it. If $|R_a|$ is less than $|D_a|$, the agent will continue roughly toward the destination and, in Figure 2.7.3's example, will collide with the obstacle.

We can cope with either situation by adding a *sidestep repulsion vector* to the total repulsion R_a when the angle between R_a and D_a is more than some minimum amount (e.g., 150°). This is how we decide the direction of the sidestep repulsion vector:

- If R_a is clockwise from D_a, then we make the direction exactly 90° clockwise from D_a.
- If R_a is counter-clockwise from D_a, then we make the direction exactly 90° counter-clockwise from D_a.
- If R_a is *exactly* opposite D_a, then we just consistently use a convention; for example, we make the direction 90° clockwise from D_a. This ensures that two intelligent agents on a direct collision course will swerve in opposite directions and move past each other (as long as they are both using this algorithm).

Again, there is no correct way to decide on the magnitude of the sidestep vector, but making it proportional to $|R_a|$ is a good idea. Figure 2.7.4 shows how adding a sidestep vector fixes the problem in the last diagram by producing a desired velocity that will take us around the obstacle:

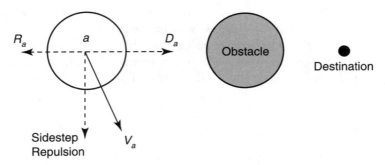

FIGURE 2.7.4   *Adding sidestep repulsion to avoid the obstacle.*

Unworkable Repulsion

In the code for `GetRepulsion()`, we calculate the angle between the destination direction and the direction to the entity. We do this to predict whether the agent will collide with that entity. What if we decide that the agent is on a collision course, and also notice that the distance to the entity is as large or larger than the distance to the destination? In other words, what if the agent is being repulsed by something on, or beyond his destination? Figure 2.7.5 shows an example of this situation.

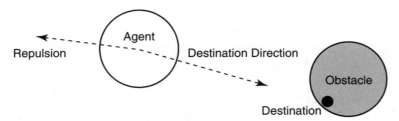

FIGURE 2.7.5   *An unworkable repulsion.*

This repulsion vector is "unworkable" in the sense that if its magnitude is large enough to matter, it will prevent the agent from reaching his destination. Even adding a sidestep repulsion vector to the total repulsion won't help here, as the agent can't go around the obstacle to get to the destination.

The solution is either to ignore this particular repulsion vector and carry on, or to give up on this destination. To make that decision, our short-range movement code should consult some higher-level AI. Here are some reasons why that AI might consider it justifiable to ignore the repulsion on an agent *a* from an entity *e* and let *a* continue:

- *e* is an obstacle, but it's small and can be pushed out of the way.
- *e* is a hazard, but *a* is fleeing from a bigger threat.
- *e* is a friendly agent whom *a* can instruct to move away from his destination.
- *e* is moving and should be clear of the destination by the time *a* reaches it.

If the AI decides to give up on the destination, the short-range movement code should flag a failure, just as if *a* had become physically stuck. The long-range movement code can then go about finding alternative routes to the long-range goal in the usual way. In other words, testing for an unworkable repulsion vector is a cheap way to discover that there is an entity blocking an agent's route, before the agent has actually collided with that entity. The agent can intelligently avert a collision by halting or using a different route.

Preventing Oscillations

If we were to implement the algorithm as outlined so far, we'd soon notice a frequently occurring aesthetic problem; namely that when there are two or more obstacles or hazards near to a moving agent, the agent will often oscillate rapidly back and forth between them in a very unnatural and unconvincing way. This is caused by the direction of repulsion changing rapidly from one movement update to the next, as illustrated in Figure 2.7.6.

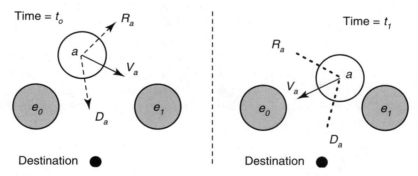

FIGURE 2.7.6   *An oscillation in velocity over two consecutive time steps.*

Figure 2.7.6 shows the repulsion on an agent *a* over two successive updates, where the game-time is first t_0 and then t_1. When the time is t_0, because *a* is nearer to entity e_0 than to entity e_1, the repulsion from e_0 dominates and *a* moves away from e_0 toward e_1. At time t_1, the opposite happens; because *a* is now nearer to e_1 than to e_0, the repulsion from e_1 dominates and a moves away from e_1 toward e_0. It's easy to imagine that this might repeat many times before the agent reaches his destination.

Our first step toward preventing an oscillation like this is to predict that it is about to happen. We can do this as follows:

- We start by calculating the repulsion-modified velocity at the current time t_0 in the usual way.
- We then use this velocity to predict a's position at the next movement update t_1.
- We also predict the position of nearby obstacles and hazards at t_1 using a's assumed velocities for those agents.
- We then feed these predicted positions into the usual routines to estimate the destination direction, repulsion, and finally the velocity of a at time t_1. (The function `GetRepulsion()` will need modifying to optionally use predicted instead of current positions.)
- If the angle between the velocity at t_0 and predicted velocity at t_1 is more than some threshold value (e.g., 90°), then we can assume that an oscillation will occur unless we do something to stop it.

We now need to decide what steps to take to prevent that oscillation. There are a number of ways to do this, but the following rules work very well in practice, and the tests are fast and simple:

- If the current repulsion at t_0 comes entirely from nonhazards, ignore the current repulsion and make a go straight to the destination. As long as our physics-level movement code copes well with collisions, this will always look more natural than oscillating.
- Otherwise, if the *predicted* repulsion at t_1 comes at least partly from hazards (so that the agent is trying to avoid hazards at both t_0 and t_1), then flag a failure, and let the long-range movement code find another route.
- Otherwise, use the current repulsion at t_0 in our velocity calculation as usual, safe in the knowledge that the repulsion at t_1 will later be ignored, avoiding an oscillation! (To see this, note that we predict that the repulsion at t_1 will involve only nonhazards, and so will be ignored by the first of these three rules when the current time becomes t_1).

Coping with Collisions

This method is a practical, fast solution to obstacle and hazard avoidance, and isn't intended to be entirely foolproof. Occasionally, collisions with entities will occur; for example, if the magnitude of a repulsion vector isn't high enough, or if we are ignoring the total repulsion to prevent an oscillation. Agents can also collide with static obstacles such as walls while avoiding dynamic ones.

The physics-level movement code should be written to cope elegantly with collisions; for example, by allowing agents to slide around obstacles where possible. It's also worth cheating whenever you can get away with it. In *The Thing*, one squad member could pass straight through another without colliding, but would try to knock him out of the way before this happened.

In the worst case, if the agent gets stuck on an obstacle, the short-range movement code should flag a failure and allow the long-range movement code to find another route to the goal.

Conclusion

This article presented a flocking style approach to dynamic obstacle and hazard avoidance in games. Repulsion vectors from nearby entities in an agent's memory are added to the agent's destination direction to calculate a desired velocity. The direction of each repulsion vector is that of the agent from the entity in question, and its magnitude is calculated heuristically. An extra sidestep repulsion vector is added when the total repulsion is roughly opposite to the destination direction. If the agent is being repulsed by an entity on or beyond the destination, then that repulsion is deemed unworkable, and either the repulsion is ignored or we flag a failure. Oscillations in velocity are preempted, and then prevented by ignoring the culprit repulsion, or by flagging a failure.

If you decide to integrate this approach into your game, you will have to resolve certain avoidance issues that are beyond the scope of this article. For example, you will need higher-level AI to make a *stationary* agent move away from any nearby hazard, such as a primed grenade that has just landed at his feet. You will probably need another approach for negotiating certain stationary obstacles and hazards, such as doors and steam jets, that are dynamic only in the sense that they can be in either blocking or nonblocking states [Hancock02]. If your agents follow spline paths to their destinations [Rabin00] you will need to decide whether to use the direction to the next point on the spline as D_a in Equation 3, or to simply ignore the spline when the agent is subject to any repulsion.

In any case, we found that this generic method naturally satisfied a multitude of specific gameplay requirements for *The Thing*, as well as making our agents move about more realistically. We hope that you can achieve similar results.

Acknowledgment

An earlier version of this algorithm was devised and implemented by Jon Robinson for *Evolva* [Artworks00].

References

[Artworks00] *Evolva*, Computer Artworks/Virgin Interactive, 2000, see *www.computerartworks.com*

[Artworks02] *The Thing*, Computer Artworks/Black Label Games, 2002, see *www.computerartworks.com*

[Hancock02] Hancock, John, "Navigating Doors, Elevators, Ledges, and Other Obstacles," *AI Game Programming Wisdom*, Charles River Media, 2002.

[Matthews02] Mathews, James, "Basic A* Pathfinding Made Simple," *AI Game Programming Wisdom*, Charles River Media, 2002.

[Rabin00] Rabin, Steve, "A* Aesthetic Optimizations," *Game Programming Gems*, Charles River Media, 2000.

[Reynolds87] Reynolds, C.W., "Flocks, Herds, and Schools: A Distributed Behavioral Model," in *Computer Graphics*, 21(4), SIGGRAPH '87 Conference Proceedings, pp. 25–34, 1987.

[Reynolds03] Craig Reynold's Web site, *www.red3d.com/cwr*

[Stout00] Stout, Bryan, "The Basics of A* for Path Planning," *Game Programming Gems*, Charles River Media, 2000.

[Woodcock00] Woodcock, Steven, "Flocking: A Simple Technique for Simulating Group Behavior," *Game Programming Gems*, Charles River Media, 2000.

2.8

Intelligent Steering Using PID Controllers

Euan Forrester—Electronic Arts Black Box

euan@ea.com, euan_forrester@pobox.com

To achieve the realism demanded by many of today's games, physics simulations have become more complex and accurate. Although realistic physics simulations are often rewarding for human players to control, they can be frustrating from an AI programmer's perspective. As these simulations become more complex, the effects of a given input to the system become less clear, and it becomes more difficult to write a simple if . . . then . . . else logic tree to cope with every possible circumstance. Thus, new methods of controlling objects operating under these rules must be developed.

In the context of game AI, the primary use for such control is in the steering of objects operating under the constraints of a physics system. This article details a solution to this problem by applying an engineering algorithm known as a Proportional-Integral-Derivative (PID) controller that has been used for over 50 years [Willis99].

PID Controllers Explained

PID controllers are feedback-based algorithms primarily used in engineering applications to control an output variable to minimize the difference between a measured value and a desired value. For example, a thermostat might adjust the output of a furnace to hold the temperature of the house at a specified value. This algorithm works equally well whether or not the desired value varies with time.

The difference between the measured value and the desired value is called the *error*. The output is the sum of three terms:

- The first term is *proportional* to the current error.
- The second term is proportional to the *integral* of the error.
- The last term is proportional to the *derivative* of the error.

So, the equations are:

$$error(t) = measured(t) - desired(t)$$

$$output(t + 1) = c_p \cdot error(t) + c_i \cdot \int error(t)\, dt + c_d \cdot \frac{d}{dt} error(t)$$

Where:

$output(t)$	is the output at time t
$measured(t)$	is the measured value at time t
$desired(t)$	is the desired value at time t
c_p, c_i, c_d	are the proportional, integral, and derivative coefficients

Although the preceding equation looks intimidating, each term is easy to calculate in practice. The proportional term is simply the current value of the error. The integral term can be approximated by storing the last several values of the error, multiplied by their associated time steps, in an array. It is then the sum of all of the values in the array. The derivative term can be approximated by taking the current error, subtracting the previous error, and dividing by the time step.

ON THE CD

A demo with source code that implements the preceding description can be found on the accompanying CD-ROM.

These controllers are referred to as being *feedback-based* because they are iterative. Their output is applied to the system, and the results of this application are taken as input, in the form of *measured(t)*, for the next iteration. This process continues for the life of the system.

A PID controller, then, models the behavior of one aspect of a system. Thus, it can be a great deal simpler than the system itself. This simplicity is what makes it suitable for AI programming.

The difficulty in implementing a PID controller is clearly not in the algorithm itself. Instead, it is in choosing the weights associated with each term, known as *tuning* the controller. A great deal of care must be taken in tuning the weights to achieve the effect desired of the system. Although no generalized process exists for this tuning, some advice will be presented later.

PID Controllers Applied

To help understand how these abstract pieces fit together, let us consider the problem of steering a missile. We want the missile to fly realistically, and so it will be moved by a complex physics system. Thus, it will have many physical properties, such as mass, an inertia tensor, lift, drag, and so forth. It will be steered by moving a rudder located at its rear. The angle of the rudder will be controlled directly by the output of our PID controller. We will define a right-handed local coordinate system, with the X-axis pointing along the missile's direction of travel.

For the purposes of this example, we will consider only the 2D, top-down, aspect of this problem. Thus, we will only be concerned with rotations around the missile's

Z-axis. However, extending the example into 3D by including rotations around the Y-axis is easily accomplished with the addition of a second PID controller, assuming that control about each axis is independent.

It should be apparent from the preceding description that the effects of a given input to the system (moving the missile's rudder) at a given time are quite unclear. We will assume that the physics calculations are sufficiently time-consuming that we cannot simply query for the missile's position and velocity at a time in the future.

Mapping the Missile's Steering to the PID Controller

To accomplish this, we must define the error that is being minimized. One way to do this is to define a position in space that the missile is trying to steer toward, called a *steer-to* point. This position could be fixed, like a stationary target, or moving, like an enemy aircraft or a point along a spline that the missile is trying to follow. Since we desire the missile to be traveling directly toward the steer-to point, we can define the desired value as being the angle between the center of the missile and the steer-to point. Of course, when we compute the steer-to point, we must ensure that it is some minimum distance ahead of the missile, to avoid exaggerating the error as the missile approaches the target. We will then define the measured value as the current angle of the missile's velocity. The velocity is used, instead of the angle the missile is currently

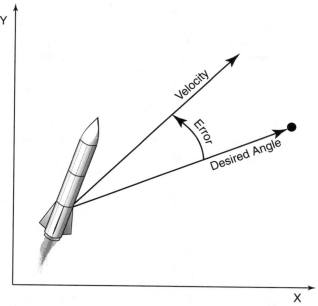

FIGURE 2.8.1 *The missile's velocity and desired angle. Image courtesy of Ryan Bedard.*

facing, in order to ensure that the missile will travel toward the target instead of merely facing toward it (see Figure 2.8.1).

Effects of the Proportional, Integral, and Derivative Terms

Before we can discuss how to tune the three PID coefficients, we must first have a general understanding of their effects.

The proportional term varies with the current size of the error. The greater the difference between the desired and actual angles of the missile, the farther we turn the rudder. As the missile starts to point more toward the desired angle, we turn the rudder less. So, it sounds like this is all we would need to control our missile. However, there are three problems associated with using proportional-only controllers:

1. **Asymptotic behavior:** If we choose our proportional coefficient to be a small number, as our error approaches zero, so will our steering input. This will result in eventually turning to point in the correct direction, but the behavior will be asymptotic. We desire the missile to turn sharply and smoothly, not slowly and lazily.

2. **Positive feedback:** If we choose our proportional coefficient to be a large number, to ensure that our steering input is a reasonable size even when the error is small, the steering input will be greatly exaggerated when the error is large. This will cause the missile to swerve wildly toward the steer-to point, only to overshoot it because it will be unable to overcome its angular momentum in time. The result is a series of oscillations, known as *positive feedback* or *ringing*, instead of a smooth turn.

3. **Steady state error:** If forces not controlled by the rudder, such as wind, are affecting the missile's velocity, it might never reach its desired angle. If a crosswind blows our missile off course, the error will begin to grow. Because the error is growing, the rudder will turn farther. However, the rudder will only turn as far as the point where the force of the wind is balanced by the force from the rudder. At this point, the error will be constant, and so the rudder will remain at a constant angle. Thus, the missile will be unable to get back on course. This is known as *steady state* or *offset* error.

The integral term can deal with the first and third problems. In these cases, individual errors are insufficient to steer the missile in the correct direction quickly enough, or even at all. However, when summed over time, they will add up and will be able to have a greater impact. It should also be remembered that if the error started off large and has recently become smaller, the integral term will have a "memory" of the larger values, and will continue to push the system in the same direction.

The derivative term can deal with the second problem. Because it varies with the rate of change of the error, it can be used to dampen the effects of the proportional term. If the missile turns too sharply toward the target, the error will be rapidly getting smaller. Its derivative, then, will have a large negative value. Having the proportional and derivative terms work in opposition like this ensures that we turn the missile toward the steer-to point, but never so sharply that we overshoot and turn too far. The proportional and derivative terms will not always work against each other, however. When the desired value changes, the derivative term will increase and help to "kick start" the system in the correct direction.

Tuning the PID Controller

Armed with an understanding of the effects of each of the three terms, tuning a PID controller for a game becomes an exercise in trial and error. There are several ways to speed up the process, however:

Start with the proportional coefficient. The proportional term has the largest effect on the controller's behavior. Thus, it is advisable to start by setting the other two coefficients to zero, and tuning the proportional coefficient until the controller behaves roughly as desired.

Only vary one coefficient at a time. It is clear that changing one coefficient can change the behavior of the entire system, requiring the retuning of one or both of the others. For example, if the derivative coefficient is increased to achieve more damping, the system will take longer to converge on the desired value. This will allow the integral term to grow larger than before, possibly causing overshoot. For this reason, it is recommended to hold two of the coefficients constant while achieving the desired effect with the third. Once this has been accomplished, revisit the values of the other two coefficients to adjust for the changes that have been made to the behavior of the system.

Tune the coefficients in real-time. It is extremely likely that many changes to the coefficients will need to be made before the controller behaves as desired. Thus, the process will be greatly sped up if you are able to see the effects of a given tuning right away without having to wait for the game to recompile.

Have an instant replay feature. An instant replay feature can be very helpful if the controller encounters an unlikely situation where it doesn't behave as you expect. It allows you to replay the event over and over as you tune the PID's coefficients until the results are satisfactory.

Several articles available online offer further advice on trial and error tuning, including [Popelish00, Williams95, VanDoren98a, VanDoren00].

In addition to tuning each of the coefficients, the size of the array containing the integral term must also be tuned. Other than the negligible increase in memory usage for a larger array, the only concern when tuning the array size is the length of time that a particular error will exert influence on the controller. For situations where the controller is able to quickly correct errors that appear, it makes sense to have a smaller array. Systems that are slower to respond to a given input, however, might benefit from a larger array.

Extensions to the PID Algorithm

Since the PID algorithm is so simple, it is easy to add refinements to its behavior. The following is a list of some examples:

Using variable coefficients. An object's handling characteristics can vary at different times. For example, our missile might turn sluggishly at low speeds, and sharply at high speeds. In such cases, it is helpful to make each coefficient a function of the object's speed.

Switching between PID controllers based on the object's state. If it is possible for the object to enter a different state, such as sliding sideways, it might be necessary to switch to a different PID controller to take it out of that state before it can continue steering normally. One way to accomplish this is to have the alternate controller run in parallel with the main controller, and to add a bit of logic for when to use one in place of the other. In this case, the alternate controller can try to minimize the difference between the desired angle and the angle the missile is currently facing, rather than the angle of its velocity. Using this method, however, can lead to the problem of *integral windup*: a large integral term accumulated in the inactive controller. When this controller becomes active, this large term can lead to undesired effects. A solution to this problem is to not have the controllers accumulate error values in their integral terms when inactive.

Using more complex functions of P, I, and D. There is not necessarily a need to stick with the linear functions in the equation given earlier. One example is to cap the values of each term, as a simple approximation of an asymptotic function. This can be useful to cap spikes in the derivative term that occur when the missile changes targets. However, more exotic variations are also possible, such as squaring terms, or multiplying them together, depending on the behavior desired.

Filtering input data. If the input data is noisy, it will cause the derivative term to jump around in an undesirable manner. Applying a low-pass filter, such as averaging its last several values, will smooth it out at the price of some responsiveness. More filtering can be achieved by lengthening this history. Noise in the proportional and integral terms can be filtered similarly.

Other Uses for PID Controllers

The usefulness of PID controllers is not limited to steering problems. The algorithm is general enough for a wide variety of applications. Thrust, braking, altitude, and temperature are a small set of the possible things that can be controlled using the PID algorithm. Although many of its uses to AI programmers are within the context of physics systems, creative developers will doubtless be able to find others as well.

The key to remember is that the problem must be expressible in terms of minimizing the error in a single variable. The problem must also occur over an interval of time during which a series of corrective efforts can be applied. Thus, turning a searchlight on or off would not be a good application of a PID controller because the result occurs instantly after the switch is pressed. However, applying torque to the searchlight so it points toward a particular target would be a good application.

Further Reading

As game developers, we have the luxury of adopting the trial-and-error approach to PID tuning described in this article. In the engineering world, however, this can cause expensive equipment to blow up and kill people. As a result, engineers have created various alternatives to this approach. These alternatives involve creating mathematical models of the process to be controlled, and, as such, are beyond the scope of this article. The interested reader, however, might want to learn about the Ziegler-Nichols method [VanDoren98b], as it is a popular approach that combines trial and error with a more rigorous mathematical analysis. Two other methods, Cohen-Coon and direct synthesis, are discussed in [Willis99].

Conclusion

PID controllers are a robust, easy-to-implement solution to the problem of steering physically based AI characters. Although the tuning process can seem daunting at first, it becomes much easier once a feel is gained for the effects of the three coefficients. There is also a wealth of knowledge and experience to be gained from the engineering world for those desiring a deeper understanding of the controller's workings.

The use of PID controllers is not limited to steering, however. Any problem that can be reduced to the minimization of the error in a single variable over an interval of time can be solved in this manner. This includes a wide variety of problems associated with controlling physically based objects.

Acknowledgments

This article would not have been possible without the work of Philip Ibis, whose original idea it was to apply PID controllers to steering AI characters in this manner, and Chris Robertson, who designed, implemented, and tuned many of the extensions to the algorithm.

References

[Popelish00] Popelish, John, "Visual Loop Tuning," available online at *www.tcnj.edu/~rgraham/PID/popelish.html*, 2000.

[VanDoren98a] VanDoren, Vance, "Basics of Proportional-Integral-Derivative Control," available online at *www.manufacturing.net/ctl/index.asp?layout=articleWebzine&articleId=CA186117*, 1998.

[VanDoren98b] VanDoren, Vance, "Ziegler-Nichols Methods Facilitate Loop Tuning," available online at *www.manufacturing.net/ctl/index.asp?layout=articleWebzine&articleId=CA188322*, 1998.

[VanDoren00] VanDoren, Vance, "Understanding PID Control," available online at *www.manufacturing.net/ctl/index.asp?layout=articleWebzine&articleId=CA186185*, 2000.

[Williams95] Williams, Charles, "Tuning a PID Temperature Controller," available online at *newton.ex.ac.uk/teaching/CDHW/Feedback/Setup-PID.html*, 1995.

[Willis99] Willis, Mark, "Proportional-Integral-Derivative Control," available online at *lorien.ncl.ac.uk/ming/pid/PID.pdf*, 1999.

2.9

An AI Approach to Creating an Intelligent Camera System

Phil Carlisle—Team17 Software Ltd.

pc@team17.com

While working on *Worms 3D* for Team17, we were given the task of producing a camera system capable of providing the user with the best possible view of the game action. One unique aspect of the game is that the player controls multiple individual characters, such that the camera system is continually focussing on different subjects and areas of the game world.

Requirements

We decided to look at the possibilities of using common AI concepts to help us capture that action. The requirements for the camera system can be split into two categories: user requirements and technical requirements.

User Requirements

User requirements are the most obvious to the user. Typically, these can be thought of as gameplay related.

- The camera should be responsive to user input and act in an intuitive manner.
- The camera must maintain a clear view of the currently selected character.
- When significant events happen during gameplay, the camera must strive to highlight these events to the user.
- The camera must attempt to anticipate the player's movements, such that it provides a clear view of where the character is heading.

Technical Requirements

Technical requirements are those that affect the ability of the camera to comply with the user requirements.

- It must not require pre-processing of the environment.
- It must operate correctly in a networked game.
- It must be possible to control from a design perspective.

Camera System Architecture

This section discusses the approach adopted when first creating the overall camera system, touching a little on how it fits in with the game architecture as well as its benefits and drawbacks.

The general game architecture we had decided on during the design phase of the project was based on a system of *entities* and *services*. An entity in our design was any object that existed in the game world (for our purposes, something that had a graphical presence). A service was a process or class that would provide code to handle functions requested by the entities; for example, game logic, collision, AI control, and pathfinding were services. It was clear that we would implement the camera system as a service.

Our game architecture was based on a messaging system to reduce dependencies between code modules and to facilitate the network functionality.

The camera system was designed as a central "camera manager" service, with individual "camera" objects stored in a list (actually an STL vector) of camera objects. The input into the camera system was handled by the camera manager, which accepted input messages and turned them into control signals for the individual camera objects. These camera objects serve as a storage class for the variables needed for a particular camera to be set up in the engine (e.g., position, look at, field of view, and so on). They also provide update functions so that each camera can have separate behaviors. In a typical game update cycle, the camera manager updates the "currently active" camera object. At any time, the game objects can signal the camera manager to change which camera is the active camera (also, cameras themselves can do the same).

Steering Behaviors

Because of the requirement for the camera system to function within a fully dynamic environment, it had to be a real-time system, which meant we couldn't pre-process the environment. As a result, we drew inspiration from Craig Reynolds' work on steering behaviors [Reynolds99]. As you'll see, some of the techniques presented in this article resemble Craig's classical steering behaviors, but have been modified to keep the camera within parameters and away from obstacles. Some of the more recognizable steering behaviors used in the camera system are arrival (to slow the camera down as it draws near its target) and coherence (to attract the camera toward its target).

Avoiding Occlusion

Given one of the main criteria of the camera system was to maintain a clear view of the current character, we had to provide an implementation that would allow the camera to avoid occlusion. Due to the dynamic nature of the environment, we could not implement any type of attraction points, a common technique used in games to draw a camera toward a known "good" viewpoint.

As it is, we developed a system using raycast collisions that worked well.

FIGURE 2.9.1 *A typical game camera placement.*

As seen in Figure 2.9.1, a typical method of implementing a third-person camera would be to simply cast out a ray from the character into the world in the direction of the camera's position. Then, set the camera's position to the location of any collision point between the two. This method works, but is very much prone to sudden movements in the camera, which we found unacceptable.

Our implementation overcomes this problem. Instead of a single raycast, it casts out a number of rays, which help guide the camera around obstructions in order to maintain a good view of the character. The first four rays are cast out from the character to points at either side and above and below the camera, as shown in Figure 2.9.2. These rays are then used to determine two things:

- Should the camera move away from an obstacle?
- Should the camera distance be shortened?

If any of these four rays collides with an object, then the camera is susceptible to being blocked in the near future. To keep the camera away from potential problems, the camera must be impulsed in the opposite direction of the camera-to-collision vector.

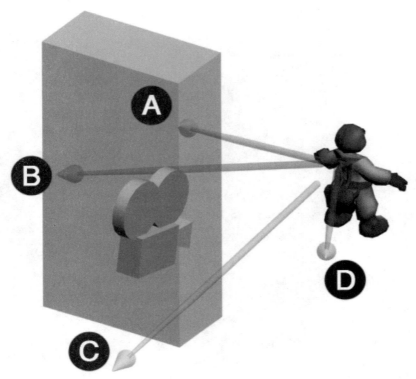

FIGURE 2.9.2   *Raycasts to detect imminent occlusion of the camera. Note that ray B is intersecting the block, which could potentially occlude the camera.*

Smoothing

There are circumstances where all four rays could be colliding (e.g., the character has moved into a long tunnel). To prevent oscillation (where a collision causes an impulse, which then causes a collision to occur on the opposite side, causing the opposite impulse and so on), we must produce an "overall" impulse vector from all of the impulse checks and apply a damping force.

To allow the user to continue to move the camera in the direction that could potentially block the view, we apply a camera movement impulse that is larger than any possible impulse from the ray collision tests. Because we know that the camera would become blocked by simply rotating, we also apply a shortening of the character-to-camera distance in proportion to the distance of the collision point from the character. This is also interpolated to provide a smooth transition for the camera movement.

Camera Transitions

In our particular game, camera transitions were possible at any time. For example, one of the available weapons was an option to switch to another character. Transitioning between one character and another in a dynamic environment is a nontrivial task. The possibility of occlusion is very high.

Initially, we implemented a straightforward transition system that interpolated between one camera and the next (each character having a logical camera associated with it). This worked reasonably well; however, there were issues of occlusion and the camera would move through solid objects. This was unacceptable, so we tried several other methods. The problem we encountered was that while it was relatively simple to predict a path for a character walking on solid objects (e.g., a landscape), it is actually harder to predict a path through empty space.

One possible solution is to create a space tree (such as a Binary Space Partition tree) and use that to indicate possible path nodes for the camera that lay "outside" solid volumes. However, we opted for a simpler solution to the problem. When the camera needed to switch from one character to another, it first cut to an orbiting camera showing the whole environment, and then cut back to the next character. This allowed us to give some context to the transition between one character and the next because essentially users could see where they transitioned from and where they were transitioning to.

User Input

The camera system itself was controlled via a message passing system. Each user input was translated into different input-mappings via a translation service. This allowed us to have different control inputs on different platforms still controlling the camera with the same input message. Typically, the user input was simply digital off-on signals for beginning rotations; however, it was possible to apply an analog force to the camera as well. We also allowed the input translations service to map the analog controllers onto digital inputs.

Typically, the user inputs would simply apply a change in value to a rotation or elevation angle. Unfortunately, this made it impossible to obtain fine control (e.g., if the value change was too great, it was impossible to aim at someone; if it were too small, it was too slow for the user). The response to this issue was to include a method of ramping up the speed of inputs over time, such that as a controller was held in a direction, the value applied would be increased over time. This allowed us to have fine-grained control with small "nudges" of the controller, or faster more responsive controls if an input button was held down.

Camera Events

It was a requirement from the design that the camera should respond to certain game events (e.g., explosions) and that the camera be able to have certain effects applied to it, such as shake, white out, and so on. This was handled with a system of camera override events. In essence, a camera event was created when a message was received that something that would cause an event had happened. For example, if an explosion occurred within a given radius, a camera event message would be sent that would then cause a camera event to override the normal positioning of the camera by applying a jittering function to the camera's final calculated position. In essence, camera events are simply additions or alterations to the current camera, rather than an encompassing camera behavior. Camera events were also required to temporarily focus the user's attention on a specific area of the environment (e.g., when an important game event occurred).

Scripting

Because of the message-based nature of the camera system design, it was relatively trivial to include a set of mechanics that allowed our designers to control the camera via our script interface. We simply provided the script interface (in this case, LUA) a method of sending messages with parameters, which were then handled by the camera manager service. This interface also allowed the designers to create camera paths by scripting a system to define path nodes and then allowing a message to instruct a specified camera to follow a given named path.

Further Work

During the initial design stages for the camera system, it was envisioned that there would be an overall AI system used to control the camera system. This AI would have been used to prioritize incoming camera event messages, influencing the camera view to capture more visible events. In the final implementation, we were able to achieve some measure of success; however, due to project time constraints, we were unable to completely overcome some of the issues facing the game camera system.

For any dynamic camera system, it would be useful to use ideas from [Hawkins02] to incorporate camera knowledge used in films into game camera systems, especially when trying to portray a more cinematic effect.

Conclusion

Creating a camera system that can react to a dynamic environment was our goal. In our implementation, we achieved this by creating our own camera-specific steering behaviors that, coupled with a raycast collision system, we used to guide the camera position. We also implemented a camera manager "service" that used rules from film camera work to allow us to respond to interesting events during gameplay. Finally, we implemented a camera scripting language that allowed our designers to control the camera system in order to provide entertaining in-game camera movements for scripted sequences.

All these systems together allowed us to ship a game with a very reactive and interesting camera. Given a little extra time, it would have been useful to include more "film-like" rules to control camera transitions; however, the system we implemented more than fulfilled our goals.

References

[Hawkins02] Hawkins, Brian, "Creating an Event-Driven Cinematic Camera," *Game Developer Magazine*, October 2002, available online at *www.gamasutra.com/features/20030108/hawkins_01.htm*

[Reynolds99] Reynolds, Craig, "Steering Behaviors for Autonomous Characters," *Game Developers Conference*, 1999, available online at *www.red3d.com/cwr/*, also on the *AI Game Programming Wisdom 2* CD-ROM.

GROUP MOVEMENT, TACTICS, AND PLANNING

3.1

Constraining Autonomous Character Behavior with Human Concepts

Jeff Orkin—Monolith Productions

jorkin@blarg.net

A current trend in game AI is the move from scripted to autonomous character behavior. Autonomous behavior offers several benefits. Autonomous characters can handle unexpected events that a script might not have anticipated, producing emergent gameplay. Level designers can focus on creating worlds packed with opportunities for characters to showcase their behaviors, rather than getting bogged down scripting the actions of individual characters.

Various articles, including [Blumberg01] and [O'Brien02], have described how to design goal-based autonomous behavior, where characters select the most relevant behavior based on their desires, sensory input, and proximity to objects of interest. In theory, it sounds simple enough to drop a character with a palette of goals into a level filled with tagged objects, and let him take care of himself. In practice, there are many additional factors that need to be considered to get believable behavior from an autonomous character. During the development of the first-person spy game *No One Lives Forever 2: A Spy in H.A.R.M.'s Way (NOLF2)* [Monolith02], we found it necessary to imbue our characters with the understanding of a number of human concepts in order to get believable behavior. This article does not describe a specific implementation of a goal-based behavior system. Instead, it presents a number of factors that should be considered as inputs into the relevancy calculation of a character's goals, to produce the most believable decisions.

Emergent Gameplay

Emergent gameplay is born when players have the freedom to explore and solve problems in any way they choose, and the game world responds appropriately. For this style of gameplay to be possible, the game design must provide the player with a set of tools to interact with well-defined gameplay mechanics. Rewarding the player for creativity and exploration creates more depth to the gameplay, and draws the player into an immersive experience. The tremendous success of *Grand Theft Auto 3*'s [Rockstar01] open-ended "sandbox" style game design is a testament to the game players' satisfaction with emergent gameplay. AI systems in particular must provide satisfying responses to anything a player might do. Autonomous behavior allows characters to handle unpredictable player actions far more gracefully than scripted behavior can.

Players of *NOLF2* recounted stories on Web forums about emergent gameplay they experienced. *NOLF2* follows a linear story, but each level gives players freedom to explore and choose how to overcome obstacles. Players take on the role of international super-spy Cate Archer. The game starts in Japan where Cate meets a contact, Yamata-san, who gives her a first mission. Cate needs to infiltrate a village guarded by fierce ninjas and photograph a secret meeting. Yamata-san is armed for self-defense, in the unlikely scenario that Cate lures a ninja all the way down to the start of the level. A *NOLF2* player on the Web posted a clever approach to overcoming the difficulty of fighting the ninjas in the village. The player used Cate's tazer to knock out Yamata-san and carry him into the village to an area with lots of enemies. Upon waking, Yamata-san disposes of the ninjas far more deftly than the player could have at the start of the game. The player used the game mechanics of the tazer and carrying bodies, and was rewarded by Yamata-san reacting appropriately by fighting the ninjas that surrounded him when he woke up. Yamata-san handled the situation autonomously, without a script defining how to react to the unanticipated situation of waking up from a tazer shock in a hostile environment. A minor character in the game design took a major role in this player's experience due to the player's decisions.

Controlling the Chaos

Characters in *NOLF2* employ the same autonomous behavior systems in combat and noncombat situations. When no threat is present, characters exhibit behavior inspired by *The Sims* [Maxis00]. They are constantly active, wandering about, interacting with the environment. Their activities include working in offices, napping on beds, turning on radios, drinking from water fountains, and using the restroom. Figure 3.1.1 illustrates how opportunities for interaction are represented in the game world.

NOLF2 game designer Craig Hubbard and lead level designer John Mulkey recognized the importance of autonomous behavior in a spy game. Hubbard explains, "The main goal was to make the characters *live* in the environment instead of just standing around waiting for the player to show up. Because you have the option of sneaking around, we felt it was critical that the game have a life of its own. You can spend a lot of time spying on NPCs and plotting your next move, so they need to do interesting things" [PCG02].

We were initially optimistic that if we filled a level with autonomous characters and tagged objects of interest, the game would take care of itself. As Mulkey liked to say, "Just wind it up and go!" Instead, we were greeted with chaos. Characters were wandering to unexpected places, at unexpected times, and would generally overreact to any disturbance.

For example, we placed a character in an office, and expected him to work with the nearby desk and filing cabinets. Instead, he wandered across the level to work in a

FIGURE 3.1.1 *A character surrounded by opportunities, in the form of AI nodes that indicate where a character can stand to interact with objects of interest. See Color Plates 3 and 4 for additional examples. © 2002. Reprinted with permission from Monolith Productions, Inc.*

different office. This was due to a character at a guard post outside who had decided he wanted to do some office work, but was nowhere near an office. The guard claimed the nearest office, forcing the other character to find a new office. In addition, if any character in the level heard a noise, he would run around alerting his allies. In no time, the player would be bombarded by every enemy in the entire level.

We had achieved autonomy, but the behavior was not believable, and more importantly for a game, the behavior was not fun. It is the art of good level design to use the systems provided by engineers as tools to craft something compelling and fun. Our autonomous systems did not allow the level designers any input into the characters' decisions, and we did not want to take the step backwards of using command and scripts to add control. The solution was to impart our characters with understanding of various human concepts, and allow level designers to modify properties of the environment to affect the behavior of the characters. To adequately control behavior, our characters needed to understand the concepts of ownership, dependency, relevance, responsibility, priority, consciousness, expected state, and presence of others. The rest of this article describes these concepts in more depth; using problems we encountered to illustrate their need, and describes the solutions we employed on *NOLF2*. These concepts provide characters with a rich understanding of their surroundings, leading to believable and satisfying autonomous behavior.

Ownership

The excessive wandering of our characters was caused by the fact that all objects of interest were up for grabs. If one character decided to get up from his desk to use the restroom, another character might notice the vacant desk and immediately sit down and start working. When the first character returned and found his desk occupied, he would have to walk somewhere else in search of a vacant office. In the real world, a person has his own office. He works at his own desk, rather than at the first vacant desk he encounters. Our characters needed to understand the concept of ownership.

Our simple implementation of ownership involves grouping objects into sets, and assigning a set to a single character. One character might own a desk, file cabinet, and a water fountain. If that character dies or otherwise exits the level, another character can claim the set. A character can only own one set of objects at a time. A better solution might be to allow objects to be part of multiple overlapping sets, so that some objects like a water fountain or urinal can be shared. Other options include having a world set for public objects, or leaving public objects out of any set. For our purposes, the simple solution worked, and players did not seem to notice.

Dependency

There are often dependencies between real-world objects. A cannon needs to be loaded with shells before it can be fired. Coffee needs to be poured from the pot before it can be consumed from a cup. The security code needs to be entered before the door can be opened. The *NOLF2* level designers got a little carried away, and decided that characters should wash their hands in the sink after using the restroom. The problem this introduced was that characters did not know that the sink should only be used *after* the toilet. Sometimes, a character would use the sink first. Other times, a character would use the toilet, then return to a desk, and then go to use the sink. It appeared that he did not realize how dirty his hands were until he got back to his office.

One possible remedy to this dependency problem is to combine using the toilet and using the sink into one atomic, inseparable behavior. This solution eliminates the dependency problem, but comes at the cost of flexibility. Characters in *NOLF2* use bathrooms, but also relieve themselves in the great outdoors, where there are no sinks. If the toilet and sink are tightly coupled, the bathroom behavior cannot be reused outdoors.

Ideally, the game content authoring tools should allow for the explicit specification of dependencies between objects. This could be accomplished with the addition of a simple dependency parameter on the object that references another object by ID or by type. In *NOLF2*, we employ a more ad hoc solution. The sink object is disabled until after a character uses the toilet, at which time all other objects are disabled and the sink is enabled. After using the sink, the sink is disabled, and the other objects are re-enabled.

Responsibility

In a world filled with opportunities, how is a character to decide what to do? Imagine a military compound, where characters sleep, eat, train, stand guard, do vehicle maintenance, office work, janitorial work, and scientific research. A typical person is not a jack-of-all-trades. People specialize depending on their field of expertise.

Enemies in *NOLF2* sound alarms and call for help when a threat is detected. Reinforcements rush in, but if they fail to find danger, they either exit the level or blend in. Blending in is accomplished by claiming a set of objects left vacant by a fallen ally. If characters do not discriminate about the types of vacancies, an armed soldier might decide to do some research with a microscope, which looks out of place. Characters need to understand their purpose in the world. Armed soldiers are responsible for taking guarding posts, leaving research to scientists.

Objects in *NOLF2* can optionally be tagged with the class of character that is allowed to interact with it. Untagged objects can be used by anyone. For example, everyone can use the water fountain, but only scientists can use microscopes. A more flexible system might be to allow objects to be tagged with a specific character, a character class, or a set of character classes. Some objects might be invisible to the player, and some can have additional properties. A guard post is not a physical object, but is instead a location with a radius.

Some responsibilities imply something about location. A soldier at a guard post is responsible for guarding a specific area. Tethering characters to portions of the level prevents the player from getting overwhelmed by enemies, and keeps the level from emptying in response to the first disturbance created. It makes sense that a soldier responsible for guarding a gate would go alert when he hears gunfire, but not immediately run toward the sound, abandoning his responsibility.

It is worth noting that while radii are simple, convenient means of defining space, they are not ideal for constraining behavior. As a radius is enlarged to include some desired location, it often ends up including a great deal of undesirable area too. If possible, a more precise option is to tie a behavior such as guarding to a specific region of the world. A region can be defined as list of rooms, buildings, or other spaces. Regions can be defined hierarchically to contain sub-regions. AI systems might be able to leverage spatial data already existing in other game systems such as collision detection and triggers.

Relevance

A modern computer game falls somewhere between a simulation and a drama created to entertain an audience. The player takes an active role as a story unfolds around him or her. AI controlled characters are actors in this dramatic production. The autonomy of the characters produces improvisation among the actors, but they need to have some awareness of the intended experience for the player.

Dynamic music is tied to characters' moods in *NOLF2*, to add tension and give the player clues that danger might be near. This generalized system produced some humorous results at first. Siberian levels are populated with rabbits, whose simple behavior includes goals of fleeing from the player. When a rabbit spotted someone, his panic raised the music to a maximum intensity, making chasing a rabbit a very dramatic event. Rabbits needed to understand their relevance to the story as a whole, or irrelevance as the case may be. A simple solution to this specific problem is to apply an optional ceiling to the music intensity that a class of characters can request.

Priority

It is likely that a character will be presented with multiple opportunities simultaneously. He will need some means of determining which opportunity is the highest priority at any given time. For example, if a character is faced with an armed enemy and a steaming cup of coffee, he should realize that defending himself is more important than having a drink.

Behaviors in *NOLF2* break down into three categories: relaxed, investigative, and aggressive. A character's intelligence is most convincing when he favors investigative behaviors over relaxed behaviors, and aggressive behaviors over all others. Within each category, more specific behaviors take a higher priority over more general behaviors. Investigating a dead body takes priority over going generally alert. Firing at an enemy from behind cover takes priority over standing still and firing. Relative priorities at a detailed level are at the designer's discretion. Ties between behaviors with matching priorities can be broken randomly or arbitrarily.

A behavior with a high priority implies urgency. Characters can use animation to express this urgency, and communicate it to the player. *NOLF2* characters stand up faster from chairs and beds when alerted to a threat, and abruptly toss cigarettes aside rather than casually putting them out with their feet.

The priority of a behavior needs to persist until the behavior completes. We had a problem in *NOLF2* if a character noticed a dead body and started to walk over to it, but was then drawn away to chase an enemy. After the enemy evaded him, he would search a bit and then give up and return to relaxed activities of filing paperwork while an ally laid dead on his floor. In a goal-based system, the highest priority goal takes control of the character's behavior. The priority of the CheckBody behavior needs to persist until a character has visited each body that he has previously seen. When characters in *NOLF2* check on allies and determine they are dead, they dispose of the bodies from the level.

State of Consciousness

The example in the preceding section about priority makes an assumption about the character's understanding of the concept of consciousness. In order for a character to decide to check on an ally's fallen body, he first must recognize that his ally is not conscious. This is accomplished in *NOLF2* by emitting a stimulus from unconscious characters. Other characters sense the stimulus using a trigger system similar to that described in [Orkin02], and run over to investigate. Checking the current health of the source of the stimulus determines the investigator's course of action. The investigator can either kick a knocked-out ally to wake him, or dispose of a dead ally's body.

It is equally important for a character to understand his or her own level of consciousness. A sleeping or knocked-out character needs to ignore most sensory input, and choose from a much smaller set of possible actions. The actions might include snoring, and waking up. Overlooking this need led to an amusing bug during development of *NOLF2*. If the player used the tazer on one of the scientists in Cate's UNITY headquarters, the victim would pass out, but still respond to the player. While lying lifeless on the ground, the scientist would say, "Hi Cate, Mildred said to say thank you for the flowers." Furthermore, if a character realizes that he was unconscious in the recent past, he can behave believably suspicious or disoriented when waking.

Expected State

Consciousness is really a specific example of the more general concept of expected state. A character that knows the normal set of states for his allies can just as easily recognize that they are caught in a bear trap or in hysterics from laughing gas, as he can recognize that they are unconscious. *NOLF2* got a great deal of mileage out of applying the concept of expected state to everything in the world that could change state. Broadcasting stimuli from objects that change state allow our characters to respond to changes, additions, and subtractions from the world.

The possibilities for exploiting this concept are endless. Examples of recognizing state changes in *NOLF2* include characters noticing open doors and drawers, knocked over bottles, broken windows, and lights turned on or off. Footprints are additions to the expected state of the world. If a character runs from a threat to get backup, and finds that his allies are not where he expects them, he can respond to the subtraction of his allies from the world with an "Oh no!"

The same method described previously to broadcast the presence of an unconscious character can be used to alert characters to a change of state on any object. Whoever changes the state of an object from its default state is responsible for registering a stimulus with the general-purpose trigger system [Orkin02]. The current state is stored as a member of an object, and set to an enumerated value. The state of an object at level-load time is its default state. The stimulus can be cleared if someone reverts the state of the object back to its default state. Characters keep track of which stimuli they have already observed, so they only respond once per stimulus instance.

Once a character recognizes that something is not in an expected state, he can respond in a number of ways. He can walk over for a closer look, or even return the object to its expected state, by closing a drawer, for example. A single disturbance might not warrant any further action. Instead, a character can keep track of what he has observed, and respond after enough occurrences have accumulated. A single bottle knocked over might not be cause for alarm, but 10 broken bottles might be very alarming. A character can turn on the lights in a dark room to get a better look at a disturbance, and his knowledge of the expected state of the lights will lead him to turn off the lights on his way out.

Presence of Others

It looks smart when a character turns off the lights as he leaves a room, but it looks considerably less smart when he turns off the lights while others are still in the room. Characters need to take into account the presence of other characters and modify their behavior accordingly. The article "Simple Techniques for Coordinated Behavior" [Orkin04] in this book goes into more detail on possible solutions for getting characters to take each other into account.

The Introspective Character

The previously described factors can be summarized as a list of questions that a character can ask him or herself during the process of goal-based action selection.

Ownership: "Is this object mine to use?"
Dependency: "Is there anything I need to do before using this object?"
Responsibility: "What is my purpose in life?"
Relevance: "How will my actions affect the player's experience?"
Priority: "What is most important right now?"
Consciousness: "Am I awake?"
Expected State: "Has anything changed?"
Presence of Others: "How will this action affect other characters?"

Additional Factors

This article described a number of concepts necessary to produce believable autonomous behavior, but has certainly not covered everything. In addition to the preceding concepts, we found that it would have been helpful for characters to have a better understanding of spatial relationships, and of their own internal feelings. Spatial relationships encompass a number of concepts such as the difference between inside and outside, and how rooms, hallways, and floors of a building connect. Basing decisions off internal needs, desires, and revelations allows a character to go far beyond simple reactive behavior. The point is simply that the more a character understands, the more believably he can respond to his surroundings, adding more depth to the gameplay experience.

References

[Blumberg01] Blumberg, B., Burke, R., Isla, D., and Downie, M., "CreatureSmarts: The Art and Architecture of a Virtual Brain," *Proceedings of the Game Developers Conference (GDC 2001)*: pp. 147–166.
[Maxis00] *The Sims*, Maxis/Electronic Arts Inc., 2000. See *thesims.ea.com/*

[Monolith02] *No One Lives Forever 2: A Spy in H.A.R.M.'s Way*, Monolith Productions/Sierra Entertainment, Inc., 2002. Toolkit and SDK available at *nolf2.sierra.com/*

[O'Brien02] O'Brien, John, "A Flexible Goal-Based Planning Architecture," *AI Game Programming Wisdom*, Charles River Media, 2002.

[Orkin02] Orkin, Jeff, "A General-Purpose Trigger System," *AI Game Programming Wisdom*, Charles River Media, 2002.

[Orkin04] Orkin, Jeff, "Simple Techniques for Coordinated Behavior," *AI Game Programming Wisdom 2*, Charles River Media, 2004.

[PCG02] *PC Gamer*. Imagine Media, September 2002.

[Rockstar01] *Grand Theft Auto III*, Rockstar Games/Take-Two Interactive Software, Inc., 2001. See *www.rockstargames.com/*

3.2

Simple Techniques for Coordinated Behavior

Jeff Orkin—Monolith Productions

jorkin@blarg.net

A number of common problems arise when developing AI systems for combat with multiple enemies. Agents block each other's line-of-fire. Agents follow the exact same path to a target, often clumping up at a destination. Some agents are oblivious to a threat even though others nearby are getting shot or killed. Multiple agents decide to do the exact same action or animation simultaneously. These problems would seem to require some type of group behavior layer dealing with complex higher-level reasoning. In fact, these problems can be solved with simple techniques that use existing systems and leverage information that individual agents already have.

No One Lives Forever 2 (NOLF2) [Monolith02] received kudos from critics and game players for improvements in coordinated behavior. Our tight development schedule did not allow for the implementation of a group behavior layer, but we were able to solve the problems previously described by leveraging existing information in our pathfinding, vision, and sensory systems. The addition of a simple blackboard gave us a means to share this information among multiple agents. There are limits to the amount of coordination that can be achieved without a dedicated group behavior layer, but our techniques got us a lot of "bang for the buck" in terms of the players' perception of coordination. Agents in *NOLF2* split up and take different paths to targets, surround enemies, duck and dodge out of each other's way, and warn each other of danger.

"Split Up!"

When agents' decisions are driven by the same logic, nearby agents will tend to go to the same place at the same time. Multiple agents that are investigating the same noise, or chasing the same threat will often take the same path to their target. This leads to crowding en route and at the destination. Staggering timing and offsetting waypoint positions can alleviate the situation somewhat, but does not attack the fundamental problem. The heart of the problem is that the agents are running the same shortest path algorithm, causing nearby agents to follow the exact same path to a destination.

Ideally, agents would take different paths to the same destination, to guarantee that they do not form a crowd or conga line.

Reservations

If agents are running the same algorithm to find the shortest path to a destination, how can we entice them to choose different paths? The shortest path can also be thought of as the least costly path, so the key is making a path appear more costly when another agent is already taking it.

One effective technique for altering the cost of a path based on other agents' paths is to allow agents to reserve pathfinding nodes for themselves. An agent planning a path reserves a single node along his path as his own. Other agents planning paths avoid using reserved nodes if at all possible. A reserved node is not relinquished until the agent who reserved it completes his path, or plans a new path. The specific implementation of this technique depends on the pathfinding data structures for a particular game.

NOLF2 builds paths out of adjacent axis-aligned rectangular volumes of arbitrary sizes. Agents can move freely inside of a volume. Paths consist of waypoints on the edges between connected volumes. When an agent plans a path, he reserves the volume *before* the destination volume. Other agents' planning paths consider reserved volumes to have a much higher cost than unreserved volumes. This causes them to choose alternate paths if they exist. If no alternate paths exist, the other agents will use the reserved volume.

Why do we reserve the volume *before* the destination, instead of the destination itself? All agents heading to the same place need to reach the same destination volume. Reserving the volume just before the destination forces agents to try to find alternate routes that lead to the same final volume. The result is that agents arrive from different directions whenever possible. It is worth reiterating the point that the agent reserves only *one* volume and not the entire path. This technique leads the agent to proactively find alternate routes, rather than reactively avoiding obstacles at the last minute (see Figure 3.2.1).

Agents appear to be cooperating when they spread out and approach a target from different directions. A player in a room might find agents entering from multiple doors. If a player runs down an alleyway behind a building, he might find agents coming from the other direction, heading him off at the pass. This simple technique is surprisingly effective in creating the illusion of coordinated behavior. Reviewers of *NOLF2* noted the enemy's ability to both surround and flush out the player. In reality, the agents are simply taking different paths. Color Plates 5 and 6 illustrate this technique with screenshots from *NOLF2*.

As you might have already noted, if the destination volume has only one neighbor, this technique will be ineffective in spreading out the agents. This is an acceptable limitation, because junctions are more common than dead ends, and in the case of dead ends, crowding is more understandable.

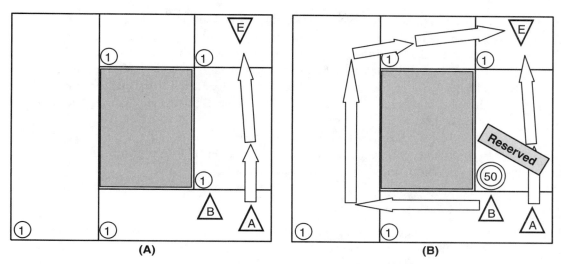

FIGURE 3.2.1 *Agents A and B are pathfinding to enemy E. Initially, all pathfinding volumes have a cost of 1, circled in their bottom left corners. (A) Agent A plans a direct path to E, and reserves the volume before the destination. (B) Agent B plans a different path to E, because the reserved volume appears to be very expensive.*

Maximum Occupancy

The reservation technique works better in combat scenarios than in investigative situations. In a combat situation, agents approach from different directions, but stop to fire their weapons when they get close enough to their target. Their firing range prevents them from converging on a single point. If agents are investigating a disturbing sound, like a bottle breaking or coin dropping, they might crowd as they converge on the specific position of the sound.

Using a similar reservation technique to that described previously, the first agent to reach the volume containing the disturbance can flag it as occupied for the investigation. Additional agents who arrive later stop at the edge of the occupied volume and peer in suspiciously, but do not crowd the initial investigator. The distance between the investigator and the other agents does depend on the size of the volume, but this should not be a problem as all points inside of a convex volume are visible from the edge. It is believable that an agent would stop when he can see an ally already investigating the space.

Blackboard Communication

The techniques described so far might appear to add a great deal of overhead to the pathfinding data structures. The use of a simple blackboard, like that described in [Isla02], eliminates the need to add any data to the pathfinding data structures themselves. A blackboard is a shared object that allows inter-agent communication through posting and querying public information.

It might seem simpler to store the shared data inside of game objects such as pathfinding volumes, but there are several advantages to using a centralized blackboard. In addition to relieving the objects of the overhead needed for sharing data, a blackboard also provides a common location and interface for accessing the data, making the code base more maintainable as it ages and scales. Finally, centralizing the shared data minimizes the impact of inevitable agent design changes that affect the inter-agent data sharing requirements.

Our blackboard in *NOLF2* allows agents to post records, remove records, query records, and count records. A record consists of an ID for the posting agent, an ID for a target object, and some generic four-byte data.

```
// A record on the blackboard.
struct BlackboardRecord
{
      BBRecordType eType;
      ObjectID idPoster;
      ObjectID idTarget;
      int nData;
};

// The shared blackboard.
class CBlackboard
{
public :
      void PostBBRecord( BBRecordType eType, ObjectID    idPoster,
            ObjectID idTarget, int nData );
      void RemoveBBRecord( BBRecordType eType, ObjectID idPoster );
      void RemoveAllBBRecords( BBRecordType eType );
      int CountBBRecords( BBRecordType eType, ObjectID idTarget );
      BlackboardRecord* GetBBRecord( BBRecordType eType,
            ObjectID idTarget );
protected:
      BlackboardRecord* m_aBBRecords[MAX_BB];
};
```

An agent planning a path clears any previously reserved volumes, and reserves the volume before the destination like this:

```
g_pBlackboard->RemoveBBRecord( kBB_ReservedVolume, myID );
g_pBlackboard->PostBBRecord( kBB_ReservedVolume, myID,
      volumeID, NULL );
```

While planning a path, other agents will check if a volume is reserved, and apply a cost penalty if it is.

```
float fCost = pVolume->fCost;
if( g_pBlackboard-> GetBBRecord( kBB_ReservedVolume, volumeID )
{
   fCost *= 50.f;
}
```

This specific example illustrates how the blackboard can be used to keep track of occupied space, but that is just one of many applications. A blackboard can facilitate coordinating timing, sharing world objects, and varying actions and animations among multiple agents.

"Get Out of My Way!"

So, now we have agents splitting up and ambushing targets from different directions, but we still have problems. Once the mayhem of combat begins, the player and agents move about erratically looking for good cover and firing positions. It is inevitable that agents will get in each other's way, blocking lines of fire. It would take a complex system to constantly recalculate the optimal position for every agent, and we have already determined that we do not have a group behavior layer. Our agents are deciding where to go autonomously, without any knowledge of the big picture. Given this predicament, we are better off trying to deal gracefully with obstruction when it occurs than trying to prevent it from occurring.

When an agent finds his line-of-fire obstructed by an ally, there are four ways to resolve the situation.

1. The obstructed agent can do nothing.
2. The obstructed agent can fire anyway, either killing or going through his ally.
3. The obstructed agent can move.
4. The obstructed agent's ally can move.

The first two options are far from optimal, as they will either make the agents look stupid, or expose the fact that agents can shoot through each other. We employ the last two options on *NOLF2*, using moves that the agents already have in their animation sets.

The first step toward resolving the obstruction situation is to determine that an agent's line-of-fire is blocked. Presumably, this is already taken care of by the line-of-sight checks used to determine if a target is obscured by any of the game objects or level geometry. The next step is to determine if the obstructing object is an ally. If the vision system keeps track of an identifier for the obstructing object, then it is easy to check whether this object is an agent of a specified alignment.

Once the agent knows who is in his way, he can request that his ally ducks. If the request is granted, the ally crouches and continues firing while the requesting agent fires over his head. Problem solved! The ally might be busy, however, reloading his weapon, or just standing up from a crouch. If this is the case, the requester himself moves by doing a step or roll to either side. If there is a maximum time an agent is allowed to crouch, then these moves can be combined. One agent ducks to get out of another's way, and after the crouch timer has expired he stands back up and the agent behind him steps or rolls aside. This produces a dynamic environment where agents are constantly in motion, trying to get a clear shot, and no one stands idle behind someone else for more than a split second.

The preceding solution works well with ranged weapons, but does not make as much sense if the agents are using close-range melee weapons. In this case, we can employ an alternate yet similar approach. Rather than requesting that allies duck, agents can request that allies step or roll to the side. The result is a mob of agents that take turns thrashing an enemy in a round-robin fashion. Each one takes a few swings, and then steps or rolls to the side to let someone else get a shot. This solution really needs to be witnessed in "God" mode to be fully appreciated.

"Get Down!"

Our agents are splitting up, and keeping out of each other's way, but their limited set of combat behaviors makes for monotonous gameplay. It would be nice to add some pizzazz to the agents' repertoires by adding some special behaviors to specific types of characters. In *NOLF2*, our soldiers have an AttackProne behavior. When the right situation presents itself, an agent drops to his belly and fires from a safer position. The agent shows some intelligence in his decision to make himself more difficult to hit. If every agent encountered exhibits this behavior, it looks less like intelligence and more like a robotic reaction. When multiple agents go prone simultaneously, it looks comical.

Again, our blackboard can help our agents share information and coordinate. When an agent goes prone, he posts the current time to the blackboard in a record of type kBB_ProneTime. When another agent recognizes an opportunity to go prone, he first checks the blackboard for kBB_ProneTime records. If someone else has gone prone recently, he decides to do something else instead. Every time someone posts a new kBB_ProneTime, he first removes any previous posting.

The previous example illustrates how a blackboard can be used to coordinate the timing of a behavior across all agents. A similar approach can be used to constrain a behavior to only activate based on behaviors of other agents. In *NOLF2*, ninjas jump onto rooftops and attack the player from above. This behavior only activates if there are already two ninjas attacking the player, and none on the roof. Agents post kBB_Attack and kBB_AttackFromRoof messages to the blackboard. These messages include the ID of the attacker, and the ID of the target. A ninja can query the blackboard to count how many agents are attacking the same target, and how many agents are already on the roof. When the constraints are met, the ninja jumps onto the roof.

"What's Going On?"

We have come a long way toward convincing the player that agents are aware of each other, but we have still left one opportunity to break the illusion of coordination. Agents need to react appropriately to an ally's distress or agitation. Nothing looks worse than an agent standing idle and emotionless while his comrade takes damage, or runs by chasing an enemy. The same sensory trigger system [Orkin02] used by agents to detect the enemy can be used to detect each other.

Assuming a system is in place to keep track of existing audio and visual stimuli, and alert agents of relevant stimuli, this system can be used to allow agents to notice their allies. When an agent detects danger or takes damage, he emits an audible stimulus for his excitement or pain. This stimulus wakes up anyone in earshot. Any agent who is aware of danger emits a persistent visible stimulus that tracks his own position. When this visible stimulus enters the field of view of a relaxed ally, it alerts the ally of danger. The stimulus can contain an identifier that specifies exactly what information the agent is trying to convey. The identifier can indicate that the agent is aware of an enemy, in pain, caught in a bear trap, or in laughing-gas-induced hysterics.

Say It Loud and Clear

You might have noticed that the preceding sections are titled with quotations. These exclamations are examples of things agents can say to highlight the fact that they are actively cooperating with one another. Players might already notice the coordinated behavior, but either way, verbalizing the events will seal the deal on the illusion. When agents announce their intentions, it verifies that their behavior is coordinated rather than coincidental. It would be a shame for players not to recognize all that hard work.

In reality, agents are not verbalizing their intentions. Instead, they are announcing decisions that a group of agents has already committed to. For example, one agent grants another's request to duck out of his way, and *then* the obstructed agent yells, "Get out of my way!" An agent finds an alternate path to a target, and *then* yells "Split up!" The agents are leveraging the work that they have already done to arrange the coordination. The player will never perceive that the decision was actually made a fraction of a second before the verbalization.

Conclusion

This article illustrates how a significant degree of coordination can be achieved without the addition of a group behavior layer. Explore the possibilities of leveraging and sharing existing information in your own games. Your games' AI systems might afford different opportunities for coordination than those previously described. There are, of course, limits to what can be achieved through these techniques. If detailed choreography between agents is required, a centralized approach, like that described in [van der Sterren02], might be a more appropriate choice.

References

[Isla02] Isla, Damian, and Blumberg, Bruce "Blackboard Architectures," *AI Game Programming Wisdom*, Charles River Media, 2002.

[Monolith02] *No One Lives Forever 2: A Spy in H.A.R.M.'s Way*, Monolith Productions/Sierra Entertainment, Inc., 2002. Toolkit and SDK available at *nolf2.sierra.com/*

[Orkin02] Orkin, Jeff, "A General-Purpose Trigger System," *AI Game Programming Wisdom*, Charles River Media, 2002.

[van der Sterren02] van der Sterren, William, "Squad Tactics: Planned Maneuvers," *AI Game Programming Wisdom*, Charles River Media, 2002.

3.3

Team Member AI in an FPS

John Reynolds—Creative Asylum Ltd.

john@creative-asylum.com

The use of teammates has become very popular amongst the first- and third-person action genres in recent years, in both the simulation and arcade sub-genres.

However, implementing convincing teammates who will not get in your way while you are shooting, nor disappear into a far corner of the map, is quite an involved process. By implementing some key rules it is possible to create teammates who can usefully back you up in the thick of the action, follow instructions reliably, and survive with you until the end of the game.

In this article, we first look at the principles that a non-player character (NPC) should adhere to. We then look at ways of implementing these within a game. Included on the accompanying CD-ROM is a demo that shows these concepts in action.

ON THE CD

Correct Positioning

The correct positioning of the NPCs in relation to the player is an important aspect of simulating intelligence. Getting this wrong will frustrate the player and seriously hinder gameplay. In this section, we examine ways in which a teammate can avoid the player's field of view and line-of-fire, why a teammate should not stand between the player and a target, and how the teammate's body stance can affect its positioning.

The NPC should avoid moving into the player's field of view, as this could obscure important details the player should see. Moving into the player's line-of-fire is even worse, as it could result in the player hitting a teammate instead of the enemy. The angle that NPCs should leave clear for the player's field of view is a matter of balance. Teammates being visible from time to time can build the feeling of being part of a team. However, we must consider the accuracy of the player's weapon. Fully automatic guns can be quite inaccurate after a few rounds, and therefore a wider field of fire is necessary to avoid friendly fire.

A second area must also remain clear—the area between the player and a target. There might be several targets but, as far as is possible, the player should have a clear line-of-sight to each of them. Otherwise, the player will be frustrated if he or she is forced to move to find the target. This also gives the player the opportunity to be the first to shoot at the target, which is important if the player is to feel involved and in control. Figure 3.3.1 shows the two areas that must be clear: the player's field of view and the player's line-of-sight to the target.

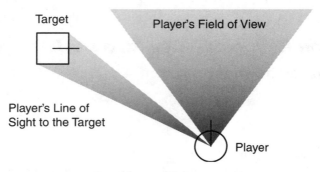

FIGURE 3.3.1   *Areas for an NPC to avoid.*

If the player turns to face a teammate, then the teammate should move to allow the player to see past. However, this can result in a lot of unnatural shuffling of NPC team members as they each clamor out of the player's line-of-sight. Realistically, team members would move as little as possible, because movement catches the eye and hinders spotting and targeting actual enemies.

The body stance of the player and NPCs can also be important. If an NPC is crouching or crawling, then it would be safer to pass in front of the player (since the NPC has a less obstructive profile). However, this should be avoided as, depending on the terrain, it is still possible to obscure the player's field of view, and the NPC is still at risk of friendly fire as it is just below the player's line-of-fire.

Correct Movement

Now that we have examined where a teammate should be positioned, let's look at how they should move. We will examine both how they should move around the player and how they should move to a waypoint. We also cover issues such as levels of threat, straying from the team, use of caution, team context, and speed of movement.

Where there are multiple targets, the risk of being positioned between the player and the target is increased. Moving out of the way can impose its own problems, because moving away from one target might place the NPC in front of another. There are two approaches to solving this problem. The first, illustrated in Figure 3.3.2a, is to consider all the targets and find the smaller angle that would lead to a clear view for the player, and then move in that direction. The second, illustrated in Figure 3.3.2b, is to consider the direction the player is looking and move away from the player's current viewing direction. This might give the longest route in some cases, but would mean the NPC never has to cross the player's line-of-sight.

Unfortunately, the previous algorithm does not take into account the levels of threat a target presents. Proximity, level of awareness, and readiness to fire are all fac-

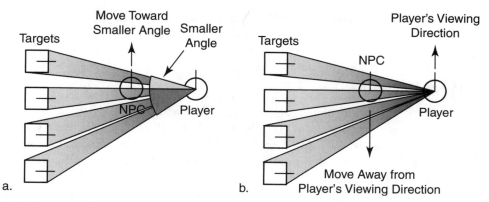

FIGURE 3.3.2 *Two options for how the NPC can step out of the player's line-of-fire. (a) The NPC travels in the direction of the smaller angle. (b) The NPC travels away from the player's viewing direction.*

tors that might change the order in which the player chooses his or her target. These factors should act as a filter to which targets a teammate should keep clear for the player. For example, if a teammate is currently standing between the player and an enemy patrol 500 meters away, he should not reposition himself between the player and an advancing soldier 10 meters away.

It might be possible for an enemy target to either retreat, or to attempt to maneuver around the team to gain a strategic advantage. In either case, team members might want to pursue the target. This can lead to team members straying some distance, potentially into enemy territory, without anyone else from the team to back them up. Therefore, it is worthwhile to set a maximum distance in which a team member can stray from the rest of the team. Players will not want the enemy base on full alert by the time they get there, nor will they want to spend time scouring the map for their missing teammate.

All movement should be done with appropriate caution. NPCs should not be the first to go around corners, into rooms, or over the brow of a hill unless ordered to do so. If so, they should use tactical strategies, avoiding risking themselves or the rest of the team. Descriptions on achieving this are found in [van der Sterren02a] and [van der Sterren02b].

Team members should also respect the current context of the situation. If the player wants to avoid conflict by using stealth tactics, the NPC members should not engage the targets upon seeing them. Many games tackle this problem by allowing the user to set a context for a team, and then team members will adhere to the player's choice of context. For stealth modes, there will usually be an automatic change of context triggered by either the player firing, or the team being fired upon.

NPC teammates should move at approximately the same speed as the player. This avoids the situation whereby the player must keep stopping to let the rest of the team catch up. However, when moving, the team should lag just behind to give the player a clear view around them, and to be on immediate hand should the player need support.

Correct Behavior

Simulating intelligent behavior, in this context, is largely rule-based and focuses on the strategic aspects of both the individual NPC and the team as a whole. The goal is to present the illusion that the teammates are professional, trained soldiers. We will examine three behaviors that are common to the genre: use of cover, selective firing, and reloading.

If there is cover available, to shield itself from a target or hide behind in stealth, the NPC should use it. Favoring the use of cover and shadow within the pathfinding algorithm will make teammates appear to think strategically. There will be exceptions, of course, when the team should advance with all haste. However, the NPCs should get their cues from the player. A description of how to use cover and shadow with a waypoint system can be found in [Lidén02].

Team members should be selective as to when they fire. They should generally only fire when the target is within range and in view. This might mean giving up trying to hit a target after firing a number of rounds and waiting until conditions have changed. For example, if the target is proving too difficult to hit, then the NPC might want to wait until it is closer or more exposed.

In the more realistic games, teammates should also fire in controlled bursts, as a human would, to try to maintain accuracy and conserve ammunition. Having accurate teammates is a design consideration, as it will affect gameplay. Assigning low reaction times can compensate for high accuracy, but can also have the undesirable effect of making the teammates appear unaware and therefore less intelligent. In addition, avoid setting lower reaction times than the enemy, as it will inevitably cause teammates to lose in battle. Reaction times are discussed in more detail in the section *The Player Is the Most Important*.

The teammate should watch the number of rounds it has fired, and use every safe opportunity to reload. This would mean that after every engagement with the enemy, when things are calmer, the teammate should reload. When reloading, it is best to find some cover and stay still behind the cover until the reloading is complete. If the teammate is in a prolonged gun battle and does run low on ammunition, it would be appropriate for the teammate to withdraw a little to let another teammate with more ammo take its place in the firing line. This requires staggering the firing across the team so that only one teammate runs out of ammunition at any one time. It is also important that there is a team member nearby to keep up the attack while the other reloads.

Supporting the Player

Depending on the style of game, the NPCs might support the player in different ways. Some styles, such as Capture the Flag, require the NPCs to work more or less autonomously, assisting the players only in achieving their ultimate goal. However, in other styles, the NPCs must work as a close team supporting the players in their every movement. We will look at this second style more closely, covering the following topics: protecting the rear, reporting to the player, selecting a target, and responding to orders.

At least one NPC in the team should protect the sides of the player from enemies. The player doesn't have good peripheral vision and therefore must be protected accordingly.

If a threat is seen, it should be reported so that the player has the opportunity to choose the appropriate action. This might be to engage the enemy (after all, it is their game), or perhaps to tell the team to hold their fire. If the team is in the middle of a fire fight, then reporting a sighting is less important and it might be appropriate for the NPC to attack the target and leave the rest of the team to attack theirs.

Cues such as sightings, hearing a suspicious sound, or even reporting a "hunch" can be used to inform the player of his or her surroundings and help guide the player through the game. Reporting is usually done through audio; for example, a radio message. Visual cues, such as an exclamation mark above an NPC's head, are also effective, as they allow the player to see which teammate reported something.

As mentioned earlier, the player will probably be attacking targets based on their level of threat. This should also be the criterion when selecting a target for a teammate to engage. Unless there is only a single threat, the teammates should engage targets other than the player's. One effective method is for teammates to engage the targets that are at the largest angle from the player's line of sight. This means that the NPCs are attacking targets that are either outside of the player's field of view, or at the edges of the screen, allowing the player to attack the targets he or she can see clearly.

The player must be able to issue orders to the team, and the team members must appear to be professional enough to carry out the orders without compromising themselves or the rest of the team. A list of common orders is given in Table 3.3.1.

Table 3.3.1 Orders Common to the FPS Genre

Order	Immediate Action Required?	Whole Team Required?
Cover Me	No	No
I Need Backup	Yes	No
Attack My Target	Yes	No
Close In	No	Yes
Spread Out	No	Yes
Move To Waypoint	No	Yes
Hold	Yes	Yes

When designing the AI behavior, it is important to decide which of the orders require a response from the whole team, which require an immediate response, and the duration of each order. Sensible settings for these factors will help make the team function effectively, sustain the illusion of intelligence, and keep the player happy.

The Player Is the Most Important

The player must be allowed to play the game, and the team should compliment the experience, not hinder it. We will now examine some more specific ways in which the NPC teammates can help keep the playing experience pleasurable, including the choice of weapon, collection of objects, and reaction times.

NPC teammates should select their weapons based on the player's current weaponry. It would not be much fun for the player to be outgunned by his teammates. Not only does this give the player the impression that he or she is not the most important player in the team, it can also detract from the gameplay. A teammate who constantly annihilates the enemy with a rocket launcher would be no fun to play with.

If the game features objects that can be collected, such as medical kits, power-ups, or new weapons, ensure that the player gets the first chance to collect the item. An NPC teammate should only take the item once the player has passed it by. If the team consists of several NPCs, then allow the most needy NPC to collect it.

Reaction times must be set carefully. In practice, there are two types of reaction time. The first is when an enemy has been seen but provides no immediate threat. In this case, the NPC should report the sighting to the team, and the player would have the opportunity to react. The second is when the team finds itself under attack. In this circumstance, the players would want the NPCs to fire quickly to avoid losing a team member, or indeed being killed themselves.

Implementation

An effective way of implementing the techniques described in this article is to use a layered approach, as shown in Figure 3.3.3. The lower the layer, the higher the priority.

Player Awareness

The first priority for any NPC team member is to stay out of the player's way. The player's position, orientation, current target, and possible targets must all be taken into consideration before doing anything.

If there are multiple members in the team, then each NPC should avoid moving into the line of sight of the other NPCs. An effective method for achieving this is to have a hierarchy of teammates. Each teammate avoids entering the line of sight of the player and each teammate above it in the hierarchy. This system ensures that NPCs do not fight over positions.

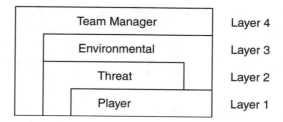

FIGURE 3.3.3 *The Implementation Hierarchy allows the NPCs to examine their current situation from different perspectives, each with its own priority level.*

The team manager, described later, will ensure that other aspects of team management are controlled.

Threat Awareness

The NPC should always be looking out for targets using a line-of-sight algorithm. If a target is seen, heard, or suspected it should be reported. However, if the team is too busy to provide backup, then the target should be engaged.

Despite always looking out for targets, and engaging targets if applicable, the priority for movement is always with the player awareness layer.

Environmental Awareness

This layer causes NPCs to consider their surroundings and behave correctly and tactically within the environment. This would include identifying anything that can be used for cover or any areas that are not permissible because they are too exposed or too dangerous. This layer will also be used to make sure the NPC is not straying too far from the player.

Team Manager

The team manager layer is shared by all the teammates, and has access to all the data for each members of the team. It ensures that the team members work as a team, however many there are. Each NPC will query the team manager to find information, such as which direction and angle range it should be covering, which teammates it should be helping, waypoint information, and whether it is allowed to pick up an item. This must be done frequently to keep each NPC up to date with changes.

The environmental awareness level also consults the team manager to obtain information on how far it can venture from the player; and at the threat awareness level to control the rate of fire to avoid multiple NPCs running out of ammunition simultaneously.

The team manager should never consider the player when processing information for the NPC. With the exception of simulations, the team manager must consider the player too unpredictable. Therefore, as an example, NPC teammates must cover the area the player is also covering, as the player might look away at any point.

All the orders made by the player should be directed to the team manager, which will filter the implications down to each NPC as they become able to respond to the order.

Finding an Available NPC

An NPC team member will often be required to carry out an order. When the team is under attack, it will be difficult to find an available team member, as every NPC should be covering the area, supporting other team members, or engaging the enemy. However, algorithmically some NPCs will be more available than others.

The attributes that make up the equation include:

N = Number of enemies in covering area.
O = Number of enemies within range.
P = Number of enemies threatening team.
Q = Supporting another team member (1=True, 0=False). This is multiplied by infinity to ensure a busy teammate is never selected.

$$Availability = (1 + N)(1 + O)(1 + P) + (Q\infty)$$

Lower numbers indicate greater availability. If all team members have availability above a threshold value (which will be game and context specific), then any requests for help must be declined.

Fire Staggering

Fire staggering, ensuring that two NPCs in close proximity do not run out of ammunition at the same time, will usually occur naturally. NPCs should not be targeting the same enemies or firing the same number of rounds at the target. The team manager should also monitor the levels of ammunition and, if necessary, temporarily widen the covering area of one NPC and shorten another's area to allow one NPC to conserve ammunition. Once the NPC runs out, the other will cover the entire area while the first reloads. This ensures that all NPCs use their entire magazine during a prolonged encounter and that there is always an NPC with ammunition engaging the threat.

Demo on the CD-ROM

ON THE CD

The demo included on the accompanying CD-ROM allows you to control a player while your teammates position themselves as best they can in order to adhere to their positioning rules (which can be toggled on and off). The demo is a great tool to get a feel for how teammates should move around an unpredictable human player.

Conclusion

Using a set of rules to control the NPCs as individuals and using a team manager to control them as a team is a simple and effective solution to coordinating NPC teammates.

Intelligent NPCs make excellent teammates that can improve the gameplay experience, allowing the design to accommodate many new and interesting features.

As the player grows to trust the actions of the team, and with the help of good design and storyboarding, a bond between the player and the team might well emerge. This could provide a far deeper experience for the players as they explore the game world with their NPC friends.

References

[Dawson02] Dawson, Chad, "Formations," *AI Game Programming Wisdom*, Charles River Media, 2002.

[Lidén02] Lidén, Lars, "Strategic and Tactical Reasoning with Waypoints," *AI Game Programming Wisdom*, Charles River Media, 2002.

[Pelletier01] Pelletier, B., Gummelt, M., and Monroe, J., "Postmortem: Raven Software's *Star Trek: Voyager–Elite Force*," *Game Developer Magazine*, available online at *www.gamasutra.com/features/20010207/pellertier_01.htm*, 2001.

[van der Sterren02a] van de Sterren, William, "Squad Tactics: Team AI and Emergent Maneuvers," *AI Game Programming Wisdom*, Charles River Media, 2002.

[van der Sterren02b] van de Sterren, William, "Squad Tactics: Planned Maneuvers," *AI Game Programming Wisdom*, Charles River Media, 2002.

3.4

Applying Goal-Oriented Action Planning to Games

Jeff Orkin—Monolith Productions

jorkin@blarg.net

A number of games have implemented characters with goal-directed decision-making capabilities. A goal-directed character displays some measure of intelligence by autonomously deciding to activate the behavior that will satisfy the most relevant goal at any instance. Goal-Oriented Action Planning (GOAP) is a decision-making architecture that takes the next step, and allows characters to decide not only what to do, but how to do it. But why would we want to empower our characters with so much freedom?

A character that formulates his own plan to satisfy his goals exhibits less repetitive, predictable behavior, and can adapt his actions to custom fit his current situation. In addition, the structured nature of a GOAP architecture facilitates authoring, maintaining, and reusing behaviors.

No One Lives Forever 2: A Spy in H.A.R.M.'s Way (NOLF2) [Monolith02] is one example of a game that contains goal-directed autonomous characters, but no planning capabilities. Characters in *NOLF2* constantly re-evaluate their goals, and select the most relevant goal to control their behavior. The active goal determines the character's behavior through a hard-coded sequence of state transitions.

This article explores how games can benefit from the addition of a real-time planning system, using problems encountered during the development of *NOLF2* to illustrate these points.

Defining Terms

Before we can discuss the benefits of GOAP, we first need to define some terminology. An agent uses a *planner* to *formulate* a sequence of *actions* that will satisfy some *goal*. We need to define what we mean by the terms *goal*, *action*, *plan*, and *formulate*.

Goal

A *goal* is any condition that an agent wants to satisfy. An agent might have any number of goals. Characters in *NOLF2* typically have about 25 goals. At any instant, one goal is active, controlling the character's behavior. A goal knows how to calculate its current relevance, and knows when it has been satisfied.

Goals in *NOLF2* fall into three categories: relaxed, investigative, and aggressive. Relaxed goals include passive goals such as Sleep, Work, and Patrol. Investigative goals include the more suspicious Investigate and Search. Aggressive goals are used for combat situations, like Chase, Charge, and AttackFromCover.

While conceptually similar, there is one key difference between the goals employed by *NOLF2* and the goals referred to by GOAP. *NOLF2*'s goals include an embedded plan. Once a goal is activated, the character runs through a predetermined sequence of steps, hard-coded into the goal. The embedded plan can contain conditional branches, but these branches are predetermined at the time the goal is authored. Goals in GOAP do not include a plan. Instead, they simply define what conditions need to be met to satisfy the goal. The steps used to reach these satisfaction conditions are determined in real-time.

Plan

The *plan* is simply the name for a sequence of actions. A plan that satisfies a goal refers to the valid sequence of actions that will take a character from some starting state to some state that satisfies the goal.

Action

An *action* is a single, atomic step within a plan that makes a character do *something*. Some possible actions include GotoPoint, ActivateObject, DrawWeapon, ReloadWeapon, and Attack. The duration of an action might be short or infinitely long. The Reload-Weapon action will complete as soon as the character finishes a reload animation. The Attack action might continue infinitely, until the target is dead.

Each action knows when it is valid to run, and what it will do to the game world. In other words, an action knows its *preconditions* and *effects*. Preconditions and effects provide a mechanism for chaining actions into a valid sequence. For example, Attack has a precondition that the character's weapon is loaded. The effect of ReloadWeapon is that the weapon is loaded. It is easy to see that ReloadWeapon followed by Attack is a valid sequence of actions. Each action might have any number of preconditions and effects.

A GOAP system does not replace the need for a finite-state machine (FSM) [Fu04], but greatly simplifies the required FSM. A plan is a sequence of actions, where each action represents a state transition. By separating the state transition logic from the states themselves, the underlying FSM can be much simpler. For example, Dodge and ReloadWeapon are different actions that both set the character's state to Animate, and specify an animation to play. Rather than having a Patrol or Wander state, a GOAP system can formulate a plan that instructs the character to use to the Goto state to move between a number of patrol points. Ultimately, the Goto and Animate states cover most of things that characters do; they just do them for different reasons. Actions define when to transition into and out of a state, and what happens to the game world as a result of this transition.

Plan Formulation

A character generates a plan in real-time by supplying some goal to satisfy to a system called a *planner*. The planner searches the space of actions for a sequence that will take the character from his starting state to his goal state. This process is referred to as *formulating* a plan. If the planner is successful, it returns a plan for the character to follow to direct his behavior. The character follows this plan to completion, invalidation, or until another goal becomes more relevant. If another goal activates, or the plan in progress becomes invalid for any reason, the character aborts the current plan and formulates a new one.

Figure 3.4.1 depicts an abstract illustration of the planning process. The rectangles represent the start and goal states, and each circle represents an action. The goal in Figure 3.4.1 is to kill an enemy. Therefore, the goal state is the state of the world in which the enemy is dead. The planner needs to find a sequence of actions for the character that will take the world from a state in which is the enemy is alive to a state in which the enemy is dead.

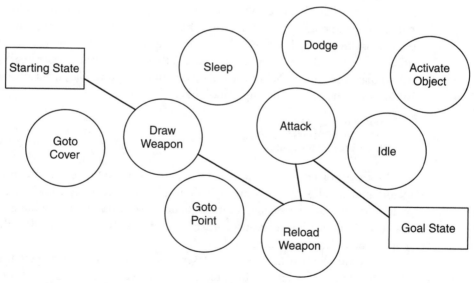

FIGURE 3.4.1 *The plan formulation process.*

This process looks suspiciously like pathfinding! In a sense, that's exactly what it is. The planner needs to find a path through the space of actions that will take the character from his starting state to some goal state. Each action is a step on that path that changes the state of the world in some way. Preconditions of the actions determine when it is valid to move from one action to the next.

In many cases, more than one valid plan exists. The planner only needs to find one of them. Similar to navigational pathfinding, the planner's search algorithm can be provided with hints to guide the search. For example, costs can be associated with actions, leading the planner to find the least costly sequence of actions, rather than any arbitrary sequence.

All of this searching sounds like a lot of work. Is it worth it? Now that we have defined our terms, we can discuss the benefits of this decision-making process.

The Benefits of GOAP

There are benefits at both development and runtime. Characters in the game can exhibit more varied, complex, and interesting behaviors using GOAP. The code behind the behaviors is more structured, reusable, and maintainable.

Benefits to Runtime Behavior

A character that determines his own plan at runtime can custom fit his actions to his current surroundings, and dynamically find alternate solutions to problems. This is best illustrated with an example.

Imagine that character X detects an enemy whom he wants to eliminate. Ordinarily, the best course of action would be to draw a loaded weapon and fire it at the enemy. In this case, however, X has no weapon, or maybe no ammunition, so he needs to find an alternate solution. Luckily, there is a mounted laser nearby that X can use to blast the enemy. X can formulate a plan to go to the laser, activate it, and use it to zap someone. The plan might look like:

```
GotoPoint(laser)
ActivateObject(laser)
MountedAttack(laser)
```

Problem solved! Character X fed the planner his KillEnemy goal, and the planner formulated a valid plan to satisfy it. The planner hit a dead end when it tried to include the action DrawWeapon in its sequence, because DrawWeapon has a precondition that the character has a weapon. Instead, it found an alternate plan that does not require the character to have a weapon.

But wait! What if the mounted laser requires power, and the generator is turned off? The planner can handle this situation just as well. The valid plan for this situation involves first going to the generator and turning it on, and then using the laser. The plan might look like:

```
GotoPoint(generator)
ActivateObject(generator)
GotoPoint(laser)
```

```
ActivateObject(laser)
MountedAttack(laser)
```

The GOAP decision-making architecture allows character X to handle dependencies that may not have been anticipated at the time of the behavior development.

Benefits to Development

Handling every possible situation in hand-authored code or scripts quickly becomes difficult to manage. Imagine the code for a `KillEnemy` goal with an embedded plan that handles the situation described previously. The goal's embedded plan needs to handle characters with or without weapons, plus finding, navigating to, and activating alternate means of destruction.

It might be tempting to break down the `KillEnemy` goal into smaller goals, such as `KillEnemyArmed`, `KillEnemyMounted`. This is essentially what we did for *NOLF2*, but the proliferation of goals has its own problems. More goals means more code to maintain, and revisit with each design change.

Seemingly innocent design additions caused headaches during the development of *NOLF2*. Examples of these additions included drawing and holstering weapons, turning on lights when entering dark rooms, and activating security keypads before opening doors. Each of these additions required revisiting the code of every goal to ensure that the embedded plan could handle the new requirements.

GOAP offers a much more elegant structure that better accommodates change. The addition of design requirements is handled by adding actions, and preconditions to related actions. This is more intuitive, and touches less code than revisiting every goal. For example, requiring characters to turn on lights in dark rooms before entering can be handled by adding a precondition to the `GotoPoint` action that requires the lights to be on in the destination. Due to this precondition, every goal that results in moving the character transparently handles turning on the lights in dark rooms before entering.

Furthermore, GOAP provides the guarantee of valid plans. Hand-coded embedded plans can contain mistakes. A developer might code a sequence of actions that cannot follow each other. For example, a character might be instructed to fire a weapon, without ever being told to first draw a weapon. This situation cannot arise in a plan dynamically generated through a GOAP system, because the preconditions on the actions prevent the planner from formulating an invalid plan.

Benefits to Variety

The structure imposed by GOAP is ideal for creating a variety of character types who exhibit different behaviors, and even share behaviors across multiple projects. The planner is provided with a pool of actions from which to search for a plan. This pool does not necessarily have to be the complete pool of all existing actions. Different character types might use subsets of the complete pool, leading to a variety of behaviors.

NOLF2 has a number of different character types, including Soldiers, Mimes, Ninjas, Super Soldiers, and Bunnies. We tried to share as much of the AI code as possible between all of these character types. This sometimes led to undesirable branching in the code for behaviors. One instance of undesirable branching was related to how characters handle closed doors. A human stops at a door, opens it, and walks through, while a cyborg Super Soldier smashes the door off its hinges and continues walking. The code that handles going through a door needs a branch to check if this is a character that smashes doors.

A GOAP system can handle this situation more elegantly, by providing each character type with a different action to accomplish the same effect. A human character can use the OpenDoor action, while a Super Soldier uses the SmashDoor action. Both actions have the same effect. They both open a path that was previously blocked by a door.

There are other solutions to the smashing versus opening the door problem, but none as flexible as the GOAP solution. For example, OpenDoor and SmashDoor could be states derived from a base HandleDoor class. Using a state class hierarchy like this, a designer can assign states to slots, such as the HandleDoor slot, creating character types that handle doors in different ways. However, what if we want a character that opens doors when relaxed, and smashes doors when agitated? The state class hierarchy solution needs an external mechanism to swap out the state in HandleDoor slot under certain conditions. The GOAP solution allows a character to have both the OpenDoor and SmashDoor actions at all times. An additional precondition on each action for the required mood allows the character to select the appropriate action to handle the door in real-time, without any external intervention.

Implementation Considerations

Now that you have seen the benefits, and are excited about the prospect of applying GOAP to games, you need to be aware of some good and bad news. The bad news is that there are a couple of challenges involved in implementing a GOAP system. The first challenge is determining the best method for searching the space of actions. The second challenge is one of world representation. In order to formulate a plan, the planner must be able to represent the state of the world in a compact and concise form. Both of these topics are large areas of research in academia, and a complete discussion of them is beyond the scope of this article. The good news is that we can stick to simple solutions for the domain of games. The rest of this article presents some reasonable solutions to these challenges that make sense for game development.

Planner Search

Earlier we observed that the planning process is remarkably similar to navigational pathfinding. These processes are so similar, in fact, that we can use the same algorithm for both of them! The planner's search can be driven by an algorithm that most game AI developers are already intimately familiar with; namely, A*. Although many game developers think of A* as a pathfinding algorithm, it is actually a general-purpose search algorithm. If A* is implemented in a modular fashion, like that described by [Higgins02a], the bulk of the code for the algorithm can be shared between the navigation system and the planner. The planner just needs to implement its own classes for A*'s node, map, and goal.

The A* algorithm requires the calculation of the cost of a node, and the heuristic distance from a node to the goal. Nodes in the planner's search represent states of the world, with edges representing actions between them. The cost of a node can be calculated as the sum of the costs of the actions that take the world to the state represented by the node. The cost of each action can vary, where lower-cost actions are more preferable. The heuristic distance can be calculated as the sum of the number of unsatisfied properties of the goal state.

We have two choices when searching with A*. We can search forward, starting at our current state and searching for a path to the goal state, or we can search backward from the goal to the starting state. Let's first examine how a forward search would work for the previously described situation where an unarmed character wants to eliminate an enemy with a mounted laser that requires power. The forward search will first tell the character to go to the laser with the GotoPoint action, and then tell the character to use the laser with the AttackMounted action. The precondition on AttackMounted will fail if the power is off. It will take an exhaustive brute-force search to come up with the valid plan that will first send the character to turn on the generator, and then use the laser.

A regressive search is more efficient and intuitive. Searching backward will start at the goal, and find that the AttackMounted action will satisfy the goal. From there, the search will continue for actions that will satisfy the preconditions of the Attack-Mounted action. The preconditions will lead the character step by step to the final plan of first activating the generator, and then using the laser.

World Representation

In order to search the space of actions, the planner needs to represent the state of the world in some way that lets it easily apply the preconditions and effects of actions, and recognize when it has reached the goal state. One compact way to represent the state of the world is with a list of world property structures that contain an enumerated attribute key, a value, and a handle to a subject.

```
struct SWorldProperty
{
    GAME_OBJECT_ID hSubjectID;
    WORLD_PROP_KEY eKey;

    union value
    {
        bool    bValue;
        float   fValue;
        int     nValue;
        ...
    };
};
```

So, if we wanted to describe the state of the world that will satisfy the KillEnemy goal, we would supply the goal state with a property that looks like this:

```
SWorldProperty Prop;
Prop.hSubjectID = hShooterID;
Prop.eKey = kTargetIsDead;
Prop.bValue = true;
```

Representing every aspect of the world in this way would be an overwhelming and impractical task, but this is unnecessary. We only need to represent the minimal set of properties of the world state that are relevant to the goal that the planner is trying to satisfy. If the planner is trying to satisfy the KillEnemy goal, it does not need to know the shooter's health, current location, or anything else. The planner does not even need to know whom the shooter is trying to kill! It just needs to find a sequence of actions that will lead to this shooter's target getting killed, whomever that target might be.

As the planner adds actions, the goal state grows as preconditions of the actions are appended to the goal's satisfaction state. Figure 3.4.2 illustrates a planner's regressive search to satisfy the KillEnemy goal. The search successfully completes when the current state matches the goal state. The goal state grows as actions add their preconditions. The current state grows accordingly as the planner searches for additional actions that will satisfy the additional goal properties.

In each step of the regressive search, the planner tries to find an action that has an effect that will satisfy one of the unsatisfied goal conditions. A property of the world is considered unsatisfied when the goal state's property has a different value from the current state's property. Often, actions that solve one of the unsatisfied conditions add additional preconditions to be satisfied. When the search completes, we can see that a valid plan to satisfy the KillEnemy goal is:

```
DrawWeapon
LoadWeapon
Attack
```

The planning example illustrated in Figure 3.4.2 consists of actions that have constant Boolean values for preconditions and effects, but it is important to point out that preconditions and effects can also represented by variables. The planner solves for these variables as it regresses from the goal. Variables add power and flexibility to the planner, as it can now satisfy more general preconditions. For example, a Goto action with the effect of moving a character to a variable destination is far more powerful than a Goto action that moves to a constant, predetermined location.

Actions can use the previously described world state representation to represent their preconditions and effects. For example, the constructor for the Attack action defines its preconditions and effects like this:

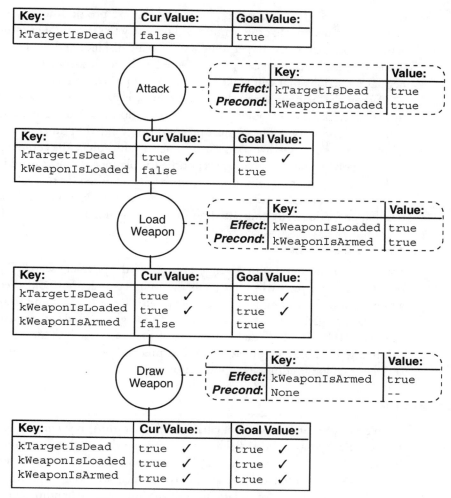

FIGURE 3.4.2 *The planner's regressive search.*

```
CAIActionAttack::CAIActionAttack()
{
    m_nNumPreconditions = 1;
    m_Preconditions[0].eKey = kWeaponIsLoaded;
    m_Preconditions[0].bValue = true;

    m_nNumEffects = 1;
    m_Effects[0].eKey = kTargetIsDead;
    m_Effects[0].bValue = true;
}
```

Actions only need to specify preconditions in this symbolic manner if they are going to factor into the planner's search. There might be additional preconditions that can be called *context* preconditions. A context precondition is something that needs to be true, but that the planner will never try to satisfy. For example, the Attack action might require the target to be within some distance and field of view. This is a more complex check than can be represented with an enumerated value, and the planner has no actions that will make this true if it is not true already.

When the planner is searching for actions, it calls two separate functions. One function checks the symbolic planner preconditions, and the other checks freeform context preconditions. The context precondition validation function can contain any arbitrary piece of code that results in a Boolean value. Since the context preconditions for an action will be re-evaluated every time the planner attempts to add this action to a plan, it is important to minimize the processing required for this validation. Possible optimizations include caching results from previous validations, and looking up values that are periodically computed outside of the planner.

Planner Optimization

Some consideration must be given to optimizing the planner's search. The complexity of formulating a plan will increase as the number of actions, and preconditions on actions grow. We can attack this problem with some of the same strategies used to optimize navigational pathfinding. These strategies include optimizing the search algorithm [Higgins02b], caching results of previous searches, and distributing plan formulation over several updates. Context preconditions can also be used to truncate searches that are heading down unfruitful paths.

Conclusion

With each new game released, the bar is set higher for AI behavior. As expectations for the complexity of character behavior rises, we need to look toward more structured, formalized solutions to creating scalable, maintainable, and reusable decision-making systems. Goal-oriented action planning is one such solution. By letting go of the reins and allowing games to formulate plans at runtime, we are handing over key decisions to those who are in the best position to make them—the characters themselves.

References

[AIPS02] AIPS'02, *Conference on AI Planning & Scheduling*, information about AIPS 2002 available online at *www.laas.fr/aips/*, 2002.

[Fu04] Fu, Dan, and Houlette, Ryan, "The Ultimate Guide to FSMs in Games," *AI Game Programming Wisdom 2*, Charles River Media, 2004.

[Higgins02a] Higgins, Dan, "Generic A* Pathfinding," *AI Game Programming Wisdom*, Charles River Media, 2002.

[Higgins02b] Higgins, Dan, "How to Achieve Lightning-Fast A*," *AI Game Programming Wisdom*, Charles River Media, 2002.

[IPC02] 2002 IPC, *International Planning Competition*, information about IPC 2002 available online at *www.dur.ac.uk/d.p.long/competition.html*, 2002.

[McDermott98] McDermott, Drew, *Planning Domain Description Language*, information about PDDL2.1 available online at *www.dur.ac.uk/d.p.long/IPC/pddl.html*, 1998.

[Monolith02] *No One Lives Forever 2: A Spy in H.A.R.M.'s Way*, Monolith Productions/Sierra Entertainment, Inc., 2002. Toolkit and SDK available at *nolf2.sierra.com/*

[Nilsson98] Nilsson, Nils J., *Artificial Intelligence: A New Synthesis*, Morgan Kaufmann, 1998.

[Russell02] Russell, Stuart, and Norvig, Peter, *Artificial Intelligence: A Modern Approach (Second Edition)*, Prentice-Hall, Inc., 2002.

3.5

Hierarchical Planning in Dynamic Worlds

Neil Wallace—Black & White Studios / Lionhead Studios

nwallace@lionhead.com

In classical planning, there is a clear distinction between formulating a plan and executing it. This distinction is based on the assumption that the world remains in the same state between the planning and the execution of the plan. For example, an agent might plan to throw a grenade at another agent; however, by the time the plan is formulated, the other agent might already be too close and the plan must be abandoned. Clearly, if we want to create plans within a dynamic world, we can't assume that the world remains the same between planning and plan execution. This article looks at how hierarchical planners can be used to plan effectively within dynamic worlds. In addition, it will be shown how hierarchical planners can be extended to deal with the problem of agent cooperation.

Why Do We Need to Plan?

Traditionally, agents within games have tended to be reactive rather than deliberative; that is, they react to situations that arise directly by performing a single action (or hard-coded sequence of actions) rather than planning a sequence of actions and then carrying out this plan.

There are several problems with the reactive approach:

- The reactive approach relies on developers thinking of possible situations that might arise and how the agents should react to these situations. Planning eliminates this problem by introducing the ability for agents to solve problems themselves rather than having pre-canned solutions from the developer. Game worlds are growing increasingly complex and dynamic, which compounds the problem of having to think of possible situations that might arise and write behaviors to deal with them.

- The reactive approach makes it very difficult to deal with complex situations where the agent must perform a number of actions to achieve its goal.

- The reactive approach does not allow much scope for complex cooperative behavior between agents that can be tightly coordinated.

Classical Planning

Classical AI planners function by treating planning as a search problem and attempt to find a plan that takes them from the current world state to some desired world state. However, one cannot possibly describe the world state completely, so instead, classical planners such as STRIPS [Filkes71] describe the world instead in terms of the propositions that are currently known to be true. Planning then becomes the process whereby given the set of propositions that are currently true (Σ), a plan α is found that makes the set of goal propositions (Ω) true.

The plan is a sequence of *operators* that have the following features:

A precondition list: The precondition list is a set of propositions that must be true in order to apply the operator (e.g., to move from point A to point B, it is necessary to be at point A).

An add list: The add list is a set of propositions that will be added when the operator is applied (e.g., an agent moving from A to B would add the proposition that the agent is at B).

A delete list: The delete list is a set of propositions that will be removed when the operator is applied (in the previous example, the delete list would be the proposition that the agent is at point A).

Limitations

Classical AI planning systems maintain a distinction between the actual *planning* of a plan and the *execution* of the plan. An agent will formulate a plan and then carry out all the actions to satisfy this plan. It is implicit in making this distinction that classical AI systems assume that the world in which they act will not change between planning and completing execution of a plan, which is a limitation for games.

Hierarchical Planning

A hierarchical planner differs from a classical planner in that it does not simply consider a single problem space; rather, it employs a hierarchy of abstract problem spaces, called *abstraction spaces* [Knoblock91]. Rather than attempting to solve a problem in the original problem space, the *ground space* [Knoblock91], a hierarchical planner first formulates a plan in the most abstract problem space. This plan cannot be carried out directly since it is expressed in high-level terms. Instead, the plan must be refined in order to produce a complete plan in terms of ground level operators—actions that the agent can carry out directly. This can be thought of as similar to the way we plan: we first formulate a high-level plan, perhaps simply consisting of our current state and our desired state. This plan is then fleshed out to provide details of how each of the objectives and sub-objectives are to be achieved; we first decide *what* we want to achieve before considering *how* to best achieve it.

Hierarchical Task Networks

To look at some of the features of hierarchical planers we will look at *hierarchical task networks* (HTNs); however, the principles shown are applicable to the more general hierarchical planning problem.

Figure 3.5.1 shows an example of an HTN. It consists of nodes representing tasks and two types of edges. *Reduction links* [Paolucci00] describe the decomposition from an abstract task into less abstract subtasks. *Provision/outcome links* [Paolucci00] are used to propagate values between tasks; they show dependencies between the outcome of tasks and the ability to perform others. An example of this is shown in Figure 3.5.2; the task T (representing killing an agent) might be reduced to acquiring a weapon (T1) and attacking the agent with the weapon (T2). This reduction has a provisional link, meaning that T1 must be performed before T2 so that the weapon found in T1 propagates to T2.

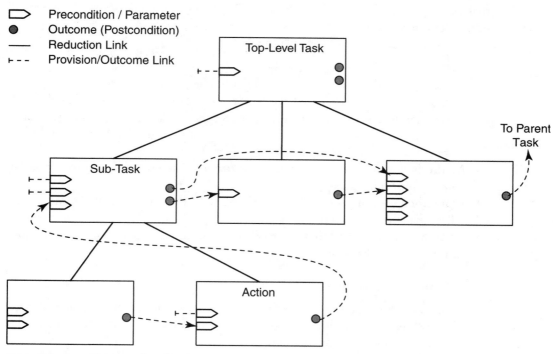

FIGURE 3.5.1 *A hierarchical task network.*

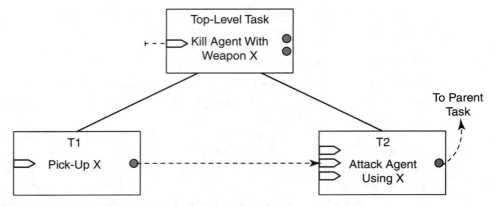

FIGURE 3.5.2   *Decomposition of a hierarchical task network.*

Unlike classical STRIPS style planners, which try to find a sequence of actions that take us from our initial state to our goal state, HTN planners search for plans that accomplish *task networks* [Erol95]. HTN planners use *problem reduction* search rather than state space search.

The components of an HTN planner are:

- **Tasks:** Tasks fall into two categories:
  Primitive tasks (also called *actions*), which can be performed directly.
  Non-primitive tasks (also called *compound tasks*), which cannot be executed directly since they represent activities that can be expanded to primitive tasks in multiple ways. For example, if an agent wants to get a certain object, he might be able to buy it, borrow it, or steal it.
- **Methods (also called *task reduction schemas*):** Methods are used to *expand* or *reduce* nonprimitive tasks.
- **Operators:** Operators in HTN planning are like those in classical planning; they tell us the effects of each task.
- **Critics:** Critics are used to remove conflicts within the plan at the earliest opportunity to reduce backtracking.

Task Reduction in HTNs

Expanding or reducing nonprimitive tasks is done by finding a method that is capable of accomplishing the nonprimitive task. The nonprimitive task is then replaced by the task network produced by the method.

In mapping a nonprimitive task *t* to a task-network *n*, a method will specify constraints within *n*. These constraints are not only ordering constraints on the tasks within *n*, but also inheritance information specifying how the provisions of *t* become the provisions of the tasks within *n*.

Conflict Resolution in HTNs

Interactions between tasks might lead to a plan that contains conflicts; for example, using up all of a particular resource early in a plan might prohibit the agent from being able to carry out a task later in the plan. Critics are used to identify these conflicts as early as possible, since we can spot the conflicts as they occur rather than wait until a complete plan is formed. This considerably reduces the amount of backtracking required. A detailed discussion of critics can be found in [Tate90].

The HTN Planning Procedure

A number of different systems have been devised for HTN planning, [Erol95] provides the following procedure that captures the essence of these:

1. Input a planning problem P.
2. If P contains only primitive tasks, then resolve the conflicts in P and return the result. If the conflicts cannot be resolved, return failure.
3. Choose a nonprimitive task *t* in P.
4. Choose a method *m* to reduce *t*.
5. Replace *t* with the task network produced by applying *m*.
6. Use critics to find the interactions among the tasks in P, and suggest ways to handle them.
7. Apply one of the ways suggested in step 6.
8. Go to step 2.

HTN planning works by iteratively reducing nonprimitive tasks and resolving conflicts until a plan is found that is free from conflicts and contains only primitive tasks.

Partial Replanning

Partial replanning is one of the most powerful features of HTN planning. It enables us to adapt plans that become invalid (either during planning or during execution) rather than having to completely replan. For example, if an agent walks to a hardware store with the intention of buying a spanner only to find that they are out of stock, he should look for another item, such as a monkey wrench, that can perform the same function rather than completely replanning.

This partial replanning is necessary during the planning stage so that critics can be employed effectively, it allows a conflict to be detected, the offending part of the plan can be removed, and a new part planned to replace it. This ability to partially replan is also useful when conflicts arise at plan execution time.

Since plans have a tree structure, it is a simple task to decide which parts of the plan have become invalid and to replan for these parts.

Replanning Example

Let us assume that we have two agents, *A* and *B*. Agent *A* wants to kill agent *B*, and between the two agents lies a knife. Agent *A* starts with his planning problem "Kill

Agent"; however, this plan cannot be carried out directly as it is not expressed in a low enough level to be carried out by the agent. It must be reduced to simpler actions by applying *methods*. The first method the agent might try to apply is "Attack with Weapon." This method replaces the agent's existing task "Kill Agent" with the sequence of actions "Pick up Weapon" and "Attack Agent with Weapon" (as shown in Figure 3.5.2).

Now suppose that agent *B* gets to the knife first so that agent *A* is unable to carry out his action "Pick up Knife" and must replan. If agent *A* must kill agent *B* as part of a larger plan (e.g., killing a guard to gain entry to a secured compound), only the invalid part of the overall plan needs to be reconsidered. For example, agent *A* would not need to reconsider again how he is going to get into the compound—his plan to kill the guard is still valid—only the method chosen to achieve this plan has become invalid. The upshot of this is that agent *A* can use an alternative method rather than "Attack with Weapon" (provided it produces the same effects that are required as pre-conditions; in this case, that it will kill the guard). Possible alternatives would be a method such as "Attack with Bare Hands" or, if applicable, agent *A* can attempt to replan using the same "Attack with Weapon" method, but with a different object (e.g., with the gun he just spotted).

Performance of Hierarchical Planners

Since hierarchical planners use multiple levels of abstraction, the planning at any particular level of abstraction is a fairly simple task. This is largely due to the fact that at any given level, the number of applicable operators is considerably smaller than the total number of operators. This reduction in the search space at each planning level results in a considerable reduction in complexity compared with planning only at the ground level. Under an ideal decomposition of a problem, hierarchical problem solving reduces the worst-case complexity of the search from exponential to linear time [Knoblock91].

Planning Agent Cooperation

Planning in a dynamic world is made even more difficult if agents must cooperate in order to achieve a shared goal. This is due to the interactions between the agents; one agent's actions might invalidate the plan of another agent, or one agent's plans might be dependent on the progress of another agent's plan. While the solution to the multi-agent problem is beyond the scope of this article, some direction is provided as to where the solution might lie.

There are two parts to the multi-agent problem: eliminating conflicts and coordinating plans. Lansky proposes one method for eliminating conflicts within cooperative plans by localizing plan effects to individual agents (by reducing or eliminating interactions) [Lansky90]. Meanwhile, Georgeff offers one possible way in which the problem of coordinating plans might be resolved by introducing *synchronization actions* [Georgeff83]. These two methods each deal with one particular aspect of the cooperation problem. By localizing plan effects, conflicts are avoided. By introducing synchronization actions, cooperating agents are able to coordinate their actions.

Coordinating Hierarchical Plans

The coordination of a hierarchical plan can be done at several levels as shown in Figure 3.5.3. If we are to coordinate the plan at the most abstract level, the coordination is much easier since the plans at this level are much simpler. However, if we require very tight coordination, it might be necessary to coordinate at a less abstract level since those more abstract levels might not provide a suitable description of the plan. Clearly, there is a tradeoff between the ease of coordination and the crispness of the coordination.

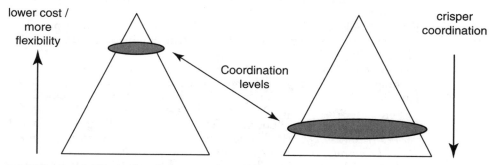

FIGURE 3.5.3 *Hierarchical plan coordination at multiple levels.*

It should be noted that if we want to coordinate plans at the abstract level, we must have some notion of how these abstract plans can be refined. [Clement99] does this by deriving summary information that captures the external preconditions and the effects of their refinement.

Conclusion

In this article, we demonstrated the shortcoming of classical AI planners and showed that hierarchical planning offers several key benefits over classical AI planning:

- Since planning is performed at multiple levels within the hierarchy, the planning at each level is much simpler than if we attempt to plan at a single level.
- The hierarchical nature of the planner also translates to a significant reduction in the search space, as invalid plans can often be ruled out at the top level of the planning hierarchy and so are never considered for expansion by the lower levels.
- Hierarchical planners better support replanning on the fly, and as a result are much more suitable for planning within dynamic worlds. They can even be adapted to deal with the difficult problems encountered when planning agent cooperation.

References

[Armano01] Armano, G., Cherchi, G., and Vargiu, E., "An Agent Architecture for Planning in a Dynamic Environment," *AI*IA 2001: Advances in Artificial Intelligence, 7th Congress of the Italian Association for Artificial Intelligence*, 2001.

[Clement99] Clement, B., and Durfee, E., "Top-Down Search for Coordinating the Hierarchical Plans of Multiple Agents," *Proceedings of the Third International Conference on Autonomous Agents*, pp. 252–259, 1999, available online at *ai.eecs.umich.edu/people/durfee/COABS/aa99.pdf*

[Erol94] Kutluthan, Erol, Hendler, James, and Nau, Dana S., "HTN Planning: Complexity and Expressivity," *Proceedings of the Twelfth National Conference on Artificial Intelligence (AAAI-94)*, 1994.

[Erol95] Erol, K., Hendler, J., and Nau, D., "Semantics for Hierarchical Task-Network Planning," *technical report TR 95-9, The Institute for Systems Research*, 1995, available online at *techreports.isr.umd.edu/TechReports/ISR/1995/TR_95-9/TR_95-9.phtml*

[Filkes71] Filkes, R.E., and Nilsonn, N.J., "STRIPS: A New Approach to the Application of Theorum Proving to Problem Solving," *Artificial Intelligence 2*, pp. 189–208, 1971.

[Georgeff83] Georgeff, M.P., "Communication and Interaction in Multiagent Planning," *Proceedings of the Third National Conference on AI*, pp. 125–129, 1983.

[Knoblock91] Knoblock, Craig, "Search Reduction in Hierarchical Problem Solving," *Proceedings of the Ninth National Conference on Artificial Intelligence*, 1991.

[Lansky90] Lansky, A., "Localized Search for Controlling Automated Reasoning," *Proceedings of DARPA Workshop on Innovative approaches to Planning, Scheduling and Control*, pp. 115–125, 1990.

[Paolucci00] Paolucci, M., Shehory, O., and Sycara, K., "Interleaving Planning and Execution in a Multiagent Team Planning Environment," *technical report CMU-RI-TR-00-01, Robotics Institute, Carnegie Mellon University*, 2000, available online at *www.ri.cmu.edu/pubs/pub_3274.html*

[Tate90] Tate, A., Hendler, J., and Drummond, D., "AI Planning: Systems and Techniques," *AI Magazine*, 1990.

[Tate00] Tate, Austin, Levine, John, Jarvis, Peter, and Dalton, Jeff, "Using AI Planning Technology for Army Small Unit Operations," *Artificial Intelligence Planning Systems*, 2000.

3.6

Goal-Directed Behavior Using Composite Tasks

Eric Dybsand—Glacier Edge Technology

edybs@ix.netcom.com

Goal-directed behavior is a widely used and powerful tool for increasing the believability of the actions for the non-player characters (NPCs or agents) or computer programmed opponents (CPOs) found in computer games. Agents and CPOs with a sense of purpose produce the appearance of believability to the human player who observes them. This sense of purpose is established through the use of goal direction.

The increase in agent and CPO action believability contributes to the player's enjoyment of the game. This article introduces various forms of goal-directed behavior while offering examples of their use in commercial computer games, simulations, and academic research projects. One implementation of goal directed behavior, called the *composite task*, is examined as it is applied to a military tactical combat simulator (to also be released as a commercial computer wargame).

What Is Goal-Directed Behavior?

Goal-directed behavior is a technique by which agents or CPOs will execute a series of actions or exhibit a set of behaviors that attempt to accomplish a specific objective or goal. A goal could be described as behavior as simple as *eating* or *survival* [Woodcock 01], whereby an agent will attempt to seek a specific type of agent for consumption or where the agent being pursued as food will attempt to avoid the seeking agent. Yet a goal could be complex like *create the largest economy* for a CPO in a game like the classic *Civilization*. Such a goal requires the completion of multiple, complex steps (or sub-goals).

The simple goal in Figure 3.6.1 illustrates a simple state transition. The agent transitions from the state of being "Hungry" to a state of being "Satisfied" by achieving the goal of "Obtain Food."

Figure 3.6.2 is an example of a more complex goal-directed behavior; the CPO has transitioned from a state of "Need Hover Tank" to a state of "Have Hover Tank" by accomplishing the goal of "Build Hover Tank," which required the achieving of multiple sub-goals.

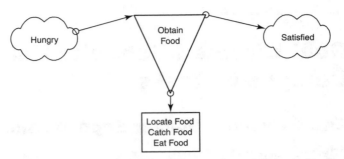

FIGURE 3.6.1   *An expression of a simple goal (Obtain Food).*

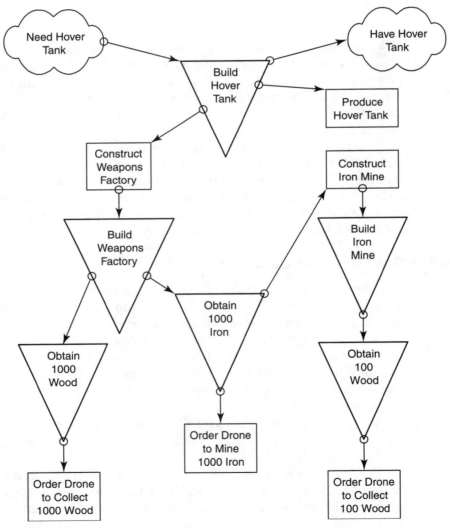

FIGURE 3.6.2   *An expression of a complex goal.*

As the complexity of a goal increases, so typically do the number of the sub-goals of the goal. Therefore, the challenge to the computer game AI developer is to implement a system that will manage goals in a flexible and efficient manner.

To this end, a number of successful implementations of goal-directed behavior have been developed and deployed for use in computer games. In his work with *Quake I* and *Quake II* bots, John Laird's team designed and implemented a complex goal-directed system using Soar technology [Laird00a], whereby goals were expressed in terms of conditions that in turn helped to select *operators* that were proposed and then executed. The Soar operators could be primitive actions (e.g., *Catch Food*) or internal actions or more abstract goals [Laird00b]. In essence, the conditions describe the state of the world and the states of the entities operating within the world, which for all intents and purposes, are what goals really are.

Working with *Quake III*, van Wavern categorized short-term goals as those goals achieved while attempting to accomplish long-term goals. In any *Quake* game, the primary long-term goal of the bots is to win the game. Van Wavern notes that the bots are given a variety of intermediate-term goals to accomplish for that purpose. Shorter-term goals, such as *coming up for air*, while swimming toward a longer-term goal location, is another example of how he used goal-directed behavior [van Wavern01]. The shorter-term goal *coming up for air*, was introduced to the bots as it entered the state of *need air*.

In *Age of Empires II*, the *Strategic Numbers* and *Rules* in the AI Script personality files used by the CPO of that game, formed conditional states that could be considered goals. For example, a *Strategic Number* such as *sn-wood-gather-percentage* could express the percentage of the villagers to be assigned to wood-gathering actions, and used in a rule in which it was part of the condition or part of the result of the state of the condition [Ratchev99]. Here is an example of such a conditional goal:

```
(defrule
(goal resource-needed WOOD)
(current-age == dark-age)
(civilian-population >= 10)
(not (strategic-number sn-wood-gatherer-percentage == 40) )
=>
(set-strategic-number sn-wood-gatherer-percentage 40)
(set-strategic-number sn-food-gatherer-percentage 60) )
```

A goal of *needing wood* is defined by the previous rule. This goal has conditions attached to it declaring the *age* (historical time period) it is to be applied within, the *count of population* to consider, and the *count of current population that are already gathering wood*. The goal expressed by the previous rule is achieved by setting the level of population to be used for gathering wood and gathering food.

Composite Tasks 101

In 1995, during the development of the CPO for *Enemy Nations*, a real-time strategy game, a *Goal/Task System* was designed and implemented to provide goal-directed behavior for hundreds of agents in real-time. A Goal in *Enemy Nations* declared a State and a Condition that could be evaluated for completion. Multiple Goals could be combined as Sub-Goals of a Goal, to describe the accomplishments needed to complete that Goal. Goals could be accomplished by completing Tasks that were associated to the Goals. Tasks were completed by the agents carrying out Actions that were associated with specific types of Tasks.

During the research in 2001, for the design of the CPO for the *CSXII Tactical Combat Simulator* for the U.S. Army Infantry Company Commander School [CSXII01], it became apparent that there was a need for an extremely flexible goal-directed system. This system was needed to manage the hundreds of agents that were performing the roles of soldiers, civilians, and enemy troops during the simulation. As a result of this need, the Composite Task concept evolved from the Goal/Task System of *Enemy Nations*.

The Composite Task concept is intended to provide more flexible goal-directed behavior control and management for hundreds of agents in a real-time environment because of its simplicity of design, data-driven content, and generalized evaluation processes.

To understand how Composite Tasks help to manage and control the goal directed behavior of agents, we begin with some definitions:

- A Composite Task is a task that is accomplished by completing other Composite Tasks and/or Component Tasks (referred to as a simple Task).
- A simple Task is completed by executing a series of Actions
- An Action is behavior performed by an agent.

As these definitions suggest, the foundation of this concept begins with a Task that is eventually accomplished by the behavior of agents carrying out Actions. Actions are behaviors such as gather, move, pick up, shoot, turn, jump, build, produce, fly, and so on. Actions are typically very game specific, and will be further defined and exemplified later in this section.

A sequence or selection of Actions can be packaged to accomplish a specific Task. This means that the associated Actions are components of that Task. And thus, an agent can determine how to complete a particular Task, by analyzing and executing the component Actions of a given Task. An example of a Task could be the simple *Obtain Food* task described at the beginning of the article. In the next section, Tasks will be declared as C++ objects, and it will become obvious that any number of Actions can be components of a Task, thus making it possible to declare fairly complex Tasks.

However, the really complex Tasks are best described by Composite Tasks, as a collection of other Composite Tasks and/or just simple Tasks.

A Composite Task can be treated as a component of another Composite Task, creating a hierarchy of complex tasks. Likewise, other simpler Tasks can be associated with a Composite Task, and they too are referred to as components of the Composite Task.

This might seem a bit confusing, so to go over this again: all tasks are made up of components (*Note: for this meaning, "components" is always lower cased*). Component Tasks (referred to as simple Tasks) are made up of components that are Actions. Composite Tasks are made up of components that can be either other Composite Tasks or simple Tasks.

A design such as this creates enormous flexibility in associating behaviors with accomplishments, and low-level goals with other intermediate or top-level goals.

Implementing Composite Tasks

Now let's look a little closer at how Composite Tasks can be implemented.

We begin with defining what an Action object is. As described previously, an Action represents a low-level behavior, performed by an agent, to accomplish some task. To do so, the Action object has to indicate what that behavior will be. In our C++ tAction class declaration that follows, the m_iCommand member of the class indicates this behavior. The behavior can be altered by one or more parameters applied to the interpretation of the m_iCommand. These parameters are located in the m_vParameters vector member. Finally, the tAction object can be uniquely identified with the m_iID member.

```
// the low-level behavior object
//
class tAction {
    int    m_iID;           // unique ID of the object
    int    m_iCommand;      // token identifier of behavior
    vector<int> m_vParameters;    // behavior parameters
};
```

A process (later called an *Action Handler*) within the game will need to interpret the value of the tAction::m_iCommand in order to execute the behavior required for this particular Action. During the execution, the contents of the tAction::m_vParameters vector could be used to alter a particular occurrence of that behavior.

An example of this usage would be for the low-level behavior of gathering wood, which could be specified by the tAction::m_iCommand containing the value interpreted as "gather." The tAction::m_iID would contain a value used to identify this Action as a "gather wood" action, and that m_iID value would be found in the parameters of a Component Task (see later in this section). That m_iID value would be used to locate this specific tAction object, which might be stored in a container (an STL map container—see [Boer00] for details on using STL in computer games). The tAction::m_vParameters vector might contain a token that indicates that "wood" is to be the target of the "gather" action. The tAction::m_vParameters vector parameters could be updated by the interpretation process before the Action was executed, with an additional parameter token of "quantity" and parameter value of "1000," which would mean for the agent executing this Action to perform the specific Action of "gathering 1000 wood." Not all of the parameter tokens need to be pairs either.

Some parameter tokens could be singletons that act as switches and flags during the execution of the task.

Next, we go up a level in the concept, and declare the Task object.

```
// the general task object
//
class tTask {
    enum {
            // types of tasks
            kComposite,
            kComponent,
            // task status flags
            kCompleted,
            kIncomplete,
            kInactive
    }

    // unique id of this instance of a task type
    int m_iID;
    // an identifier for a specific task type
    int m_iTaskType;
    // indicates this is a composite or component task
    int  m_iType;
    // current status of the task
    int  m_iStatus;
    // m_iID of parent task of this task
    int  m_iParent;
    // indicate how important this task is to complete
    int  m_iSuccess;
    // values to use to alter the completion of the task
    vector<int> m_vParams;
    // IDs of tasks or actions that complete this task
    vector<int> m_vComponents;
    // tokens that indicate task will terminate
    vector<int> m_vTerminate;
    // tokens that indicate task has completed
    vector<int> m_vCompletion;
};
```

The tTask objects would also be stored in some container, accessible by the use of the tTask::m_iID. We rely on a separate unique identifier ID (tTask::m_iID) and a separate task type identifier ID (tTask::m_iTaskType) so that it is possible to declare multiple instances of the same type of task, each capable of completing similar, but different, goals. Therefore, the m_iTaskType identifies the type of task (such an approach allows declaring a "build factory" and a "build bridge" task separately, each with similar processes but with entirely different sub-goals). The m_iType is an indicator that the tTask is a Composite Task or a Component Task (referred to as a simple Task). As a Composite Task, the contents of the m_vComponents vector will be interpreted as tTask::m_iIDs, while as a simple Task, those contents will be interpreted as tAction::m_iIDs. Another indicator member is the m_iStatus value that reflects that this instance of a Task is *completed, incomplete,* or *inactive.* The m_iParent member contains the tTask::m_iID of the task for which this instance of a Task is a Component Task. Thus, the highest level Composite Task has a zero value for m_iParent, because it has no parent tasks. The m_iSuccess member is useful for indicating how important a Task is to the completion of its parent Composite Task. Any meaningful value can be used to represent that the Task absolutely must be completed in order to complete the parent Composite Task, and then scale the value downward from there to represent lesser levels of importance.

Finally, we get to the vectors. The m_vParams contains tokens interpreted to determine how to complete the task. The m_vComponents was mentioned previously and its contents are interpreted based on the value of the m_iType of the tTask object. In addition, the order of items in the vector indicates the priority of completion for the Tasks or Actions identified by this Task's components. The m_vTerminate contains tokens that are interpreted for the termination conditions for a Task, when it is not possible to be completed. And lastly, the m_vCompletion contains tokens that are interpreted for the completion conditions of the Task. These last two vectors allow for a Task to be terminated because it is no longer possible to complete the Task and to specify to the executing process when the Task is considered complete.

The *tokens* referred to previously can be as simple as enum values or as complex as unique IDs to a tParameter object that contains additional data and information. The reader can select the approach most applicable to the reader's game needs, and only need to be concerned with ensuring that the executing process is developed in a way that it is able to execute the behavior or evaluation in a manner consistent with the desired behavior. Since this a very common practice in computer game development, no more time will be spent on discussing tokens.

To summarize, the tAction and tTask objects provide for the organization of data that describe the completion of complex goals. The members of the tAction objects are processed by an *Action Handler*, which interprets the values of the object and executes specific behavior appropriately. The data provided by the tTask objects are processed by a *Task Handler* routine (unique by tTask::m_iType). This data describes how a task is broken down into sub-goals and actions, and offers runtime parameters that affect its execution, as well as data that defines when the task can be terminated without completion, or when the task is actually considered completed. Additional details describing the *Action Handler* and *Task Handler* are beyond the scope of this article.

A Composite Task Implementation

Full Spectrum Command

As noted earlier, the Composite Task concept was designed for the purpose of managing complex goal directed behavior for a tactical combat simulator developed for the U.S. Army. The simulator is publicly referred to as *Full Spectrum Command* (*FSC*).

FSC [CSXII02] is designed to be a training tool used by the Infantry Company Commander School, to exercise the student's (U.S. Army Captains preparing to take command of light infantry companies) planning and tactical decision-making skills in a Military Operations in Urban Terrain (MOUT) environment. The student is placed in command of (up to) a company-sized detachment of modern soldiers, and is presented with a variety of MOUT tactical combat situations, created by instructors. The student generates a plan, based on U.S. Army doctrine and the Operations Order (OPORD) that defines the student's mission, and task organizes the elements of the student's forces, and assigns orders (tasks) to complete the mission. Then, *FSC* processes the student's plan in real-time with a first-person perspective, executes the simulation, allows the student limited input and modification of the plan (no Rambo-like participation typically found in first-person shooter type games), and when the mission is terminated or completed, *FSC* provides the student and instructor with After Action Review reporting and analysis.

The Composite Task concept was developed to manage the agents representing the various maneuver elements and soldiers that are under the command of the student. The U.S. Army relies on extremely deterministic Courses of Action (COA) and Battle Drills for performing specific combat-related tasks in a consistent manner. The COA are essentially very complex goals that must be completed. The COA are also made up of a number of other COA and Battle Drills, which must be completed (usually in a prescribed sequence) in order to achieve the completion of the highest level COA. The Battle Drills consisted of prescribed sequences of actions and tasks that were to be completed, in order to appropriately execute the drill.

Thus, the Composite Task provided a means to represent the COA and Battle Drills as data that could be interpreted by *Task* and *Action Handler* processes inside the AI Engine and therefore allow the agents to be managed appropriately while achieving goals.

Conclusion

The obvious advantages to such a data-driven approach to goal-directed behavior, as using Composite Tasks for Goal Directed Behavior, are:

- The ability to expand the encoding of complex tasking.
- The ability to incorporate flexible task completion and termination considerations.
- The ability to vary the execution of task accomplishment at runtime.

Most important, goal direction provides the illusion of a sense of purpose for the behavior of agents and CPOs. By suggesting to the player observing their actions, that these artificial entities have a purposeful intent to their behaviors, an increase in the agent's believability occurs.

References

[Boer00] Boer, James, "Using the STL in Game Programming," *Game Programming Gems*, Charles River Media, 2000.

[CSXII02] *CSXII Tactical Combat Simulator* (also called *Full Spectrum Command*) Developed by Quicksilver Software, Inc. in association with Legless Productions, Inc. for the Institute of Creative Technology, UCLA, for the Infantry Company Captains Training Course, Fort Benning, U.S. Army, under the auspices of STRICOM and the Future Combat Systems program, 2002.

[Laird00a] Laird, John, "The Soar Tutorial, Part V," *The Soar Quakebot*, available online at *ftp.eecs.umich.edu/~soar/tutorial.html*, 2000.

[Laird00b] Laird, John, "It Knows What You're Going to Do: Adding Anticipation to a Quakebot," *AAAI 2000 Spring Symposium on Artificial Intelligence and Interactive Entertainment, Technical Report SS-00-02*, AAAI Press, 2000, pp. 41–50.

[Ratchev99] Ratchev, Stoyan, "Computer Player Strategy Builder Guide," *AI Expert Documentation—Age of Empires II: The Age of Kings*, Ensembles Studios, 1999.

[van Wavern01] van Wavern, J.M.P., *The Quake III Arena Bot*, Delft University of Technology Masters Thesis, June 2001, available online at *www.kbs.twi.tudelft.nl/Publications/MSc/2001-VanWaveren-MSc.html*

[Woodcock01] Woodcock, Steven, "Flocking with Teeth: Predators and Prey," *Game Programming Gems 2*, Charles River Media, 2001.

AI ANIMATION CONTROL

4.1

Simplified Animation Selection

Chris Hargrove—Gas Powered Games

chargrove@gaspowered.com

This article describes an animation selection mechanism for determining the active animations of characters. The animation selection is based on a narrow set of discrete inputs and events, in a manner that's easy to manipulate for both artists and AI programmers. The system allows for just a few simple inputs (such as a character's cardinal movement direction, posture, and weapon type) and isolated triggered events (such as waves or taunts) to determine the entire animation state of a character at a given time, even in the presence of hundreds of animations from which to choose. Unlike many other systems, the approach described in this article directly supports characters that can run multiple interdependent animations simultaneously, via the use of more than one animation channel.

The animation channels, input names and values, and control-flow "actions" are all configurable via a simple artist-friendly scripting language, allowing the artist to take nearly full control over the animation selection pipeline. The AI programmer's job is made easier due to the simplified conduit between a character's abstract behavior and its animation inputs. The result is an animation selection scheme that gives the artist a level of control usually only available to programmers, without losing the simplicity and flexibility of other data-driven approaches. This system was used in the animation architecture for *Unreal II: The Awakening*, successfully exposing an enormous amount of animation content in a form that the programmers could manage.

The Problem

On many projects, AI animation selection code is frequently taking more time and effort to develop than the rest of the actual AI work.

For the development of 3D games, traditionally artists such as modelers and animators have created mesh assets with animations, and the job of using these animations on a given character has rested (to a large degree) on a programmer. Frequently, this is the same programmer responsible for the underlying AI for the given character, due to the often close relationship between a character's actions and its visual representation.

Only a few short years ago, the programming burden of hooking up animations in this way was not considered that big of a deal. The number of animations to contend with was relatively small, usually with only one animation channel, and very simple conditions under which each animation was used. Eventually, for many developers, the number of animations and conditions increased to the point that a more general solution to the problem was necessary. Fortunately, the fact that only one animation channel was involved made it relatively painless to move the selection process over to highly effective table-based data-driven approaches [Orkin02].

Times are changing quickly, though. As requirements continue to rise, more and more game animation systems are allowing characters to run multiple animations at the same time (such as walking with the lower body while shooting with the upper body), setting many animation selection solutions right back to square one. The table-driven approaches might work initially (just have one table per channel and treat them independently), but this often turns out to be less than ideal when trying to contend with necessary interdependencies between channels. Even if the dependency issue is ignored, the frequent addition of more animations and animation channels can cause even a well-designed table approach to collapse, leaving the AI programmer to pick up the pieces.

This is a big problem, as many developers (both programmers and artists) have noticed. So, how do we alleviate this problem without crippling our animation capabilities in the process? How do we allow the AI programmer to work with a complex animation set easily (even across multiple channels), without a lot of time-consuming labor necessary to make characters look the way the animator intended? How do we give animators the kind of selection control they want, instead of forcing this control onto programmers who, by and large, don't even want it in the first place?

When it comes down to it, there's one question we need to answer: Is it possible to let the animators themselves handle the bulk of the selection process, to where the AI programmer can spend as little time as possible dealing with this issue and can focus almost entirely on the AI itself?

Inputs and Outputs

In order to determine a general-purpose effective approach to the animation selection problem, let's look at the animation selector as an algorithm we need to fill, based on a given set of inputs and outputs.

The phrase "animation selection" already gives us our basic output: the animation(s) that should be playing on our character, with one animation per animation channel. A character that plays only one animation at a time has only a single channel and hence only a single animation returned by the selector, while a character with upper and lower body channels will have two animations returned, and so on.

So, there's our output. Now what about the inputs? In many animation selection schemes, the inputs are things like animation channel "slot names." These slots represent abstract animation categories (like "walk" or "idle") that a number of actual concrete animations can fill, or other simple markers/conditions used to identify the desired animation for the channel in broad terms. In this type of system, an animation table can be made that maps the available concrete animations (rows) to their abstract slots and other selection criteria for their use (columns). The selector then picks an animation for each channel from the list of matching candidate rows within the animation table, and you're done. There are many ways to structure an animation table, but the goal in most cases is the same: a reduction of the number of animation names that the AI code has to deal with.

Approaches like this (which we'll just call *slot systems*) are often quite effective for single-channel animation systems, as there is only one channel to worry about, and the slots and conditions tend to be relatively simple to define.

Unfortunately, things become considerably more complicated when working with multiple channels. Since slot names are what's used by the backing code (usually tied directly into the AI code), the addition of a new slot name or a new animation channel can have dramatic repercussions in terms of programming. Multiple channel systems also tend to have quite a large number of special case situations, such as disabling one channel when a specific animation is playing on another channel, or using a different slot in a given channel to avoid conflicts with another. These types of special case dependencies between different channels end up resulting in highly fragile code, which is very difficult to maintain, let alone extend.

The conclusion then is that slot-based selection systems don't scale very well as the number of channels and slots increases. So, let's step back a bit. To get away from this whole "slot" idea and look at the input issue from a fresh perspective, we're going to introduce a constraint:

The AI code should not know or care how many animation channels a character uses.

In other words, to make sure this whole "channel slot" idea is essentially killed off on the programming side, we're going to try to minimize the direct use of channels altogether. By not assuming what channels there are or how many we need to deal with, we eliminate slots entirely and force the inputs to the animation selector to be more general.

So, what kind of "general" inputs are we talking about? Well, how about the same types of variables that a slot-based animation selector would need to know about in order to pick slots in the first place? After all, if the AI is going to choose the slots for the various animation channels of a character, it obviously has to know about factors that affect those slot choices. These inputs are based on character state, and might include things such as movement direction, current stance or posture, and alertness level.

If we look at the inputs required to determine what should be playing on all the given channels, in general we'll find that the number of inputs is far, far less than the number of slots they in turn choose from (which, in turn, is far less than the number of total available animations). A set of just a few input variables can translate into tens or hundreds of slots, and hundreds or even thousands of animations.

Unfortunately, some types of animations aren't as easily selected from character inputs like those mentioned previously. This includes triggered one-shot "event" animations, such as the character waving, sneezing, dying, and so on. In terms of the complexity of the animation selection problem, these animations are certainly easier to select, since they correspond directly to matching in-game events. We need these types of animations integrated into the regular selection system, though (so that they can cooperate with the system's default behavior), while still keeping away from direct channel manipulation within the AI code if possible. This cooperation (like allowing event animations to override default animations) requires that the character maintain a small amount of animation selection state information, such as how much time remains on a given override (in order to determine when the event animation is done).

In summary, we want an animation selector that can determine the animations that should be playing on all of a character's channels, based on a small set of input variables, an occasional one-shot event, and a bit of current animation selection state information. The translation of this information into individual animations playing back on individual channels is done behind the scenes, away from the AI code. Ideally, if the rules of the selector could be controlled by the artist(s) responsible for the character's animations in the first place, it would provide a clean separation of concerns between the artists who create the character's body, and the programmers who create the character's mind.

Bring in the Agent

The remainder of this article describes one possible implementation of such a selection mechanism, based on the use of a small artist-friendly scripting language. While the language is not necessarily trivial to implement (depending on your familiarity with writing scripting language compilers), the result can still pay for itself almost immediately, due to the incredible reduction in complexity of the animation system interaction within the AI code.

Animation selectors in this example are referred to as *animation agents*, based on the dictionary definition of an agent as "one who is authorized to act for or in place of another, as a representative, emissary, or official." Our animation agents act as emissaries, selecting animations on behalf of the character.

The agents are defined by text written in an *agent language*. The agent language resembles general-purpose programming languages in some respects, but it is kept simple in order to improve ease of use by artists and other nonprogrammers [Poiker02]. The actual grammar of an agent language is merely an implementation detail, so we'll focus on the general structure of such a language rather than going into parser land (plenty of resources are available on the topic of writing parsers, such as [Aho86]).

An agent language file is composed of several blocks of various different types, with each block somewhat resembling a function from a traditional programming language. There are four different types of blocks: Channels, Inputs, Transition, and Action. The typical layout of an agent language file is shown in Figure 4.1.1.

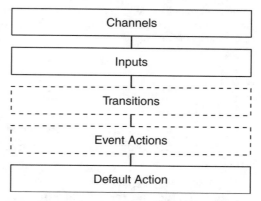

FIGURE 4.1.1 *Agent language file layout.*
Dashed lines indicate optional blocks.

Channels Block

The file starts out with one Channels block, listing the artist-determined names of all the animation channels used by the character, in channel index order (where the first name becomes the first animation channel, the second name is the second channel, and so on). In many multiple-channel animation systems, later channels stack on top of earlier ones as subsets, so an example three-channel configuration might look like this:

```
channels
{
    AnimAllBody;
    AnimUpperBody;
    AnimHead;
    // ...and so on
}
```

Inputs Block

The Inputs block contains definitions for the variable inputs available to the agent. In theory, these could be generic variables such as integers, floats, strings, and so on. Unfortunately, the added complexity of having arbitrary input data types tends to cause more problems than benefits (for programmers as well as artists). Instead, we restrict the inputs to being simple enumerations of a name with a few allowed values. This retains the vast majority of the input flexibility needed from the selection system, while dramatically simplifying both the creation and usage of the agent language. An example input configuration for a soldier might look like this:

```
inputs
{
    Direction = None, Forward, Backward, Left, Right;
    Posture = Stand, Crouch, Prone;
    Speed = Walk, Run;
    WeaponType = None, OneHand, TwoHand, Shoulder;
    // ...add more inputs as necessary
}
```

The reason these are called "inputs" rather than "variables" is because they're only variables to the outside, not to the agent. Input values are *read-only* within the agent, so the AI does not have to worry about whether the agent will change any of the values it assigns. The AI programmer (or an associated content developer) has control over the assignment of these input values, while the agent author has control over how the values are used.

The actual names and values of inputs must be agreed upon by both the creator of the agent language file and the AI programmer. The usage of unexpected input data on either side should be treated in the same manner as other content deviations (in other words, whether you choose to silently fail in this situation or complain loudly is up to you).

Action Blocks

Action blocks make up the vast majority of an agent language file, as they comprise the bulk of what defines an agent. Action blocks are analogous to functions in a programming language, with a few restrictions. They have no parameters, and no return value. Their entire purpose is to alter the state of the various animation channels, based on the current state of various inputs.

There is always at least one action in the agent language file, named "Default." Agent actions can always be called directly from the outside, in response to triggered events like those mentioned previously (waving, taunting, and so forth). The Default action is a bit different, however, as it is automatically called on the character once per frame. This default processing action provides the state of the animation channels based on the given inputs, assuming that the relevant animation channels are not still bound to other animations due to some type of event.

The next section is dedicated entirely to the contents of actions, but just to set the stage, the following is a fragment of an example Default action using some of the soldier inputs listed previously. The double-slash comments provide an overview of what's happening, and the next section will dive into more of the details.

```
action Default
{
    // Describe default behavior of all-body channel
    set(1) AnimAllBody
    {
        if (Direction = None)
        {
```

```
            // If the Direction input is currently
            // set to None, randomly choose between
            // two different animations, with one
            // being nine times more likely to occur
            // than the other
            random
            {
                chance 9 anim "IdleCommon";
                chance 1
                {
                    anim "IdleRare";

                    // If the rare idle is chosen,
                    // Use double-brace empty block
                    // syntax to prevent upper body
                    // from doing its default behavior
                    set(1) AnimUpperBody {}
                }

                // Keep the random value chosen for
                // this "random" block for the length
                // of the selected idle animation
                keepchance 1.0;
            }

            blend 0.5;
        }
        else
        {
            // If the Direction is not None, go ahead
            // and run or walk depending on the Speed
            // input.  The "str" syntax provides a
            // string argument as a concatenation of
            // constant strings and current input
            // values.
            if (Speed = Run)
            {
                anim str("Running", Direction);
                blend 0.1;
            }
            else
            {
                anim str("Walking", Direction);
                blend 0.2;
            }
        }
    }
    // Describe default behavior of upper-body channel
    set(1) AnimUpperBody
    {
        if ((WeaponType = None) or (Speed = Walk))
            anim "ArmsDown";
        else if (WeaponType = Shoulder)
            anim "ArmsHigh";
        else
```

```
                anim "ArmsNormal";

            blend 0.25;
        }
    }
```

Transition Blocks

Transition blocks are optional blocks associated with inputs, which contain agent language actions that should be called automatically in response to input changes. When used, the switch of an input from one value to another by the AI code results in an automatic one-shot "event" action call, used to play in between transition animations when available. A transition block is named after the input it monitors, and is filled with statements using the keywords "from" and "to," resulting in the given actions being called whenever the appropriate change is detected.

```
transition Posture
{
    from Stand to Prone = ProneDrop;
    from Prone to Stand = ProneRise;
    // ...more transitions here
}
```

Actions

Most of what makes up an agent comes from the action blocks in an agent language file. Programmers will recognize the basic structure of an action due to its similarities with functions. Unlike general-purpose functions, though, actions have a very specific intent: the modification of animation channel state.

We've defined our animation selection output as the set of animations (one per channel) that should be playing at the given point in time. Actually *playing* those animations is the responsibility of another component of the animation system, however. For this reason, our agents only need to worry about what they think should be playing on the given animation channels, not necessarily what actually *is* playing. Even though you'd want to make sure the two stay synchronized, there's still a definite benefit to this approach, since the agent only needs to keep track of its internal animation channel state to do its job.

Once per frame, the animation system can look at the channel data for the agent, and if the animation currently playing on a given channel is different from the one that the agent says should be playing, it starts playing the new animation. When a new animation is started, the system can take advantage of various other pieces of per-channel information stored with the agent, perhaps including blending factors, playback rate multipliers, flags indicating whether the played animation should loop, and so forth.

The purpose of actions is to modify this "desired" animation channel state, using several different types of language statements.

Control Flow Statements

There are only a few statements for branching control flow supported in the agent language. The most important ones are the "if-else" selection statements, which use simple expressions just like in a programming language, with a few modifications to promote nonprogrammer accessibility (e.g., the use of = instead of ==, and the words "and" and "or" instead of && and ||). Since our language also only supports simple enumerated inputs, we also only need the equality and inequality operators; there's no need for other less-than/greater-than relational operators. The left side of a given equality/inequality comparison is an input name, and the right side is one of the input's possible values.

The next control flow construct is the "random-chance" block, similar in syntax to "switch-case" blocks in C. The "random" keyword is analogous to "switch," and identifies the overall block where random selection can occur. Within this block, each "chance" is like a "case," and is followed by an "odds" number and the given statement to potentially execute. The odds of all the chances are added up to reflect the probability of any given chance being selected. See the Default action example from the previous section for an example use of this construct.

Finally, the action language should also support the "return" and "call" statements. The return should act just like a void-function return in C (return from the action immediately), and "call *someActionName*" should be used to call into other actions as subroutines (keeping in mind that actions have no parameters, so a more sophisticated function calling syntax is not required). Agents often have a nontrivial amount of shared logic used in different branches of execution, so the use of common subroutine actions and call statements can be just as beneficial in the agent language as it is in conventional programming languages.

Channel Block Statements

Another category of statements is the two "channel block" statement constructs, which we call "set" and "force."

The purpose of actions is to modify animation channel state, and the "set" and "force" statements are a big part of that, as they serve two purposes. First, they identify the channel that should be manipulated by the statement that follows (often a compound statement delimited by braces), and second, they check whether the given statement should be executed in the first place.

As part of an agent's animation channel state, the agent keeps track of two pieces of "binding" information: the "binding time" (a floating-point time value), and a "binding level" (a non-negative integer). The basic idea is this: when a channel gets its state assigned, it is "bound" for a given amount of time, and at a given level of priority (the binding level). The binding time is a timer that counts down, and as long as the channel has binding time remaining on it, its state cannot be changed again unless it is overridden. Whether such an override can occur depends on the current binding level, the new desired binding level, and which of the two channel block statements ("set" or "force") was used. The "set" command will only successfully override if the new binding level is greater than the current one, while the "force" command will override if the new level is greater *or equal* to the current one.

By default, every channel is "unbound" at binding level 0. What this means is that any "set" or "force" statement that comes in will succeed. If it succeeds, the given channel scope is entered, the channel is restored to its default state, and the commands inside (the "channel commands" discussed next) are used to change the state from these defaults. Once the channel scope exits, the block becomes "bound" at a binding level greater than zero, indicated by the "set" or "force" command (the Default action example uses "set(1)" to indicate that the channel should be bound at level 1). This binding level acts like a lock, and until the lock is released, no other channel blocks will be able to change the channel's state.

The lock becomes released when either the binding time runs out on its own, or the channel's binding is overridden. In the first situation, the binding time ticks down every frame and when it hits zero, the binding level is reduced to zero. The binding time can be assigned within the channel block via the "keep" command listed in Table 4.1.1, but it defaults to zero. What's interesting, though, is the fact that since the binding time is only updated once per frame, even a binding time of zero is *still* a valid binding, until the next frame when the timer is checked again (which, being zero, causes the binding level to be reset). This means that "set" and "force" commands without a binding time provided will still have a binding time of one frame, no matter what. This is a good thing, as we'll see shortly.

Both the "set" and "force" constructs can override an existing binding depending on the current binding level and the one provided with the command. The "set" command will only succeed if the new level provided is greater than the current binding. This means that if, inside a given action, two "set" blocks exist back to back at the same binding level, then the second one is guaranteed to fail (the block will not be entered) because it is not capable of overriding the binding established by the first block. On the other hand, "force" blocks will override even if the binding level is the same, so if two "force" blocks were back to back at the same binding level, and the first one succeeded, then the second one would also succeed and cancel out everything the first one did.

This whole set/force thing might seem like an odd system at first, but it allows for an enormous amount of control. Default animation behavior can be specified in the Default action using "set(1)" blocks with no binding time, so that all the bindings will last only one frame and will only occur if no other (more pressing) animations want to be played (since set(1) is as low a binding priority as you can ask for). Dependencies between channels can be expressed by sprinkling appropriate set/force blocks inside other such blocks. For example, the Default action example has a line:

```
set(1) AnimUpperBody {}
```

within one of the branches in the AnimAllBody block. The double-brace empty statement effectively clears out the channel to its defaults, effectively setting it to "no animation." Since this set block happens *before* the regular AnimUpperBody default behavior section, it prevents the regular processing from occurring. In effect, it's saying "if I need to play the IdleRare animation on the all-body channel, then I want to prevent any animation from playing on the upper-body channel." This kind of dependency control allows for all types of otherwise painful special case scenarios to be expressed easily as a standard feature of the selection language.

In addition to the Default behavior, binding times allow event animations (like waving) to be expressed simply as "force" blocks using the "keep" command. The command "keep" takes a time value that acts as a multiplier of the time the channel's animation takes, so "keep 1.0" means "keep this channel bound for exactly the length of the animation I just provided." For example, a waving action might look something like this:

```
action WaveOnce
{
    force(1) AnimUpperBody
    {
        anim "Wave";
        blend 0.2;
        looping 0;
        keep 1.0;
    }
}
```

The AI code could then safely call the "WaveOnce" action any time it liked, and since a binding time was provided, the binding with the "Wave" animation would remain effective over the next several frames (for as long as the animation lasted), and the agent's desired animation for the AnimUpperBody channel would be reflected accordingly. What's nice is that the WaveOnce action could specify bindings on multiple channels, possibly using random selection with random-chance blocks, and the AI code doesn't have to care. All it needs to know are the action names associated with the handful of specific events it cares about (ones that cannot be handled in default behavior), and the agent will take care of the rest.

Channel Command Statements

The final set of statements needing mention are the channel commands themselves. These are the commands that, once a channel block is entered, allow the channel state to change from its default behavior. Some common commands are listed in Table 4.1.1, although others can easily be added depending on the features of your animation system (such as the ability to choose a starting animation frame, or commands to set other various channel flags that are available). Note that all of the commands listed are only applicable inside a set/force block, except for "keepchance," which is associated with random-chance blocks instead (but was listed in the table due to its similarity to "keep").

Table 4.1.1   List of Common Channel Commands Used in Actions

Command Parameters	Description
anim "*animname*"	Set current animation for channel. Defaults to none.
blend *blendTime*	Set the blending time in seconds for the channel, used when current animation for the channel is different from the previous animation and a switch is required. Defaults to zero (no blending).
rate *rateMultiplier*	Set the animation playback rate multiplier for the channel, used to play the animation at a rate different than originally specified. Defaults to 1.0 (no rate adjustment).
looping *loopFlagBoolean*	Set whether the channel is supposed to loop its associated animation. If not, the channel freezes the animation at the last frame once the frame is passed. Defaults to true (looping is enabled).
keep *time*	Sets the binding time for the channel to a given time, as a multiple of the channel's animation length (if present), or in seconds. Defaults to zero (no time; one frame only).
keepchance *time*	Used only in random blocks; keeps choosing the same chance item for the given amount of time, as a multiple of the channel's animation length (if present), or in seconds. To support this feature, the agent state must keep track of the current values of all random blocks present, and keepchance time remaining for each.

Debugging Agent Behavior

Since agent language text does have some "programming" aspects to it, it makes sense to wonder whether agents can feasibly be debugged, if unexpected animation behavior occurs. Fortunately, the answer is yes.

When a channel becomes bound (at a given binding level), it is easy to record the action the channel is in at the time of binding, and keep this information along with the binding time and level. Then, if debugging becomes necessary, a quick inspection of an agent's current input values, along with its channels and their bindings (time, level, and the action responsible for it), is almost always sufficient to identify problems quickly and easily. There's no need for any type of full-blown "agent debugger," since the agent is not capable of writing input values (only reading them), and aside from the inputs, the binding information is the only other data involved in determining the fate of the agent's various channels.

Theory and Practice

When considering various approaches to a development problem, it's important to distinguish between theoretical solutions, and proven ones. The animation selection system described in this article was used successfully on *Unreal II: The Awakening*, and proved itself very effective even in the context of extremely complex meshes with an enormous amount of animation data. Many of the humanoid meshes had more than 10 simultaneous animation channels and hundreds of animations from which to choose (some hand-animated, some procedurally generated at runtime).

Had the project stuck with a more conventional "slot" system, the AI code would have become overwhelmed by the weight of such a monstrous data set. With the agent system in place, however, the character animations could be controlled almost entirely with just a handful of inputs and less than 20 special event actions. The narrow interface between the agent and the AI code gave the artists the kind of animation selection influence they were looking for (via the agent language), and at the same time removed much of the animation concerns from the AI code, allowing the AI programmer to focus on other things.

Conclusion

As the detail and complexity of our game characters increases, animation systems must improve to take the resulting increase in animation data into account. Animation selection might have been practically an afterthought back when everyone was working with just a single animation channel and only a few animations, but modern content requirements make the problem much less trivial to solve. If left unchecked, the problem can spiral out of control, often leaving the AI programmer to deal with the aftermath.

This article discussed an animation selection mechanism that allows the AI programmer to remain focused on AI, and at the same time allows the artists responsible for animating a character to gain a greater amount of control over how those animations are used. The effort required to implement the system initially is a bit more than with other more conventional approaches, but the cost of this effort is more than made up for by the productivity and quality benefits gained from its use.

References

[Aho86] Aho, Alfred V., Sethi, Ravi, and Ullman, Jeffery D., *Compilers: Principles, Techniques, and Tools*, Addison-Wesley, 1986.

[Orkin02] Orkin, Jeff, "A Data-Driven Architecture for Animation Selection," *AI Game Programming Wisdom*, Charles River Media, 2002.

[Poiker02] Poiker, Falko, "Creating Scripting Languages for Nonprogrammers," *AI Game Programming Wisdom*, Charles River Media, 2002.

4.2

Pluggable Animations

Chris Hargrove—Gas Powered Games

chargrove@gaspowered.com

This article discusses an extensible plug-in based animation pipeline that combines the handling of precreated and dynamically generated (procedural) animation facilities into a single unified mechanism. This allows artists and AI programmers to take advantage of procedural animation effects in the same manner as regular animations, adding an additional level of flexibility and control when creating characters. The described pipeline has been successfully applied in practice, acting as the backbone of the animation architecture and tool set for *Unreal II: The Awakening*.

Animation sequences are created based on a set of "abilities" that activate and deactivate at different points in time within the animation's length. These abilities can perform any number of effects on the character, from a simple application of precreated animation frame data, to a complex on-the-fly inverse kinematics (IK) operation using external "satellite" points in space provided by an external source, to esoteric visual effects like bone attachment manipulation and vertex deformation. The abilities themselves are provided as plug-ins, and new abilities can be added during the development process (or in some cases even afterward, by mod authors) without changing the core of the animation pipeline. The process of creating these types of animations can be made friendly to artists without much effort, via a simple GUI dialog box based primarily around a single list view control.

Down with Programmer Art

It's been said many times that the key word in *artificial intelligence* is *artificial*. It's no surprise then that AI in games often focuses on improving the illusion of a game character's intelligence, rather than the actual intelligence itself. For many games, a large part of this illusion rests on outward appearances. After all, the way a character looks and acts can be just as important, if not more so, than the way the character thinks underneath.

As the detail level of our game characters has increased, so has their animation requirements. These days, to make our virtual beings appear convincing, precreated animation (either hand-animated or motion-captured) now must often be combined with dynamic procedural effects. Examples such as head/body aiming, lip-syncing, and physics-based "ragdoll" animation are becoming more and more commonplace in modern games.

Unfortunately, for many developers, these types of procedural animation requirements don't mix well with the traditional art pipeline and tool set. As a result, these procedural animations tend to be implemented and tweaked entirely by programmers (via callbacks or other circumventing measures) rather than artists, with the expected less-than-ideal outcome.

In today's competitive game industry, "programmer art" is generally something to be avoided, and that goes just as much for animation as it does for any other type of art content. To allow artists to have control over procedural animations as well as precreated ones, the animation systems and tool sets for our games need to be structured accordingly.

Pluggable Sequences

To combine precreated and procedural animation into a unified system, there needs to be some type of concept of an animation sequence that supports them both. While one's first thought might be to implement some type of animation sequence base class, inherited by both types of animations, in reality this creates a "one or the other" scenario that only partially solves the problem. Ideally, we'd like to have our animation sequences be capable of supporting both precreated *and* procedural animations together at the same time (to handle effects which require both), or combinations of multiple procedural effects.

To accomplish this, we take our theoretical base class and move it into its own construct, which we'll call an "ability," acting as an element of animation functionality. The sequences themselves then become nothing but compositions of abilities, which are evaluated in series each frame to perform the sequence's behavior for the frame.

In operating system terms, we can think of a running sequence as a "process" of some kind, composed of one or more "threads" of execution. While real operating systems handle thread execution order in a variety of ways, for our purposes these "threads" have fixed indices and operate in order of their index. Thread 0 goes before Thread 1 goes before Thread 2, and so forth. A sequence can have any number of threads.

Each of these "threads" in the sequence can have one "ability" running on it at one time. The thread acts like a socket, which abilities can plug themselves in and out of over the course of the sequence. A thread could have the same ability for the entire sequence, or it could decide to switch to another ability part of the way through, or it decide to stop being useful entirely by using the "none" ability (which, as one would guess, does nothing).

Abilities are implemented as concrete subclasses of an abstract ability base class. The abilities have parameters, associated as meta-data with the ability class. This parameter meta-data (including things like parameter names, data types, and descriptions) is used to expose the parameters to the sequence editing tools used by the artists.

Each ability only has three operations: Init, Evaluate, and Exit. An instance of an ability is created at the moment it is needed by a thread, and it is destroyed as soon as the thread switches to another ability or the sequence ends. The Init method is called on the ability when it is created, and Exit is called before it is destroyed (optionally these can be implemented as a constructor and destructor pair if desired). The Evaluate method is called every frame in which the ability object is active, in order for it to perform its part of the animation sequence.

Example Abilities

One important ability (arguably the very first one that should be implemented) is the "Apply Precreated Animation" ability, which refers to a given set of precreated animation data from an artist, and applies it to the mesh running the sequence. This allows a normal "classic" animation to be represented as a sequence with only one thread, using only the Apply Precreated Animation ability for the entire duration of the sequence.

Other procedural abilities can be made, performing similar kinds of operations as the precreated animation ability, but at runtime. These include anything from simple "Bone Rotator" and "Bone Scaler" abilities, to complex "IK Reach" or "Look At" support, and so on (a good overview of IK techniques can be found in [Lander99]).

Some abilities might not do anything on their own, but merely act as modifiers for other abilities that occur on subsequent threads. One example is a "Bone Filter" ability that enables or disables bones for processing by later abilities. Bone Filter can be implemented in a variety of ways, although one simple implementation takes an array of strings as parameters, with each string containing a bone name and some modifier characters. The modifiers indicate whether the bone should be enabled or disabled, and whether the change should be applied to the bone's children as well.

Finally, a "Child Sequence" ability can be created to spawn a "child process" of another full-blown animation sequence within the thread. This ability invites the reuse of common thread behaviors, by isolating these behaviors into their own sequences specifically for use by this ability (e.g., a sequence with a Bone Filter for the upper body of a character could be used as a child in any upper body sequence). The Child Sequence ability permits infinite nesting of sequences within threads within sequences, allowing sequences to be composed to any level of complexity desired. An example of this type of recursive configuration is shown in Figure 4.2.1.

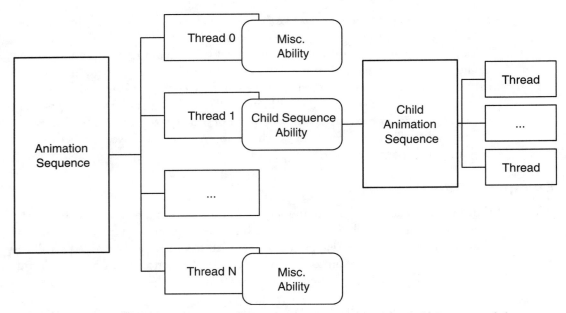

FIGURE 4.2.1 *Sequence/Thread hierarchy demonstrating recursion via Child Sequence ability.*

External Parameters

While many abilities are capable of acting on their own using the parameter information given to them, some might rely on data provided by outside sources. A "Look At" ability needs to know where to look, an "IK Reach" ability needs to know where to reach, and so on.

While this information can be provided in any number of ways (many of which are quite easy to implement), it's important to plan for this feature in one way or another, to avoid accidentally ruling out a very useful category of abilities. For the Look At and IK cases, one easy implementation is to have your character support a set of named "satellite" points in world space, which can be accessed by name on the fly. On the ability side, the name can be specified in some kind of "SatelliteName" string parameter. Then at game time, the AI code can specify the actual world location of these points via the same names (the artist and programmer must agree on the names to use). The ability can then transform the satellite points into mesh space and work with them accordingly.

Editing Tools

Due to the straightforward compositional nature of these sequences, creating a sequence editor is a relatively simple matter of creating a small dialog box with a list view control. Figure 4.2.2 is a screen shot of an example sequence editing box, similar in nature to the one used in *Unreal II: The Awakening's* external mesh editing tool. Changing activation frames, thread indices, abilities, and parameters is performed easily just by double-clicking the given fields in the list view, which in turn provides editing boxes, drop-down ability menus, and so on.

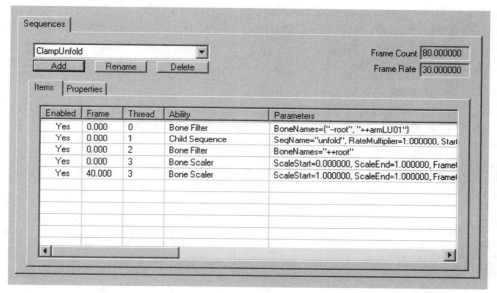

FIGURE 4.2.2 *Example dialog box for a sequence editor.*

In Figure 4.2.2, the "Bone Filter" and "Child Sequence" abilities are analogous to the abilities described previously with the same names, and "Bone Scaler" is an ability that scales one or more bones either instantly or over time. The resulting sequence uses the filters to execute a child "unfold" sequence on only one bone branch within the mesh (named "armLU01"). In addition, the sequence scales up the clamp at the end of this arm, going from scale 0 to 1 over the first 40 frames and then holding at 1 over the last 40 (both Bone Scaler abilities take the clamp bone name as a parameter, although this is offscreen in the figure).

Conclusion

This article discussed an animation pipeline based on sequences made from small pluggable animation abilities. By treating an animation as a composition of these abilities, both precreated and on-the-fly animation behaviors can be combined quickly and easily. The use of simple editing tools allows content developers full control over the parameters driving procedural animations, allowing access to these parameters to go beyond typical programmer-only restrictions. The result is a powerful and extensible animation framework for your artists, and in turn, more life for your characters.

References

[Lander99] Lander, Jeff, "*Real-time Inverse Kinematics* Handout," available online at *www.darwin3d.com/confpage.htm*, March 1999.

4.3

Intelligent Movement Animation for NPCs

Greg Alt—Surreal Software
Kristin King

galt@eskimo.com, kaking@eskimo.com

Most games have a system for moving non-player characters (NPCs) and an animation system that lets you play specified animations for characters. But how do you integrate steering behaviors while avoiding problems like "skating" (having your orcs look like they're ice skating because their feet aren't connecting with the ground) or "popping" (when the switch from one animation to another is jarring)? And how do you know which animation to play and how fast to play it?

This article describes an intelligent character animation system used in the PC and PS2 versions of *Fellowship of the Ring* as well as two upcoming games from Surreal Software. First, it briefly explains steering behaviors and animation systems. Next, it describes the middle layer between them, which includes a system for movement, a set of movement animation behaviors, and an animation controller. Finally, it gives some tips on "gotchas" that can come up during implementation of the middle layer along with some further enhancements that can be implemented.

Steering Behaviors

Steering behaviors [Reynolds99] are an important part of making NPC movement appear intelligent, smooth, and natural. A steering behavior is part of a hierarchical finite-state machine or other system of behaviors to control an NPC's actions. Once each frame, the steering behavior takes some information about the NPC's environment and provides a steering acceleration to influence the NPC's movement to pursue some simple goal, such as moving toward another character, steering around obstacles, or staying in formation.

However, in order to have seemingly intelligent movement, it is not enough to have steering behaviors controlling an NPC's movement. The NPC needs to have a goal (a reason for moving somewhere) and a way to get there. Therefore, a higher-level AI system needs to take an NPC's goals and use them to decide which steering behaviors to use and which locations the NPC will move toward or away from.

Steering behaviors, therefore, provide a powerful abstraction for game AI. High-level AI systems don't need to know about the low-level details of NPC movement and the NPC's environment—they can just specify the target location and which steering behaviors to use to get there; the steering behaviors take care of the rest. At the same time, the lower-level NPC movement system doesn't need to know any of the details of why and how the NPC wants to move. Instead, the system continuously gets an acceleration vector from the steering behaviors and moves accordingly. If there are multiple steering behaviors, the multiple acceleration vectors are combined to create a single acceleration vector for each update.

Another nice thing about steering behaviors is that you can combine simple steering behaviors to build a complex behavior. Behaviors such as Pursue, Evade, or Arrival try to steer the NPC toward or away from a specific target, while behaviors like Separation and Obstacle Avoidance can influence an NPC's movement along the way to a target [Reynolds99]. By combining multiple simple steering behaviors, you can build up complex behavior, such as chasing a target while attempting to stay in formation and dodging obstacles. The resulting NPC movement can appear intelligent as well as smooth and natural.

Animation System

An animation system [Woodland00, Watt00] is needed to bring characters to life—to make them run, jump, or swing a sword. A skeletal animation system does this by moving the character's skeleton. When the character is "skinned" [Hagland00] before being rendered, the moving bones move a character's vertices, which moves its "skin," creating the effect of movement.

Each animation contains a set of *keyframes*, or animation data for a specified frame. For each keyframe, the animator specifies the appropriate positions for bones (or, in vertex animation, vertices). The animation system then interpolates between the keyframes by picking appropriate positions for all the frames in between.

Interface Provided by the Animation System

Having animations for characters is all well and good, but how do you choose how fast to play each animation or which animation to use? The animation system just does what it's told by other systems. However, for the system described in this article to work, the animation system interface needs to provide several things (described more fully in the *Animation Controller* section later in this article):

- The ability to change the animation. For example, when the NPC speeds up, the animation system needs to be able to change from walk to run.
- The ability to set the speed factor of an animation, speeding the animation up when the character needs to move faster, or slowing it down when the character needs to move slower.
- The ability to set the animation time, so the animation system can start an animation in the middle. For example, when the animation system changes from

walk to run, it needs to be able to start the run animation at the point that most closely matches the walk animation at the moment it changed.

- The ability to query for information from an animation's data, such as its length in seconds and its associated translation velocity.
- The ability to query for properties of a currently playing animation on a specific character, such as the current animation time, meaning how many seconds the character is into an animation.

The Middle Layer

Together, the steering behaviors and the animation system decide where the NPC will go and what it will look like when it goes there. However, there is a gap between the two. First, how do you move the NPC? The steering behaviors only generate acceleration vectors; they don't do the moving. Second, how does the animation system find out which animation to play, how fast to play it (to avoid skating), and at what point in the animation to start playing it (to avoid popping)? Figure 4.3.1 shows a high-level view of the middle layer between the steering behaviors and the animation system.

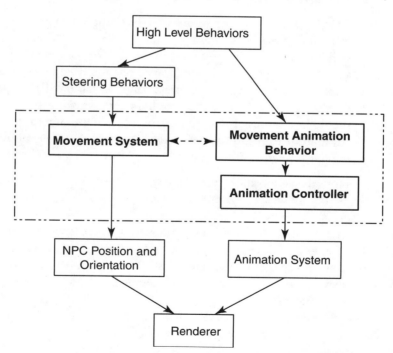

FIGURE 4.3.1 *How the movement system, movement animation behavior, and animation controller work together.*

There are three parts to the solution: the movement system, the movement animation behavior, and the animation controller. Briefly, they work together like this:

- The movement system gets the acceleration vector from the steering behaviors, and then updates the current velocity and generates the NPC's new position and orientation to move the NPC.
- The movement animation behavior chooses the appropriate animation, speed, and the point at which to start the animation.
- The animation controller uses the animation system's interface and provides a simpler, higher-level interface so that the movement animation behavior can change the animation as appropriate, set the speed, and choose the correct position in the animation.

Let's take a closer look at these three parts.

Movement System

Figure 4.3.2 shows a high-level view of how the movement system fits into the overall system described in this article. The movement system receives acceleration vectors from the steering system. It also obtains the following information from the movement animation behavior:

- **Speed thresholds:** The points at which the movement system should switch from one animation to another. For example, if the NPC is transitioning between walking and stopping, you need thresholds for the walking-to-stopped transition and for the stopped-to-walking transition. You need two thresholds for each transition to create a hysteresis, preventing oscillation if the speed is close to the threshold. For example, the threshold for switching from running to walking should be a bit lower than the threshold from walking to running.
- **Animation translation speeds:** The speeds a character should move when playing the animation at full speed.

From the acceleration vector, the speed thresholds, and the animation translation speeds, the movement system creates a movement translation vector, which it then uses to move the NPC.

The movement system is implemented with the MovementSystem class, which acts as an engine and drive train to move and orient an NPC in the world. Each NPC has an instance of the MovementSystem class as a member. After an NPC has updated all of its behaviors, it calls MovementSystem member functions to act on the results of the steering behaviors.

Before any functions are called, the movement animation behavior will have already initialized the movement system by providing speed thresholds and animation translation speeds.

First, the NPC calls the UpdateVelocity() member function to take a weighted average of all the steering behavior accelerations for the frame, limit the acceleration if it exceeds the maximum, and apply the final acceleration to the NPC's velocity. The UpdateVelocity() member function checks the new velocity to see if it is greater than

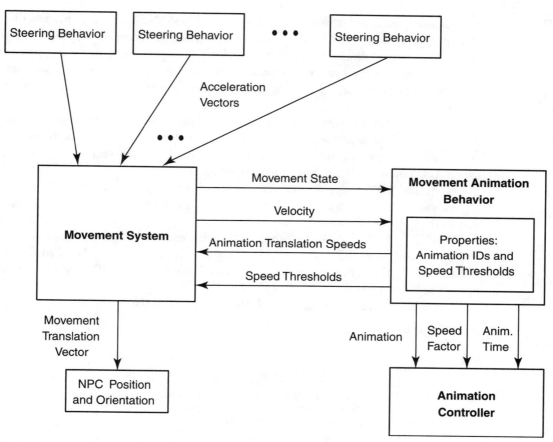

FIGURE 4.3.2 *The interfaces for the movement system, movement animation behavior, and animation controller.*

the maximum speed. If so, or if the change in velocity would cause the NPC to turn too quickly, UpdateVelocity() might limit the velocity or the change in velocity.

After UpdateVelocity() calculates the velocity, it updates the movement state (an enum that could be eStopped, eTurningLeft, eTurningRight, eWalking, or eRunning) by comparing the old movement state to the new velocity magnitude and speed thresholds. For example, if the old movement state is eWalking, the velocity magnitude is compared against the rWalkToStoppedThreshold and rWalkToRunThreshold speed thresholds. If the velocity magnitude is less than rWalkToStoppedThreshold, the new movement state will be eStopped. The new movement state will then be available when the movement animation behavior queries it in the next frame.

Next, the NPC calls GenerateMovement(), which returns the movement translation vector that corresponds to the current velocity and the time since the last update. If the fForceFullSpeedFlag flag is set, then GenerateMovement() ignores the current velocity magnitude and instead uses the full translation speed of the animation that corresponds to the current movement state. Using the full translation speed has the visual effect, for example, of the NPC suddenly changing from being stopped to walking at full walking speed. Additionally, if the current movement state is eStopped, the movement translation vector needs to be zero length to prevent NPCs from sliding.

The GenerateMovement() member function also changes the FacingDirection vector to align to movement, or, if the movement state is eStopped, turns the vFacingDirection vector toward the vDesiredFacingDirection vector, and sets the movement state to eTurningLeft or eTurningRight.

Next, the NPC calls ApplyMovement() and passes it the translation vector. ApplyMovement() translates the NPC object in the game world and updates its position in the game.

Finally, the NPC calls ApplyRotation(), which rotates the NPC object to orient its forward axis along the vFacingDirection vector. This causes the NPC to always face the direction it is moving, rather than sliding sideways. The NPC's movement is now done for this frame.

The following pseudocode shows the MovementSystem class.

```
class MovementSystem
{
public:
    void UpdateVelocity();
    VECTOR3D GenerateMovement();
    void ApplyMovement(const VECTOR3D &vMove);
    void ApplyRotation();
    void  SetThresholds(float rWalkToStop,
        float rStopToWalk, float rRunToWalk,
        float rWalkToRun);
    EMoveState GetMovementState();
    float GetSpeed();
    bool IsForceFullSpeed();

private:
    float rWalkToStoppedThreshold;
    float rStoppedToWalkThreshold;
    float rRunToWalkThreshold;
    float rWalkToRunThreshold;
    EMoveState eCurrentState;
    VECTOR3D vVelocity;
    VECTOR3D vFacingDirection;
    VECTOR3D vDesiredFacingDirection;
    DynamicArray<VECTOR3D> daAccelerations;
    DynamicArray<float> daAccelerationWeights;
    bool fForceFullSpeedFlag;
    GameObject *pOwner; // to update position/rotation
};
```

Movement Animation Behavior

The movement animation behavior system makes sure that the animation being played and the way it is being played are appropriate, given the NPC's current movement. This behavior would be at the lowest level of a hierarchical state machine or behavior system. (We won't discuss it here, but higher up in the hierarchy would be some sort of general movement behavior that handles pathfinding and uses steering behaviors to move the NPC to a new target position.)

Figure 4.3.2, earlier in this article, shows a high-level view of how the movement animation behavior shares information with the movement system and how it uses the animation controller. It gets the movement state and velocity from the movement system, and it gets the animation IDs and speed thresholds from designer parameters. Based on this information, it uses the animation controller to change the animation, set the speed factor, and set the animation time.

When the movement animation behavior is started by a higher-level movement behavior, it calls its `Start()` member function. This function initializes the behavior by taking parameters specified by the game designer and passing them on to the NPC's movement system and animation controller. These parameters specify a style or manner of movement. Each parameter set needs the following:

- Animation IDs for all the animations, including the stopped, walking, running, turning left, and turning right animations.
- Speed thresholds for transitions between animations.

As we discussed in the *Movement System* section, the movement system needs to know the speed thresholds for switching between the `eStopped`, `eWalking`, and `eRunning` movement states. The animation controller needs to know the animation IDs for the stopped, walking, running, turning left, and turning right animations.

Every frame after that, the movement animation behavior calls its `Update()` member function. First, `Update()` gets the current movement state from the NPC's `MovementSystem` member.

Next, `Update()` chooses the corresponding animation ID from the movement animation behavior parameters.

After that, if the movement state is a stationary one, such as `eStopped`, `eTurningLeft`, or `eTurningRight`, and if the proper animation is not already playing, then `Update()` uses the `ChangeAnimation()` member function in the `Animation-Controller` class to change to the proper animation. `Update()` starts the new animation at the beginning and uses the `SetSpeedFactor()` member function in the `AnimationController` class to play the animation at a speed factor of 1.0. At this point, the animation is fully set up, so `Update()` returns.

Alternately, if the movement state is `eWalking` or `eRunning`, then `Update()` checks whether the new animation has changed since the last frame. If so, then `Update()` specifies an appropriate starting time by using the `SetAnimationTime()` member function in the `AnimationController` class. For example, if the NPC is 75 percent through a walking cycle and needs to switch to running, `Update()` starts the run cycle at 75 percent as well. If the animation has changed, the NPC uses the `ChangeAnimation()` and `SetAnimationTime()` member functions of the `AnimationController` class to change to the new animation at the appropriate starting position.

Finally, `Update()` sets the speed factor of the animation so that the animation matches the NPC's velocity. If the movement system's `fForceFullSpeedFlag` is set, `Update()` plays the animation at speed factor 1.0. Otherwise, `Update()` plays the animation at the speed factor represented by the current speed (as reported by the `MovementSystem`) divided by the translation speed of the animation.

Animation Controller

Earlier in this article, we talked about the interface that the animation system needs to provide. The `AnimationController` class uses that interface to let an individual NPC control its animation. An instance of this will be a member of the main NPC class and will provide a simple bridge between an NPC's behaviors, such as the movement animation behavior, and the game engine's animation system.

`AnimationController` has three main member functions to influence the animation being played by its owner. The `ChangeAnimation()` member function changes the animation the NPC is playing. `SetSpeedFactor()` speeds up or slows down the animation. `SetAnimationTime()` specifies the point to start playing an animation.

`AnimationController` also has three other member functions to get information about an animation or about the state of the current playing animation. `GetTranslationSpeed()` returns the speed that a character should move when playing the specified animation at full speed in meters per second or whatever units you use for speed. `GetLength()` returns the time it takes to play one cycle of the specified animation at full speed. `GetCurrentAnimationTime()` gets the current animation playing time for the character.

The following pseudocode shows the `AnimationController` class.

```
class AnimationController
{
public:
    void ChangeAnimation(AnimationID idAnim);
    void SetSpeedFactor(float rSpeed);
    void SetAnimationTime(float rTime);

    float GetTranslationSpeed(AnimationID idAnim);
    float GetLength(AnimationID idAnim);
    float GetCurrentAnimationTime();

private:
    GameObject *pOwner; // to access animation system
};
```

Gotchas

To make the intelligent movement animation system work effectively, with NPCs moving smoothly and naturally, watch out for three key gotchas.

First, not only steering behaviors but also collision response can affect movement. A collision response can cause an NPC to move in a different direction or a shorter distance than attempted. If the NPC moves in a different direction, the NPC can slide sideways while bumping into an object. If the NPC moves a shorter distance (or if the move is canceled entirely by the collision response), the NPC could either play its walk animation slowly or appear to walk in place against an object. Another option is for the NPC to stop when its movement is cut short, but this can result in an NPC getting stuck on objects—improving the look of the animation at the expense of gameplay and making the NPC look less than intelligent.

Second, although animations look best when played at 100-percent speed, playing an animation at 100-percent speed has disadvantages. The first disadvantage is that forcing an NPC to move at two discrete speeds can interfere with steering behaviors. Some steering behaviors rely on the NPC being able to slow down or speed up slightly; for example, to avoid colliding with moving objects or to maintain a formation with other NPCs. Forcing NPCs to move only at discrete walk or run speed would make the NPCs bump into objects and break formation, and would also cause a slow oscillation between walking and running when a speed in the middle is appropriate. The second disadvantage is that NPC movement will look less natural, as the NPC will switch abruptly between the two speeds, rather than smoothly varying them. Take these issues into consideration when deciding whether a specific NPC should be set to force the full animation speed, or whether the movement animation behavior should be allowed to vary the animation speed factor.

Third, if your animation system supports blending when transitioning between two different animations, then another issue comes up. Although it's a good idea to interpolate between the walking and running or walking and stopped animations to prevent a jarring pop at the transition, if you're not careful, interpolating can cause the NPC to skate during the transition. The key to solving this problem is to ensure that the animation is played at an appropriate speed to compensate for the fact that full translation speed varies during the transition.

Future Enhancements

The movement system and movement animation behaviors described here will handle basic NPC movement, but there are plenty of possible enhancements. We'll discuss a couple.

Different Movement Axes

Instead of just having one movement axis, you can have four: forward, backward, left, and right. The movement system can keep track of the current movement axis and change it, so the NPC can strafe sideways or walk backward. The decision to change the movement axis would be made by a higher-level movement behavior. For example, if the NPC decides to move to a location a short distance directly behind it, the MoveToPoint behavior can cause the NPC to walk backward a step or two without turning. This looks much better than having the NPC first do a 180-degree turn and then take a step or two to end up facing in the opposite direction. Moreover, having four axes can make NPC movement look much more natural when making small adjustments, as when an NPC companion steps out of the way of the player.

Additional Animation

If an NPC has a relatively fast run and a slow walk, this can cause some problems. Since animations look best when played close to full speed, the NPC can look bad when moving at a speed between walking and running. If there is a point at which speeding up the walk and slowing down the run both look bad, you might consider adding an additional animation in the middle to fill the gap, either a fast walk, a slow run, or a jog. This would require adding a new movement state and additional thresholds.

Conclusion

With the intelligent NPC movement animation system described in this article, you can make full use of steering behaviors and make the NPC look good in the process. The movement system moves and orients an NPC in the world, getting information from the animation system to make sure that the movement state is appropriate for the speed at which an animation is designed. At the same time, the movement animation behavior gets information from the movement system about which animation should be played and how fast. As a result, the NPC always appears smooth and natural, without skating or popping. There are some things to look out for, like handling the animation during a collision. With this system in place, your orcs can put away their ice skates and focus on where they're going to get their next meal.

References

[Hagland00] Hagland, Torgeir, "A Fast and Simple Skinning Technique," *Game Programming Gems*, Charles River Media, 2000.

[Reynolds99] Reynolds, C. W., "Steering Behaviors for Autonomous Characters," *GDC 1999 Conference Proceedings*, Miller Freeman Game Group, 1999, pp. 763–782, *www.red.com/cwr/steer*, also on the *AI Game Programming Wisdom 2* CD-ROM.

[Reynolds00] Reynolds, Craig, "Interaction with Groups of Autonomous Characters," *GDC 2000 Conference Proceedings*, CMP Game Media Group, 2000, pp. 449–460.

[Watt00] Watt, Alan, and Policarpo, Fabio, *3D Games: Real-Time Rendering and Software Technology*, ACM Press, 2000.

[Woodcock00] Woodcock, Steve, "Flocking: A Simple Technique for Simulating Group Behavior," *Game Programming Gems*, Charles River Media, 2000.

[Woodland00] Woodland, Ryan, "Filling the Gaps—Advanced Animation Using Stitching and Skinning," *Game Programming Gems*, Charles River Media, 2000.

STATE MACHINES

The Ultimate Guide to FSMs in Games

Dan Fu and Ryan Houlette—Stottler Henke Associates, Inc.

fu@stottlerhenke.com,
houlette@stottlerhenke.com

Finite-state machines (FSMs) are without a doubt the most commonly used technology in game AI programming today. They are conceptually simple, efficient, easily extensible, and yet powerful enough to handle a wide variety of situations. Because of their many good qualities, FSMs have become an indispensable tool in the game programmer's toolbox. Perhaps you've already used them in your games, and now you're looking to further explore their capabilities. This article will help you push your FSMs further. Perhaps you need a solution to a thorny FSM problem. This article will show you how to surmount the limitations of FSMs. Or perhaps you simply don't know anything about FSMs, but you've heard they can be useful. This article will teach you the basics.

While many excellent articles have been written about FSMs in games (see the *References* section for some examples), these articles generally focus on a single aspect of or enhancement to FSMs. This article, by contrast, offers a broad overview of the topic, starting with the plain-vanilla FSM and ranging all the way to its more exotic augmentations. It is intended to serve as a roadmap of the many possible applications for FSMs, and as a consolidated jumping-off point for further research. We hope that it will also spark your imagination and lead you to create your own innovative uses for FSMs in games.

The Basic Finite-State Machine

Formally, the finite-state machine (or finite-state automaton) starts in its simplest form as a construct from computational theory, defined as a set of states S, an input vocabulary I, and a transition function T(s,i) mapping a state and an input to another state. The machine designates a single initial state designated as the *start* state, and zero or more *accepting* states. After the FSM processes all input, the ending state's identification as an accepting state dictates whether the machine accepts the input or not.

Less abstractly, an FSM is a concise, nonlinear description of how an object can change its state over time, possibly in response to events in its environment. Its practical use departs from the theoretical definition in four ways. First, because it's intuitive to think of each state as representing some desired behavior, each state has corresponding code so that as the object's state changes, its behavior changes accordingly. Second, the monolithic transition function T resides across states. Each state can be said to "know" the conditions under which it should transition to a different state. Third, the notion of an accepting state is irrelevant. In its place, accepting states are generally interpreted as the end of execution for the FSM. From here, another FSM gets invoked by the game to handle further input. Fourth, the input continues indefinitely until the FSM is no longer needed, or the game ends. The practical FSM isn't about recognizing a language—it's all about driving behavior.

FSMs are often depicted graphically using flowchart-like diagrams in which states and transitions are drawn as rectangles and arrows—so often, in fact, that the Unified Modeling Language (UML) reserves one of its nine diagram types just for state machines [Fowler00].

Because game character behavior can be modeled (in most cases) as a sequence of different character "mental states"—where change in state is driven by the actions of the player or other characters, or possibly some features of the game world—game programmers often find that finite-state machines are a natural choice for defining character AI. Figure 5.1.1 shows such an FSM-based behavior where the states describe how the character will act, and the transitions between states represent the "decisions" that the character makes about what it should do next. This "decision-action" model is straightforward enough to appeal to the nonprogrammers on the game development team (such as level designers), yet impressively powerful. FSMs also lend themselves to being quickly sketched out during design and prototyping, and even better, they can be easily and efficiently implemented.

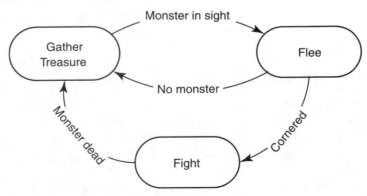

FIGURE 5.1.1   *Example of an FSM as a diagram.*

Defining FSMs

Now that we've covered the basic motivation for using FSMs, let's turn our attention to the ways in which FSMs can be implemented. You can write an FSM in three ways. The first, and perhaps most obvious, is to simply code one up. This is the most common, straightforward way to track state information. The second way is to create a macro-assisted FSM language, which, while ultimately code, is much more readable and maintainable. The last way is to create a custom FSM scripting language that describes a state machine. In this section, we consider the three ways of defining an FSM.

Coding an FSM

Consider the following code segment, adapted from an article [Rabin02a]:

```
void RunLogic( int *state )
{
    switch( *state )
    {
        case 0:  //Wander
            Wander();
            if( SeeEnemy() ) *state = 1;
            if( Dead() ) *state = 2;
            break;
        case 1:  //Attack
            Attack();
            *state = 0;
            if( Dead() ) *state = 2;
            break;
        case 2:  //Dead
            SlowlyRot();
            break;
    }
}
```

This function keeps track of three states. Each state corresponds to a single action that gets called each time the function is invoked. After the action, a state change might be in order. The logic is simple and easy to debug. Unfortunately, numerous problems crop up in practice if we adopt this method if only because the implementation is ad hoc. Imagine one team member adhering to the convention of "one state and its transitions per case," as in the preceding code, while another team member micro-optimizes by moving the "If Dead()" transitions to a single catch-all statement at the end of the function. Such an optimization would not technically be wrong, but it would certainly be confusing to the other developers. The problem here is that, modulo FSM coding guidelines, there is no prescribed structure.

Another coded method described by Eric Dybsand [Dybsand00] employs C++ classes to rigidly track states. We can build an FSM by allocating an FSM class, and then populating it with state instances that will refer to each other in transitions.

Methods for querying the current state and providing an input to effect a transition are provided. Because the input is a single value—an integer—the code must somehow encapsulate the transition logic to determine the integer. A possible solution could be:

```
void RunLogic( FSM* fsm )
{
      // Do action based on current state and
      // determine the next input.
      int input = 0;
      switch( fsm->GetStateID() )
      {
            case 0:  //Wander
                  Wander();
                  if( SeeEnemy() ) input = SEE_ENEMY;
                  if( Dead() ) input = DEAD;
                  break;
            case 1:  //Attack
                  Attack();
                  input = WANDER;
                  if( Dead() ) input = DEAD;
                  break;
            case 2:  //Dead
                  SlowlyRot();
                  break;
      }

      // Do state transition based on computed input
      fsm->StateTransition(input);
}
```

Here we can see that the transition logic, immediately succeeding the action, ultimately sets the value of the input variable in the three cases, after which the FSM handles the transition.

While it might seem tempting to decouple the state actions and transition logic, it would be a mistake for two reasons. First, if you're trying to understand a state and want to see its immediate transitions, you'd want the logic right there after the action. Having the logic in disparate pieces of code would force you to assemble the FSM "big picture" in your head, oscillating between action and transition code. The second reason is that you'll end up doing a lot of work calculating an input that won't matter. States usually don't have more than a handful of transitions apiece even though the amount of aggregate data referenced is huge. By calculating an input suitable for all states all the time, your transition logic will quickly become a bottleneck. Remember: FSMs tend to grow, not shrink. Over time, this is a potential liability.

In practice, you'll most likely implement a middle ground between *Mealy* and *Moore* machines. A Mealy machine is an FSM whose actions are performed on transitions, while a Moore machine's actions reside in states. Virtually all game developers lean toward the Moore model because it's more intuitive to think of a game character as being in a state doing something with events prompting it to do something else.

However, on transitions, or within the transition code, there's often good reason to insert an action.

Writing an FSM with an FSM Language

Previously, we noted a lack of structure when coding a state machine. Because state machines can be so trivial to implement at first, a likely breakdown in structure can come down to bury you during crunch time when state machines are at their largest and most complex. A great way to retain structure is through the use of an FSM language.

In [Rabin02a], Steve Rabin presents a state machine language that employs six C-style macro definitions plus a C++ class. With it, we can define the earlier FSM example using just four macros (BeginStateMachine, State, OnUpdate, and EndStateMachine) and one member function (SetState), like so:

```
bool MyStateMachine::States( StateMachineEvent event,
                             int state )
{
BeginStateMachine
    State(0)
        OnUpdate
            Wander();
            if( SeeEnemy() ) SetState(1);
            if( Dead() ) SetState(2);
    State(1)
        OnUpdate
            Attack();
            SetState(0);
            if( Dead() ) SetState(2);
    State(2)
        OnUpdate
            RotSlowly();
EndStateMachine
}
```

As you might have guessed, the macros reference the seemingly unused function arguments, event and state. Mostly, the macros are an expansion into if-then-else statements. For example, State(1) will check if state equals 1. If it does, then the indented block will execute, starting with OnUpdate, which activates on a regular game tick. As an aside, there exist two additional sibling macros, OnEnter and OnExit, which execute once when entering and exiting the state, respectively.

Defining a state machine through the use of macros has three beneficial properties:

- **Structure:** All your state machines will follow the same consistent format. With a shallow learning curve, other programmers can get up to speed quickly.
- **Readability:** The developer can write concise yet easily understood code. Much of the lower-level detail condenses in favor of focusing reader attention on state actions and transition logic.

- **Debugging:** The programmer's attention will be solely on the action and transitions—not the otherwise distracting macro expansions.

Perhaps the best practical feature of this FSM language is its simplicity: it only adds six new keywords to your code. This language helps you be more productive, while still providing C++ access to game engine internals. While you might be tempted to add additional macros to suit your particular needs, be aware that this kind of distilled parsimony is hard to maintain, and, as with scripting languages, it's important to determine requirements before instituting fundamental changes.

ON THE CD

If you want to experiment with this solution, the source code is on the accompanying CD-ROM.

Writing a Data-Driven FSM

So far we've examined two code-based approaches to FSM implementation, one with and one without macros. We're now ready to introduce the last way to write an FSM: using a data-driven approach. As the name might imply, the design is marked by the authoring of data that is ultimately a form that can power an FSM—fuel for an engine, if you will.

Scripting languages are one example of a data-driven approach. The developer writes in a scripting language, and then saves work to a text file. From there, the file contents are transformed into either a standard language like C++ or bytecode. The C++ version will be further translated into a machine language through a standard compiler, whereas the bytecode will be interpreted by the engine.

Figure 5.1.2, adapted from [Fu02], shows one way you can incorporate an FSM scripting language into a game. On the left are the team members who use an AI editing tool to write the FSMs. Typically, the editor is either pure text [Rosado03, Yiskis03] or a visual graph with text [Fu02, Carlisle02].

Aside from the language used in the editor, the team members will need to declare a native condition and action library. This is a vocabulary subset of the scripting language for game-specific conditions and actions. The team uses the vocabulary to describe the transition logic between states as well as action execution. An example transition logic could be SeeEnemy() and CloseToEnemy(), while an example action could be Attack().

With a complete FSM script, the compiler transforms the script into bytecode for the script engine [Berger02a]. The script engine executes the bytecode, acting in concert with the game engine. It is the script engine that will prescribe an Attack, or ask for the results of a SeeEnemy query from the game engine. See [Berger02b, Houlette01] for engine implementation information.

The interface between the script and game engines facilitates the binding between vocabulary and game world [Berger02c]. The vocabulary keywords, bandied about freely in the editing tool, must at some point be bound to functions in game engine code that ultimately do what is advertised. Thus, the interface is a "glue layer" that implements the condition and action vocabulary in the game world, returning the

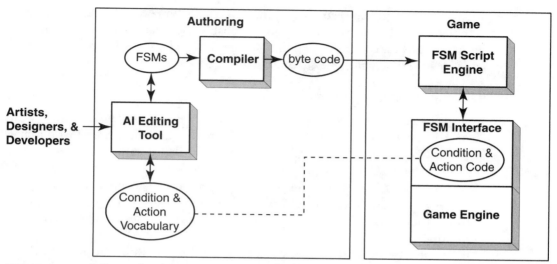

FIGURE 5.1.2 *Relationship between authoring, script engine, and game engine.*

results to the scripting engine. Usually, the vocabulary will see considerable change early in the development cycle, eventually stabilizing after sample prototypes have been created.

As with any scripting language, the decision to create an FSM scripting language should not be taken lightly. For everything you might expect to benefit from a scripting language—accelerated productivity, contributions from artists and designers, ease of use, and extensibility—there are just as many pitfalls [Pelletier01, Tozour02a]. Perhaps the riskiest proposition is that a good amount of manpower, measured in months, must be committed up front to language design and engine implementation before realizing any tangible results. As it is, you'd be wise to perform a requirements analysis anyway. What will take time is the design of a language that exposes the transition logic and actions adequately, while maintaining a fundamental simplicity—one that enables users to quickly synthesize powerful FSMs, while allowing them to remain oblivious to all the minute game engine details. If you're in a prototyping stage where you don't know all your requirements, or suspect they will change unpredictably, you're better off with one of three strategies: a programming language masquerading as a scripting language; a macro-assisted language that retains readable structure while conferring direct access to game engine data structures; or a hybrid combination of high-level scripting language controlling coded FSMs.

Integrating FSMs with Your Game

Deciding how you will define FSM logic is an important first step to using finite-state machines in your game, but there are a few other design decisions to be made before your FSM architecture is complete. You will need to select an FSM processing model;

you must also determine how the actions associated with FSM states actually interact with the rest of the game engine. You will probably also need to consider how to optimize your FSM architecture for efficient execution. The following sections address these issues and present some common solutions.

Processing Models for FSMs

As we have seen, a finite-state machine can define the conditions under which a game character changes from one behavioral state to another, and the actions that the character takes in each state. For this to be anything more than a static definition, though, the game engine needs to actually process the FSM—that is, evaluate the transition conditions for the current state and perform any associated actions—while the game is running. When and how the FSMs should be processed will depend on the exact needs of your game. The three most common FSM processing models are polling, event-driven, and multithreaded.

The polling model is the most straightforward of the three. In this model, the game engine simply processes each FSM at regular time intervals, where the length of the intervals is generally tied either to the frame rate (e.g., the FSM executes every three frames) or to some desired "FSM update frequency" (e.g., the FSM should update five times per second). Exactly how much an FSM can accomplish within the scope of a single processing cycle is at your discretion. One common approach is to allow an FSM to make no more than one state transition in a processing cycle. Another method is to give each FSM a time bound that it cannot exceed during its processing; the FSM must stop checking for state transitions after the time expires. (Preemptive time-bounded implementations are also possible but much more complex.)

The polling model is extremely easy to implement and debug. Its very simplicity can lead to inefficiency, however, since FSMs are always processed regardless of whether there is anything for them to do. Imagine, for example, a Little Red Riding Hood character who is in the *GoingToGrandmasHouse* state. She will remain in that state until she sees a wolf. There is thus no reason to process Little Red Riding Hood's FSM until a wolf is within her visual range. A polling system, though, would continue to process that FSM regardless of whether a wolf was anywhere near, which might be expensive if the evaluation of the *SeesWolf* condition requires complex computations (such as line-of-sight tests). Of course, careful design of your FSMs can mitigate this problem by minimizing the transition-checking costs for commonly used states.

The event-driven model is designed precisely to solve this problem of wasted FSM processing. In this model, an FSM is only processed when it is relevant—that is, when something has happened in the game world that might provoke a state transition. The game engine thus requires special infrastructure to keep track of the conditions under which each FSM is relevant and to determine when those conditions have been met. A typical implementation would be to use a publish-subscribe messaging system (also known as the Observer pattern) that allows the game engine to send event messages to individual FSMs. Different events correspond to different types of occurrences in the game world, such as Little Red Riding Hood seeing the wolf, or the woodcutter hitting the wolf with his axe. At any given instant, an FSM subscribes only to the events that have the potential to change the current state. When an event is generated by the game, the FSMs subscribed to that event are all processed. The other FSMs are not processed, since nothing has changed in the game world that could possibly affect them.

Because of its "as-needed" approach to FSM processing, the event-driven model has the potential to be much more efficient than polling. The tradeoff, of course, is that the additional infrastructure incurs processing overhead that increases with the number of events tracked. There is thus a tricky balance to be struck between making your events too fine-grained (resulting in lots of events and high messaging overhead) and making them too coarse-grained (resulting in few events but also low efficiency gains for FSM processing). In addition, implementing the messaging infrastructure is a nontrivial task, although once it has been built it can often be exploited by other parts of the game engine.

Both the polling and the event-driven models assume that finite-state machines will be intermittently and serially processed. The multithreading model takes a very different tack. In this model, each FSM is assigned to its own thread for processing, and the game engine runs in another separate thread. All FSM processing is thus effectively concurrent and continuous. This means that communication between FSMs and the game engine must be thread-safe, using standard locking and synchronization mechanisms.

The primary benefit of this approach is the conceptual elegance of treating the FSMs as autonomous agents that can constantly and independently examine and react to their environment. However, the use of threads imposes a considerable overhead on the game engine, particularly if the game has many simultaneous characters active. Moreover, multithreaded programming is notoriously difficult: small synchronization mistakes can lead to very subtle and difficult-to-reproduce bugs.

A variant of the multithreaded model is to use *microthreads* for FSM processing [Dawson01, Carter01]. A microthread is essentially a lightweight virtual thread managed internally by the game engine rather than by the operating system. Microthreads can be substantially more efficient than full-fledged threads, but building a microthreading architecture is no easy feat. In addition, microthreading requires an FSM implementation that is preemptible, which is difficult to achieve with hard-coded FSMs. (Interpreted data-driven FSMs tend to be naturally preemptible.)

Interfacing with the Game Engine

Part of the attraction of using FSMs lies in their ability to encapsulate complex behavior logic and keep it separate from the rest of the game engine. In the end, though, there must be some mechanism that enables the FSMs to query and act upon the game world. (After all, the most intelligent character in the world is just so much wasted development time if the player can't actually *see* the character doing anything intelligent.) For example, consider the Little Red Riding Hood FSM in the previous section. When a state in that FSM invokes an action such as `FleeWolf()`, somehow this must trigger the corresponding sequence of character movement, animations, sounds, and so on within the game.

The most obvious way to interface with the game engine is simply to code each action as a separate function and then have the states directly call these functions. This is the approach discussed previously in the *Coding an FSM* section, and it yields tightly coupled, completely hard-coded FSM-game interaction. It also has the advantage of making it very easy to parameterize actions with arbitrary arguments. The weakness of this approach lies in its rigidity: Every change to an action implementation requires recompilation of the entire system.

In a slightly more sophisticated variant of this scheme, the direct calls to action functions are replaced by calls to function pointers (see also [Farris02]). These pointers are stored in a special container object that is either globally available as a singleton or passed in to the FSM code. One common implementation is to keep all of the function pointers in a big array and use an enumerated type to reference individual functions:

```
actionFunctions[kFleeWolf]()
```

Another technique involves wrapping each function pointer in a method, so that the FSM invokes an action by calling the corresponding container method:

```
actionFunctions->FleeWolf()
```

While on the surface this approach seems little different from direct function calls (and indeed adds what appears to be unnecessary complexity), the extra layer of indirection actually adds a great deal of flexibility. For one thing, it allows action implementations to be moved out of the main code body and into a DLL, thereby modularizing the system and reducing the amount of recompilation required. This in turn makes it trivial to vary action implementations by merely exchanging DLLs. There is also the less tangible design benefit of having all character actions grouped together in a single class rather than cluttering up the namespace as global functions.

The two preceding techniques work well with code-based FSM implementations, but a somewhat different approach is needed for data-driven FSMs, which, existing beyond the realm of the C++ compiler, cannot directly invoke C++ functions. The FSM script engine must therefore furnish some way for the FSMs to "virtually" invoke actions using their unique identifiers. Internally, the FSM engine will have code analogous to the following:

```
int FSM_Engine::DoAction(int actionId, vector<ActionArg> params)
{
    switch( actionId )
```

```
        {
                case kFleeWolf:
                        // make character flee
                        break;
                ...
        }
}
```

Each time the FSM script specifies that the character should perform an action, the FSM engine calls the DoAction() method with the corresponding action identifier and parameter vector. Note that while this approach does entail additional overhead, it also offers the most flexibility, since FSMs can be modified while the game is running without any need for code changes.

Efficiency and Optimization

In general, finite-state machines are among the most efficient technologies available to the game AI programmer. There is always room for optimization in the world of game development, though, so in this section we'll look at several techniques for making your FSMs faster. These techniques can be organized into two main groups: those that manage the amount of time spent processing FSMs, and those that actually reduce the computational cost of processing the FSM.

For time management, perhaps the most effective technique is what we'll call *scheduled processing*. This is based on the observation that all game characters do not necessarily need to be updated with the same frequency. For example, in our Little Red Riding Hood game, the wolf is one of the main characters, so he probably needs to be updated very frequently (say, 10 times per second). The woodcutter's magic axe, on the other hand, which does nothing but make occasional witty comments, can get by with an update every 30 seconds. Processing its FSM more frequently is a waste of CPU time. We can do better by assigning a priority to each character and then scheduling FSM processing based on those priorities, thereby ensuring that every character gets updated as often as it needs but no more.

While the scheduled processing model is an easy way to get significant performance gains, it can result in uneven CPU usage by the game AI subsystem, since the number of FSMs processed (and the time required to process each one) can vary wildly from frame to frame. We can improve on this model by incorporating a *load-balancing* algorithm that attempts to schedule FSM processing so that it takes a constant amount of time per frame. Such algorithms estimate how long a given FSM's processing will take by collecting statistics about past performance and extrapolating. It is impossible, of course, to perfectly smooth out the CPU load, but there are relatively easy-to-implement algorithms that work well in practice [Alexander02].

Another way to limit the amount of time spent processing FSMs is to place a bound on the time spent in the AI subsystem on each game frame. When that bound is exceeded, no more FSMs can be processed on that frame. Within a given frame, each FSM can itself be time-bounded, as described in the section on polling. For even more fine-grained control, you can opt for an interruptible FSM implementation, which allows an FSM to stop in the middle of processing when its time runs out and then pick up where it left off at the next opportunity.

The second category of optimizations consists of techniques for making FSMs run faster. Because the basic infrastructure of the finite-state machine is fairly light-weight, it is difficult to obtain drastic speedups by optimizing it. Individual FSMs can benefit from optimization at a design level, which involves arranging states and transitions to minimize the evaluation of expensive conditions. To get systemic performance improvements, though, adoption of a *level-of-detail* (or LOD) FSM scheme is probably your best bet [Brockington02].

Level-of-Detail FSMs

The fundamental idea behind LOD systems is the notion that it is acceptable to make approximations when calculating how the game world should look or act *if the player won't notice the difference*. For example, a 3D graphics engine might be able to use less-detailed textures and character models for elements of the scene that are distant from the camera since the player can't make out fine detail at a distance anyway. The same principle applies to game AI: characters outside of the player's perceptual range can take shortcuts in their computations knowing that as long as their behavior remains the same at a macro level the player won't be able to tell.

When constructing an LOD system, there are three key design issues to address. First, you should decide how many levels of detail are appropriate for your game. What the right number is depends both on how much development time you have available and the extent to which your AI design lends itself to approximation. Keep in mind that unlike in graphics, where the creation of levels of detail can be largely automated using preprocessing tools, each AI level of detail will most likely require individual design and implementation.

Second, you must determine your LOD selection policy, which determines which level of detail is used for a given character at a given time. A basic algorithm is to choose the level of detail based on the character's distance from the player, effectively creating concentric rings of increasing approximation. If your game world is divided into regions or areas, these might help make the determination. Whether the character is currently visible to the player can also strongly affect the choice of level of detail. Of course, both the visibility and location of a character are likely to change over time; consequently, your LOD system needs to allow characters to move from one level of detail to another, ideally without any obvious discontinuities in character behavior. It should probably also have safeguards against "thrashing" between two levels of detail, which can occur, for example, when a character loiters near the boundary of a LOD region.

The third step in designing a LOD system for game AI is determining what kinds of approximations you can usefully make in your FSMs. Often the most expensive part of FSM processing is the evaluation of transition logic, so one LOD strategy is to identify the most costly transition computations and then provide several implementations of each, where one is the exact, highest-detail version and the others use cheaper, less accurate algorithms. A variant is to have each character's FSM cache and reuse the results of its own costly computations, refreshing the cache with frequency proportional to the current level of detail.

Level-of-detail processing does not have to be limited to the scope of an individual function, however, but can apply to an entire FSM. In such a scheme, a character might run a complex FSM when in close proximity to the player, then switch to progressively less sophisticated versions of the same behavior as the player moves farther away, ultimately running only a bare-bones path-following FSM when out of the player's view. This type of LOD system gives the developer complete control over the complexity of each level of detail on a character-by-character basis. At the same time, it can double or triple the number of FSMs that must be created. Authoring a character behavior for multiple levels of detail is not necessarily an easy task, either, since the transition from an FSM at one level of detail to an FSM at another level of detail should be smooth and imperceptible.

Extending the Basic FSM

Up to this point we've limited our discussion to the implementation issues surrounding the plain-vanilla FSM. There are many, many extensions to the basic FSM available, however, and they can be combined as needed to create a custom FSM architecture that meets the specific needs of your games. In this section, we will talk briefly about some of the more useful and interesting extensions.

Extending States

As we have seen, each state in an FSM generally has some code or script associated with it that causes a game character to take certain actions. As long as the character remains in that state, it will continue to execute that action code. In some cases, though, you might not want a character to repeatedly perform a given action, or you might want to ensure that a character always performs a given action before going into a given state. For example, the knight should always draw his sword before going into the Duel state. One way to handle this is via an *OnEnter* block, which is nothing more than a section of code (or script) associated with a particular state that is executed exactly once each time that state is entered. It is also possible to have *OnExit* blocks, which are executed exactly once as the FSM leaves the current state. *OnExit* blocks are useful for doing any necessary state-specific cleanup or animations.

Stacks and FSMs

There are a number of FSM variants that use a stack data structure to greatly enhance the capabilities of the FSM. One such variant adds a stack-based "history" to the FSM so that it can remember the sequence of states that it has passed through and retrace its steps at will [Tozour04]. As transitions are followed, states are pushed on and popped off the history stack. This makes it easy to create characters with a memory who can stop what they are currently doing to handle a sudden change in situation, and then return to what they were originally doing once the situation has been addressed.

An even more powerful stack-based variant is the *hierarchical FSM*, in which each state can actually invoke an entire FSM of its own [Houlette01]. When an FSM transitions into such a hierarchical state, the state's FSM is instantiated and run as a fully independent state machine, with its own data separate from the parent FSM, as shown in Figure 5.1.3.

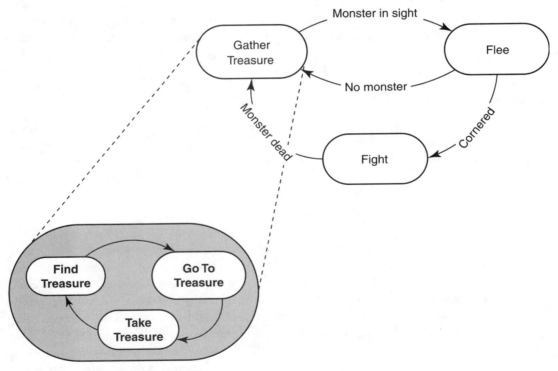

FIGURE 5.1.3   *A hierarchical FSM.*

The chain of currently invoked FSMs for a given character is stored in a stack (see Figure 5.1.4, where only the topmost FSM is "active"; that is, controlling the character's actions). When the topmost FSM reaches an accepting (or "final") state, it is popped from the stack, and the new topmost FSM becomes active.

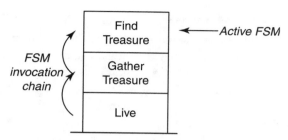

FIGURE 5.1.4   *Stack of currently-invoked FSMs for a single character.*

Hierarchical FSMs have a couple of advantages that tend to make their added complexity worthwhile. For one thing, they allow large, complex character behaviors to be broken down into smaller, more understandable, and more maintainable chunks. As your FSMs grow and become more complex, the ability to refactor and decompose FSMs in this way can be invaluable. In addition, hierarchical FSMs allow you to avoid duplication of FSM code (or script), since you can extract common sub-behaviors out into separate FSMs that can be referenced by many other FSMs.

Polymorphic FSMs

While hierarchical FSMs provide modular building blocks out of which we can construct new, more complex FSMs, their long-term use will eventually introduce a proliferation of similar behaviors, often with minor changes introduced for new types of entities. Because of the references made in an FSM to other FSMs, minor changes introduced at an abstract level frequently lead to a propagation of necessary changes to the lower-level FSMs. For example, we might want to model squad tactics using squad roles and levels of aggression. When attacking, the generic "Combat" behavior would dispatch a specialized version based on, say, a rifleman role and high aggression. The invoked FSM might be called "Combat_Rifleman_High." Likely, the lower-level FSMs will also need specialized versions as well. The unfortunate result is a bigger FSM library with no particular way for the user to simplify it through refactoring.

To handle the growth of the FSM library while simplifying the construction of specialized behavior, we can create a *polymorphic* extension so that a single Combat FSM can entertain multiple versions [Fu02]. Exactly which version gets invoked depends on the set of attribute-value pairs—in this case, the role is "rifleman" and aggression is "high"—that describe each individual soldier. In essence, we have attached a little bit of state information to the game character so as to simplify authoring of multiple FSMs. The FSM engine, when invoking a Combat FSM for a game character, will always consult the character's attributes to select a specialized FSM.

Fuzzy State Machines

A variation of finite-state machines called "fuzzy automata" or "fuzzy state machines" (FuSMs for short) combines the ideas of fuzzy logic [McCuskey00] with finite-state machines. Fuzzy logic is an extension of traditional Boolean logic where there exists the notion of partial truth; that is, false and true are extremes on a spectrum—commonly between zero and one—where there are values in between. Usually when people speak of fuzzy logic, they're talking about computing degrees of membership in sets.

Carrying the notion of fuzzy sets over to finite-state machines, a fuzzy state machine considers multiple states to be the current state; in fact, you could say that a FuSM is in all of its states simultaneously, to greater or lesser degrees, with a vector of numbers—indicating membership in each set/state—constituting the current state [Dybsand01, Klir95]. Although fuzzy automata have their uses in other industries, they are rare in video games. Little literature exists documenting any implementation, although there are a smattering of games that employ fuzzy inference, such as Activision's *Call to Power* [Woodcock99]. While the technology might be construed as fuzzy automata, it is more correctly classified as a fuzzy expert system—an example of a rule-based system—which is an altogether different approach to game AI.

Coordinating Multiple FSMs

Although much can be done with individual FSMs, sometimes it is convenient (or even essential) to have two or more FSMs working in concert. If you are building a game where characters act as a team (such as in a tactical FPS or most sports games), you almost certainly will need to establish coordination between multiple FSMs belonging to different characters. The simplest way to implement coordination is an implicit approach where individual team members, each with its own FSM, behave in a coordinated manner without any explicit "goals" or "tasks." The apparent complexity of character actions is an emergent property, finely tuned through gameplay [Snavely02, van der Sterren02a]. In military terms, this is the "tactical" level of execution. The next step up, called "operational," has an explicit representation for goals and plans. Typically, there exists a hidden character that observes the game world, decides what the team should do, and issues commands to team members through a messaging mechanism [van der Sterren02b] or direct manipulation of each team member's FSM queue.

Multiple FSMs can also be used within a single character, although this is somewhat less common. It can be extremely handy, though, for modeling very complex behavior such as that of a fighter pilot, who simultaneously is steering the plane, navigating, monitoring sensors for threats, communicating with friendly forces, and firing weapons. Combining all of this into a single FSM would be nearly impossible since it involves many simultaneous decision-making processes, and even if it were feasible, the resulting FSM would most likely be a tangled, unmaintainable mess. A much cleaner approach is simply to use several FSMs running in parallel within a single character, each of which handles one aspect of being a fighter pilot. Thus, you might have a steering FSM, a communications FSM, and a weapons control FSM, all of which are coordinated by a separate "commander" FSM. With this multi-FSM approach, you get simultaneous execution of the different behavioral subsystems for free, without having to manually build it into a single huge, massively interleaved FSM.

For the most part, coordination between multiple FSMs, whether inter- or intra-character, is similar to multithreaded programming. You must provide mechanisms such as semaphores or mutexes that FSMs can use to synchronize their actions. Generally, a framework for sharing information between FSMs is also important. A basic message-passing scheme is one option and can also double as a synchronization mechanism. Another common scheme is to provide shared memory spaces (sometime called *blackboards*) that can be written to and read from by multiple FSMs [Isla02, Orkin04]. Whatever your implementation, be wary of the usual pitfalls of multithreaded programming: deadlocks, race conditions, and simultaneous access to the same data by multiple FSMs.

Debugging FSMs

Errors can lurk in even the simplest FSM, regardless of how much forethought and design you put into it. Although in theory you might be able to track down AI bugs using your favorite C++ debugger, in practice this becomes a nightmare when you have hundreds of FSMs, each with dozens of states, all intimately interacting with other portions of the game engine. Be prudent, therefore, and build debugging facilities into your AI architecture from the beginning. It will save untold amounts of frustration and time.

At the very minimum, you should include logging facilities in your FSM architecture, preferably with a variable verbosity setting, so that after spotting a bug, you can trace the sequence of events that led up to it. Even if you have more sophisticated debugging facilities, simple logging can still be extremely useful, although it is strictly limited to after-the-fact analysis. If you want to be able to peer into the state of the AI engine while it is running, a console window with a basic command-line interface can give interactive access to a huge amount of data. It also gives you the power to interactively change the state of an FSM while the game is running to test hypotheses or possible fixes.

Another handy technique is to provide hooks into the game engine so that AI state information can be displayed in the game world itself [Tozour02b]. For example, in debug mode, game characters could be annotated with colors, symbols, or text that summarizes the current status of their FSMs. This technique makes it possible to debug a faulty behavior by following the character around in the game world and observing the changing annotations.

Summary

In this article, we provided a broad overview of how FSMs are used in games: the computational model, implementation, processing, optimizations, extensions, and debugging. What follows is a rundown of the salient points.

We started by describing the basic finite-state machine computational model, which basically consists of states and transitions. From there, we discussed three ways in which state machines can be implemented: hard coded, hard coded with macro assist, and scripting language. Hard coding is straightforward, but brittle and prone to bugs. Using macros in code helps organize the code, improves readability, and aids in debugging. The last method, a scripting language, is good to implement, as long as you do it correctly.

There are three processing models used for implementing FSMs in games. A polling approach is simplest, but can possibly lead to inefficiencies. Event-based systems are the most efficient, but require special infrastructure built into the game engine (as opposed to the AI engine). A thread-based approach involves separate threads for game engine and AI. Implementation, although conceptually intuitive, is nontrivial, and could lead to inefficiencies.

There are three ways to implement the interface between an FSM and game engine. The first consists of direct hard-coded function invocations. The second employs function pointers or callbacks. The last method, used for data-driven implementations, relies on unique identifiers that correspond to cases in a switch statement.

Although finite-state machines connote efficiency, their implementation often calls for optimization. One technique is to schedule processing so that FSMs do not get updated much more than necessary. Still, this is a rough approximation. Load-balancing can monitor FSM processing and prescribe schedules according to past performance. Time-bounded FSMs can be interrupted and re-entered. Another technique is to use a level-of-detail scheme that determines the necessary amount of processing so that the game player is none the wiser.

There were five extensions made to the basic FSM model. For states, "OnEnter" and "OnExit" blocks can be used for initialization and cleanup, respectively. Stack-based FSMs, perhaps more akin to push-down automata, allow characters to retain some "memory" of what they were doing so as to resume their activity later. Polymorphism was introduced as an object-oriented way to write state machines where we treat the character as the "object" and let the engine decide which version to run. We also defined fuzzy state machines, and covered multiple FSMs either for team-based AI or intra-character.

The last topic we covered on FSMs was debugging. Three methods were introduced: logging for after-action analysis, interactive debugging using a console or GUI, and annotations through the game world.

Conclusion

By now you realize that finite-state machines are much more useful than a regular expression would otherwise suggest. Obviously, a game FSM as described here is much more powerful than a theoretical FSM. Nevertheless, the basic notions of state and transition are the simplest to comprehend compared to any other approach to game AI. This, we believe, is the major reason why FSMs are so ubiquitous in games. The underlying computational model is simple, yet powerful enough to handle a wide range of desired behavior. Together with the numerous extensions we presented, FSMs have surpassed what one might normally expect from an FSM-based approach to game AI, yet still retain the essence of a simple machine.

Of course, FSMs aren't going to solve all your AI needs. Basic capabilities such as pathfinding, reasoning, or learning aren't really meant to be handled by FSMs (and probably shouldn't be). Still, the FSM will remain one big indispensable tool in the game programmer's toolbox. Finite-state machine work in the game community continually matures. The next three articles in this section show that FSMs are moving toward sophisticated computational and knowledge representation models that overcome deficiencies of traditionally implemented FSMs, yet maintain accessibility to designers and developers. This, we believe, is a good thing. Even though you can be extremely productive with FSMs, there's always room for improvement, and there's good reason to believe that the practical use of FSMs will remain on the cutting edge.

References

[Alexander02] Alexander, Bob, "An Architecture Based on Load-Balancing," *AI Game Programming Wisdom*, Charles River Media, 2002.

[Berger02a] Berger, Lee, "Scripting: Overview and Code Generation," *AI Game Programming Wisdom*, Charles River Media, 2002.

[Berger02b] Berger, Lee, "Scripting: The Interpreter Engine," *AI Game Programming Wisdom*, Charles River Media, 2002.

[Berger02c] Berger, Lee, "Scripting: System Integration," *AI Game Programming Wisdom*, Charles River Media, 2002.

[Brockington02] Brockington, Mark, "Level-of-Detail AI for a Large Role-Playing Game," *AI Game Programming Wisdom*, Charles River Media, 2002.

[Carlisle02] Carlisle, Phil, "Designing a GUI Tool to Aid in the Development of FSMs," *AI Game Programming Wisdom*, Charles River Media, 2002.

[Carter01] Carter, Simon, "Managing AI with Micro-Threads," *Game Programming Gems 2*, Charles River Media, 2001.

[Dawson01] Dawson, Bruce, "Micro-Threads for Game Object AI," *Game Programming Gems 2*, Charles River Media, 2001.

[Dybsand00] Dybsand, Eric, "A Finite-State Machine Class," *Game Programming Gems*, Charles River Media, 2000.

[Dybsand01] Dybsand, Eric, "A Generic Fuzzy State Machine in C++," *Game Programming Gems 2*, Charles River Media, 2001.

[Farris02] Farris, Charles, "Function Pointer-based, Embedded FSMs," *Game Programming Gems 3*, Charles River Media, 2002.

[Fowler00] Fowler, Martin, and Scott, Kendall, *UML Distilled*, Addison-Wesley, 2000.

[Fu02] Fu, Daniel, and Houlette, Ryan, "Putting AI in Entertainment: An AI Authoring Tool for Simulation and Games," IEEE Intelligent Systems 17(4):81–84, 2001. *www.computer.org/ intelligent/ ex2002/ x4toc.htm*

[Grossman03] Grossman, Austin (ed.), *Postmortems from Game Developer*, CMP Books, San Francisco, 2003.

[Houlette01] Houlette, Ryan, Fu, Daniel, and Ross, David, "Towards an AI Behavior Toolkit for Games," AAAI Spring Symposium on AI and Interactive Entertainment, 2001. *www.qrg.northwestern.edu/ aigames.org/ 2001papers.html*

[Isla02] Isla, Damian, and Blumberg, Bruce, "Blackboard Architectures," *AI Game Programming Wisdom*, Charles River Media, 2002.

[Klir95] Klir, George J., and Yuan, Bo, *Fuzzy Sets & Fuzzy Logic: Theory & Applications*, Prentice Hall, 1995.

[McCuskey00] McCuskey, Mason, "Fuzzy Logic for Video Games," *Game Programming Gems*, Charles River Media, 2000.

[Orkin04] Orkin, Jeff, "Simple Techniques for Coordinated Behavior," *AI Game Programming Wisdom 2*, Charles River Media, 2004.

[Pelletier01] Pelletier, Brian, Gummelt, Michael, and Monroe, James, "Postmortem: Raven Software's Star Trek: Voyager—Elite Force," *Game Developer Magazine*, January, 2001. Also appears in [Grossman03].

[Rabin00] Rabin, Steve, "Designing a General Robust AI Engine," *Game Programming Gems*, Charles River Media, 2000.

[Rabin02a] Rabin, Steve, "Implementing a State Machine Language," *AI Game Programming Wisdom*, Charles River Media, 2002.

[Rabin02b] Rabin, Steve, "Enhancing a State Machine Language through Messaging," *AI Game Programming Wisdom*, Charles River Media, 2002.

[Rosado04] Rosado, Gilberto, "Implementing a Data-Driven Finite-State Machine," *AI Game Programming Wisdom 2*, Charles River Media, 2004.

[Snavely02] Snavely, P.J., "Agent Cooperation in FSMs for Baseball," *AI Game Programming Wisdom*, Charles River Media, 2002.

[Tozour02a] Tozour, Paul, "The Perils of AI Scripting," *AI Game Programming Wisdom*, Charles River Media, 2002.

[Tozour02b] Tozour, Paul, "Building an AI Diagnostic Toolset," *AI Game Programming Wisdom*, Charles River Media, 2002.

[Tozour04] Tozour, Paul, "Stack-based Finite-State Machines," *AI Game Programming Wisdom 2*, Charles River Media, 2004.

[van der Sterren02a] van der Sterren, William, "Squad Tactics: Team AI and Emergent Maneuvers," *AI Game Programming Wisdom*, Charles River Media, 2002.

[van der Sterren02b] van der Sterren, William, "Squad Tactics: Planned Maneuvers," *AI Game Programming Wisdom*, Charles River Media, 2002.

[Woodcock99] Woodcock, Steve, "Game AI: The State of the Industry," *Game Developer Magazine*, August, 1999.

[Yiskis04] Yiskis, Eric, "Finite-State Machine Scripting Language for Designers," *AI Game Programming Wisdom 2*, Charles River Media, 2004.

Stack-Based Finite-State Machines

Paul Tozour—Retro Studios

gehn29@yahoo.com

The *finite-state machine* (FSM) is a simple and very popular technique for modeling AI behaviors. A finite-state machine consists of a finite number of *states* connected via *transitions* [Fu03]. Each state represents a behavior that the AI character can execute.

Let's imagine we want to model behaviors for a guard character in a "first-person sneaker" game such as the seminal sneaker *Thief: The Dark Project* [LGS98]. Normally, the guard is idle, and he will simply stand around and guard the area. The level designer might also decide to assign him to a patrol, which will cause the guard to walk around the level on a scripted patrol path.

The guard will spend most of his time "idling" or following a patrol path. The player can stimulate the guard by making noise or allowing the guard to see him. If the guard is stimulated sufficiently, he will attempt to find the player by searching the area. As soon as the guard can see the player clearly, he will draw his sword and engage in combat. Figure 5.2.1 demonstrates what this finite-state machine might look like.

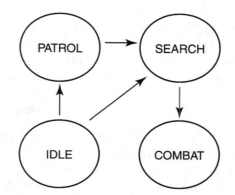

FIGURE 5.2.1 *A simple finite-state machine for a guard in a stealth-oriented game.*

Backtracking

The FSM shown in Figure 5.2.1 may appear correct, but it has one major flaw: it only models behavior transitions in the forward direction. Once the guard enters the Combat state, there's no way for him to leave combat, so he will continue to swing his sword long after the player has escaped. In the real world, we would need to add more transitions to allow the guard to exit combat and resume searching if the player escapes. Similarly, if the guard searches for a while and fails to find the player, he needs to either resume his patrol or return to his guard post.

This raises an interesting question. Imagine that our guard hears the player's footsteps and begins searching for him (that is, he enters the Search state). After a thorough search, he fails to uncover anything suspicious. At this point, how does the guard know whether to go back to his patrol or return to standing guard? He needs some way to remember whether he was idling or patrolling, and in either case, he must remember the spot he was guarding or the section of the patrol path he was walking on.

It would be possible to do this with a traditional finite-state machine, but it would be very cumbersome. We would need to make duplicate versions of the Search and Combat states depending on whether we entered the Search state from an Idle state or a Patrol state. For example, we'd need to make SearchFromPatrol and CombatFromPatrol for the cases where we entered Search and Combat from a Patrol state, and SearchFromIdle and CombatFromIdle to handle entering those states from Idle.

Clearly, trying to solve our problem by cloning existing states would quickly lead to a combinatorial explosion of new states as our finite-state machine grew more complex.

The State Stack

The crux of the problem is that a traditional FSM can only track a single state. As soon as you perform a transition, all information about previous states is lost.

We can fix this by enhancing our FSMs with a *state stack*. Whenever we perform a state transition, we allow the option of pushing the new state onto the top of a stack. The previous state remains in the stack, waiting to be reactivated. At any given moment, only the topmost state in the stack is active. To return to the previous behavior, all we need to do is pop the topmost state off the stack. The next lowest state thus becomes the active state and resumes execution.

This also allows us to support three possible types of transitions between states:

- **Push:** Push the target state onto the top of the stack.
- **Pop:** Pop this state off the stack.
- **Replace:** Replace the current state with the target state as the topmost state in the stack. This is equivalent to a "pop" immediately followed by a "push."

Note that stack-based FSMs are essentially identical to a form of context-free languages called *push-down automata* (PDA) [Autebert97].

It's important to remember that a stack-based finite-state machine is merely an extension of the concept of a standard FSM. You can always implement a standard FSM within a stack-based FSM by using only "replace" transitions.

Let's return to our hypothetical guard. He begins in the Idle state and then goes into the Patrol state. We therefore push the Patrol state onto the stack: Patrol is now the topmost state, and Idle is below it. When he begins searching for the player, he pushes the Search state, and when he enters combat, he pushes the Combat state. Figure 5.2.2 shows what the guard's state stack looks like at this point.

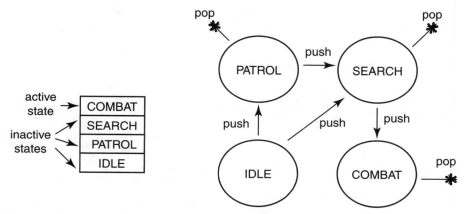

FIGURE 5.2.2 *A sample state stack (left) for a stack-based FSM (right).*

Let's imagine that at a certain point in combat, the player manages to escape. We therefore pop the Combat state off the stack. Search now becomes the active state, and the guard resumes his search of the area. After a thorough search, he fails to find the player, so he pops Search off the stack and resumes his Patrol at the appropriate patrol point. Furthermore, if we assume the patrol is noncircular, once the guard reaches the end of the patrol path, he returns to the Idle state and begins guarding the area.

Conclusion

Finite-state machines are a simple and powerful method for modeling AI behaviors. However, they do not have any inherent support for resuming past behaviors by backtracking along the FSM graph. A stack-based finite-state machine corrects this deficiency by adding a state stack and adding new transition types that allow us to specify how the stack should be manipulated when a transition occurs.

References

[Autebert97] Autebert, Jean-Michel, Berstel, Jean, and Boasson, Luc, "Context-free Languages and Pushdown Automata," *Handbook of Formal Languages*, Volume I, Chapter 3. Springer Verlag, Berlin Heidelberg, 1997.

[Fu03] Fu, Dan, and Houlette, Ryan, "The Ultimate Guide to FSMs in Games," *AI Game Programming Wisdom 2*, Charles River Media, 2003.

[LGS98] *Thief: The Dark Project,* Looking Glass Studios/Eidos Interactive, 1998. See *www.eidosinteractive.com*

5.3

Implementing a Data-Driven Finite-State Machine

Gilberto Rosado—DigiPen Institute of Technology

grosado@digipen.edu, grosado716@hotmail.com

*F**inite-state machines* (FSMs) are very popular for implementing game AI character behavior. FSMs are used to specify what AI characters should be doing at any given time and how they should react to in-game events and player actions. Even though FSMs are most commonly associated with AI programming, they are perfectly suitable for other programming problems that require dynamic behavior at runtime.

When programming the dynamic behavior of AI characters, it is desirable to keep as much of the logic out of the code as it is possible. By being able to specify an FSM's state transition logic from outside of the program, the AI designer can quickly tweak an AI character's behavior without having to recompile any source code. Another benefit to this approach is that two or more AI characters can have different behaviors, but share the exact same code; just use different data files to define each character's behavior.

This article presents a bit of wisdom on how to implement a data-driven state machine. A data-driven FSM implementation should be able to:

- Instantiate a custom FSM whose states and state transition logic are defined in an external data file.
- Provide functionality for state-specific callback functions for entering, updating, and exiting a state.
- Handle the addition of possible states with minimal coding.

The Structure of a Finite-State Machine

Before considering how to implement an FSM class, it is important to define the structure of an FSM. An FSM is a collection of states that define the current behavior of the AI character, as well as the conditions that will effect a transition to another state. A transition is represented by a set of conditions, and an output state for the FSM to transition to when the conditions are met. Conditions drive the FSM, as they define the logic for state transitions. Conditions can be defined as a Boolean expression involving game variables, such as player health or enemy distance. For example, if an FSM was in a Chase Enemy state, then it might transition into an Attack Enemy state when the condition is met of being within 10 meters of the enemy. For more on the theory behind FSMs, see [Fu04].

Figure 5.3.1 shows an example of a finite-state machine that models the behavior of a hypothetical AI character in an action game. The FSM states are shown by rectangles. Each state has a number of transitions, shown as circles with arrows pointing to an output state. Each transition has a number indicating the order in which it must be evaluated when testing for a change of state. Inside of a transition is a set of conditions that must evaluate to true in order for the state machine to enter to a new state.

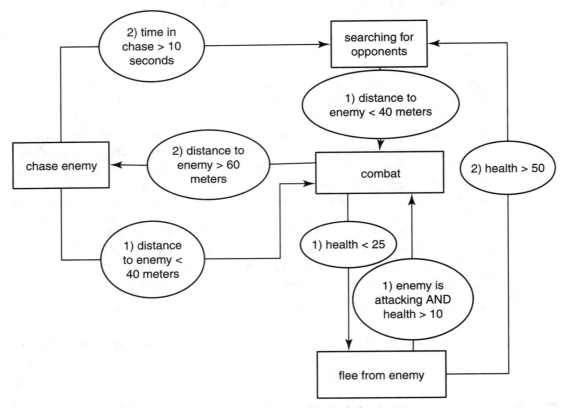

FIGURE 5.3.1   *Finite-state machine diagram of a hypothetical character.*

An FSM can be defined in text format. We will define a single state using the following format:

```
[STATE_NUMBER]
STATE = STATE_NAME
CONDITION_NUMBER_VARIABLE = FSM_VARIABLE
CONDITION_NUMBER_FUNC = FSM_FUNCTION
```

```
CONDITION_NUMBER_VAL = VALUE
OUTPUT_STATE_NUMBER = OUTPUT_STATE_NAME
```

The FSM file format illustrated in this article supports conjunction of conditions; for example, condition1 AND condition2 must evaluate to true. Disjunction (condition1 OR condition2) can be achieved by using two separate conditions with the same output state. Using our FSM file format, the FSM's flee state from Figure 5.3.1 can be defined like so:

```
[STATE_2]
STATE = FLEE
CONDITION_0_VAR = ENEMY_STATE
CONDITION_0_FUNC = EQUALS
CONDITION_0_VAL = ATTACKING_ME

CONDITION_0_1_VAR = HEALTH
CONDITION_0_1_FUNC = GREATER_THAN
CONDITION_0_1_VAL = 10
OUTPUT_STATE_0 = COMBAT

CONDITION_1_VAR = HEALTH
CONDITION_1_FUNC = GREATER_THAN
CONDITION_1_VAL = 50
OUTPUT_STATE_1 = SEARCHING
```

Loading the FSM Files

In the implementation presented in the sample code, the names of the states, variables, and functions are stored in C/C++ enums. When loading the input file, string comparisons are performed in order to find the appropriate enum value for the state, function, or variable name. This could be a potential problem, since adding a state name or variable type to the enums could require adding code to the loading function. However, it is easy to automate the string comparison functions by using some of the C macro tricks illustrated in Steve Rabin's article "Finding Redeeming Value in C-Style Macros" [Rabin02b]. This method is illustrated in the sample code.

The Condition and Transition Classes

The FSMCondition and FSMTransition class definitions come directly from the FSM file format. We will look at the FSM state class further along in this article, but for now remember that the FSM state class will have a collection of FSMTransitions that it will use to determine if there needs to be a state change based on the current status of the FSM's owner. The following are C++ classes for the FSM transitions and conditions:

```
class FSMCondition
{
public:
    FSM_VARIABLES variable;
```

```
        FSM_FUNCTIONS function;
        int value;

    bool ConditionFulfilled(int value)
    {
        switch (function)
        {
            case EQUALS:
                return input_value == value;

            case NOT_EQUALS:
                return input_value != value;

            case GREATER_THAN:
                return input_value > value;

            case LESS_THAN:
                    return input_value < value;

            default:
                return false;
        }
    }
    };

    class FSMTransition
    {
    public:
        //container of FSMConditions
        std::vector<FSMCondition> m_conditions;
        FSM_STATE_NAME           m_outputState;

        //adds a condition to the transition
        void AddCondition(FSMCondition condition)
        {
            m_conditions.push_back(condition);
        }

        //sets the output state variable
        void SetOutputState(FSM_STATE_NAME output_state);

        //returns the first condition
        std::vector<FSMCondition>::iterator
        GetConditionsBegin()
        {
            return m_conditions.begin();
        }

        //returns the end iterator of condition container
        std::vector<FSMCondition>::iterator
        GetConditionsEnd()
        {
            return m_conditions.end();
        }
    };
```

Special attention should be given to the `FSMCondition::ConditionFulfilled()` function, which will be used when evaluating state transitions. `ConditionFulfilled()` compares the input value against its own condition value using the condition function and returns true if the condition has been met. While the implementation presented here shows only simple functions such as greater than, less than, and equals, it can be modified to implement any other function that takes an input value and has a Boolean return value.

The `FSMTransition` class contains a collection of `FSMCondition` objects, and provides a way to iterate through all of the them through the `GetConditionsBegin()` and `GetConditionsEnd()` member functions. These two functions will allow the FSM class to test all of the conditions contained within the current state's collection of `FSMTransition` objects, and effect a change of state once all of the conditions of a particular state transition evaluate to true.

Implementing the FSM State Objects (TFSMState)

To implement a data-driven FSM, it is important for the FSM state objects to be able to dynamically allocate FSM transition objects at runtime. Therefore, an `AddFSMTransition()` function will be required. It is possible to store pointers to `FSMTransition` objects, or just store the `FSMTransition` objects in the FSM state class itself using a Standard Template Library (STL) container. An STL container is preferred for the FSM state class, since using STL requires no memory management by the programmer.

Whatever container the FSM state class uses to keep the `FSMTransition` objects, it is important that it maintains them in the order in which they were inserted, as that is the order in which the `FSMTransitions` will be evaluated at runtime. Both the STL `std::list` and `std::vector` containers provide this functionality.

Adding State-Specific Code to the FSM State Class

When implementing any state machine class, it is important to be able to specify specific sections of code to execute while entering or exiting a state. This is necessary if a state might need to allocate memory or change some of the class' member variables on entering a state or if cleanup needs to be done when exiting out of state. One might also want to have some code be performed every game tick while the state machine is in a particular state.

A common approach for executing state specific code is the "switch statement implementation." There are potential problems when using the "switch" implementation such as forgetting breaks and, for FSMs with many states, potentially slow execution. Approaches that are more elegant include creating mini state machine languages [Rabin00, Rabin02a] and using function pointers [Farris02]. For this particular implementation, a method similar to the one presented in [Farris02] is used.

The `OnEnter()`, `OnUpdate()`, and `OnExit()` functions associated with each state will be implemented in the classes that have a state machine object as a member variable. In order for the TFSMState class to be able to call these class-specific functions, it must use pointers to member functions. A problem with using pointers to member functions is that you must know the name of the class that implements the function, as well as have a pointer to an instance of that class. However, this problem can be solved by using templates. (See [Farris02] for a discussion of using pointers to member functions.)

The following is the partial definition of the template class TFSMState:

```
template <class T>
class TFSMState
{
    typedef std::vector<FSMTransition> TransitionVector;
    TransitionVector m_transitionsVector;

    FSM_STATE_NAME m_stateName;

public:
    //get iterator to the first transition
    TransitionVector::iterator GetTransitionsBegin();

    //get the end iterator of the transitions
    TransitionVector::iterator GetTransitionsEnd();

    //add a transition to the state
    void AddFSMTransition(FSMTransition transition);

    //sets the functions associated with this state
    void SetStateFunctions(T* pInstance, PMemFunc pOnEnter,
    PMemFunc pOnUpdate, PMemFunc pOnExit);

    //calls the OnEnter, OnExit, or OnUpdate functions
    //using the pointers to member functions
    void OnEnter();
    void OnUpdate();
    void OnExit();
};
```

GetTransitionsBegin() and GetTransitionsEnd() provide access to the FSMTransition container through std::iterators. These functions will allow the FSM class to iterate through all of the FSMTransitions of the current state in order to test if there needs to be a change of state.

SetFunctions() is used to store pointers to member functions that will be called when entering, exiting, and updating a state. The first parameter is the *this* pointer of the class that owns the functions, and the other parameters are the respective callback functions.

The Finite-State Machine Class (TFSM)

The FSM class is the top-level class of the data-driven FSM architecture, as well as the only FSM-related class that the client needs to use. Its functions include instantiating a unique FSM based on the FSM data file, evaluating the current state's transition conditions, and calling the OnEnter(), OnUpdate(), and OnExit() state functions during state transitions and game updates.

The TFSM class stores an STL map of TFSMStates with the state name enum value as the key. The STL map container stores value-data pairs that are sorted according to the value, hence called the "key." In addition, the STL map retrieval algorithm is $O(lg(n))$, providing for inexpensive look-ups at runtime. For in-depth discussion on the STL map containers, consult either [Stroustrup97] or [Boer00].

Since our TFSMState objects are templates, the FSM class must be a template also. This is required in order to use pointers to member functions from arbitrary classes. The following is the partial definition for the TFSM class:

```
template <class T>
class TFSM
{
    typedef TFSMState<T> State;
    typedef map<FSM_STATE_NAME, State, less<int>
    StateMap;

    //map containing all states of this FSM
    StateMap m_statesMap;

    //name of current state
    FSM_STATE_NAME m_currentState;

    //adds a new state to the state machine
    void AddState( State new_state );

    //keep a map of variable callback functions,
    //using the name of the variable as the key
    typedef int(T::*PIFUNC)(void);
    typedef map<FSM_VARIABLES, PIFUNC> IntVariableMap;
    IntVariableMap m_intVariableMap;

public:
    //sets the OnEnter, OnUpdate, and OnExit functions
    //of the FSM states
    void AddStateFunctions(T* p_instance,
    FSM_STATE_NAME state_name,
    PFUNC p_OnEnter, PFUNC p_OnUpdate,
    PFUNC p_OnExit);

    //adds a callback function to get the current
    //state of a variable
    void AddVariableFunction(T* p_instance,
    FSM_VARIABLES var_name, PIFUNC var_func);

    //evaluates the transitions of the active state to
    //see if there need to be a state change
    FSM_STATE_NAME EvaluateCurrentStateTransitions();

    //Executes the OnUpdate() function for the active
```

```
        //state
        void ExecuteStateMachine();

        void LoadStateMachine(LPCSTR file_name);
    };
```

The AddStateFunctions() method is used to set the OnEnter(), OnExit(), and OnUpdate() functions for the state specified in the second parameter. This function would be called, after loading the state machine, for every state that the FSM wants to handle.

The member variable, m_intVariableMap, is an STL std::map that stores pointers to member functions returning int (with the FSM variable type as the key) used to get the current value of the variables that will be used when evaluating state transitions. A downside of this approach is the many accessor functions that will have to be written for the TFSM to be able to access the current state of the object using the TFSM class. However, this approach completely automates the state transition evaluation process. It is important to note that while the return type of these functions is int, a container of functions returning other types such as float or bool can be used as well.

The EvaluateCurrentStateTransitions() function handles all the transitions from one state to another. The function iterates through all of the FSMTransitions of the active TFSMState object. For all FSMTransitions of the current state, all of the FSMConditions are evaluated. If, for any FSMTransition, all of its conditions are met, then the TFSM class will effect a state change.

The last member function listed, LoadStateMachine(), loads the finite-state machine logic from an external data file. When loading the state machine from a file, one can instantiate a local TFSMState, add transitions to it by using the TFSMState's AddTransition() function, and pass it by value into the AddState() function, where it will be copied into the TFSM's map of TFSMStates.

Using the TFSM Class

To use the TFSM class, one must declare an instance of it using the name of the class that owns it as the template parameter. The FSM data file is then read at initialization time, and the state-specific functions and variable accessor functions are defined. Let us look at an example of a class that has an instance of a TFSM and how it uses it. For simplicity, a class representing a flashing light bulb is shown. The following is the partial definition of the CLightBulb class:

```
class CLightBulb
{
public :
    //declare the TFSM object
    TFSM<CLightBulb> m_stateMachine;

    //on state functions
```

```
                    void BeginOnState();
                    void UpdateOnState();
                    void ExitOnState();

                    //off state functions
                    void BeginOffState();
                    void UpdateOffState();
                    void ExitOffState();

                    //accessor function to get the time since the
                    //light bulb was turned on or off
                    int GetTime();

                    //constructor
                    CLightBulb()
                    {
                        //load state machine file
                        m_stateMachine.LoadStateMachine("light.fsm");

                        //define functions for on state
                        m_stateMachine.AddStateFunctions(this,FSMS_ON,
                        BeginOnState, UpdateOnState, ExitOnState);

                        //define functions for off state
                        m_stateMachine.AddStateFunctions(this,
                        FSMS_OFF, BeginOffState, UpdateOffState,
                        ExitOffState);

                        //define function to get the time variable
                        m_stateMachine.AddVariableFunction(this, TIME,
                        GetTime);
                    }

                    void Update()
                    {
                        //evaluates the state transitions of the
                        //active state
                        m_stateMachine.
                        EvaluateCurrentStateTransitions();

                        //call the active state's update function
                        m_stateMachine.ExecuteStateMachine();
                    }
                };
```

Here is the FSM data file for the light bulb:

```
 [STATE_0]
STATE = FSMS_ON
CONDITION_0_VAR = TIME
CONDITION_0_FUNC = GREATER_THAN
CONDITION_0_VAL = 1000
OUTPUT_STATE_0 = FSMS_OFF
```

```
[STATE_1]
STATE = FSMS_OFF
CONDITION_0_VAR = TIME
CONDITION_0_FUNC = GREATER_THAN
CONDITION_0_VAL = 1000
OUTPUT_STATE_0 = FSMS_ON
```

The light bulb FSM data file defines two states: ON and OFF. Both states have a condition of time being greater than 1000 milliseconds in order for the FSM to transition to the output state.

Enhancements

Some possible enhancements to this finite-state machine implementation include more complex transition functions, and more value types for the condition variables such as float or strings for enumerated ranges, like those in fuzzy logic. The addition of probabilities in state transitions would be a great enhancement to the architecture. Another enhancement would be to implement a visual editor to aid in the making of the state machine files. Using an editor would eliminate potential mistakes in the state machine's files such as spelling errors. Another method of eliminating errors in the files would be to use a preprocessing program that checks the file's validity.

Conclusion

Undoubtedly, finite-state machines are useful for many programming tasks, especially game AI programming. This article presented an FSM class that allows developers to define state transition logic through outside data, allowing for dynamic behavior as well as quick tweaking of state machine logic, all without having to recompile the game. The TFSM class allows functions to be specified for use when entering and exiting states as well as for code to be executed per game tick, allowing for clean and modular coding. While any addition of states or conditional variables will require additional coding, once they are set up, the state transition logic can be changed through the data files.

While the FSM class presented here is not as full featured as a scripting language, it strikes a nice balance between the game code and data-driven programmability. Whatever approach you decide to take in implementing an FSM class, do not overlook the power that a data-driven design can bring to your state machines.

ON THE CD

The code provided on the accompanying CD-ROM has the full TFSM implementation, as well as the light bulb example. Another example of a TFSM state machine is in the source code, in which the main() function is implemented using a data-driven FSM. When running the application, try experimenting with the ".fsm" file to change the time between light bulb flashes, application time of execution, and application update frequency.

References

[Boer00] Boer, James, "Using the STL in Game Programming," *Game Programming Gems*, Charles River Media, 2000.

[Farris02] Farris, Charles, "Function Pointer-Based, Embedded Finite State Machines," *Game Programming Gems 3*, Charles River Media, 2002.

[Fu04] Fu, Dan, and Houlette, Ryan, "The Ultimate Guide to FSMs in Games," *AI Game Programming Wisdom 2*, Charles River Media, 2004.

[Rabin00] Rabin, Steve, "Designing a General Robust AI Engine," *Game Programming Gems*, Charles River Media, 2000.

[Rabin02a] Rabin, Steve, "Implementing a State Machine Language," *AI Game Programming Wisdom*, Charles River Media, 2002.

[Rabin02b] Rabin, Steve, "Finding Redeeming Value in C-Style Macros," *Game Programming Gems 3*, Charles River Media, 2002.

[Stroustrup97] Stroustrup, Bjarne, *The C++ Programming Language*, Third Edition, Addison-Wesley Longman, 1998.

5.4

Finite-State Machine Scripting Language for Designers

Eric Yiskis—Sammy Studios

erk1024@hotmail.com

Giving better tools to game designers leads to better games; this is especially true with AI, which embodies much of the gameplay. AI is often implemented with finite-state machines (FSMs) [LaMothe02, Fu04] or layers of finite-state machines [Yiskis04], making it difficult for the game designers to edit. Graphical approaches have been attempted with limited success. Once you have more than a handful of states and transitions, the diagram of the system becomes a rat's nest of jumbled, confusing lines.

This article describes how to create a high-level custom scripting language with finite-state machine qualities built into the grammar. This allows the designer to create states and transitions in an intuitive way, without having to understand and implement the FSM algorithm. Through the use of blocking commands, the language is able to communicate with other FSM layers in the system. The language can *push* and *pop* states, extending the system to a pushdown automata (PDA). This is useful for reducing the number of states and it permits the system to remember states.

Design Assumptions

There are a wide variety of finite-state machine implementations. Looking at a collection of FSMs for AI, recurring patterns can be recognized (see Figure 5.4.1). Often the states are grouped and transitioned sequentially as they are completed. Each state in the sequence has the same set of transitions: if you see an enemy, attack; if you hear a noise, investigate; if you are low on health, flee.

In designing a language to represent such finite-state machines, we want to incorporate support for these recurring patterns into the language's syntax to assist designers in creating the AI. This leads to the design assumptions discussed next.

High-Level Sequential Commands

The designers are implementing high-level logic: normal behavior, reactions to events, and tactics used against the player. In most cases, this takes the form of a sequence of actions. Here is the sequence from Figure 5.4.1:

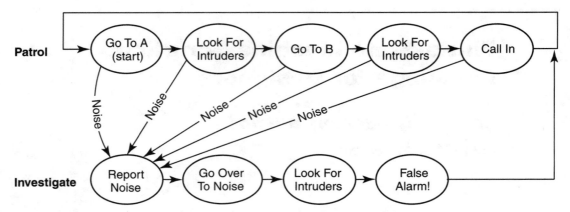

FIGURE 5.4.1   *Example of an AI finite-state machine. Each oval represents a state with arrows representing transitions.*

    1) Go to location "A"
    2) Look for intruders for two seconds
    3) Go to location "B"
    4) Look for intruders for two seconds
    5) Call in on the radio: "Sector 3 secure!"
    6) Repeat

Each of the steps in the sequence is going to take many frames (passes through the main game loop) to achieve. We certainly don't want the designer to write code such as:

```
switch(step) {
    case 1:
        if (GoToLocation("A") == kDone) then
            step = 2;
        break;
```

The point of writing a scripting language to create FSMs is to free the designer from having to manage state information. The solution is to use blocking commands. We write a command "go to location" that blocks until the character is within a threshold distance to the desired location.

Behaviors

In the Patrol sequence, transitions to a different sequence are generally the same no matter which step the sequence is in. For example, if the guard hears a suspicious noise, it doesn't matter if the guard is performing "Look for intruders" or "Go to location B," the reaction is going to be the same: investigate the sound. To simplify this, we need a way to associate a single transition with a set of states.

Transitions, if triggered, must happen immediately even though the sequence is currently blocked on one of its commands. This means the transitions must be tested every frame during gameplay.

It makes sense to group a sequence of states together with a common set of transitions in to a single behavior state. While a behavior executes, it carries out the sequence one step at a time, and every frame it checks for transitions to another behavior. This arrangement makes the state diagram (and implementation) much cleaner and easier to conceptualize (see Figure 5.4.2).

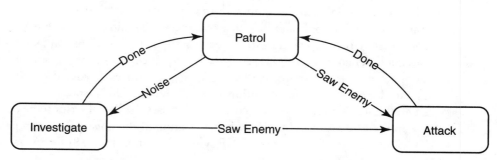

FIGURE 5.4.2 *Behaviors simplify the state diagram. Each box represents a behavior.*

The Grammar

With behaviors as our building block, we design a language to implement them. Inside each behavior script is a section of code that can take sequential commands, and a section for the transitions. We model the syntax after a language that already exists—like BASIC—to make it easier for someone with programming experience. Here is an example script for the Patrol behavior:

```
Behavior Patrol
begin

variable
    integer targetActor

transition
    # Listen for a noise
    if (SuspiciousNoise())
        switch ("Investigate",NoiseLocation())

    # Look for enemies
    set targetActor to LookFor(alive,enemy)
    if (targetActor)
        switch ("Attack",targetActor)

sequence

    # Patrol
```

```
        do forever
        begin
            goto GetLocation("WaypointA") walk
            idle 2
            goto GetLocation("WaypointB") walk
            idle 2
            playanimation "RadioCheckIn"
        end
    end
```

The goto, idle, and playanimation commands are all blocking commands. There can be nonblocking commands in the sequence section as well. However, in the transition section, only nonblocking commands are allowed. There has to be a variable section before the transition section so that transitions can set and retrieve variables. When this script is executed, the sequence section goes from one command to another as they complete. During this time (on each pass through the game's update loop), the entire transition section executes. If "suspicious noise" becomes true, the switch command is executed. This causes the Patrol script to be dumped and the Investigate script to be run with the location of the noise passed as a parameter.

The next listing is a sample BNF syntax definition [Aho88] for the language.

```
FSM Language Grammar

Notes:
 0..n* means zero or any number of a syntax elements.
 Anything in brackets [ ] is optional.
 A backslash "\" continues the previous line.

<script> ::         behavior <identifier> [(<var decl list>)] \
                    begin [variable 0..n*<variable decl>] \
                    [transition 0..n<command>] sequence \
                    0..n*<command> end

<variable decl> ::  <type> <identifier>
<type> ::           integer
                    float
                    vector

<var decl list> ::  <variable decl>
                    <var decl list>, <variable decl>

<command> ::        do forever <command>
                    if (<expr>) then <command> [else <command>]
                    begin 0..n*<command> end
                    switch( <expr list> )
                    exit

<expr> ::           <predef func>
                    <constant>

<expr list> ::      <expr>
                    <expr list>, <expr>
```

```
<predef func> ::      LookFor(<lookfor adj. list>)
                      SuspiciousNoise()
                      NoiseLocation()
```

Implementation

With the grammar in hand, the compiler and virtual machine classes can be implemented. The techniques required to implement the compiler are beyond the scope of this article; there are many good books on the subject [Mak96, Aho88]. Let's assume that the compiler generates a binary executable and a symbol table. The compiler first parses the transition section (if present), and puts an exit instruction at the end of it. A flag is stored there if no transition section exists. The compiler saves the location of the start of the sequence section and parses it.

The execution is "re-entrant," which means that each time through the game's update loop, the virtual machine continues running the script where it left off. First, it runs the entire transition section, and then it starts executing the sequence section with a program counter saved from the previous execution. Here is the pseudocode to execute a behavior:

```
if (state == kSwitch)
{
    delete current script
    setup new script
    SavedProgramCounter = StartOfSequenceBlock
    state = kRunning
}

if (TransitionBlockFlag)
{
    pInstruction = CodeBuffer
    while (state == kRunning)
        state = Execute(pInstruction)
}

if (state == kSwitch)
    return;

pInstruction = SavedProgramCounter
while (state == kRunning)
    state = Execute(pInstruction)

SavedProgramCounter = pInstruction
```

In this code, a pointer to the current instruction acts as the program counter. When Execute() is called, it modifies the instruction pointer. Usually, Execute() just advances the pointer to the next instruction. In the case of a blocking command, the pointer is only advanced if the instruction is complete. In a loop, Execute() conditionally sets the pointer to the top of the loop [Berger02].

Switch-script commands can occur in either the transition or the sequence section. If a switch is executed in the transition section, the virtual machine exits and starts up the new script in the next update pass. Nonblocking infinite loops will stall the game, so the sequence section must contain a blocking command or an explicit call to exit inside loops. In the case of the patrol script, goto and idle are both blocking commands so even though the loop is infinite (do forever), the script will not stall the game. To be safe, the virtual machine can check the number of instructions executed in a single frame, and if the number becomes too great (~1000), the script can be halted.

Remembering Behaviors

When AI is implemented with an FSM, the character switches states in response to events. The problem is that the character forgets what it was doing before the events occurred. One solution to this is to divide up the character's behaviors into layers. For example, with the guard, there could be a layer of "normal activity." On this layer, the guard patrols, gossips with other guards, and does other guard-like duties. The next layer consists of "engage enemy" activity: investigating, attacking, or responding to an alarm if one sounds. When the character is finished "engaging the enemy," we want it to go back to what it was doing in the "normal activity" layer (see Figure 5.4.3).

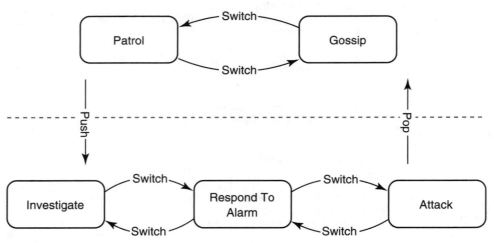

FIGURE 5.4.3   *Using a pushdown automata (PDA) to make layers.*

To implement this in the scripting language, we add the ability to push and pop scripts as well as switch. Any time a behavior in the "normal activity" layer detects an enemy, it pushes the new behavior on to the stack. The behavior it pushes might switch to another "engage" behavior before the enemy is dispatched. As soon as there are no enemies in the area, the engage behavior pops itself off the stack to return to the "normal activity."

With the ability to push and pop states, the system is technically now a PDA. To implement this in the virtual machine, it has a stack on which the symbol table and program counter for dormant scripts are stored. Whenever it executes, it simply runs the script at the top of the stack.

Sample Code

ON THE CD

Sample code for the compiler and virtual machine objects is supplied on the accompanying CD-ROM. It implements the PDA version of the system. Many implementation details couldn't be covered in this article, so take the opportunity to look through the code.

Conclusion

Looking at typical AI FSMs, there are design patterns that occur repeatedly. We can use these patterns to make a custom scripting language that is both powerful and approachable for designers. Through the use of blocking commands, sequences, and shared transitions, complex AI can be written without the scaffolding that usually accompanies FSM creation. The architecture can be further extended into a PDA so that characters have better memory of previous behaviors.

References

[Aho88] Aho, A., Sethi, R., and Ullman, J., "Syntax Definition," *Compilers: Principles, Techniques and Tools*, 1988.

[Berger02] Berger, Lee, "Scripting: The Interpreter Engine," *AI Game Programming Wisdom*, Charles River Media, 2002.

[Fu04] Fu, Dan, and Houlette, Ryan, "The Ultimate Guide to FSMs in Games," *AI Game Programming Wisdom 2*, Charles River Media, 2004.

[LaMothe02] LaMothe, André, "Finite State Machines," *Tricks of the Windows Game Programming Gurus Second Edition*, Sams Publishing (Macmillian), 2002, pp. 737–742.

[Mak96] Mak, Ronald, *Writing Compilers and Interpreters, An Applied Approach Using C++ (Second Edition)*, 1996.

[Yiskis04] Yiskis, Eric, "A Subsumption Architecture for Character-Based Games," *AI Game Programming Wisdom 2*, Charles River Media, 2004.

A Subsumption Architecture for Character-Based Games

Eric Yiskis—Sammy Studios

erk1024@hotmail.com

> **subsume** (*transitive verb*)
>
> *"To classify, include, or incorporate in a more comprehensive category or under a general principle."*
>
> —The American Heritage® Dictionary of the English Language, Fourth Edition

Character-based games use the most complex AI we can devise. Our goal is to make the AI opponents move, react, and think like real human beings—and as computers are not yet sentient, this can be a daunting task. We must write code to answer everything from high-level issues such as "How do I flank a group of soldiers behind cover?" to very low-level issues such as "Where do I put my foot in order to walk?" Implementing the solutions to these issues as a monolithic state machine or set of heuristics leads to fragile AI and a system that is hard to extend and maintain.

A subsumption architecture [Arkin98] cleanly decomposes the implementation into concurrently executing layers of finite-state machines (FSMs) [Fu04, LaMothe02]. Lower layers take care of immediate goals, and upper layers take care of long-term goals. The architecture solves three major problems with character AI: interruptions causing a character to forget what it was doing, characters getting stuck on obsolete goals, and robust handling of animation and character physics.

Robotic Roots

In 1986, Rodney Brooks published a paper describing a radical new approach to robot AI, emphasizing ongoing interaction with the environment. Previous approaches centered on more and more accurate internal representations of the physical world. Brooks disagreed with this approach; he considered the world to be too dynamic and complex to be maintained inside a robot. His approach was that "the world is its own best model" and concentrated on making his robots operate by sensing the changing environment. He built a robot called "Allen" with a simple three-level subsumption architecture [Brooks90]:

The bottom layer let the robot avoid both static and dynamic obstacles using sonar range detectors. When approached too closely, Allen would scurry away from any objects it detected. The inverse square of the distance to each obstacle was used to determine how fast the robot should go. Additionally, Allen would come to an abrupt halt if there were objects directly in its path. With only this layer active, Allen would sit in place until approached.

The middle layer caused Allen to randomly wander about. Allen would pick a direction and travel for approximately 10 seconds. this desire was combined with the obstacle avoidance layer through vector addition. In this way the obstacle avoidance part of the bottom layer was subsumed; however, the halt reflex continued to operate unchanged.

The top layer used sonar to find distant places for Allen to explore. If a "distant place" was found, it generated a heading which suppressed the direction of the wander layer. This direction was summed with the bottom layer's obstacle avoidance vector; therefore, the physical robot did not blindly follow the desires of the top layer.

This is a very simple example of the architecture, but it demonstrates many of its strengths. We could summarize the layers as *obstacle avoidance, random wandering,* and *exploring.* The robot doesn't collide with things because the obstacle avoidance layer takes precedence over (suppresses) higher layers. However, when there are no obstacles to avoid, the upper layers subsume control in order to achieve the loftier goals of exploring the area. The random wandering layer is an example of *action modification*; it takes the goal of the exploration layer and modifies it so the robot will have a better chance at finding a route to "distant places."

Subsumption Architecture in a Game

There are a variety of ways to use a subsumption architecture in a game. However, some general design rules should be followed.

Low to High Goals

The lowest layer handles the most immediate goals (e.g., to walk forward one step). Layers are built from the bottom up, so the lowest layer is the first to be implemented, and additional layers are not built until each lower layer is tested. Each layer above that handles progressively longer-term goals until the highest layer implements the *high-level goals* (e.g., destroy hostile forces in the area).

Layer Responsibilities

Each layer should have a clearly defined responsibility. For example, the first layer of the Allen robot was to avoid obstacles. No other layers were allowed to subvert this function. This helps robustness because the code to implement a responsibility is centralized, instead of being scattered (and probably copied) throughout the code.

Layer Communication

Upper layers must achieve their goals by issuing requests to the layer directly below it. Upper layers are not allowed to bypass a layer in order to change the state of the character. For example, the layer that is responsible for navigation is not allowed to set animations directly (which is the responsibility of the *movement* layer). If layers are bypassed, two pieces of code will fight for control over some aspect of a character.

Upper layers get status information from lower layers in a non-implementation specific manner (through polling or events). Upper layers should not know or care about individual states in a lower layer. For example, the navigation layer would ask the movement layer "are you standing?" This is true even if the movement layer is currently in a state with the character reloading his gun as part of an "idle" sequence. In some cases, upper layers only want to know the status of a request in terms of "in progress," "succeeded," or "failed."

Concurrent Execution

All the layers run in parallel. In most games, characters are sent an "update" message for every pass through the main loop. Each layer should receive an update call, starting with the bottom layer. Upper layers must not block indefinitely waiting for a lower layer to complete a task. Otherwise, a character is likely to stall if a minor goal can't be achieved. At the very least, upper layers should time out. Upper layers should recognize if the situation has changed, and that a previously requested goal is now invalid or impossible.

Example Layer Set

Consider an imaginary game called *Shuriken*. This is a third-person fighting game with one ranged weapon type, the throwing star. This game has a main character, Mr. Lee, fighting various teams of thugs, guards, and boss characters. Assume there are pre-existing collision and animation systems. The layers for this game are shown in Figure 6.1.1.

Movement Layer

The first thing to implement is a finite-state machine to control the movement and animation of our characters. All the characters in this game share the same basic set of movements. We can customize the characters by giving different modifiers for strength, speed, jump height, and durability. The movement layer is responsible for interpreting input and adhering to the physical rules of the game. This input can come from either a player holding a game controller or from the AI code. This layer has one state per animation (we assume that the animation system will blend between animations).

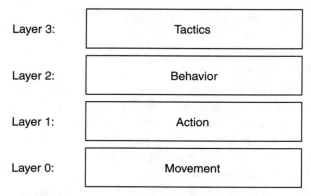

FIGURE 6.1.1   *Initial layer set for the game* Shuriken.

The movement FSM enforces animation constraints, as shown in Figure 6.1.2. For example, a character cannot go directly from the Fall state to the Stand state; it must first pass through the Land state. It also selectively responds to input: if the character is standing and it receives an analog input vector (from a joystick), it starts to run. However, while the character is being knocked back, it ignores input. Input can also come in the form of events; if the character is hit by punch, it will play a Knock Back state animation and slide the character back a step.

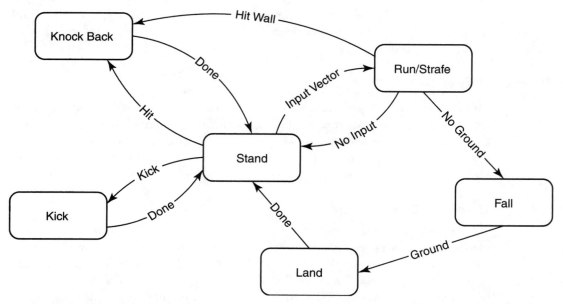

FIGURE 6.1.2   *Simplified movement layer FSM.*

The movement FSM enforces physical constraints. If the character is running and slams into a wall, it is stopped and a Knock Back is played. If the character loses contact with the ground, it falls. Each state is responsible for moving the character as well as playing the appropriate animation. The Fall state would accelerate the character downward and look for a ground surface.

Action Layer

The movement layer contains all of the building blocks for actions. Actions are short-term goals we need the character to achieve. Actions occur for a finite period of time. Unlike motions, actions can succeed or fail. Some actions in *Shuriken* are Goto, Fight, and Die.

The Goto action asks the navigation system: how do I get from my location to location X? The navigation system responds with a list of waypoints. The action then sends requests to the motion layer, such as "run, turn, run, run, climb down ladder, run, stop!"

Actions such as Fight have a time limit: "fight enemy X for Y seconds." The action will return a status of "failed" if the enemy can't be engaged, or return "succeeded" if the enemy dies or the enemy is engaged until the time limit.

Why is Die an action and not just an animation? Death can be complicated. The character might die while fighting. It might fall to its death, or die while falling or jumping. The Die action looks at the situation and chooses between different death options in the movement layer.

Behavior Layer

Behaviors are goals with indefinite time periods, and are constructed out of actions. Examples of behaviors in *Shuriken* are Patrol, Investigate Noise, and Attack Enemy X. The Patrol behavior is just a simple sequence of actions:

1. Go to location A
2. Look around
3. Go to location B
4. Call in: Alpha Sector Secure!
5. Go to location C
6. Repeat

In the case of the Attack Enemy behavior, the behavior constructs a series of actions in order to fight the intended target. This might include pursuing the character, collecting nearby weapons, or looking for advantageous spots to attack from and moving to them. The attack behavior doesn't necessarily fail if one of its actions fails. For example, while the character is navigating to its chosen "attack location," the location might become occupied. The behavior can just look for a different spot from which to attack.

Tactical Layer

With the other layers implemented, *Shuriken* characters are ready to employ high-level tactics and some simple planning. In *Shuriken*, a Guard character only has one tactical state: Defend Area. The pseudocode for Defend Area might look like this:

```
Update()
{
    if (low health)
    {
        request Retreat behavior
        return
    }

    if (behavior in progress) && (not timed out)
        return

    if (no enemy spotted)
    {
        request Patrol behavior
        return
    }
    else
    {
        if (no alarm)
        {
            if (close to enemies)
                request Retreat behavior
            else
                request Sound Alarm behavior
            return
        }

        request Attack Enemy behavior
        return
    }

    if (suspicious noise)
        request Investigate Noise behavior

} // Update()
```

This function would be called each time the character receives an update message. More complex characters might have multiple states in their tactical layer. Notice that if the character is investigating a noise and sees an enemy, it might retreat to sound an alarm or it might attack immediately. When the Investigate Noise behavior was being written, it would have seemed to make sense that if an enemy were discovered, it should be attacked. However, pushing that decision into the tactical layer (the layer above it) allows for more interesting AI. In general, each layer should not make its own state change decisions. Instead, allow upper layers to make state changes through requests.

Implications

With a base set of layers in place, we can look at how this solves some common problems with AI driven characters. Lower layers ignore the wishes of upper layers in order to enforce the rules of the game. This keeps the rule-enforcing code centralized, easy to debug, and hard to inadvertently break with higher-level AI code.

Because state is stored at every layer, the character remembers what it was doing even if setbacks occur. If a guard is in the Attack Enemy behavior and is suddenly knocked down, the attack behavior will request the action layer to pursue the enemy, and the action layer figures out which movements are needed to get there.

With concurrently executing layers, the character won't get stuck on a minor task. If a character is pursuing an enemy and the enemy is destroyed, the tactics layer notices and requests the Patrol behavior. This has a cascading effect where all of the (now obsolete) lower-level goals are switched to new, valid ones. If higher-level goals waited for lower-level goals to finish, then the character would run over to the spot where the enemy perished—for no real purpose.

Multiple Modules Per Layer

One of the features of our imaginary game is the ability to throw shurikens (throwing stars). Characters should be able to throw while running, jumping, and falling. Looking at the movement layer FSM, there doesn't seem to be a clean way to add throwing. One might consider adding states: running and throwing, standing and throwing, falling and throwing, until each combination of motions are accounted for. This not only doubles all the states in the system, it also doesn't work very well. The reason is that a throw might overlap a movement state transition. For example, the character could be running, initiate a throw, and then jump. The state logic doesn't handle this, and neither does the current full-body animation system.

The solution is to split the character into two parts, legs and torso that can be animated independently. Using the previous example, the character is running (using a full-body animation), and the throw is activated. The throw animation is overlaid on the torso. Then the character jumps, which is no problem. The jump animation replaces the run animation, but the throw continues on the torso until it completes. To control this, the movement layer must be split as well (see Figure 6.1.3).

In most cases, the two movement modules operate independently. However, when a movement requires control over the entire body (e.g., a Kick movement), the torso module is suppressed. Suppression of modules can happen in a couple of ways. One way is that lower layers just ignore requests by upper layers. Modules can explicitly suppress each other through a message or method call.

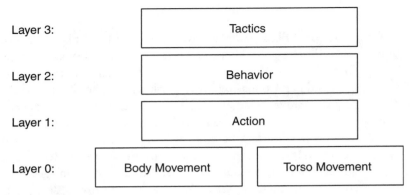

FIGURE 6.1.3 *Multiple movement modules in Layer 0.*

Planning and Teamwork

Consider the "Defend Area" tactical state. If we break down the logic into steps, it would look like this:

If you see an enemy:

Step A: Retreat to a safe distance.
Step B: Sound the alarm.
Step C: Attack the enemy.

This constitutes an implied plan for the character; it doesn't look like a plan because it has been broken up into pieces. Each piece has clearly defined entry and exit conditions. The advantage of breaking it up is that the plan can be entered at any step. For example, if an enemy is spotted and the alarm is already activated, then the character goes directly to attacking. If the enemy is killed, then the "enemy spotted" condition goes false and the character goes back to patrolling.

Consider the case when there are three guards in an area, and an enemy is spotted. An alarm button is mounted on one wall. One guard is near the alarm button. When the enemy is spotted, the guard near the button will press it. Because the alarm has been sounded, the other guards will switch to attacking, even though they will have initially gone for the button. If another guard enters the room, he would attack immediately. Without a plan broken into pieces, all four guards would have run over to press the same button, making them look stupid or mechanical.

Notice that this spontaneous teamwork was not explicitly implemented; it emerged from the design of the tactics layer. It is also robust; if the first guard is killed before it is able to press the button, the other guards will continue to try to press the button until the alarm is activated.

Conclusion

A subsumption architecture addresses many common problems associated with character AI and provides a structure that integrates low- and high-level goal achievement. The architecture creates robust characters that react well to rapidly changing conditions. It can be extended by adding more layers for higher levels of strategy, or by adding multiple modules per layer to meet the needs of the game's design. If plans are well designed, individuals can enter plans "in the middle" and exit obsolete plans because of the architecture's constant sensing of the situation; this leads to spontaneous teamwork if multiple characters have access to the same plan.

References

[Arkin98] Arkin, Ronald C., *Behavior Based Robotics*, MIT Press, 1998, pp. 130–140.

[Brooks90] Brooks, Rodney A., "Elephants Don't Play Chess," *Designing Autonomous Agents, Theory and Practice from Biology to Engineering and Back*, MIT Press, 1994, pp. 3–15.

[Fu04] Fu, Dan, and Houlette, Ryan, "The Ultimate Guide to FSMs in Games," *AI Game Programming Wisdom 2*, Charles River Media, 2004.

[LaMothe02] LaMothe, André, "Finite State Machines," *Tricks of the Windows Game Programming Gurus Second Edition*, Sams Publishing (Macmillian), 2002, pp. 737–742.

6.2

An Architecture for A-Life

Nick Porcino—LucasArts

nporcino@lucasarts.com

This article presents Insect AI, a straightforward architecture, notation, and design methodology for agent design. Insect AI is a design tool for programmers and nonprogrammers alike, and can be easily tuned to generate specific behaviors.

Insect AI agents exhibit a number of interesting properties that satisfy the characteristics of motivated behavior as defined in the ethological literature—behaviors can be grouped and sequenced, the agents are goal directed, behavior can change based on the internal state of the agent, and behaviors can persist if stimuli are removed [Davis76].

The agents are easy to implement, and are computationally inexpensive. Insect AIs have found their way into a number of games already [Bombad01].

As Smart as a Bug

John von Neumann observed that the description of intelligence might be more complicated than the system that realizes it [von Neumann58]. Instead of aiming for a complete system description or set of algorithms, Insect AI uses emergent behaviors—behaviors that have not been explicitly specified at the level of the system's implementation. Simple systems can generate complex behavior as the result of the interactions of reflexes and the environment [Reynolds87, Brooks86, Sims00].

Insects demonstrate a wide variety of interesting and successful behaviors, yet their nervous systems are simple. A typical insect like a bee has around a hundred thousand neurons, about half of which are dedicated to the reduction of sensory information into useful signals. Of the remainder, less than a thousand are motor neurons, and even fewer are control neurons that moderate signals between the cerebral ganglion and the motor neurons. There are individual neurons that activate and deactivate specific behaviors [Guthrie80]. It is possible to analyze behaviors in terms of simple computational units and create simulations of the behaviors. This approach is known as *computational neuroethology*.

Computational Neuroethology versus
Neural Networks

Although both Insect AI and neural networks attempt to mimic the functional success of biological nervous systems, Insect AI is not a neural network in the traditional sense. Typical neural network methods model large numbers of regularly connected identical neurons with no feedback. A learning method such as back propagation with gradient descent is performed on an associated Lyapunov energy function, and through this process a neural network converges on a solution.

In contrast, Insect AI circuits and behaviors are explicitly designed. Inspiration is taken from the study of simple invertebrate neuronal networks with small numbers of dedicated neurons whose interconnections are fairly easy to ascertain or deduce. Invertebrate neuronal networks are real-time control systems, and are ideally adapted by nature for successful survival behaviors, and are thus of interest to game programmers!

Principles of Distributed Control

W.J. Davis contributed greatly to neuroethology [Davis76]. He demonstrated how behaviors could be distributed across many simple units and listed several organizing principles, some of which are described here. These principles prove very useful when designing agents that are as smart as a bug.

- Command neurons, once activated, can invoke behaviors that outlast the original stimulus. A creature that creeps toward light can keep creeping even if the light is momentarily removed.
- The source of information should be connected as directly as possible to the units that use it. This keeps circuits simple and fast. A reflex circuit meant to draw a limb away from heat should be connected directly from the heat sensors to the actuators, without going all the way back to the brain (or an arbitrating algorithm or heuristic) for processing.
- Reflexes should self-govern and run autonomously. In nature, neurons exist that suppress behaviors that would otherwise occur spontaneously. Severing a leech's cerebral ganglion from its nerve chord causes it to swim continuously. The female preying mantis decapitates the male to elicit copulatory behavior [Guthrie80].
- Sensory feedback should be used to make behaviors self-calibrating. A leg controller doesn't need to be driven by an inverse kinematic solution, but instead can be driven by joint angle and load sensors.
- Specialization in a homogenous network can be maintained by controlling the circuit's relationship to incoming data, so the same circuit can accomplish different tasks simply by changing the inputs. A chase behavior could follow either a sound or a light by switching the input.
- Sensors with a nonlinear response are particularly useful. If a joint angle sensor signals not an angle, but a response that increases nonlinearly at the limits of motion, the signal functions analogously to pain. Such a signal can provide both

an imperative signal to reflexes to compensate the motion, and input to a learning system that can adapt the reflex to avoid the pain signal in the future.

- Learning is distributed throughout the entire system, rather than localized in one place. If a limb is injured, local learning can adjust the motion of the affected limb, while the rest of the system continues to function normally. Reinforcement learning and Q-Learning work quite well in these systems [Watkins89].
- Some behaviors are cooperative, but others must be hierarchical. An insect can balance behaviors such as *move to light* and *collect food*, but an escape reflex must override everything. Cooperative decision making can be implemented by a weighted sum of inputs. In a boid model, both cooperative and hierarchical decisions are used. There are several reflexes: *avoid collisions*, *move to center*, *match speeds*, and *move to goal* [Reynolds87]. While most of the reflexes can be summed since they all have similar behavioral priority, *avoid collisions* dominates in times of crisis by shutting off the other reflexes.

Pattern Generation

So far, we have examined reflex behaviors that are driven directly by environmental or command stimulus. Another category of behavior is characterized by the repetition of a sequence of events. Moving a leg, coordinating multiple legs, and patrolling a series of waypoints are all forms of pattern generation.

Surprisingly, patterns driven by pacemaker cells are rare in nature. Instead, neurons are connected reciprocally in pairs or groups such that each neuron inhibits its neighbor [Laurent88]. Every neuron tries to fire, that firing suppresses neighboring neurons, and patterns naturally arise as each neuron settles into an oscillation where it fires at a time maximally distant from the time its neighbors fire.

This pattern gives rise to one of the most common neural architectures in invertebrates—the ladder. Imagine a centipede with a neuron connected to each leg. Each neuron is connected to the neuron on the opposite side of the body, and to its fore and aft neighbors, forming a ladder of inhibitory links. This simple structure gives rise to the wave pattern commonly observed to move down the legs of a centipede, or the rippling wave seen in some fishes' fins. A ladder of six neurons is sufficient to generate all known straight-line walking patterns observed in insects [Porcino90]. This circuit can be put to great use controlling the walking animations of many types of creatures and robots.

Components of Insect AI

The following sections introduce the components of Insect AI and their notation. The primary design goal of the notation is that it be simple to remember, obvious to read in a diagram, and easy to draw so that Insect AIs can be sketched out and revised rapidly. The components and their representations have been derived from practical experience earned over a great many AI design tasks by a number of people, including high school students! Implementation is straightforward and adapts easily to methods like C++ polymorphic objects, or streamlined SIMD-oriented data structures.

Signals

Signals are the information flows between the components of Insect AI. All signals have an activation component, and might have other components as well, such as steering. In general, signals range between 0 and 1, or −1 and 1. No matter how many components a signal has, they are always indicated by a single line. If the direction of flow isn't clear, an arrowhead can be used. If an Insect AI component has a control input, the activation component of a signal is the value that drives it.

Sensors

Sensors can respond to any type of input or object in a game—power ups, player joystick inputs, the location of a teammate, and so on. Sensors can be directional (capturing a direction and a magnitude), or nondirectional (capturing only a magnitude). An icon within the sensor indicates the quantity or object the sensor responds to. A directional sensor is denoted by a half circle; a nondirectional sensor by a box (see Figure 6.2.1).

FIGURE 6.2.1 *Sensors are represented by an icon representing the sensed quantity. The semi-circle indicates a directional sensor; the box indicates a nondirectional sensor. The sensor on the left senses the presence and direction of friendly agents. The sensor on the right detects only light magnitude.*

Activation is a behaviorally significant quantity. A value of 0 means no activity, 0.5 could be considered strong enough to pay some attention to, and a value of 1 would indicate maximum activation. Sensors can be tuned to indicate importance; a less important sensor could be clamped so that its output never actually reaches 1.

The outputs of a directional sensor are *steering*, *pitch* (in a 3D environment), and *activation*. The nondirectional sensor outputs *activation* only. The *steering* value ranges from −1 for hard left and +1 for hard right, with 0 being neutral. An agent that can maneuver in three dimensions would also have a *pitch* value, with −1 being full pitch down, and +1 being full pitch up.

Buffers

Buffers are used to introduce hysteresis and delay into an AI's behavior. The output of a buffer tracks the input at a rate determined by an adaptation constant and controlled by a simple linear interpolation equation. A buffer following a light sensor can prolong a light sensor's activation if the light is momentarily interrupted, allowing the AI to continue what it was doing for a few moments as if the light was still there (see Figure 6.2.2).

FIGURE 6.2.2 *Buffers provide a signal delay, the output of the buffer tracks the input. In this example, a light sensor's output is smoothed by a buffer.*

Sum and Average

Sum and average units provide simple mechanisms for consensus decision making. A weighted unit differs from an ordinary unit in that each input is multiplied by a different constant value before performing the sum or average. A convenient notational shorthand for the weights is to use small circles for less important inputs, and large circles for more important inputs. The weights typically need tuning by the programmer or a learning system, so an indication of relative importance is all the designer typically specifies during the design phase (see Figure 6.2.3).

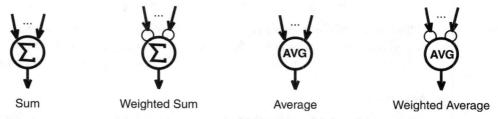

| Sum | Weighted Sum | Average | Weighted Average |

FIGURE 6.2.3 *Sum and Average units. The small circles indicate weights on the inputs.*

Functions

In general, functions operate on the activation component of a signal. Many different functions are possible; multiplicative and threshold functions are very commonly used. The multiplicative function has a control input indicated by the small circle (see Figure 6.2.4), an input, and an output. Typical functions can compute inversions, Gaussian weighting, and so on. The icon within the circle is a simple graphical representation of the function. The number of inputs depends on the function being computed. Many useful gates don't have control inputs; this class of gates includes multiplicative constants, inverters, and threshold units.

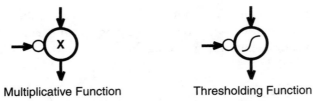

Multiplicative Function   **Thresholding Function**

FIGURE 6.2.4   *Sample functions. In both, the signal enters at the top, is transformed, and then output at the bottom. The signal input at the small circle is a parameter of the function.*

Switches

Switches have one or more input signals, an output, and most have a control input. Figure 6.2.5a shows a switch where a 0 signal on the control input selects the left input, and a signal closer to 1 selects the right input. Hysteresis is introduced to reduce chatter. The switch selects 1 whenever the control signal rises above a value of 0.55, and 0 when the signal subsequently falls back below a 0.45 value. If no signal is present on a switch, the output is 0. That situation would arise on the switch of Figure 6.2.5c, which outputs a signal only if the control input is 0.

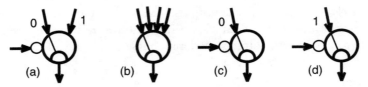

(a)   (b)   (c)   (d)

FIGURE 6.2.5   *Some switches. (a) Two inputs, indicated by 0 and 1, selected by the control input on the small circle. (b) Winner takes all; only the signal with the highest activation passes through. (c) Passes the signal if the control input is 0. (d) Passes on 1.*

Actuators

Actuators are output mechanisms. Actuators are always at the end of a signal, and are drawn as a box containing an icon indicating what it does. Besides the obvious motors and claws, a number of imaginative actuators are possible. Some examples are a steerable jet engine for boids, an output to a debugging monitor, and control inputs to a joypad—very useful for substituting an AI when no human Player Two is around (see Figure 6.2.6).

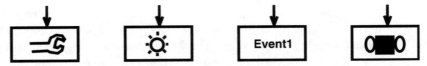

FIGURE 6.2.6   *Sample actuators. From left to right, they are a claw, a light, an abstract game event, and a motor with two steerable wheels.*

Some Examples

Valentino Braitenberg's pioneering book *Vehicles* introduced a number of key concepts in computational neuroethology [Braitenberg84]. Some of his vehicles are shown in Figure 6.2.7, redrawn using Insect AI notation.

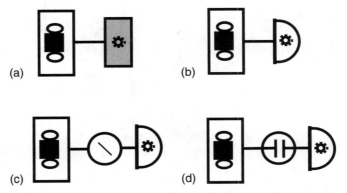

FIGURE 6.2.7   *Some Braitenberg-style vehicles: (a) light sensitive, (b) light seeking, (c) light avoiding—the function is an inverter, and (d) persistent light seeking.*

The simplest agent we can create is one that links a sensor to an actuator. If a light magnitude sensor drives a motor, we create an agent that goes faster in response to increasing light levels (Figure 6.2.7a). If we link a directional light sensor to a steering input, the agent will drive straight toward a light getting faster as it goes (Figure 6.2.7b). If we put an inverting function between the light sensor and the motor, we get an agent that drives quickly out of dark spots and comes to rest near a light source (Figure 6.2.7c). Adding a buffer between the sensor and actuator will cause the agent to continue to move toward the light even if the light source is momentarily interrupted (Figure 6.2.7d). This type of mechanism can sometimes eliminate the need for trajectory prediction.

The famous boid flocking model [Reynolds87] has no global algorithm; rather, flocking boids make decisions locally in individual agents. The important contribution of the boid model was to show that cooperative group behavior could emerge in a system that didn't explicitly encode it. Cooperative group behavior is a characteristic of manifest interest to game programmers. Figure 6.2.8 shows a boid drawn using the Insect AI notation.

The *move to center of group* and *match velocity with neighbors* simply sum their outputs and pass them through to the motor. In Reynold's model, the output of *avoid collisions* is summed with the other signals. In Figure 6.2.8, the *avoid collisions* sensor output is simply switched out except when a collision is imminent. The hysteresis on the switch greatly reduces the steering oscillation that can arise with this setup. A switch or sum should be selected according to whether a collision is allowable or not.

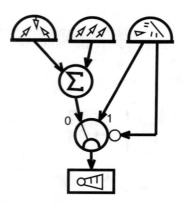

FIGURE 6.2.8   *A simple boid. The sensors from left to right are* move to center of group, match velocity with neighbors, *and* avoid collisions.

Implementation of Walking

Consider an insect's walking reflex. Insects have a variety of complex gaits ranging from one leg stepping at a time to a fast alternating tripod where three legs swing at the same time, leaving the other three in a stable configuration on the ground. Insects can negotiate arbitrary terrain, they can recover quickly from a fall, and they can continue to walk even after they've lost a leg.

A simple physics model and control circuit can make an agent walk over irregular terrain. The leg controlling circuit in Figure 6.2.9 is based on data in [Laurent88], and was derived in [Porcino90].

The circuit is self-starting once the legs of the insect are bearing weight. The reflex works as follows:

1. When the foot is first planted, the load sensor on the bottom of the foot contacts the ground, generating a *push* reflex that plants the foot more strongly and thrusts the body forward. It simultaneously suppresses the *swing-lift* reflex.
2. Soon the leg is extended toward the rear of the animal. The leg is almost ready to lift and swing back. Other legs begin to carry weight; pressure on the load sensor is decreased. This gradually stops the *push* reflex and allows the leg to be lifted and swung forward in preparation for another step.
3. When the lifted leg is swung all the way forward, the forward angle sensor starts the *depress* and *push* reflexes, which restarts the cycle at the first step.

This sequence is easy to create and tune because it is self-limiting through the joint angle sensor, and self-calibrating due to the load sensors in the feet—a leg won't be raised if it is still carrying a load. The logarithmic response of the *forward angle* sen-

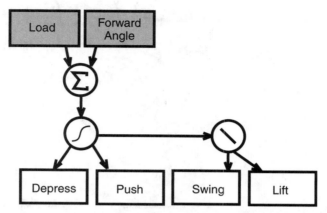

FIGURE 6.2.9 *A leg controller. The* Forward Angle *sensor has a logarithmic response that increases the farther forward the leg moves,* Load *indicates a load sensor in the foot. Depress and Lift are actuators that raise and lower the leg, Push and Swing are actuators that push the leg to the rear, and pull it forward. The activation of* Load *and* Forward Angle *are summed. The function following the summation is a thresholding unit; the function on the right is an inverter.*

sor acts as a pain signal if the leg is swung too far forward, ensuring that the leg will always get pushed to the ground to restart the cycle.

To generate a coordinating gait between several legs, a slightly more complex circuit is required. The Swing and Lift reflex must be suppressed by the neighboring legs' swing and lift reflexes to produce the ladder architecture described earlier in this article. The gaits that result are adaptive to the conditions of the physical simulation and are biologically correct. A further enhancement to the circuit allows speed control on the *push* reflex. Adjusting the speed differentially between the two sides of the insect will steer it.

An Artificial Cockroach

The cockroach of [Beer89] is a well-studied Insect AI. This agent has two basic reflexes: *locomotion* and *eating*. These reflexes are driven by a few switches and sensors. An internal energy monitor is most active when the insect is hungry, and there is a food sensor near the mouth. Both sensors activate logarithmically as per Davis' principles. Figure 6.2.10 shows Beer's cockroach reinterpreted using the Insect AI notation.

The *wander* and *collision avoidance* sensors are sufficient to allow the cockroach to make its way around obstacles and into new areas where food might be available. No explicit pathfinding is designed into the system. The output of *wander* is not tied to any environmental stimulus; it simply generates a time varying steering signal.

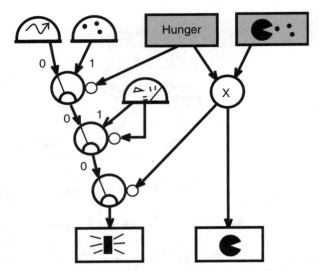

FIGURE 6.2.10   *The artificial cockroach circuit. The sensors from left to right are* wander, move to food, avoid collisions, hunger, *and* food near mouth. *The actuators at the bottom are* locomotion *and* eating. *The function containing an "x" is a multiplier. The switch on locomotion passes the steering signal only when its control input is zero.*

If the hunger sensor becomes active, *wander* is switched off in favor of *move to food*. When the agent is hungry and food is located, *food near mouth* activates the *eat* behavior and suppresses the movement reflexes. Eating continues until *mouth near food* becomes inactive, or until *hunger* becomes quiet.

This agent, although not much more complicated than a boid, exhibits goal-directed behavior (find food when hungry) in addition to its reflexive behavioral repertoire (wander and follow edges). It groups and sequences behaviors (move to food, eat the food). It changes its behavior based on internal state (find food only when hungry). Behaviors persist if stimuli are removed (if food is removed, the insect will go looking for more food). The full behavior of this agent is not explicitly defined anywhere in the system, but instead emerges from the interactions of simple behaviors and reflexes.

Conclusion

Insect AI opens the door to using results from the neuroethological literature, and can be used to create agents that are as smart as a bug. The Insect AI methodology has proven itself flexible and easy to use. The resulting agents are robust, and computationally efficient. The notation is easily extensible to accommodate the particulars of a new game or simulation feature, and is easily mastered by nonprogrammers.

COLOR PLATE 1

COLOR PLATE 2

COLOR PLATES 1 & 2 Scenes from *Soldier of Fortune 2*. A character vaults over an obstacle (Plate 1). A character rappels down thanks to embedded navigation behavior (Plate 2). From the article "Jumping, Climbing, and Tactical Reasoning: How to Get More Out of a Navigation System." Images courtesy of Ben Geisler and Christopher Reed.

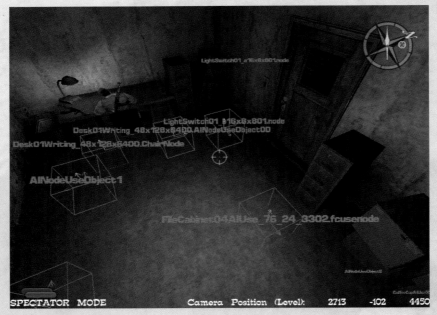

COLOR PLATE 3

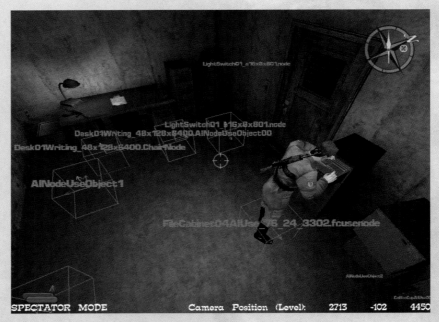

COLOR PLATE 4

COLOR PLATES 3 & 4   Characters in *No One Lives Forever 2* interact with their environment. AI Nodes indicate where a character can stand to interact with objects of interest. (Plate 3) The soldier sits at a desk. (Plate 4) The soldier ruffles through a file cabinet. From the article "Constraining Autonomous Character Behavior with Human Concepts." © 2002. Reprinted with permission from Monolith Productions, Inc.

COLOR PLATE 5

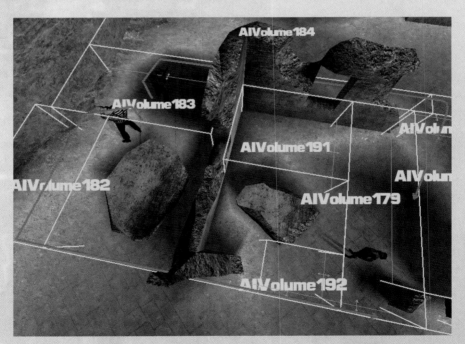

COLOR PLATE 6

COLOR PLATES 5 & 6 Scenes from *No One Lives Forever 2*. (Plate 5) A mime and a soldier detect the player behind a wall (first-person perspective). (Plate 6) The mime and soldier split up, using a technique described in the article "Simple Techniques for Coordinated Behavior." The red lines indicate the paths planned from AIVolume183 to AIVolume179 (top-down third-person perspective). © 2002. Reprinted with permission from Monolith Productions, Inc.

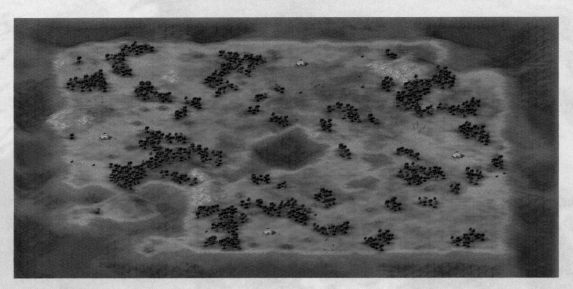

COLOR PLATE 7

COLOR PLATES 7-10   These four images are randomly generated maps from *Empire Earth* (4096 x 2048, 24 bit). Examples of four different map types are shown, along with four different epochs and two different environments. Each map was generated for four players. From the article "Random Map Generation for Strategy Games." © 2003. Reprinted with permission from Stainless Steel Studios.

COLOR PLATE 8

COLOR PLATE 9 Image from "Random Map Generation for Strategy Games" article.

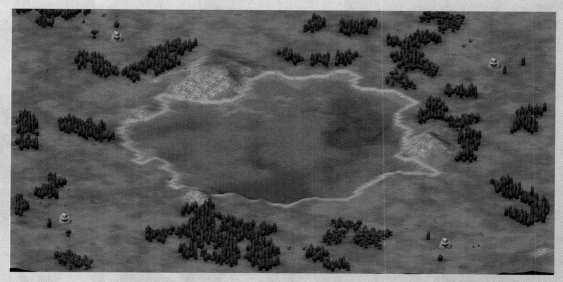

COLOR PLATE 10 Image from "Random Map Generation for Strategy Games" article.

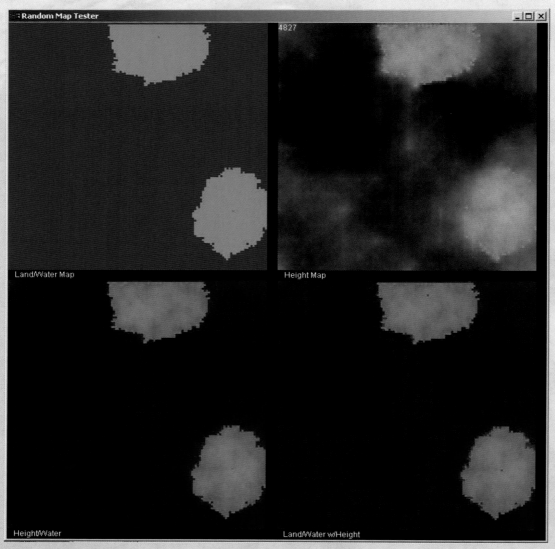

COLOR PLATE 11 An *Empire Earth* test application written to visualize the map generation process. There are four panes in which different textures are shown. These textures correspond to different 2D arrays generated to create the map. Shown in the panes are the land water array, the height map array, the land water array combined with the height map array, and a final array representing the combination of all of the arrays. From the article "Random Map Generation for Strategy Games." © 2003. Reprinted with permission from Stainless Steel Studios.

COLOR PLATE 12   A screenshot of the demo program included on the CD-ROM for the article "Designing a Multi-Tiered AI Framework." The demo is an example of the basic architecture as described in this article. There is a sample game situation that can be loaded into the framework, where the blue player is concerned with resource gathering while its yellow opponents are more aggressive.

COLOR PLATE 13   Jenna's avoidance planning is displayed as she approaches a particularly nasty piece of track. The graphical debug display makes it easy to visualize the obstacles to be avoided (*red*), those she is clear of (*green*) and the region to stay away from (*orange*). The change in color vivacity highlights the range to the obstacle in question. From the article "The Art of Surviving a Simulation Title." © 2003. Reprinted with permission from Particle Systems.

COLOR PLATE 14   While debugging Jenna's plan for movement (*green*) as she tries to move smoothly toward the ideal line (*red*) it is noticed that she is both dummying the player in front and giving an annoyed gesture to the left – but why? From the article "The Art of Surviving a Simulation Title." © 2003. Reprinted with permission from Particle Systems.

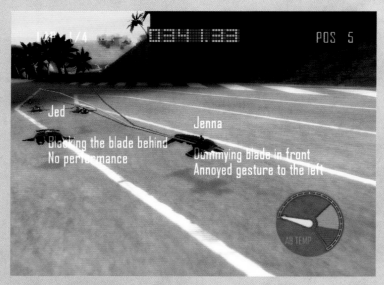

COLOR PLATE 15.   With the simulation frozen in time, and Jed's maneuver and animation status displayed, we see the reason. He is trying to block Jenna, she has noticed and she is not particularly happy. From the article "The Art of Surviving a Simulation Title." © 2003. Reprinted with permission from Particle Systems.

References

[Beer89] Beer, Randall D., Chiel, Hillel J., and Sterling, Leon S., "Heterogeneous Neural Networks for Adaptive Behavior in Dynamic Environments," in *Advances in Neural Information Processing Systems*, vol. 1, Morgan Kaufman Publishers, 1989.

[Bombad01] Lucas Learning, *Star Wars Super Bombad Racing*, 2001.

[Braitenberg84] Braitenberg, Valentino, *Vehicles: Experiments in Synthetic Psychology*, MIT Press, Cambridge, 1984.

[Brooks86] Brooks, Rodney A., "A Robust Layered Control System for a Mobile Robot," *IEEE Journal of Robotics and Automation*, vol. RA-2, no. 1, March 1986, pp. 14–23.

[Davis76] Davis, William J., "Organizational Concepts in the Central Motor Networks of Invertebrates," *Neural Control of Locomotion*, R.M. Herman, S. Grillner, P.S.G. Stein, & D.G. Stuart (Eds.), Plenum Press, New York, 1976, pp. 265–292.

[Guthrie80] Guthrie, D.M., *Neuroethology: An Introduction*, Blackwell Scientific Publications, Oxford, 1980.

[Laurent88] Laurent, Gilles, and Hustert, Reinhold, "Motor Neuronal Receptive Fields Delimit Patterns of Motor Activity During Locomotion of the Locust," in *Journal of Neuroscience*, vol. 8, no. 11, Nov. 1988, pp. 4349–4366.

[Porcino90] Porcino, Nick, "A Neural Network Controller for Hexapod Locomotion," *Proceedings of the International Joint Conference on Neural Networks*, San Diego, 1990, pp. I, 189–194.

[Reynolds87] Reynolds, Craig W., "Flocks, Herds, and Schools: A Distributed Behavioural Model," *ACM Computer Graphics (SIGGRAPH)*, vol. 21, no. 4, July 1987, pp. 25–34, *www.red3d.com/cwr/boids*

[Sims00] Maxis, *The Sims*, *www.maxis.com*, 2000.

[von Neumann58] von Neumann, John, *The Computer and the Brain*, MIT Press, 1958.

[Watkins89] Watkins, C., *Learning from Delayed Rewards*, Thesis, University of Cambridge, England, 1989.

6.3

A Flexible Tagging System for AI Resource Selection

Paul Tozour—Retro Studios

gehn29@yahoo.com

Game AI agents have two primary means of communicating with the player: they can perform animations, and they can play audio files. That is, they can move, and they can speak.

Admittedly, this oversimplifies the situation quite a bit. Game AI characters can also interact with objects in the game world, and techniques such as procedural animation allow you an extraordinary amount of flexibility in controlling the way your characters move. Fundamentally, however, game AI agents primarily express themselves to the player through sound and movement.

This article addresses the problem of selecting content for an AI agent to execute. The system we describe serves as an interface between the AI code and the underlying resource system. It allows you to both design and query AI-related resources at arbitrary levels of specificity, from fully generic to highly specialized. This system is primarily useful for selecting sounds and animations, but it has many other potential uses as well.

We'll begin by addressing sounds specifically and then discuss how to apply this system to animations.

AI Audio System

Game AI characters use sounds for several purposes. Sounds can broadcast an AI agent's current state ("I'm attacking!" "Guess he got away . . ."), acknowledge player actions ("I'm hit!"), and fill in dead space ("Sure is boring around here . . . just standing guard all day long . . .").

The simplest approach to designing an AI audio system is to build a list of any significant changes to an AI agent's internal state that the agent needs to communicate to the player. You can then map each such change to a set of one or more sound cues. For an AI system based on finite-state machines [Fu04], these changes occur whenever an AI's behavioral finite-state machine performs a state transition.

For example:

[alert state]
All right, come on out! Where are you hiding, villain?

[took hit]
Aaaarrrgh! I'm hit!!!

[lost track of player]
Ah well, I guess he got away.

This is a good start, but what we really want is to be able to define our resources such that they cover a broad range between the most general and the most specific.

Imagine you're developing a stealth-oriented game. At a certain point in the game, the player is ambushed by guards and narrowly escapes with his life. While fleeing, he runs through the dining room and into the library and accidentally knocks over a bookshelf as he enters the room. Imagine further that another guard could see the player fleeing this way, turn to another guard, and say:

> *"I saw a man over there! He was carrying a sword and bleeding heavily. I saw him walk out of the dining room and into the library and knock over a bookshelf. Let's get him!"*

Clearly, this level of specificity is obscenely impractical, if not impossible. Outside of a text-to-speech (TTS) system that could convert any arbitrary text string to human-like speech [Nuance03], any system that would allow your game characters to regularly respond at this level of detail would require you to record an absurd number of audio files. In this example alone, there are far too many permutations—what type of weapon the player is holding, whether or not he's bleeding, what rooms he's entered or exited, what kind of furniture he's knocked over, and even whether the player is male or female.

However, it *is* possible to create AI audio files at this level of specificity. The key is to remember that we can't possibly cover all of the possible permutations of variables, so we'll have to settle for a combination of audio cues at various levels of specificity, ranging from the most specific (as in the previous example) to the most generic. Whenever an AI character attempts to play an audio cue, it will search for the most specific audio cue it can possibly use in the current situation.

In many cases, this means we'll have to gradually relax our specifications until we find an appropriate resource. This will often force us to settle for very generic audio cues (such as "I'm hit!" or "Guess he got away"). But every once in a while, it will allow our characters to use highly situation-specific audio cues that describe the situation in much more intimate detail. Those are the "magic moments" in a game when the game begins to shift the player's sense of gameplay beyond mere state-space exploration and task fulfillment and push the level of interaction toward a sense of communion of human and artificial minds. These are the moments that make the user say, "Wow—I can't believe the game actually noticed that!"

Building a Tag Vocabulary

We can support this type of flexible resource matching by describing each resource with a set of *tags*, or qualifiers that specify how that resource should be used. Then, whenever we need to play a sound or an animation, we search the resource database to find the resource whose tags best describe what we're looking for.

There are two types of tags: *value tags* and *enumerated tags*.

A *value tag* is always expressed by itself. A resource either has this tag or it doesn't. For example, an AI character can specify the "NearAlly" tag when it is close to another character that it considers an ally.

An *enumerated tag* has a set of allowable values and can express only one of those values. For example, a tag such as "PlayerGender:[Male,Female]" in the tag vocabulary tells the system that a resource can be tagged with either "PlayerGender:Male" or "PlayerGender:Female," but not both.

The first step in planning our AI audio system is to define a *vocabulary*. This is a list of the allowable tags that we will use to specify resources. A simple vocabulary might look something like this:

```
NearAlly
HasSeenPlayer
PlayerGender:[Male,Female]
AIState:[Idle,Searching,Attacking]
AreaType:[Barracks,Office,Kitchen,Mess Hall,Outdoors]
Morale:[Demoralized,Medium,Gung-Ho]
Voice:[Guard01,Guard02,Priest01,Skeleton01,Goblin01]
```

Tagging AI Resources

After we define our vocabulary, we can begin designing our resources. We begin at the most general level, with generic audio cues that describe only the AI's current behavior state, and proceed to more specific audio cues that take additional situational factors into account—that is, resources that have more tag qualifiers. The following sample audio cues give an idea of how we can use these tags to describe resources.

AIState:Idle
Not much goin' on around here . . .

AIState:Searching
Hello? Is someone out there?

AIState:Searching, HasSeenPlayer
All right, I know you're out there. Come on out, wherever you are!

AIState:Searching, NearAlly
There's an intruder about. I'm quite certain of it.

AIState:Searching, NearAlly, HasSeenPlayer
Keep your eyes peeled—I saw an intruder about.

AIState:Searching, NearAlly, HasSeenPlayer, PlayerGender:Male

There's a man around here somewhere. I saw him with my own eyes!

AIState:Searching, NearAlly, HasSeenPlayer, PlayerGender:Female

There's a woman around here somewhere. I saw her with my own eyes!

When an AI agent wants to play an audio cue, it will always use the most specific possible AI cue from the set of available AI audio resources.

Thus, if a character is searching, is near an ally, and has seen the player previously and knows that she is female, it will prefer to use "There's a woman around here somewhere. I saw her with my own eyes!" rather than the more generic "Hello? Is someone out there?"

Executing Tag Queries

Let's assume we've recorded a set of AI audio resources and have tagged them properly. We can now consider the structure of the code that will select a resource. We do this by building a *tag query*, which is a list of tags we want to search for.

The tag query has a special syntax. We use the "+" symbol here to denote a *required* tag: that is, an asset *must* have this tag in order to become a candidate for matching. We use the "?" character to denote an *optional* tag. An optional tag tells the tag system to rank a matching resource more highly if it contains the specified tag. However, unlike required tags, a resource can still be selected even if it does not match any optional tags.

For any given tag query, we use the following simple algorithm to select a matching resource:

1. Begin with the set of all available resources.
2. Rule out any resources that do not include *all* of the required tags in the query set.
3. Rank the remaining resources in terms of those that match the greatest number of optional tags.
4. Rank the remaining resources from step 3 in terms of those with the least number of additional tags (that is, tags on the resource that are not specified as required or optional tags in the query).
5. If more than one resource is ranked highest at this point, select the least recently used resource. If there is more than one resource that has never been used, select randomly from among the highest-ranked resources.

The most desirable asset is the one that matches all of the required tags in the query list, matches as many of the optional tags as possible, and has the least number of extraneous (unspecified) tags.

To see how this works, imagine we have a guard that has heard some noises and has begun searching the area for the player. However, the guard has not yet actually seen the player. Also, there happens to be another character nearby, and that character is friendly toward the guard.

We will therefore create a tag query that looks like this:

+AIState:Searching ?NearAlly

Note that the "HasSeenPlayer" and "PlayerGender" tags are not included in this tag query, since the AI has not seen the player and does not know his or her gender.

Also, note that we use a question mark for "NearAlly" to indicate that this is an optional tag. This is a way of telling the system that we'd prefer to use sounds that are appropriate when near an allied AI, but we'll be satisfied with more generic AI cues if we have to.

Now take another look at the list of sample AI audio cues presented in the *Tagging AI Resources* section. We will use these seven sounds as our example AI audio resource set.

First, we execute rules 1 and 2 from our algorithm. Rule 2 disqualifies the first sound ("Not much goin' on around here . . ."), since this resource is tagged with "AIState:Idle" instead of "AIState:Searching." We then execute rule 3, which ranks the last four sounds higher than all the others, since they all include "NearAlly." Finally, we execute rule 4, which gives the last three sounds a lower ranking, since they all include extra tags that we did not specify in the tag query.

The sound we end up with is therefore:

AIState:Searching, NearAlly
"There's an intruder about. I'm quite certain of it."

Building a Tag Query

One nice benefit of this type of tagging system is that it makes it extremely easy to play sounds from our code. The following sample function `CreateTagQuery()` shows how to do this. `CreateTagQuery()` does nothing more than accept a query object—typically represented as a string—and automatically append additional specifier tags.

```
void AI::CreateTagQuery(TagQuery& query) const
{
    AddTags_CharacterVoice(query);
    AddTags_LocationType(query);
    AddTags_PlayerGender(query);
    // etc.
}
```

`CreateTagQuery()` allows you to pass in a primitive tag query such as "+AIState:Alert," and the function will automatically analyze the current situation and automatically append all the appropriate tags ("+Voice," "+Location," "+PlayerGender," etc.) in order to construct a fully qualified tag query. This makes it very simple to play AI sounds, since `CreateTagQuery()` does most of the work.

Each of the individual `AddTags_x()` functions examines some aspect of the AI character's state or the current game state and appends the appropriate tags to the growing tag query string. For example, `AddTags_CharacterVoice()` might look like this:

```
void AI::AddTags_CharacterVoice(TagQuery& query) const
{
    query += "+Voice:";

    switch (m_Type)
    {
        case AI_GUARD01: query += "guard01"; break;
        case AI_GOBLIN01: query += "goblin01"; break;
        // etc.
    }
}
```

Obviously, this code is provided only for the sake of explanation; you would want to use a much more data-driven solution than the code shown here. That is, a real implementation would store data such as a character's type ("guard01," "goblin01") in game data files rather than using a big, hard-coded switch-case statement.

Tagging Animations

Up to this point, we've focused exclusively on using the tagging system to look up AI audio resources. We now consider how you can use it to select animations.

AI animation systems typically organize animation resources into some number of *poses* or *stances*, which are sets of animations that all begin and end at the same character pose. For example, if a character is in the "HoldingOneHandedSword" pose, we create a set of animations related to one-handed sword usage such that we can play the animations in any sequential order. This is very similar to a finite-state machine, in which each "state" of the finite-state machine contains a set of animations appropriate for that stance or pose.

We can then use special transition animations to transition between states—for example, a "draw sword" animation to transition from the "unarmed" stance to the "holding a sword" stance, and a "sheathe sword" animation for the opposite.

The following sample tag vocabulary shows an example of the tags we might use to describe animations.

```
Pose:[Standing,Sitting,HoldingSword,HoldingBow,Dead]
Action:[Idling,Moving,Attacking]
MovementDirection:[Forward,Backward,Left,Right]
MovementSpeed:[Creep,Walk,Run]
Character:[Guard,Civilian,Monster]
Mood:[Normal,Angry,Surprised,Fearful,Sad]
Limping:[LeftLeg,RightLeg]
HoldingShield
```

Thus, for any given animation, we would use the "Pose" and "Action" tags to specify the character's current pose and the action the character is attempting to perform, along with some number of additional tag specifiers depending on the character's current state. For example, the tag set for a guard's unarmed forward walk animation might look like this:

```
Pose:Standing
Action:Moving
MovementDirection:Forward
MovementSpeed:Walk
Mood:Normal
Character:Guard
```

Building a Decision Tree

At this point, some readers might be wondering why we don't simply build a decision tree instead of using tags. We could design a tree such that at each level, we branch into several possible descendants based on the value of a single tag or the absence of that tag. The actual audio resources would be placed at the leaves of the tree. Figure 6.3.1 shows how this would work.

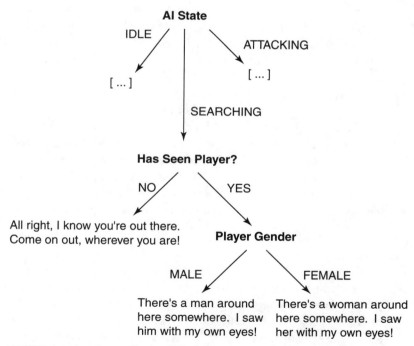

FIGURE 6.3.1 *A greatly simplified decision tree for three of the sounds in our example.*

In many cases, a decision tree is a useful structure for conceptualizing the design of our tag vocabularies. However, there are also many cases where a tree structure is a poor fit for the problem.

Using our sample vocabulary, sometimes we might want to pick a sound based on the PlayerGender tag, sometimes we'd want to select a sound based on the AreaType, sometimes we'd want to discriminate based on Morale, and sometimes we'd want to describe sounds with combinations of two of those factors, or all three at once. In such cases, it's very unclear which of our three qualifiers—PlayerGender, Morale, and AreaType—should be higher in the tree. These three specifiers are completely orthogonal to each other—there is no inherent ranking between them.

A sparse matrix is a better metaphor. Each tag qualifier is one dimension of the matrix. Thus, if we wanted to, we could create an audio cue that specified values for all seven of the tags in our sample vocabulary (NearAlly, HasSeenPlayer, PlayerGender, and so forth).

However, decision trees are nonetheless an excellent way to optimize tag lookup in the implementation.

The algorithm described in this article for matching resources to a tag query (in the previous section *Executing Tag Queries*) requires us to look through our entire resource set in order to pick a resource. Clearly, with a large number of resources, this lookup will be very slow unless we find a way to optimize our search.

Fortunately, there are a number of excellent classifier algorithms, notably ID3 and C4.5 [Quinlan93], which can take arbitrary data sets consisting of (multiple input values $\Rightarrow$ single output value) mappings and automatically construct optimized decision trees from them.

This is a perfect fit for our problem, as we can easily provide a complete set of (tag set) $\Rightarrow$ (resource) mappings for all of our resources.

Thus, it's possible to build a tag lookup system that will automatically analyze your entire audio or animation resource set, build an optimized decision tree data structure based on the tags attached to all of your resources, and save this decision tree as a special data file that your game engine can read. This gives you the freedom to design a highly flexible database of resources based entirely on tags, while also providing the fast resource lookup that decision trees can provide.

Conclusion

As the game industry evolves toward open-ended simulations based on emergent behaviors, it becomes increasingly difficult to create content that's tightly fitted to the current game state and the player's current circumstances. This is precisely because such simulations dramatically expand the possibilities for gameplay and make the current game state at any moment far less predictable [Pacotti03].

Although it might not be possible to create content that will match all of the possible game states in such an open-ended game world, the tagging system proposed here allows you to create content that will fit *some* of the possible game states *some* of the time.

Acknowledgments

The author would like to acknowledge the programming staff of now-defunct Looking Glass Studios as the originators of the tagging system presented in this article.

References

[Fu04] Fu, Daniel, and Houlette, Ryan, "The Ultimate Guide to FSMs in Games," *AI Game Programming Wisdom 2*, Charles River Media, 2004.

[Nuance03] Nuance VocalizerTM 2.0, *www.nuance.com/prodserv/prodvocalizer.html*

[Pacotti03] Pacotti, Sheldon, "Toward Massively Responsive Conversations," available online at *www.gdconf.com/archives/2003/Pacotti_Sheldon.ppt*, March 2003.

[Quinlan93] Quinlan, J. Ross, *C4.5: Programs for Machine Learning*, Morgan Kaufmann, 1993.

6.4

Motivational Graphs: A New Architecture for Complex Behavior Simulation

Emmanuel Chiva, Julien Devade, Jean-Yves Donnart, Stéphane Maruéjouls— MASA Group

emmanuel.chiva@masagroup.net,
julien.devade@masagroup.net,
jean-yves.donnart@masagroup.net,
stephane.maruejouls@masagroup.net

Being a game character is not an easy job. Apart from moving around, you also have to interact with the player in a natural way, look alive, communicate, and on top of it all, stay alive. In the last decade, game developers have came up with a number of ways of dealing with such complexity.

In this article, we introduce a new architecture that incorporates ideas borrowed from biology, cognitive science, and behavioral science. Applied to game development, it enables designers and developers to easily describe, model, and implement realistic autonomous software agents. This architecture is called a *motivational graph*. It is a hybrid between rule-based approaches and connectionist systems. Specifically, it uses concepts such as activity propagation to trigger modules within a hyperconnected graph.

We will attempt to demonstrate the benefits of this approach: multitasking, opportunism, tradeoff, emergence and easy factorization for increased productivity. The main goal is not to design intelligent agents, but rather to demonstrate how an entity can be adaptive and, above all, exhibit realistic behaviors from the player's point of view.

Decision Systems—Symbolic AI versus Situated Agents

Symbolic AI has been and is still today used extensively in games. Problem-solving techniques are often top-down, recursively decomposing each problem into a list of sub-problems that are easier to solve. Such techniques need the world to be described as a set of symbolic attributes. As a consequence, symbolic AI needs an environmental description in the form of a set of discrete states.

A nonexhaustive description of symbolic AI techniques would include finite-state machines (FSMs), fuzzy finite-state machines (FFSMs), expert systems (ESs), decision trees, and graphs.

FSMs, FFSMs, and ESs are easy to implement and need little CPU resources. They do a reasonable job of modeling the entity, but often result in deterministic and predictable behaviors. Decision trees and other classical algorithms, on the other hand, provide a good set of methods, often expensive in terms of CPU cycles, which allows the development of smart behaviors. However, they are often limited in their ability to adapt, since they only deal with sets of discrete situations.

Recently, new methods, originating from academic research have appeared, aimed at providing techniques allowing the implementation of high-level, adaptive behaviors. These include artificial life [Langton97], animats [Meyer96], behavioral approach [Maes92], multi-agent systems [Gasser89], and so forth.

These methods are innovative because they consider the entity as "situated" in its environment and whose behaviors aim to satisfy their goals and motivations according to their local perceptions, their internal state, and the communication they receive (hence the name "situated agents"). The main advantage of this "bottom-up" approach is to show some level of autonomous adaptation in the sense that they can generate action sequences that can be considered as emergent behaviors (in other words, not explicitly programmed). Motivational graphs belong to this category.

Motivational Graphs

In some newer games, characters show action selection capabilities: they are motivated and exhibit an internal state that varies according to their performances in the game (most of the time, killing the player is a strong motivation).

From a behavioral sciences point of view, a motivation can be viewed as an internal variable that accounts for both the internal state of the entity and for the stimuli it receives [McFarland93]. It is used to trigger behaviors that define possible goals for the entity. By reaching such goals, the entity tries to maintain the variable in an "acceptable" state, thus "satisfying the motivation." In that respect, a motivational system can be viewed as a dynamic system, able to generate its own goals and assess its own needs.

For example, a hungry (*motivation*) mouse is looking for food by exploring its environment (*behavior*), particularly the garbage area (*goal*) known as a good meal-provider. Eating will increase its food level (*internal state*) and thus satisfy its hunger.

Many existing attempts to solve the goal generation problem proved to be only reactive (as opposed to "cognitive") and difficult to fine-tune when there are many conflicting motivations. This often results in either oscillations or hacks in the system to avoid choosing between contradictory goals. Motivational graphs have been developed to allow a better management resulting in more realistic behaviors. This is especially true when:

- The entity can select behaviors that are compromises between its conflicting motivations, and opportunistically switch goals, to account for any unpredicted event.
- Behaviors can be organized hierarchically; the entity can choose to maintain its current behavior when needed, using persistence mechanisms.
- The entity is able to exhibit emergent behaviors that are not explicitly programmed.

We will describe the principles of a motivational graph before giving some examples of how it can be applied to game bot development and its advantages.

General Principle

Figure 6.4.1 compares a motivational graph (right) with a more classical decision tree-based algorithm for action selection (left).

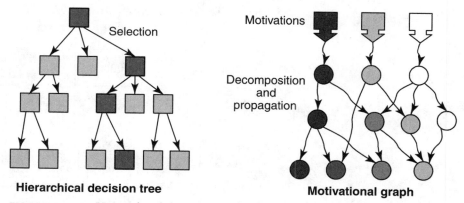

FIGURE 6.4.1   *Hierarchical decision tree versus a motivational graph.*

In a traditional decision tree, nodes are goal-states that can be decomposed and leafs are state change operators that represent the decisions the entity makes. Each decomposition implies a selection that requires decision rules (e.g., evaluation functions) associated with the states. A recursive decomposition in the decision tree allows the generation of the action plan.

Here is the most important aspect of a motivational graph. In such a graph, motivations generate an activation that is propagated in a behavioral network until it reaches the final nodes. These nodes correspond to the elementary actions that directly link to the physical actions of the entity.

Motivational graphs inherit from both neural networks and rule-based systems. Globally, they can be viewed as networks in which energy is propagated. However, nodes, instead of being neurons, are sets of rules that define the strength of the connections.

The key advantages are:

- It becomes possible to process many tasks or action plans in parallel since the activation is propagated throughout the entire graph.
- Decision rules are simpler since they model the way activation is propagated instead of defining the way goals are decomposed.
- Only a few rules are needed to give the entity a complex behavior since its state is not defined by a single node but by the entire graph.

From a game development point of view, another key feature is that such systems are highly modular—a property that allows programming complex behaviors while avoiding the pitfall of combinatorial explosion.

Motivational Graphs Exhibit Modularity

To illustrate this property, let us focus on three examples. Figure 6.4.2 compares a finite-state machine and a motivational graph. The goal is to add a reflex action (*Reflex Action*) in a predefined behavioral sequence (*Beh1, Beh2, Beh3*).

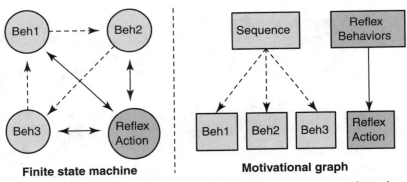

Finite state machine   **Motivational graph**

FIGURE 6.4.2   *Comparison between an FSM and a motivational graph.*

The FSM requires a transition rule to be programmed for each state (transition from *Beh i* to the *Reflex Action*) as well as a reverse transition rule that gets the "token" back to *Beh i* once the *Reflex Action* has been completed. This requires the developer to program six rules.

A motivational graph (as shown in Figure 6.4.2—right-hand side) can process the *Reflex Action* and the behavioral sequence in parallel. Triggering the *Reflex Action* therefore only requires one rule, which competes with the current behavior. The latter remains active and can automatically regain control as soon as the *Reflex Action* is completed.

Figure 6.4.3 compares how a mission is decomposed by either a decision tree (left) or a motivational graph (right).

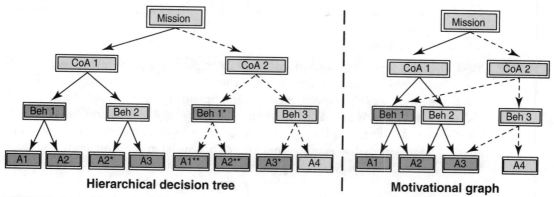

FIGURE 6.4.3 *Motivational graphs modularity—comparison with a hierarchical decision tree.*

Using a decision tree, the developer must program each module (behavior or action) separately, since the algorithm requires decomposing recursively each behavior in sub-behaviors, before choosing the appropriate elementary action. The fact that some modules are very similar is not exploited (e.g., *Beh1*, *Beh1**).

In a motivational graph, each module has its own autonomy and can participate to the instantiation of several different behaviors; for example, the *Beh1* behavior allows implementing both courses of actions *CoA1* and *CoA2*.

Figure 6.4.4 illustrates how a motivational graph can be modularly updated. Once again, let's take the example of our decision tree. With such an algorithm, any change in the situation requires the tree to be completely evaluated.

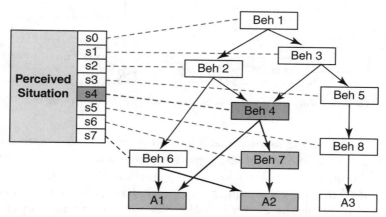

FIGURE 6.4.4 *A motivational graph can be modularly updated.*

In a motivational graph, only a few situation elements are considered in order to update the activation modulation. Take the example of the situation element *s4*. This element is used by the behavior *Beh4* only and is therefore only updated at the *Beh4* level (and, in this case, at the level of its sub-behaviors and actions: *Beh7*, *A1* and *A2*).

A Simplified Example

Modularity properties of motivational graphs also provide a convenient way of developing compromise behaviors. Let's suppose character A sees two characters, B (friend) and C (enemy). Let's also consider that A can implement three actions: *Attack*, *Avoid*, and *GoTo* and has two contradictory motivations: *Fighting enemies* and *Safeguard*.

Figure 6.4.5 illustrates how to implement this simple agent using a motivational graph. The presence of an enemy generates activity at the motivation level. Both conflicting motivations *Safeguard* and *Fighting enemies* are activated. Activation is propagated to the behaviors *Protect_itself()* and *Fight()*, respectively.

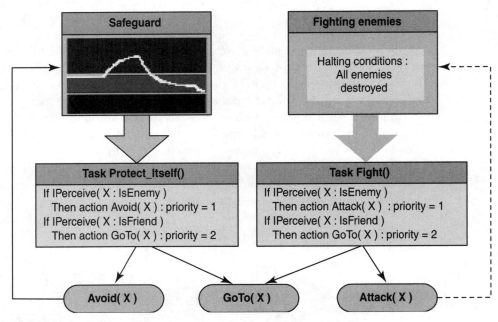

FIGURE 6.4.5 *Internal functioning: example showing trade-off.*

Using the motivational graph formalism, the developer decomposes these two behaviors into possible elementary actions (these will be triggered when the rule conditions within each module are activated). In the present example, the *IPerceive(X : Att)* condition is a request that allows identifying the list of perceived characters X characterized by the *Att* attribute. The value of this attribute and the priority of the rule define the potential of the associated action. In each behavior, two rules will be triggered to activate the elementary actions:

- *Avoid(B)* and *GoTo(C)* for the behavior *Protect_itself*
- *Attack(B)* and *GoTo(C)* for the behavior *Fight*

If the enemy is perceived as too strong (respectively too weak), the action *Avoid(B)* (respectively *Attack(B)*) will be selected due to a higher priority. If the balance of power is less obvious, the *GoTo(C)* action will be selected as a trade-off between attacking and avoiding (even if this action is considered a lesser priority by each behavior on its own).

In such a situation, a hierarchical decision tree would have chosen the strongest behavior (*Protect_itself()* or *Fight()*) and would have then selected the action with the highest priority (*Avoid(B)* or *Attack(B)*).

Applications: Motivational Graphs in an FPS Bot

ON THE CD

After this rather theoretical introduction, we will see how to apply motivational graphs to bot management. We decided to take the example of an FPS game environment in which we will build the graph step by step and illustrate the resulting key advantages (see the accompanying CD-ROM for the corresponding AVIs).

Problem Specifications

The problem here is to develop a bot that can perform three main tasks:

- Stay alive (collecting life bonuses and armor)
- Destroy its enemies (collecting weapons and ammo)
- Fulfill its mission (capture the enemy flag)

While this appears to be a simple problem, the main difficulty is to combine player orders and bot needs, and still account for the environment (walls and objects).

Mission Definition

The bot's mission is to capture the enemy flag. Let's begin by considering a simple bot that does not take into account its environment. Armor, ammo, weapons, and life bonuses are ignored: the bot tries to fulfill its task using the shortest possible path. It uses the game engine to define the best route and then "blindly" follows it. Figure 6.4.6 illustrates this behavior—the two trajectories correspond to two different starting positions.

Introducing Motivation and Personality

We can now configure the bot motivational graph so that it tries to simultaneously protect itself and destroy its enemies. Figure 6.4.7 shows the resulting motivational

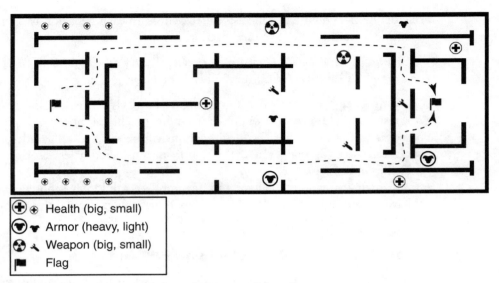

FIGURE 6.4.6   *Bot trajectories—shortest possible path.*

structure. On the top is personality (survival instinct and aggressiveness), and on the bottom are the four motivational blocks that can trigger the bot's behaviors.

Now the bot will consider its own needs and take them into account to improve its behavior. In the following sections, we will show the resulting behavior as it can be observed in the simulation.

Motivations and Opportunism

The bot still has the same mission to capture the enemy flag. This mission is the main task; however, the new bot exhibits some degree of autonomy. The bot will try to fulfill its motivations as long as the main task is not affected.

In the following example (shown in Figure 6.4.8), the bot exhibits an opportunistic behavior. It always tries to take the shortest route; however, it remains reactive to the objects that could help satisfy its motivations: life, armor, weapons, and ammo. The result is that the trajectory can be slightly modified when the bot sees an object and decides to go for it. Incidentally, such diversions can result in a new trajectory, since the bot can recompute its path whenever needed.

Multitasking and Trade-Offs

Competition between motivations: In this example, the bot has been released from the strong constraint: it can freely choose between its motivations and its mission. The resulting behavior is more autonomous. According to its preferences and its initial state, the bot can deliberately choose to go and seek bonuses before capturing the enemy flag.

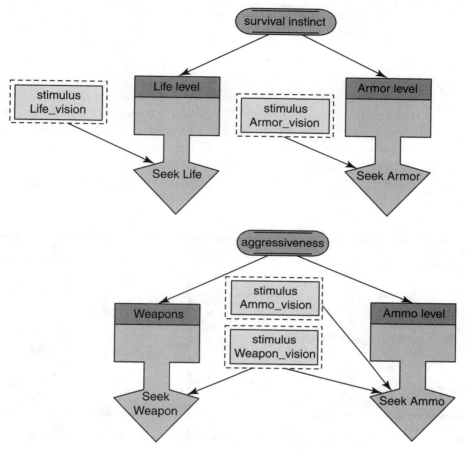

FIGURE 6.4.7 *Graph with internal states, stimuli and motivations.*

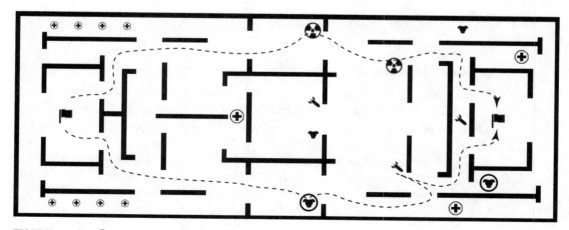

FIGURE 6.4.8 *Bot trajectories as they satisfy their motivations on route to the flag.*

Trade-offs between motivations: If several goals and motivations must be fulfilled simultaneously, the bot tries to make trade-offs. As an example (see Figure 6.4.9), the trajectory number 1 corresponds to an aggressive bot that is mainly interested in weapons: it seeks the most powerful weapon available and only then goes for the enemy flag. The trajectory marked 2 corresponds to a careful bot that first goes for the "mega-armor" before fulfilling its mission. The third trajectory corresponds to a bot that equally seeks weapons and armor. The resulting behavior is that the bot seeks a place where it can find both weapons and armor (even if these are not the best the bot could find), simultaneously fulfilling its motivations and completing its main task.

The interesting part is that this trade-off behavior can be obtained without having to explicitly program it.

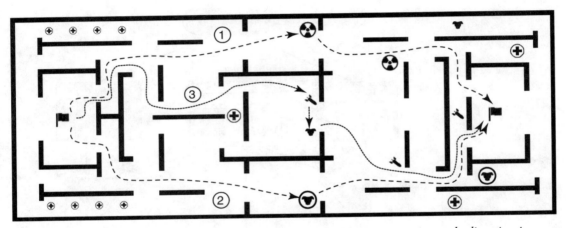

FIGURE 6.4.9   *Motivated behaviors and trade-offs at work. Bot 1 is aggressive, only diverting its path for weapons. Bot 2 is careful, picking up armor on the way to the flag. Bot 3 is interested equally in weapons and armor, finding a way to incorporate both desires on its way to the flag.*

Motivated Pathfinding

Finally, instead of using the entire motivated graph to determine the bot's actions, it is possible to introduce pathfinding capabilities by plugging some motivated behaviors into a modified pathfinder, thus enabling the bot to take into account items that satisfy its motivations while computing its way.

As shown in Figure 6.4.10, the resulting bot uses paths that rapidly lead it to the enemy flag while capturing life and armor according to its motivations. The balancing mechanism is emergent and therefore does not need extensive programming.

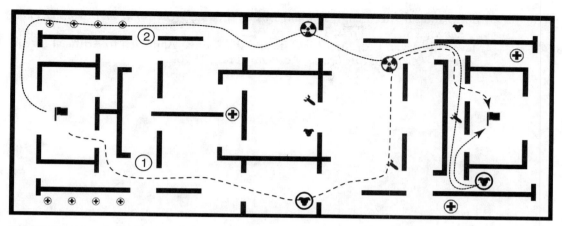

FIGURE 6.4.10 *According to its personality and motivations, the bot plans an optimized path that already takes everything into account, instead of making diversions.*

Conclusion

What we presented here is a high-level introduction to motivational graphs as generic tools for implementing complex behaviors.

Beyond FPS games, motivational graphs are naturally adapted to the implementation of virtual worlds and online games where the number of possible situations encountered is potentially infinite. The ability to decompose and plan behaviors as well as the close integration with pathfinding allows obtaining elaborate NPCs for RTS and tactical shooters games.

Key advantages are the savings in terms of development time, easy implementation of realistic and complex behaviors, and factorization of rules avoiding combinatorial explosion. This technology allows the developer to spend less time programming and more time perfecting the gameplay.

References

[Gasser89] Gasser, L., and Huhns, M.N., *Distributed Artificial Intelligence*, Morgan Kauffman, 1989.

[Goldberg89] Goldberg, D.E., *Genetic Algorithms in Search Optimization and Machine Learning*, Addison-Wesley, 1989.

[Holland86] Holland, J.H., "Escaping Brittleness: The Possibilities of General-Purpose Learning Algorithms Applied to Parallel Rule-Based Systems," *Machine Learning: An Artificial Intelligence Approach, Volume 2*, Morgan Kaufmann, 1986.

[Langton97] Langton C.G., *Artificial Life. An Overview*, The MIT Press, 1997.

[Maes92] Maes, P., "Behavior-Based Artificial Intelligence," *From Animals to Animats 2. Proceedings of the 2nd Int. Conf. on Simulation of Adaptive Behavior*, The MIT Press, 1992.

[McFarland93] McFarland. D., and Bösser, T., *Intelligent Behavior in Animals and Robots*, The MIT Press, 1993.

[Meyer96] Meyer, J.A., "Artificial Life and the Animat Approach to Artificial Intelligence," *Artificial Intelligence*, Academic Press, 1996.

6.5

Minimizing Agent Processing in *Conflict: Desert Storm*

Sebastian Grinke—Pivotal Games

seb.grinke@pivotalgames.com

Modern game AI demands efficient use of processor resources. While a great deal has been written about sophisticated level-of-detail AI routines [Brockington02], few have discussed simpler approaches that can often produce adequate results with less development effort.

Around halfway through the development of *Conflict: Desert Storm (CDS)*, we discovered that the number of enemies required to populate the large game maps, and the amount of processing taken up by those enemies (especially line-of-sight ray casts) was slowing the frame rate of the game to an unacceptable level. Moreover, the problem was exacerbated by allowing the player to control four independent game characters (who could roam the map freely) in both the cooperative and single-player game modes. Unfortunately, each enemy had a large processing overhead and there had to be enough enemies in the game world for all of the player characters to fight simultaneously.

To remedy this problem, we used a variety of optimization techniques. Some were aimed at reducing the processing performed by each agent [McLean02]; however, this article focuses on how we managed to minimize the number of enemy agents processed per frame. Our first step was to freeze distant enemies and page out enemies in areas unoccupied by player characters. We then stepped back a level from programming optimizations and modified the design of the game. One change was to spawn enemies close to the player, instead of populating the world with patrolling enemies that went unnoticed. Another change was to keep enemies close to the player to give the illusion of there being more enemies than actually existed.

The outcome was a game that not only ran faster, but also had more enemies per map and was therefore more exciting for the player. It is interesting that solving what was essentially a technical problem also had the beneficial side effect of improving the gameplay.

Freezing Distant Enemies

The first optimization we added was freezing distant enemies as shown in Figure 6.5.1. Enemies in the game detect how far they are from the nearest player character. If this distance is greater than the fog distance (the distance at which the enemy can no longer be seen) for more than a short time delay, a flag is set and the code freezes the enemy. The time delay was added to prevent enemies who are running toward the player from being frozen as the player retreats.

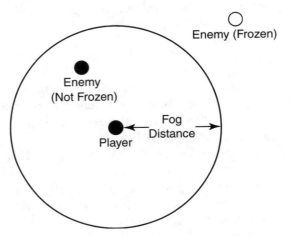

FIGURE 6.5.1   *Enemies outside of the fog distance are frozen.*

There are some exceptions. The code will not freeze enemies who are falling, playing a death animation, or performing an important game action such as running to an alarm point (usually indicated by a flag toggled on and off elsewhere in the AI). It is important to eliminate any indications that enemies are being frozen when out of range.

The only processing done on a frozen enemy is the distance check, so that the enemy can be "thawed out" at the right time. Note that there might be some issues to consider when an enemy is unfrozen. Do your enemy agents have any form of memory? If so it might be somewhat out of date. If you find this to be a problem, you can store the time an enemy was frozen, and write a thawing out function that uses the elapsed time to update the enemy's memory and behavior.

Paging Out Enemies

Many games store the enemies in some form of list, and different sections of code (such as the renderer, the AI, and collision detection) loop through this list processing them. If we remove enemies from the list, the game speed is improved in two ways.

First, the amount of processing required by any list operation is reduced. Second, the list itself fits in a smaller memory footprint and can be cached more easily by the processors.

We used a paging technique to keep the number of enemies in our active list to a minimum. Each game map was split into areas. An area was defined as a list of geometry zones (sections of the game map that are separated by portal rendering boundaries) as shown in Figure 6.5.2. When there are no player characters in an area, we swap the enemies belonging to that area to an inactive list. While in this list, the enemies are not processed at all. When a player-controlled character enters an area, any enemies in the inactive list for that area are swapped back into the active list and carry on as they were.

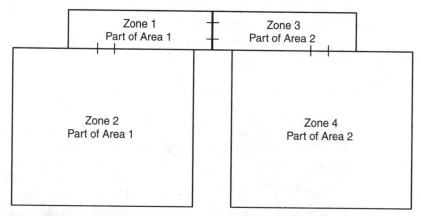

FIGURE 6.5.2   *Dividing a map into areas for the purposes of paging enemies in and out.*

The advantage of this is that it sometimes allows us to page out enemies while they are relatively near the player character. Frozen enemies are also paged out, which reduces the number of distance checks we have to do per frame.

Note that there might be cases where it is undesirable for an enemy to be paged out (e.g., an enemy who is running to raise the alarm). In this case, it is possible to flag the enemy so that it does not get paged out.

Obviously, we cannot allow the player to see an enemy being paged in or out. We achieved this by limiting the movement of our enemies to places that could not be seen from foreign areas as shown in Figure 6.5.3. We then added special enemies who did not belong to any area and were therefore never paged out. These special enemies were used to fill out the empty space between areas and in special cases where an enemy had to be able to go from area to area. For example, in the last level of the game there is an enemy general who has to flee from one end of the map to the other, with the player in pursuit. The general is not attached to any area.

There are other solutions to this problem. It would have been possible to write code that allowed enemies to move from one area to another, by jumping between the various area lists. We avoided this, as we wanted to guarantee that the number of enemies being processed at any one time was below a certain limit. It would also be possible to keep enemies in adjacent areas active. Unfortunately, our maps were not suited to this, as it would require much smaller areas.

If the player characters in an area are not under player control (and therefore not being observed by any players), we can use an additional trick. In this situation, the player will notice if all of the enemies in an area are paged out, as his character will not be fighting them. The player might not, however, notice if some of the enemies are paged out. In fact, in *CDS*, only one enemy is kept active for each player character in this situation. For this to work without the player noticing, it is important to choose the right enemy. We ordered the enemies in an area according to their importance. If any enemy is fighting the player character, he is chosen. If no enemies are engaging the player, then the first (and therefore most important) living enemy in the list is used.

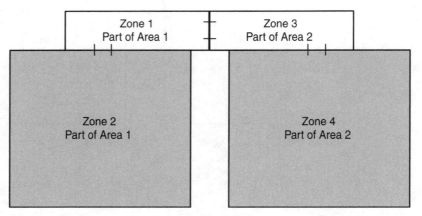

FIGURE 6.5.3   *Enemies are not allowed to move outside of the shaded rooms.*

Spawn Points

Spawn points are a good way of adding enemies to a game without slowing it down. Designers place the spawn points on the game maps using an in-house editor. The basic idea is that the points spawn new enemies into the game world when the player is not looking.

This system has several advantages over just having all the enemies patrol the map from the beginning. First, and most importantly, the number of enemies active in the game world at any one time can be kept below a minimum threshold—if there are too many active enemies, no new ones are spawned. This not only keeps the game speed up, but also has the added advantage of regulating how many enemies are attacking the player at any one time, which is an important design consideration.

We can also use the spawn points to control the geographical distribution of our enemies in such a way that they are created near the player characters. This gives the impression that there are many more enemies in the game world than there really are. This is done by not spawning enemies further away than a maximum distance from the nearest player character. For the same reason, in *CDS* the code does not spawn enemies if they are attached to an inactive area.

It is also possible to use spawn points to respawn the same enemy over and over again, which avoids having to allocate and free memory while the game is running. We do this by attaching one or more enemies to a spawn point. The spawn point remains inactive while any of the enemies belonging to it are alive. Once they are all dead, the spawn point becomes active again, and the enemies can be respawned into the game world.

To avoid the player seeing an enemy being spawned, each spawn point can be attached to one or more regions in the game world. When a player character enters one of these regions (which can be a sphere or box placed in the game editor) the spawn point is permanently disabled. This also gets around the problem of enemies spawning in parts of the map that the player has already visited.

Spawn points can also be hooked into other areas of the game. For example, in *CDS* each level script has the ability to enable and disable spawn points, which allows us to do things like spawn more enemies when an alarm is raised or the player completes an objective.

One final consideration is that it is not necessary to update the spawn system every frame. The update routine, which decides when to spawn new enemies, has to perform distance checks between the spawn points and the player characters. As a consequence of this it has some processing overhead. We found that there was no noticeable difference in only calling this routine once a second.

Retaining Player Proximity

We also found it advantageous to alter our AI to keep the enemies near the player characters as much as possible. This is another useful trick in making the game maps appear more populated than they really are.

There are two very simple ways of achieving this. If enemies are randomly patrolling, they can be made to walk between waypoints that are within a minimum radius of a player character. Similarly, if they are searching, they can select search points that gradually home in on a player character [McLean04].

Diagnostics

While implementing these solutions, we found it very useful to write some simple diagnostics display code so that we could see which areas and enemies were active and why. We also added color particle displays to tag enemies in the game world as frozen, unable to freeze, and so forth. This saved time in debugging the code we had written. As standard practice, good AI diagnostics should be implemented whenever possible [Tozour02].

Conclusion

The key to minimizing agent processing in *Conflict: Desert Storm* was to reduce the number of enemies processed per frame. Rather than write a complex level-of-detail system, we opted instead to use a combination of simpler techniques and found this approach very effective in saving development time. In solving this technical problem, we also managed to improve the design of the game, which was an unexpected yet beneficial side effect.

References

[Brockington02] Brockington, Mark, "Level-of-Detail AI for a Large Role-Playing Game," *AI Game Programming Wisdom*, Charles River Media 2002.

[McLean02] McLean, Alex W., "An Efficient AI Architecture Using Prioritized Task Categories," *AI Game Programming Wisdom*, Charles River Media 2002.

[McLean04] McLean, Alex W., "Hunting Down the Player in a Convincing Manner," *AI Game Programming Wisdom 2*, Charles River Media 2004.

[Tozour02] Tozour, Paul, "Building an AI Diagnostic Toolset," *AI Game Programming Wisdom*, Charles River Media 2002.

FPS, RTS, AND STRATEGY AI

7.1

Using a Spatial Database for Runtime Spatial Analysis

Paul Tozour—Retro Studios

gehn29@yahoo.com

Many games require AI characters to reason about their physical environment. For example, combat AI systems in action games require combatants to take cover from enemy fire and execute various tactical maneuvers that take the dynamic environment into account. Stealth-oriented "first-person sneaker" games, such as *Thief: The Dark Project* [LGS98], require characters to perform a search of an area looking for the player.

Some types of behaviors, such as scripted action sequences and NPC patrol paths, are simple and predictable enough that level designers can effectively plan them using a linear script. However, this level of designer control breaks down when characters need to interact with the player directly. The moment a character enters combat or begins searching for the player, the gameplay must become vastly more interactive, and scripting is no longer feasible. Highly interactive AI behaviors require a much higher level of abstraction that allows AI units to perform some amount of reasoning about their environment.

Static and Dynamic Representations

Some AI developers have attempted to guide AIs' spatial reasoning by providing tools for designers to place "hints" in the game world [Lidén02]. Other developers have created systems that can analyze a game world and build a data structure that AIs can use to reason about the environment [van der Sterren01].

However, these kinds of tools only take the static environment into account, so this type of analysis can only address some of our concerns. There are many situations where AIs need to perform spatial reasoning about the *dynamic* aspects of the current game state in order to select an appropriate behavioral response.

The game world is continuously changing—bullets are flying, guards are rushing about and screaming, giant robots are firing high-powered weapons, and grenades are exploding and collapsing stacks of barrels that collide with poison gas canisters that then detonate and kill the guards. We can't hope to reason about such situations with data structures that only account for the permanently fixed aspects of the game world.

Influence mapping [Tozour01] is a good example of this type of dynamic spatial reasoning. Influence maps allow you to reason about the relative strengths of opposing forces in different areas and pinpoint the implicit boundaries of control between those factions.

This article discusses some of the other ways that game AIs can reason about their environment. We propose a *spatial database* that allows you to store any number of different types of relevant spatial data at runtime and combine that data in any number of ways to perform decision-making.

The Spatial Database

The spatial database consists of a two-dimensional (2D) grid overlaid on top of the game world. Each cell of the grid can contain many different flavors of data. Think of this as multiple independent layers superimposed on the same grid, with each layer containing a different type of data (see Figure 7.1.1).

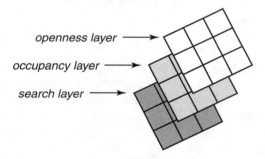

FIGURE 7.1.1 *Part of a spatial database with three arbitrarily chosen layers.*

The spatial database layers can contain both static and dynamic data. Some of the most useful types of data layers include:

- A static *openness layer* for representing proximity to static obstacles
- A static *cover layer* to represent locations where AIs can take cover from weapon fire
- A dynamic *area searching layer* for AIs who need to actively search an area for a possible intruder in a game that includes a stealth component
- A dynamic *area occupancy layer* to represent the occupancy level of different areas
- A dynamic *line-of-fire layer* to represent the direction various AI combatants are aiming with ranged weapons
- A dynamic *light level layer* to represent how bright or dark different parts of the game world are at any given point in time

This layer-based approach allows you to combine multiple layers to compute composite desirability values for a number of different tasks. For example, you can form a "combat desirability layer" by combining a number of different layers—the openness layer, the static cover layer, the area occupancy layer, as many others as necessary—to dynamically construct a new layer that represents the desirability of moving to any given cell in combat.

If each cell in the desirability layer contains a value indicating how wise it would be for an AI to move to that cell, then an AI unit only needs to look through the cells nearby, pick the cell with the highest value, and move to it.

Figure 7.1.2 shows an example of what this might look like, using the algorithm *desirability = openness * occupancy * static_cover*, where each of the "openness" and "occupancy" and "static_cover" layers contain normalized floating-point values. A value of 0 indicates the least desirable value, and 1 indicates the most desirable. For example, the openness layer would contain a 0 value for grid cells situated inside a wall or another static obstacle, with a gradient of values closer to 1 for cells farther from the wall. The occupancy layer would contain values closer to 0 for areas more highly populated by AI units. The static cover layer would typically contain cell values of 0 or 1 when in and out of cover, depending on whether the AI is attempting to enter cover or remain exposed.

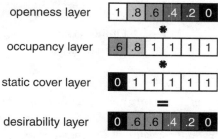

FIGURE 7.1.2 *Calculating a desirability layer.*

This kind of shared data structure has the additional benefit that it allows us to implicitly coordinate the behavior of multiple AIs. Quite often, we don't need complex high-level reasoning to make multiple AI agents work together—we can create emergent behavioral coordination simply by virtue of using shared data structures [Orkin04].

Obviously, this kind of 2D representation won't work for every type of game world. Three-dimensional game environments, such as typical first-person shooter (FPS) game worlds, often consist of multiple vertical levels, and a 2D grid will not be able to handle these types of environments easily. For the sake of simplicity, we'll postpone discussion of the potential solutions to these problems until the end of this article.

The Openness Layer

Imagine that we've created a game AI character with a number of combat tactics at his disposal. Each "tactic" consists of a small set of predefined behaviors for attacking a single opponent. Some of these tactics, such as "Circle of Death," require a certain minimum amount of open space in order to execute them properly.

This puts us in a quandary. If we aren't careful, we could end up doing a Circle of Death in a tight hallway, and our AIs will end up strafing into the walls. Clearly, our AI characters need some way to ask the question, "How much space do I have?"

We can solve this by creating an "openness" layer in the spatial database. Each cell of the openness layer will contain a numeric value that indicates how close it is to a wall or another immovable, impassable object (see Figure 7.1.3).

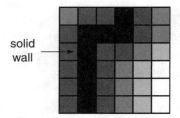

solid
wall →

FIGURE 7.1.3   *Part of an openness layer.*

For each cell in the openness layer, we determine whether that cell is "blocked"—usually by performing some type of line testing against the world geometry. If a cell is blocked, we assign it a value of 0; otherwise, we give it a value of 1.

We then propagate the influence of each 0-value cell to all of its neighbors. For each 1-value cell adjacent to a cell with a value less than 1, we lower that cell's value accordingly, depending on the neighboring cell's value. There are many ways to perform this propagation, but for now, let's assume we add a constant value—for example, 0.2. To see how this works, imagine we have a row of four cells with values (0, 1, 1, 1). In the propagation phase, these values would become (0, 0.2, 1, 1), then (0, 0.2, 0.4, 1), and finally (0, 0.2, 0.4, 0.6).

This is essentially an influence map [Tozour01] that describes the influence of static obstacles on the game world. A cell's value indicates its proximity to static obstacles—whether it is inside a wall, close to a wall, or in the middle of a large room.

As a side benefit, this also allows you to determine the open space gradient between any two neighboring cells—that is, the direction of increasing or decreasing openness. An AI can look at a single cell and its four immediate neighbors and use the differences between their openness values to determine what direction points toward the middle of the room (toward cells with higher openness), or what direction points toward the walls (toward lower openness values).

The Area Occupancy Layer

Many strategy games, particularly real-time strategy (RTS) games such as *WarCraft 3* [Blizzard02], include a "fog-of-war" feature, in which each unit makes a part of the world visible within a fixed radius around its location.

This is usually implemented using an influence mapping approach. Each unit in the game propagates some amount of influence in a "fog-of-war grid" in some (typically circular) area around itself—that is, it adds a fixed value to all the cells within its visibility radius. Any cells with nonzero values are visible through the fog-of-war. Units must update these fog-of-war grid values whenever they move and when they are created or destroyed.

This system also has advantages for games outside the strategy genre. It's often useful for AIs to know how highly populated any given part of the world is at any given moment. In a game with fog-of-war, we get this automatically: any area *not* under fog-of-war must have a unit nearby.

We can make an "occupancy layer" in the spatial database to achieve the same effect. Each AI fills in a gradient around itself with values that indicate how close it is to that cell. Figure 7.1.4 shows an example.

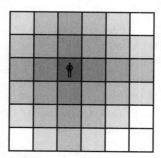

FIGURE 7.1.4   *The area occupancy layer.*

The key benefit of an occupancy grid is that it gives us a quick and easy way to query any location in the game world and determine the extent to which it is populated by AI units. Cells will have higher values if they are closer to more AI agents. Thus, our hypothetical combatant can also take this into account when determining whether it can perform the "Circle of Death" tactic, and can avoid strafing into crowded areas by simply querying the area occupancy layer in addition to the openness layer.

The main difference between an occupancy layer and a typical fog-of-war grid is that a fog-of-war grid can hold constant values for each AI unit regardless of the distance between the AI unit and the corresponding cell, while area occupancy must indicate the general distance to each AI unit.

The Area Search Layer

In stealth-oriented games such as *Thief: The Dark Project* [LGS98], AI characters often need to search an area while attempting to find the player. This requires some amount of spatial reasoning, since characters need to remember where they have previously searched so they can create the illusion of methodically searching every part of a room. In addition, multiple AI characters searching the same area should coordinate their search to avoid redundant search patterns and take one another's actions into account.

The effect we want is essentially identical to a "hidden map" feature. Many strategy games begin with a map that is completely black except for the area around your initial cities and armies. As you send scouting parties out to explore the map, your units "uncover" additional areas of the map within a fixed radius around each unit. Note that this is different from a fog-of-war effect. Where a fog-of-war effect shows the areas that are *currently* visible, the hidden map indicates whether an area has *ever* been seen at any point in the past.

In a strategy game, it's very easy to develop an AI algorithm that will automatically scout the map and uncover the hidden map areas. Simply overlay a large grid on top of the game world, where each cell in the grid holds a Boolean value (or a single bit in an integer representation) indicating whether or not a given player's units have ever seen that cell. Your AI searching code can then select the first available scouting party, find the nearest cell marked as "not seen," and send the scouting party to that cell.

Searching in stealth-oriented "sneaker" games can work almost exactly the same way. When a guard begins a search, he can consider the surrounding area to be under a "hidden map," and thus ensure that he performs a thorough search of the area by uncovering each part in turn.

We begin by initializing the "area search layer" to zero values. As the NPC moves around the area, he can determine whether he has an unblocked line-of-sight to all the cells within a limited viewing arc in front of his point of view. As he searches, we increment the values of any cells in his view arc.

However, a stealth game area-search system is somewhat different from a strategy game hidden map feature because a guard who is searching for an intruder typically begins the search with some clues to help inform his search. He has probably seen the player, heard footsteps, seen a dead body, or heard the sound of water arrows putting out torches, so he probably has a pretty good idea where to begin.

It's possible to implement this by maintaining a persistent database of all of the "evidence" the guard has observed—all of the stimuli the guard has noticed in the past, along with any associated data, such as the time and location when the stimuli occurred [Orkin02]—and bias the search toward that evidence.

As the search continues, the search database can gradually "decay" and allow AIs to once again search areas they have already searched. In practice, it's often useful to perform this decay randomly to make the search patterns less predictable. An entirely uniform decay pattern can cause the guard to repeatedly search the same area in exactly the same pattern.

This system also allows you to automatically coordinate the activities of multiple searchers simply by virtue of sharing the same search layer. If three guards are searching a room, each guard will automatically know where the other two have searched and will avoid searching the same areas again. In many respects, this is equivalent to emergent agent coordination using a blackboard architecture [Isla02, Orkin04].

The Line-of-Fire Layer

Many game genres feature combat with ranged weapons, and in some cases, this introduces the possibility that AIs can accidentally shoot one another. Although there are a number of steps you can take to reduce the probability of these kinds of accidents [Tozour02], the first step is to make sure AIs don't stand in one another's line-of-fire in the first place.

The "line-of-fire layer" has a nonzero value for each cell that's in some AI unit's line-of-fire toward its target. Whenever an AI agent begins aiming a ranged weapon, it propagates some positive influence value along the cells in a straight line toward its target. AIs can then query this layer and avoid navigating into cells that have nonzero values. Figure 7.1.5 shows what this might look like for a game world with two shooters.

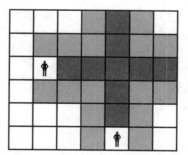

FIGURE 7.1.5 *The line-of-fire grid.*

Note that this could potentially cause AIs to take their own lines of fire into account, thus preventing them from moving forward. It's easy to solve this by having each AI agent ignore its own contribution to the line-of-fire layer by temporarily subtracting its own contribution before reading any values from the line-of-fire layer.

The Light Level Layer

Many modern 3D games feature dynamic lighting systems in which multiple light sources illuminate the environment and cast shadows simultaneously. In such games, there is sometimes a need for AI characters to factor the current lighting level into their behavior. For example, a game might feature a character that prefers to avoid the light (a vampire, perhaps), or one that prefers to avoid darkness (such as a guard who's particularly leery of vampires).

We can easily factor this into our composite desirability calculations by creating a "light level layer." Each light source can propagate its influence—depending on its current radius, lighting type, intensity, and so on—onto this light level layer, such that each cell indicates the current light intensity at that location.

Handling 3D Environments

Three-dimensional environments pose a particular challenge for this approach, as a single 2D grid will not be able to adequately represent areas where there are multiple vertically overlapping parts of the game world.

In most cases, we can address this by breaking the grid up into smaller sub-grids and allowing any number of sub-grids at each (x, y) location. For example, you can break a 1000x1000 grid into a grid of 100x100 separate sub-grids, where each sub-grid is 10x10 cells. At any given location in the world, we can place any number of sub-grids at different heights at the same (x, y) location. Assuming that our game world doesn't change too dramatically at runtime, we can create a tool in the game's world editor to statically analyze the game world and determine how many sub-grids are required at each (x, y) location and the appropriate Z (height) value for each sub-grid.

This approach will generally work well for most standard 3D environments—that is, anything that more or less resembles human architecture. Although any particular sub-grid might not exactly match the geometry of the corresponding part of the level, this will not usually pose much of a problem, as the spatial database is intended more as a general heuristic to inform AI decision-making, rather than a critical data structure—such as a pathfinding database—which must precisely match the geometry of the game world.

Optimizations

In this section, we discuss a number of potential memory and performance optimizations.

In the worst case, this type of spatial database system could be a performance nightmare. With a large enough grid at a very high resolution and a sufficiently large number of AI units updating their influence over large parts of the database, we might need to update a huge number of cells every frame. Even worse, much of this updating will be a waste of time, since many of these cells will never actually be used to inform AI decision-making.

However, we shouldn't take the spatial database metaphor too literally. There are a huge number of potential optimizations depending on the character of your game and its particular performance and memory constraints.

First, we can tune the relative size of the grid cells. Although using a higher-resolution grid—that is, more grid cells—will give us better accuracy and will sometimes lead to better AI decision-making, there's clearly a point of diminishing returns, at which point making the grid cells smaller will give us little or no benefit. Using larger cells will make the spatial database require less memory and allow for faster spatial database updates, since there will be fewer cells in each layer to update for any given modification to the spatial database.

Some layers of the spatial database are entirely static and don't need to be recalculated at runtime. For example, there's no reason to calculate the openness layer at runtime when it only takes static obstacles into account. It's much easier to precompute this layer using an automated tool within the game's world editor.

Furthermore, static spatial database layers often lend themselves well to data-compression techniques. In particular, run-length encoding (RLE encoding) and Lempel-Ziv compression can often dramatically reduce the memory footprint of static spatial database layers. Additionally, if we're using a spatial database composed of multiple sub-grids in a 3D environment, we can often compress each individual sub-grid and avoid decompressing it until it's actually queried.

In the case of dynamic spatial database layers, we can often take advantage of the fact that these layers will typically be sparse—that is, they will mostly consist of 0 values throughout most of the game. This is particularly well suited to the multiple-sub-grid approach, where we can easily optimize each sub-grid out of existence if all of its cells contain the same value.

In some cases, we can also optimize the way we compute our composite desirability layer values. These computations will often take the form of a purely multiplicative equation such as $desirability = a * b * c \ldots$ We can take advantage of the fact that if any of the multipliers is 0, the final desirability value will also be 0. Thus, as soon as we discover that any value in the equation is 0, we can forgo the remainder of the calculation.

We also don't necessarily need to update all of the spatial database grid layers every game tick. Quite often, we can use a "lazy" approach and compute the value of a spatial database layer cell only when it is actually queried. For example, imagine we want to compute a combat movement desirability heuristic for the "Circle of Death" tactic. However, a key aspect of the Circle of Death tactic in our game is that it only really works well within 10 to 20 meters of the target, and therefore we will only need to update the cells within that 10–20 meter radius.

Conclusion

As games become increasingly complex and game worlds include larger numbers of AI agents and dynamic objects, it becomes increasingly important for AIs to be able to reason about their physical environment. A spatial database allows you to perform reasoning about the dynamic aspects of your game world on a spatial level. Furthermore, a spatial database allows you to implicitly coordinate the activities of multiple AI agents by virtue of sharing a single data structure.

References

[Blizzard02] *WarCraft III: Reign of Chaos*, Blizzard Entertainment, 2002. See *www. blizzard.com*

[Isla02] Isla, Damian, and Blumberg, Bruce, "Blackboard Architectures," *AI Game Programming Wisdom*, Charles River Media, 2002.

[LGS98] *Thief: The Dark Project*, Looking Glass Studios/Eidos Interactive, 1998. See *www.eidosinteractive.com*

[Lidén02] Lidén, Lars, "Strategic and Tactical Reasoning with Waypoints," *AI Game Programming Wisdom*, Charles River Media, 2002.

[Orkin02] Orkin, Jeff, "A General-Purpose Trigger System," *AI Game Programming Wisdom*, Charles River Media, 2002.

[Orkin04] Orkin, Jeff, "Simple Techniques for Coordinated Behavior," *AI Game Programming Wisdom 2*, Charles River Media, 2004.

[Tozour01] Tozour, Paul, "Influence Mapping," *Game Programming Gems 2*, Charles River Media, 2001.

[Tozour02] Tozour, Paul, "The Basics of Ranged Weapon Combat," *AI Game Programming Wisdom*, Charles River Media, 2002.

[van der Sterren01] van der Sterren, William, "Terrain Reasoning for 3D Action Games," *Game Programming Gems 2*, Charles River Media, 2001.

7.2

Performing Qualitative Terrain Analysis in *Master of Orion 3*

Kevin Dill, Alex Sramek—Quicksilver Software, Inc.

lanorolen@yahoo.com,
alex_ai@bluepineapple.com

One challenge for many strategy game AIs is the need to perform qualitative terrain analysis. By qualitative, we mean that the analysis is based on fundamental differences between different types of locations—for instance, areas that are visible to our opponents, areas that are impassable, or areas vulnerable to enemy fire. In *Master of Orion 3* (a galactic strategy game), we identify stars that are inside or outside of our empire's borders, those that are threatened by our opponents, and those that are contested (shared with an opponent). This information is used to identify locations where we need to concentrate our defenses and to help us expand into areas that minimize our defensive needs while maximizing the territory we control.

In this article, we present the algorithms used to make the qualitative distinctions given in the preceding paragraph and the ways in which the AI uses that information. The lessons we would most like the reader to take away from this article are not the specifics of the algorithms used, but rather the thought processes involved in applying qualitative reasoning to terrain analysis. The important questions to address are: what are the qualitative distinctions we should look for, how can we recognize them, and what uses can the AI make of that information? Our algorithms are but a single example of how these questions can be answered.

Background

Master of Orion 3 (*MOO3*) is a turn-based strategy game in which human and computer players build empires and vie for control of the galaxy. The map of the galaxy consists of up to 256 star systems that are connected by star lanes. Virtually all travel takes place along these lanes. Each star system can have up to eight planets that vary in desirability for each species. For the purposes of this discussion, we use the terms "star" and "system" interchangeably, although they have slightly different connotations in the game. Each player, computer or human, starts with control of one or more planets in a single system. They know the relative positions of the other stars but they do not have any information about star lanes or stars they have not explored. Once a star has been explored, however, the player who explored it is privy to all information about that star from that point forward.

Our goal is to provide the AI with a good measure of the strategic value of a star's location when choosing areas for colonization or conquest, rather than simply selecting locations on the basis of proximity to our homeworld or economic value. As a simple example, imagine that there is one star through which space ships from the outside must pass to reach our empire. That star is extremely valuable to us because we can concentrate all of our defensive power in a single location. We'll want the AI to use this principle any time multiple stars can be protected by defending a few pivotal locations.

Our first task is to analyze the terrain to determine whether a given star is inside or outside of our borders, whether it is contested, and whether another empire threatens it. Using this information, we can generate a priority for colonizing or conquering that star's planets. For example, a star that increases the territory we control by placing new stars inside our borders is often more valuable than one that is already inside our borders. Conversely, a star outside of our borders that does not protect any other stars is generally a liability. We might establish a colony at this latter star, but only if the planet there is so attractive that it justifies the strategic cost. Identifying threatened colonies also allows us to concentrate our defenses at the locations that are vulnerable to attack. In the interests of brevity, this article focuses on the decision-making process for selecting new colonies, but the other decisions use similar methods.

The Building Blocks—Free Spaces and Corridors

Many games, particularly strategy games, have maps characterized by relatively large open spaces containing strategically valuable locations such as resources or cities. These areas are often connected by comparatively narrow passages. [Forbus02] describes the open areas as free spaces and the connecting passages as corridors.

Two important characteristics should be remembered if the terrain analysis is to be useful. First, each corridor should always be treated as a one-dimensional entity that connects exactly two free spaces. In other words, if we draw a Voronoi diagram [Okabe92] for the map, any place where edges of that diagram meet should be part of a free space even if it is a small one. Second, the strategic value of corridors should be the sole result of the way they connect free spaces. Valuable locations such as resources or cities should always be inside of a free space even if there are only one or two corridors to that free space.

In *MOO3* we were fortunate enough to have this terrain analysis handed to us by the game design. The free spaces of *MOO3* are the stars, and the corridors are star lanes. For other games, extracting this information might not be so easy, but we believe that a variety of techniques could work. Two suggestions are to use an analysis similar to that presented in [Forbus02], or simply have the designers specify them.

Analyzing the Terrain

Conceptually, we define a star as being inside our borders if every path along the star lanes that lead away from that star arrives eventually at another of our colonies without passing through any unexplored stars. This is true whether we have colonies at that star or not. To keep the computations tractable and ensure that our colonies stay in reasonable proximity to one another, we limit the number of star lanes that we will traverse during this computation. A star is threatened if it is outside our borders or if there is a path from a colony belonging to another civilization to that star that does not pass through a star that we control.

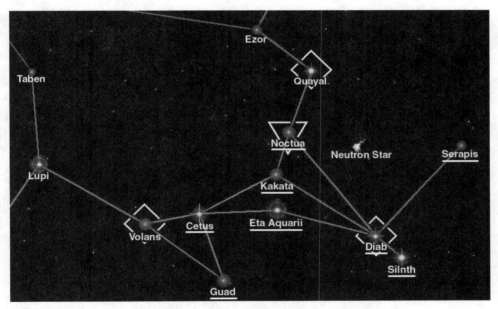

FIGURE 7.2.1   *A section of the galaxy map with stars and star lanes displayed.*

As an example, consider the section of a galaxy map shown in Figure 7.2.1. Suppose that our empire, designated with diamonds, began at Diab and has established additional colonies at Volans and Quayal. Further suppose that an opponent has established a colony at Noctua (designated with a triangle). In that case, all of the underlined stars are inside our borders. This is because the only way to get to those stars from the rest of the galaxy is through stars that we control—either Volans or Quayal. Note that our border stars are not considered to be inside of our borders. Furthermore, due to the enemy colony at Noctua, all stars other than Silnth and Serapis are threatened. Silnth and Serapis are protected by Diab. If we were to eliminate the enemy colony at Noctus, then none of the stars inside our borders would be threatened. Alternately, if we were to establish a colony at Kakata, then Cetus, Eta Aquarii, and Guad would no longer be threatened.

Internally we store the status of star lanes rather than stars. Getting the information on a star is fairly simple. A star is threatened if any of its star lanes are threatened; it is inside our borders if all of its star lanes are inside our borders. For those who would like a better look at how this process functions in code, the terrain analysis code from *MOO3* is available on this book's CD-ROM along with a utility to create and update galaxies.

ON THE CD

Selecting New Colonies

The vast majority of AI decisions in *MOO3* are made by what we call the "ping pong ball squared" method. Using this method, we first determine the possible actions we could take and assign a priority to each. Next, we assign probabilities to each action based on its priority and then randomly select one. A simple way to conceptualize this is that we throw a number of ping pong balls equal to each action's priority into a hopper and then select one ping pong ball at random. In some cases, we square all of the priorities to increase the likelihood of selecting one of the "better" choices.

Clearly, given this relatively simple model for decision making, the art of AI design is found in assigning appropriate priorities to each action while eliminating those actions that shouldn't even be considered. In the case of the colonization AI, we keep a list of all the vacant planets we know about. Whenever a colony ship becomes available, we go through this list and assign a priority to each planet. The base value for this priority reflects the expected economic value of that planet to the AI's empire. This is then multiplied by a variety of strategic modifiers. Finally, we eliminate the clearly inappropriate locations by ignoring planets with comparatively low priorities.

A slightly simplified version of the decision process for selecting strategic modifiers is given here:

- Start with a base multiplier of 1.0.
- If we already have one or more colonies at the star in question:
  - If another civilization has a colony there, then this is a contested system and we should try to strengthen our claim. Multiply by 1.5.
  - Otherwise, we have already claimed this system—better to claim new systems first, and fill in our borders later. Multiply by 0.8.
- Otherwise, if another civilization has established a claim in this system, then we would prefer to avoid a border conflict. Multiply by 0.3.
- Otherwise, check if the star is inside our borders. If so, we have a slight preference for expanding outside our borders. Multiply by 0.9.
- Otherwise, this star can only be an unclaimed star that is outside our borders. Stars like this can be a liability if they don't protect any other stars because they increase the size of our border (and thus the number of places we must defend). However, if they allow us to place a claim on a significant amount of new territory and/or reduce the overall size of our border, then they can be extremely valuable.

- First, multiply by 0.5. This calculation reflects the fact that a star outside our borders gives our enemies a new place to attack. If this star protects other stars, then other multipliers (given below) will offset this multiplier.
- For each star that has enemy colonies that would now be inside our borders, multiply by 0.3. This factor has the effect of discouraging us from colonizing stars inside other empire's borders.
- If a colony at this star will not place any foreign colonies inside of our borders, then consider how much new territory this would allow us to claim and how many of our current border systems would become interior systems.
  - Start with a base multiplier of 1.0.
  - For each unclaimed star that is outside our current borders but would be inside our new borders, add 0.25.
  - For each of our systems that is currently outside our borders but would be inside our new borders, add 1.
  - If our homeworld would become an interior system as a result of placing a colony here, add an additional 1 because of the importance of protecting that particular system.
  - Multiply by the sum of these factors.

To increase the effect of these calculations, we combine all of the preceding modifiers and square them, and then multiply the result by the economic value of the planet to get the overall priority. We eliminate planets whose priority is less than half the priority of the "best" choice. This discourages the AI from making obviously stupid decisions because of a bad roll of the dice.

Results

The best results were achieved in the way AI-controlled empires grow. Our goal was to encourage the development of distinct borders where one empire ends and the next begins, without having to hard code them. Prior to implementing this AI, we found that empires tended to intermingle. One reason for this is that often a planet that is useless to one empire is attractive to another. For example, an empire of humans isn't likely to place colonies on the local gas giants, but a neighboring civilization of aliens might prefer those planets. Even when we gave a preference for building new colonies close to existing colonies, there was nothing to prevent empires from intermingling their colonies. Once the AI described previously was implemented, we began to see expansion that made much more sense. The AIs were no longer aggressive in a way that had been both tactically unsound and frustrating to human players.

Early in the game the AIs expand, colonizing primarily those systems that allow them to claim new territory without infringing on the territory of their neighbors (unless the economic value of the planet in question is greater than the strategic cost). Later, as good planets become scarce in the unclaimed portions of the map, empires will colonize the better planets inside their borders. Finally, when they have few remaining choices, they might intermingle. Because of the large number of other factors that go into the decision, as well as the random element, the decision-making process is not completely obvious or predictable as the game is played. However, the effect is clear if the game is allowed to run for a while and then the AI's expansion is examined.

Interestingly, one of the complaints from the play-testers was that when they allowed the AI to select their colonies (which is an option in *MOO3*), they were unable to understand why it chose the ones it did. They were frustrated by the fact that it would ignore a juicy colony in a system they'd already colonized in favor of some other planet whose value was not immediately obvious to them. As a result, we had to turn the strategic portion of the colonization AI off for the human player.

There are two other decisions that use our terrain analysis. First, it affects production choices by allowing us to boost the priority for building local defenses (such as missile bases or orbital weapon platforms) on planets in threatened systems. This emphasis allows the AI to use its resources more efficiently, although it is not particularly visible to the player nor is it the dominant factor in determining how strong the defenses at any particular planet will be.

The final use of the terrain analysis is in the selection of targets for our attacks. We wanted the AI to be more likely to attack enemy planets inside its borders and most likely to attack those in contested systems. The intention behind these priorities was to create the sense of a border conflict—that is, fighting springs up because of this border dispute, and the urgency of the attack decreases once the dispute has been resolved one way or the other. Unfortunately, this isn't all that apparent to the player. Another criticism of this portion of the AI is that it doesn't look for strategic opportunities. In retrospect, it would have been fairly simple to recognize systems that would allow us to consolidate our border if we capture them or that would expose the enemy's juicier interior systems to attack.

There was some discussion of having the diplomatic AI use our terrain analysis in support of the border conflicts previously mentioned. Currently, if another civilization has planets inside the AI's borders, the diplomatic relations are not affected. It would have been nice to have the diplomatic AI express its displeasure when it detected a dispute, or even issue demands for the surrender of the disputed territory if relations deteriorate. When relations are good, the AI could attempt to negotiate peaceful settlements in which one or the other side would cede the disputed planets in return for some form of compensation.

Beyond Border Recognition—Other Uses for Corridors and Free Spaces

As previously discussed, the core of *MOO3*'s terrain analysis is the recognition that there is a fundamental distinction between the free spaces where our resources must be defended and the corridors between them. Our AI is able to detect and reason about the borders of the area controlled by each player on the basis of this analysis.

This is only one of a myriad of uses for this information that a typical real-time strategy or turn-based strategy game could have. Consider the following other uses, for example:

- We can often defend a free space much more efficiently by defending each of the exits of the threatened corridors that lead to it rather than waiting for the enemy to move its forces into the free space. Further, because the corridors are generally narrower than the free spaces, we can bring more of our units into action at any particular time than the enemy, giving us a tactical advantage at those locations.
- If we can place scouts some distance down each corridor, we can have advance warning of an attack. This can allow us to defend multiple corridors with a single force by placing them in a position where they can defend whichever corridor comes under attack.
- When attacking, narrow terrain might not allow us to bring sufficient force to overwhelm the defenders in any particular corridor. In this case, it might behoove us to launch simultaneous attacks down multiple corridors to force the enemy to split their forces.

The appropriate applications of this information are obviously game specific, but it should be clear that there are far more than the relatively simple ones we used in *MOO3*.

Conclusion

In the opening paragraphs of this article, we suggested three questions that AI programmers might ask while designing their AI: what are the qualitative distinctions we should look for, how can we recognize them, and what uses can the AI make of that information. For *MOO3*, we determined that we wanted to be able to identify areas that are inside our borders, those that are threatened by an opposing civilization, and those that are contested. Doing this required the use of a higher-level qualitative distinction—the distinction between the large open spaces where resources are located (free spaces) and the narrower passages that connect them (corridors). This analysis was then used to identify strategically important locations for colonization, attack, and defense.

References

[Forbus02] Forbus, K., Mahoney, J.V., and Dill, K., "How Qualitative Spatial Reasoning Can Improve Strategy Game AIs," *IEEE Intelligent Systems*, July/August 2002.

[Okabe92] Okabe, Boots, and Sugihara, *Spatial Tessellations: Concepts and Applications of Voronoi Diagrams*, John Wiley & Sons, 1992.

7.3

The Unique Challenges of Turn-Based AI

Soren Johnson—Firaxis Games
sjohnson@firaxis.com

In many ways, turn-based AI is similar to its real-time sibling. In fact, real-time games are usually split into "micro-turns" invisible to the user, so the coding challenges are not fundamentally different. However, splitting up the decision-making process into discrete steps creates some unique challenges for a turn-based AI programmer. This article examines these problems based on practical examples from the development of the AI for *Civilization III*.

Unequal Time

The most obvious challenge for turn-based AI is that the user can have an infinite amount of time to conduct a turn. The player can conduct extensive micro-management—an advantage not available in a real-time game. Unlike the human player, turn-based AI's game time is usually limited to a few seconds per turn. This time discrepancy encourages the most competitive players to spend as much time as possible micro-managing their empire to out-perform the AI.

From an engineer's point of view, the only way to address this time discrepancy is to write a better AI. However, from a designer's point of view, the core problem is not an issue of time but an issue of game mechanics, which can be addressed at the beginning of a project.

One of our high-level design goals for *Civilization III* was to reduce the amount of time required to play a full turn. Our belief was that previous *Civilization* games were unnecessarily long, and we could concentrate the fun by simplifying a number of game concepts.

For example, in *Civilization III*, unit upkeep is paid on a national level, coming directly out of the empire's treasury. In previous versions, units were attached to a "home city" that was responsible for providing the upkeep. The original intention behind this rule was simply to provide a counter-balance for maintaining a large military.

By simplifying this rule, we took a level of micro-management out of the game without sacrificing the rule's original purpose. Historically, the AI had suffered in comparison to the human when trying to manage its units' home cities, especially humans willing to spend the time to micro-manage which units were attached to which city. Thus, the new rules both sped up the game and decreased the effect of the unequal time discrepancy between the AI and the user.

The time gap was also lessened by exerting a concerted effort on closing rule loopholes, especially exploits made possible by the turn-based environment. One new feature in *Civilization III* was a one-time production bonus from chopping down a forest. However, forests could be replanted, which quickly led to a strategy known as "lumberjacking"—having workers repeatedly chop down and replant forests in the same location, receiving the same production bonus each time.

This unanticipated exploit was only possible in a turn-based environment because lumberjacking would not have been cost efficient if time had been a factor. Further, the practice put the AI at a disadvantage, since lumberjacking was not part of its strategy set. We solved the problem in a patch by dictating that each tile on the map could only produce one deforestation bonus over the course of a game. Alternately, we could have written lumberjacking into the AI, but given our high-level goal of discouraging time-consuming "micro" strategies, eliminating the exploit made more sense.

Automated Decisions

Because many users might prefer to spend as *little* time as possible conducting their turns, the AI must also be capable of automating decisions for the user. As these choices are very discrete (e.g., build a library or a swordsman?), the time-conscious user's enjoyment depends greatly on the AI (such as the city governors) making the right decisions for the player.

In *Civilization III*, we implemented a learning algorithm to help the city governors make decisions tailored to the current player. Every unit and building is given a positive or negative weight depending on the user's decisions and non-decisions.

More specifically, manually choosing a unit or building produces a strong positive weight. Switching production away from a unit or building generates a moderate negative weight. Allowing a unit or building to be finished adds a weak positive weight. Further, the weights slowly move toward zero with each progressive turn.

Thus, the governors' decisions are heavily influenced by the user's recent tendencies. Building a few temples will prompt the governors to prefer temples in other cities. Switching production to military units will encourage the governors to start gearing up for war. By basing these decisions on the user's choices—and not on what a hard-coded AI determines is best for the player—the system is more likely to manage the user's empire in a helpful manner.

We employed a more direct method to ensure that worker automation was helpful to the player. Although a "full automation" mode was included, which gave the AI total control over the worker, "safe automation" was also available. The latter mode prevents the AI from altering terrain improvements previously built by the user. The automated worker would never, for example, replace a mine with irrigation. This mode encourages users to trust the automated options available, greatly reducing the amount of time required to manage an empire.

Predictability

Another critical challenge for turn-based AI is predictability. As the gameplay has a discrete order (unlike a more chaotic real-time strategy game), the AI is highly vulnerable to recognizable patterns. Indeed, while a good number of contemporary games use scripting to simulate intelligent behavior, *Civilization III* is almost entirely script-less.

Instead, the AI uses a combination of fuzzy logic and probabilistic reasoning to manage most of its decisions, including diplomatic initiatives, research paths, city production, and attack routes. This combination provides intelligent yet unpredictable decisions by assigning weights to a variety of inputs, adding some probabilistic noise, and finally reaching a "best guess" solution.

The AI's memory model provides a good example of this process. A wide assortment of user actions are recorded in the memory of the AI, from declarations of war to broken trade deals to tribute demands. Each of these actions is assigned a weight that determines the AI's attitude toward the player. For example, while violating a diplomatic agreement might make the AI "annoyed," a nuclear attack will likely produce a "furious" opponent.

Further, the AI's memory slowly decays as the game progresses, forgiving the player's past transgressions. The rate at which actions are forgotten depends on the type of offense. While capturing a city might upset the AI for 20 to 30 turns, razing the city will likely be remembered for the duration of the game.

Sometimes, very simple factors can lead to the appearance of advanced reasoning. For example, the calculation that determines whom the AI decides to attack includes a variable representing the distance between the AI's capital and the player's closest city. A smaller distance will increase the likelihood of an AI attack. This factor has been perceived as a high-level desire for "manifest destiny"—that the AI will strike back against users trying to settle within its regional area.

Thus, the decision-making processes encourage intelligent behavior without the predictability of a script-based AI. Fuzzy logic provides discrete weights for a wide range of inputs, while probabilistic reasoning ensures that even with identical states, the AI will exhibit a variety of behaviors.

Cheating

Although cheating is regrettably a standard tool for AI programmers, cheating is a dangerous choice in a turn-based environment. Because the game turns can be deconstructed and repeated as often as the user wishes, cheating is almost impossible to hide. Therefore, the editor provided with *Civilization III* exposed the vast majority of gameplay cheats employed by the AI. We included difficulty levels with cheating, without cheating, and with cheats in the human's favor. Further, by providing access to the AI cheats in the editor, we allowed the user to adjust the AI bonuses as desired.

However, the greatest risk cheating introduces into a turn-based game is opening an unexpected hole for the human to exploit. A number of information cheats in *Civilization III*—which gave the AI access to information it should not have—were discovered by our user community and then used to control the AI's decision-making process.

For example, the AI would mark undefended cities as strategic targets, even if they were beyond its legal sight range. Two exploits resulted from this information cheat. First, the user could lay a trap for the AI by leaving an undefended "decoy" city deep within the human's territory. The AI would bypass border cities and charge into the interior, exposing its troops to a human ambush. The second exploit involved amphibious invasions. The human would move units in and out of cities along the coast, forcing the AI's invasion force into a never-ending movement cycle, changing its landing target every turn.

Although these abuses were both fixed in AI patches, their existence reveals that AI cheating—especially in easily dissectible turn-based games—is not necessarily a one-way street. Thus, cheating should be viewed as a tool of last resort when designing AI within a turn-based environment.

Competitive Balance

A standard game of *Civilization III* pits the human against a number of AI-controlled opponents. Ideally, the AI will be blind to which opponent is human, viewing each rival with an equal amount of inherent hostility. Indeed, the user will interpret any sign that the AIs are ganging up against the human as simply a different form of cheating.

Competitive balance must remain a high priority for an AI programmer, following the rule that an AI should be "fun" above all else. Hence, when determining whom to attack, the AI does not consider whether a rival is human-controlled. Ensuring competitive balance is especially important in a turn-based game because the discrete environment allows—and perhaps even encourages—reverse-engineering of the AI's decision-making process.

An anti-human bias would be very difficult to hide within a turn-based environment. However, the AI programmer will have a difficult task ensuring that the AIs treat each other like they would treat the human when the latter is an unknown element. For example, the human might expect the AIs to only make "fair" deals with each other, always demanding reasonable prices for their tradable items. Nonetheless, some skilled human player will often trade goods for much less than their full value under the right circumstances.

How can we allow the AI to have the same flexibility without giving the impression that the AIs are making deals "on the cheap" with each other? Unfortunately, this question is almost impossible to answer empirically, which could lead to accusations of AI cheating even if we are only trying to model intelligent human behavior. Ultimately, we chose to expose the number controlling the flexibility of AI-to-AI negotiations in the editor, accepting that the "fairness" of such a factor will always be purely subjective.

Conclusion

Writing a turn-based AI presents a number of unique challenges. The common thread uniting these separate issues is the user's complete control over the game's speed. Players willing to invest extreme amounts of time and players looking to streamline their gaming experience present two very different challenges not faced in a real-time environment. Furthermore, the ability to micro-analyze a turn-based AI makes predictability, cheating, and competitive balance extremely important issues. Hopefully, understanding these unique challenges before beginning to design and code a turn-based AI will make the task much easier.

References

[Kirby02] Kirby, Neil, "Solving the Right Problem," *AI Game Programming Wisdom*, Charles River Media, 2002.

[Scott02a] Scott, Bob, "Architecting a Game AI," *AI Game Programming Wisdom*, Charles River Media, 2002.

[Scott02b] Scott, Bob, "Architecting an RTS AI," *AI Game Programming Wisdom*, Charles River Media, 2002.

Random Map Generation for Strategy Games

Shawn Shoemaker—Stainless Steel Studios

shansolox@yahoo.com

While there are numerous articles dedicated to the generation of random maps for games, such as [LeckyThompson99], there is little published information on random maps for strategy games in particular. This subset of map generation presents distinct challenges as evident by the relatively few games that implement them. While the techniques described here can be used to create maps suitable for any type of game, this system is specifically designed to create a variety of successful random maps for real-time strategy games. This article describes the random map generation implemented in the RTS game *Empire Earth* (*EE*) developed by Stainless Steel Studios.

Problem Statement

The central problem is to develop a system capable of generating maps for a tile-based, real-time strategy game supporting 2 to 16 players. The maps must be fair in terms of land per player and resources per player. Maps must not give a strategic advantage to one particular player. Given a seed, a number of players, and a map size, random map generation must be predictable and reproducible. Maps of the same size, type, and number of players should appear similar while allowing for different game outcomes. A large variety of map layouts must be supported. Maps must be developed for both the hard-core RTS audience as well as the more casual empire-building audience. The map generation should be (relatively) quick in terms of processing time and take advantage of available system memory, as many in-game systems will not be running while maps are generated. Seven different types of maps must be created: continental, large islands, small islands, highlands, plains, tournament islands, and mediterranean. Color Plates 7 through 10 are examples of completed four player maps: continental, highlands, large islands, and mediterranean, respectively. Maps must allow for manipulation by designers. Six different sizes of maps must be supported: tiny, small, medium, large, huge, and gigantic.

Solution Overview

The random map generator in *EE* consists of one DLL and 50+ script files. The architecture allows for a different map generation DLL to be specified through scripting (although in *EE*, this was never pursued). There are seven scripts for each map type. The inputs to map generation are the number of players, the number of teams, the map size, the map climate, the type of random map, and the random number seed.

First, players are placed on a blank map. Teams are placed adjacent to each other and enemies are placed somewhat symmetrically opposed about the map. Land is then grown for each player. Areas that are not land are encoded as water. There are various restrictions to land growth based on the map type. Within this player land, areas of land that must be flat are then grown. Flat areas provide land that players can build buildings on. The height map is then generated to give elevation to the map. The grown land, flat land, and height map are then combined to create varied elevation matching the land and flatness restrictions.

The map is then processed for cliffs and other terrain analysis. Next, resources such as gold, iron, stone, and berries are placed in each of the player-owned lands. As wood is abundant and restricts pathfinding, forests are placed after the other resources. The map is then painted with terrain textures in a fractal-generated pattern. Next, the initial units (in the case of *EE*, a Capital building and some number of citizens) are generated for each player offset from that player's starting location. World player units such as fish and animal herds are placed on the map next. This completes the map generation process. The following sections focus on the interesting areas of this process.

Test Application

Early in the implementation, a test application was written to visualize the generation process as it developed. Additionally, the map generation was not yet integrated into the game engine. As shown in Color Plate 11, this test application had four panes in which different textures were shown. These textures correspond to different 2D arrays generated to create the map. The application is generic enough to allow visualization of any of the arrays generated. Color Plate 11 shows the test application displaying the land water array, the height map array, the land water array combined with the height map array, and a final array representing the combination of all of the arrays. In addition to the arrays shown, the final array also combines the flat map array (not shown) and results from the height map filter. This final array provides a preview of the map generation results.

Scripts

To enable designers to manipulate random map attribute values, a scripting language was developed. This included development of a basic text parser and data structures to contain this information. Please refer to [Berger02a, Berger02b, Berger02c, Poiker02] for information on implementing scripting languages. In the scripts, *attributes* such as number of resources per player, maximum height of the height map, and player land allocation could be set. Scripts proved quite useful in that small changes could yield different map variations such as an island map and a continental map. To make the scripts even more versatile, the parser was extended to support things such as `#defines` and `#ifdefs`.

Climate was also set through the scripts. Different climates would result in different terrain texture sets, forest tree sets, and animals present on the map. Scripts also allowed for incremental development of different map types. Work on island maps could commence once continental maps were already in the game. As new maps required new attributes, those attributes were added to the parser and the matching code added to the map generator. This ability to extend the map generation through script attributes has also benefited future projects. Diehard fans of *EE* were even able to "create" new map types of their own through the creation of new map scripts. This, of course, was an undocumented feature.

As map development continued and new attributes were added, the scripts became quite lengthy. There was one master script for each type of random map, and one script for each size of that type of map. For example, the continental map type had the following files: continental, small continental, medium continental, large continental, huge continental, and gigantic continental. In each of these scripts, there were subsections defining values for a particular number of players (*EE* random maps supported 16 players as well). In addition, the number of map attributes recognized by the parser had also grown. Scripts became increasingly difficult to manage.

User manuals were created to help the designers understand the random maps and all of the attributes available to them. Additional tools were developed to ease the editing of attributes throughout all of the files. Ultimately, designers had some difficulty making the best use of the scripts, as they are designers and not programmers. Generally, when new map types were designed, programmers would initially create the scripts, with some decent default map attribute values. Designers would then tweak the maps to fit their vision.

Player Placement

One of the first steps in map generation is to place the players about the map. Player placement is very important, as it has a huge impact on the next step in which land is grown for players. The algorithm used begins by inscribing one large disk on the map. This disk has inner and outer radii specified as attributes. One random location per player is then chosen inside the disk (within the inner and outer radii). The closest of these player points are then pushed apart. This process repeats until the distribution of points becomes sufficiently optimal. A map attribute specifies how optimal the solution should be, with the optimal solution evenly placing the players about the map. Although this algorithm does produce somewhat predictable player locations, this is exactly what is desired to keep the maps balanced for the hard-core audience. The map attributes do allow for a large variation of location distributions.

When locations are spread fairly about the map, they are then assigned to players. If the game has teams, the players on the same teams are given adjacent map locations.

A great deal of the map generation is based around players, such as resource distribution. Since designers were very happy with the layout of player land and their resources, they wanted additional areas of the map to have a similar layout. Dummy players were created to address this, which are players created for the sole purpose of map generation and never appear in the game. They are placed after the real players, so as to not take the perfect locations. To keep dummy players' land away from the real players, they are placed on the inside or outside of the real player disk. Their land is grown after the real players' to ensure that they do not starve real players for land. Dummy players also have resources placed on their land. Designers found dummy players to be quite useful—for example, dummy players allow island maps with unclaimed, resource-rich, center islands (perfect for colonizing) to exist.

Clump Details

As land is a resource in strategy games, fair land allocation is certainly a priority. Land also needs a natural appearance. To address these concerns, land is grown in the map generator in *clumps*. What follows is a brief discussion of how the clump class functions and how the class was used in different portions of the map generation process. This discussion is more of an overview of clumps than the details on the particular implementation.

Clumps have many different parameters, most of which are set through attributes. These attributes include values such as clump size, number of clumps, and clump chaos level. Clumps grow until they reach their clump size. They can grow in two different ways. One growth method, the *completion method*, grows the clump, tile by tile, to completion. The other method, the *step method*, grows the clump one tile per iteration. Figure 7.4.1 demonstrates clump growth using the step method. During growth, each clump maintains a list of the current edge tiles. One of these edge tiles is chosen at random. If the edge tile candidate passes the particular clump tile validation, the clump is grown to include that tile. Should the edge tile candidate fail the clump tile validation, another edge is considered. An iteration in the step method is complete once a clump has grown by one tile.

When clumps have completed their growth, or they cannot grow any larger, a new clump is created. The new clump is located some distance away at a random angle, which is influenced by the chaos level of the clump. New clumps are created until the specified number of clumps (of clump size) is achieved. In the case where a clump cannot grow further, a new clump, of limited size, is created to attempt to make up for the incomplete growth of the original clump.

Land Clumps (clumps class)

In the land growth phase of map generation, a land clump is created for each player. The clump's first tile is the player's starting tile. Each player's clump then attempts to

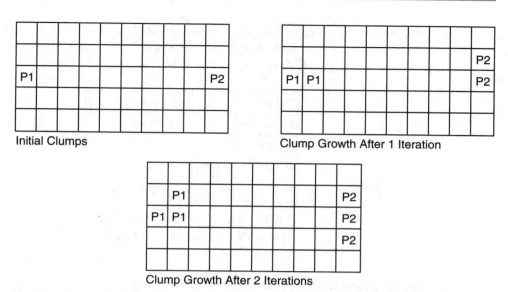

FIGURE 7.4.1 *Clump growth using the step method. P1 and P2 represent each player's tiles.*

grow one tile. This growth uses the step method to ensure that each player's clumps get an equal chance to grow and that no one player's clumps surround another players starting position, thus starving them of land. This demonstrates the importance of the player placement on the map. Players that are too close to each other are likely to run out of space for their clumps to expand. Various clump tile validation rules are employed to determine the next valid tile for any clump, and for land growth, successful growth tiles are those that are close to the player's starting position. As all successful growth tile candidates are edges of the current clump, new player land always grows adjacent to existing player land.

Land clumps assign values to the 2D land water array. This array is initialized as all water tiles. As new tiles are designated as player-owned land through the land clump growth, that player's enumerated value is written into the land water array. As new tiles are evaluated for a particular clump during its growth, the land water array is one of the values used for clump tile validation. This means that a player's clump cannot expand to claim tiles belonging to another player. Additional tile validation rules address specific issues with player land. For example, a validation rule that prevents peninsulas will restrict tiles that are too far from a player's starting position.

Island Land Clumps (`islandclumps` class)

Different map types use different clump tile validation rules. Island maps require that a new land tile for a player is not within some tile distance from another player's land, while land maps allow players' land to be adjacent to an enemy player's land. Through attributes, island maps make use of the `islandclumps` class (derived from `clumps`) and grow using the step growth method. Figure 7.4.2 shows the result of `islandclumps` growth for a small two-player map. Notice the two-tile minimum distance separating the land for each player. Each player's clump has also grown to the size of 19 tiles.

P1	P1					P2	P2	P2	P2	P2
P1	P1	P1	P1			P2	P2	P2	P2	
P1	P1	P1	P1				P2	P2	P2	
P1	P1	P1	P1	P1			P2	P2	P2	
P1	P1	P1	P1			P2	P2	P2	P2	

FIGURE 7.4.2 *Complete island clump growth. P1 and P2 represent each player's tiles.*

Flat Elevation Clumps (`flatclumps` class)

Areas of flat land are grown using `flatclumps`, which is also derived from `clumps`. Flat clumps complete the 2D flat land array. These clumps are grown using the completion growth method and are only allowed to grow in that player's existing land. Flat clumps ensure that each player has an adequate amount of land that is free from elevation so that he or she can build buildings. Figure 7.4.3 shows the results of complete flat clump growth in the results of the island growth from Figure 7.4.2. Note that each player now has five tiles that will be flat.

P1	P1					P2	P2	P2	P2	P2
P1	P1	P1	P1			P2	P2	F	F	
F	F	F	P1				P2	F	F	
P1	F	F	P1	P1			P2	F	P2	
P1	P1	P1	P1			P2	P2	P2	P2	

FIGURE 7.4.3 *Complete flat clump growth. P1 and P2 represent each player's tiles. F represents a flat tile.*

Height Map Details

Once the land is grown, realistic terrain is then added. Fractals—the diamond square fractal in particular—are a quick and easy way to generate realistic looking elevation [Bourke02]. The diamond square algorithm as described in [Martz97] and [Shankel00] was implemented in a small amount of time. Map attributes expose parameters of the fractal such as minimum, maximum, and initial elevation. The 2D height map array is the output of the fractal. This process creates varied terrain; however, some of the noise in the resultant fractal was not desired. A simple filter was added to help smooth out these jagged terrain artifacts.

As the height map was combined with the land water array, some height map values were altered to fit the more important land water allocation. Array values that appear as land in the land water array but had water elevation values in the height map are increased in a way to both preserve some sort of natural look as well as to create land where it was needed. This process also goes the other way as elevations in the height map decoded as land but listed as water in the land water array are lowered to water elevation values. For locations specified as flat in the flat land array, height map values are ignored and the terrain is set to the flat elevation map attribute. The filter again worked to smooth out possible cliffs created from the flat land influence.

Resource Allocation

Next, resources (berries, iron, gold, stone, and wildlife) are placed. Resources are placed on a per-player basis, with each player receiving the same number of each type of resource. Resources are placed within rings centered on the player's starting location. The number of each resource and the size of the rings are map attributes. To place the resource, random locations within the rings are considered until an acceptable resource location is found or the number of search iterations elapses.

However, there are several reasons why a randomly chosen location for a resource might fail. One reason is that certain resources cannot be placed on particular terrain features. Moreover, resources are also restricted in their minimum distance to other resources. Additional rules prevent resources from being placed too close to player starting locations, as this provides an economic advantage.

Trees are the last resource to place, as they are plentiful and also restrict pathfinding. Luckily, the clump class lends itself perfectly toward the creation of forests. The number of forests per player, the size of the forests, and the number of clumps per forest are all specified as map attributes. Unlike most resources, player-owned land does not restrict forest growth. The class treeclumps was derived from the clump class, thus making forests a collection of clumps. Forests are not allowed to grow near other forests, and specific areas of the map are marked as forest free.

Conclusion

This article provided an introductory overview of random map generation for strategy games. The process detailed was successful in creating a good variety of mostly fair maps. While generating fair maps remains a difficult task, there are a few points worth reiterating. First, reproducible maps—made possible by the random number seed—are excellent for development and debugging. Next, the scripting system described allows for rapid prototyping of maps as well as offloading programming tasks onto game designers. The scripting system also allows for a great variety of maps due to its flexible and extensible nature. Lastly, the natural look of the maps was achieved by use of the self-similar height map and the organic clump class.

Unfortunately, this design is far from perfect. Processing times for some maps can be quite large. There is also no concept of placing particular terrain features on the map, which might exist in a "super tile" design (in which large, predesigned areas of map are simply placed onto an existing blank map). Super tile designs can benefit from fairer and more visually pleasing terrain features and a more cohesive look to the overall map. Furthermore, while the scripts were incredibly powerful, they forced designers to program. Often, programmers ended up creating rough versions of new maps, as too much knowledge of the generation process was required to create a new map type. *EE* maps would have benefited from more terrain analysis earlier in the map creation process. Maps could be created in which players had vastly different numbers of chokepoints or even no access to other players. The resource placement system often created maps with resource advantages. This design was also quite a burden on the development schedule.

These issues aside, this system is far from obsolete. With few modifications, the system detailed can create an even larger variety of maps. In an island map with teams, the land for team members could be allowed to grow together. Adjusting the elevations of an island map can create canyon maps similar to those found in *StarCraft*. Varying the parameters of an island map can also create river maps. The resource placement system could also benefit from some sort of grid-based resource placement scheme.

References

[Berger02a] Berger, Lee, "Scripting: Overview and Code Generation," *AI Game Programming Wisdom*, Charles River Media, 2002.

[Berger02b] Berger, Lee, "Scripting: The Interpreter Engine," *AI Game Programming Wisdom*, Charles River Media, 2002.

[Berger02c] Berger, Lee, "Scripting: System Integration," *AI Game Programming Wisdom*, Charles River Media, 2002.

[Bourke02] Bourke, Paul, "Fractals, Chaos," available online at *astronomy.swin.edu.au/~pbourke/fractals/*, 2002.

[LeckyThompson99] Lecky-Thompson, Guy W., "Generating Random Terrain," available online at *www.gamasutra.com/features/19990917/infinite_04.htm*, 1999.

[LeckyThompson00] Lecky-Thompson, Guy W., "Real-Time Realistic Terrain Generation," *Game Programming Gems*, Charles River Media, 2000.

[Martz97] Martz, Paul, "Generating Random Fractal Terrain," available online at *www.gameprogrammer.com/fractal.html*, 1997.

[Poiker02] Poiker, Falko, "Creating Scripting Languages for Nonprogrammers," *AI Game Programming Wisdom*, Charles River Media, 2002.

[Shankel00] Shankel, Jason, "Fractal Terrain Generation—Midpoint Displacement," *Game Programming Gems*, Charles River Media, 2000.

7.5

Transport Unit AI for Strategy Games

Shawn Shoemaker—Stainless Steel Studios

shansolox@yahoo.com

Unit AI refers to the micro-level artificial intelligence that controls a specific unit in a game and how that unit reacts to input from the player and the game world. Transports present a particular challenge for unit AI, as many units must work together to achieve their common goal, while attempting to minimize player frustration. This article discusses the general transport unit AI challenge and a successful solution. Land, air, naval, and building transports (such as fortresses and town centers) will be discussed, and a class hierarchy implementation will be suggested. Algorithms for the loading (including the calculation for rendezvous points) and unloading of transports will be presented as well as warnings for particular pitfalls. This article assumes some sort of finite-state machine-based unit AI system and is applicable to any game in which there are multiple units in need of transporting. This article details the transport unit AI as found in the real-time strategy (RTS) game *Empire Earth* (*EE*) developed by Stainless Steel Studios.

Problem Statement

Transports move passengers around the map. Passengers are land-based units. Air transports, land transports, naval transports, and even building transports are required. When transport and passengers are instructed to load, all units must meet together. Passengers must then go into the transports. When transports are instructed to unload at a particular point, the transports must move near that point and, once there, attempt to unload their passengers. The system must adhere to existing RTS transport standards so that the behavior for loading and unloading is what players expect. Further, headaches inherent to transport systems should be minimized.

Solution Overview

There are four main types of transports. It is assumed that land units (units that can only move on land) are the only passengers for all transports. Figure 7.5.1 details the class hierarchy for the different classes of transports. Examples of air transports are helicopters, airplanes, space ships, balloons, and winged creatures. The transport itself flies above the terrain, and is free to move anywhere on the map, while its passengers are limited to valid areas of land. Building transports cover any stationary unit, such as a bunker or a tower. Land transports abstract an armored personnel carrier, siege tower, wagon, and even a horse. Land transports are limited to generally the same type of terrain as their passengers. Examples of naval transports are ships, submarines, and water creatures. Naval transports are the most challenging to implement, as the transport can only move on water, while the passengers are limited to the land.

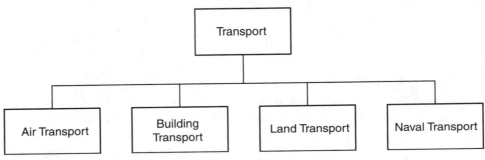

FIGURE 7.5.1   *Transport class hierarchy.*

In this solution, all units have high-level goals. These goals are often based on input from the player. Goals are broken down into small steps, and the units go about accomplishing their goals by following these small steps. This system is unit-level AI (unit AI), in this case implemented through finite-state machines (FSMs).

Loading describes the high-level goal that units are given when a player instructs those units to board a transport. Units instructed to board become passengers. Loading is complicated in that multiple units must meet as one. Units involved in loading must also have their unit AIs interact with each other. Players can also exploit loading. For example, at some point, passengers will teleport into the transport as they move from the game world to the transport's "magical" cargo location. Such exploits need to be avoided.

Unloading is the high-level goal given to a transport unit when a player instructs that transport to disembark its passengers. Unloading is complicated for a number of reasons. First, the transport must move within a certain range of its unload location, before the passengers are unloaded. Second, unloading requires some guessing as to the player's intended unload location. Often, this unload location must be modified since the particular transport could never actually move to the location indicated by the player. Lastly, unloading must prevent exploits that might allow passengers to unload on a location that they might not be able to move to otherwise, such as teleporting passengers through walls.

Finite-State Machines

FSMs form the basis of most unit AI. There is a good resource on FSMs in this book [Fu04], so only a brief overview of FSMs as they apply to this system is provided here.

As mentioned before, units in the game world have high-level goals given to them by the player. These goals can be as simple as to move to a location. To accomplish these goals, units must break the goal down into lower level manageable steps, which in this solution are referred to as *actions*. To accomplish its goal, a unit must transition from one action to another action. Actions are connected to other actions with a Boolean combination of conditions, called *triggers*. Triggers test conditions on the unit and the unit's place in the game world. Visually, the set of actions and triggers for a unit form a connected, cyclic directed graph. As a unit is updated in its current action, all of the triggers for that action are tested. If a trigger evaluates as true, the unit transitions from the current action to the next action. Once the transition has occurred, the unit does not test triggers again until the next update. If no triggers evaluate as true, the unit remains in its current action. Figure 7.5.2 shows a simple FSM, with two actions and two different triggers.

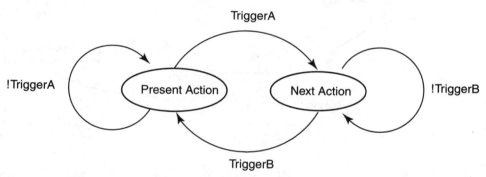

FIGURE 7.5.2   *Simple finite-state machine.*

Passenger FSM

As shown in Figure 7.5.3, passengers have it easy. Passengers cannot unload (because transports handle unloading their cargo in this solution), which simplifies the problem. When passengers are told to load into a transport, they begin in action CalculatePath and then they must move to the rendezvous point and wait for the transport to arrive. Once the transport is near, passengers load into the transport. To prevent passengers from waiting forever for their transport, they must test both for the death of their transport unit, and for the transport losing its high-level goal. Passengers must also make multiple attempts to reach the rendezvous point. Once passengers have loaded, they go to the Idle action.

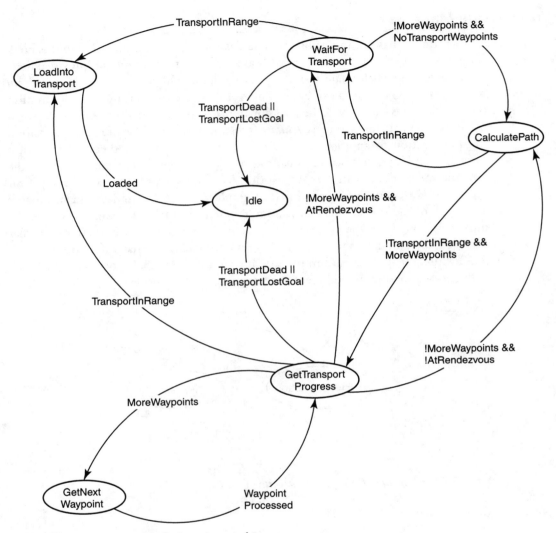

FIGURE 7.5.3   *A passenger finite-state machine.*

Transport FSM

Transport FSMs are a little more complicated. For load goals, transports must move to the rendezvous point, picking up passengers along the way. Once at the rendezvous point, transports must wait until either all passengers have loaded or there is no room for additional passengers. If a transport fills up before all passengers have loaded, those extra passengers must be informed that the transport is full.

For unload goals, transports must move to the unload point. Once within range of the unload location, the transport can attempt to unload its cargo. The transport might need to continue moving toward the unload point, although its simple *in range test* might return true (the in range test returns true if the distance between the transport and its unload location is less than the unload range of the transport). This exception will be explained in more detail later. (See Figure 7.5.4.)

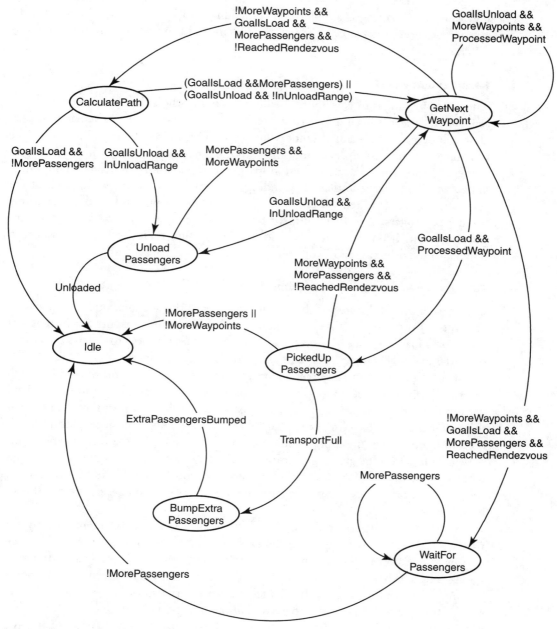

FIGURE 7.5.4 *A transport finite-state machine.*

Loading

Loading is the high-level goal for units that need to enter a transport. Both passengers and transports are given a load goal, although they each have their own role to play for this goal. As passengers come within the loading range of the transport, they load into the transport. Loading is simpler than unloading. To load, all units involved must agree on some *rendezvous point* where they will meet. Each type of transports does this differently.

Rendezvous Point

The key to loading is to determine a rendezvous point where the transport and all passengers will meet. Given a group of units and a transport, the particular transport class will determine an initial rendezvous point. This point is then validated for the passengers. If the passengers cannot move to the rendezvous point or if there are permanent blocking units at that location, the rendezvous point is adjusted. The simple adjustment considers the tiles surrounding the initial rendezvous point. Each of the surrounding tiles is tested as before, to determine if they are valid rendezvous points for the passengers. The first valid surrounding tile is then chosen as the new rendezvous point. If none of the surrounding tiles is valid, then the system has broken down and the original rendezvous point is used.

Testing for Passengers in Loading Range

Once passengers and transport begin moving toward their rendezvous point, passenger units must test to see if they are in range to load into the transport. Each transport has its own loading range. This is the distance from the transport to the passenger that potential passengers must achieve in order to load into the transport.

If the transport and passenger are on the same *continent* (an area of land in which the tiles form a connected graph, with connections corresponding to possible land pathfinding), the distance the passenger must travel to the transport is calculated. For this calculation, pathfinding (a special performance-friendly bounded pathfinder) is used to literally path the unit to the transport and then count the tiles covered. This prevents units from teleporting over impassible terrain. If the unit is not close enough with this test, the border tiles of the transport are considered. If the passenger is on one of these border tiles, the passenger is in range. This second case is generally due to building transports.

When the transport and passenger are not on the same continent (mostly for naval transports), a ray is cast from the passenger to the transport. The first shore tile on this line nearest to the passenger, referred to as the test tile, is then used for a simple distance check to the passenger. If this distance is acceptable given the transport's loading range, the distance from this test tile to the transport is next checked. The sum of these two distances must be less than the transport's loading range. If the sum of distances is still valid, then a more exact land path distance check—using the pathfinder—is performed between the passenger and the test tile. If the land path fails and the passenger is very near to the transport, one final test is used. This is a straight line-of-fire obstacle test that checks for walls and buildings blocking the passenger. This final test is used to ease naval transporting, as it results in passengers being able to load more often.

Air Transports

Air transports move without regard to terrain or collisions, and as they are generally faster than passengers, air transports do most of the moving when loading up passengers. The passenger nearest to the transport is determined. The rendezvous point is then set to this nearest passenger's location. All units involved head toward this location, with most of the burden resting on the air transport reaching the rendezvous point.

Building Transports

As building transports cannot move, passengers must meet at the building. Therefore, the rendezvous point is simply the location of the building.

Land Transports

The transport and passengers will meet somewhere between one another. First, the nearest passenger to the transport is determined (this assumes that the other potential passengers are close to this passenger). Next, a line is cast from the nearest passenger to the transport. Tiles underneath the line are determined. One of these tiles on the line is then selected as the rendezvous point based on the transport and nearest passenger's relative maximum velocities. The goal in selecting this tile is to try to make both passenger and transport travel the same distance because their speeds are nearly equal.

Naval Transports

Naval transports come to get the passengers. Terrain analysis, as detailed in [Higgins02], is crucial here, as a location is needed that both land and naval units can reach. For this reason, there are two rendezvous points: one land tile for the passengers, and one water tile for the transport. The distance between these two rendezvous points must be less than, or equal to, the transport's load range. If the transport and all of the passengers are already on the same continent, then the transport is on a shore tile, and all passengers move to a tile adjacent to the transport. If the units are on different continents, then both groups must move to meet each other. The shore tile closest to the passengers is chosen as the land rendezvous point. A water tile adjacent to the land rendezvous point is then determined. Both rendezvous points are then adjusted so that both transport and passengers can reach them.

Unloading

Unloading is the high-level goal given to transports to disembark their passengers. Players give the transport a particular location in which to unload. The *unload point* is then modified so that it is a location that the transport can actually reach. The transport then tries to get as close as it can to the unload point. Once the transport is within its unload range from the unload point, the passengers can exit the transport. As passengers exit, they use *sub-tile placement* to keep them from colliding with other passengers, other units, and terrain features. Sub-tile placement generates valid terrain locations for an input unit that will not result in that unit colliding with any surrounding units. Further, sub-tile placement prevents units from "teleporting" through walls or buildings.

Testing for Transports in Unload Range

Once the transport begins moving toward its unload location, it performs simple distance checks to the unload point. When this simple distance check is less than the unload range of the transport, the transport can attempt to let passengers out. As unloading essentially teleports units from the transport's location to another location, it is very important to prevent unloading exploits. When a transport attempts to unload passengers, it tests to see if its first passenger can path to the unload point from the transport's current location. As mentioned previously, this test actually uses the pathfinder to obtain a realistic path distance.

Unload Point

Selection of the unload point (UP) is key to the unloading process. As shown in Figure 7.5.5, given the transport point (T) and the player's clicked point (CP), there are actually three unload points: the transport destination point (TDP), the first passenger point (FPP), and the unload point. The transport destination point is where the transport must move to for the cargo to unload. The first passenger point is the first tile that is adjacent to the transport destination point on which cargo can pathfind. Finally, the unload point is the ultimate destination of the cargo.

Each transport class determines these three points in different ways, which will be discussed later. Once each point is chosen, it must be validated for the particular passengers and transport. This validation involves specific pathfinding tile requirements for the units as well as more general terrain analysis (such as continent testing and so forth). The points must also be reachable, or nearly reachable, by the particular unit. The final unload point can even be changed from the player's clicked point to achieve these requirements. For example, a naval transport is instructed to unload (by the player's clicked point) five tiles inland while its unload range is three tiles. Obviously, the unload point must be modified, as shown in Figure 7.5.5, because the transport cannot unload a distance of five tiles.

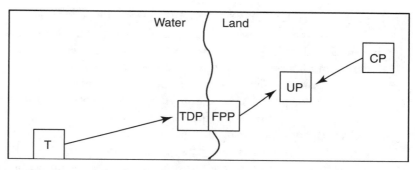

FIGURE 7.5.5 *The three unload points.*

Air Transports

Since air transports are not restricted in their pathfinding, the transport destination point does not constrain the other points. Therefore, the first passenger point and the unload point are equal and subject to the pathfinding constraints of land units. These two points need to be modified for the passengers due to terrain obstacles, units, or pathfinding restrictions. This design relies on the sub-tile placement code to keep unloading passengers from colliding with existing units as well as keeping them off invalid terrain.

Building Transports

As building transports are immobile, all three points are the same as the building's location. While this violates the rule that the first passenger point and the unload point must be valid for the passengers, the sub-tile placement code can handle this. Again, the sub-tile placement code is used to ensure that passengers do not place on top of other units or invalid terrain. This placement code is the same code used to place new units that are produced in factory buildings, so units placed using this code have the same appearance as those just produced out of a building.

Land Transports

As land transports have the same pathfinding restrictions as their cargo, the transport destination point, the first passenger point, and the unload point are all equal to the player's clicked point. The land pathfinder is used to determine actual passenger path distance when it is time to unload. In *EE*, another pathfinder was used when the siege tower attempted to unload. This pathfinder would allow placement over exactly one wall unit, as this was the special power of the siege tower.

Naval Transports

Naval unloading is a challenge. Given the player's clicked point, the closest water tile to that location is determined as the transport destination point. An adjacent land tile to the transport destination is then chosen as the first passenger point. As the first passenger point and the player's clicked point could be quite a distance from each other, the unload point is generally modified from the player's clicked location. A line is drawn from the first passenger point to the player's clicked point. Tiles along the line are then considered potential unload points. The selected unload point is then the closest tile to the player's clicked point that is still within the unload range, as imposed by the transport destination point and the first passenger point.

Once the transport is in range of the unload point, it attempts to unload a passenger. While this test generally uses the pathfinder, in this case, the transport can still be in the water. Therefore, the test sums the "teleportation" distance from the transport's tile to the first passenger point, and then uses the pathfinder for the remaining land path distance to the unload point.

Conclusion

This system is very good for naval unloading, an area that has always been the source of much player frustration. Air and land transports also work well. Add this system to a group-level goal system similar to that found in [Dawson02], and the unloading of a group of transports is quite successful. This system also supports special design requirements, such as the requirement that passengers can unload through a wall when transported by a siege tower. There is also much reuse possible in this system. For example, the garrisoning system in *Empire Earth*, in which citizens go to work inside various resource drop-off buildings, makes use of much of the transport code.

Unfortunately, this system is still not perfect. Transports still represent a headache to players. Dealing with multiple transports is particularly bad. When multiple transports try to load, many can determine the same or nearby rendezvous points, and thus cut each other off as they attempt to move there. Naval transports are particularly bad at this due to the difficulties with naval pathfinding (large rectangular units moving on a square mesh). Similar problems occur when many transports are instructed to unload at the same location. The group-level goal system did help, but often the solution was not optimal. Much of this is due to the challenge of guessing what the player wants and expects. Perhaps the micromanagement required for transports is simply too great, and a micro-less solution, as found in *Rise of Nations*, would be better.

With little modification, this transport system can be expanded to create a Tunnel Network as found in *C&C Generals* or a Nydus Canal from *StarCraft*. Additional processing could be performed when calculating the unload point. Presently, the unload point is mostly based on pathfinding restrictions of the transport unit. It could be expanded to also take the passengers' pathfinding restrictions into account. Unfortunately, most pathfinding tests are quite expensive.

References

[Dawson02] Dawson, Chad, "Formations," *AI Game Programming Wisdom*, Charles River Media, 2002.

[Fu04] Fu, Dan, and Houlette, Ryan, "The Ultimate Guide to FSMs in Games," *AI Game Programming Wisdom 2*, Charles River Media, 2004.

[Higgins02] Higgins, Dan, "Terrain Analysis in an RTS—The Hidden Giant," *Game Programming Gems 3*, Charles River Media, 2002.

7.6

Wall Building for RTS Games

Mario Grimani—Sony Online Entertainment

mgrimani@soe.sony.com, mariogrimani@yahoo.com

Many real-time strategy (RTS) games give players the ability to place passive defensive structures that act as barriers for enemy unit movement. Different games might use different representations for these structures; walls, barbed wire fences, sandbags, and force fields are just a few. Despite different appearances, as long as these structures do not behave differently we can treat them the same. For the purpose of this article, we will refer to them as walls.

Figuring out intelligent wall placement is not a trivial problem. The solution is expected to take into account locations that we want to protect while making good use of natural barriers. Other requirements might include wall cost, distance from a given location, size of the protected area, and many others. Quick-and-dirty solutions like building a rectangular wall around the given locations rarely meet anything but the most basic requirements. What we need is a simple and fast solution that is flexible enough so that we can tailor it to individual games' needs. In this article, we present a solution that meets these requirements.

A good wall-building algorithm can be very helpful. If used properly, it can make the non-player character (NPC) opponents much more formidable. For RTS games that have a map editor, adding an automated wall-building feature directly in the editor can make the level designer's job easier. With a given starting point and preset parameters, one click of a button could generate walls and reduce the need for manual editing. For games that have random map generation, wall building could be added as one of the generation phases. This feature would let us produce walls as part of the starting conditions, which would be a welcome addition to map generation.

Now that we have examined the benefits of wall building, we are ready to start examining possible solutions.

Defining the Problem

We will start by restricting the problem domain to tile-based maps. Furthermore, we will add the restriction that the obstruction footprints, which are the areas obstructed by the placement of game objects, have to be confined within the tile boundaries. Both of these restrictions are very common in today's RTS games and, as we will see, solutions that we find could be applied to some less restrictive environments.

Using a discrete domain, like tile-based maps, allows us to break walls into basic building blocks and wall segments, which we will define as follows:

A *wall segment* is a passive defensive structure that blocks unit movement over a single tile that it occupies. Two wall segments are considered adjacent when they touch along the edges (not diagonals). Free-standing wall segments can have up to four adjacent wall segments (neighbors), one in each of the major directions: North, East, South, and West. Wall segments that are part of a wall have exactly two adjacent wall segments.

Obviously, when we build a wall we are trying to protect a given location on the map by blocking the movement of enemy units. This implies that a wall has to block all access routes and cannot have breaks that would allow units to pass through. Now that the wall continuity requirements are complete and the problem space has been clarified, we are ready to define walls.

A *wall* is a set of wall segments connected together in such a way that:

- Every wall segment has exactly two unique adjacent wall segments (neighbors). It might not be obvious, but this requirement implies that wall segments are linked in circular fashion. For example, starting at any wall segment and moving along the wall in clockwise direction will lead back to the same wall segment.
- There is at least one interior tile.
- All interior tiles are connected through edges (diagonal connections do not count). For example, starting from any one interior tile and moving through adjacent interior tiles we can reach all interior tiles.

Where:

- An *interior tile* is a tile inside the walled-off area.
- An *interior area* is the set of all interior tiles for a given wall. The interior area has at least one tile. If it has more than one tile, all tiles have to be connected.

Introducing a concept of interior tiles helps us eliminate unwanted fringe situations that would needlessly complicate the algorithm. The requirement for existence and connectivity of interior area is definitely a reasonable one, and this will become more apparent as we start defining moves used by the algorithm.

Figure 7.6.1 shows examples of valid walls as well as groups of wall segments that do not form a wall. The examples clarify what configurations of wall segments are considered a wall.

Obviously, building a simple wall for a given location can be trivial—we could just wall off the location's immediate perimeter. Unfortunately, such a trivial solution is unlikely to be useful in a real game situation, so we will need more information than just the location we want to protect. We need acceptance criteria that have all

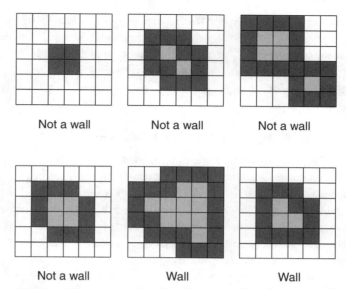

FIGURE 7.6.1 *Examples of walls and wall segments that do and do not form walls.*

desired parameters relevant to the wall we are building. The algorithm will take those criteria into account and run until the criteria are met. Some of the useful criteria parameters are minimum and/or maximum distance from the location we are trying to protect, minimum and/or maximum number of interior tiles (size of walled off area), and maximum number of wall segments (cost of building wall). When setting criteria parameters, we have to be careful not to create conflicting requirements that cannot be fulfilled.

Finally, with all this in mind we are ready to define the problem:

On a given tile map, build a wall that fits the definition, protects the given location, and meets the given acceptance criteria.

The Algorithm

Using the problem and problem domain definitions, we are ready to start working on the solution. We plan to use the greedy algorithm approach, explained next, and tailor it to fit our needs.

Greedy Algorithms

A greedy algorithm is an algorithm that tries to find an optimal solution by using a series of locally optimal steps ("best" moves at the time). Choosing locally optimal steps for the biggest immediate gain is what gave greedy algorithms their name. Since locally optimal steps are easier to generate, greedy algorithms are usually fast and fairly easy to implement. The disadvantage of this approach is that there is no guarantee that a series of locally optimal steps will yield a globally optimal final solution. Some well-designed greedy algorithms, like Dijkstra's Single-Source Shortest Path Algorithm, guarantee an optimal solution, but others do not. In our case, finding a near optimal solution, instead of the optimal one, is not necessarily a bad thing. For more information on greedy algorithms, see [Cormen01], which dedicates an entire chapter to the topic.

Building Walls Using the Greedy Method

Let's begin by defining a starting location.

A *starting location* is a given location that needs to be protected by building a wall and is used as a starting point for the wall-building algorithm.

An intuitive way of applying the greedy algorithm to the problem would be to create an initial wall around the starting location and then apply a series of "greedy" moves to wall segments until all of the criteria for wall completion have been met. In this context, a move can be defined as follows:

A *move* is the process of removing an existing wall segment and placing in it at a different location in such a way that:

- There is a net gain of exactly one tile in an area that is walled off (number of interior tiles increases by one).
- The resulting wall still meets the definition.

This definition mandates that all moves have outward direction (the first requirement), and it implies that some moves might require addition of extra wall segments (the second requirement). Now we are ready to define a set of moves that we will use to build walls.

By looking at the wall definition and its first requirement, we can see that any given wall segment and its two neighbors, a wall segment triplet, can be arranged only in a limited number of ways. We can generate all possible cases by creating all permutations of neighbors for a central wall segment: neighbor 1 to the North, neighbor 2 to the East, South, or West; neighbor 1 to the East, neighbor 2 to the South, West, or North, and so forth. The result is four groups of three cases, 12 cases total. Figure 7.6.2 shows all of the cases in groups of three. It is important to notice that the results for each group are the same as results for the previous group rotated clockwise by 90 degrees.

Next, we use the results from this exercise, and, for every arrangement of wall segment triplets, we generate all wall permutations that the triplet can be a part of. The permutations are generated by adding the new wall segments to the existing triplets, while making sure that the result still meets the first wall definition requirement. For example, in case 1 of group 1, wall segments can be added in the upper-left and the lower-right corners. Those two extra positions yield four permutations, as shown in Figure 7.6.3. Every case in every group has a different number of positions available for the placement of extra wall segments. It turns out that, using this method, every group generates a total of 17 permutations.

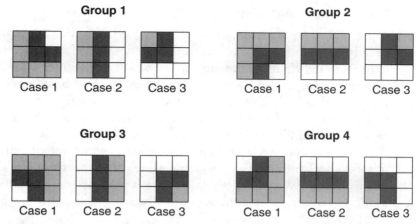

FIGURE 7.6.2 *All permutations of a wall segment (the center square in each block of nine segments) with two neighbors.*

Group 1, Case 1: four permutations

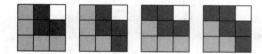

Group 1, Case 2: nine permutations

Group 1, Case 3: four permutations

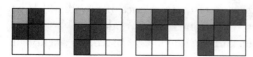

FIGURE 7.6.3 *Each group from Figure 7.6.2 generates 17 wall permutations. This figure illustrates the 17 permutations for Group 1.*

The Paradigm Shift

At this point, we are dealing with 17 cases per group with four groups total, which would give us a total of 68 cases. Although some permutations share common patterns that can help us reduce the number of cases, the situation is going to get worse with the introduction of natural barriers. Since natural barriers act similarly to wall segments (they block unit movement), their presence will greatly increase the number of possible moves. The large number of moves leads us to question whether there is a better way of handling the outward expansion. The answer lies in the realization that there is a one-to-one relationship between walls and the interior areas that they protect. In other words, for every wall, there is exactly one interior area that it surrounds, and vice versa. We can use this fact to our benefit. Instead of pushing the wall outward, we can expand the interior area. Once we are done, we can always generate a wall from the interior area data.

This paradigm shift allows us to redefine the problem and draw on graph theory to represent the problem domain as a graph with nodes. In that context, we can define the following:

A *node* is a representation of the smallest area that can be obstructed by the placement of game objects. In graph theory, a node is also called a vertex.

A *graph* is a data structure that consists of a set of nodes and a set of edges such that every edge connects precisely two corresponding nodes. A map, which defines our search space, is represented with one such graph. The *edge* not only connects two nodes, but also, through that connection, defines a path that units take when moving between those two nodes. The nodes sharing the same edge are called adjacent. During the graph traversal (a systematic processing of nodes), the adjacent nodes become the successor nodes (the next ones to process). For RTS games with tile maps, a node represents one tile, and a graph with nodes that has eight neighbors represents a map. We can assume that one wall segment blocks movement over a single node.

The new problem domain allows us to break away from the previously imposed restrictions. As a result, in this new domain, a node can have an arbitrary number of edges coming out of it, connecting it to the other nodes. How does using this new problem domain affect the existing definitions? Here is a quick rundown:

The *wall* and *wall segments* are functionally the same, but since they can be used with an arbitrary graph, the tile map restrictions are gone. Two wall segments are adjacent if they share the same edge, and a wall segment can have any number of adjacent wall segments (neighbors). The wall segments that are part of a wall still have only two neighbors, and a wall still requires at least one interior node.

An *interior node* replaces the interior tile, and the *interior area* becomes a set of all interior nodes.

We still need the *starting location* as it defines the *starting node*, which we will use as the starting point for the interior area expansion.

The *move*, due to the paradigm shift, becomes a process of adding new nodes to the interior area. The move still needs to meet the criteria that, after the move, there is an interior area gain of one node, and that the resulting wall still meets the definition.

Putting the Greedy Method to Use

With the paradigm shift to interior area expansion, we can apply the principles of greedy algorithms to the problem.

We begin by promoting the node defined by the starting location to the first interior node, thus creating an initial interior area. Next, we expand this interior area, one step at a time, by adding one node per step. The node to add is selected by the algorithm using greedy methodology, which means that at each step, the algorithm looks at nodes bordering the interior area and selects the node ranked as best by a heuristic function. To meet the greedy requirements, the heuristic function has to evaluate nodes based on immediate, locally optimal, gain. In its simplest form, the function ranks bordering nodes based on how many additional wall segments it would take to keep them walled off from the outside area. The node that requires the fewest number of wall segments is selected as the best node and added to the list of already selected interior nodes. As the algorithm progresses and the interior area grows, new nodes are promoted to interior nodes and added to this list, which we will define as follows:

A *closed list* is a collection of all interior nodes.

By definition, the closed list represents the interior area in its entirety. We call it a closed list because it contains nodes that the algorithm has finished processing. The nodes in this list have been evaluated and accepted as part of the interior area. They are never removed from the list, because moving them could fragment the interior area and undermine the assumption that all interior nodes are connected. These processed nodes can be defined in the following way:

A *closed node* is a node in the closed list. Since all nodes in the closed list are interior nodes, a closed node is also an interior node.

Since the nodes bordering the interior area are evaluated at every step, it would be inefficient to generate them every time. Instead, we generate them once and then keep them in the separate list that we modify as we go along. This list and its nodes we can define as follows:

An *open list* is a collection of all nodes that are candidates for addition to the interior area.

An *open node* is a node in the open list. Like all nodes in the open list, each open node is a candidate for the interior area.

By definition, the open list represents a perimeter of interior area, and, upon algorithm completion, every node in the open list represents a location for wall segment placement. When a node from the open list is promoted to an interior node, it is removed from the open list and added to the closed list. All nodes neighboring the promoted node not already in the open or closed list become new candidates for addition to the interior area and should be moved to the open list.

In pseudocode form, here is the essence of algorithm:

```
List OpenList   // Nodes bordering the interior area
List ClosedList // Nodes in the interior area

WallBuilder(Node              StartNode,
            AcceptanceCriteria Criteria)
{
    Node BestNode, SuccessorNode

    // Initialize lists
    reset OpenList
    reset ClosedList

    add StartNode to OpenList
    while ((OpenList is not empty) and
          (Criteria are not met))
    {
        remove best choice node BestNode from OpenList
        add BestNode to ClosedList

        for each successor SuccessorNode of BestNode
        {
            // Ignore nodes already in OpenList
            if SuccessorNode is in OpenList
                continue

            // Ignore interior nodes
            if SuccessorNode is in ClosedList
                continue

            add SuccessorNode to OpenList
        }
    }
}
// Upon exit, OpenList contains the nodes that have
// to be walled off
```

The pseudocode uses only a handful of data types. List is a generic data type that represents a collection of nodes and can be implemented in many different ways, as we will see later in the article. Node is a data structure that contains information relevant to a single node. Depending on the implementation, the node information structure might include any combination of the following: position on the map, list of neighboring nodes, obstruction data (terrain and objects), and data structure linkage fields. AcceptanceCriteria is an aggregate data structure that represents a set of variables, which define conditions for algorithm completion.

Using the Algorithm

The key to using the algorithm is understanding its three controlling functions and using them properly. The functions are *traversal function*, which finds successor nodes; *heuristic function*, which ranks open nodes; and *acceptance function*, which decides when the wall meets given criteria. The traversal and heuristic functions together control the interior area expansion. The acceptance function controls the algorithm and determines when to stop. Let's discuss each function in detail.

The *traversal function* is the function that, for each given node, gets all successor nodes and decides which ones can be used. When used to find nodes to promote to open nodes, the function has the power to block individual nodes and prevent the interior area from spreading into undesirable areas. Frequently, the traversal function is used by the heuristic function to get a list of successor nodes that will be used as part of the cost calculation.

The *heuristic function* is the function that ranks open nodes and, through the ranking process, controls the shape of the interior area expansion.

The function is trying to maximize the gain of interior area while minimizing the cost of walling it off. Since the algorithm mandates that the area gain is one node per step, the only option is to minimize the cost of adding that node. As a result, the highest ranked nodes are the ones with the lowest cost.

We mentioned before, that in its simplest form, the cost is equal to the number of wall segments needed to keep the new node walled off from the outside area. While this approach to the cost calculation works from the efficiency perspective, it tends to generate asymmetric walls that stretch in one direction. This anomaly happens because a list of successor nodes tends to be arranged in a certain order. Traversing successor nodes in this order leads to nodes at the beginning of the list getting preference over nodes with the same cost farther down the list. The preference usually leads to expansion in the general direction of the successor node at the beginning of the list. To avoid this undesirable behavior, we have to introduce another cost parameter to the heuristic function calculation: distance from the starting node. The closer a node is to the starting location, the lower its distance-related portion of the cost. Factoring in distance ensures that nodes with the same cost of walling off are selected in the proper order, with the closest nodes picked first. The benefit of this new approach is that, for the same total cost of walling off, we maximize the minimum wall distance from the starting node, which is good for defensive purposes.

With this modified heuristic function, we have to guarantee that, in all possible cases, the distance-related part is always less significant than the portion related to walling off. To achieve this, we have to multiply the cost of walling off by a constant larger than the maximum possible distance cost, which is usually the maximum distance itself. Taking these changes into account, the typical heuristic function can be described by the following formula:

$$f(n) = c \times w(n) + d(n) \tag{1}$$

where $f(n)$ is a cost function that represents the cost of adding node n to the interior area, c is a constant larger than the maximum possible distance from the starting node, $w(n)$ is the cost of walling off node n, and $d(n)$ is the distance from node n to the starting node.

The *acceptance function* checks the current set of algorithm variables against variables given as part of the acceptance criteria. If the criteria are met, the function stops the algorithm.

Taking Advantage of Natural Barriers

The wall-building algorithm would be of little use if it did not take into account natural barriers and put them to a good use. Incorporating a natural barrier into a wall can either lower the cost of walling off a certain area or allow us to wall off larger areas for the same cost. Some natural barriers tend to be indestructible so incorporating them into a wall can have defensive benefits as well. To take advantage of natural barriers, we have to modify traversal and heuristic functions.

The traversal function has to be changed so that it ignores natural barriers when looking for nodes to be promoted to open nodes. The change guarantees that no nodes obstructed by terrain are considered candidates for interior area.

The heuristic function needs to make sure that terrain obstructions are credited with their ability to block unit movement. Terrain obstructions act as free walls and should be omitted from the cost of walling off calculations. The most efficient way to implement this change is on the node traversal level. By ignoring nodes, we are effectively omitting them from the heuristic calculation. The omission reduces the cost of nodes adjacent to a natural barrier, which makes them more desirable to use. The resulting effect is that the algorithm takes advantage of natural barriers and tries to use them as free walls.

Advanced Issues

With the basic wall-building functionality in place, we are ready to explore advanced issues. Here are some of the most important ones.

Map Edges

All RTS games handle map edges in one of two different ways: they embrace them as part of the gameplay, or they hide them from the user by making them inaccessible, sometimes permanently covering them with the fog-of-war. The latter case requires an impassable terrain around the edges, to make them inaccessible. Since the impassable terrain forms a natural barrier, the wall-building algorithm is ready to handle this case. The case that is more interesting to us is embracing the map edges as part of the gameplay. How does the wall-building algorithm behave in such a situation? It turns out that the traversal and heuristic functions are ready for this case. The traversal function cannot find nodes past the map edges, so the interior area expansion will naturally stop at the edges. At the same time, the heuristic function has no cost for the area past the edges, so the nodes along the edges will have reduced cost, which will make them more attractive candidates for the interior area. In a way, the algorithm handles the area past the edges as an invisible natural barrier that, instead of having impassable nodes that we are ignoring, has no nodes at all.

The Minimum Distance Requirement

Some in-game situations might require that the wall-building algorithm generate a result where no wall segments are closer to the starting location than the specified minimum distance. Making two changes to the algorithm can make meeting the minimum distance requirement possible. First, we need to modify the heuristic function to give the highest priority to the nodes that are closer than the minimum required distance. The highest priority guarantees that no unnecessary processing is done until all the nodes are at the minimum distance. Here is what the formula for the modified heuristic function looks like:

$$f(n) = \begin{cases} 0 & \text{if } d(n) < \text{ minimum distance} \\ c \times w(n) + d(n) & \text{if } d(n) \geq \text{ minimum distance} \end{cases} \tag{2}$$

Since the function is a cost function, the formula gives high priority nodes a cost of 0.

Second, we need to modify the acceptance function to make sure that the algorithm does not stop before all nodes have reached the minimum distance. This second change is a matter of prioritizing acceptance criteria data inside the acceptance function. This minimum distance requirement is very useful in situations when there is a need to wall off an important object (e.g., a building) and keep it out of range of enemy unit fire.

The Maximum Distance Requirement

In similar fashion, we could require the algorithm to guarantee that no wall segments in the final solution are placed farther than the specified maximum distance. The simplest way to implement this is to stop the open nodes that are located at the maximum distance from becoming the interior nodes. This approach manages to stop the interior area expansion, but there are some undesirable side effects. By having a class of open nodes that are not candidates for removal from the open list, we are undermining the functionality of the open list. A much better solution is to introduce the concept of the *maximum distance list*, the list that holds nodes located at the maximum distance. When a node is ready to be added to the open list, we check its distance from the starting node. If the distance is equal to the maximum distance, the node is added to the maximum distance list instead. Upon the algorithm completion, merging the open list with the maximum distance list gives us the final solution. This requirement is useful if we want to make sure that the wall is placed within the manageable distance. Another good example are the situations where we want to make sure that the wall segments are under protective cover of tower fire.

Doors and Gates

Another addition to the wall-building algorithm could be the placement of doors and gates. Since walls are indiscriminate in their functionality of blocking unit movement, we might want to add an ability to get allied units through walls at certain strategic locations. A brute-force approach would be to blindly place gates along the wall at certain distances from each other. While this approach would solve most of the problems, it can have some very questionable worst cases. For example, gates could end up being placed against impassable objects or terrain obstructions like cliffs and forests. Moreover, without doing connectivity checks, the brute-force approach cannot guarantee that gates will lead us to all outside locations of interest. A more sophisticated approach would be to create a path [Stout00, Matthews02] from the starting location to different locations of interest outside the walled off area while ignoring walls as obstacles. The points where the path intersects with wall segments are logical placement locations for gates. For visual appeal reasons, we could merge gate placement locations that are close to each other and that lead to the same outside area.

Diagonal Walls

Some RTS games on the market have walls with wall segments that can be connected in diagonal directions as well as the four directions we have covered in this article. In those cases, an assumption is made that units cannot move diagonally between two wall segments. The algorithm can be modified to handle these cases by making two adjustments. First, we have to make sure that the cost function is ignoring the cost of walling off diagonal directions, and, second, we have to make sure that diagonal successor nodes are not added to the open list. These two adjustments will allow the wall-building algorithm to generate diagonal walls.

Conclusion

ON THE CD

Many real-time strategy games that feature wall-like structures as part of their gameplay do not incorporate wall-building algorithms. Adding such algorithms could greatly benefit NPC opponents and random map generation algorithms (if the game provides one). In this article, we provided a solution for walling off locations through the use of a greedy strategy. The solution, while non-optimal, generates high-quality walls and is not restricted to tile maps. Included on the accompanying CD-ROM is a working version of the wall-building code, based on the algorithm presented in this article. The code, along with the material presented in this article, should provide a solid foundation for writing wall-building algorithms for most RTS games.

References

[Cormen01] Cormen, Thomas H., et al., *Introduction to Algorithms, Second Edition*, MIT Press, 2001: pp. 370–404.

[Matthews02] Matthews, James, "Basic A* Pathfinding Made Simple," *AI Game Programming Wisdom*, Charles River Media, 2002.

[Pinter01] Pinter, Marco, "Toward More Realistic Pathfinding," *Gamasutra*, available online at *www.gamasutra.com/features/20010314/pinter_01.htm*, March 14, 2001.

[Stout96] Stout, Bryan, "Smart Moves: Intelligent Pathfinding," *Game Developer Magazine*, October 1996, available online at *www.gamasutra.com/features/19970801/pathfinding.htm*

[Stout00] Stout, Bryan, "The Basics of A* for Path Planning," *Game Programming Gems*, pp. 254–263, Charles River Media, 2000.

7.7

Strategic Decision-Making with Neural Networks and Influence Maps

Penny Sweetser—School of ITEE, University of Queensland

penny@itee.uq.edu.au

Influence maps provide a strategic perspective in games that allows strategic assessment and decisions to be made based on the current game state. Influence maps consist of several layers, each representing different variables in the game, layered over a geographical representation of the game map. When a decision needs to be made by the AI player, some or all of these layers are combined via a weighted sum to provide an overall idea of the suitability of each area on the map for the current decision. However, the use of a weighted sum has certain limitations.

This article explains how a neural network can be used in place of a weighted sum, to analyze the data from the influence map and make a strategic decision. First, this article summarizes influence maps, describes the current application of a weighted sum, and outlines the associated advantages and disadvantages. Following this, it explains how a neural network can be used in place of a weighted sum and the benefits and drawbacks associated with this alternative. Additionally, it goes into detail about how a neural network can be implemented for this application, illustrated with diagrams.

Influence Maps

Influence maps are used in games for strategic assessment and decision-making. An influence map provides a spatial representation of the AI agent's knowledge about the world and allows it to develop a strategic perspective of the current game state, layered on top of the underlying physical or geographical representation of the game environment [Tozour01]. Each layer of data is a repository for different information about the game world, and each cell is a database of relevant data for all the units and resources that occupy that cell. For example, the layers could store data for combat strength, vulnerable assets, area visibility, body count, resources, and passability for each cell on the map [Tozour01].

When generating an influence map, initial values first need to be calculated for each cell in each layer of the map, based on the current state of the game. That is, if a layer contained data on combat strength, then the combat strength of all the units would need to be calculated for each cell. Once these initial values are calculated, the values in each cell need to be propagated to the nearby cells, thereby spreading the influence of each cell. This influence propagation gives a much more accurate picture of the current strategic situation, as it not only shows where the units are and what they're doing, but also what they might do and the areas they potentially influence [Tozour01]. After the initial values are calculated for each layer and the influences are spread, the data can then be prepared for use in strategic assessment.

Figure 7.7.1 shows an example influence map and illustrates the propagation process. The grid in the top-left shows a possible game situation, in which tanks from two players are positioned in various grid cells. In this example, each tank for the light player will provide an influence of positive one to that cell, whereas each tank for the dark player will provide an influence of negative one.

The grid at the top-right shows how each of these tanks will spread, or propagate, their influence to the nearby cells. Only two tanks are shown for clarity. In this example, each influence value is propagated only one space in each direction and the influence is halved when it is propagated. The result of this propagation for each cell is shown in the grid on the bottom left. The cells with a positive value are influenced by the light player and the cells with negative values are influenced by the dark player. The larger the value is in the positive or negative direction, the more it is influenced by the respective player. The final grid on the bottom right shows the same influence values as the grid on the left, but the influence is illustrated in grayscale.

Influence maps can be used for strategic assessment and decision making, as their structure makes it possible to make intelligent inferences about the characteristics of different locations in the environment. For example, areas that have high strategic control can be identified, as well as weak spots in an opponent's defenses, the enemy's front, flanks and rear, prime camping locations, strategically vulnerable areas, choke points on the terrain, and other meaningful features that human players would choose through experience or intuition [Tozour01, Woodcock02].

Each layer, or set of layers, provides information about a different aspect of the game. For example, the influence map can indicate where the AI's forces are deployed, the location of the enemy, the location of the frontier, areas that are unexplored, areas where significant battles have occurred, and areas where enemies are most likely to attack in the future [Tozour01, Woodcock02]. Furthermore, when these layers are combined, they can be used to make strategic decisions about the game. For example, they can be used to make decisions about where to attack or defend, where to explore, and where to place assets for defense, resource-collection, unit-production, and research.

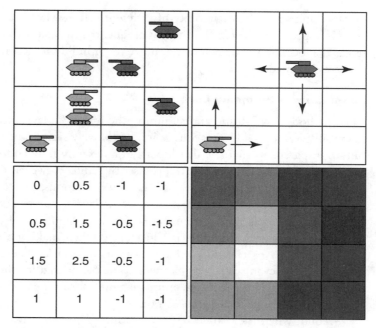

FIGURE 7.7.1 *An example influence map, illustrating an example game situation (top left), propagation (top right), resulting influence values numerically (bottom left) and in grayscale (bottom right).*

Desirability Value with a Weighted Sum

As described in the previous section, the initial value of each cell in each layer is first calculated, based on the current game state. Subsequently, the value, or influence, of each cell is propagated to other nearby cells. At this point, there needs to be some method to combine the relevant layers in order to rank the cells on the map by how good they are for the decision being made. For example, if the AI is going to select a location on the map to attack, then there needs to be some way to combine and weight the different information in the game environment that is relevant to this decision.

The method that is used to combine layers is usually a simple weighted sum. The result of this process gives a "desirability value," which estimates a cell's value with respect to a certain decision. For this calculation, the relevant layers for the current decision are chosen and multiplied by a coefficient that roughly indicates each layer's relative importance in making the decision. After the relevant layers have been selected and weighted, the resulting values are added together to determine the desirability. The result is a matrix of desirability values corresponding to the cells on the map.

By comparing the desirability of different cells, each cell can be ranked by how good it appears for the current task. Subsequently, the cell with the best value is chosen as the location to attack, defend, move to, or build on, depending on the decision that is being made.

Limitations of Summing Layers

This method of weighting and summing the influence layers to attain a final set of desirability values is advantageous as it is a relatively simple approach. Moreover, it is fully transparent in that the developer knows exactly how and why it is making its decision, as these parameters have been set by hand. However, this method of calculating the desirability values does have certain limitations.

First, the developer needs to choose which layers are relevant to the decision that is being made. This might seem like a simple task, but it often difficult to know exactly which factors an expert is considering when making a decision, such as an expert game player choosing which location to attack. Therefore, the process of choosing the relevant variables that need to be considered for the decision is a matter of trial and error. As a result, the process is time consuming and might mean that useful and important information is left out.

Second, when the chosen layers are summed together, it is possible that important information might be lost. For example, consider a situation in which the AI has units in a certain cell that are adding a positive influence, while the human player has units in the same cell that are adding a negative influence. When these opposing influences are added together they cancel each other out, and it seems as though there are no units adding influence in that cell. However, the information that both forces have units in this cell could be quite important to a strategic decision, but by simply adding them together it can go unnoticed.

Third, finding the correct weighting for each layer for each decision is also a matter of trial and error, and as such can require a great deal of tweaking to get right. The only way to find a suitable set of weights is to guess initial values and then hand-tune until the AI seems to be behaving reasonably.

In short, the use of a weighted sum is a relatively simple method that has worked in the past, but it is not without its perils. Using a weighted sum means that the developer will need to spend a great deal of time tweaking the weights and input variables to get the desired results, and that important information might still be lost, despite the time and effort that is applied.

Desirability Value with a Neural Network

A neural network can be used, in place of a weighted sum, to analyze the data from the influence map and make a strategic decision. The details of how to design and use this network are discussed in the next section. To begin, let's look at why this method would be suitable for this application and how it compares to a weighted sum. First, the use of a weighted sum requires the developer to choose the relevant variables.

However, this task can be automated by having the neural network determine the influencing factors. Alternatively, the neural network could be fed all the layers of the influence map for each decision, allowing it to use the relevant variables and ignore the rest. Second, the information in the individual layers will not be compromised, as occurs when the layers are added together in a weighted sum. Instead, the neural network will analyze each layer in parallel, so that situations such as both sides having forces in the same cell will be recognized. Finally, there is no need to hand-tune the coefficients that will be used to weight each layer, as is required by the weighted sum. Rather, the neural network will analyze the input variables and determine these weights during training, based on the extent to which each variable contributes to the final decision.

Computational Complexity

The major drawback with using a neural network in this application is the computational complexity that will be involved. This problem arises as the network will have a number of inputs equal to the number of layers multiplied by the number of cells on the map. Furthermore, the number of weights will be equal to the number of inputs times the number of hidden units in the neural network, making for a very large number of calculations that the network must make.

However, in most circumstances it is not necessary or desirable to analyze the entire map when making a decision. For example, if the AI were choosing a place to build a research building, then it wouldn't make much sense to consider building it in the opponent's base. Instead, the AI would most likely want to examine the area containing its own base to determine the best location for this new building. Therefore, only a small section of the map, in this case the AI player's own base, would need to be analyzed. This approach is more efficient and makes much more sense in most circumstances. It is also possible to use a lower resolution grid to reduce complexity, with fewer grid divisions and larger grid squares.

Additionally, the problem of efficiency can be minimized by training the network during development, rather than in-game. With this approach, the network will work more like a state machine, simply taking input and determining the output. This still means that it can analyze dynamic data in real-time, just that it has learned how to do this before the game is shipped. Methods of training are discussed further in the next section.

Using Neural Networks with Influence Maps

In designing the neural network that will be used to analyze the influence map data, the major points to consider are the network's inputs and outputs, the training data and training process that will be used, and the design of the network. For this application, we will use a multilayer feed-forward network [Haykin94], similar to the network described in [Sweetser04]. In this type of network there is a set of inputs, one or more hidden layers, and a set of outputs. Each unit in a layer is connected to every unit in the next layer. When the input is received by the network it is propagated forward from the input layer to the hidden layer, and then to the output layer. During training, the training examples are fed into the network and propagated forward through the network to give an estimated output, which is compared to the actual output and an error is calculated. This error is then back-propagated back through the network and the internal weights are adjusted to minimize the error.

Determining the Number of Input, Output, and Hidden Units

For the neural network to analyze the influence map, the number of input units the neural network requires will be based on the size of the game map, or section of the map, and the number of layers on the influence map. The network will require an input unit corresponding to each cell in each layer of the influence map, resulting in a total number of input units equal to the number of layers multiplied by the number of cells. Moreover, there will need to be one output unit for each cell on the influence map, so that each cell will receive a final desirability value from the network. The number of hidden units will initially be set some arbitrary number, approximately in the range of 10 to 20, which will need to be tuned to attain optimal performance. An example neural network with this structure can be seen in Figure 7.7.2.

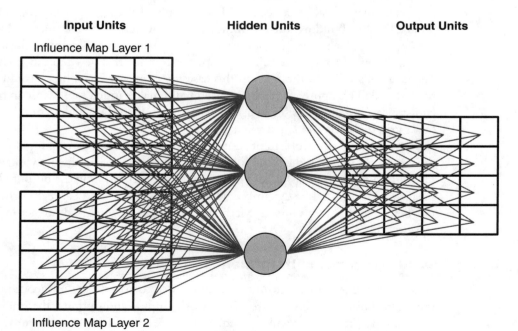

FIGURE 7.7.2 *An example multilayer feed-forward network for an influence map.*

Different Decisions and Personality

There will need to be a separate neural network for each decision that is to be made, as the set of weights will be different for each decision. However, these networks will be identical in design, the only difference being that they will be trained independently and as a result will have a different set of weights. Therefore, once the design of the network has been finalized, the same design can be used for each instance of the network, or each decision that is being made.

The best way to implement this would be to have a single neural network and separate arrays for each set of weights, so that the neural network can simply use the set of weights that corresponds to the current decision it is making. Furthermore, it is possible to have more than one set of weights for each decision, with each set of weights being the result of a different training set and therefore taking a different approach to the decision. This method could be used to simulate different personalities that the AI could have, with each personality responding differently in each situation depending on certain attributes, such as how aggressive or defensive the AI player is. Alternatively, different sets of weights could be used to simply give rise to variation in the decisions, making the AI less predictable.

Training the Neural Network

Another important decision that will need to be made for this application is how the network will be trained, in terms of what data will be used for training and whether the network will be trained in-game, during development, or both. The best option for possible sources of data would be to generate datasets from real gaming sessions with human versus human players. In this situation, a dataset could be built up based on decisions that human players made in different game states. This data could then be used to train the neural network during development, so that the system learns to mimic the human players. Subsequently, the network could be tested and tuned until a suitable level of performance is reached, at which time the weights could be locked so that the network will act as a state machine and no more learning will occur. This method would mean that the developers will know that the network will behave at a reasonable standard and require minimal computation time, even though it will not continue to learn.

Alternatively, the network could be allowed to continue to learn during play, so that it is able to adapt to the individual player and learn which strategies work best against that player. This method would require computational time either in-game or between games, using downtime on the player's computer. An alternative to the neural network learning to mimic human players would be for the developer to generate the dataset by hand, creating potential game situations and determining what the best decision would be in those situations. However, this method would be time consuming and probably not as realistic as real game situations, even though it would allow the developers to ensure that an appropriate range of game states are covered.

Moreover, these two methods of generating data could be combined so that an initial dataset is generated by human versus human play and then tweaked by the developer to ensure that there is a range of quality data in the dataset.

Conclusion

In summary, using a neural network to generate a decision from an influence map has the ability to give the appearance of a more human-like and realistic strategic AI than the conventional method of using a weighted sum. The reason for this is that the neural network will be trained to mimic expert human players, as opposed to the rough approximation that is provided by the weighted sum. Additionally, the use of a neural network automates many of the tedious processes that are involved in using a weighted sum for this purpose, such as determining coefficients and selecting relevant variables. However, it is important to note that neural networks require tuning of their own, and as such the use of a neural network will not necessarily reduce the time required in development and testing. Nonetheless, neural networks used in this application have the potential to produce AI that is far more human-like, challenging, and engaging to play.

References

[Haykin94] Simon, S., "Neural Networks: A Comprehensive Foundation," Maxwell Macmillan International, 1994.

[Sweetser04] Sweetser, P., "How to Build Neural Networks for Games," *AI Game Programming Wisdom 2*, Charles River Media, 2004.

[Tozour01] Tozour, P., "Influence Mapping," *Game Programming Gems 2*, Charles River Media, 2001.

[Woodcock02] Woodcock, S., "Recognizing Strategic Dispositions: Engaging the Enemy," *AI Game Programming Wisdom*, Charles River Media, 2002.

7.8

Multi-Tiered AI Layers and Terrain Analysis for RTS Games

Tom Kent—Atomic Games, Inc.

tick@houston.rr.com

Real-time strategy games typically handle soldier AIs individually, giving each one orders from the computer player AI. However, this structure gives the AI a large number of agents to control, reducing the resources available and greatly increasing the coding required to handle all but the simplest tactics. Complex, large-scale plans, intuitive to human players, are out of the reach of these AIs. For example, supporting a 10-man infantry squad attack with some tanks requires the careful coordination of a dozen units. Using a more complicated tactic, like a pincer movement to besiege a city from two sides, involves a great deal of special-case coding to control the vast number of required soldiers.

A relatively simple mechanism is needed to control an arbitrarily large number of units with plans of varying levels of complexity. Fortunately, this problem has been solved for thousands of years, beginning with the dawn of organized warfare. For millennia, armies have used a hierarchical chain of command to control large numbers of troops. Figure 7.8.1 shows a sample hierarchy from the U.S. Army.

Many games already collect individual soldiers into squads. Soldiers still need a basic intelligence, but long-term planning is done on the squad level. By extension, these squads can also be collected into platoons, platoons into companies, and so on. Then, an AI system is built for each tier in the hierarchy. The versatility that such groupings give is immense. For example, building a platoon from a few infantry squads and a tank automatically gives heavy weapon support to your infantry. Orchestrating scores of troops to attack a target from two directions simultaneously requires quite a bit of planning, while attacking a target with two companies from opposite directions is comparatively trivial. Additionally, such groupings eliminate the trickle effect seen in some games of individual soldiers attacking one at a time by advancing your forces en masse.

In this article, we examine the construction of these AI tiers, and then introduce terrain analysis that is specific to each AI tier. Finally, an example is provided to pull these elements together into a coherent whole.

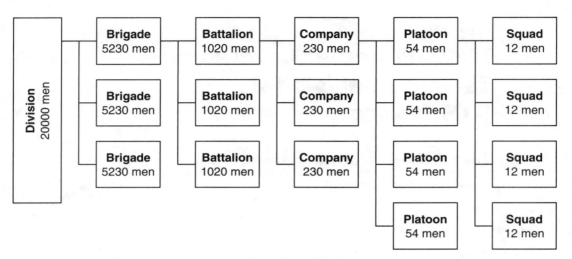

FIGURE 7.8.1   *U.S. Army organizational chart. Note, this is a generic chart that does not account for support units or variations among different branches of service.*

Some Basic Implementations

Each AI tier is designed as a separate system, but all have the same general functionality. They communicate with each other as well as think and plan. All RTS games already have a computer player AI and a soldier AI, which are the highest and lowest AI tiers in this system. However, the workload on each of these two AI layers is reduced in this system compared to most others, as some tasks are handled by intermediate AI layers.

The AIs need to communicate with superior and subordinate AI layers, as well as with other instances of the same AI type. Some messages need an immediate response, usually requests for information. However, most messages, like orders or feedback, do not need to be acted upon immediately. These types of messages are queued until the next time the AI does its planning and order processing.

The "think step" is where the AI analyzes its environment, develops tactics, and performs pathfinding. The environmental analysis is based on threat assessment and location selection. Tactical planning includes combat, target selection, and maneuvering. Pathfinding should typically use an A* algorithm [Russell02, Matthews02] on the AI's associated map to create paths based on the tactics developed. It also handles maintaining position of the subordinate AIs under its control in formations.

This system requires each AI to get a reasonable amount of time to think, but defining reasonable can be difficult. Each instance of the soldier AI needs to think often enough to react realistically to its changing environment. Higher AI layers do not need think as often and there are fewer instances of each AI, so their timing is rarely a problem. The lowest level is the most difficult to time correctly. Too much time for the soldier AI and the other AIs get no processing time; too little and there will not be enough time for each soldier to react. In practice, making sure each soldier AI gets processed about once or twice a second seems sufficient.

Moreover, it should be noted that each of the AIs above the soldier level is not associated with a specific avatar in the game [Reynolds02]. There can be squad leaders on the battlefield, but killing one will not kill the squad AI. Some games use personalities to vary the decision-making processes between different instances of an AI. For those, switching a squad's AI personality when its squad leader dies can be an interesting result.

Soldier AI

All RTS games already have at least a rudimentary soldier AI. Designing this type of AI is beyond the scope of this article, but there are plenty of resources available on the topic [van der Sterren02a]. Under a multi-tiered system, the scope of the soldier AI is reduced. The soldier's job is just to follow orders and stay alive. It also needs to report occurrences to the squad AI, like completed or failed orders or newly spotted enemies. Finally, each soldier needs to know how to select and engage a target.

Most other planning is done at a higher layer and the soldiers just follow orders. Of course, pathfinding is always necessary. However, a well-chosen series of waypoints by the squad AI results in several short paths for each soldier move, rather than a single long path, reducing the overall time and memory required.

Squad AI

Squad level AIs are already used in many games [Gibson01, van der Sterren02b]. Here, the squad AI needs to receive orders from the platoon AI, translate them into soldier orders, and distribute them to the squad members. Additionally, feedback from the squad's soldiers is evaluated. This can result in new soldier orders or be passed up to the platoon AI.

The most complex job the squad AI does is translating orders for the soldiers. Move orders need to account for the relative positions of the soldiers according to formations, terrain, and posture. For example, a crawling infantry squad evaluates thickets differently than a speeding tank does. Defend and attack orders have similar requirements. More complicated orders are built by combining basic orders, such as move into a position to shoot at the target (Move & Attack) or withdraw to a better defensive location (Move & Defend).

Platoon AI

The platoon level AI has similar tasks to the squad AI. Orders from the next highest AI level are processed and then passed down to its squads. Feedback from the squads is handed up to the higher AI or results in new squad commands being issued.

Again, message translations are where the bulk of the thinking occurs. The squad's location with respect to the rest of the platoon is the paramount concern for movement, defense, or attack. Fewer details from the lower levels are needed; general unit types and abstract offensive and defensive ratings are the main concern.

As an example, consider a World War II game in which a platoon is created with two infantry squads and a tank squad. The platoon is immediately tougher than its individual squads. The heavy firepower of the tank complements the infantry's better detection ability. The platoon AI decides on a formation [Dawson02], a triangle for this example, and the squads are positioned. The front of the platoon is the side with both infantry squads, as seen in Figure 7.8.2a. When maneuvering, the squads are issued move orders using waypoints that maintain their relative locations. A move order makes each squad wait at every waypoint until the rest of the platoon has arrived, and then they all continue on to the next waypoint. When the platoon contacts an enemy, multiple infantrymen spot and engage the enemy while the tank supports the infantrymen with its heavy firepower.

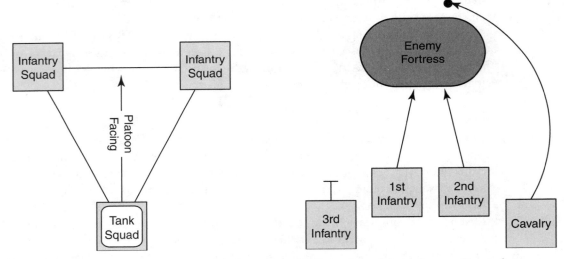

FIGURE 7.8.2   *(a) Platoon in a triangle formation. (b) Brigade assault on fortress. Two infantry companies attack, cavalry flanks, third infantry holds in reserve.*

Company AI, Brigade AI, Division AI, Army AI, et al.

Each of these layers is similar to the platoon AI, but with bigger blocks of units. Moreover, formations are less rigid, allowing for more involved tactics. Rather than simply maneuvering the brigade in formation, the brigade AI can send a company forward to scout out the enemy while the other companies are kept in reserve to support the forward company or to flank the newly engaged enemy.

The highest AI level below the computer player AI has a few more duties. Each is assigned a different portion of the world where it will operate, which affects what it does and how it does it. For example, an army AI in a forward area gets priority on the best troops, as it will most likely have to engage the enemy. While some strategic information, like first contact with the enemy or discovery of a major stronghold, is passed on to headquarters, most tactical data is analyzed and acted upon here.

For a high-level AI example, let's look at a medieval game where controlling fortresses are the goal. The AI wants to capture a fortress defended by an enemy of company-strength force. The nearest available brigade is ordered to lay siege. The brigade AI approaches the fortress while staying out of engagement range. It then sends two infantry companies directly toward the enemy while ordering the cavalry company to hook behind the fortress, cutting off reinforcements and possibly attacking the stronghold from behind, as in Figure 7.8.2b. A third infantry company is held in reserve. This example illustrates how complicated tactics can be created from a few simple orders.

Computer Player AI

The Computer Player AI (CPAI) has many roles in RTS games: civilization growth, construction, economics, research, politics, and, of course, combat. Just as in the case of soldier AIs, this is beyond the scope here, but there are a number of articles on the subject [Harmon02, Scott02]. The CPAI areas that the multi-tiered AI system will mainly impact are combat strategy, and, to a lesser extent, troop construction.

For strategy, the CPAI analyzes the relative strengths of the friendly and enemy troops and their disposition. From the troop analysis, the CPAI decides on an overall strategy—attack or defend—and deploys its armies. As the game progresses, the CPAI adjusts to the fluid battle situation, adjusting its armies as needed. Influence mapping is a powerful tool for this type of strategic planning [Woodcock02].

Construction comes in when replacing casualties. Two methods of reinforcements are available. The individual soldiers can be sent to reinforce decimated squads individually. Alternatively, the new troops can be collected into new squads, and platoons, and added en masse to armies, or even made into new armies. Both methods are useful and the individual game dictates which method is best.

The Map: Analysis and Pathfinding

All AI tiers need access to the map data, in which paths are planned, locations identified, and tactics implemented. However, each level of AI needs different information. The soldier AI wants to know details for making decisions like finding a trench to crawl into. The highest level AI only needs to know a few abstract details, like locations of strategic importance (cities and bridges, for example) and enemy troop concentrations.

The method used here has multiple maps, each having a different level of detail roughly corresponding to the size of the associated AI unit. Each larger map section collects the information from the finer detail map segments it contains. The map data consists of two types of information: dynamic and static data.

The dynamic information is mainly about troops in the battle, where they are, and what they are doing. This data needs to be updated periodically to stay current with fluid battle conditions. Updating about once or twice a second has proven successful in balancing an accurate game state without monopolizing undue processing time.

The static information consists mainly of the map data, things like the locations of roads, buildings, and other terrain features, and their effect on game elements such as pathfinding and combat. This data is set at the start of a battle and rarely changes. A destroyed bridge affects combat and pathfinding decisions, but is a unique event. The base map data is changed and the various map layers adjusted to the new situation.

Element Map

The map with the finest level of detail is built on the scale of the individual soldier, perhaps one- to three-meter squares. In some games, this is the actual map element data. In others, finer detail is available, but this scale is sufficient for AI purposes. A wall or tree seen by the player is directly represented in static map data. A soldier's path is actually calculated on this map, and things like a defend position are found. The dynamic map data tracks actual troops: an enemy sniper, a friendly archer, or even a part of a tank.

Tile Map

The next map is on the scale of a squad, about 10 meters on a side. Some games use a tile-based map during the map creation process, and this often corresponds to the size needed. Each tile collects the data from a square of 9 or 16 elements. The static tile map abstracts the information from each element to get data about movement and defense values. For example, a tile with some field elements and some trench elements has a worse movement value than one with all road elements, but a much better defense value. Squad paths are calculated on this level and the soldiers sent a series of waypoints from the squad path, limiting the length of any soldier path needed. Additionally, dynamic data on troop presence are collected. The troop data is abstract here, just the combined strength values of all the soldiers rather than a list of those troops. A second set of values is also kept for the troops known to the other side.

Mega-Tile Map

The next larger map layer is on the scale of a platoon, from 25 to 50 meters. This collects three-by-three or four-by-four squares of tiles into mega-tiles. The mega-tile map abstracts data from its tiles. The general movement and defense values are used to find paths for platoons, which are then sent to their respective squads. Both true and known troop strengths are tracked and used for planning platoon tactics.

Larger Scale Maps

Larger scale maps are built up in a similar manner, one for each AI layer. The only pathfinding essentially needed is an impassable path check, as blocking terrain is incorporated into the strategic planning, along with friendly and known enemy troop strengths.

Putting It All Together

As an example, the computer player AI tells a specific platoon to guard a pass. The platoon AI issues move orders to each of its squads, putting a scout squad in the middle of the pass, support squads to either side to attack anyone engaging the scouts, and the rest of the platoon at the rear of the pass as reserves, as in Figure 7.8.3a.

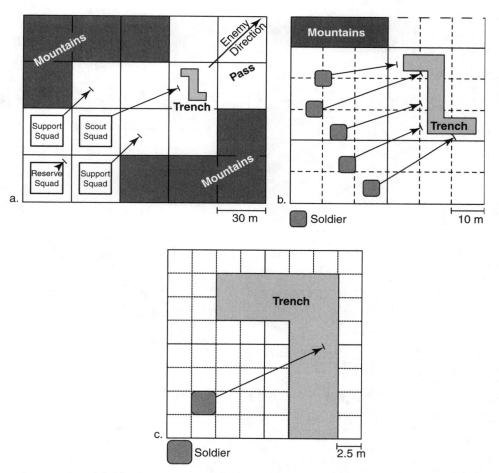

FIGURE 7.8.3   *(a) Platoon moves to defend a pass on the mega-tile map. (b) Scout squad defends pass on the tile map. (c) Scout soldier moves into trench on the element map.*

The scout squad AI is told to move to a location (the middle of the pass) and defend in a certain direction (toward the enemy) in Figure 7.8.3b. It, in turn, tells its soldiers to deploy in specific positions on its skirmish line and to face the general defend direction, with some variance to ensure maximum area coverage.

In Figure 7.8.3c, one of the soldier AIs is ordered to a certain position. This soldier AI handles moving the soldier to that position, finding the best defensive location there, and assuming a defensive posture while scanning in its defend direction.

Feedback is passed back up the chain of command. A scout sees enemy troops charging up the pass. He passes this information up to the scout squad AI. That AI tells the rest of the squad about the oncoming attackers and reports to the platoon AI that it is under attack. The platoon AI informs the support squads that the scouts are under attack and considers committing its reserves if needed. Finally, it lets the computer player AI know the enemy is attacking the pass. The message sequence is seen in Figure 7.8.4.

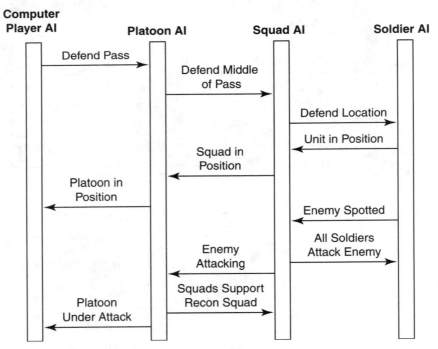

FIGURE 7.8.4 *Message sequences between AI tiers.*

This, of course, might set off another chain of commands as the CPAI decides whether to send more platoons to support the first one, let it fight alone, or even withdraw to a better defensive position. The key point here is that there are messages going up and down the chain of command, and each AI will handle the messages differently.

Conclusion

This article introduced multi-tiered AIs and gave a broad overview of how they work. The core concepts were presented, along with an example to give an idea of the interlocking system in its entirety. However, this has only scratched the surface, as there are many more topics to explore, such as the implementation of specific tactics and strategies for the tiers, the use of personalities, and time-slicing.

Ensuring that the various AIs interact seamlessly in a multi-tiered AI system can be challenging and raises issues about control and timing. However, this system reduces the level of complexity for each individual AI layer and promotes a substantial amount of code reuse. More importantly, it greatly enhances the user's sense of challenge and enjoyment by adding a variety of subtle and complex tactics for the computer player.

References

[Dawson02] Dawson, Chad, "Formations," *AI Game Programming Wisdom*, Charles River Media, 2002.

[Gibson01] Gibson, Clark, and O'Brien, John, "The Basics of Team AI," *Proceedings*, Game Developers Conference, 2001.

[Harmon02] Harmon, Vern, "An Economic Approach to Goal-Directed Reasoning in an RTS," *AI Game Programming Wisdom*, Charles River Media, 2002.

[Matthews02] Matthews, James, "Basic A* Pathfinding Made Simple," *AI Game Programming Wisdom*, Charles River Media, 2002.

[Reynolds02] Reynolds, John, "Tactical Team AI Using a Command Hierarchy," *AI Game Programming Wisdom*, Charles River Media, 2002.

[Russell02] Russell, Stuart, and Norvig, Peter, *Artificial Intelligence: A Modern Approach (Second Edition)*, Prentice Hall, 2002.

[Scott02] Scott, Bob, "Architecting an RTS AI," *AI Game Programming Wisdom*, Charles River Media, 2002.

[Stout00] Stout Bryan, "The Basics of A* for Path Planning," *Game Programming Gems*, Charles River Media, 2000.

[van der Sterren02a] van der Sterren, William, "Squad Tactics: Team AI and Emergent Maneuvers," *AI Game Programming Wisdom*, Charles River Media, 2002.

[van der Sterren02b] van der Sterren, William, "Squad Tactics: Planned Maneuvers," *AI Game Programming Wisdom*, Charles River Media, 2002.

[Woodcock02] Woodcock, Steven, "Recognizing Strategic Dispositions: Engaging the Enemy," *AI Game Programming Wisdom*, Charles River Media, 2002.

Designing a Multi-Tiered AI Framework

Michael Ramsey—2015, Inc.

miker@masterempire.com

> *"Under a good general there are no bad soldiers."*
>
> —Chinese proverb

Great AIs need the ability to plan according to an overall doctrine or methodology. Planning for military success in a game can be divided into two separate categories: strategies and tactics. While tactics cover small-scale interactions, such as scouting a battlefield or capturing an enemy city, strategies are all encompassing. Strategies can include which city to capture, what units should be involved, and when to capture the city.

The ability for an AI to manage a large number of units has always been an issue for AI developers. When these large numbers of units are coupled with the realization that they need to be driven by an AI that is more complex then just a reaction-based system, we have a situation that is overwhelming for the AI. Overwhelming the AI will lead to game situations that show gaping holes in the AI's formulation of a grand strategy. Under the right conditions, the AI can even look intelligent at times, but the holes still remain. Often, the low-level response mechanisms are sufficient, but the higher-order strategies and implementations are not.

What the Multi-Tiered AI Framework (MTAIF) provides is the mechanism to have an AI controlled by several different levels of managers. What this allows for is a quick, controlled way for an AI to make goals at a high level. Rules can be maintained on overall doctrine, as well as objectives that an AI wants to accomplish. This allows for grand strategic decisions to be made at a higher level, which then has the corresponding operational AI execute the tasks. This architecture keeps decisions separated by multiple tiers, each specializing in a specific task. This allows your strategic AI to concentrate on broader strategies, while your lower-level operational AI can concentrate on tactical situations. The MTAIF solution is a framework that once established, is easily expandable to support differing implementation methodologies.

Overview of the Multi-Tiered Framework

A diagram of the Multi-Tiered Framework is shown in Figure 7.9.1. The most crucial design rule for the MTAIF is the principle of simplicity. The reason is that you want to spend your time balancing the game's AI, not fighting with an overly burdensome framework. With this simplicity also comes the ability for the MTAIF to maintain objectives at a high level and the inherent ability to adapt to changing game situations. When a strategic AI is tasked with the function of maintaining higher-order objectives, you can write a more specialized AI at the lower levels that will focus on specific objectives.

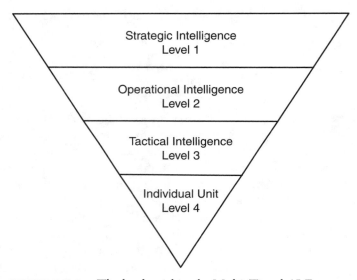

FIGURE 7.9.1   *The levels within the Multi-Tiered AI Framework.*

Strategic Intelligence (SI): This is the general knowledge of an AI's empire. This is where the grand strategy is defined through combined goals and strategies, which can include everything from resource levels, technology trees, to the AI's overall attitude, general conflict doctrine, as well as diplomatic tendencies. At this level, the AI makes general goals and plans (which can and should be modified as gameplay progresses). Then it is up to the lower management structures to interpret and implement these projects.

Operational Intelligence (OI): At the level of Operation Intelligence, the AI is concerned with implementing the general orders of the Strategic Intelligence. At the OI's disposal is any information that is needed to conduct these operations. The OI is further divided into various activity groups: land, naval, air, and space operations. The OI can also track noncombat activities such as economic and diplomatic operations. Commanders and units in the field generally use data from this level, because it is usually the most up to date and reflects their area of concern.

Tactical Intelligence (TI): Tactical Intelligence data is the information that will be readily available to your units as they explore the game world. This information can come in the form of newly encountered opponents, resources, general geography, or anything else you want the AI to be aware of. As this real-world intelligence is gathered by the game units, each unit can create information packets that are sent to a higher intelligence level. These higher levels are constructed in a way to either allow immediate action or if the situation deems necessary, communication and cooperation with other game objects.

Situational Projects

When communication needs to occur between the various objects in the framework, they occur almost exclusively through the use of Situational Projects (SP). These messages are the basic lines of communication for any type of behavior that is accomplished in a game, whether it is communication between a unit in the field and its corresponding Field Manager, or a Field Manager needing clearance to assault a newly discovered enemy complex. In the following example, as illustrated in Figure 7.9.2, there are several scouting units near enemy cities. Soldier 1 and soldier 3 are within proximity of the cities, which would cause SPs to be created by both City Managers as well as the units seeking either interdiction or avoidance orders. Depending on the AIs internal stance on aggression, diplomatic relations, and its offensive tendencies, the threatened parties might create either a combat or a diplomatic Situational Project.

Some of the different possible project types and the level at which the SPs are sent are listed in Table 7.9.1.

Table 7.9.1 Various Situational Projects Showing Which Levels They Are Sent From and Received

Situational Project Type	Level Sent	Level Received
Initiating diplomatic actions, either unilateral or bilateral	Strategic	Strategic
Massing of units	Strategic	Operational
Protection of region	Strategic	Operational
Transfer of resources	Strategic	Operational
Fortification of a location or region	Strategic	Operational
Opponent incursion	Operational	Strategic
Discovery of an opponent	Tactical	Operational
Deep strategic penetration	Tactical	Individual Unit
Strong reconnaissance	Tactical	Individual Unit
Flanking maneuver	Tactical	Individual Unit
Envelopment	Tactical	Individual Unit

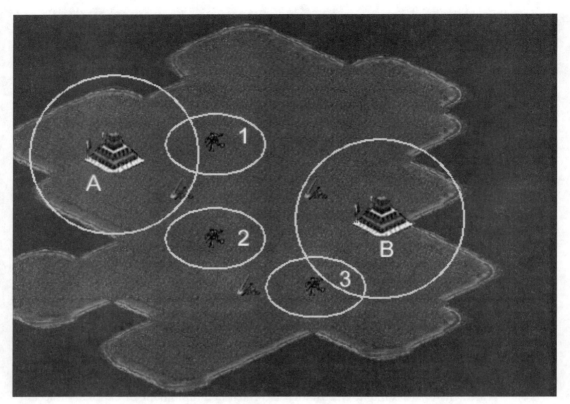

FIGURE 7.9.2   *Showing when Situational Projects (SP) would occur. In this situation, soldiers 1 and 3 would cause SPs to be created and sent by themselves and the cities.*

Force Projection

Every game object (tank, soldier, city, bridge, and so forth) has an associated value; this is its force projection. This can be also viewed as the game object's sphere of influence. This allows the AI to quickly and easily evaluate a group of units, via its force projection. In a combat situation (e.g., your lonely scout just wandered into a camp of aliens), the force projection can help determine if the unit can succeed in combat.

Situational Projects in Action

How the AI will react to an enemy incursion is influenced heavily by the offending units. If an army marches right into a city's sphere of influence and its forces are comprised of three heavy tanks, while the force projection of the city is only itself and one lonely soldier, the AI definitely better take notice of the invader and react accordingly. A sample action that an AI could take is to mass troops. The following is an example flow using the MTAIF, from the point of incursion.

- The city sends an SP from the Operational Intelligence level to the Strategic Intelligence level detailing the enemy incursion.
- The Strategic Intelligence level determines that hostilities are unwarranted and progresses to develop a salient outside the city, by massing troops. The SI then determines the required forces to repel the attack and sends an SP to the nearest cities to mass troops.
- The cities that receive these massing orders look at their appropriate Field Manager (the Field Manager that deals with the massing of units), which would then order the units to the needed city.

The Multi-Tiered Class Layout

ON THE CD

A class diagram of the MTAIF is shown in Figure 7.9.3. The MTAIF is composed of several interoperating classes that use access to a generic messaging system for communication. The core management class is the `EmpireMgr`, and holds the core implementation of the selected AI. The selected AI behavior is either `cPlayerCore` by default, or as is in the demo, `cPlayerInept` or `cPlayerResource`. The selection of this behavior defines the AI at its highest level, and how it will respond and progress throughout the game.

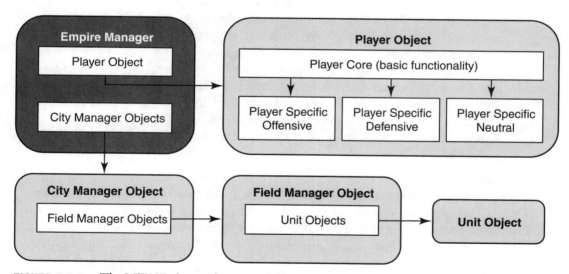

FIGURE 7.9.3 *The MTAIF class architecture. The Empire Manager class (`cEmpireMgr`) is the core object, controlling access to the Player Object (`cPlayerObject`), and the City Manager Object (`cCityMgr`). The City Manager in turn manages multiple Field Manager Objects (`cFieldMgr`), which maintain the individual Unit Objects.*

Residing inside the `cEmpireMgr` are the various `cCityMgr` objects. These objects represent the contact points the AI has throughout the game world. The contacts could be any tangible object in the world, a city, a planet, or a fortress on the edge of a frontier—basically any object that would be responsible for unit management. The cCityMgr objects form the Operational Intelligence level in the framework. They are the buffer between the high-level strategic decisions of the AIs core code and the grunt in the field who has to execute the doctrine. The management of units in the game occurs through a series of Field Managers. The cFieldMgr class is a container that encapsulates the various Situational Projects that might occur in the field. Each Field Manager is in charge of one type of Situational Project, which in turn might have numerous units under its direct supervision.

Implementation of the Core AI Framework

The cPlayerCore object is the foundation on which all other AIs are built upon. The cPlayerCore contains the basic functions that all other AIs will use. These include access to diplomacy objects, economic objects, pathfinding routines, building classes, and other utilitarian functions. Since the concentration of an instantiated AI is to focus on other behavior types, it makes sense to have all the core components that are not necessarily directly applicable extracted out to form the base class.

The core AI class also receives and posts Situational Projects (SPs) for the rest of the classes to query from. To limit the amount of posting and receiving, the cPlayerCore has the ability to grant permissions to the lower objects. These permissions allow certain decisions to be made by the lower objects without the need for constant updating. Some of the messages come in the form of diplomatic resolution issues. Once a certain stance against an opponent has been achieved, the City Managers will now have the go ahead to engage any aggressors. If the AI needs to concentrate on resource accumulation for the next two years, the City Manager now can perform that function without the constant overhead of messaging. Because many messages are being created and acted upon, there is no need to clutter the pipeline with extraneous or superfluous messages.

Empire Manager: The cEmpireMgr object is the heart at which all other components tie into. It forms and manages the access to the underlying objects, such as the cPlayerCore object. The instantiation of the AIs object is handled through a general factory. When provided with a requested AI behavior, such as a balanced, resource-hungry, or inept AI, it will allocate the object and return a pointer to the cEmpireMgr object.

```
cPlayerCore*
AllocateContestantObject(int iType,
                         cPlayerEmpire *pEmpire)
{
    cPlayerCore *pAIObject;
    switch (iType)
    {
        case BalancedAI:
            pAIObject= new cPlayerCore(pEmpire);
```

```
                    break;
            case IneptAI:
                pAIObject= new cPlayerInept(pEmpire);
                break;
            case ResourceHungryAI:
                pAIObject= new cPlayerResource(pEmpire);
                break;
            default:
                pAIObject= new cPlayerCore(pEmpire);
                break;
        }
        return pAIObject;
    }
```

The `AllocateContestantObject` is a simple factory. See [Gamma95] and [Vlissides98] for a comprehensive coverage of design patterns, such as the factory pattern.

City Manager: The City Manager is the Operational Intelligence level of the framework. Here the tactical facts are processed and either acted upon or messaged up to Strategic Intelligence level. The ability for a City Manager to act is provided by the core AI routines (as in the Strategic Intelligence level). For example, if any enemy unit has been discovered in the AI's territory, based on previous events, the SI might have already passed a doctrine that allows all units to engage immediately (if within a certain force projection threshold). This would then allow the unit to engage the belligerent.

Field Manager and Units: The Field Managers are responsible for all the units in the game. They are grouped according to unique SPs. This allows for each Field Manager to oversee only one set of unit types. This simplifies the container framework and allows decisions to be made more quickly. Units might have a lifespan associated with their current SP, and when that expires, either the City Manager will be responsible for the unit's reassignment or it will be reallocated.

Message Manager: The heart of how SPs are managed occurs here. Depending on your game, the implementation might vary from a simple list of SPs that are processed linearly each turn, to an orders dictionary that manages load-balanced SPs. When the Message Manager is just a simple list, the only overhead is the posting and processing of the messages. Since these messages are processed by individual game objects, they can be handled by different game threads. This allows much of the overhead processing time to be broken up among objects. The Field Managers are perfect thread candidates, since the units are already grouped by their SPs. When you use this approach coupled with the load balancing (discussed in the next paragraph), you have a powerful tool for advanced AI programming.

A concept that all real-time games must have is that of load balancing. This concept involves segments of an overall time amount to be allocated for specific operations. Since AIs are notorious in the amount of time that can be consumed for even basic operations (e.g., pathfinding), it's a reasonable solution for the processing of a

Situational Project and the subsequent action to occur over multiple frames. The Orders Dictionary Manager [Ramsey02] must allow for the staggering of SPs over multiple frames. The preferred method is to provide a series of linked SP containers that contain links, or references to other SP containers.

An example of a multiple SP container would be an order given to path across the world and mass troops outside an enemy fortification. The pathing itself would be broken up into multiple path requests. The world will have been partitioned into cells, and when a path traverses a cell, the individual pathing information would be stored in an SP. This also allows the breaking of larger paths into smaller segments, which in turn are computed on the fly. Only the nearest pathing cell needs to be updated, thereby postponing unnecessary computations. In effect, hierarchical pathfinding is performed using the multiple SP container.

Using Threads in the MTAIF

One of the most powerful capabilities of MTAIF is its natural support for the usage of threads. The use of threads is more complex than just having your user interface run on a second thread in the game. Here we need to have multiple threads for the Field Managers. We want to have threads that are used for SPs that require more then an immediate solution, such as the massing of units and then a subsequent order to march across the game map. Even though this is comprised of many smaller SPs, it should still be linked together in an orders dictionary. Each thread can have a varied execution length that allows a certain part of the overall SP to be executed. Some items to be aware of is that you don't want to have the thread execute on old or invalid data. Such determinations would lead to invalid results. Another potential threading problem is that unless the Thread Manager is set up correctly (with the proper hooks for accessing immediate game data), you make strategic decisions based on old SPs. Even with these added complexities and concerns, threading allows for a truly advanced AI machine.

Expanding Strategic Intelligence with Military Ideologies

At the strategic level, the MTAIF is capable of maintaining and applying real-world military ideologies. These ideologies provide a simple list of priorities that any commander should be aware of. Generally, the most valued principles are unity of command, control of an objective, flexibility, economy of force, initiative, and mass.

There are others that could be modeled [Dunnigan03], but we will concentrate on these six.

Unity of command is the desire of an empire to operate in accordance to one central leader. Obviously in real-life, this is a bit more difficult when you have supporting troops commanded by various leaders—all with their own individual experiences and understandings of a situation. This is not a concern in the MTAIF. The coupling of the distinct hierarchical levels with a messaging system allows for a clean delineation that keeps all entities under the same strategic focus, unless we want miscommunications by design in our Operational Intelligence level.

Control of an objective means having a battle plan and sticking to it. The control of an objective coupled with flexibility is not a contradiction in methodology. We want to have a definite focus on how the AI is to engage opponents, but we also want the AI to have the common sense to change its plans. An example of controlling an objective coupled with flexibility is that we have an AI ordered to take an enemy village. As the AI gets closer to the village he realizes that there is a mass of units behind the village. The AI should be flexible enough in its planning to engage the massing enemy units, and then return to the village to control the objective.

Economy of force is the concept of not putting all your resources into one military operation. Economy of force also dictates that you divide your forces appropriately among potential conflicts. For some situations the AI has to recognize, either through force projection analysis or some other means, that an overwhelming attack is necessary. This coupled with an AI maintaining a reserve to deal with any smaller operations around the battlefield—such as striking at enemy supply lines—allows the AI to maintain the initiative.

Initiative is about getting to a conflict first, with an overwhelming force, and maintaining the initiative. An AI that sits around and waits for something to happen will primarily be a reactionary-based AI. This brings us to the concept of mass. Victory is usually given to the belligerent that brings the most combat power to the battlefield. An AI that can effectively and within the scope of the defined rule set mass units and gain the initiative has the potential to be an extremely engaging opponent at the strategic level.

Application to Various Genres

Classical turn-based and real-time strategy games are perfect for this type of framework. This framework has also been implemented in a varied form for an online multiplayer game. The framework allowed for similar relationships to the ones described in this article, but used in a different setting. This allowed city scouts to see an enemy raiding party and then report back to the town mayor. The mayor would then give the go ahead for an attack or, depending on his game statistics, would refer to the Duke. If this was part of a bigger framework, the relationships would be the same at the lower level, but the Duke would report to the King. The ability to track and manage an entire kingdom or fiefdom is reduced to a series of manageable tasks.

Sports games can also benefit from using this framework. It allows the general decisions to be made by the coach (SI), the assistant coaches handle the operational intelligence, and then each of the players is his or her own Field Manager. This allows the general strategic decisions to be made by the coach, while the actual actions and results are generated by the Field Managers.

Another aspect of using a MTAIF for sports games is the use of individual players that are composed of real-life statistics. Field Managers can change at runtime by simply swapping out different AI objects. These AI objects can be more than simple statistic changes, they can be complete different AI objects that truly reflect unique behavior.

Demo and Source Code

ON THE CD

The demo program included on the accompanying CD-ROM demonstrates the basic architecture, as described in this article, without the orders dictionary. There is a sample game situation that can be loaded into the framework. The demo allows for you to see a basic game situation, where the blue player is concerned with resource gathering while its yellow opponents are more aggressive. Color Plate 12 shows the demo in action. Source code is provided for the complete AI framework.

Conclusion

Current and future games need AIs that can logically and naturally move a large number of units in accordance with an overall plan. What the MTAIF allows for is an architecture that encourages the separation of the low-level implementers and the higher-level strategy thinkers. This allows the lower-level systems to be devoid of decisions that could influence the overall grand strategy, but instead allows those grand strategies to be made by an AI that specifically manages higher-order relations. This delineation of tasks allows us to write AI code that is more focused, and allows the game simulation to be less reactionary and more proactive in its decision-making process.

References

[Dunnigan03] Dunnigan, James, *How to Make War*, Quill, 2003.
[Gamma95] Gamma, Erich, et al., *Design Patterns*, Addison Wesley, 1995.
[Noble00] Noble, J., Weir, C., and Bibby, D., *Small Memory Software: Patterns for Systems with Limited Memory*, Addison-Wesley, 2000.
[Ramsey02] Ramsey, Michael, "Simple Techniques for Complex Systems" available online at *www.masterempire.com/OpenKimono.html*, October 15, 2002.
[Vlissides98] Vlissides, John, *Pattern Hatching: Design Patterns Applied*, Addison-Wesley, 1998.

RACING AND SPORTS AI

8.1

Racing Vehicle Control Using Insect Intelligence

Alex Darby—FreeStyleGames Ltd.

alex.darby@freestylegames.com

This article gives a detailed overview of the AI system used in the PS2 racing game *Downforce* developed by Smartdog. *Downforce's* AI is based on insect intelligence and was influenced by academic research into biologically inspired AI; particularly the mechanisms used in the steering behaviors of simple animals, and architectural approaches to cognitive modeling developed for controlling robotic AI agents in chaotic real-world environments [Brooks91, Porcino04]. It was also influenced by a personal philosophical approach toward AI that takes into account the physical nature of an agent and its surrounding environment [Dennentt88, Thomas04].

Artificial Intentionality

The question of whether an object's behavior is "intelligent" depends on two things: the definition of intelligence used, and the point of view of the observer. Many noted philosophers believe that "intentionality" is what separates unintelligent action from intelligent action—that is, to be (or appear to be) intelligent, the behavior exhibited by the object must be judged as intentional [Dennett88].

In his book, *Vehicles*, Valentino Braitenberg describes a set of thought experiments using very simple robots to build up a system of what he termed "synthetic psychology" [Braitenberg84]. For example, one robot that always steers toward light might be described by an observer as "loving" light, whereas another robot that always steers away from light might be described as "hating" light—Nick Porcino's article in this book gives examples of how these simple vehicles can be implemented [Porcino04]. The vehicles used by Braitenberg in his thought experiments were carefully chosen to show how an object's behavior can be easily interpreted by an observer as intentional and emotionally driven, regardless of the simplicity of the actual internal mechanisms of the object that produce that behavior.

It follows, therefore, that anything we as AI programmers can do to make the behavior of a system appear more intentional will also make it seem more intelligent. This article proposes that it is not only whether the system is capable of solving the problems facing it, but also *how it behaves* that will ultimately determine whether the system is perceived as intentional or stupid by the player. Although the *competence* of an AI system will be judged by whether or not it provides a fair and challenging opposition to the player, other factors will affect the player's perception of the system's intentionality in the long term—and therefore, by implication, its perceived intelligence.

The Fundamental Data Abstraction: Track Space

The entire *Downforce* AI system uses a simple but monumentally useful data abstraction termed *track space*. The track space transform in essence transforms the position of the car in three dimensions into a 2D position relative to the width and length of the track. This transform effectively removes the corners, representing the track as a long strip with a width of 1.0 and potentially infinite length—similar in principle to a Mobius band.

Although it was significantly extended from its original conception, credit for inventing the idea behind the track space transform belongs to Rob Dutton, who primarily dealt with the physics and replay code on *Downforce*.

Basics of Track Space

The two components of a track space position measure the position across the width of the track and along the length of the circuit, and will be referred to as fWidthPos and fLengthPos, respectively.

fWidthPos represents the vehicle's position across the width of the track, starting at 0.0 on the left edge and going up to 1.0 at the right edge. Negative values of fWidthPos indicate the vehicle is off the track to the left, and positive values greater than 1.0 indicate the vehicle is off the track to the right.

fLengthPos is a value that represents the vehicle's position along the length of a lap of the track. It has an essentially arbitrary scale and only makes sense in terms of the specific track that the vehicle is driving on. It could be the distance in meters the car has traveled relative to the center of the track, or it could be any other measure that has an equivalent meaning.

Implementation of the Track Space Transform

The precise implementation of the track space transform will depend on the data you are using to represent your track for both the AI and for the race position tracking code. This section gives an overview of the way data is represented in *Downforce*, and the way the track space transform is calculated.

In *Downforce*, the track is represented as an array of track lines. Each track line is made up of three points: the left edge of the track, the right edge of the track, and the point where the optimum racing line crosses the line between the two edge points. The track lines are approximately evenly spaced along the track length and approximately perpendicular to both edges of the track.

The values fWidthPos and fLengthPos are both calculated as proportional distances between the four vertical planes formed by the edge points of two consecutive track lines (see Figure 8.1.1). This is accomplished using basic vector math, requiring two vector normalizations per track position—this can of course be optimized by precaching the normal vectors involved, and for further optimization the distances (and inverse of the distances) between each of the two pairs of planes can also be pre-cached.

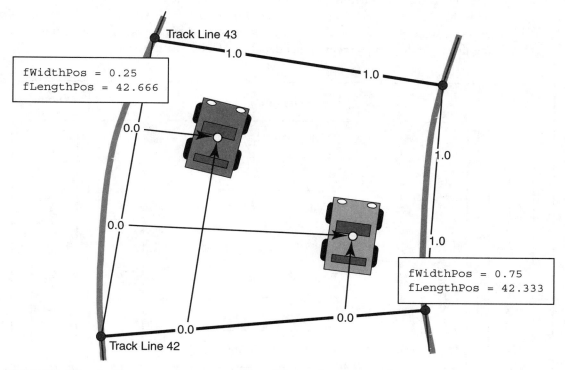

FIGURE 8.1.1   *A diagrammatic representation of the track space transform.*

The fLengthPos value in *Downforce* is made up of a whole number and a fractional component. The whole number component is incremented as the vehicle crosses each of the stored lines in the race direction, and decremented as the vehicle crosses lines in the opposite direction. The fractional component of fLengthPos is calculated as the proportion of the distance covered between the last line crossed and the next line. For example, an fLengthPos of 7.5 would indicate that the car was halfway through the seventh track section.

It should be noted that track space is unreliable for performing fine-grain collision checks. In most cases, track space is a distortion of Euclidean geometry, and collision checks would only be accurate if the car's bounding boxes were also transformed into that space. However, it is sufficiently accurate to use for calculating a meaningful likelihood of collision, but is insufficient for detecting actual collisions.

Downforce AI System Overview

The *Downforce* AI is in many respects derived from Rodney Brooks' "Subsumption Architecture" [Brooks91]. The layered approach used in the *Downforce* AI draws directly on the Brooksian methodology, and in principle this system also shares a lot with the "Insect AI" architecture [Porcino03]. There are, however, significant differences between these systems, and the links between them are often more of underlying principle than implementational detail (see Figure 8.1.2).

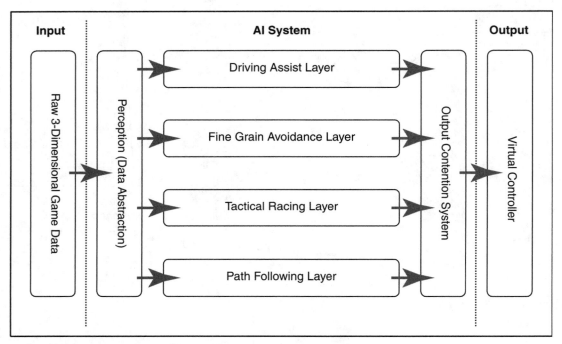

FIGURE 8.1.2   *A simple architecture diagram of the* Downforce *AI.*

Downforce's AI is primarily reactive—rather than having an internal representation of the game world, it bases its behavioral responses on the current game state each time its "perception" is updated and stores very little state dependent data. However, the biologically inspired mechanisms within *Downforce*'s system are not necessarily implemented using the same mechanisms as system made up of interacting computational building blocks like those used in Insect AI [Porcino03].

As shown in Figure 8.1.1, the core of this AI system is composed of a series of hierarchically organized *layers*. Each layer is responsible only for a specific task (or tasks) involved in the system's operation—such as choosing the optimum road position, following the chosen racing line, or avoiding collisions. The input and output interfaces for all layers are the same, which means that the system architecture is very modular.

As indicated by the gray arrows, the raw game data is processed and abstracted into "perceptual" input. All layers are run in pseudo-parallel—in other words, their code is executed serially, but the system output is not used until all layers have calculated their output. Each layer will independently examine the input data and generate an output based on its responsibilities.

The individual outputs are combined via a contention system into a final output that is used to control the AI controlled vehicle—this data is identical to the data retrieved from the game pads and used by the player to control his or her vehicle. The final output of the system—and therefore the overall behavior exhibited—is emergent from the interactions between the various layers.

Behaviors

Layers are themselves composed of smaller sub-tasks or *behaviors*. Each behavior deals with a single aspect of the task(s) that its parent layer is responsible for. The overall behavior of a layer emerges from the interactions between its constituent behaviors in much the same way that the interactions between the layers produce overall system behavior.

For example, following the ideal racing line through a corner at high speed involves two sub-tasks. The first sub-task is altering the steering input of the car to correctly follow the racing line. The second sub-task is to use the throttle and brake. Both sub-tasks must manipulate their controls in a complementary fashion to ensure that the vehicle is travelling at the maximum speed to follow the racing line without losing control.

Interaction between Layers

In addition to the output contention system, there are three main ways in which layers can interact with each other. The first and most straightforward way is to directly override the output of another layer. This is how the Driving Assist Layer operates—reducing throttle values set by other layers to stop the vehicle from losing traction. The second method is to directly affect the internal state of another layer causing its behavior to change; for example, switching a layer from a "defensive" to an "aggressive" state.

The third, and least obvious, of the three methods is for one layer to achieve its own tasks indirectly, by altering the input data used by another layer. The main advantage of this technique is that it allows high-level system tasks to be implemented in terms of lower-level ones, drastically simplifying the computations involved in the higher-level task. For example, the Road Position Layer works by choosing the optimum road position given the current positions and relative speeds of nearby vehicles.

It then dynamically changes the car's racing line and leaves the Path Following Layer to deal with following the new racing line.

Output Contention System

The system's output is a Virtual Controller that gives the AI system the same control interface to the vehicle that a player has—in its most basic form; a steering value, a braking value, and a throttle value. Since all of the layers are attempting to control the vehicle through this same interface, a contention system is required to decide which of the layers' outputs makes it into the final system output. A very simple explicit priority system is used, implemented by a combination of the execution order of layers (layers executed later have a higher priority), and a series of state dependent rules for situations that cannot be handled by the execution order priority.

Path Following Layer

The Path Following Layer is, as its name suggests, responsible for generating the correct controller inputs to cause the vehicle to follow a specific path at maximum speed. The task of path following is broken down into two sub-tasks, generating the correct steering control value and the correct speed control input value.

The Steering Control behavior is responsible for calculating a steering output to cause the vehicle to follow the racing line, and the Cornering Speed Regulation behavior is responsible for making sure the vehicle is travelling at an appropriate speed to perform the required steering without losing control. These two sub-tasks of the layer, although inextricably linked, are carried out entirely independently and the two behaviors have no communication between them whatsoever.

Behavioral Modularization

Although treating the tasks of steering and controlling the speed entirely separately might seem a little strange, it has certain advantages. These advantages come from the fact that each behavior only worries about its own responsibilities, and assumes that other behaviors will take care of everything else. The necessary synchronization between behaviors arises as a result of the fact that they are working from the same input data—for example, the racing line in the case of the path following layer.

The advantages of this conceptual task breakdown translate more or less directly into code. The decentralization of control and implicit synchronization of the sub-tasks means that substantially less special case code is required in the implementation (when compared to the situation where all aspects of the path following task are handled together explicitly and are constantly being synchronized).

This technique of relying on other behaviors to fulfil their responsibilities is used throughout the *Downforce* system, and is key to its emergent nature. Additionally, by making assumptions about the responsibilities of the other behaviors, the responsibility of each individual behavior is minimized. Reduced responsibility roughly equates to a reduced problem space, giving a reduced computational load per behavior, and consequently an overall reduction in execution time for the layer.

Steering Control

This behavior's responsibility is to calculate a steering input that will both follow the racing line and converge the vehicle onto the racing line if, for whatever reason, it strays from it.

This problem could be handled in any number of ways, and its implementation will depend strongly on the data representations used within the game. There is only one pivotal aspect to the steering control; the vehicle should look ahead along the racing line from its current position in order to generate its steering value, and the distance that it looks ahead should be increased proportionally with speed. Euan Forrester's article on PID controllers in this book gives a very good method for generating steering control inputs [Forrester04].

Cornering Speed Regulation

The first thing to point out about this behavior is that it only has responsibility for regulating the vehicle's speed with respect to the path it is trying to follow, and nothing more. Other behaviors, in other layers, are responsible for other speed regulation tasks—for example, slowing to avoid collision with other vehicles and so forth.

Speed regulation is not a massively complex problem and, like generating a steering input, could be solved using any one of a number of equally valid methods. In *Downforce*, a dead-reckoning mathematical approach was decided on using the Newtonian physical equations for bodies in circular motion. These physical equations can be applied in many different ways, but fundamentally they allow an accurate maximum speed to be calculated for any given section of track as long as the physics model being used is fairly realistic [White02].

The basic system takes the form of a state machine based around *corners*. For the purposes of this behavior, a corner is defined as "a section of track that the vehicle is unable to travel through at its current speed without losing control." This judgment is based on the racing line the car is following and the track profile (the angle of the track surface in terms of the world x and z axes).

The first of the three states is Corner Identification. In this state, the behavior simply outputs a maximum throttle value and constantly scans the track ahead for a combination of track profile and racing line that will require it to slow down, and when found this is identified as the start of a corner. The apex point of the corner is also identified at this time. The apex is identified as the first point after the start of the corner where the change in turn radius is opposite to that of the start of the corner (where the corner begins to "open out"). It should be noted that this method won't always identify the exact corner apex, but the approximation provides consistent and robust results.

When a corner is identified, the difference between the calculated maximum speed for the corner and the current speed of the vehicle is used to derive a braking distance based on applying maximum braking (again using the usual Newtonian equations). The distance to the start of the corner is then compared to the calculated braking distance, and if the vehicle is outside the braking distance it simply keeps accelerating at full throttle.

This corner identification process is performed on every update of the vehicle's AI. Since the vehicle is constantly accelerating, the start position of the corner will often change as the speed of the car increases. Obviously, the braking distance will also increase as the car accelerates, and the braking distance quickly converges with the distance to the start of the corner. As soon as the vehicle is inside the braking distance for the corner, it switches into the next state Braking For Corner.

Once the state switches into Braking For Corner, the corner's start and apex points are buffered until the corner is exited to enable the vehicle to judge when it should begin accelerating again. While in this state, the behavior outputs the maximum braking value until its speed reaches the maximum speed for the corner. Once the cornering speed is reached, the vehicle enters the third and last cornering state Cruise To Apex.

In the Cruise To Apex state, the vehicle simply applies a small percentage of the maximum throttle to ensure that its speed doesn't drop too much below the cornering speed until it reaches the apex point of the corner, at which point full throttle is again applied.

Although maximum throttle and braking values are applied indiscriminately by this behavior, the behaviors within the Driving Assist Layer will limit these values based on the vehicles' current state of wheel-spin, sideways drift, and so on to keep the car under control.

Tactical Racing Layer

Building upon the abilities of the path following layer, the Tactical Racing Layer has the responsibility for making tactical race decisions. This layer will assess the race conditions and change the speed and racing line to gain racing advantage among a pack of cars—elevating the system from an expert driver to an expert racer.

This responsibility is split into three behaviors in the *Downforce* AI. The first behavior, the Optimum Road Position, has the responsibility for evaluating the current race conditions and choosing the most appropriate road position. The second behavior is responsible for generating a new racing line, which will be used as the input for the path following layer (based on the optimum road position). The third behavior, Collision Avoidance Speed Control, has responsibility for overriding the speed control set by the path following layer in order to avoid collisions as the vehicle maneuvers into the optimum road position.

Optimum Road Position

Aside from the insect-like Brooksian basis for the layered architecture used by this system, this behavior is the most biologically inspired aspect of the system. Although it is different in specific implementation, it uses many of the same principles for input and processing of data as Nick Porcino's Insect AI [Porcino04].

Visual Perception

Each car uses four simple eye-like sensors to perceive its environment in terms of the proximity and relative speed of other cars. These sensors act very much like the eyes of a simple insect by reducing the complex environment down to a relatively small number of inputs so that it can be analyzed and reacted to.

Cars have one pair of *eyes* facing in each direction along the track. The two eyes in each pair are of different types; the first type of eye responds to the relative speed of other cars, and the second type responds to their proximity. Each eye stores a one-dimensional image that represents the entire track width, and has a resolution of 20 "perceptual pixels" (or *percepcels*). In combination, the car's four eyes give it a low-resolution image of the state of the track both ahead and behind that is used to choose the optimum road position.

The process used to generate the perceptual data stored in the car's eyes involves rendering a low-resolution one-dimensional image of the track width into each eye in terms of relative speed, or proximity, as appropriate. The process of rendering the car's eyes is made significantly less computationally expensive by pre-calculating the track space positions of all the cars.

The first step in rendering the car's eyes is to create two perception lists, each containing all the other cars within a fixed maximum distance in front and behind the current car. Each perception list is iterated through, calculating the relative speed and proximity values for each vehicle and storing each in all percepcels it projects into in the appropriate eye (see Figure 8.1.3).

Values stored in the percepcels of speed-sensing eyes are between −1.0 and 1.0, both values corresponding to a specified maximum speed difference (negative or positive, respectively). Values stored in the percepcels of proximity-sensing eyes are in the range 0.0 to 1.0 (0.0 proximity corresponding to a minimum distance from the vehicle, and 1.0 being exactly alongside).

Once this process is complete, the vehicle's four eyes are combined in a per-percepcel manner into a single *compound eye*. The specific implementation of the combination of the four eyes into a single compound eye isn't really hugely important, as the result is what matters. The key aspect of this is to end up with a compound eye where each percepcel represents the "desirability" of being at the position on the width of the road to which it corresponds.

This technique works by multiplying the value in each relative speed percepcel by the value in the corresponding proximity percepcel, and adding the result into the

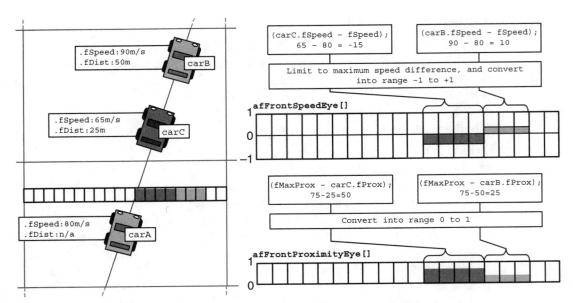

FIGURE 8.1.3   *Calculation of percepcel values for* carA*'s forward facing eyes.*

appropriate percepcel of the compound eye. This means that both faraway vehicles with large speed differences, and very close vehicles with no speed difference will basically not show up in the compound eye.

To allow us to fine-tune the effects of each eye (and each pair of eyes) on the content of the compound eye, the raw percepcel values are multiplied by constants at every stage of their combination. The basic principle involved in the combination of the four eyes into one is that any percepcel value that represents something that might be "bad" for the vehicle will have a negative effect on the corresponding percepcel in the compound eye. For example, the most negative percepcel that would ever be generated in the compound eye would probably be caused by a very nearby vehicle driving at full speed the wrong way around the track.

In *Downforce,* each eye has a scaling constant that alters the values of its percepcels before it is combined with the other eye in its pair. In addition, different constants are applied to the percepcels of the eyes sensing relative speed depending on whether their value is positive or negative; this allows the effect of relative speed on the choice of road position to change depending on the polarity of the relative speed. The combination of the two different types of eye in each pair is buffered, and the buffers from the front and back pairs of eyes are again multiplied by constants before combination.

Once the four eyes have been combined, the effect of the racing line should be added in. The racing line's effect to the compound eye should be strongly positive and should have a width in percepcels equivalent to that of a vehicle. Its effect should be centered on the percepcel that corresponds to racing line's fWidthPos position at the vehicle's steering look ahead distance (see the section *Steering Control*).

Once the racing line is added into the compound eye, choosing the optimum road position is (more or less) just a matter of choosing the most positive percepcel in the compound eye and converting that percepcel back into a corresponding track position. This works more effectively if, rather than picking a position based on an individual percepcel score, a windowed average is used—taking into account an extra half a vehicle's width either side of the central percepcel.

Depending on the physics of your game, it might also be necessary to build latency into the decision to change the choice of optimum position, since in close racing situations the most positive percepcel tends to change wildly from frame to frame. The technique used in this behavior takes a little time and experimentation to tune, so it is almost essential to have a method for editing parameters that affect it at run-time (ideally in real-time).

Path Generation

The path generation behavior has the responsibility for translating the road position identified by the Optimum Road Position behavior into a new racing line. This racing line is then used as input for the Path Following Layer allowing this layer to control the vehicle at a much higher-level, concerned with racing as opposed to driving.

The method used to generate the new racing line in *Downforce* is very simple and more than adequately efficient. Each vehicle's Path Following Layer keeps a buffered local version of the racing line currently being followed. Rather than calculating an entirely new racing line based on the ideal road position, the pre-stored "ideal racing line" is cheaply interpolated in track space toward the optimum road position as it is copied to the buffer used by the Path Following Layer.

This interpolation is performed by calculating the difference in the fWidthPos component of track space between the current optimum road position and the position of the pre-stored ideal racing line at the position it was put into the compound eye used to determine it. This difference is then added to the fWidthPos of the points being copied from the ideal racing line into the buffer used by the vehicle's Path Following Layer.

The only real complications to this process are limiting the difference applied to the ideal racing line as it is interpolated to keep the racing line within the road width. The rate of change of the racing line must also be limited so the Path Following Layer is able to follow it without losing control of the car.

Collision Avoidance Speed Control

This behavior has the responsibility for overriding the speed controls set by the Path Following Layer to avoid collisions with other vehicles—primarily front-to-back collisions from behind. This test was only done when a vehicle detected another vehicle in front of it going at a lower speed.

The test was implemented as a fairly standard predictive collision test using the instantaneous relative velocities; however, since linear velocities/accelerations do not produce accurate results for vehicles travelling on curved paths, the collision test was performed using velocities measured in the track space domain.

The distance between the vehicles was calculated, and divided by the closing speed of the rear vehicle to determine the time until a potential collision. The vehicle's relative velocities in the fWidthPos dimension of track space were then used to generate positions for the two vehicles at the time of potential collision, which were compared to determine a final "instantaneous likelihood" of collision.

Unfortunately, this still did not prove sufficiently reliable, since the vehicles are attempting to follow the racing line and the racing line is still a curved line even in track space. The method was finally refined to a high degree of accuracy by calculating the fWidthPos components of the track space velocities of the vehicles relative to the fWidthPos velocity of the racing line over the same distance in fLengthPos track space that was represented by each vehicle's velocity.

Although using instantaneous velocities to predict collisions is not the most accurate method, it is cheap, reliable, and sufficiently accurate for the purposes of this behavior. Since other behaviors are explicitly trying to steer around other cars in front that are going slower, this behavior only needs to worry about slowing the car if the chance of front-to-back collision is high.

Fine Grain Avoidance Layer

This layer's responsibility is chiefly to deal with potential collision situations where the previous layers have not adequately coped. It is much "thinner" than the previous two layers because it has a lot less calculation to do to get its job done. Two behaviors make up this layer; the first tracks the Race Priority state of the car, and the second avoids collisions (especially side-to-side collisions) in a more accurate manner than the Optimum Road Position layer.

Race Priority/Racing Etiquette

This behavior has a simple job: it tracks the "Race Priority" of the AI controlled car relative to the other cars. In a potential collision situation between two cars, Race Priority determines which car will back down—essentially a matter of professional etiquette among racing drivers. Although this is a straightforward judgement, it is a significant aspect of the AI system, since there are many occasions when two cars will both be attempting to occupy the same part of the track (especially in overtaking and blocking situations when cornering).

Race priority is decided differently based on which car is "inside" and which is "outside" with respect to the corner direction. Inside and outside are defined as follows: if the corner is to the *left*, the *inside* car is the *closest* to the *left* edge of the road, and the *outside* car is the car *farthest* from the *left* edge of the road—and vice versa for a right-hand corner.

In general, the car whose center is farthest forward will be given priority. However, when cornering, the inside car will be given priority if its center is farther forward than the back of the outside car—even though it is slightly behind the outside car.

To make the priority system seem fair to the player, in *Downforce* the player is given a significant advantage over AI in the priority calculation. An AI car only has priority over the player's car when its center is past the front of the player's car. Additionally, when cornering on the inside of an AI car, the player has priority as soon as the front of his or her car passes the back of the AI car.

Fine Grain Collision Avoidance

This behavior has responsibility for avoiding collisions that have not been avoided by the Optimum Road Position Layer—in the vast majority of these situations, the collision being avoided is a side-to-side collision. Its operation is straightforward, and it works by directly overriding the steering and speed control values generated for the car by the Path Following Layer.

The side-to-side collision avoidance is dependent on Race Priority. A vehicle will only ever perform fine grain side-to-side avoidance if it *does not* have Race Priority. The method used is as follows: if a vehicle A is attempting to steer toward a vehicle B (which has race priority over A) and is close enough that steering toward B will cause a collision, then A's steering is limited to a value that will cause it to travel parallel to the direction of B—thus preventing a collision.

In *Downforce*'s AI system, it was necessary to accommodate the fact that the steering wheels of the vehicle had a maximum rate of steer angle change. This was accomplished by increasing the distance at which the steering limit was applied from its base level in proportion to the closing velocity of the two vehicles. Additionally, any vehicle whose steering value was limited would also have its throttle scaled to approximately two-thirds of the throttle being applied by the car with Race Priority, thus giving way to that vehicle.

Front-to-back collisions are avoided by this behavior in a very similar manner to side-to-side collisions, but implemented by overriding the braking and throttle values rather than the steering value. This function of the behavior only exists because it proved very difficult to tune the parameters controlling the Collision Avoidance Speed Control behavior in the Optimum Road Position Layer so that it functioned accurately at both large and small closing speeds.

Instead of relying on Race Priority, however, this functionality is implemented so that the car behind always has responsibility for not running into a car in front of it. The throttle and braking values of the car behind are altered so that throttle is reduced, and braking increased, in proportion to its proximity and relative speed. To prevent this behavior from interfering with desirable behavioral functionality of other layers (e.g., overtaking at high closing speeds), the parameters controlling the front-to-back aspect of Fine Grain Collision Avoidance need to be carefully tuned so that it only has an effect in situations where the cars are almost touching each other.

Driving Assist Layer

The Driving Assist Layer has responsibility for controlling problems such as wheel-spin, and brakes locking so that the rest of the system doesn't have to worry about it. This responsibility is split between two behaviors: one that ensures that the car always has maximum traction under acceleration, and a second that prevents the brakes from locking under braking. These tasks are accomplished in broadly the same way as in the real automotive industry, except that we are controlling a simulated vehicle and so have access to exact measures of the spin and slip of the four wheels relative to the surface.

Traction Control

This behavior has responsibility for minimizing wheel-spin—that is, slippage of the wheel (relative to the surface is it contacting) in the lengthwise axis of the driving wheel (in *Downforce*, this is the wheel's local z-axis).

Once the wheel slip in the lengthwise axis of the wheel exceeds a threshold value, the actual amount of slip is calculated as a proportion between the threshold and a maximum slip value. This proportion is used to scale the current throttle value (generated initially by the Path Following Layer, and potentially modified by both the Optimum Road Position and Fine Grain Avoidance Layers).

It was also found necessary to set a minimum throttle value that this behavior would reduce the throttle to, when below a threshold speed, since scaling the throttle unnecessarily will result in slow acceleration especially from a standing start. This will be very important if you have a vehicle with a high power-to-weight ratio since it will tend to spin its wheels in low gears.

Depending on whether the vehicle being controlled is front, back, or four-wheel drive, it might be necessary to check the wheel spin and the wheel skid—that is, slippage of the wheel in the widthwise axis (the wheel's local x-axis). It might also be necessary to combine slip values from the front and back wheels in differing proportions to derive an optimum throttle scaling value. Additionally, for the best results, the highest of the wheel slip values should be used to calculate the throttle reduction value rather than the average slip value—unless of course the physics system allows each driven wheel to be controlled separately.

Anti-Lock Braking

This behavior was implemented using almost exactly the same code as the Traction Control system, but by scaling the brake value under braking rather than the throttle under acceleration. The most significant component of wheel slip with regard to judging the amount of wheel locking was found to be in the z-axis of the wheels.

Although preventing the wheels from locking when braking in a straight line will stop the vehicle significantly more slowly than allowing the wheels to lock, the overall reduction in braking efficiency was found to be preferable. Otherwise, the AI cars will lose control because they are forced to change their racing line under heavy braking.

Extending the Basic Architecture

Probably the most useful technique in this article is the "visual" perception based reasoning. The power of this technique is its ability to express many different aspects of the tactical choices of road position race with just one array of values (the compound eye). Without changing the algorithm for choosing the optimum road position from the compound eye, it is possible to choose a path directly in the way of a faster car coming from behind (blocking its racing line), or to explicitly follow cars close by that are going the same speed or slightly slower (drafting them). This is achieved by changing the constants that affect the combination of speed and proximity percepcels in the forward and backward facing eyes.

Taking this further, it would be possible to extend the Optimum Road Position Layer so that it could have state-specific sets of constants controlling how the four eyes are combined into the compound eye, and essentially allowing the vehicle to swap driving styles on the fly—from blocking, to straight racing, to drafting, and so on.

In addition to these basic extensions, it would also be possible to extend the compound eye so that it takes other types of data of the track's suitability. For example, if the game had racing teams it would be possible to deliberately cause it to steer to block specific opponents of its teammate by taking the team membership into account when calculating the compound eye.

Conclusion

The *Downforce* AI system architecture, and in particular the principles and techniques used within it, are suitable for a wide range of AI applications. The key features of the architecture and the advantages they offer are as follows:

- Its behavioral functionality is modular, extensible, and scalable. This helps to reduce developmental risk, and to simplify tasks like difficulty tuning by localizing variables that control specific aspects of the system's behavior.
- It uses simple but powerful representational abstractions (such as track space and insect-inspired "eyes") to both reduce the computational expense of complex decision-making, and help to predispose the system toward intelligent seeming behavior.

Systems like this, whose overall behavior is emergent, tend to exhibit robust behavior and are generally capable of coping well with unexpected situations—predisposing the system to fail gracefully and reducing the amount of special-case code.

References

[Blanchard00] Blanchard, M., Rind, F. C., and Verschure, P. F. M. J., "Collision Avoidance Using a Model of the Locust LGMD Neuron," *Robotics and Autonomous Systems* 30, pp. 17–38, 2000.

[Braitenberg84] Braitenberg, Valentino, *Vehicles: Experiments in Synthetic Psychology*, A Bradford Book/The MIT Press, 1984.

[Brooks91] Brooks, R.A., "How to Build Complete Creatures Rather than Isolated Cognitive Simulators," in K. VanLehn (ed.), *Architectures for Intelligence*, pp. 225–239, Lawrence Erlbaum Associates, Hillsdale, NJ, 1991.

[Dennett88] Dennett, Daniel C., "Evolution, Error and Intentionality," *Sourcebook on the Foundations of Artificial Intelligence*, New Mexico University Press 1988.

[Forrester04] Forrester, Euan, "Intelligent Steering Using PID Controllers," *AI Game Programming Wisdom 2*, Charles River Media, 2004.

[Möller98] Möller, R., Lambrinos, D., Pfeifer, R., Labhart, T., and Wehner, R. "Modeling Ant Navigation with an Autonomous Agent," *From Animals to Animats 5*, MIT Press 1998.

[Porcino04] Porcino, Nick, "An Architecture for A-Life," *AI Game Programming Wisdom 2*, Charles River Media, 2004.

[Thomas04] Thomas, Dale, "New Paradigms in Artificial Intelligence," *AI Game Programming Wisdom 2*, Charles River Media, 2004.

[Webb00] Webb, B., and Scutt, T., "A Simple Latency Dependent Spiking Neuron Model of Cricket Phonotaxis," *BiologicalCybernetics* 82, pp. 247–269, 2000.

[White02] White, Richard, "Maximum and Minimum Speeds of Car on Banked Turn with Friction," available online at *www.crashwhite.com/physicstutoring/sampleproblems/sampleproblemch6/spch6no3.html*, October, 2002.

8.2

Fast and Efficient Approximation of Racing Lines

John Manslow

john@jmanslow.fsnet.co.uk

The original *AI Game Programming Wisdom* book contained a series of three articles [Biasillo02a, Biasillo02b, Biasillo02c] that described many of the techniques used to control AI vehicles racing around a track, assuming that an approximation to the track's racing line was available. The articles suggested that such an approximation could be obtained by recording the path taken by an AI vehicle while it was under the control of a competent human player.

While this is a fast and efficient way of producing accurate approximations to racing lines, it cannot be used for randomly generated or player created tracks, making it difficult for developers to provide competent and convincing AI opponents to race on them. This article solves this problem by describing a fast and efficient technique for automatically generating approximations to racing lines.

Racing Lines in Games

It is important that AI controlled vehicles follow some approximation to a track's racing line for two reasons:

- Real vehicles being controlled by real racing drivers follow the racing line, so AI controlled vehicles must also do so to maintain suspension of disbelief.
- The racing line is the path that allows the AI to drive around the racetrack as quickly as possible and thus present the greatest challenge to the player.

Finding an approximation to a racing line is not easy, however, because racing lines are a complex interplay of the physics of the vehicles being raced, and the details of the shape of the track [Anderson93, Bechman91].

Some games have attempted to overcome this difficulty by restricting random and player created tracks to being assembled from predefined segments (curves, straights, s-curves, and so forth) with precomputed racing lines. This approach has two major limitations:

- It provides a less satisfying experience for players who want to drive random tracks or design their own because of the lack of variety in the predefined segments.
- A racing line cannot be produced by plugging together predefined sections of racing line because each section of racing line is context dependent—it changes depending on what comes before it and what comes after.

The following section describes how the racing line of any track can be quickly and efficiently approximated by a line of minimum curvature.

Lines of Minimum Curvature

To simplify the problem of finding an approximate racing line, this article ignores the details of the physics of the vehicles being raced and instead seeks an approximation to the path of minimum curvature along the track. This is limited as an approximation to the real racing line because it has no sense of the direction in which a vehicle is traveling or its speed. This can produce errors in the way the approximation trades curvature in one part of the track off against curvature further along.

Despite its disadvantages, however, the path of minimum curvature can be approximated quickly, efficiently, and reliably, and follows true racing lines accurately enough to create the illusion of intelligence and offer the player a challenging opponent. Further justification for using a path of minimum curvature comes from the fact that the maximum speed that a vehicle can drive along a curve without sliding is inversely proportional to its curvature. If a vehicle's inertia is ignored, therefore, a path of minimum curvature is the path that it can travel at maximum speed without sliding.

Approximating Lines of Minimum Curvature

An approximation to a track's racing line can be represented by a series of points (as described in [Biasillo02c]) placed at regular intervals along the track. The algorithm in this article is initialized by placing these points at the track's center, and their positions are iteratively updated to form successively more accurate approximations. At any time, the curvature of the approximation can be measured by the sums of the squares of the angles between the vectors joining adjacent points.

By repeatedly applying small forces to every set of three contiguous points in the approximation, as shown in Figure 8.2.1, it is possible to gradually reduce its curvature. Figure 8.2.1 shows three points in a racing line, labeled A, B, and C, which are joined by the vectors AB and BC. The vectors AB and BC make an angle α, which contributes to the total curvature of the line. Applying a small force f proportional to α to the points A, B, and C, as shown in the figure, causes the points to move in such a way that α is reduced. This process is repeated for all sets of three contiguous points in the racing line until the reduction in total curvature produced by one pass along the entire racing line becomes small.

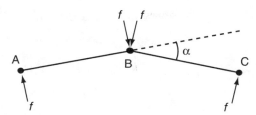

FIGURE 8.2.1 *How to apply forces to points on a racing line to reduce its curvature.*

The previous procedure can lead to the points in the approximation being unevenly distributed along the length of the track, since the forces applied to A and C are orthogonal to the vectors AB and BC, but the net force applied to B has components that tend to shorten them.

To prevent this, the vectors between adjacent points are given a spring-like property so that they apply restoring forces to the points at their ends that are in the direction of the vector and proportional to the difference between its current length and its original (ideal) length. This is illustrated in Figure 8.2.2 where the vector AB has length l rather than l_{ideal}, and so a restorative force proportional to the difference between l and l_{ideal} is applied to the vector's endpoints A and B.

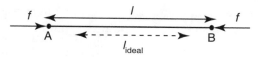

FIGURE 8.2.2 *How to apply forces to regulate the length of each section of racing line.*

Finally, each point on the approximation must be constrained to lie within the bounds of the track. This can be accomplished simply by placing any point that strays beyond the track back onto its boundary.

This does not produce discontinuities in the line because neighboring points will be adjusted in the next pass of the algorithm. Repeated application of the three steps described previously will produce successively more accurate approximations to a track's racing line. The CD-ROM that accompanies this book contains an implementation of the algorithm, with source code, that shows it approximating racing lines on randomly generated racetracks.

Although the algorithm is iterative, it is quite efficient, scaling as $O(n)$ for an n-point approximation. It can approximate the racing line of a track using 300 points in around five seconds on an Intel Celeron PC running at 500MHz. Although the demonstration implementation shows the algorithm operating on nonlooped tracks, it can equally well be applied to looped tracks simply by connecting the first and last points in the racing line.

ON THE CD

Variations on Lines of Minimum Curvature

The algorithm described in this article is very flexible and many modifications can be made to it that change the nature of the approximations it produces. For example, the equation for the force applied to points A, B, and C in Figure 8.2.1 can be changed to almost anything, provided that the force retains the same sign as α. Some equations will allow the approximation to be found more quickly than others, and each will produce a slightly different path around the track.

For example, choosing f to be +1 if α is positive and −1 if α is negative produces a shortest path irrespective of its curvature. Similarly, setting f to be equal to the cube of α forces the algorithm to work harder at reducing the curvature of the sharpest corners of the racing line by introducing additional curvature into previously straight sections. The code on the accompanying CD-ROM illustrates further enhancements to the basic algorithm that allow it to take account of the direction in which the vehicle will be traveling, and asymmetries between acceleration and braking.

ON THE CD

Conclusion

This article described a solution to the difficult problem of approximating racing lines for random and player created tracks. The solution starts with a series of points placed along the center of the track, which represent a rough approximation to the racing line, and iteratively updates the points' positions, at each step increasing the accuracy of the approximation to the path of minimum curvature. The basic algorithm is fast and stable, and can easily be modified to produce racing lines with a variety of characteristics.

References

[Anderson93] Anderson, George, *Winning: A Race Drivers Handbook*, Motorbooks International, 1993.

[Bechman91] Beckman, Brian, "The Physics of Racing," available online at *www.miata.net/sport/Physics/*, 1991.

[Biasillo02a] Biasillo, Gari, "Representing a Racetrack for the AI," *AI Game Programming Wisdom*, Charles River Media, 2002.

[Biasillo02b] Biasillo, Gari, "Racing AI Logic," *AI Game Programming Wisdom*, Charles River Media, 2002.

[Biasillo02c] Biasillo, Gari, "Training an AI to Race," *AI Game Programming Wisdom*, Charles River Media, 2002.

The Art of Surviving a Simulation Title

Dr. Brett Laming—Argonaut Sheffield

brett@argonaut-sheffield.com

While AI is both exciting and rewarding, it can be a tough field to specialize in. Although scripting languages and data files sensibly pass much of the higher-level functionality over to designers [Rabin00], it is still common practice to leave the lower-level requirements to a single programmer. This programmer must ensure that the basic building blocks of the AI work, and continue to work, in an appropriate manner.

In the case of titles involving the physical simulation of one or more vehicles, simulation titles for short, good low-level AI is essential. The complex nature of these simulation titles means that AI tends toward a more mathematical approach, focused toward lower-level control rather than higher-level behavior. Creating an optimal and realistic system for controlling the AI and maintaining it throughout the length of a project can be quite a task, especially for a programmer new to the field.

This article aims to simplify the task of writing simulation AI by providing a number of guidelines. Adopted, for the most part, after working on the space simulation *Independence War 2* (*I-War 2*), these guidelines have also brought success to the futuristic racing game *Powerdrome*.

Simulation AI

AI is viewed as a high-risk area, especially in simulations. In conjunction with the physics, it forms the prerequisite of the single-player game. Producers and publishers alike want to see AI in the game and working as soon as possible because it reassures them that the project is progressing. Likewise, if it breaks, they want to see it fixed, quickly, because the single-player game ultimately depends on it.

Simulation AI is particularly fragile, encompassing the frailties of both the physics and gameplay on which it is founded. Approaching milestone deliverables, this fragility is compounded as new functionality gets put in place quickly. With little or no time for AI repair or retuning, the AI never quite works, is always trailing behind, and is generally regarded as problematic.

There is a good chance that simulation AI will never escape this fragility. Because of its dependencies, the AI will break, even if left alone. Yet by carefully planning the

AI foundations, preparing for the worst, and knowing when not to overcomplicate things, life will be a little easier when the inevitable happens.

Design and Implementation

Unfortunately, there are no set rules to successful design and implementation of AI. Each genre and title is different. Generally, the best approaches come from experience, whether personal, gleaned from others, or based on foundation papers such as [Biasillo02], who offers a good architecture for racing AI.

The guidelines presented here are based on higher-level design philosophies that have proved useful and have worked in the past. In addition, a number of lower-level guidelines, especially important to AI, warrant a special mention:

- Prevent typographical errors by minimizing code repetition. Make use of abstraction at every possible level. This is especially true of repeated code that makes use of <, >, +, and -, all of which are easily mistyped.
- The complexity of the AI will often mean that individual details of its implementation are forgotten. Sensible naming conventions and comments are great aids for refreshing memory. Keep them relevant and up to date—misleading comments or badly named variables can do more harm than good.
- Try to code as neatly as possible, even when experimenting. If you have to go back and tidy code, resist the temptation to rewrite it—this will often introduce more errors. Instead, change it in place and test as you go.

Create a Prototype

Prototypes are vital—especially for new AI. They reassure everyone on the team that your ideas work, and they provide immediate pre-production content for any prospective publisher. At this stage, the goal is proof of concept; if the concept isn't working, throw it away and rethink. Allow for this contingency and think about investing a couple of extra hours here and there—after all, with a good design you will more than recover this time during subsequent milestones.

Pre-production time should be spent trying out as many ideas as possible, so it is wise to get an AI test harness up and running quickly. By making use of previous titles, existing engines, or third-party software, time can be spent concentrating on the AI and not its supporting code.

I-War 2 reused the principles of *I-War* for its AI prototype. The *Powerdrome* test harness was a simple 2D application written in *OpenGL*. It is worth bearing in mind that 2D prototypes are often easier to understand, quicker to produce, and can usually be converted to 3D with relative ease.

Test the Code

With all the scheduling questions involved in writing AI, it is often difficult to justify spending extra time testing newly written code that appears functional. However, as additional features increase the complexity of the AI, it is important to ensure that any resulting problems are a direct consequence of the latest changes and not some previously untested functionality.

For example, at one stage in *I-War 2* a designer noticed that the AI steering code seemed to steer a spaceship away from its desired direction. Revisions to the steering code were immediately examined to find the culprit. Unfortunately, the cause turned out to be a "matrix to quaternion" method that had not been thoroughly tested and didn't hold for that spaceship's particular orientation—a problem that could have been averted with careful testing of the underlying support functions.

In an ideal world, testing would consolidate every bit of code that got written, but realistically this is not feasible. After all, some functionality is too complex to cover all possible test conditions. Nonetheless, when working with vectors, matrices, and other mathematical constructs—the very building blocks of the AI—it is fairly straightforward to accurately verify their functionality. Each needs to be tested thoroughly with a range of values, not just those it might be obtaining from the game at the present time. Math classes should go even further and have associated unit tests written for them. This allows us to check their integrity should anyone try to optimize them later.

As a final note, it is worth mentioned the pitfall of relying on the rest of the team to perform exhaustive AI testing. Although this allows you to keep AI functionality progressing, it is a dangerous strategy. Often, when someone else does spot an error, the AI has moved sufficiently far ahead that the original mistake has become obfuscated by the latest changes.

Force the AI to Steer through the Player's Interface

With increased processing power, the need for real-world physics in simulation games is quickly becoming a competitive requirement. Real-world physics appeals to players because it approximates observations that are made in real life. While players might have never flown a space ship, for example, their Newtonian experience of the real world has already given them an impression of what should and shouldn't be possible.

It stands to reason, therefore, that deviation from this realism is going to break a player's immersion in the game. As immersion is a key factor in the longevity of a simulation game, its maintenance is important. If the AI breaks the natural constraints imposed by the physics, in sight of the player, then it will quickly be spotted. If it maintains these constraints, then it helps preserve the illusion of being no different in capability from a human player.

The easiest way of enforcing this realism is to constrain the AI in exactly the same way as the player. To do this, the AI should use the same collection of inputs, or *yoke*, that is available to the player. While forcing the AI to use the same yoke is a lot tougher than cheating, it has a distinct number of advantages:

- First, it maintains a clean divide from gameplay. A human-controlled player will set his or her yoke from an input device. The AI will fill in the yoke of any computer players. The underlying gameplay code just needs to accept its control inputs in the form of the shared yoke.

- Further, the yoke facilitates good AI design, encouraging thinking in terms of the human approach (*how much do we want to accelerate?*) rather than the procedural approach, (*where should we be now?*). It also allows for seamless interchangeability of player and AI control by the game. This was used to good effect by both the autopilots in *I-War 2* and the victory lap control of the player vehicle in *Powerdrome*.

- Finally, assuming any special advantages for the AI are kept to a minimum, it provides an insight at any time into how the AI would handle the player's situation using the same game state. This could have many exciting connotations for the future, opening up the possibility of sophisticated tutorials that teach you to fly, or guide you around during docking procedures, while being fault tolerant of your mistakes.

Layer the Design

It is important to create your AI using a layered approach, a point that has been recognized by the strategy genre for a while [Woodcock01]. Just as a yoke forms the interface between AI and simulation, most AI designs can be broken down into clear levels, each with its own minimal interface to the next level of behavior. With a layered approach it is easy to break down the work into manageable chunks. By artificially providing the minimal amount of information required at each divide, we give ourselves a method for systematically testing the AI from the ground up.

One such design that has served us well in the past is shown in Figure 8.3.1. While an in-depth discussion of this architecture is beyond this article, it should give you an idea about where some natural divides of an AI system might lie.

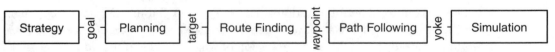

FIGURE 8.3.1   *A layered design strategy for simulation AI.*

A high-level strategy module sets a goal. A plan is then drawn up to achieve this goal. The result of this plan is a target position. Route finding plots a course to this position using waypoints. Path following achieves each waypoint by computing the relevant yoke over time. Each yoke update is passed to the simulation, which then updates the state of the game world.

The important point to this design, as we discussed previously for the yoke, is that each layer does not need to know how its input was obtained. The choice of waypoint passed to the path following module, for example, could have come from a predefined route, an A* algorithm, or from a test case written for debugging purposes.

The goal given to planning could have come from an AI fleet commander or the user issuing an order.

Let the Computer Do the Work

Regardless of how the low-level AI is written, the result is generally a complex solution of equations with n unknowns. All of these will need fitting with sensible values. Tuning these values by hand is delicate, time-consuming, and often infeasible. With time being such a valuable commodity, anything that can help alleviate the need for this process is obviously advantageous.

To illustrate, *Powerdrome*, for example, used a key value (*catchup*) to determine the competitiveness of the AI around the track. While the final value was eventually set by hand, the initial value was found by allowing the AI to race around the track a number of times with a number of different *catchup* values and recording the associated lap times. By deciding what the average lap time should be for each track and competition, we could then cross-reference to get a value that kept the AI competitive at the right level.

Obtaining values directly from the game like this often removes the need for, and insecurity of, more general adaptive methods. Manually directing the search for key values using our knowledge of the AI mechanics allows us to, reasonably independently, calculate the relevant parameters in the quickest possible time.

Debugging Strategies for Anomalous Behavior

At some point in the project, the AI is likely to exhibit anomalous behavior, at which time other people will politely inform you that it is "broken." At this stage it is important for you to find the root of the problem as efficiently and quickly as possible.

The key to fast diagnosis is having tools already in place that make this job easier. Being able to pause the game at a point in time, access debug displays, and systematically turn on and off AI functionality is invaluable. These tools are essential to gain the time to concentrate on higher-level behavior while minimizing time spent on lower-level problems.

Time and time again, good runtime debugging support has meant the difference between quick diagnoses and protracted debugging sessions. While not strictly AI, its analysis here will hopefully reflect the importance of getting it right.

Use Text and Graphical Debugging Mechanisms

AI runtime debugging in *I-War 2* consisted of a few full screens of text giving such information as position, velocity, and orientation for any object in the world. It was both painful to use and difficult to decipher.

While text debugging is easy to get working, graphical debug displays convey data far more effectively, especially in a 3D game like *Powerdrome* (Color Plate 13). As creating a library for these displays often means a welcome break from the AI, it is worth spending time getting it right.

First, the debug library should be easy and intuitive to use. If we are concentrating on writing AI, then adding information to a debug screen should require no more than a couple of lines of code. Requiring anything more extensive will risk disrupting the programmer's line of thought.

The library should support both low-level and high-level drawing primitives. Low-level primitives might consist of lines, rectangles, and text. High-level primitives might consist of spheres, cubes, or splines. If no high-level primitive fits, then we can use a combination of lower-level primitives to obtain a similar result without much time loss.

When text is required, it should be displayed at the position of its context as in Color Plate 14. While this often requires a little more effort to get working, it provides immediate insight into what the information actually applies to.

Finally, we do not want to be spending time manipulating data into acceptable forms. If we want to draw a square, for example, we want to be able to draw it regardless of whether it is expressed as four points or a width and height. The debug library should provide support for all common forms in which data can be represented. This helps keep the overhead for adding debugging info as low as possible.

Selectively Enable Debugging Aids

If the runtime debug information for *Powerdrome* was displayed in its entirety, the result would be a horrible, confusing mess. By building in the ability to switch on and off parts of the display it is possible to focus on what is actually interesting at the time. An extensible flag approach means that newly categorized debug information can be added quickly.

The same flag structure also allows components of the AI to be turned on and off. This allows us to see how the AI functions with or without them. During problem diagnosis, this is invaluable. Consider, for example, an AI player with its avoidance routines turned off that drives around a track in a smooth line, albeit hitting things. If the same AI player keeps wobbling around the smooth line with avoidance turned on, then it is easy to hypothesize that avoidance is causing the wobble.

On a final note, to be truly useful for debugging, we need to be able to turn human-controlled players over to the AI and vice versa. Doing so allows us to observe the AI through our characters' eyes and follow them around, rather than trying to observe all their behavior from the outside. It also allows us to manually maneuver the AI into situations that we want to observe it in.

Capture Anomalies with a Pause Feature

Anomalous low-level AI behavior is often subtle, infrequent, and over in seconds. If it is not caught immediately, it might not be seen under the same circumstances again.

Examples of these short-duration anomalies crop up time and time again, so it's a good idea to get a system in place to catch them. The core component of this system is the ability to freeze time in an instance and have a good look around. One solution is to separate AI thinking, the decision as to what it should do, from the actual simulation, the application of its decision. By using the game's pause functionality, it is then possible to turn off simulation while keeping the rest of the game, including the AI and camera, ticking over.

Provided the AI is mostly deterministic (it will, after all, be under constant computation), you should then be able to capture that moment in time and get a feel for what is happening (Color Plate 14). By making use of debug support, switching on and off various AI components and using the in-game cameras to have a good look around, it should be possible to analyze any anomalous or unexpected behavior (Color Plate 15).

Graphically Track the History of Parameters and Variables

There are often moments when we want to know why various AI parameters adopted the values they did. As these parameters can often change in a split second, there is little or no time available to pause the simulation. With each parameter often having many dependencies, it can be difficult to trace the causal event. However, in simulation AI, finding these events is important, especially if they cause the AI control system to become unstable.

A useful tip is to keep a graphical history of these parameters and their dependent variables over a short period of time. This allows us to see the gradual decay and rise of a value as well as any spikes in its behavior. More importantly, it allows us to see a parameter's relationship with its dependent variables, and which variable is the first to cause related problems.

It is important to display these variable histories at both the same scale and position across the screen. This will let you take in the relationships between them at a glance. One particularly useful parameter is frame rate. Many AI factors implicitly depend on the current frame rate and, with new features being added all the time, it is useful to see the impact this is having on the AI.

Make the AI Visible to the Player

Personally speaking, one of the most difficult challenges of game AI is knowing when to stop. At some point, the complexity of the AI will have become such that adding anything else will do it more harm than good. In other words, the risk of breaking the current AI and adding more time to the schedule will outweigh the benefit of new functionality.

This stage is usually reached when the AI has grown so complex that it has become impossible to hypothesize on the impact new functionality will have. At this point in time it is a good idea to stop and consolidate what already exists. By communicating sensible by-products of AI calculations, it is often possible to give the illusion of greater complexity with little or no work.

Let Intelligence Be in the Eye of the Beholder

With increased complexity, the boundary between explicitly recognizing what the AI is doing and hypothesizing about what it could be doing begins to blur. Once this boundary has been reached, informal focus testing to find out what is missing is often a far better approach than implementation of aspects that are actually missing.

For example, approaching an important project milestone, the *Powerdrome* driver AI had the ability to perform block and overtake maneuvers. Both blocking and overtaking were constrained by common sense. Overtaking, for example, would only happen if the way ahead were clear.

In addition, the *Powerdrome* character would also be sent relevant animation cues to indicate maneuver intentions. If the AI were blocking on the left, for example, the character would receive an animation cue to look behind and to the left.

At one stage, a tester said that he had just seen an AI player "dummy" the player ahead and slip through on the opposite side. Dummying is the process of moving to one side while preparing to overtake quickly on the other, fooling drivers who are trying to block into moving toward the wrong side.

Unfortunately, dummying had not been implemented yet. What this tester was actually seeing was the AI trying to overtake on the right, being blocked by the AI driver in front and overtaking on the left due to the lack of space.

Hence, provided the AI performs sufficiently varied actions that seem sensible to the player, such as not overtaking until the way ahead is clear, emergent behavior will cause players to create their own contexts regardless of whether those contexts were intentional.

Illustrate Your Hard Work

Interesting AI was going on behind the scenes in both *I-War 2* and *Powerdrome*. The problem with *I-War 2* was that this intelligence was never communicated, although the data was readily available. As such, players were oblivious to its existence and concentrated instead on aspects of the AI that did not get the time they deserved.

Half-Life, on the other hand, is made really special by the coordinated communication of the marine squads. Likewise, the flight simulator *Flight Unlimited 2* is made special by showing off its runway route finding using taxiing instructions. Both make use of data that has to be calculated anyway.

If we endeavor to make our AI think like human players, then, regardless of success, a human-like flow of thought is defined. Explicitly communicating this flow of thought is an easy way to give our AI some character. Letting the player know what the AI is attempting to do might convince that player that the AI is trying to do something sensible.

For example, a computer-controlled driver in *Powerdrome* who engages his after-burner going into a sharp corner initially projects an image of being dumb. If the same computer driver waves his fist in visible agitation just prior to the corner then the situation is not as clear cut. Instead of the players thinking, "That's really dumb," they now think "He was a bit annoyed—what happened there? Rage?" In product reviews, it is this type of reasoning that could make the difference between slighted or praised AI.

Conclusion

Creating good AI for a simulation title is a challenge. This article presented some general guidelines that make this challenge easier. It covered creating the foundations from fire fighting to knowing how to make the most of what you've got. While these guidelines cannot guarantee you absolute success, they can at least point you in the right direction.

References

[Biasillo02] Biasillo, Gari, "Representing a Racetrack for the AI," *AI Game Programming Wisdom*, Charles River Media, 2002.

[Rabin00] Rabin, Steve, "The Magic of Data-Driven Design," *Game Programming Gems*, Charles River Media, 2000.

[Woodcock01] Woodcock, Steve, "Game AI: The State of the Industry," available online at *www.gamasutra.com/features/20001101/woodcock_01.htm*, November 1, 2001.

8.4

Dead Reckoning in Sports and Strategy Games

François Dominic Laramée

francoislaramee@videotron.ca

For a game AI, predicting the behavior of the human player is one of the keys to success, whether the human is the AI's partner or its opponent. Dead reckoning (DR) algorithms can help in one aspect of this effort, namely predicting motion. While the applications of such a mechanism in military simulations are obvious (e.g., the AI can only attack effectively if it knows where the enemy will be located at the time of the attack), dead reckoning can also be used in sports games, where the human player and its AI teammates must exchange the ball or the puck every few seconds. Furthermore, the method can help offset the effects of latency in online games.

This article outlines the principles of dead reckoning and how an AI can apply them to these various domains of behavior.

Origins of Dead Reckoning

Dead reckoning was originally developed as a tool for navigators. For example, a sailor can use dead reckoning techniques to estimate the position of his ship, given its original position, intended course, and recorded speed, without taking wind or current into consideration [Auxetrain03, Navigate99]. Obviously, the more important the effect of these outside factors in a real-life situation, the less reliable the estimate provided by dead reckoning. Still, in cases where more precise methods are impractical— for example, when navigating in heavy fog without the assistance of a global positioning satellite system—dead reckoning can at least provide enough information to steer clear of the most dangerous obstacles.

Of course, if you can estimate your current position given only your original location and trajectory, you can do the same for any other object for which you know the same information. In the military domain, dead reckoning is often used to estimate movements of enemy fleets and troops between instances of visual, radar, or spy satellite contact. In recent years, the same principles were also applied to the design of autonomous robots [Borenstein94, NASA96].

Equations for Dead Reckoning

It is possible to implement dead reckoning with several levels of sophistication, depending on the properties of the object being tracked. This article describes inertial motion, pseudo-Brownian motion, and kinematics.

Inertia

At the most basic level, dead reckoning reduces to Newton's first law of motion: knowing an object's position and speed, we can assume that the object will continue to travel in a straight line. Therefore, future positions can be computed with the simple equation:

$$P_t = P_0 + vt \tag{1}$$

where P_t is the position of the object at time t, P_0 is its original position, and v is its velocity vector. The first derivative of this equation tells us that, for every time step of the simulation, we simply have to increment the object's current position by v; the easiest way to do so in a 2D or 3D world is to increment each component of the position vector separately:

$$P_{x,t+1} = P_{x,t} + v_x$$
$$P_{y,t+1} = P_{y,t} + v_y$$
$$P_{z,t+1} = P_{z,t} + v_z \tag{2}$$

For objects deprived of self-determination and relatively free of outside influence, like an asteroid, a derelict spaceship, or a hockey player who has been knocked down on the ice, this very simple model is sufficient. In fact, since human players can't hope to do much better themselves, the model might even be too good; for example, in cases where an AI bot is shooting at the human player. In these cases, it might become necessary to insert evaluation errors into the calculation, for example by making the estimate of the human's velocity a normal random variable, with a mean equal to the actual velocity and a variance that depends on the game's difficulty level.

Pseudo-Brownian Motion

If an object is extremely maneuverable, like a UFO or a mosquito, it is impossible to predict its velocity vector over lengthy periods with any level of reliability. The same phenomenon occurs when the object's movement is dominated by overwhelming outside factors. As a result, from an independent observer's point of view, such objects behave more or less as if they were subject to random Brownian motion.

In a true Brownian scenario, predicting a precise position for a particle in a fluid is impossible. The best that can be done, assuming that the object's initial position and the magnitude of its velocity vector are known, is to compute the average displacement among a number of such particles [Weisstein03]. This value depends on the temperature of the medium, its dynamic viscosity, and Boltzmann's constant. In the case of the UFO that can do anything it pleases, including fly in a straight line, all that can be done is calculate the radius of a spherical region of space in which it could have moved. In the case of a floating mine, a straight trajectory is highly improbable, and so it might be reasonable to assume that the mine will not have wandered away from its original location by more than half (or even the square root) of the distance it would have covered had it moved straight.

Kinematics

If the object's initial velocity v is unknown, it can be computed from observation: plot a curve of its position for an arbitrary interval, and compute speed as the first derivative of the position curve.

However, if you need a more sophisticated estimate of the object's future trajectory, you can add an estimate of its acceleration vector to the mix. Several methods can be used to estimate the acceleration parameter:

- For a ballistic missile, this acceleration is simply gravity, plus the effects of air and/or water resistance if necessary.
- For an enemy ship in an eighteenth-century naval warfare simulation, the acceleration vector applied on an enemy ship as a result of the effects of current will be identical to that suffered by the AI's own ship, unless the sea is particularly turbulent or the battle is being fought in a storm. Thus, this factor cancels out.
- For the human player's avatar, acceleration can be derived from the buttons being pressed.
- For other objects, it can be computed as the second derivative of the curve describing the object's position.

Once we have the acceleration in addition to the initial position and velocity, we can compute dead reckoning positions using the classical kinematics equation:

$$P = P_0 + v_0 t + 0.5 a t^2 \tag{3}$$

where P is the new position estimate at time t, P_0 is the initial position, v_0 is the initial velocity, and a is the acceleration vector. Differentiating this equation over t yields a position increment at time t equal to $v_0 + at$. Alternatively, we can adopt a two-step approach, first incrementing the velocity vector by a, and then applying Equation 1 or Equation 2 to update position; this approach has the added advantage of giving us an accurate estimate of the object's velocity vector at any given time.

Dead Reckoning in Sports Games

We can apply dead reckoning to team sports games; for example, in these two situations:

- When the AI is trying to shoot the ball or the puck past an active human obstacle; for example, a soccer goalie, a hockey defenseman, or an NFL cornerback.
- When the AI is trying to pass the ball or the puck to the human player.

In both cases, the AI should apply dead reckoning to compute the most likely trajectory of the human player's avatar. The agent can then fire away from the goaltender's probable position, or target a pass that will intercept a human partner's trajectory at a suitable location.

For example, in a hockey game, the AI could look at the dead reckoning parameters for both the human player and the other AIs on the ice to determine whether the human's current trajectory is likely to take him to an open spot shortly. If so, the AI can time a pass so that the puck will reach that spot at the same time as the player. In an American football game, the AI calculating how to throw the ball to a human receiver will need to take the third dimension into consideration (so that the ball will intercept the receiver's trajectory at a point where it is between, say, one meter and three meters from the ground), but the principle remains the same.

Dead Reckoning in Military Simulations

Since dead reckoning has its origins in the military world, it is hardly surprising that many of its most obvious applications are in combat games. For example:

- In a World War II scenario, the human player flies a reconnaissance plane over an enemy fleet. The fleet's position, velocity, and likely heading can be determined from the recon data, and its future positions estimated by DR. A bombing raid can then be planned effectively.
- In a contemporary war scenario, a DR assistant can help the human player determine the targets of an incoming missile attack, and guide his anti-missile defense decisions: which interceptor missiles to fire, in what order, and so forth.
- In a submarine simulation, the player is piloting his sub through a mined harbor. The floating mines are equipped with electronic countermeasures, so that they blink in and out of radar contact. DR is used to determine the volumes into which the mines might have wandered since radar contact was lost, and therefore help the player choose a safe course.

In most cases, the same DR techniques can be used both by a noncheating enemy AI that must estimate the positions of the human player's units, and by the human player's own AI instruments and underlings.

Dead Reckoning in Online Games

Finally, there are ways to use dead reckoning to mitigate the effects of network latency in a multiplayer online game [Aronson97]. Aronson's method incorporates the following steps:

1. Each player periodically broadcasts a packet containing his avatar's location, velocity, and acceleration.
2. During the intervals between packets, each machine runs a dead reckoning algorithm to compute the approximate positions and orientations of all other players.

3. When a new incoming packet from another player is received, the local state of the world is updated accordingly, and the process starts anew.

Since the information on which the dead reckoning calculations are based is perfect (because no one is actually trying to hide it), the discrepancies between real position and calculated position will remain small. This is the case as long as each participant broadcasts a new packet reasonably often and the velocity of the objects isn't so high that any amount of error correction will be insufficient. Here, "reasonably often" is a relative term that depends on the game's domain. For naval warfare, where unit movement is slow and course changes take time, errors will accumulate so slowly that receiving one packet every five seconds might be sufficient for the calculations to appear flawless. In a jet fighter battle, however, the state of the world will have to be updated three to five times per second, or the errors will quickly become noticeable.

Inferring Goals

It is also possible to infer an agent's intention and goals from the type of observations that are made in this article [Huber93]. Huber represents the physical world as a quadtree in which cells can contain the locations of agents and of worthwhile objectives in the area. A belief network connects these locations, so that observation of an agent's position and trajectory over time can result in identification of its possible goals—and direct the observer's own interception strategy.

Correcting Errors

A fundamental issue in dead reckoning systems is that the translational error between the real position of an agent and the estimate provided by DR can become unbounded with time. However, it is possible to impose a constant bound on this error [Graves97], provided that an "evidence grid" (in other words, an a priori map of the features of the area being traversed) is available:

- The agent computing its own position examines its immediate surroundings, calculating a local short-term map.
- This short-term map is compared with the a priori map using pattern recognition techniques.
- Small, incremental corrections are applied to the agent's trajectory on the fly.

Interestingly, when the a priori map contains imperfect information about the area, Graves' experiments show that adding a learning mechanism to modify the map during execution only provides marginal performance improvement. In a real-time scenario, such minimal improvement might not justify the cost in execution time or the implementation effort.

Conclusion

Dead reckoning is an easy way to predict the trajectories of objects. In a game context, it can be used by an AI trying to guess the behavior of a human player. It can also help an AI assistant provide a human commander with information similar to what could be obtained in the real world. In both cases, since the AI bases its decisions on information that is readily available to the human player, there is no appearance of cheating.

Better yet, since dead reckoning takes $O(n)$ time, where n is the number of objects tracked by the algorithm, and each object requires but a handful of arithmetic operations per time step, this more realistic behavior is obtained at very little cost in execution time.

References

[Aronson97] Aronson, Jesse, "Dead Reckoning: Latency Hiding for Networked Games," available online at *www.gamasutra.com/features/19970919/aronson_01. htm*, Sept. 19, 1997.

[Auxetrain03] United States Coast Guard Auxiliary training program, "Dead Reckoning," available online at *www.auxetrain.org/Nav1.html*, 2003.

[Borenstein94] Borenstein, Johann, "Internal Correction of Dead-Reckoning Errors with the Smart Encoder Trailer," *Proceedings of the International Conference on Intelligent Robots and Systems (IROS '94)*, 1994, pp. 127–134. Also available online at *www.eecs.umich.edu/~johannb/paper53.pdf*

[Graves97] Graves, Kevin, Adams, William, and Schultz, Alan, "Continuous Localization in Changing Environments," *1997 IEEE International Symposium on Computational Intelligence in Robotics and Automation*, 1997, available online at *citeseer.nj.nec.com/graves97continuou.html*

[Huber93] Huber, Marcus J., and Durfee, Edmund H., "Observational Uncertainty in Plan Recognition Among Interacting Robots," *Proceedings of the IJCAI Workshop on Dynamically Interacting Robots*, 1993, available online at *citeseer.nj.nec. com/huber93observational.html*

[NASA96] NASA Space Telerobotics Program, "Dead Reckoning for Walking Robots," 1996, available online at *ranier.hq.nasa.gov/telerobotics_page/Technologies/0403.html*

[Navigate99] Navigate! Society, "Dead Reckoning and Fixes," 1999, available online at *home.att.net/~agligani/navigation/dead.htm*

[Weisstein03] Weisstein, Eric, "Brownian Motion," 2003, available online at *scienceworld.wolfram.com/physics/BrownianMotion.html*

8.5

Building a Sports AI Architecture

Terry Wellmann—High Voltage Software

terry.wellmann@high-voltage.com

Real sports teams spend countless hours practicing together with two main goals in mind. The first is to improve the skills and abilities of the individual athletes. The second is to train a group of independently thinking individuals how to function as a cohesive unit. The key to success is to have individuals instinctively react to the current situation in a manner that is predictable by their teammates.

While simulating the abilities of an athlete is a simple, straightforward problem to solve, simulating cohesive group decision-making is considerably more difficult. This article focuses on the sport of basketball (with lessons from the *NBA Inside Drive* series [NBA02, NBA03, NBA04]); however, the concepts presented here are applicable to a wide variety of games. Hopefully with the help of this article you will gain a better understanding of the things to consider when building a sports AI architecture and you will have all of the tools necessary to successfully design an AI system that is easy to understand, build, maintain, and extend.

As you sit down to plan your AI architecture, keep the following goals in mind:

- Keep it simple. There is no need to add complexity to a system if it does not add to the user's experience.
- Break your decisions down into various levels of responsibility; do not try to do everything at one level.
- Spend some time planning your architecture. The more time and thought you put into it, the easier it will be to build.
- Do not be afraid of making mistakes. Developing AI is not easy to do, especially for sports games where the user knows all of the rules and is very familiar with how the sport is played.
- Do not underestimate the power of randomness. Randomness brings your AI to life and allows the user playing your game to observe behaviors that are more complex than they actually are.

Agent Plans

One of the first tasks in designing any sports game AI is to identify the high-level decisions your agents are going to have to make. For our purposes, we will be referring to these high-level decisions as plans. One very important thing to keep in mind here is to keep this breakdown simple and group the common decisions together. If you try to enumerate every decision that needs to be made, you will quickly end up with an overwhelming number of plans.

For the game of basketball, the plan list is straightforward. Examples of offensive, defensive, and shared plans include pass, shoot, drive to the basket, run the play, rescue a trapped ball handler, position the defender, double team the ball handler, steal the ball, intercept a pass, block a shot, take a charge, rebound, get set up for an inbound, get set up for a free throw, and so forth. For the purpose of this article, our focus is not on the details of any individual plan, but rather how the plan is a vital component in the architecture.

The following code example for the class `AgentPlan` shows what your basic plan functions are. The `AgentPlan` class serves as a base class for all plans. Each individual plan will have additional functions and state variables that are unique to the particular high-level decision being managed.

```
class AgentPlan
{
    ...
    float EvaluateInitiation();
    float EvaluateContinuation();
    void Initiate();
    void Update();
    ...
}
```

The `EvaluateInitiation()` function is responsible for evaluating how desirable it is for this plan to execute. The `EvaluateContinuation()` function is responsible for evaluating how desirable it is for the plan to continue to be used if it is currently executing. The `Initiate()` function is called to perform initialization or one-time decision-making each time the plan is initiated. The `Update()` function is called for every iteration of the agent's AI tick and is responsible for carrying out the plan.

Making the distinction between plan initiation and continuation is important, as you generally want to evaluate a different set of conditions to govern the use of the plan if it is currently being used.

One key thing to note about the `EvaluateInitiation()` and `Evaluate-Continuation()` functions is the fact that they return floating-point values. This small detail will allow you to build a complex system where several plans can be compared against each other to determine which one should be used for the current situation. As we will see in the *Team Management* section, it also provides a quick and easy way to expand your AI system with new plans, as each plan is essentially a building block in a complex system. Keep in mind that each plan is independently responsible for evaluating the current situation to determine how appropriate it is to be used—this is the real power of the plan.

While this type of decision-making is very powerful, be careful how you use it. You are going to want to establish a set of guidelines to make your development process smoother. In general, a good rule of thumb is to keep your evaluation values between −1.0 and 1.0. Only consider using or continuing to use a plan if the evaluation value is greater than or equal to 0.0. Sometimes, you need to strongly encourage or force the initiation of a plan, in these cases return a value larger than 1.0 for the EvaluateInitiation() function.

In practice, you will find that many of your plans do not need complex logic to determine if they should be used for a given situation, where other plans seem to be tightly interrelated. For the plans that are simple, returning an arbitrary positive value is sufficient, but keep in mind, the larger the value, the more likely the plan will be chosen. For the plans that seem to be interrelated, the best practice is to treat each decision without consideration for the others in the system; we discuss a better way to handle this type of decision-making resolution in the *Team Management* section.

Team Management

Now that you have identified several plans that will be responsible for making decisions for each agent, you need to design a way to organize them for the situations where they will be used. The game of basketball can easily be described as set of common states, offensive states, and defensive states, each with distinct responsibilities and clear transition points. Each state encapsulates a different goal and set of responsibilities that direct the overall goals of the AI agents in the game.

Using a finite-state machine provides a simple, yet powerful framework for your architecture. Each state is responsible for making team-level decisions that affect each of the AI agents. The core sets of states are the offensive and defensive states. These states mirror each other (e.g., there is an offensive inbound and a defensive inbound state) and are responsible for managing all aspects of game play that a user can interact with. The offensive and defensive states are as follows:

- **Inbound:** Responsible for getting the ball in play.
- **Transition:** Responsible for getting the ball into the frontcourt.
- **Frontcourt:** Responsible for managing the attempts to score.
- **Rebound:** Responsible for rebounding the ball after it has been shot.
- **Recover loose ball:** Responsible for recovering a ball that has been knocked loose or was not successfully rebounded in the air.
- **Free throw:** Responsible for managing the free throw attempts.

The common states are responsible for managing neutral situations where the ball is not in play and neither team is on offense or defense. They are as follows:

- **Pregame:** Coordinates the team and player introductions.
- **Tip-off:** Coordinates the tip-off.
- **Time-out:** Coordinates the time-out.
- **Quarter break:** Coordinates the breaks from quarter to quarter.
- **Substitution:** Coordinates the player substitutions.
- **Post game:** Coordinates post game celebrations.

Figure 8.5.1 shows the state organization and flow of the states previously described. You will notice that the main offensive and defensive states such as the transition, frontcourt, rebound, and recover loose ball form a complete circle and are able to run without additional interaction. The additional offensive and defensive states, as well as the common states are triggered based on a game event, such as a made shot, a foul, a violation, a time-out, or the end of a quarter.

Now that we have identified the various states of our system, we will take a closer look at the key responsibilities of a state. For purposes of this article, we are going to look at the frontcourt offense state, as it is the most complex. The following code listing shows key elements of the state.

```
class FrontCourtOffense : public TeamStateBase
{
    protected:
        enum TBallHandlerPlans
        {
            eBallHandlerShot,
            eBallHandlerPass,
            eBallHandlerDrive,
            eBallHandlerPlayMovement,
            ...
        };

        enum TNonBallHandlerPlans
        {
            eNonBallHandlerRescueBallHandler,
            eNonBallHandlerGetOpenForPass,
            eNonBallHandlerSetPick,
            eNonBallHandlerPlayMovement,
            ...
        };

    public:
        ...
        int Update(int);
        void ReInit(void);
        ...
};
```

The key elements of the FrontCourtOffense class are the two enumerated types that define a priority order for evaluating agent plans, and the update function.

The ReInit() function is called each time a state becomes active. This gives you an opportunity to make any one-time decisions such as picking a play and doing

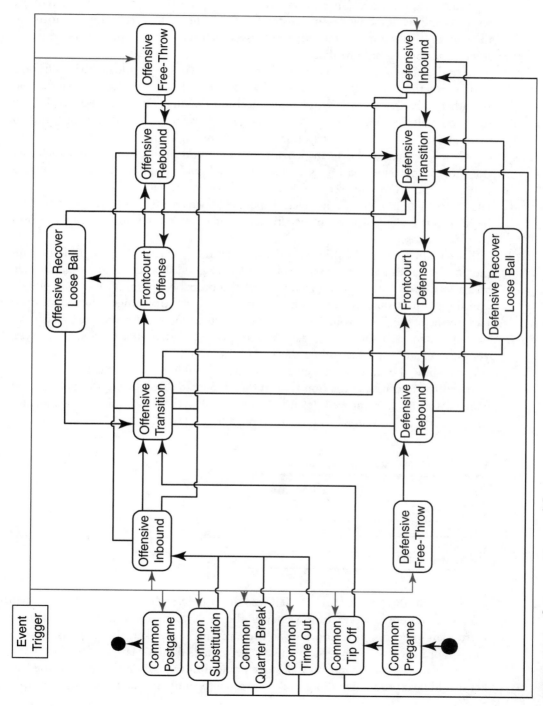

FIGURE 8.5.1 *State transitions and flow.*

general state re-initialization. The `Update()` function is called for every iteration of the AI tick and is responsible for executing the state logic. The simplest form of the `Update()` function is a loop that processes each AI agent on the team and determines what plan should be used.

For the sake of code simplicity, it is a good idea to break your logic into additional update functions (not shown)—one to handle the ball handler decision-making and the other to handle the non-ball handler decision-making. The main reason why you want to break the code up is that each function will work with a different set of agent plans and, as you will see shortly, it is easier to handle plan resolution.

When evaluating the agent plans, you want to do so in priority order such that the most important decision is evaluated first. Looking at the `TBallHandlerPlans` enumeration, you will see an order of `eBallHandlerShot`, `eBallHandlerPass`, `eBallhandlerDrive`, and finally `eBallhandlerPlayMovement`. This order is important because in the event that two plans return an equal evaluation value, the higher-priority plan is chosen.

Sometimes, using the priority order for plan resolution is not enough. For example, imagine a situation where the ball handler is a good shooter, he just stole the ball, and has an open breakaway down the court. You probably do not want him to pull up and shoot a jump shot as soon as he gets into good shooting range if he has an open path to the basket. You would prefer him to continue to drive toward the basket until he can execute a higher percentage dunk or lay-up. To handle situations like these, you need to add some additional checks to your evaluation loop.

Handling the aforementioned example is simple if you assume that the drive plan only returns a positive evaluation value if the player can drive toward the basket—this generally means he's not well defended. For the sake of this example, we will assume the plan evaluation values as shown in Table 8.5.1.

Table 8.5.1   Plan Evaluation Values

Plan	Plan Evaluation Value
Shot Plan	0.5
Pass Plan	−0.1
Drive Plan	0.1
Play Movement Plan	0.0

Based on the priority rule of plan resolution previously described, the shot plan would be chosen; however, from watching the AI perform, we realize that every time there is an opportunity to continue to drive toward the basket, the AI pulls up for a jump shot instead of going for the higher percentage dunk or lay-up. Since we know that the drive plan only returns a positive evaluation value if driving toward the basket would be a productive thing to do, we can add some simple if-then logic to override our plan selection.

The following pseudocode shows what the FrontCourtOffense::Update() logic is for evaluating and applying the best plan.

```
for (each plan to evaluate)
{
    // get the proper evaluation value
    if (planToCheck == currentPlan)
    {
        evalValue = EvaluateContinuation();
    }
    else
    {
        evalValue = EvaluateInitiation();
    }

    // is the current plan the best option?
    // this is simple priority order plan selection
    if (evalValue > bestEvalValue)
    {
        bestEvalValue = evalValue;
        bestPlan = currentPlan;
    }
    // handle situations the priority method can't
    // this check handles cases where we may want to
    // override the shot plan
    else if (bestEvalValue > 0.0f && bestPlan == shot)
    {
        // is the drive plan a valid option?
        if (currentPlan == drive && evalValue > 0.0f)
        {
            // set the best plan to drive, but
            // leave the bestEval value set to
            // its current value
            bestPlan = drive;
        }
    }
}

// if the best plan is the current plan, update it
// otherwise initiate the new plan
if (bestPlan == currentPlan)
{
    currentPlan->Update();
}
else
{
    currentPlan->vInitiate();
}
```

While the brute-force method just described for picking a plan is not as nice as we would like, it is a necessary evil that will help keep the individual plans much simpler, as they don't need to take into account the responsibilities of other plans—this achieves one of our primary goals when building an AI system: keep the plans simple.

This method of plan resolution also pushes the decision-making up to a higher level, the team management level, where more knowledge about the overall situation is known. Once again, this helps to achieve a primary objective by building a simple, easy-to-maintain AI system.

Agent AI

Now that we have identified our key plans and have organized them into states, we have the ability to make high-level decisions that are appropriate to the situation. As previously mentioned, our agent plans are responsible for evaluating the current situation and determining how appropriate it is for the plan to be used, but we never discussed how that decision was made. Continuing our theme of separating the logic into different levels of responsibility, we will tackle the last piece of the high-level AI architecture: the agent AI.

The agent AI level is nothing more than a well thought-out collection of utility functions and data used by the plans to evaluate and execute the thing they represent. If we take a closer look at the requirements for the shot plan, we quickly see that we need three things. The first thing is a way to determine what the potential success chance is of the player making the shot from his current location on the court. The second thing is to determine what type of a shot should be performed, such as a jump shot, dunk or a lay-up. The third thing is a way to tell the player to perform the selected shot with the specified success chance.

Determining a player's success chance is straightforward. First, you need to determine the best chance of success based on the player's skill and abilities, which are easily represented by ratings values. Next, you need to determine if any penalties need to be applied. Penalties can consider a variety of factors, but in the case of shooting success, the biggest one is the defensive pressure on the shooter. The better he is defended, the harder it will be for him to get a good shot off.

When picking the type of shot to perform, you first want to evaluate the likelihood that the player will attempt a dunk. If the dunk cannot be performed because the player is too far from the basket, he does not have a clear path to the basket, or he physically cannot dunk, you want to check to see if he can do a lay-up. The necessary checks to determine if the player can do a lay-up are similar to the ones used for a dunk, except you do not need to worry about the player's ability, as every basketball player is able to perform them. Finally, if the checks to perform a dunk or lay-up fail, your last option is to perform a jump shot.

The final elements of the high-level agent AI are the command issuing functions. These functions serve two main purposes. The primary purpose is to provide a place within the high-level AI to make any decisions that require more thought or logic than a simple random number. An example of this type of decision would be determining what classification of dunks could be attempted; for example, making the decision whether a player can perform a flashy dunk such as a 360, or having him stick to the basic dunks. The secondary purpose of these functions is to provide a wrapper to the agent mechanics that we will discuss shortly. By isolating the code responsible for issuing commands to the agent mechanics, you make it very easy to refine and add additional information to the command being given without being forced to touch a lot of code.

Agent Mechanics

The final piece of your AI architecture is the agent mechanics system. We consider the mechanics system as low-level AI, but do not let this classification confuse you about its overall importance. Without it, you have no way to move players around the court to do the things the high-level AI wants them to do. The mechanics system is something beyond the scope of this article, but we will touch on a few key points.

The primary purpose of the mechanics system is to manage and select the animations that are used. Additionally, the mechanics system is allowed to make simple decisions that require nothing more than a random number. It is important to understand this distinction, as it will keep your overall AI architecture clean and easier to maintain. By restricting all critical decision-making that requires knowledge of the situation or access to player skills and attributes ratings to the high-level, you keep your AI code cleaner and easier to maintain.

When designing your mechanics system, think about the types of commands you would want to give to someone who knows nothing about the game of basketball but could follow directions if they were clear and concise. Some of the commands on your list would include walk, jog, run, stand, stumble, fall, pass, catch, pick up ball, shoot, steal, rebound, block, and so forth. Breaking the commands down in this fashion makes it easy to interface the high-level and low-level AI systems.

Conclusion

Sports, in general, present a unique set of challenges to AI programmers. The rules are well defined and allow little room for creativity. Professional athletes have personalities and playing styles that are recognized by millions of fans. The goal of the AI programmer is to provide the user with an interactive experience that captures the abilities, personalities, and emotions of the athletes being simulated.

The concepts we discussed here with agent plans, team management, agent AI, and agent mechanics can be applied to any sport and a broad range of games. For example, plans could easily be chained together to produce more complex decisions or could be responsible for controlling a large number of agents in a strategy game. Do not be afraid to experiment with these concepts and mold them into something that suits your needs.

Remember, AI development is all about good planning and trial and error. Experienced AI programmers will quickly tell you that they did not get it right the first time and they are always learning and discovering better ways to do things.

References

[NBA02] NBA Inside Drive 2002, *www.xbox.com/nbainsidedrive2002/*
[NBA03] NBA Inside Drive 2003, *www.xbox.com/nbainsidedrive2003/*
[NBA04] NBA Inside Drive 2004, *www.xbox.com/nbainsidedrive2004/*

SCRIPTING

9.1

Optimized Script Execution

Alex Herz—Lionhead Ltd.

aherz@lionhead.com

Today's games require stunning graphics to attract players. Most of the CPU time (usually far more than 50 percent) is spent displaying impressive visuals. Another big portion of the processing time must be dedicated to physics calculations to enable the player to interact with this world. Finally, any cycles left are used for AI. Therefore, complex AI calculations must be distributed over many frames to minimize the CPU load during any particular frame. The faster your AI is executed, the more non-player characters (NPCs) your game can support and the more impressive each will be.

Many AI implementations incorporate runtime interpreted scripts in one form or another. Increasing the script interpretation speed will be highly beneficial to the overall AI performance for these systems. This article shows several methods to increase the script execution speed up to full CPU speed (~one script instruction per CPU cycle). By avoiding just-in-time (JIT) compilation, it won't be necessary to actually compile down to native code, which would require a dedicated backend for each possible target platform.

Script Opcode Post Optimization Using Patterns

Custom script compilers tend to produce highly unoptimized code. Many developers are weary of compile time optimizations because they tend to require resource management customized for the target machine. Another reason is that the complexity of the compiler debugging and verification increases dramatically with optimized code. Simple, unoptimized code can be generated and tested with far less effort.

This section presents an easy way to speed up the script execution of unoptimized code without customizing to the target platform and without complicating debugging. The main strategy will be to reduce the number of instructions used. Another key strategy will be to keep a clear separation between the compiler and optimizer. This will aid in the development of the optimizer because the compiler generated code can be validated before being passed to the optimizer. Any errors found in the code output of the optimizer must have been added in the optimizer stage.

If your script system supports debug information, you will want to separate the optimization stage from the actual compilation, as well. Optimizers often change the layout of the code to take advantage of specific features of the target machine. This invalidates the coherency between the machine code, the debug information, and the high-level language, as well as many assumptions a debugger can make about the code. Therefore, it should be possible to generate an unoptimized version for debugging purposes by bypassing the optimizer stage.

When looking at the "assembly" output of your compiler you will find many patterns.

Generally, the compiler will generate the same code pattern to load the address of a variable, call a function, and so forth. For some special cases it might be viable to revisit the portion of the compiler that creates the corresponding code. For other situations, like loading the address of a variable, the code cannot be optimized at compile time. The compiler does not know how the address is going to be used later in the code or if it can merge the address load with another instruction. The result is that your compiler will unnecessarily recalculate/load addresses that have just been used, mainly because it must take the most conservative stance and make no assumptions.

By knowing your "assembly" language, you will be able to find repetitive or very similar pieces of compiler-generated code that could easily be merged into a more efficient form. After finishing the script compilation, an optimizer can scan the file for the opcode combinations (or patterns) you identify and replace them with an optimized version.

In the same run, it can check if there are addresses that are calculated several times. After the first address calculation, the address should be saved in a spare register, and all matching address calculations should be replaced by a reference to the register.

These methods might shorten your code by up to 50 percent. That is half the amount of script opcodes to parse and execute. Therefore, your script will run at almost twice the speed (assuming decoding script opcodes is the bottleneck of your virtual machine [VM]).

Optimizing Non-Branched, Constant Scripts

Non-branched scripts consist of a list of commands that are executed in the order stated from beginning to end, every time the script is run. We assume for this section that the script does not refer to any non-constant data, or in other words, no variables used in the script will change. In real-world applications, most scripts will contain branches and will refer to non-constant data. Therefore, later sections of this article will show how to transform any script into a non-branched static script, such that the optimizations presented here can be applied to any script. Furthermore, this technique requires that your script implementation allows calling native (CPU opcode compiled) functions. Normally, native function calls are used to pass all game-relevant data back to the game.

If a script is known to be non-branching and constant, all of the native function calls can be intercepted inside the VM [Berger02]. Each intercepted call is stored as a function pointer along with all of the arguments for that specific function in a big list called the *execute list*. Because of the constant nature of the script, the arguments passed to the functions will remain the same every time the script is executed, and the order in which the functions are executed is constant as well because there is no branching. The next time the script is executed, the VM can traverse the execute list instead of interpreting the script opcodes again.

For each item in the execute list, the function arguments are pushed onto the stack of the native application corresponding to the calling convention of the native function. Afterward, the function pointer is called. Obviously, the stack has to be restored afterward.

An easy way to accomplish this on an x86 machine is to save a copy of the stack pointer in a static variable before pushing the arguments and later copying the old value back. This method will satisfy the __cdecl and __stdcall conventions for win-tel C/C++ code. Functions with different calling conventions must be handled differently. For the sake of simplicity, the script can be restricted to __cdecl and __stdcall conventions. If a class's member function is defined as __cdecl, then the function can be called like a normal __cdecl function after the "this" pointer has been pushed as the first argument. If no calling convention is applied to a member function, then a compiler-specific convention is used.

Running an execute list has hardly any overhead compared to running native code and will outperform most JIT compilations because all of the irrelevant operations are discarded automatically. This solution is far less error prone and straightforward to implement, even for already implemented scripting systems.

Optimizing Branched Scripts

Branched scripts are scripts with conditional jumps that can't be predicted at compile time. Depending on memory constraints, a branched script can be turned into a non-branched constant script (see next section) or it has to be interpreted. In the latter case, the execution speed depends on both the time needed to decode a script opcode and the time needed to execute it. Generally, decoding takes far more time, as an input stream must be parsed; whereas executing the command directly translates into a few native opcodes.

When compiling the script into script opcodes, the compiler outputs an encoded stream of binary data [Berger02]. Using a *jump table* can radically decrease the time needed to decode this stream when the script is executed. The jump table contains the offset of the native opcodes executing a certain script opcode. Using a jump table, the compiler can output a stream of addresses instead of encoded instructions.

When running the script, the VM merely needs to read the next address from the compiled script into the instruction pointer of the CPU. As the address points to a piece of native code that executes the specific script instruction, there is no need to decode the compiler-generated instruction.

The time needed to decode a script opcode is reduced to a memory read followed by an unconditional jump (about two to three cycles on most Intel machines).

Assuming Intel 386 functionality of the VM, the worst-case script opcode execution time will average about 15 CPU cycles for commands with an indirection using a jump table, as shown in the following example.

Example (decoded script assembly command):

```
mov [vm_reg0],vm_reg1
```

Actions performed by the VM to execute this script command (using x86 asm):

```
; get content of virtual machine register 0 into eax
mov eax, [ecx+0]    ; ecx points to the table of
                    ; virtual machine registers,
                    ; approx. 3 cycles
; get content of virtual machine register 1 into ebx
mov ebx, [ecx+4]    ; approx. 3 cycles

; solve the indirection required by the sample opcode
mov [eax], ebx      ; approx. 3 cycles

; increment our virtual machine's instruction pointer
add edx,4           ; edx points the script opcodes
                    ; approx. 1 cycle

; transfer program control to the next opcode handler
jump [edx]          ; approx. 3 cycles
```

Using this technique, most of the time is actually spent executing the script opcode rather than parsing it. To gain even more speed, the stack pointer can be set to point to the VM's stack segment, and the native push and pop instructions can be used to implement stack operations.

Unfortunately, this method has one big drawback: it highly restricts the flexibility of the VM. There must be a unique implementation (jump table value) for each script opcode combination (the previous example shows the execution of one sample script opcode combination). Although most of the VM could be auto generated by a custom tool, you still have to restrict the number of possible opcode combinations to a viable number. The biggest factor here is the number of registers available. If all registers can be combined with each other, you will have a minimum of $(n_{commands} * n_{registers}!)$ script opcode combinations. If the number of opcode combinations cannot be reduced to a viable amount, then a hybrid between opcode parsing and the jump table method can be used. In this technique, a jump table entry is generated for a group of opcode combinations, and the compiler places another piece of opcode after the jump table entry. This additional piece encodes exactly which opcode combination the compiler is referring to.

In summary, the best results are achieved if pure jump table opcodes are used for the most commonly executed instructions. A combined jump table/parse approach for the less common commands should be used to minimize the size of the jump table.

One final note: The script opcodes (jump table values) change whenever the VM's code is changed, so all scripts must be recompiled after the VM has been modified.

Compiling Branched Scripts into Non-Branched Scripts

As shown previously, execute lists are a convenient way to increase script opcode execution speed for static scripts without the need of writing a JIT compiler for all target platforms. This section describes how to compile dynamic scripts into static ones, so the same optimizations can be applied. Furthermore, this process is useful if the target platform is not a VM but a real-world processor that doesn't support any type of branching (like pixel and vertex shaders on GeForce3 or 4 class cards).

The following example illustrates a branched script function defining a response for when a "Monster" sees or hears the player. In addition to the player position (a 3D vector called "pos"), the function has two arguments indicating how the "Monster" senses the player.

```
Monster::PlayerSpotted(bool hear_player,
                       bool see_player, float* pos)
{
    if(!see_player)
    {
        if(hear_player)
        {
            //we have heard something..check out
            //situation..keep an eye on the place
            FocusAttention(pos); //native function
        }
        else
        {
            //someone told us about the
            //player (monster friend or so)
            //let's help our friends
            WalkTo(pos); //native function
        }
    }
    else
    {
        //we can see the enemy..let's kill him!
        ShootAt(pos); //native function
    }
}
```

This simple example shows a script function that includes branching based on external arguments. To make this a static script, the compiler generates several versions of it. All of the branching is dependant on the two Boolean function arguments. Each Boolean has two possible states, true and false. Thus, there are 2^2 possible combinations of the two arguments.

The compiler generates the code for each possibility and removes the branching code in each case. The code for hear_player = true and see_player = false would be reduced to:

```
Monster::PlayerSpotted(bool hear_player=true,
                       bool see_player=false,
                       float* pos)
{
    FocusAttention(pos);
}
```

This leaves us with a very short and non-branched script that can be optimized using execute lists.

Runtime Evaluation for Execute Lists

When using execute lists, all references to non-constant data will be lost because the list only stores the data actually passed to a native function the first time the script is executed. Therefore, if the script dereferences an indirection to a pointer and passes the dereferenced value to a function, then the actual dereferencing will take place only once when the script is parsed and turned into an execute list. Every time the execute list is executed, the value stored in the list (and not the value the pointer currently points to) is passed as a function argument.

This problem can be solved by passing pointers to all native functions called by the script and having the function solve the indirection. Unfortunately, this leads to additional problems and performance penalties because each native function has to verify the passed pointer and dereference it, even if just a constant value was passed.

Runtime Indirection

A *runtime indirection* can deliver an elegant way to get around the previously presented problems. As the execute list stores nothing but function pointers and arguments, the compiler has to express any operation that is vital to the script in terms of calls to native functions.

To have a pointer dereferenced (which is passed to a function stored in an execute list) at runtime, the VM must supply a native function that takes the pointer as an argument, dereferences the pointer, and replaces the old argument stored in the execute list with the result. The script compiler has to output a call to this function rather than placing script opcodes to dereference the pointer in the binary output stream. This compiler generated function call will be stored in the execute list so that the operation is not lost.

The execute list must be expanded to store information whether the function arguments use a runtime indirection or the plain value from the arguments stored in the execute list. This helps the VM decide where to acquire the argument from.

Runtime Branching

The branching inside a script that depends on external arguments can be removed by compiling different versions of a script, as shown previously. If a script contains branching based on local variables or member variables, a different method must be applied, as insufficient information about these conditions is available at compile time.

As shown in the previous section, all critical operations must be expressed using native function calls in order to convert them into an execute list. Therefore, another native function is supplied by the VM, which evaluates Boolean expressions and changes the execution order of the execute list depending on the result of this function.

The script compiler uses this function to solve all non-predictable branches to make the script execute list compatible.

Conclusion

This article showed how a dedicated script compiler in conjunction with a VM can produce script code that requires little or no parsing at runtime. When using an execute list (neglecting the time spent to copy function arguments from the execute list to the stack), the overall performance of the script code should be almost equivalent to natively compiled code.

References

[Berger02] Berger, Lee, "Scripting: The Interpreter Engine," *AI Game Programming Wisdom*, Charles River Media, 2002.

9.2

Advanced Script Debugging

Alex Herz—Lionhead Ltd.

aherz@lionhead.com

Today's demand for even better non-player character (NPC) behavior requires scripts with increased complexity. Most existing script systems, however, support a rather poor debug mechanism, if any. This is insufficient to create bug-free and highly complex scripts for NPCs. Formerly, proper debugging support for scripts has been considered a dream [Tozour02]. Now, this dream becomes reality.

This article shows how to create a custom debugger for a Win32-based, virtual machine (VM) driven script system. This custom debugger includes the following capabilities:

- Breakpoints
- Variable watch
- Register watch
- Memory watch
- Call stack
- Step-by-step execution in assembly
- Step-by-step execution in high-level scripting language

These enhanced debug capabilities will lead to shorter development times of complex scripts, as errors inside the scripts can be tracked down and corrected far quicker.

Exchanging Debug Information

Your debugger needs to communicate with the VM to retrieve debug information. An easy way to establish this communication on a Win32 system is to use the debug support provided by the operating system.

Debugging a Process

To start debugging, the debugger creates a new process that uses the VM to execute scripts (a game running scripts, for example) using the `CreateProcess()` function. The `DEBUG_PROCESS` parameter has to be passed to the function in order to receive debug events from this process:

```
STARTUPINFO                    si;
PROCESS_INFORMATION            pi;
si.cb                = sizeof (si);
si.lpReserved        = NULL;
si.lpDesktop         = NULL;
si.lpTitle           = NULL;
si.dwX               = 0;
si.dwY               = 0;
si.dwXSize           = 0;
si.dwYSize           = 0;
si.dwXCountChars     = 0;
si.dwYCountChars     = 0;
si.dwFillAttribute   = 0;
si.dwFlags           = 0;
si.wShowWindow       = 0;
si.cbReserved2       = 0;
si.lpReserved2       = NULL;

// create debug process on module name
if (!CreateProcess (executable,//path to exe
    parameters,//commandline for the exe
     (LPSECURITY_ATTRIBUTES)NULL,
     (LPSECURITY_ATTRIBUTES)NULL,
     FALSE,
     DEBUG_PROCESS| CREATE_NEW_CONSOLE,
     NULL,
     path,//working directory for exe
     &si,
     &pi))
     {
         Error("Failed to start debug process");
     }

//close unused handles
CloseHandle(pi.hThread);
CloseHandle(pi.hProcess);
```

How to handle the debug events is shown in the next code listing.

The VM and the debugger act like a client/server system where the client (the VM) sends string messages to the server (the debugger). The VM sends all messages (like a breakpoint hit) using the OutputDebugString() function. When OutputDebugString() is called by a process that is being debugged, the WaitForDebugEvent() function returns OUTPUT_DEBUG_STRING_EVENT to the debugging application.

The following code listing shows an example loop that processes the most important debug events, including the OUTPUT_DEBUG_STRING_EVENT. The reaction to this event is handled inside the HandleVirtualMachineEvent() function, which we discuss in more detail later. This loop should be executed in a separate thread to keep the debugger from stalling while waiting for debug events.

```
DWORD      n_processes=0;
bool       b_finished=0;
HANDLE     ProcessHandle =
OpenProcess(PROCESS_ALL_ACCESS,NULL,pi.dwProcessId);
//pi.dwProcessId returned by CreateProcess()
//acquire read/write permission
while(!b_finished)
{
    DEBUG_EVENT DebugEv;
    //doesn't return before another debug event was
    //created by the application being debugged
    WaitForDebugEvent(&DebugEv, INFINITE);

    DWORD dwContinueStatus = DBG_CONTINUE;
    //examine the debug event
    switch (DebugEv.dwDebugEventCode)
    {
        case EXCEPTION_DEBUG_EVENT:
        //pass any exception back to the VM
        dwContinueStatus=DBG_EXCEPTION_NOT_HANDLED;
        break;
        case CREATE_PROCESS_DEBUG_EVENT:
            n_processes++;
        break;
        case EXIT_PROCESS_DEBUG_EVENT:
        //keep track of the processes so we can stop
        //debugging when the last one has exited
            n_processes--;
            if(!n_processes)b_finished=true;
        break;
        case LOAD_DLL_DEBUG_EVENT:
        //close new handle to avoid locking the file
            CloseHandle(DebugEv.u.LoadDll.hFile);
        break;
        case OUTPUT_DEBUG_STRING_EVENT:
        //handle events send by the virtual machine
        HandleVirtualMechineEvent(ProcessHandle
        ,DebugEv);
        break;
    }
    //allow the debugged application to continue
    //running until the next debug event occurs
    ContinueDebugEvent(DebugEv.dwProcessId,
    DebugEv.dwThreadId, dwContinueStatus);
}
CloseHandle(ProcessHandle);//close the handle
```

Interacting with the VM

Using the `ProcessHandle` and the `DebugEv` parameters passed to `HandleVirtualMachi-neEvent()`, the string sent by the VM using `OutputDebugString()` is acquired from the VM's process memory using `ReadProcessMemory()`:

```
void HandleVirtualMachineEvent(HANDLE handle, DEBUG_EVENT DebugEv)
    {
            //alloc the string
char* VM_MSG = (char*)
malloc(DebugEv.u.DebugString.nDebugStringLength+1);

            DWORD size;
            //read from VM's memory
bool success = ReadProcessMemory(ProcessHandle,
DebugEv.u.DebugString.lpDebugStringData,
VM_MSG,DebugEv.u.DebugString.nDebugStringLength, &size);

            if(success)
            {
//NULL delimit it
VM_MSG[DebugEv.u.DebugString.nDebugStringLength] =0;

//Parse the string message send by the
//virtual machine and react to it!

            }
            }
```

Generally, `ReadProcessMemory()` enables the debugger to read from the memory of the debugged application. `WriteProcessMemory()` is allowed to write into the process memory of a process that was opened with write permission.

Now that the debugger is able to receive events from the VM, it can react to exceptions raised by the VM. Using a simple text-based protocol, the VM can notify the debugger of access violations, breakpoints, and other information.

Information to be passed to the VM is written into the VM's process memory. The VM needs to provide memory buffers the debugger can write into. In addition, the debugger needs to know where these memory buffers are. Therefore, the VM sends the addresses of these buffers to the debugging application. The following example shows how to create a buffer and how to send the required information to the debugging application.

```
DWORD*      BreakLineBuffer=new DWORD[MAX_BREAK_BUF];
char        info[255]="";
sprintf(info,"BreakLineBufferAddress: %d, Len: %d", BreakLineBuffer,
MAX_BREAK_BUF*sizeof(DWORD));
OutputDebugString(info);
```

The debugger parses the string sent using `OutputDebugString()` to acquire the size and address (inside the VM's process memory) of the buffer. Obviously, any protocol of your choice can by applied when sending the information. Using this information and `WriteProcessMemory()`, the VM's buffer can be filled from the debugging application.

Setting Breakpoints

When the VM's process is started, it sends the addresses of the internal list of breakpoint lines and the address of the breakpoint counter to the debugging application. Using these addresses and `WriteProcessMemory()`, the breakpoints used by the VM can be updated whenever the user of the debugger activates or deactivates a breakpoint in the source code.

As the breakpoint counter is updated from the debugger, the VM simply reads the value of the breakpoint counter while decoding the script instructions, and checks if the currently executed instruction corresponds to one of the entries in the breakpoint list. When this occurs, a breakpoint exception is sent to the debugger using `OutputDebugString()`, which includes the source file and line where the exception was raised.

Normally, the debugger responds to this breakpoint event by loading the specified source file and marking the source code line given.

Note: Debuggers for native binaries normally inject a piece of code that raises an interrupt at the location they want to place a breakpoint. The `__asm int 3` instruction raises a breakpoint exception that would be caught in the debug loop shown previously, although it would need to be handled in a different way. Generally, native debuggers work in the same way as the debugger presented in this article, but they communicate using the exceptions provided by the operating system rather than using `OutputDebugString()`.

Additional debug information must be included in the binary script file, in order to match up the correct script instructions with the exact file and line of the breakpoints in the debugger.

Enhancing the Tool Pipeline for Debug Support

To be able to debug a script, additional information needs to be stored in the compiled script binary. A link from the compiled script to the original source files is required to upload the files to the Integrated Development Environment (IDE) used to debug the script (aka the debugger). Step-by-step execution requires a link from each source code line to the opcodes generated for that line of code. Using this link, the VM can match script instructions to certain script code files and lines.

Debug Information

An easy way to include the file and line information (required to add high-level breakpoints to the VM) is to have the script compiler output two numeric identifiers after each script instruction (this corresponds to the program database used to debug native applications). These identifiers encode the source file and line from which the instruction was generated. The file identifier is an index into a table also stored in the compiled script file, which contains a list of all files used to generate the script. The line identifier simply represents the source line number.

This information should be generated only if the script is compiled in debug mode. In release mode, the information is omitted to speed up the script opcode parsing.

As a result, the compiled script needs to include information whether the debug information is available so that the VM can skip parsing the debug information if it is unavailable. If it is available, the VM reads the file and line identifiers after each script opcode and matches them against the breakpoint tables.

Handling Breakpoints

To guarantee that the VM and the IDE use the same file identifiers, the VM must send the file identifiers along with the filenames to the IDE, before running the script. Using this information, the IDE can set up the VM internal breakpoint tables properly using `WriteProcessMemory()`.

Variable Watch

To support variable watching, the compiled script needs to store a table of all variables used when the script was compiled, including their scopes and relative addresses.

This table is sent to the IDE when the script is loaded along with address of the loaded script's data segment and the address of the VM's stack pointer. Using this information, the IDE is able to calculate the address of any variable. The variable's relative address is looked up in the debug information table (DIT) previously sent by the VM and added to the address of either the data segment (for global variables) or to the contents of the VM's stack pointer for both local variables and function arguments (assuming an Intel x86 similar VM structure). Whether a variable is stored globally or relative to the stack pointer is determined from the variable's scope stored in the DIT.

To be able to view members of structs or classes, the DIT should include the relative address of all members. These can then be simply added to the class' or struct's address, calculated using the method presented in the last paragraph. The actual value is obtained from the calculated address using `ReadProcessMemory()`.

Call Stack

By storing the relative addresses of all functions in the DIT and having the VM send the address of the code segment and the address of the VM's instruction pointer, the IDE can calculate the name of the function currently being executed. The VM sends an additional event every time a script function is called or exited. Using these events and the DIT, the IDE can keep track of the current call stack.

Step-by-Step Execution

To support step-by-step execution, the VM needs to be capable of running in different modes. In "normal mode," the VM simply keeps executing script instructions until the script is finished or an exception occurs, which is sent to the IDE. In this mode, only an error like an access violation or a breakpoint stops the script execution.

Step-by-Step Assembly Execution

If the VM is set to "step-by-step assembly execution mode," then it sends a breakpoint exception after every script instruction decoded to the IDE. Normally, the IDE will read the instruction near the VM's instruction pointer (using `ReadProcessMemory()`), translate them into a human-readable format, and display them with the current instruction highlighted.

Register Watch

To be able to display the contents of the VM's registers, the VM needs to send the address of these registers at load time so that the IDE can update its knowledge of the register contents after having caught an exception. This mode can be used even if no debug information is available.

Memory Watch

When debugging a script at assembly level, a memory watch is handy. This can be implemented by having the VM send the address of the script's data segment to the IDE at load time. By reading this address when the IDE receives an exception, it can supply the user with a snapshot of the current memory layout.

Step-by-Step High-Level Execution

In "step-by-step high-level execution mode," the VM acts exactly as if it was in the "step-by-step assembly execution mode," with one exception. The breakpoint exception is sent only if the VM detects that the line or file debug information of the current instruction differs from the information of the previous executed instruction. This way, the IDE receives the breakpoint exception whenever a new source code line is about to be executed.

Step Over Execution

Using the "step-by-step high-level execution" mode presented in the previous section, the VM will step into each function call. Often, it is desired to step over a function call rather than into it. To accomplish this, the VM is set to "step over execution mode." In this mode, the VM operates just like in "step-by-step high-level execution mode," but does not throw a breakpoint exception if the call stack depth of the currently executed code differs from the call stack depth of the last thrown breakpoint exception.

Obviously, the "step over execution" needs to be implemented for both assembly and high-level modes. The IDE changes the current execution mode by writing to the address of the mode ID value inside the VM, which needs to be provided by the VM at load time. Therefore, whenever the VM has decoded an instruction, it checks for the current execution mode and generates the corresponding exceptions.

Conclusion

The methods presented to send debug events using `OutputDebugString()` from a VM to an IDE can be easily applied to any existing VM. In combination with any text-editing tool that is capable of running the debug loop, a powerful script IDE can be created.

In addition, being able to examine the current VM state together with an assembly-level view of the script binary is especially helpful to find and correct script compiler bugs.

References

[Tozour02] Tozour, Paul, "The Perils of AI Scripting," *AI Game Programming Wisdom*, Charles River Media, 2002.

9.3

Adding Error Reporting to Scripting Languages

Jeff Orkin—Monolith Productions

jorkin@blarg.net

Custom scripting languages are a controversial game development tool. Scripting languages empower nonprogrammers by moving game AI logic out of the C++ code. While this empowerment certainly comes with some risks (see "The Perils of AI Scripting" [Tozour02]), the benefits are that additional team members can create behaviors, designers can tweak AI more directly, and the AI logic is more accessible to the mod community. The most common complaint about scripting languages is that they are difficult to debug. This concern is exacerbated if nonprogrammers intend to write scripts. If the scripting language compiler or interpreter only gives feedback like "syntax error," nonprogrammers are not going to get very far. Fortunately, this problem is easily solved. The same techniques used to define the grammar of valid syntax can be used to identify and report scripting errors in plain English.

The most common and easiest way to create a scripting language interpreter or compiler is to use the tools Lex and Yacc (or the free Flex and Bison [Flex95, Bison95]). Lex is a lexical analyzer that tokenizes the script file. Yacc (an acronym for Yet Another Compiler Compiler) parses the script file for valid syntax, defined by a grammar provided by the developer. When Yacc comes across a sequence of tokens that do not match the patterns defined in the grammar, Yacc generates a syntax error. The key to providing scripters with valuable feedback about their errors is to tap into what Yacc is already doing.

This article gives step-by-step instructions for adding informative error reporting to a scripting language compiler developed with Lex and Yacc. It is assumed that the reader has a general familiarity with the process of developing a language with Lex and Yacc. The sample language was developed with MKS Lex and Yacc [MKS95], but these techniques should be valid with any version of Lex and Yacc, or Flex and Bison. These same steps could be taken to add error reporting to an interpreter, rather than a compiler. The result of these steps is a compiler that outputs errors as informative as those found in a mature compiler like Microsoft Visual C++®.

A Simple Language

The language developed for this article is named Simple, as it is intentionally simplistic. The complete Simple language Lex and Yacc input files, and C++ files for a compiler framework that uses their output can be found on the CD-ROM accompanying this book. This article highlights relevant excerpts.

The syntax for Simple follows C/C++ syntax, and the language has only a handful of features. Scripts can:

- Declare local variables
- Assign integer values to variables
- Add and subtract values
- Compare values with '>' and '<'
- Check "if" statements
- Call game-engine functions (with no parameters, again for simplicity)

The language is limited enough to fully define within the pages of this article, yet still offers plenty of opportunity for users to write invalid scripts. A valid Simple script might look like this:

```
int x;
int y;
y = 0;
x = SomeFunction() - 5;
if( x > OtherFunction() )
    y = 3;
```

As minimal as this script looks, imagine all of the things that could have gone wrong. Let's list everything that could go wrong, and then determine how to catch each of these errors and report them to the user in an easily understood manner.

- Semicolons could be omitted.
- Parentheses could be omitted.
- Unrecognized characters could be included.
- Unrecognized keywords could be included.
- Functions could be misspelled.
- Undeclared variables could be used.
- Variables could be declared more than once.

Each of these errors is easy enough to make due to typos, copying and pasting, or unfamiliarity with the correct syntax. The compiler should be able to report each of these problems illustrated in the following invalid script:

```
int x;
int x;
y = 0;
x = SomeFuncion() - 5
If( x , OtherFunction()
    y = 3;
```

Lex and Simple.l

Valid tokens for the Simple language are defined in Simple.l, as shown in the following code listing:

```
// Look up text in symbol table. Return the
// type as VARIABLE, FUNCTION, or a key word.
// If this is a new variable, add it to the table.
[a-zA-Z_][a-zA-Z0-9_:]* {
        return CCompiler::LookUpSymbol(yytext, VARIABLE);
        }

// Recognize strings of digits as integers.
-?[0-9]+ {
        yylval.ivalue = (int) strtol(yytext, (char **) 0,
                    *yytext=='0' ? 8 : 10);
        return INTEGER;
        }

// Recognize specific characters.
[-()<>=+;] {
        return yylval.ivalue = *yytext;
        }

// Skip white space.
[ \t\n]+     ;
```

The preceding code tells Lex about recognizable characters and strings of characters. Strings of digits form integers. Strings of letters and digits form symbol names. The compiler looks up symbol names in its symbol table to determine if the symbol is a variable name, function name, or keyword. If the compiler cannot find a matching keyword or function name in the symbol table, it assumes that the string is a variable name. This point will be important later.

Yacc and Simple.y

Valid syntax for the language is provided to Yacc in the grammar defined in Simple.y, as shown here:

```
// Declare variables before the rest of the code.
program:
      program declaration
    | program statement { CCompiler::GenerateCode($2);}
    | program error ';'  { yyerrok(); }
    | /* NULL */
    ;

// Declare a local variable.
declaration:
    INT_TYPE VARIABLE ';'
        { CCompiler::DeclareVar($1, $2); }
    ;
```

```
// Define valid statements.
statement:
     simplestatement ';'
   | IF '(' expression ')' statement
     { $$ = new CNode(IF,$3,$5); }
   | function ';'
   ;

simplestatement:
     VARIABLE '=' expression
       { $$ = new CNode('=', new CNode(VARIABLE, $1),
         $3); }
   ;

// Call a function.
function:
     FUNCTION '(' ')'
       { $$ = new CNode(FUNCTION, $1); }
   ;

// Define an expression.
expression:
     INTEGER { $$ = new CNode(INTEGER,    $1); }
   | VARIABLE      { $$ = new CNode(VARIABLE,    $1); }
   | function
   | expression '+' expression
     { binary: $$ = new CNode($2, $1, $3); }
   | expression '-' expression        { goto binary; }
   | expression '<' expression        { goto binary; }
   | expression '>' expression        { goto binary; }
   | '(' expression ')'        { $$ = $2; }
   ;
```

A script can contain any number of variable declarations, followed by any number of statements. A statement can be an assignment, function call, or "if" statement. An assignment or "if" statement can contain expressions. An expression can be an integer, variable, function call, or a pair of expressions joined by a mathematical or comparison operator.

Reporting Errors with `yyerror()`

Running Lex and Yacc with the input files Simple.l and Simple.y produces C++ code and header files for the parser and scanner that get compiled into the Simple language's compiler. The code generated by Lex and Yacc parses a script and scans for recognized sequences of tokens. When an unrecognized sequence is encountered, the scanner calls a member function called `yyerror()`. The function `yyerror()` prints "syntax error" to standard output.

The default behavior of `yyerror()` is not ideal. The error is vague, and printing errors to standard output prevents them from being logged, or displayed within another application. Fortunately, the default `yyerror()` function can be overridden with a more useful version. This is accomplished by deriving a custom scanner class from the one Lex produces, and overriding the default `yyerror()` function.

```
void yyerror(char *fmt, ...)
{
   va_list va;
   va_start(va, fmt);

   // Print a formatted error message.
   (void) vfprintf(m_pErrorFile, fmt, va);

   // Print a copy of the offending line.
   char buff[1000];
   GetLine(yylineno-1, buff);
   fprintf(m_pErrorFile,
      "\t%d: %s\n", yylineno, buff);
   va_end(va);
}
```

The enhanced `yyerror()` prints a formatted error message to a specified error file, complete with the line number and a copy of the offending line. The error file can be stored as a log, or displayed through another application, such as an IDE.

Identifying Specific Errors

If the Simple compiler is run on the invalid script that we created earlier, the first reported error will be:

```
Syntax error
4: x = SomeFuncion() - 5
```

This still does not tell us exactly what is wrong with this line of code, but at least narrows it down to which line has the problem. The next step is to identify specific errors, and pass more informative messages to `yyerror()`. Our goal is to get an error like this:

```
Error: Statements must end with ';'.
4: x = SomeFuncion() - 5
```

Unknown Character Errors

Lex is scanning each character and string of characters, to determine which tokens they represent. With one addition to the end of Simple.l, we can take advantage of what Lex is already doing, and produce errors for unrecognized characters.

```
   yyerror("Error: Unknown character '%c'", *yytext);
```

If none of the previous rules in Simple.l recognized the token, then we have discovered an unrecognized character. On line 5 of the invalid script, a ',' was typed instead of a '<'. An honest mistake, sharing the same key on the keyboard. A comma has no meaning in the Simple language. With the preceding addition to Simple.l, the compiler will give this informative error message:

```
Error: Unknown character ','.
5: if( x , OtherFunction()
```

Missing Semicolon Errors

Similarly, Yacc creates a parser that looks for recognized patterns of tokens. We can exploit this pattern matching to find invalid syntax. If we append the grammar for a valid statement with cases for statements without semicolons, we can trap the missing semicolon error.

```
statement:
    simplestatement ';'
  | IF '(' expression ')' statement
    { $$ = new CNode(IF,$3,$5); }
  | function ';'

  // Catch errors.
  | simplestatement { missing_semicolon: $$ = new
    CNode(INVALID_OP,(long)MISSING_SEMICOLON); }
  | function { goto missing_semicolon; }
```

When the parser recognizes a statement without an ending semicolon, it creates a parse tree node with the operator INVALID_OP. The parameter for the invalid operator is a token describing the error as missing a semicolon. The same technique can be used to identify missing parentheses. When the compiler comes across this node in the parse tree, it calls yyerror() to output this error message:

```
Error: Statements must end with ';'.
4: x = SomeFuncion() - 5
```

Misspelled Function and Keyword Errors

Remember earlier we said that when the compiler looks up a string of characters in its symbol table, if it does not find a matching keyword or function name, it will treat the string as a variable name. This behavior can be used to identify errors with misspelled or unrecognized function names and keywords. Anywhere we want to catch an unrecognized function name or keyword, we can use the token VARIABLE in Simple.y. For example, to catch an unrecognized function name:

```
function:
    FUNCTION '(' ')'
        { $$ = new CNode(FUNCTION, $1); }

    // Catch errors.
    | VARIABLE '(' ')'
        { $$ = new CNode(FUNCTION, $1); }
```

If a function name is not in the symbol table's list of functions, `LookUpSymbol()` will return the `VARIABLE` token. The preceding code will match a variable with parentheses, and add it to the parse tree as a function. When evaluating the parse tree, the compiler will respond to the fact that the symbol's token is a `VARIABLE` rather than a `FUNCTION` and output this error message:

```
Error: Unrecognized function name 'SomeFunction'.
4: x = SomeFuncion() — 5
```

The same technique can be used to catch errors with keywords. By adding code to Simple.y to match a `VARIABLE` token where there should be an `IF` token, we can catch the error on line 5 of our script where there is an incorrectly capitalized "If" where there should be an all lowercase "if."

Undeclared and Redeclared Variable Errors

Some errors are not identifiable through pattern matching. The parser can recognize valid variable declarations and assignment statements, but it has no way of knowing if the variable has been declared once, twice, or not at all. In these cases, it is up to the compiler to check its symbol table to determine if the variable in question has been previously declared. If a script is trying to declare a variable that already exists, or use a variable that does not exist, the compiler can call `yyerror()` with an appropriate error message. For our invalid script, the compiler should generate these errors:

```
Error: Redeclaration of variable 'x'.
2: int x;
Error: Undeclared variable: 'y'.
6:   y = 3;
```

Further Information

The error reporting techniques described in this article complement techniques described in other sources for developing a compiler or interpreter, and integrating the scripting language with a game engine. For more in-depth coverage of scripting language development, see [Berger02, Bilas00, Levine90, Kaplan94].

Conclusion

A scripting language that reports errors to users in plain English becomes less of a peril to game development. The techniques described in this article enable users to harness the power of a custom language by giving them comprehendible insight into problems encountered by the compiler or interpreter. Implementing these techniques does not require any additional skills or tools. The same pattern matching that Lex and Yacc are already performing can identify both correct syntax and incorrect syntax, and allow the compiler or interpreter to react appropriately to either case.

References

[Berger02] Berger, Lee, "Scripting: Overview and Code Generation," *AI Game Programming Wisdom*, Charles River Media, 2002.

[Bilas00] Bilas, Scott, "A Generic Function-Binding Interface," *Game Programming Gems*, Charles River Media, 2000.

[Bison95] Free Software Foundation, available online at *www.gnu.org/software/bison/bison.html*, 1995.

[Flex95] Free Software Foundation, available online at *www.gnu.org/software/flex/flex.html*, 1995.

[Kaplan94] Kaplan, Randy, *Constructing Language Processors for Little Languages*, John Wiley & Sons, Inc., 1994.

[Levine90] Levine, John, et al., *lex & yacc*, O'Reilly & Associates, Inc., 1990.

[MKS95] *MKS LEX & YACC*, Mortice Kern Systems Inc., 1995. See *www.mks.com/*

[Tozour02] Tozour, Paul, "The Perils of AI Scripting," *AI Game Programming Wisdom*, Charles River Media, 2002.

Empowering Designers: Defining Fuzzy Logic Behavior through Excel-Based Spreadsheets

P.J. Snavely—Sony Computer Entertainment America

pj_snavely@playstation.sony.com

The key to any successful software development cycle is the proper use of time and resources—everybody knows this to be true in some way. Currently in the gaming industry, it is very common to see a game designer and an AI programmer working together to implement a test-fix-test cycle of development. Wouldn't it be fantastic to design a system that puts decision-making, rule-based systems in the hands of game designers in such a way that the designer can freely make changes and see them reflected immediately?

Over the course of this article, we'll be exploring how to divide up these responsibilities and how even the most nontechnical of team members can be a vital asset to your AI development and maintenance. Furthermore, we'll also cover some of the basics of how to use and communicate the principles of fuzzy logic, and look at some ideas on basic integration of designers' visions into your complex decision-making system.

Fuzzy Set Theory

Fuzzy sets are a fairly common item in most computer science classes in your general computer science college education these days. However, their use has been previously limited only to the technical community. The job falls to the engineers on a project to communicate a way for designers to take full advantage of fuzzy set theory as a valid method of game design.

Basics

Fuzzy set theory is a way of expressing uncertainty when describing whether an object's value is contained within a set of values. In the traditional sense of sets and Venn diagrams, we're used to describing this behavior in a binary fashion. For example, take the proposition "Paul has big feet." If Paul wears a size 9 shoe, is this true? Set theory and conventional programming logic tells us that this must either be true or false. Consider Figure 9.4.1, which is a typical Venn diagram of normal set theory.

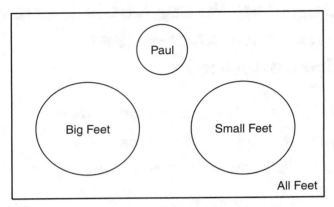

FIGURE 9.4.1   *Conventional set theory and Paul's size 9 shoes.*

Fuzzy set theory has no mutually exclusive states like those seen in Figure 9.4.1. When presented with a question such as "Does Paul have big feet?" we can answer with a degree of uncertainty rather than a purely binary "Yes" or "No." Fuzzy set theory provides us with a perfect way to express "maybe" in a numeric fashion. Figure 9.4.2 provides a fuzzy set approach to the same question.

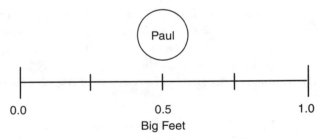

FIGURE 9.4.2   *Fuzzy set theory and Paul's size 9 shoes.*

Note also in the preceding example that we can pin Paul's shoe size down to a specific value (0.58, for example), or we can use a traditional range of values to represent the answer to this question (0.45 to 0.61).

Communication

Game designers often use fuzzy set theory in one way or another, but most times have no idea that this is what they are actually doing. As the driving force for intelligent systems contained within the game, it falls to the engineers to communicate this gap in understanding. Words such as "good" or "bad" are often used as descriptive terms for various things in games—player's health, pitcher's stamina, or Shaquille O'Neal's three-point shooting ability. The key is to translate these terms into numeric values that we can use for decision making.

Application

Let's take the example of a baseball game—many of the decisions made by the manager are based on different factors. For the purpose of this example, let's suppose that your assignment is to implement the managerial decision-making process for bunting. In a typical baseball game, bunting can happen in a variety of different situations. A typical bunt is designed to advance a runner while sacrificing an out—it's a fairly common baseball occurrence when a batter with poor skill is at bat. The document written by a nontechnical game designer describes the various situations when a team should bunt, and it contains the following list of factors:

- Number of outs (0, 1, or 2)
- Runners on base (First, Second, Third, and various combinations)
- Difference in score (Close or Not Close)
- Batter Skill Level (Good or Bad)
- Next Batter Skill Level (Good or Bad)
- Inning (Early, Late, or Extra)

Now, for most games, that would pretty much be the end of the engineer/designer interaction until the testing phase. At that point, there would be a ton of dialog and testing—mostly trying to figure out why a certain batter either did or did not bunt in the given situation. It's not the easiest cycle, but unfortunately it is one that development teams are usually stuck with.

The point at which to take advantage of the designer's knowledge and skills is right before you start the integration of the decision-making process. While a majority of designers will give you the situations in a list form, the easier way for this to be handled (and we'll see why later) is a Microsoft Excel spreadsheet. Given this approach, we could easily see every possible entry handled as shown in Table 9.4.1.

Table 9.4.1 Sample Entries for Brute-Force Managerial Bunting AI

Outs	Runners	Score	Batter Skill	Next Batter Skill	Inning	Bunt?
0	None	Close	Good	Good	Early	No
0	First	Close	Good	Good	Early	No
0	First	Close	Bad	Good	Early	Yes
0	First	Close	Bad	Good	Late	Yes

That gives the designer a lot of entries to fill out (514, to be exact), given all the combinations. Do we really want to offload that much work with that high of a risk of error? Not really—it's a good start, but we can simplify this.

Let's assume that your game has some type of application of ratings to determine a couple of the items in Table 9.4.1—Batter Skill and Next Batter Skill, to be specific. How does a "good" or "bad" rating translate from this spreadsheet of data to a classification of a player? That is a question entirely determined by the needs of the application. The two main keys that determine this are the range of the values themselves and the number of fuzzy categories the designer would like to implement.

What we have right now is the perfect example of the set diagram in Figure 9.4.1—what happens to the batters who have a skill level that could be either good or bad, depending on the definition? If we put in a static arbitrary cutoff point, (e.g., 75 on a scale of 50 to 100), we run the very real possibility of that value changing after extensive testing. Some of the other categories can also be converted into fuzzy sets. These give designers a significant tool to work with—they are no longer stuck with concrete definitions of what "early" and "late" mean when using these to define innings. Here's a way we could redefine the sets:

- **Difference in score:** Use the minimum and maximum values as 0.0 and 1.0, with ties represented as a value of 0.5 (interpolate values between the minimum and maximum).
- **Batter skill:** Use the minimum and maximum values as 0.0 and 1.0, with the average represented as a value of 0.5 (interpolate values in between).
- **Next batter skill:** Same as batter skill.
- **Inning:** Use 0.0 to represent the first inning, with 1.0 representing anything from the ninth inning and beyond.

After communicating this to the designer, we could very easily end up with a spreadsheet that makes more sense (see Table 9.4.2).

Table 9.4.2 Sample Entries for Translated Brute-Force Managerial Bunting AI

Outs	Runners	Score	Batter Skill	Next Batter Skill	Inning	Bunt?
0	None	0.5	> 0.5	> 0.5	0.33	No
0	First	0.5	> 0.5	> 0.5	0.33	No
0	First	0.5	< 0.5	> 0.5	0.33	Yes
0	First	0.5	< 0.5	> 0.5	0.78	Yes

There are a couple of important things to note here. First, we are no longer limited to one table entry per situation—we can combine table entries merely by providing ranges instead of discrete values. Second, since we're already dealing with ranges, we can now enhance the bunt column in the same way, further allowing the designer to customize how often the AI bunts given that particular situation. Our final spreadsheet might look something like Table 9.4.3.

Table 9.4.3   Sample Entries for Fuzzy Set Managerial Bunting AI

Outs	Runners	Score	Batter Skill	Next Batter Skill	Inning	Bunt?
0	None	0.5	0.0 – 0.5	0 – 0.5	0.33	0
0	First	0.5	0.0 – 0.5	0 – 0.5	0.33	0
0	First	0.5	0.0 – 0.5	0 – 0.5	0.33 – 0.78	1

Now we've really got something we can work with. Gone is the bulky document with the various scattered outlines of when we should bunt—we've replaced this with something we can work with, and these numbers form the basis of what we can implement.

So, how do we take this spreadsheet and convert it into something we can use? Obviously, we aren't going to put this data into a table within our code base—that's not designer-friendly or any way to go about writing clean code. Instead, we'll use something that's actually built into the applications within Microsoft Office.

Visual Basic for Applications

Visual Basic® for Applications (VBA) is an amazing tool supported by most standard office applications. The fascinating thing about VBA is that when it is hosted within Excel (as in our case), it will allow us a means of accessing Excel's fundamental object model [Lomax98]. This is true about a host of other applications as well, including Microsoft Word and Microsoft Outlook®. VBA is rapidly growing as a way to customize applications for individual needs.

Integration of VBA

VBA can help us with our task as well—we can use a simple little VBA routine to cycle through the entries within our spreadsheet and provide us with a data structure that we can read in and evaluate in real-time. We can actually integrate a data export tool into Excel, and allow the designer to export and change this data at will.

This has some fairly large and obvious advantages. Once the code has been written to read in and make decisions based on the exported data, there is an established data pipeline. We've changed the application from being programmer-driven to being designer-driven. As there is no code change required to import new data into the game, this is something that the designer can be let loose on. In the end, as long as the code works, you've offloaded all of the logic implementation.

Getting Started

Getting started with the Visual Basic Editor in Excel is beyond the scope of this article, but for those interested in finding out more on how to customize Excel for your needs, there are a number of good references available, such as [Walkenbach01].

Exporting Data

ON THE CD

For the sake of simplicity, the spreadsheet can be made as basic as necessary. The VBA subroutine that follows is an extremely simplistic function that writes the data to a file in a binary format. There is an example of similar VBA code on the accompanying CD-ROM—it will also provide a binary export from a very basic spreadsheet with no ranges.

```
Sub OutputBuntsToBinary()

Open "TestBuntExport" For Binary As #1

For BuntCounter = 2 To 11        'Rows for bunt scenarios
    For ColumnCounter = 1 To 6   'Columns of data

        'Write a byte for each column

        Put #1, , CByte(Worksheets(1).Cells(BuntCounter,
ColumnCounter))

    Next ColumnCounter
Next BuntCounter

Close #1

End Sub
```

Output

Looking at the sample output from what was generated (not taking into account necessary byte alignment), we can read in data that will express situations and corresponding bunt values. This data can then change as frequently as necessary, and the code will remain the same.

Game Implementation

Let's assume the following structure is filled while reading in these structures from our binary export from Excel:

```
struct sBuntSituation
    {
        char mScore,
        char mInning,
        char mCurHitter,
        char mNextHitter,
        char mRunnersOn,
        char mBunt
    };
```

Since we know all of the values in sBuntSituation currently, it is an extremely simple process to write a comparison function to determine if the current situation matches the export from Excel. We'll call this function CompareBuntSituations() and we'll skip the actual code for this, as it is too simple to be listed here. We'll further assume that we're currently working with two sBuntSituation structures—one that contains current data (mCurSit), and one that contains the one we're going to compare (lCompareSit). If we get a TRUE return value, we can then determine if we should bunt based on the exported bunt percentage (mBunt).

```
if(CompareBuntSituations(mCurSit, lCompareSit))
    {
        mBatterBunting = FALSE;

        if(rand()%100 < lCompareSit.mBunt)
            mBatterBunting = TRUE;
    }
```

Pitfalls

As with any method where data is controlled outside of the programming staff, the same type of problems exist. Here are some basic recommendations on how to safeguard and expedite the changing of your game's data:

- Put the spreadsheets in whatever method of source control your team uses. Treat them exactly as you would treat any code file.
- Don't combine multiple tables and macros into one workbook within Excel. More often than not, it is infinitely easier to edit values, re-export, and then test the current exported data.
- Keep it simple—remember that you aren't dealing with other programmers, so make exporting and changing values as straightforward and as painless as possible.
- Be flexible with requests—if there's something that will save somebody days of work and updating for two hours of your time, find a way to get it in.
- Keep exhaustive documentation and comment your code religiously. Any type of two-step process like this is going to require heavy documentation on both ends (including your VBA export).

Other Applications

Realistically, there are places all over your project to use this sort of multipronged attack. The more a code base can be data-driven, the happier and less stressed everybody is going to be at the end of the project.

There are myriad applications within sports games, including player behaviors, logic decisions for personnel movement, any manager decision in baseball (hit and run, stealing, changing pitchers, etc.), play-calling in football games, defenses in basketball games, and a slew of other uses. In nonsports games, you can use this to define anything that currently uses a table in your code base: NPC actions in role-playing games, character behaviors in fighting games, AI decision making in real-time strategy games, and things of this nature. The vision remains the same—a game that's done well ahead of schedule, with only data to tweak. The method outlined here does that, by achieving a better distribution of the workload.

Conclusion

Fuzzy set theory is a basic concept that can be applied to a wide range of data types. The key, as an AI programmer, is to be able to translate those fuzzy values into a discrete range. Given this, we can now apply it to a variety of different types of behaviors and situations. This flexibility allows the application to become more data-driven and less reliant on changes in the code base.

VBA is one vehicle that can be used to bridge the gap between designer and game. Using a straightforward export, we can learn to rely more on applications outside of the development environment. Do not be afraid to take the initiative and try new things to expedite the development process. As always, the most important thing to remember is to be creative.

References

[Buckley02] Buckley, James J., and Eslami, Esfandiar, *An Introduction to Fuzzy Logic and Fuzzy Sets (Advances in Soft Computing)*, Physica Verlag, 2002.

[Lomax98] Lomax, Paul, *VB & VBA in a Nutshell*, O'Reilly & Associates, Inc., 1998.

[Pedrycz 98] Pedrycz, Witold, and Gomide, Fernando, *An Introduction to Fuzzy Sets: Analysis and Design (Complex Adaptive Systems)*, MIT Press, 1998.

[Russell02] Russell, Stuart, and Norvig, Peter, *Artificial Intelligence: A Modern Approach (Second Edition)*, Prentice Hall, 2002.

[Walkenbach01] Walkenbach, John, *Excel 2002 Power Programming with VBA*, John Wiley & Sons, 2001.

9.5

A Modular Camera Architecture for Intelligent Control

Sandeep V. Kharkar—Microsoft Corporation

eltoro_the_deep@hotmail.com

Cameras play a vital role in the user experience of any game. A robust camera solution can make the difference between a game that is awkward to play and a game that plays smoothly and feels great. Unfortunately, cameras tend to be a low-priority item in many game development schedules, and the effort is limited to the point where the cameras stop being a nuisance. One of the reasons why the effort stops early is the lack of a solid architecture that allows rapid data-driven experimentation with camera behaviors.

This article presents a component-based, data-driven camera architecture that allows nonprogrammers to take over the development of camera behavior once the behavior components are functionally complete. The architecture will demonstrate the use of common AI techniques to enhance the robustness and creativity of the camera solution for any game. The techniques presented in this article will primarily benefit games that have a third-person perspective; however, useful tips for other types of games will also be provided. The code for the underlying architecture is included on the accompanying CD-ROM.

ON THE CD

Traditional Camera Architectures

Camera solutions in games are usually limited to a few monolithic camera behaviors that work well for expected player behavior. However, during play-testing, players do what is least expected of them and break the camera in unexpected ways. Each new special case is worked into the camera solution, making it progressively more fragile. When the game goes into final production, the camera code is barely recognizable from the original design and has become a mass of special case considerations. It is so fragile that the developer is forced to make the tradeoff between fixing the latest special case problem (perhaps breaking some other special case) or leaving the problem in and hoping the player will not discover it!

The problem with the traditional camera solution is that it focuses more on the subject than the camera. A game camera should be thought of as a primary character in the game and given the same amount of focus as the player avatar. The camera architecture should be based on modular lightweight behaviors, allow for easy addition of new behaviors, and provide mechanisms to switch between them. An architecture that accomplishes all of this is presented in the next section. For a list of interesting camera behaviors and rules for switching between them, see [Kharkar02].

The Proposed Architecture

The camera architecture presented in this article achieves two main goals: easy addition of new functionality in terms of behaviors, and smart, data-driven switching mechanisms. In addition, it achieves two secondary goals: reuse and variety. This section covers the core design of the architecture and extensibility, and the rest is handled in following sections.

The architecture assumes that a basic camera class is available. A vector camera is used in the example, the details of which are outside the scope of this article. For an excellent explanation of a vector camera, see [Paull00].

The core design of the architecture consists of two classes: a Camera Controller class and a Camera Control Fragment class.

The Camera Control Fragment

The camera control fragment class is where all the action takes place. This is the equivalent of a camera behavior. The control fragment is a simple mathematic processor that updates the camera every frame. It receives the camera's current matrix and modifies it as per the encoded behavior, generating the camera's next position and orientation. The fragment should be removed from the intricacies of the game. Any interaction with the game or request for game data is channeled through the Camera Controller. This makes the control fragment a generic and reusable piece of code that can be used across projects—more on that in a later section.

The Camera Controller

The Camera Controller is a container and manager for the vector camera and the camera control fragments. It is responsible for the creation/destruction, ordering, activation, and updates of control fragments. It is also the fragments' gateway to the rest of the game. On initialization, the controller will create the available fragments and put them into a specified order in which their updates should be called. Then, at each update, the controller will cascade the camera's current matrix through the fragments and generate a new matrix for the camera.

The ease with which new camera behaviors can be created and added in this system should be immediately apparent. However, the system has its limitations; the order of updates is static and decided at load time, and there are no mechanisms to switch fragments on and off. That brings us to our next section.

Adding AI Techniques

As mentioned in the previous section, the basic architecture has some inherent flaws and limitations. The primary flaw among these is the lack of flexibility. Adding AI techniques to the basic architecture removes the limitations and turns it into an elegant solution for both programmers and designers. The following sub-sections enumerate the different AI techniques that can be used to make this possible. The readers can then select and apply the techniques that best suit their particular application.

Rules

Adding a set of rules that turn control fragments on and off is a powerful and simple technique to enhance the basic solution. Rules can be applied just to the Camera Controller or to the Camera Control Fragments as well. If the rule set is restricted to the controller, it can evaluate a set of rules before processing the updates of the fragments. This rule set can dictate which fragments will be used for the next update cycle. If fragments can have rule sets, they can dictate when they are deactivated based on their own rules. A sample rule would be "if the camera is less than n units from the subject, then activate the move-away fragment" with the move-away fragment evaluating the rule "if the camera distance from the subject is greater than m, then deactivate."

A variant on this is the use of fuzzy rules. Fuzzy rules are not as clearly defined as the one in the preceding example. They would use terms like, "too close," or "not too far," in the rules rather than the fixed distance measures. The advantage they have over fixed rules is that they add flexibility and make for a more organic experience.

The advantage of using rules is their simplicity. Rules can be implemented with `if` - `else` sets directly in code without any external data format. The lack of an easy data-driven approach is also the downside of using rules. Moreover, rules do not allow easy reordering of the fragments. This approach is useful for applications with a small set of fragments and limited need for switching and reordering. For some good discussions on rule-based and fuzzy systems, see [McCuskey00, Dybsand01, Zarozinski01, Christian02].

State Machines

Another technique that can add dynamism to the basic architecture is a simple state machine. The controller can own a state machine with a rule set dictating the traversal from state to state. Each state can specify a list of fragments that are active for that state and the order in which they should be updated. When the controller enters a state, it would fill a pointer list with the active fragments for the state, in the specified order.

Using a state machine overcomes the limitations of just using rule sets. It allows for easy switching and reordering. State machines, particularly in this application, would also be very easy to data-drive. A finite-state machine class is presented in

[Dybsand00], and a data-driven state machine example is in [Rosado04]. For a general overview of FSMs in this book, see [Fu04].

Messaging

When using rules with state machines, the Camera Controller needs to keep track of game data locally and poll for data updates each frame. If there are many influences in the game that affect camera behavior, this can turn into an unnecessary overhead. Messaging between the game and the Camera Controller can be an effective means of decreasing this overhead. Key events and actors in the game can send messages to the Camera Controller. These messages can then be used to trigger the rule system or to switch states of the controller. For two very useful articles in the context of messaging and state machines, see [Rabin02a] and [Rabin02b].

Scripting

Scripting is the final evolution of this architecture. If you have access to a scripting engine that you can drop into this system, you will have the ultimate tool not only for great-looking cameras during gameplay, but also for scripting replays without writing special-case code for the myriad of situations. Using scripts you can determine which game events will trigger messages sent to the Camera Controller. Scripting will also allow you to abstract the messaging, switching, and ordering tasks out of the code. The creative part of the endeavor can then be handled by designers and you can focus on creating fragments for other interesting behaviors.

Unfortunately, discussing the details of scripting is outside the scope of this article. For an excellent set of articles on scripting, see Section 10 of *AI Game Programming Wisdom* [AIGPW02] or [Yiskis04].

Putting It All Together

Now that the possibilities have been presented, let us put the pieces of the puzzle together.

- A set of fragments with behavior parameters specified in external data files.
- A state machine defined in data that traverses states using messages and dictates fragment activation and ordering.
- A Camera Controller that reads the data files and creates fragments and the state machine.
- A simple messaging system that allows game events to trigger messages sent to the Camera Controller.
- A scripting engine that allows a designer to determine how and when all these pieces will communicate.

Future Work

Typically, this architecture is implemented in a way that control fragments are complete encapsulated behaviors. However, fragments created in this manner can still end up as monolithic monsters that are difficult to tame. However, if you think of the camera control fragments as individual components of a behavior, it puts an interesting twist on the solution.

When a camera is updated, there are three components to *most* behaviors: update position, update height with respect to terrain, and update look-at and field-of-view to make sure that the subject is in view. Moreover, in most cases, the three updates are performed in the order in which they are mentioned. If the fragments are limited to performing only one of the three updates, it simplifies them even more. It also allows you to mix and match them in interesting ways to create new behaviors. The Camera Controller is modified to have three lists of fragments, one for each type. However, the active fragment list can still be created out of order to handle special circumstances. This experimental extension has worked well in the short run, but more experimentation and refinement is needed.

Reuse and Sharing

To allow game developers to continue to innovate, code reuse must figure into our software development mindset. There is the obvious danger of getting stuck with old code just for the sake of reuse, but when used wisely, it will free up our time to innovate.

In that spirit, the architecture presented is designed with reuse and sharing in mind. The Camera Controller and the Camera Control Fragment classes are designed to handle the core functionality of the architecture, but they are meant to be subclassed before use. Keep in mind that the fragments are to be kept independent of the intricacies of game data and use the derived controller as their gateway to the specific application. With this approach, multiple simultaneous projects could innovate and create new behaviors in derived classes. However, because the interaction between the controller and the fragments happens in the core using the base classes, the behaviors could potentially be a shared resource.

Conclusion

Camera work has an interesting twisted nature; if done right, *no one* will notice the cameras, but *everyone* will notice the slightest flaw! Camera solutions that focus on the subject rather than the camera itself are doomed for failure, no matter how well intentioned or how well staffed. To succeed in creating a camera that complements the gameplay and wows the audience during a replay, it needs to be based on an architecture that allows rapid data-driven experimentation with camera behaviors. A nimble, flexible, extensible, and data-driven camera architecture can allow a developer to continue to innovate technically, while leaving the creative aspect of cameras in the hands of designers. This article presented one such architecture.

When thinking about cameras it is essential for developers to stay away from big monolithic camera behaviors that are difficult to manage. Therefore, remember to think small, innovate, and create. Don't forget that cameras are as much a creative effort [Mascelli98] as they are a technical one, so involve the creative people up front, provide them with the tools they need to do their work, and watch how satisfying and rewarding it is when no one notices your efforts!

References

[AIGPW02] Rabin, Steve (ed.), *AI Game Programming Wisdom*, Charles River Media, 2002.

[Christian02] Christian, Mike, "A Simple Inference Engine for a Rule-Based Architecture," *AI Game Programming Wisdom*, Charles River Media, 2002.

[Dybsand00] Dybsand, Eric, "A Finite-State Machine Class," *Game Programming Gems*, Charles River Media, 2000.

[Dybsand01] Dybsand, Eric, "A Generic Fuzzy State Machine in C++," *Game Programming Gems 2*, Charles River Media, 2001.

[Fu04] Fu, Dan, and Houlette, Ryan, "The Ultimate Guide to FSMs in Games," *AI Game Programming Wisdom 2*, Charles River Media, 2004.

[Kharkar02] Kharkar, Sandeep, "Camera AI for Replays," *AI Game Programming Wisdom*, Charles River Media, 2002.

[Mascelli98] Mascelli, Joseph V., *The Five C's of Cinematography: Motion Picture Filming Techniques*, Silman-James Press, 1998.

[McCuskey00] McCuskey, Mason, "Fuzzy Logic for Video Games," *Game Programming Gems*, Charles River Media, 2000.

[Paull00] Paull, David, "The Vector Camera," *Game Programming Gems*, Charles River Media, 2000.

[Rabin02a] Rabin, Steve, "Implementing a State Machine Language," *AI Game Programming Wisdom*, Charles River Media, 2002.

[Rabin02b] Rabin, Steve, "Enhancing a State Machine Language through Messaging," *AI Game Programming Wisdom*, Charles River Media, 2002.

[Rosado04] Rosado, Gilbert, "Implementing a Data-Driven Finite-State Machine," *AI Game Programming Wisdom 2*, Charles River Media, 2004.

[Yiskis04] Yiskis, Eric, "Finite-State Machine Scripting Language for Game Designers," *AI Game Programming Wisdom 2*, Charles River Media, 2004.

[Zarozinski01] Zarozinski, Michael, "Imploding Combinatorial Explosion in a Fuzzy System," *Game Programming Gems 2*, Charles River Media, 2001.

LEARNING

10.1

Player Modeling for Adaptive Games

Ryan Houlette—Stottler

Henke Associates, Inc.

houlette@stottlerhenke.com

When we say that a game has "good AI," we typically mean that the characters in the game exhibit consistent and realistic behavior, reacting appropriately to the actions of the player and other characters. For certain genres of games—for example, first-person shooters and real-time strategy games—"good AI" also refers to the ability of the game to challenge the player on a tactical and strategic level. While these are certainly worthy and important goals to strive for in your game, they tend to overshadow a third, seldom-mentioned component of good game AI: the capacity to adapt over time to the quirks and habits of a particular player.

An adaptive AI can drastically increase the replayability of your game, and make the game experience much more intense and personalized for the players. Nonetheless, most games today are limited to what might be called "manually adaptive AI"; in other words, the game provides difficulty sliders and configuration parameters that allow the player to directly control how game characters act at some very coarse level. While this isn't a great solution, it certainly seems much less daunting than introducing costly (and often finicky) machine-learning algorithms into your game.

Although many learning algorithms are computationally expensive enough to make game programmers run screaming, there are some approaches that are relatively lightweight, simple, and flexible enough to be useful. One in particular is a technique we call *player modeling*, borrowed from the similar notion of "student modeling" in intelligent tutoring system research. The basic idea is simple: the game maintains a profile of each player that captures the skills, weaknesses, preferences, and other characteristics of that player. This model is updated by the game as it interacts with the player. In turn, the game AI can query the player model to determine how best to adapt its behavior to that particular player, such as by asking which of several possible tactics will be most challenging to the player. Using player modeling, a game's AI can adapt both during the course of a single play as well as over multiple sessions, resulting in a computer opponent that changes and evolves with time to suit the player.

This article first defines the player model concept in more detail and then discusses strategies for designing a model to suit your game. It then presents a basic player model implementation. Subsequent sections describe how to actually integrate the modeling system with your game, including both how to update the model and how to make use of the information that it contains. The remainder of the article presents several advanced concepts, including a hierarchical player model, alternate model update methods, and other uses for the player model.

Designing the Player Model

The core of any player modeling system is, as you might expect, the model itself. This is essentially a collection of numeric attributes, or *traits*, that describe the playing style of an individual player. Each trait characterizes a single aspect of the player's behavior in the game, often associated with a particular strategy, maneuver, or skill. Depending on your perspective, a trait can be viewed as a measure of the player's knowledge and proficiency in a certain area, or it can be seen as a summary of the player's habits and preferences.

For example, in the player model for a first-person shooter game you might have a trait called "UsesSmokeGrenades" that tracks the player's use of smoke grenades to provide cover. Under "habits and preferences" model semantics, if Player A has a high value for that trait in his model, it would indicate that he often uses smoke grenades (perhaps because he likes to use them). If you prefer the "knowledge and proficiency" semantics, you would interpret a high value for this trait to mean that Player A is very good at using smoke grenades for cover. The difference is subtle, but it will affect the types of traits that you choose for your model. Choose the semantics that you feel most comfortable with and that make the most sense for your game.

Another important decision to make when designing your player model is how fine-grained you want the traits to be. For example, the "UsesSmokeGrenades" trait from the preceding example is a very coarse characterization of player behavior that does not take into account the game-world context of the player's actions. A more fine-grained model might include several different traits for smoke grenade use, each keeping track of the player's use of smoke grenades in a different situation: while retreating, while entering a building, while covering a teammate, and so on. More detailed models tend to be more useful because they can offer information about the player's behavior that is relevant to the current game context; however, detailed models also generally take longer to design and are more computationally costly to update.

Picking the right set of traits for your player model is, like much of game development, more of an art than a science. No one player model will work for all games—genre, setting, level of realism, and a hundred other factors will affect your choices. A general rule of thumb, however, is that every important aspect of gameplay should be captured somehow in the model. If your game features a great deal of haggling with shopkeepers, for example, then you should probably have some traits that model that facet of the player's play style (e.g., "MakesCounterOffers," "WillRefuseToBuy").

Another rule of thumb is that the design of the player model should be tied closely to the design of the game AI. Remember that the entire point of doing player modeling is to help the game AI adapt its behavior to the player. To that end, pick traits that complement the strategies, tactics, maneuvers, and capabilities of the AI. For example, in a real-time strategy (RTS) game where the enemy AI recognizes and exploits map chokepoints, you might want to have model traits that measure the player's own awareness of and ability to avoid chokepoints: "AvoidsMovingThrough-EnemyChokepoints," "FortifiesOwnChokepoints." Conversely, you can also include traits for player tactics that your AI is particularly vulnerable to. If your RTS AI doesn't handle attacks on two fronts well, the player trait "AttacksOnTwoFronts" would enable the AI to remember that Player B often uses this tactic and hence should be attacked early.

If you are still early in the game design phase and have not yet determined the strategies and capabilities for your AI, then you can take a more top-down approach, first choosing the traits for the player model and then using those traits to help define the requirements specification for the game AI. This allows you to tightly integrate adaptivity into the AI from the start, ensuring that all significant aspects of player-AI interaction will be modeled.

Play-testing is also an invaluable tool for refining your player modeling scheme. It is during play-testing that you will empirically verify which traits most effectively model player behavior as well as which traits are most useful for building adaptive, interesting AI. You most likely will also find during play-testing that players are acting in ways that you hadn't anticipated, and you will probably want to add or modify some model traits to capture this unexpected behavior and bring it into the scope of the game's adaptivity. For more advice on using play-testing to tune and validate your AI, refer to the "Artificial Stupidity: The Art of Intentional Mistakes" article in this book [Lidén03].

A Simple Implementation

At its most basic level, a player model is a statistical record of the frequency of some interesting subset of player actions. Any player modeling system must therefore provide some mechanism capable of observing the player and updating the statistical record appropriately. It must also provide an interface via which the game AI can query the model for specific information about the player. There are obviously a variety of ways that such a system could be implemented; we'll start by looking at a minimal version.

```
class PlayerModel {
public:
    enum ETrait {
        kUsesSmokeGrenades,
        kAlwaysRuns,
        kCanDoTrickyJumps
    };
```

```
        void Initialize();
        void UpdateTrait(ETrait trait,float observeValue);
        float GetTrait(ETrait trait);

    private:
        vector<float> _traitValues;
    };
```

This `PlayerModel` class stores a simple array of player traits. Each trait is represented by a floating-point value between 0 and 1, where 0 roughly means "the player never does this" and 1 means "the player always does this." All traits are initially given the value 0.5 to reflect lack of knowledge.

To query the model for a specific trait's value, we need only look up the appropriate entry in the array:

```
    float PlayerModel::GetTrait(ETrait trait) {
        return _traitValues[trait];
    }
```

The update method for the model is somewhat more complicated:

```
    float PlayerModel::UpdateTrait(ETrait trait,
                                   float observeValue) {
        float currValue = _traitValues[trait];
        float delta = observeValue – currValue;
        float weightedDelta = kLEARNING_RATE * delta;
        traitValues[trait] += weightedDelta;
    }
```

This algorithm is based upon the least mean squares (LMS) training rule commonly used in machine learning [Mitchell97], shown in Equation 1.

$$traitValue = \alpha \cdot observedValue + (1 - \alpha) \cdot traitValue \qquad (1)$$

According to this algorithm, the current trait value in the player model is the game's best guess about the player's true play style, and each call to `UpdateTrait()` is a piece of evidence that should be used to refine that best guess. Because players do not necessarily act completely consistently, however, not every piece of evidence will be "correct," and thus we limit the extent to which a single call to `UpdateTrait()` can influence the model. This is the role of the `kLEARNING_RATE` constant, which ranges between 0 and 1. The smaller its value, the more evidence will be required to change the player model. Typical values are between 0.1 and 0.3.

Updating the Model

There are two steps involved in each model update: detecting when an update should be made, and then telling the model to update itself. To detect when the player model should be updated, the game must be able to recognize that the player has taken (or failed to take) a specific action or sequence of actions corresponding to a particular trait. Suppose that the player model for a first-person shooter includes the trait "CanDoTrickyJumps," which indicates that the player is capable of performing difficult jumping feats such as jumping from roof to roof. The game must therefore provide some mechanism to determine when the player has successfully made (or failed) a difficult jump. The most straightforward approach would be simply to hard-code this tricky-jump-detection routine and invoke it each time the player jumps. As long as the detection routine is reasonably efficient and not invoked with excessive frequency, it should not impact game performance.

Sometimes, the detection routine for a trait might be unavoidably expensive. For example, determining whether a player is good at spotting enemies who are hidden in shadow (in a first-person shooter) requires the game to compute the visibility of all nearby enemies, which entails costly processing of scene geometry. In such cases, it might be possible to share the computational burden with the game AI code, which might already be performing some of these calculations. Often, the code that the AI uses to decide when a particular strategy is applicable can be easily generalized to also detect when the player is trying that same strategy (or failing to try it when it's the best choice). Clever caching of past computations can also help reduce the cost of your detection algorithms.

If it is impossible to speed up your detection routines, there are still ways to incorporate player modeling in your game without bringing your frame rate to a halt. One possible solution is to queue up player actions for later background processing by the modeling system. Of course, this is difficult for traits that require a large amount of contextual information to detect (such as 3D scene geometry). Another approach is to simply write a log of the necessary information and handle all model updates between game sessions (which, of course, eliminates the possibility of in-game adaptation).

Once the game has determined that the player model should be updated, all that remains to do is to call the model's UpdateTrait() method to request that it update the trait in question. This method takes two parameters, a trait identifier and a floating-point number $0 \leq x \leq 1$ that specifies the direction in which to update the trait. Generally, a value of 0 indicates that the player has failed to execute the action or strategy in question, while a value of 1 indicates successful and/or appropriate use of that action or strategy. Intermediate values can be used to represent varying degrees of success or failure. For example, a successful difficult jump in our previous example might result in the following update:

```
model.UpdateTrait(PlayerModel::kCanDoTrickyJumps,1.0);
```

Using the Model with Your AI

Once your player model has been implemented and is being updated by the game, you can begin putting it to use in your AI. To retrieve the value for a specified trait, simply call the GetTrait() method with the appropriate index; for example:

```
model.GetTrait(PlayerModel::kCanDoTrickyJumps);
```

This code retrieves the value of the player's "CanDoTrickyJumps" trait. A game character might query this trait when trying to decide on an escape route away from the player. If the player has a low "CanDoTrickyJumps" value, the character might choose a route with lots of difficult leaps from roof to roof, knowing that the player most likely will not navigate that route successfully. Otherwise, the character might be forced to take the more dangerous route through the sewers.

In general, you can think of the player model as a type of persistent game memory that enables game AI to be less episodic and more aware of its past interactions with the player. There are two main ways to make use of this memory. One is to employ it as a predictive tool, querying it to determine how the player will most likely react if the AI chooses a particular strategy. Suppose, for example, that in your role-playing game, Player B has a high value for the trait "UsesRangedWeaponsAgainst-Wizards." This indicates that when Player B has fought wizards in previous encounters, he has almost always used his longbow to pick them off from a distance rather than engaging them in melee combat. Knowing this, the AI might well decide to have its wizard magically protect himself from arrows before attacking Player B, thereby reducing the effectiveness of the player's "killer" strategy. From Player B's perspective, it looks like the game is getting smarter.

The other main way to use the player model is to look for apparent deficiencies in the player's skills and knowledge that can be exploited by the AI. This is often a good approach when your player model contains many traits that correspond directly to your AI's strategies. Imagine a strategy game where Player C has a low value for the trait "FlankingAttack." This means that Player C has never executed a flanking maneuver during battle and thus is perhaps not familiar with the idea. The AI opponent might, armed with this knowledge, therefore choose a flanking attack in the hopes of throwing Player C off balance and defeating him. In a more friendly game, this same knowledge could also be used to provide automated advice to a novice player.

Hierarchical Player Models

Most of the examples that we presented up to this point have dealt with fairly low-level traits. This is primarily because our simple player model implementation only permits us to track player characteristics that are concrete enough to be easily recognized. It is possible, however, to build a more sophisticated model that can represent higher-level, more abstract aspects of player behavior. Instead of storing the player traits in a flat list, we organize them into a tree as shown in Figure 10.1.1. In this hierarchical model, each leaf denotes a *concrete* trait that the game can update by watching the player's actions (as previously described). An internal node of the tree is an *abstract* trait that summarizes the skills or preferences stored in its children. Abstract traits are never directly updated by the game, but instead compute their values as an average of the values of their child traits. Thus, a player who earns high values for the concrete traits "AvoidsCamera," "AvoidsGuards," and "MovesSilently" will automatically gain a high value for the "Stealthy" abstract trait.

The introduction of abstract traits in the player model permits the AI to make broad adjustments to its behavior to ensure that the player continues to be challenged and engaged by the game. Consider the example shown in Figure 10.1.1. If a player has a high value for the abstract trait "Stealthy" but a low value for "CloseCombat," the AI might conclude that the player prefers to sneak around rather than fight. To make sure that the game remains challenging, the AI might increase the watchfulness of the enemy soldiers so that they're more likely to spot the player as he sneaks by. Alternately, the AI might recalibrate a mission so that there are fewer combat encounters and more guard patrols, furnishing more opportunities for the player to enjoy his favorite elements of the game.

The hierarchical player model requires a slightly more complex data structure:

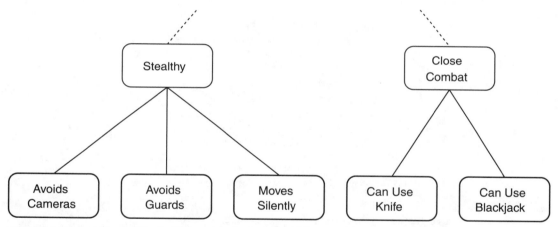

FIGURE 10.1.1 *Example of a hierarchical player model.*

```
class HPlayerModel {
public:
    enum ETrait {
        kUsesSmokeGrenades,
        kAlwaysRuns,
        kCanDoTrickyJumps
    };

    void Initialize();
    void UpdateTrait(ETrait trait,float observeValue);
    float GetTrait(ETrait trait);

private:
    HModelNode* FindNode(ETrait trait);
    HModelNode* _root;
```

```
};

class HModelNode {
public:
    void Initialize();
    void UpdateTrait(float observeValue);
    float GetTrait(ETrait trait);

private:
    void Propagate(float oldContrib,float newContrib);
    ETrait _traitId;
    float _traitValue;
    HModelNode* _parent;
    vector<HModelNode*> _children;
};
```

Moreover, the update algorithm should propagate changes in the leaves up through the rest of the tree:

```
void HPlayerModel::UpdateTrait(ETrait trait,
                               float observeValue) {
    HModelNode* leaf = FindNode(trait);
    leaf->UpdateTrait(observeValue);
}

void HModelNode::UpdateTrait(float observeValue) {
    float delta = observeValue - _traitValue;
    float weightedDelta = kLEARNING_RATE * delta;
    float newValue = _traitValue + weightedDelta;
    if (_parent != NULL)
        _parent->Propagate(_traitValue,newValue);
    _traitValue = newValue;
}

void HModelNode::Propagate(float oldContrib,
                           float newContrib) {
    int numChild = _children.size();
    float noContrib = _traitValue*numChild-oldContrib;
    float newValue = (noContrib+newContrib)/numChild;
    if (_parent != NULL)
        _parent->Propagate(_traitValue,newValue);
    _traitValue = newValue;
}
```

To query the hierarchical model for a specific trait's value, GetTrait() performs a tree search for the node with that trait's unique identifier. To speed up queries, the model could also maintain a hashtable, indexed by trait identifier, that points to the appropriate tree nodes.

An Alternative Model Update Method

In the player modeling system described thus far, model updates are managed purely by hard-coded trait detection routines. While this is certainly the most straightforward solution, it tends to lead to player modeling code being dispersed throughout your game's source wherever player actions are processed, which is both inelegant and a maintenance headache. In addition, it means that each modification to the structure of the player model (such as adding, removing, or modifying a trait) requires a code change and thus a rebuild of the game.

There is an alternative solution, however, that eliminates many of these problems: implement the trait-detection routines as a collection of finite-state machines. In this scheme, each concrete trait is associated with a single finite-state machine that encapsulates within its states and transitions the algorithm for determining when that trait should be updated. These finite-state machines monitor the stream of player and AI actions, updating the player model when the necessary conditions are satisfied.

The finite-state machine-based player modeling system can be constructed in an entirely data-driven fashion, so that the specifications for the machines and for the model itself can all be loaded from a file dynamically. This decouples the player model from the code and the build process, allowing a fast test-and-tune cycle. In addition, visual tools can be used to author the finite-state machines, which will make the trait-detection algorithms significantly easier to understand and modify.

Other methods for statistically modeling player behavior are also available. In particular, models constructed using N-grams (probabilistic directed graphs that describe the frequency of various sequences of player actions) or histograms can be both computationally efficient and an effective way to add adaptability to your games [Laramée02, Mommersteeg02].

Other Uses for the Player Model

Although the primary motivation for building a player modeling system is generally the desire to add an adaptive component to your game AI, there are several other potential benefits. For example, once you've implemented player modeling in your game, you can easily allow a player to export his player model for use in other games. Imagine that player installing your latest game—and having it already know about his quirks, skills, and playing style! No two games will have the exact same player model, of course, simply because the low-level actions available to the player vary from game to game; thus model sharing would be mostly limited to common abstract traits. Nonetheless, for games in the same genre (or the same series), that overlap should be considerable.

Another interesting option is to allow the player to view the contents of his own player model from within the game. The model representation is fairly intuitive, and if given a good graphical presentation it could easily serve as a detailed form of player feedback. Exposing the model does, however, have the possible drawback of revealing some of the AI's secrets, if the two are tightly integrated.

Conclusion

We described a methodology for implementing a general player modeling system. Player modeling is a lightweight but powerful learning algorithm that can be used to enhance your game's AI by enabling it to adapt to the skills and tendencies of individual players. The basic concept is flexible enough that it can be applied to practically any game, and it can be easily extended to work with a wide variety of other artificial intelligence techniques.

References

[Beal02] Beal, C., Beck, J., Westbrook, D., Atkin, M., and Cohen, P., "Intelligent Modeling of the User in Interactive Entertainment," *AAAI Stanford Spring Symposium*, 2002, available online at *www-unix.oit.umass.edu/~cbeal/papers/AAAISS02Slides.pdf* and *www-unix.oit.umass.edu/~cbeal/papers/AAAISS02.pdf*

[Houlette03] Houlette, Ryan, Kalton, Annaka, and Cramer, Michael, "An Architecture for Predictable Mixed-Initiative Planning," *NASA Phase II SBIR Final Technical Report* (Jan 2003).

[Laramée02] Laramée, François, "Using N-Gram Statistical Models to Predict Player Behavior," *AI Game Programming Wisdom*, Charles River Media, 2002.

[Lidén04] Lidén, Lars, "Artificial Stupidity: The Art of Intentional Mistakes," *AI Game Programming Wisdom 2*, Charles River Media, 2004.

[Mitchell97] Mitchell, Tom, *Machine Learning*, McGraw-Hill, 1997, pp. 10–11.

[Mommersteeg02] Mommersteeg, Fri, "Pattern Recognition with Sequential Prediction," *AI Game Programming Wisdom*, Charles River Media, 2002.

10.2

Constructing a Decision Tree Based on Past Experience

Dan Fu and Ryan Houlette—Stottler

Henke Associates, Inc.

fu@stottlerhenke.com,
houlette@stottlerhenke.com

In recent years, dating back to the release of *Black & White* in 2001, decision trees have gained popularity within the game development community as a practical learning method that can help an AI adapt to the player. Instead of picking from a canned set of reactions to player action, the AI has the opportunity to do something much more powerful: anticipate the player's action before he acts. The implications of this AI "holy grail" are numerous, the most important being that the AI can continually challenge the player by adapting to his behavior, thus prolonging interest in the game. No longer can the player learn a simple technique and use it repeatedly until boredom sets in; sure, he might use it for a while, but as the AI learns from its experience, the player will want to explore new ways to win. Moreover, as he discovers these winning methods, the AI will eventually adapt to those as well to further challenge the player. Now that's a game AI!

Now, before you get all excited and think that we're about to feed you this manna, our three aims in this article are much more modest. First, we're going to discuss a decision tree learning algorithm—probably the best-known to AI folk—called ID3 [Quinlan86]. In a nutshell, ID3 creates a decision tree that identifies the telltale features of an experience to predict its outcome. Our second aim is to describe ID3's role in *Black & White* by expanding on Richard Evans' article in the first edition of *AI Game Programming Wisdom* [Evans02]. Our last aim is to discuss some important aspects and extensions to the approach, and to describe the sample code included on the CD-ROM, which implements a simple form of ID3.

ON THE CD

Decision Tree Basics

Before jumping into the algorithm, let's first cover some basic decision tree concepts and terminology. Decision tree learning is an example of an *inductive learning task*: Create a hypothesis based on particular instances that makes general conclusions. For example, say we work in the Bay Area of California, and, like most workers, we drive to work. Because commute times can be significant, we want to predict our commute time. To tackle this learning problem, we will first record our experiences, and then attempt to make general conclusions about commute times.

We start by describing our experiences under various *attributes* like:

- **Hour of departure:** What time you leave for work (8, 9, or 10 A.M.).
- **Weather:** The weather that morning (Sunny, Cloudy, Rainy).
- **Accidents:** Whether any accidents on the road were reported (Yes or No).
- **Stalls:** Whether any cars stalled on the road (Yes or No).
- **Commute time:** How long you drove (Short, Medium, or Long).

Each attribute has a range of discrete values. For example, the weather can be one of sunny, cloudy, or rainy. When describing a single driving experience, we pick one value for each of the five attributes.

After a few weeks of driving, we record the following data as shown in Table 10.2.1. There are a total of 13 examples, each with its values for the attributes defined previously. The *target attribute* that's of interest here is the Commute time.

Table 10.2.1   Examples of Driving Experiences

Example	Attributes				Target
	Hour	Weather	Accident	Stall	Commute
D1	8 A.M.	Sunny	No	No	Long
D2	8 A.M.	Cloudy	No	Yes	Long
D3	10 A.M.	Sunny	No	No	Short
D4	9 A.M.	Rainy	Yes	No	Long
D5	9 A.M.	Sunny	Yes	Yes	Long
D6	10 A.M.	Sunny	No	No	Short
D7	10 A.M.	Cloudy	No	No	Short
D8	9 A.M.	Rainy	No	No	Medium
D9	9 A.M.	Sunny	Yes	No	Long
D10	10 A.M.	Cloudy	Yes	Yes	Long
D11	10 A.M.	Rainy	No	No	Short
D12	8 A.M.	Cloudy	Yes	No	Long
D13	9 A.M.	Sunny	No	No	Medium

Can we say anything about the expected commute tomorrow morning when it's 9 A.M., sunny outside, no accidents have happened, and no car stalls happened? To answer this question, we need a decision tree. Figure 10.2.1 shows such a tree. Starting from the root with our example, we check the "Hour" attribute in question, and then traverse down the branch with the corresponding value. In this case, the next attribute will be "Accident." This process—checking the attribute value and traversing a branch—repeats until a leaf value has been reached. Here, the leaf value is "Medium"; thus we can expect a medium length commuting time.

See that the decision tree explains the training set in Table 10.2.1; thus we have a hypothesis consistent with the data. Not only that, but the hypothesis makes general conclusions by predicting a commute time for instances not in the training set, such as our question about tomorrow's commute.

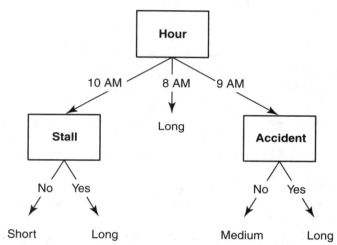

FIGURE 10.2.1 *A decision tree for expected commute time.*

In more formal terms, what we're really doing here is learning an approximation function. Let us cast each example as a pair $\langle (x, f(x)) \rangle$, where x are the actual values for attributes like hour of departure and weather, and $f(x)$ is the commute time. We are creating a hypothesis function $h(x)$ that equals $f(x)$ for all x in our training set. What's useful here is that h can be applied to any instance y not in the original set, thereby making general conclusions about $f(y)$.

A guiding principle of most inductive learning work is *Occam's Razor*. It states that given a number of competing hypotheses, the simplest one is preferable. See that the tree in Figure 10.2.1 does not reference the Weather attribute at all. This means that the attribute isn't vital to determining commute time. Indeed, predicting commute time for any instance in Table 10.2.1 amounts to checking at most two attribute values. Note that each leaf in our tree could be replaced with a sub-tree to check for weather values, but ultimately all the leaves in the sub-tree will have the exact same value as the supplanted leaf.

Learning a Decision Tree

In this section, we present a way to construct a decision tree. We will describe the ideas behind the basic algorithm and describe the ID3 heuristic.

Constructing a Decision Tree

The basic intuition for most decision tree learning algorithms is that at each decision point in the partially constructed tree we ask, "What is the best attribute that will split the examples?" That attribute will be the attribute for the node, and the immediate branches will each have a distinct value for the attribute. The algorithm partitions the examples and assigns each to its respective child node. This process repeats for each child recursively. Figure 10.2.2 illustrates the algorithm used to create a decision tree.

---

node **LearnTree**(*examples, targetAttribute, attributes*)
    examples is the training set
    targetAttribute is what to learn
    attributes is the set of available attributes
    returns a tree node
begin
    if all the *examples* have the same *targetAttribute* value,
        return a leaf with that value
    else if the set of *attributes* is empty,
        return a leaf with the most common *targetAttribute* value among examples
    else begin
        A = the best attribute among *attributes* having a range of values $v_1, v_2, \ldots, v_k$
        Partition examples according to their value for A into sets $S_1, S_2, \ldots, S_k$
        Create a decision node N with attribute A
        for i=1 to k
            begin
                Attach a branch B to node N with test v_i
                if S_i has elements (is non-empty),
                    Attach B to LearnTree(S_i, *targetAttribute, attributes* – {A});
                else
                    Attach B to a leaf node with most common *targetAttribute*
            end
        return decision node N
    end
end

FIGURE 10.2.2   *A decision tree learning algorithm.*

    The LearnTree function is initially called with the full set of training instances, the target attribute, and the set of attributes available to choose from. It proceeds by choosing the best attribute to split the instances and then creating a corresponding decision node. Going back to our earlier commuting time example, Figure 10.2.3

shows a decision tree after choosing "Hour" as the best attribute to split examples. The function annotates each node with the set of remaining examples (shown in curly braces) and a histogram count of the examples according to the target attribute (shown in brackets). The root shows "[4 S, 2 M, 7 L]," meaning that there are four examples with commute time "Short," two "Medium," and seven "Long."

Observe that the algorithm recursion stops when one of three base conditions is true:

- All the examples have the same target attribute value.
- There are no more attributes.
- There are no more examples.

When the first condition holds, we have a set of examples where the ancestor attributes and corresponding branch values, as well as the target attribute and value, are identical across examples. The second condition holds when there are inconsistencies in the training set; in other words, when there are at least two examples having identical values for all but the target attribute. Here, we make a guess as to what the predicted value should be by computing the most popular *targetAttribute* value. The third condition holds when there could conceivably be examples in the future, but none in the training set.

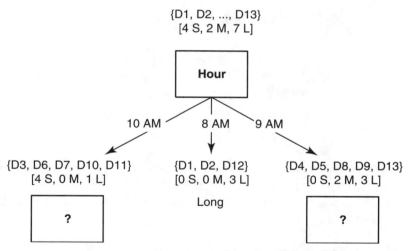

FIGURE 10.2.3 *The partially constructed decision tree after splitting with attribute Hour.*

The ID3 Heuristic

After viewing the algorithm, you might be wondering exactly how we identify the "best attribute." The answer to this question resides with ID3's heuristic, which quantifies how valuable an attribute will be with respect to the remaining examples. Intuitively, we want a heuristic that will help partition the examples such that most of the Short, Medium, and Long commute examples will be allocated to their own sub-trees.

The solution to this problem comes from Shannon's information theory. ID3's heuristic favors the best reduction in *entropy*, which quantifies the variation in a set of examples with respect to target attribute values. A set of examples whose Commute time value are all Short has zero entropy, while a set of examples with equal number of Short, Medium, and Long will have highest entropy. Keeping with the terms from the algorithm in Figure 10.2.2, entropy is defined as:

$$Entropy(S) = \sum_{i=1}^{l} -\frac{|S_i|}{|S|} \log_2 \frac{|S_i|}{|S|} \tag{1}$$

where S is the set of examples, S_i is a subset of S with value v_i under the target attribute, and l is the size of the range of the target attribute. The entropy of the training set from Table 10.2.1 would be:

$$-\frac{4}{13} \log_2 \frac{4}{13} - \frac{2}{13} \log_2 \frac{2}{13} - \frac{7}{13} \log_2 \frac{7}{13} = 1.41956 \tag{2}$$

When we consider a candidate attribute A, our expected entropy from the partition is the weighted sum of subset entropies:

$$\sum_{i=1}^{k} \frac{|S_i|}{|S|} Entropy(S_i) \tag{3}$$

where k is the size of the range of attribute A.

The attribute that has the minimal expected entropy from Expression 3 is the best attribute. Conversely, this attribute will maximize the *information gain*, defined as:

$$Entropy(S) - \sum_{i=1}^{k} \frac{|S_i|}{|S|} Entropy(S_i) \tag{4}$$

For the root of our decision tree, we would calculate the following in Table 10.2.2 to determine that the Hour attribute has the lowest expected entropy, and therefore the highest information gain. See Expression 2 to derive the third column values in the table.

Table 10.2.2   Expected Entropy and Information Gain for the Root of the Decision Tree

Attribute	Expected Entropy	Information Gain
Hour	0.65110	0.768449
Weather	1.28884	0.130719
Accident	0.92307	0.496479
Stall	1.17071	0.248842

Discussion

There are a couple of issues worth discussing now that we've covered the basic algorithm. The first has to do with ID3's performance; the second has to do with discrete values. First, even though the ID3 heuristic seems good, it does not guarantee the smallest possible decision tree. Unlike other well-known greedy algorithms, ID3 commits to selecting an attribute based on expected entropy reduction—not the actual reduction. If we wanted to determine the optimal tree, we would have to enumerate the selection of attributes, rendering this method unworkable. Thus, much work in this vein of research has focused on creation of better heuristics.

The second issue worth discussing is that we have consistently been using discrete values. Unlike, say, neural networks, which map arbitrary numerical inputs to numerical outputs, the decision tree learning method only makes use of symbolic data. We could not, for example, make a prediction on commute time if we left at 9:45 A.M.— we would have to round the time to either 9 or 10 A.M. We could have recorded departure times at finer granularity down to the second, resulting in 13 unique values. Unfortunately, ID3 tends to favor "bushy" trees: it would pick this new departure time attribute as the root of the decision tree, if only because the expected entropy would be extremely low. Then we'd have 13 branches leading to just as many leaves. That tree will not have much predictive use for our problem in practice. There do exist methods to address this problem. We'll discuss this extension in a later section.

ID3's Role in *Black & White*

Perhaps the first successful use of a decision tree was in the game *Black & White* developed by Lionhead Studios and released in 2001. A description of the game's AI appeared in [Evans01] and [Evans02]. In the game, there is a Creature that learns from the player's actions and feedback. In order to make general conclusions about the player's feedback and preferences, the Creature dynamically recalculates a decision tree that best explains the player's preferences, allowing the Creature to eventually emulate its idol.

As an example, one decision tree was formed to explain the player's reactions to the Creature's attacks on various towns. Table 10.2.3 reproduces the training set presented in [Evans02]. The first thing you might notice is the numerical values for the target attribute Feedback. Although we could interpret the numerical values as unique symbols, the original article showed the values at leaves to be approximations of the training feedback values, thus there was some discretization of the target attribute values. *K-means clustering* [Shapiro01] is one such standard technique wherein we identify the number of clusters (k) we want to create, and an algorithm attempts to successively associate (or disassociate) instances with clusters until the associations stabilize around k centroids.

Table 10.2.3   Examples of Player Feedback

Example	Attributes			Target
	Allegiance	Defense	Tribe	Feedback
D1	Friendly	Weak	Celtic	−1.0
D2	Enemy	Weak	Celtic	+0.4
D3	Friendly	Strong	Norse	−1.0
D4	Enemy	Strong	Norse	−0.2
D5	Friendly	Weak	Greek	−1.0
D6	Enemy	Medium	Greek	+0.2
D7	Enemy	Strong	Greek	−0.4
D8	Enemy	Medium	Aztec	0.0
D9	Friendly	Weak	Aztec	−1.0

If we declare four goal clusters, then the technique might create clusters centered at −1, 0.4, 0.1, and −0.3 in a one-dimensional cluster space. The respective memberships for each cluster would be {D1, D3, D5, D9}, {D2}, {D6, D8}, and {D4, D7}. Using the four cardinal values for the target attribute, the ID3 algorithm described here will generate an identical decision tree as shown in Figure 10.2.4.

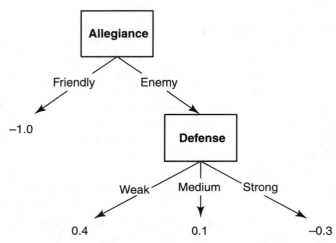

FIGURE 10.2.4   *Decision tree for expected player feedback.*

Once the decision tree has been formed, the Creature, when contemplating attacking a town, can use the tree to predict the player's reaction. In fact, if all the Creature was interested in was always attaining the two best feedbacks, it can easily create a logical expression to tell it whether to attack or not:

$$((Allegiance\ =\ Enemy)\ \wedge\ (Defense\ =\ Weak))\ \vee$$

$$((Allegiance\ =\ Enemy)\ \wedge\ (Defense\ =\ Medium)) \tag{5}$$

Notice that decision trees can easily be encoded as logical expressions for efficient application.

An Extension for Continuous Values

Earlier in this article we discussed our reliance on discrete values. In this section, we present a method for extending our algorithm to handle continuous values. In our basic decision tree, the decision at each inner node relies on an equality relationship between the example's value for the attribute and the branch's value. Now let's suppose we used continuous values (say microseconds) for the departure time. The key insight here is to use an inequality test on two branches. For example, the tests on the two branches could be "Hour < 9 A.M." and "Hour >= 9 A.M." corresponding to leaving before or on/after 9 A.M., respectively. Our choice of 9 A.M. is what's referred to as a *cut point*. Thresholding based on a cut point is a standard way of establishing intervals on data.

You might ask, how did we pick the value 9 A.M.? Well, the answer is that we pick values from the training set. In fact, for each continuous attribute we can pick as many unique values in the training set. However, that means the space of attributes to contemplate at each decision point can be as big as the training set size! That's scary. Fortunately, there has been work done to reduce the number of candidate attributes. One important observation [Fayyad92] is that any optimal cut point for an attribute must reside in a subset of points called *boundary points*. Suppose we create a sorted list of instances according to their values for the candidate attribute in question. A boundary point is defined as being a value along this single dimension between two adjacent instances having different target attribute values.

In worst case, the number of boundary points is nearly the number of instances. We can imagine a binary-valued target attribute that has alternating 0s and 1s along the dimension in question, but this case tends not to arise in practice. One case worth mentioning is when multiple instances have identical candidate attribute values and differing target attribute values. In this case, the boundary points will reside on the sides of the sorted group. This case can arise frequently when values are integers.

Example Code

ON THE CD

The example code included on the accompanying CD-ROM implements the ID3 algorithm in the executable ID3.exe. It reads in a flat data tab-delimited file of attributes, training set, and testing set. It outputs the decision tree in depth-first order, and then proceeds to classify instances of the testing set. See readme.html for more information.

Project files are included for use with Visual C++ 6.0. The files ID3.[h,cpp] contain the relevant ID3 code. Main.cpp contains the main function. You can find most of the documentation for the code in ID3.h and in the html directory under index.html. Here are some of the major classes to get you started:

- **Attribute:** Holds attribute information such as its name and the range of allowable values. Attributes are created when processing the training dataset. They are assumed to persist for the `DecisionTree` class. Many of the entropy functions reside here.
- **Value:** Every example will have a set of attributes, each with its own value. This class holds the value stored as a string.
- **Example:** A vector of values. It also contains format information for I/O.
- **Node, InnerNode,** and **Leaf:** Node is an abstract class and the other two are subclasses. A decision tree is formed using these classes.
- **DecisionTree:** Contains the ID3 algorithm.

There are three sample data input files:

- **Traffic.txt:** The motivating example for predicting commute time.
- **Bw.txt:** The example for *Black & White*.
- **Tennis.txt:** The example from the original ID3 article [Quinlan86].

Conclusion

By now we hope you realize that decision trees can help your game AI identify structure within a training set by providing a small tree that embodies an inductive hypothesis. Decision trees are a rather elegant way of learning, and can easily expose their logic. Further, the decision criteria are much easier to understand than a neural network or genetic algorithm representation. That is not to say that ID3 should be the game developer's leading brand learning technology; rather, that decision trees have their own strengths and place in the learning field, making them a powerful tool to fit certain problems. We demonstrated that decision trees are most efficient for symbolic discrete values, although there are some nice results that can speed up the learning process when values are continuous.

A more in-depth examination of the decision tree learning done in *Black & White* showed some minor clustering extensions needed to make the target attribute discrete. From there, the inductive learning task was a straightforward application of the basic algorithm presented.

One important issue, perhaps for future articles, we neglected is the question of how a decision tree, in general, can improve game AI. Creating a decision tree is really just a step toward improving the game AI. As with the prophetess Cassandra, just because you can predict the future doesn't mean you can change it beforehand. Perhaps the next step for the game development community is to form a theory of how the game AI should affect the future. We believe that decision trees represent a promising step in the right direction.

References

[Evans01] Evans, Richard, "The Future of AI in Games: A Personal View," *Game Developer Magazine*, August 2001, pp. 46–49, 2001.

[Evans02] Evans, Richard, "Varieties of Learning," *AI Game Programming Wisdom*, Charles River Media, 2002.

[Fayyad92] Fayyad, Usama M., and Irani, Keki B., "On the Handling of Continuous-Valued Attributes in Decision Tree Generation," *Machine Learning 8*, pp. 87–102, 1992.

[Quinlan86] Quinlan, J.R., "Induction of Decision Trees," *Machine Learning 1*, pp. 81–106, 1986.

[Shapiro01] Shapiro, Linda G., and Stockman, George C., *Computer Vision*, Prentice Hall, 2001.

10.3

Understanding Pattern Recognition Methods

Timo Kaukoranta, Jouni Smed, and Harri Hakonen—
Department of Information Technology,
University of Turku, Finland
jouni.smed@it.utu.fi, harri.hakonen@it.utu.fi

As game worlds resemble the real world more closely, their increasing complexity requires effective and reliable pattern recognition. Computer games encompass a variety of problems involving pattern recognition, including enemy evaluation and prediction, coaching, group coordination, terrain analysis, and learning. The task of pattern recognition is to abstract relevant information from the game world and, based on the retrieved information, construct concepts and deduce patterns for the use of higher level reasoning and decision-making systems.

The plan of this article is twofold. First, we analyze what is required from pattern recognition in computer games. We conclude that it can act in different roles, which in turn affect the choice of a method and its implementation. Second, we review a branch of pattern recognition techniques arising from soft computing. Our intention is to clarify where these methods should be used.

Pattern Recognition and Decision-Making

An artificial intelligence (AI) system comprises two parts: *pattern recognition* and *decision-making system* (see Figure 10.3.1). The world, which can be real or simulated, consists of primitive events and states (phenomena) that are passed to the pattern recognition. The information abstracted from the current (and possibly the previous) phenomena is then forwarded to the decision-making system. The world allows a set of possible actions, and the decision-making system chooses the ones to carry out.

Because game worlds exist only virtually, computer games differ from usual pattern recognition applications. We can omit certain problems that affect real-world pattern recognition, like coping with noisy sensor data or unreliable actuators. This does not mean that the game world is wholly deterministic—if it were, we would

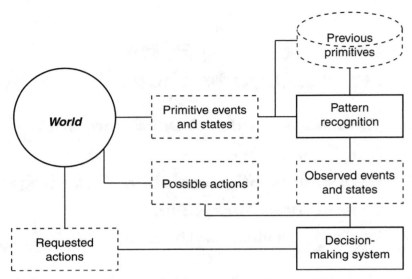

FIGURE 10.3.1   *Relationship between the world, pattern recognition, and decision-making.*

hardly need a decision-making system. The two sources of indeterminism are the built-in randomness and the human players' actions in the game world.

Although AI techniques usually refer to the decision-making system, pattern recognition forms a well-defined and equally important problem area. In the following sections, we approach it from two perspectives. In the functional approach, we analyze where pattern recognition is used and what roles it plays in a computer game. This gives us an indication of the suitable methods for each problem type. In the methodological approach, we review the methods for realizing pattern recognition. Our focus is in soft computing, which enables the pattern recognition to cope with approximations and uncertainties that the ever more complex game worlds promise to provide.

Functional Approach

In computer games, pattern recognition can act in different roles [Kaukoranta03], such as reading the game in an ice hockey match, identifying threats during a campaign, or recognizing Proppian fairy tale patterns in story generation. The roles depend on the level of decision-making, the stance toward the player, and the use of the modeled knowledge. These attributes set boundaries for the computational complexity and the quality required from the result of the pattern recognition method.

Level of Decision-Making

A classical division of decision-making problems discerns three levels:

- Strategic
- Tactical
- Operational

As we saw in Figure 10.3.1, pattern recognition is associated with decision-making. Hence, the suitability of a pattern recognition method depends on the level of decision-making it is associated with. Let us now list features and problems that are characteristic to each level.

On the *strategic level*, decisions are made for a long period of time and are based on a large amount of data. The nature of the decisions is usually speculative what-if scenarios, and the cost of a wrong decision is high. For example, a strategy for a war remains stable and should be based on all available information. Instead of considering the interactions of the soldiers in the field, the terrain is analyzed to sort out regions that provide an advantage (e.g., hills provide an upper hand for defense, whereas narrow passages suit for ambushes). This information is then used in planning the maneuvers to minimize the risks and to maximize the effect. A poor decision at this level dooms every soldier. Clearly, some details must be left out in the process, and this quantization always includes a possibility that some vital information is lost. To avoid quantization problems, the results of pattern recognition should be as high quality as possible. This is not an unreasonable demand, because strategic decisions are infrequent and the computing can be done offline or in the background.

The *tactical level* acts as an intermediary between strategic and operational levels. Tactical decisions usually consider a group of entities and their cooperation. For example, the decisions for a battle concentrate only on the engaging platoons and the conditions in the battleground. They weigh and predict events in the current focus points and dominated areas and, based on the advantages gained on the strategic level, resolve the conflicts as they occur. Ultimately, the aim of tactical decisions is to follow through the plan made on the strategic level. Although tactical decisions affect directly a limited set of entities, a poor decision can escalate to ruin the chosen strategy. Because tactical decisions are made more frequently than strategic, pattern recognition has less time to use. The results must be delivered in real-time and their quality cannot be as high as on the strategic level.

Operational level is concrete and closely connected with the properties of the game world. Although the number of decision-making entities in this level is high, the decisions consist of choosing short-term actions among a given set of alternatives. For example, a soldier must decide whether to shoot, dodge, or charge. Because the computational power must be divided among numerous atomic entities, the pattern recognition method must be reactive and run in real-time.

Let us consider soccer as an example of the levels. On the strategic level, there are the choices of how to win the game—whether to play offensively or defensively. On the tactical level, the choices concern carrying out the strategy the best possible way—whether to use man-marking defense or space-marking defense. On the operational level, the choices are simple and concrete—where should the player position itself and if it has the ball, whether to dribble it, kick it to the goal, or pass it to another player. The problem is how to choose what to do (decision-making) and on what grounds (pattern recognition). It is fairly simple on the operational level—dribble if you have an opening, pass if you can do it safely—but it gets increasingly difficult as the level of abstraction raises.

Stance Toward the Player

The computer-controlled player can have three stances toward the human player:

- Enemy
- Ally
- Neutral

A computer-controlled enemy provides challenge, and it must demonstrate intelligent (or at least purposeful) behavior. The purpose of pattern recognition is to aid computer's decision-making, and we can use quick-and-dirty methods—or even allow slight cheating—when the human player cannot observe the enemy's actions.

When the computer acts as an ally, the pattern recognition method must adjust to the human point of view. Now, the end result is passed to a human player instead of conveying it to a decision-making system. For example, a computer-controlled reconnaissance officer should provide intelligence in a visually *accessible format* rather than overwhelm the player with lists of raw variable values. In addition to accessibility, the human players require *consistency*, and even incomplete information (as long as it remains consistent) can have some value to them.

The computer has a neutral stance when it acts as an *observer* (e.g., camera director or commentator) or a *referee* (e.g., judging rule violations in a sports game). Pattern recognition depends on the context and conventions of the role. In a sports game, for example, the camera director program must heed the camera placements and cuts dictated by television practice. Refereeing provides another type of challenge, because some rules can be hard to judge. For example, in soccer the referee can allow the play to continue "when the team against which an offense has been committed will benefit from such an advantage" and penalize "the original offense if the anticipated advantage does not ensue at that time" [FIFA03]. To implement this in a computer game would require pattern recognition that can interpret (possibly complex) causal relationships between the offense and subsequent events.

Use of the Modeled Knowledge

Based on the information provided by pattern recognition, the decision-making system forms a model about the world. The complexity of the world can be simplified with *generators*, which label the events and states with symbols. For example, the punches in a boxing game can go through a generator that produces symbols "jab," "uppercut," "cross," and "hook." Now, we can construct a model for the behavior of the generator from the generated symbol sequence. Modeling recognizes the underlying dependencies between symbols, which are typically stronger between symbols that are close to each other. Often, a short-term history is sufficient, but the model gets more accurate if we increase the length of the modeling context at the cost of running time.

The decision-making system can use the modeled knowledge in two ways to do temporal reasoning:

- Prediction
- Production

In *prediction*, we want to know what symbol the generator will produce next. By storing the previous primitives, we can use pattern recognition to do preparatory prediction [Mommersteeg02, Laramée02a]. The observation passed to the decision-making system can be a probability distribution of the occurred symbols rather than a single symbol. For example, if the aforementioned generator models opponent's punches, pattern recognition can now provide the decision-making system with probabilities of the opponent's next punch, which is used to calculate an effective counteraction.

In *production*, we use the model of a generator to produce symbols. This is no longer pattern recognition, but decision-making in the form of pattern generation. For example, we can model the punch series of a real-world boxer, and use the model when selecting the next punch for a computer-controlled boxer. Another possibility is to take the model prepared for predicting the human players' moves and use their own moves against them—in other words, fight fire with fire.

As the interchangeable roles of prediction and production point out, the separation of pattern recognition and decision-making is not always clear cut. Nevertheless, the distribution of responsibilities helps us, when we begin to examine the methods.

Methodological Approach

Soft computing is a term coined by professor Lotfi Zadeh to describe methodologies that try to solve problems arising from the complexity of the natural world. They include probabilistic reasoning (such as genetic algorithms and Bayesian networks), neural networks, and fuzzy logic. Whereas conventional hard computing is founded on precision and categorizing, soft computing stresses the tolerance for approximation, partial truth, imprecision, and uncertainty. As computer games become ever more complex, the methods of hard computing are becoming less effective. Consequently, there has been a trend among game developers to adapt soft computing methods in the AI design: genetic algorithms [Laramée02b], Bayesian networks [Tozour02], neural networks [LaMothe00, Champandard02], and fuzzy logic [McCuskey00, Zarozinski01, Alexander02].

We do not strictly adhere to Zadeh's classification, but discuss soft computing methods related to optimization, adaptation, and uncertainty. One can readily see that they seem to have counterparts in the human mind: imagination does

optimization, memory learns by adaptation, and data from the senses is always somewhat uncertain. It is no wonder, then, that soft computing is sometimes called computational intelligence.

Optimization

The term *optimization* literally means the making the best of something. Mathematically speaking, optimization problems comprise three elements: an *objective function*
that we want to minimize or maximize, a *set of variables* that affect the value of the
objective function, and a *set of constraints* that limits the set of feasible variable values
(see Figure 10.3.2). The goal is to find among the feasible solutions the one that gives
an optimum value of the objective function.

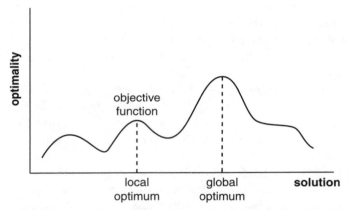

FIGURE 10.3.2   *An objective function gives the optimality of a
solution. The goal is to find the global optimum, but the search
space is usually scattered with local optima.*

Pattern recognition can be formed as an optimization problem provided that we
have a (preferably noncomplex) objective function to rank the solution candidates.
Since optimization algorithms work iteratively, they are usually time consuming and
are therefore used offline or during preprocessing. For example, to balance civiliza-
tions and units in *Age of Empires*, battles with different troop combinations were
tested by using a combat comparison simulator [Street01]. Here, the attributes (such
as armor, hit points, damage, and range) are the variables, which are constrained by
the range of allowed values. The objective function is to minimize the difference of
the number of victories in the simulator battles, and the attributes are changed to
even out discrepancies.

The use of optimization techniques assumes an inherent knowledge of the problem domain. Usually we can make good use of this knowledge by implementing
heuristic rules to guide the search for more optimal variable values. Heuristics attack

the dominating variables. For example, if archers seem to have an upper hand in the combat simulator, our heuristic rule increases the damage done by their counter-unit. The problem with this type of hill-climbing heuristic, which iteratively tries to find a better solution among the neighboring solution candidates, is that the search can get stuck in a local optimum before finding the global optimum (see Figure 10.3.2). For example, instead of increasing the damage of the counter-unit, a better balance could be achieved by increasing the range of their weapons. To escape the lure of local optima, a gamut of approaches have been developed with the likes of tabu search [Glover89] and simulated annealing [Kirkpatrick83].

Local optima can be avoided by having multiple search traces instead of one. *Genetic algorithms* have a population of candidate solutions, which go through stages resembling natural selection [Goldberg89]. The objective function is used to weed out the weak candidates, thus letting the best ones breed a new population. The variable values of the solution are encoded in the genes. Genetic algorithms work well when the variables are independent from each other, because the genetic operations like crossover and mutation are more likely to produce feasible solutions. In the worst case, the variables have strong dependencies (e.g., they form a sequence), and most of the offspring would not represent a feasible solution.

Swarm algorithms, which are based on flocking algorithms, present another approach with multiple search traces [Kennedy01]. Whereas in genetic algorithms the solution is encoded in the population, in swarm algorithms the members of the population "fly" in the search space. Because of avoidance, they keep a minimum distance to each other and cover a larger area than a single search trace, and because they fly as a swarm, they tend to progress as a unit toward better solutions. As a way to escape local optima, the members can never slow down under a minimum velocity, which can allow them to fly past and free from local optimum, especially if it is crowded.

The suitability of optimization methods depends mainly on the level of decision-making. When making strategic analysis, we have to scrutinize a vast amount of data. Consequently, there are many variables and (combinatorial) interdependencies between variables. In their natural state, the problems are computationally hard to tackle, but if we weaken our criterion for optimality by, for example, reducing interdependencies, genetic algorithms become a viable option. Although the problem setting in the tactical level is somewhat easier—there are less interdependent variables and simpler combinatorial problems—the method must be more responsive. Due to the computational demand inherent in making the method more responsive, multiple search traces are not useful and we should devise heuristic search rules. The reactivity of the operational level dictates that we can only solve problems with a few variables or a simple objective function.

Adaptation

Adaptation can be defined as an ability to make appropriate responses to changed or changing circumstances. In a sense, adaptation resembles learning a skill in the real world: when we learn to ride a bike, we do not receive, for example, the physical formulae describing the motions and forces involved. Instead, we get simple—and possibly painful—feedback of success or failure. Based on this, we adapt our behavior and try again until we get it right.

Generally speaking, the difference between adaptation and optimization is that optimization searches for a solution for a given function, whereas adaptation searches for a function behind given solutions (see Figure 10.3.3). The assumption behind this is that the more the function adapts to the problem domain, the better it corresponds to the originator of the modeled data. Adaptation is useful when the affecting factors or mechanisms behind the phenomena are unknown or dynamic. The downside is that we have to sample the search space to cover it sufficiently, and the more dimensions (that is, measured attributes) it has, the sparser our sample gets due to combinatorial explosion.

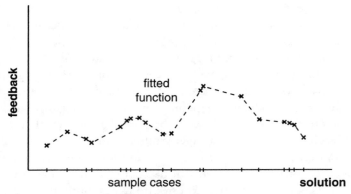

FIGURE 10.3.3   *To model the underlying generator, solution samples are fitted to a function according to the feedback.*

Since the task of pattern recognition is to abstract significant observations and rules from the given data, it can be usually formed as an adaptation problem. In other words, a pattern recognition method is initially a blank slate, which then begins to adapt to the characteristics of the world. This learning process involves self-modification according to the response from the environment. For example, influence maps [Tozour01] are a simple and statistical way to implement adaptive pattern recognition. Based on experience, we change the values: if we get casualties at some point, we decrease its value to avoid it in the future; otherwise, if it has turned out to be safe, we increase its value.

Neural networks provide us a method to adapt in situations where we do not have background knowledge of dependencies [Freeman91]. They work in two different operation modes: training and execution. These are separate phases in supervised learning, where a trainer provides feedback for all sample cases, and the neural network constructs an input-output mapping accordingly. In unsupervised learning (like self-organizing maps [Kohonen95]), the neural network adapts to the structure inherent in the input without any a priori classification of observations. If the input is a time series, hidden Markov models [Rabiner86] turn out to be useful because they can adapt to recurring structures.

We can use supervised or unsupervised learning chiefly in the strategic level due to their computational demands. The tactical level, however, is more dynamic and the results of pattern recognition are less thorough. Here, we should use methods such as hidden Markov models that yield results whose credibility can be evaluated. On the operational level, there are two possibilities: we have stochastic interpretation for input data, or we use a ready-adapted neural network. One feature is common to all levels: even after we have learned a skill, we can still try to hone it to perfection.

Uncertainty

The dictionary gives us two meanings for the word *uncertainty*: something that is uncertain, or the state of being uncertain. In the first case, we usually talk about probability (like the outcome of a dice), whereas in the latter case, the uncertainty concerns our own abilities to classify objects. If you draw a circle freehand, there is uncertainty about whether it is a circle. However, that uncertainty has nothing to do with probability. This *possibilistic* uncertainty brings forth problems of classification, and we face them every day. In the purest form, they are *sorites* paradoxes, like when a heap of sand ceases to be a heap if we remove one grain of sand at a time from it.

Fuzzy sets tackle the problem by acknowledging uncertainty and allowing elements to have a partial membership in a set [Ross95]. In contrast to crisp sets with Boolean memberships, fuzzy sets admit that some information is better than no information. However, one should always bear in mind that fuzzy sets depend on the context: there can be no universal agreement on a membership function, for example, on small (cars, humans, nebulae), and, subjectively speaking, a small car can be something completely different for a basketball player than for a racehorse jockey.

Fuzziness is not a solution method in itself, but we can use it in both optimization and adaptation to cope with uncertainty. In optimization, we can describe the objective function using an aggregation of fuzzy sets (see Figure 10.3.4), and in adaptation, the feedback can be in the form of fuzzy numbers [Herrera97]. In effect, fuzziness allows us to do more fine-grained evaluations. These hybrid systems (e.g., fuzzy neural nets or fuzzy genetic algorithms) are the core of soft computing.

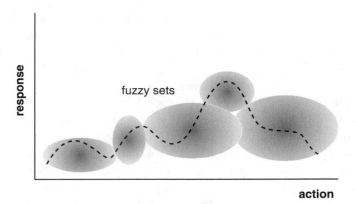

FIGURE 10.3.4   *Uncertain or complex dependencies can be modeled with fuzzy sets that cover the solution space.*

Conclusion

We observed pattern recognition from functional and methodological perspectives. The context of use defines the role of pattern recognition, which in turn affects the choice of a method. Soft computing provides a smorgasbord of methods for doing optimization, adaptation, and coping with uncertainty. These methods are steadily inching toward computer games, and their true potential will be revealed when we learn where they serve us best.

In memory of Timo Kaukoranta (1968–2002).

References

[Alexander02] Alexander, T., "An Optimized Fuzzy Logic Architecture for Decision-Making," *AI Game Programming Wisdom*, Charles River Media, 2002.

[Champandard02] Champandard, A.J., "The Dark Art of Neural Networks," *AI Game Programming Wisdom*, Charles River Media, 2002.

[FIFA03] Federation Internationale de Football Association, "Laws of the Game," available online at *www.fifa.com/refs/laws_E.html*, February 2003.

[Freeman91] Freeman, J.A., and Skapura, D.M., *Neural Networks: Algorithms, Applications, and Programming Techniques*, Addison-Wesley, 1991.

[Glover89] Glover, F., "Tabu Search—Part I," *ORSA Journal of Computing*, vol. 1, no. 3, pp. 190–206, available online at *joc.pubs.informs.org/BackIssues/Vol001/Vol001No03Paper06.pdf*, 1989.

[Goldberg89] Goldberg, D.E., *Genetic Algorithms in Search, Optimization, and Machine Learning*, Addison-Wesley, 1989.

[Herrera97] Herrera, F., and Verdegay, J.L., "Fuzzy Sets and Operations Research: Perspectives," *Fuzzy Sets and Systems*, vol. 90, no. 2, pp. 207–218, 1997.

[Kaukoranta03] Kaukoranta, T., Smed, J., and Hakonen, H., "Role of Pattern Recognition in Computer Games," *Proceedings of the 2nd International Conference on Application and Development of Computer Games*, pp. 189–194, 2003.

[Kennedy01] Kennedy, J., Eberhart, R.C., and Shi, Y., *Swarm Intelligence*, Morgan Kaufmann, 2001.

[Kirkpatrick83] Kirkpatrick, S., Gelatt, C.D., and Vecchi, M.P., "Optimization by Simulated Annealing," *Science*, vol. 220, no. 4598, pp. 671–680, May 1983.

[Kohonen95] Kohonen, T., *Self-Organizing Maps*, Springer-Verlag, 1995.

[LaMothe00] LaMothe, A., "A Neural-Net Primer," *Game Programming Gems*, Charles River Media, 2000.

[Laramée02a] Laramée, F.D., "Using N-Gram Statistical Models to Predict Player Behavior," *AI Game Programming Wisdom*, Charles River Media, 2002.

[Laramée02b] Laramée, F.D., "Genetic Algorithms: Evolving the Perfect Troll," *AI Game Programming Wisdom*, Charles River Media, 2002.

[McCuskey00] McCuskey, M., "Fuzzy Logic for Video Games," *Game Programming Gems*, Charles River Media, 2000.

[Mommersteeg02] Mommersteeg, F., "Pattern Recognition with Sequential Prediction," *AI Game Programming Wisdom*, Charles River Media, 2002.

[Rabiner86] Rabiner, L.R., and Juang, B.H., "An Introduction to Hidden Markov Models," *IEEE Acoustics, Speech, and Signal Processing Magazine*, vol. 3, no. 1, pp. 4–16, 1986.

[Ross95] Ross, T.J., *Fuzzy Logic with Engineering Applications*, McGraw-Hill, 1995.

[Street01] Street, G., Petersen, S., and Kidd, M., "How to Balance a Real Time Strategy Game: Lessons from the Age of Empires Series," Game Developers Conference, 2001.

[Tozour01] Tozour, P., "Influence Mapping," *Game Programming Gems 2*, Charles River Media, 2001.

[Tozour02] Tozour, P., "Introduction to Bayesian Networks and Reasoning Under Uncertainty," *AI Game Programming Wisdom*, Charles River Media, 2002.

[Zarozinski01] Zarozinski, M., "Imploding Combinatorial Explosion in a Fuzzy System," *Game Programming Gems 2*, Charles River Media, 2001.

10.4

Using Reinforcement Learning to Solve AI Control Problems

John Manslow

john@jmanslow.fsnet.co.uk

When creating the AI for a game, it is frequently necessary to solve complex and difficult control problems. For example, the AI cars in a racing game respond to signals from their controllers according to the complex dynamics of a physics simulation, and yet their controllers must, preferably without cheating, control the cars in such a way as to prevent them from crashing while simultaneously maximizing their average speed.

These types of problems have typically been addressed using rule-based controllers that must endlessly be tweaked and tested to produce a useful approximation to the desired behavior. This article describes how reinforcement learning can be used to automatically produce controllers that are not limited by the AI designer's understanding of a control problem, and require minimal development effort.

Reinforcement Learning in Games

Reinforcement learning (RL) provides a framework within which an AI that receives rewards and punishments in response to its actions can adapt its behavior to maximize the frequency and magnitudes of its rewards and minimize the frequency and magnitudes of its punishments. By providing rewards and punishments at the appropriate times, RL can be used to allow an AI to solve a wide variety of difficult and complex problems.

RL has enabled computers to teach themselves how to play many classic games such as Go, Checkers, Chess, Othello, and Backgammon, and card games like Poker and Blackjack. In the case of Backgammon in particular, RL achieved a stunning success by discovering an opening move better than that preferred by the world's best players, and thereby changed the way the game is played at the very highest level [Sutton98].

RL has great potential to help the developers of AI for video games because:

- The same RL engine can be used to solve a wide variety of unrelated problems, ranging from producing a competent Chess player, controlling an aircraft to fly as low as possible to avoid radar without crashing, controlling AI vehicles to follow paths specified as a series of waypoints, controlling the movements of dogfighting aircraft, to producing a competent player of a real-time strategy game.

- Provided that the problem is set up correctly, RL is likely to find a close to optimal solution with minimal development effort. For example, this article shows how to produce a controller for the steering of a car by providing the AI with punishments whenever the car crashes. Once the problem is formulated in this way, RL can be left to derive an appropriate controller by trial and error.

- It can find optimal behaviors even in situations where the effect of an action might not be immediately apparent—either because its effect has a strong stochastic component, or because its effect is delayed. Either of these can make the manual creation of even a moderately competent AI extremely difficult.

- It learns as an AI interacts with the game world, making it suitable for use both during development and to facilitate in-game learning once a game is complete.

ON THE CD

The following section introduces the application that is included on the accompanying CD-ROM to demonstrate how RL can be used to solve real problems in game development. More detailed information can be found by referring to the comments in the source code.

An Example Application: Controlling an AI Car

To show how reinforcement learning can be used to solve real problems in game AI, this article considers the problem of controlling the steering of a simulated racing car in such a way that it drives randomly generated tracks without crashing. There are basically two ways in which such a controller would normally be produced by AI developers:

- Hand written rules would be used to translate information about the car's state into control actions. Regardless of whether conventional crisp or fuzzy rules are used, this is a laborious process in which the rules must be endlessly revised to find a good trade-off between the speed of the car and the chances of it crashing, and ultimately produces only an approximate solution.

- The actions taken by a competent human player can be recorded as he or she controls the car and some statistical model (such as a neural network) used to capture the relationship between the car's state and the player's control actions so that they can be reproduced by the AI. This typically requires less development time and can produce higher performing and more organic controllers, but is ultimately limited by the human player who is being imitated.

The RL method described here requires much less development effort than the manual construction of a series of rules, and its performance is not limited by imitating any particular player. RL is therefore likely to produce a controller that offers a better trade-off between the average speed of the car and the probability of it crashing than any of the alternative ways of producing a controller.

To demonstrate RL, the software on the accompanying CD-ROM generates random racetracks along which the AI must drive a simulated car as quickly as possible without crashing. The physics of the car are simulated using a simple spring mass physics engine that allows the car's rear wheels to slide when cornering at high speed. A detailed description of the physics simulation can be found in the comments in the code, and an excellent analysis of the physics of racing cars more generally can be found at [Beckman91].

The tracks are represented to the AI as a series of straight segments as described in detail in [Biasillo02], except that guide paths for racing lines and overtaking lines are not needed and have been omitted. The specifics of what information the AI extracts from the track in order to work out how to control the car will be discussed later. First, it is necessary to consider when RL should be used and introduce the basic principles that lie at its heart.

When Should Reinforcement Learning Be Used?

RL is an extremely powerful technique that allows an AI to discover optimal behaviors in a game world through its interactions and experiences within it. Before trying to develop an RL-based solution to an AI problem, however, it is worth considering the following questions:

- Do we already know the solution to this problem and can simply hard code it? For example, the effectiveness of different weapons at different ranges in an FPS is known and fixed before a game is shipped, so trying to learn this information is a waste of time. (Or is it? Perhaps some players will be poor at dodging slow-moving projectiles making them more effective than expected at long range.)
- Do we have any other techniques that can solve this problem? Although RL can be used to find the shortest path between two points in a maze, it should never be used for this purpose, because specialized pathfinding algorithms like A* will solve the same problem thousands of times more quickly, and are easier to code.
- Can the problem be posed in a way that RL can work with? That is, can the game world be represented to the AI as a series of states that have (probably stochastic) transitions between them? Can you work out when rewards should be given so that an AI that seeks the rewards solves the problem you want it to? This question is considered in detail later.
- Can the problem be solved using some form of indirect adaptation? Indirect adaptation refers to the collection of statistics from the game world and the use of those statistics to modify the AI's behavior in preprogrammed ways. For example, a bot in an FPS might record how often it's been killed in each location, and use this information to bias its pathfinding. This type of learning is usually more efficient and easier to control than RL, and is often preferable for in-game learning. For a comprehensive discussion of all the issues involved in using in-game learning and adaptation, see [Manslow02].

Before discussing the specifics of how RL is used in the demonstration application, the following section introduces the fundamentals of one of the most popular, powerful, and intuitive forms of RL: Q-learning.

Reinforcement Learning Fundamentals

RL assumes that an AI performs actions in a game world in which it occasionally receives rewards. The world is assumed to be characterized by discrete states, in each of which the AI can take a finite number of discrete actions. Q-learning attempts to estimate the reward that the AI will, on average, receive if it takes a specific action in a specific state. These estimates are computed as the AI interacts with its environment, and RL can therefore be used when an AI must learn during a game.

Let us assume that an AI takes action a when the game world is in state s, receives reward r, and observes that the game world moves to state s_{new}. If the AI had previously estimated the reward for taking action a in state s to be $Q_{old}(a,s)$, it can improve that estimate by updating it to $Q_{new}(a,s)$ where:

$$Q_{new}(a,s) = Q_{old}(a,s) + \alpha[r + \gamma \max_a[Q(a,s_{new})] - Q_{old}(a,s)] \qquad (1)$$

The symbol α is a learning rate parameter that controls how quickly the AI updates its estimates, and γ is a discount factor. One application of Equation 1 is called a backup because it propagates information about the rewards that can be reached from the new state back up to the preceding state where it is associated with the action that was taken.

The learning rate parameter lies in the range [0,1] ,and the larger its value, the faster the AI learns. Learning too quickly is not always a good thing, however, because if the rewards or state transitions have a random component, the AI might have to revisit each state and take each action many times before it can know what reward it can expect for taking each action in each state. Allowing an AI to learn more slowly, therefore, often allows it to perform better in the long run.

The discount factor also lies in the range [0,1] and controls how long term a view the AI takes of its actions. For example, if the discount factor is small, say 0.1, the AI will display a strong preference for taking actions that lead to small but immediate rewards over ones that will ultimately lead to much larger rewards that can only be reached after many state transitions. If the discount factor is large, say 0.99, the AI will focus on trying to reach large rewards even though they might be many state transitions away, and not be distracted by smaller rewards that are easier to obtain.

As well as providing a means for estimating the reward that an AI will receive as a result of taking a particular action in a particular state, RL also prescribes a way of selecting an action based on that information. Specifically, in each state, the AI should usually select the action that is expected to give the highest reward, but occasionally choose another action completely at random. Choosing random actions in this way allows the AI to learn new things by experimenting with new behaviors.

More formally, the AI should, with probability ε, choose the action a in state s for which $Q(a,s)$ is maximized, and some other random action with probability 1-ε. The value of ε controls the trade-off the AI makes between exploring the effects of random actions in the game world and exploiting what it has already learned by doing what it thinks to be best based on its experiences so far.

Although the basics of RL theory assume a game world characterized by discrete states and actions, RL can equally well be applied in continuous environments (such as the car controlling example described in this article) with continuous actions. RL can usually be applied in continuous environments simply by sampling them at discrete points in time to create the impression of discrete states, and continuous actions can be accommodated by making $Q(a,s)$ a continuous function of a.

Breaking Down the Problem

It is important to break the problem of developing an AI down into many small subproblems that can easily be understood and solved individually. This is no less true when RL is being used to create an AI because:

- It makes it easier to debug the learning process. If the AI is trying and failing to learn many things at once, it is difficult to know why it is failing. Allowing it to solve subproblems separately allows its performance on each to be assessed independently.
- The information the AI requires from the game world and the parameters that control its learning might need to be different for each subproblem. Separating the subproblems allows the learning of each to be optimized independently.

The example problem that RL is used to solve in this article is to control a binary signal applied to a car that instructs it to steer left or steer right. RL could also be used to control the acceleration and braking of the car by providing another binary signal that instructs it to accelerate or brake. Between these two subproblems, however, there is a subtle dependency that complicates any attempt to learn how to solve either of them. That is, the best way to steer changes with the car's speed, which itself changes with the acceleration and braking signals sent to the car.

This type of dependency can make it difficult to solve any of the interacting subproblems by any technique, not just RL. The difficulty arises because the dependency would prevent the steering controller being optimized independently of the acceleration and braking controller, because any change to one affects the performance of the other. The removal of such dependencies greatly simplifies each subproblem, reducing the time required to solve them, and improving the reliability with which solutions can be found.

To isolate the subproblem of learning steering from that of learning acceleration and braking, RL is used to learn how to steer a car traveling at a wide range of random but fixed speeds. The car was placed on a track and its speed was limited to some random value by using a simple rule to control acceleration and braking. When the car crashed or reached the end of the track, a new random track was generated, the car was placed at its start, and a new random speed was chosen. This allowed RL to learn to steer the car at all speeds without also having to learn how to accelerate and brake.

Next, the controller that RL produced for steering could be fixed and RL given the task of learning when to accelerate and brake. To do this, the car would be placed at the start of a track and RL would be allowed to control its acceleration and braking while its steering was controlled by the controller that was produced earlier. When the car crashed or reached the end of the track, a new random track would be generated, and the car placed at its start ready for a new run.

Once it has been decided how an AI is to be broken down, and to which parts RL will be applied, a decision needs to be made as to what information RL will need from the game world to solve each subproblem.

Determining What State Information RL Requires

RL learns to estimate the rewards that an AI will receive, on average, as a result of taking action a in state s. To do this successfully, the AI must have access to information about the state of the game world that:

- Allows it to identify those states where rewards are available.
- Allows it to predict the evolution of the game world toward states where rewards are available. If this condition is not satisfied, RL will be unable to work out how to change the state of the game world to move toward a reward state.

Neither of these conditions needs to be satisfied completely; RL will still work if there appears to be a random component to the transitions between states or to the rewards, because the state information is not sufficient to predict either with certainty. Indeed, some random component is always to be expected, not least as a result of the actions of the player.

When deciding what information to provide to RL from the game world, try to:

- Present as little information as possible that is as relevant as possible. Including irrelevant information increases the number of states that RL must explore before finding rewards and hence slows learning.
- Use what you know about the game world and what you want the AI to learn to help you select relevant information. For example, don't include information about the weather in a game world if it doesn't affect the game's mechanics.
- Use what you know about the game world and what you want the AI to learn to structure the state space. If you know that the AI should always take the same action in two different states of the game world, try to represent those states so that they appear the same to the AI. Similarly, if states require different actions, make sure they have different representations.

- Don't be afraid to use abstract representations of the game world. For example, a single abstract indicator of the strength of an enemy in an RTS might provide more information than many individual indicators relating to specific aspects of it.

Deciding what information RL needs about the state of the game world is one of the most difficult parts of developing an RL solution, and several different state representations usually need to be tried to find one that works well. In the demo on the accompanying CD-ROM, it was found, with a little trial and error, that RL needs information about the speed of the car, how much it is sliding, how far it is from the center of the track, and the curvature of the track 5 and 15 segments in front of the car.

ON THE CD

Now that subproblems have been identified that RL can be used to solve, and we have decided what information we are going to extract from the game world to represent its state, we need to decide how RL is going to store its estimated $Q(a,s)$ values—that is, how it's going to associate the reward it can expect to receive for taking a specific action in a specific state with the state-action pair a and s.

Associating Rewards with State-Action Pairs

Any way of associating an expected reward Q with an action a and a state s can be used with RL, provided that the estimated rewards can be updated according to Equation 1 when the need arises. The two most popular choices, however, are lookup tables and neural networks. Lookup tables have the following advantages over neural networks:

- RL is known to be stable and to converge to the optimal policy when lookup tables are used. That means that RL will learn the best action to take in each state. By contrast, RL might fail to learn when used with neural networks.
- RL can learn very quickly and efficiently when used with lookup tables. When combined with neural networks, RL tends to learn rather slowly and must receive each reward many hundreds or thousands of times.

Lookup tables have the following disadvantages when compared to neural networks:

- Neural networks are effective with large numbers of inputs of different types, allowing lots of information from the game world to be represented, whereas lookup tables become impractical when more than two or three variables are extracted from the game world.
- Neural networks can accept all types of inputs without any special preprocessing, whereas continuous variables must be quantized for use with a lookup table. This quantization risks removing important information from the variables, limiting the AI's performance or preventing it from learning altogether.
- Neural networks can generalize intelligently, allowing them to correctly assess the values of states of the game world that the AI has not yet experienced. Standard

lookup tables have no generalization ability, so the AI will have to visit the states corresponding to every entry in the table to have any idea of their values.

Which technique is used to associate estimated rewards with state-action pairs (and there are many more than the two discussed here—see [Sutton98]) depends largely on where RL is going to be used. If the AI must learn in-game, lookup tables are more attractive than neural networks because of their speed and reliability.

If learning is to occur outside of the game and the AI requires lots of information from the game world, neural networks might be preferred because the slow speed and lack of guaranteed convergence when RL is combined with neural networks no longer matters. If learning fails on any particular run, the program can be restarted from a new random seed and left until the AI learns what is required of it. See [Manslow01] for a detailed description of how to apply neural networks in practice.

ON THE CD

Neural networks are used in the software on the accompanying CD-ROM because learning does not occur during gameplay, and the steering AI requires several inputs to successfully control the car. It is also likely to be less obvious to most readers how to apply Equation 1 to a neural network than to the entries of a lookup table.

At this point, we have decided what RL is going to learn, what state information it needs from the game world to learn it, and how it will relate states and actions to the estimates of the rewards it will receive. All that needs to be decided now is when the AI will be rewarded, and how large the rewards need to be.

Providing Rewards and Punishments at the Proper Times

RL knows nothing about the real problem it is being used to solve—it just tries to maximize the rewards it receives. Providing rewards at the correct times is therefore vital if RL is to solve the problem we actually want it to. In general, rewards are provided when:

- The AI achieves its objective or the AI's opponent finds itself in a state where it can't achieve its objective. These types of reward are compulsory because they define the AI's ultimate aim.
- The AI does something that we know increases the chances of it achieving its objective. These "guide" rewards are optional and can accelerate learning by guiding RL toward states where the AI can achieve its objective.

Negative rewards have the effect of punishments in that RL attempts to avoid states where negative rewards are available. Negative rewards are provided when:

- The AI's opponent achieves its objective or the AI finds itself in a state where it can't achieve its objective. These types of reward are compulsory because they also define the AI's ultimate aim.
- The AI does something that we know increases the chances of the AI's opponent achieving its objectives. These negative "guide" rewards are optional and can accelerate learning by guiding RL away from states that the AI should avoid.

All applications of RL include either the first or the third type of reward because they are provided whenever the AI completely succeeds or completely fails, and hence indicate directly what the AI should aim to achieve. For example, to learn steering, RL receives a negative reward of −1.0 in any state where the car crashes because, if the game world reaches such a state, the AI has failed in its objective of keeping the car on the road.

Sometimes, only a very small proportion of states correspond to a complete success or failure. For example, if RL was used to produce the AI for an RTS, success or failure might depend solely on whether the AI wins or loses a game. Only a very small proportion of the states of the game world might correspond to victory or defeat, however, meaning that it would take a large number of games for RL to work out which actions taken in which states lead to which outcomes.

Adding the second and fourth type of reward can help to guide RL toward actions that we know tend to increase the likelihood of the AI succeeding, in a similar way that the heuristic in A* helps to guide the search for a shortest path. In the case of the RTS AI, for example, we could provide small rewards for collecting resources, building military units, or attacking the player, because we know that all these things tend to increase the chances of the AI winning.

Care must be taken when using these types of rewards, however, to make sure that they are so small that they guide the AI but do not directly control it. From Equation 1 it is apparent that, for each state we move away from a complete success or failure, the reward associated with it is multiplied by the discount factor. For example, assuming that an AI is given a reward of r for a success, n states away that reward looks as small as $r(\gamma)^n$, which is only 0.02 for $n = 11$ and typical values of $r = 1.0$, $\gamma = 0.7$.

If we were providing guide rewards of 0.02 or larger when an RTS AI collected resources, for example, the AI would be directly controlled by the guide rewards until it was within 10 states of victory or defeat. This is the case because farther from the end of the game, the rewards provided to guide the AI are larger than those propagated back from states where the actually AI wins or loses. The AI would therefore do nothing but collect resources right up until the end of the game.

Rewards that are intended purely to guide RL should therefore be kept very small so that they do not dominate the rewards associated with the real successes and failures of the AI. Guide rewards could be applied if RL was used to control the acceleration and braking of a car to encourage acceleration and discourage braking, to maximize the car's speed.

To do this, a small positive reward of 0.000025 could be given to the AI every time it accelerates, and a small negative reward of −0.000025 provided every time it brakes. These guide rewards would encourage the AI always to accelerate but are sufficiently small that they would be overridden more than 30 states away from any state where the AI would crash. This should leave enough time for the AI to brake and avoid crashing.

Although everything that is necessary to assemble an RL application has now been covered, the following section discusses some of the technical details associated with the parameters that control learning, the learning rate α, the discount factor γ, and the best action selection probability ε. Adjusting these parameters can help optimize the speed and reliability of the learning.

Setting the Parameters that Control Learning

In many applications of RL, the parameters that control it are fixed at nominal values such as $\alpha = 0.1$, $\gamma = 0.7$, and $\varepsilon = 0.9$, which often work well in practice. There are some exceptions, however, which will be considered for each parameter in turn:

Learning Rate (α)

If an RL AI operates in an environment where there are many stochastic rewards and state transitions, the rewards it associates with particular actions in particular states will be noisy, making it difficult for the AI to consistently choose the best actions.

Because the magnitude of the noise can be reduced by lowering the learning rate parameter, some RL applications that are not required to learn continuously start off with a large learning rate of, say 1.0, and gradually reduce it to 0.0. This allows the AI to estimate the general value of state-action pairs $Q(a,s)$ very quickly and then gradually reduce the noise on those estimates so as to select the optimal action in each state with increasing reliability.

One theoretically sound way to reduce α (which is consistent with the convergence proofs for RL) is to let the learning rate on the nth step of the algorithm be determined by $\alpha_n = k_1/(k_2+n)$, where k_1 and k_2 are positive constants. In practice, this might reduce α so slowly that it takes a long time for the behavior of the AI to stabilize. Scaling α as $\alpha_n = (k)^n$ where $k < 1.0$ is therefore sometimes preferred even though it might cause RL to converge to suboptimal behaviors.

The AI that learns to steer is exposed only to deterministic rewards and state transitions, and hence works well with a fixed learning rate. A little experimentation revealed that the AI was particularly effective with a learning rate of $\alpha = 0.2$, which is its default value in the demonstration application on the accompanying CD-ROM.

ON THE CD

Discount Factor (γ)

It was stated earlier that the discount factor controls from how far away states where rewards are available will attract the AI. In some applications, it might be found that the default value of $\gamma = 0.7$ will produce an AI that takes too short-term a view of its actions. Increasing γ toward 1.0 will force the AI to take a long-term view, ignoring some immediate rewards to collect larger rewards later in the game.

Increasing γ might particularly be necessary in large state spaces, where rewards are relatively sparse, or when guide rewards are used. In these cases, larger values of γ can help to stop the AI focusing on collecting excessively large guide rewards to the exclusion of achieving its ultimate objective. The discount factor is left at its nominal default value of 0.7 in both the demonstrations on the accompanying CD-ROM.

ON THE CD

Best Action Selection Probability (ε)

In some applications of RL, the probability that the AI selects the best action in each state is gradually increased to 1.0. This slowly reduces the number of random actions the AI takes and allows it to focus on exploiting what it has learned by taking the best action more often.

The best action selection probability is left at a nominal default value of 0.8 in the demonstration application on the accompanying CD-ROM. Before the steering controller was placed in a game, however, this probability would be set to 1.0 (unless the AI was expected to continue to learn) so that the controller would always take the best action in every state.

Conclusion

RL is a technique that allows AIs to gradually improve their behavior in a game world. This is done as the AI interacts with the game world, making it suitable both as a tool to aid in the development of an AI prior to a game shipping, and for use in AIs that adapt during gameplay. RL can produce near optimal AIs in environments where manual creation of an AI is difficult, such as when the effects of the AI's actions are delayed or random, and will work in continuous and discrete environments with continuous or discrete actions.

The interested reader is strongly recommended to review the code on the accompanying CD-ROM, since the code comments discuss many of the details of the implementation that are not covered in the book, and the RL implementation on the CD-ROM can be applied elsewhere with minimal modification. This article described only a basic implementation of one type of RL, and the reader is directed to [Sutton98] for further information on the many enhancements to the basic algorithm that can dramatically improve its learning performance.

References

[Beckman91] Beckman, Brian, "The Physics of Racing," available online at *www.miata.net/sport/Physics/*, 1991.

[Biasillo02] Biasillo, Gari, "Training an AI to Race," *AI Game Programming Wisdom*, Charles River Media, 2002.

[Manslow01] Manslow, John, "Using a Neural Network in a Game: A Concrete Example," *Game Programming Gems 2*, Charles River Media, 2001.

[Manslow02] Manslow, John, "Adaptation and Learning," *AI Game Programming Wisdom*, Charles River Media, 2002.

[Sutton98] Sutton, Richard, *Reinforcement Learning: An Introduction*, MIT Press, 1998. Available online at *www-anw.cs.umass.edu/~rich/book/the-book.html*

10.5

Getting Around the Limits of Machine Learning

Neil Kirby—Lucent Technologies
Bell Laboratories
nak@lucent.com

To some AI programmers, the Holy Grail of AI would be a game that learns in the field and gets better the more it is played. Multiplayer network games especially would become challenging to the most skillful players as the AI learns and uses the best plays from the best players. This article examines some of the limitations of machine learning and some of the ways around them.

First is an analysis section giving four fundamental questions and two divisions of the problem space. This sets the stage for three example games to study. Following them are sections discussing limits to learning and ways of mitigating them. In conclusion, we note that while there are serious limits to machine learning, games are getting around them.

Analysis

At the most basic level, game AI responds to input and generates output. The limitations of machine learning as part of a game AI thus can have at least three categories: inputs, outputs, and the ability to respond. Learning itself gives us a fourth category. These broad categories can be expressed as a set of basic questions.

1. Is it cheap to *see* (recognize) the thing to be learned from? The AI must be able to use the input.
2. Is it cheap to *store* the knowledge? The algorithm used to respond to the inputs has to coexist with the resource limits imposed by the rest of the game.
3. Is it cheap to *use* the knowledge? Not only do the algorithms used to respond have to perform well, but also the output that is generated must be usable by the system.

If the answer to all three is affirmative, this might be a good place for learning by the AI. There is also a fourth fundamental question not to lose sight of.

4. Does learning make the game *better*?

This article also makes two major divisions in the problem space of machine learning in games. The first is to look at what will be termed *implicit* versus *explicit* learning. The second is to divide games that learn in the field from those that learn only while in development. Both of these divisions have a profound impact on how learning is handled in games.

For our purposes, implicit learning occurs when the game by itself decides to learn something. In the most general cases, implicit learning is usually seen as a very hard problem; if programming machine learning is hard, programming machine-directed machine learning is far harder. Implicit learning is also seen as having the highest potential payoff in the form of a game that gets better the more it is played.

Explicit learning occurs when the program is told it should learn something, usually by the player. Explicit learning provides a solution to question #1; is it cheap to recognize the thing to be learned from? The answer is yes because the player is doing the hard work. While solving a hard problem, explicit learning is not a universal solution. It requires player involvement, a direct impact on gameplay, bringing us to look at question #4, does learning make the game better?

The second division is whether the game learns in the field. Learning in the field is seen as highly desirable from a feature point of view, but risky from a quality assurance point of view. As used here, learning in the field is meant to imply learning *while the game is being played*. Issues of game design and resource availability prevent helper programs from assisting with the learning task outside of playtime.

Examples of Learning in Games

To illustrate, we will look at the learning in three different games: *Black & White*, *Command & Conquer Renegade*, and *Re-Volt*.

Black & White

Black & White (*B&W*) uses explicit learning in the field, making the solution to question #1 rather straightforward. When the player rewards or punishes his creature, the program goes back to the last thing the creature did and applies the learning to that activity. It is proven by example that the learning is cheap enough to store (question #2) and use (question #3) because the game runs well on target machines. Details on how creatures in *Black & White* learn can be found in [Evans02]. The use of explicit learning is fully integrated as a major part of gameplay, addressing question #4 in the affirmative. Learning clearly makes the game better. The player's creature becomes customized to the player's desires by learning what the player wants it to do and not do.

Continuing the analysis, *Black & White* learns in the field, giving rise to potential quality assurance problems. To avoid such problems, the creatures in *Black & White* were programmed with innate behaviors that constrain learning. Testing on the project began early and the testing process was fully integrated into the development process from the beginning [Barnes02]. Creatures in *Black & White* can learn strange behaviors that the players teach them, but that is correct since they are supposed to do what the player bids them.

Command & Conquer Renegade

C&C Renegade has a feature that is turned off in the shipping version of the game [Hjelstrom02]. The code tracks player movements from area to area. A player might shoot a window out and leap through the opening from one area to a new area. Prior to this, the two areas had no valid path between them. The code notes that the two areas are now connected (since the player successfully jumped between them), updates the pathfinder, and now AI units can use the new path. This feature was not enabled in the shipping version of the game because there was not time to implement it fully and not due to any fundamental flaws [Smith02].

This is learning on a far smaller scale than *B&W*, but the same type of analysis can be applied. It categorizes as implicit learning in the field. Going through the previous four questions yields affirmative answers to all of them. The event to learn from is computationally easy to recognize. The learning is essentially free to store since the pathfinder already stores exactly this kind of data. The learning is free to use since it is just a new value for data already in the pathfinder. It can be argued that the learning would make the game better as well. If the player shoots a second story window out and leaps onto a truck parked below, an AI-driven character in hot pursuit would follow the same path instead of using the stairs, making it seem more intelligent. This capability of learning in the field would not have raised any quality assurance concerns; the game engine would prevent the player from making illegal paths.

Re-Volt

In [Biasillo02], Gari Biasillo describes a genetic algorithm used when developing *Re-Volt* to tune the handling characteristics of racecars on racetracks. The designer ran a tuning algorithm and the AI changed tuning parameters and selected toward those that reduced the lap times. The tracks and the car settings for them do not change after the game ships. This method categorizes as implicit learning, but not in the field. This categorization is typical of most uses of learning algorithms mentioned in the AI Roundtables over the last six years at the Game Developers Conferences [Woodcock01]. If learning algorithms were going to be used at all, it was going to be in a controlled way.

Doing the analysis, we find that shorter lap times make it clear when new settings are better. The data is already present in the control code, so storing the new knowledge takes up no incremental space. Using the new knowledge as the game runs is at no incremental cost as well. However, the tuning run itself is not without cost, and the article mentions methods to minimize the time the runs take. Tuning the cars well clearly makes the game better.

Limits to Learning

Limits to learning will be dealt with in terms of the first three questions. The discussion is limited to enumerating the various limits so that a fuller treatment can be given to dealing with the limits.

It can be hard for games to recognize something to learn from. Games tend to simulate believable worlds, whether real or imaginary. A good simulation quickly gives rise to problems similar to those troubling computers dealing with the real world. Realistic inputs are noisy. Some outcomes have time-related dependencies that must be included in order to learn the true lesson. Some systems will learn the wrong things from correct examples. Many signals have a high data rate compared to the rate at which they supply useful information.

Some learning algorithms are too expensive to update while a game is running. The expense can come from using a large amount of data, storing a large amount of data, or performing a large amount of processing on the data. Regarding fuzzy logic, Bart Kosko cautions, "Supervised networks do have drawbacks. Tuning such systems can take hours or days of computer time" [Kosko93]. Neural networks, in this next example used for analyzing music in real time, have their own problems. "Neural networks are justly famous for their computational demands. [. . .] Once a network is trained, however, its classification work is quite fast, certainly fast enough to be used as part of a real-time analysis environment" [Rowe01].

Knowledge can be too expensive for a game to use. For example, neural networks grow in CPU demand as the size of the network grows. While Rowe found their performance at classifying music to be fast enough, a decade earlier this was not always the case. "The majority of networks are simulated on sequential machines, giving rise to a very rapid increase in processing time requirements as the size of the problem grows. This is particularly true when simulating networks which use Boltzman machines or those which use back-propagation" [Davalo91].

Good Knowledge Representation
Helps Everywhere

Knowledge representation can play a key role in making learning systems work well. In a wide variety of disciplines, preprocessing input signals can lower the data rate and provide better inputs to the learning algorithm both as it is learning and as it is being used.

Consider various ways of coding music. One channel of CD-quality music requires 88.2 thousand bytes of data per second regardless of content. Most MIDI musical scores need far, far less. MIDI is roughly a few events per note, and most music is roughly a few notes per second. Printed sheet music gets by at about one event per note.

Speech recognizers take audio signals with a data rate of between 8 and 88 KB/sec and reduce it to a 10 to 20 bytes/sec text stream. The pieces of information recovered from the data stream are often referred to as *features*. Along the way, recognizers compute a handful of features from frames of hundreds of samples. Finding the right features to learn from is important enough that some researchers are working on automating the task of feature selection [Turian96, Markovitch02].

As a general rule, the higher the level of representation, the easier the knowledge will be to work with, although it might be more expensive to acquire. There is a danger that potentially important data will be lost in the reduction process. Nuances of a live musical performance will not be present in a MIDI score. Any user of e-mail is aware of the limitations of text transcriptions when sarcasm, hyperbole, or subtleties are involved.

Seeing More Clearly

The immediacy of the present can make it easier for an AI to detect a learning experience. Learning that involves the past can be harder to recognize. Even when presented with correct data, AI can learn the wrong things.

As It Happens—Dealing with the Present

All three game examples recognize a learning experience relatively easily. The explicit one (*B&W*) has to be able to tie feedback to behavior temporally, which is relatively straightforward. It is the occasional source of player frustration if they are delayed in getting feedback to their creature before it does something else. In general, games with explicit learning should have few difficulties recognizing when to learn—the player is telling them.

The *C&C Renegade* feature shows the value of data reduction and knowledge representation. The real input stream that is driving the learning is the movement of the player; when it is novel, the AI learns. That input stream is a real-time, mouse-and-keyboard kind of data flow. The analysis does not happen directly on the raw input stream. Constantly moving position data is reduced to the more meaningful information of area. Areas mean something to the pathfinder, and area connectivity is something that the pathfinder stores. *This type of data reduction and knowledge representation makes this learning possible.* While the example is very specific to the way the game was designed, other experts can exploit their own domain knowledge to look for similar transformations that will create learning opportunities in their games.

Re-Volt has no trouble recognizing improvements. The lap timer is a perfect differentiator of relative merit. The controlled environment of the tuning runs prevents outside noise from interfering with the tests. Games with clear differentiators of merit such as these should of course exploit them.

Causal Chains—Dealing with the Past

One of the very hardest things for learning systems to deal with is recognizing key precursors that brought about an experience to be learned from. This is not much of a problem for games where the current game state does not lose too much generality for having potentially different possible prior histories. This is perfectly true of Backgammon and can be mostly true of, for example, racing games. The current positions, vectors, and state of the racers care little how they were arrived at. This is not true of many strategy games where an outcome to learn from has long chains of required precursor events. *In such games, history must be stored so that the AI can learn from it.*

A strategy game that is supposed to learn will have to be able to do the difficult task of seeing backward down causal chains to see the key enablers. The fact that they are games and not in the real world can provide some solutions. The abstractions that make the game simulation workable at all are a great benefit to the AI. Compared to the real world, the AI can have perfect information of the past. It would need to be an acceptable form of "cheating" for the AI to go back into otherwise hidden player data in order to analyze player successes that it legitimately saw. Unlike the real world, the data is there—as long as it was stored!

Storing historical data has uses beyond making the AI able to learn the right things. That same data is a source of debugging data for testing and especially for regression testing. Always logging history data might well be justified on benefits to testing alone, regardless of whether the learning feature it enables makes it into the shipping version of the game.

The saying, "For want of a nail the shoe was lost. For want of a shoe a horse was lost. For want of a horse a rider was lost. For want of a rider the battle was lost. For want of the battle a kingdom was lost" suggests that the game should track nails to keep from losing kingdoms. The required tracking, monitoring, and recording of minutia is in direct conflict with the desire to perform data reductions and to work at higher levels of abstraction! The same need to reduce what could be a voluminous flood of data to "just the good stuff" for debugging and testing is present in the AI as well. In addition, the analysis capability that the AI needs should be quite useful when extended as a debugging aid. As always, this logging capability needs to be designed in up front, and globally included in all the areas of the project.

Seeing the Wrong Thing in the Right Examples

Instance-based learning methods such as neural nets and Markov models can sometimes learn the wrong thing from correct data. They can also have difficulty if they are not trained with data that is "difficult" to classify. Moreover, they can have problems when dealing with data that is hard to differentiate even when trained with it.

To illustrate, according to Hubert Dreyfus, a military system designed to tell if there were military ground vehicles present among trees, as seen from aerial photographs, had no trouble with the photographs it was trained with. Further testing showed poor performance. Analysis showed that the system had learned how to tell sunny day photos (which incidentally happened to have tanks in them) from cloudy day photos (of civilian vegetation). A different system designed to classify the gender of people in photographs had great difficulty with long-haired male rock stars until it was trained with them as well as the population at large. And a speech recognition system for German had a hard time with the first three numbers, "eins, zwei, drei." They all have the same vowel, they have similar consonants, and even native German speakers have trouble with "zwei" and "drei." The system was changed so that instead of modeling the best representations of the number, it maximized the ability to differentiate them. The system had a slightly harder time always correctly recognizing a digit when it heard one, but it was far less likely to hear the wrong thing.

There are common threads here. The first is that testing can often show if a learning system is underperforming. This is of little comfort for those contemplating systems that learn in the field, other than reinforcing the need to include ways to ensure that the system does not learn the wrong things and to provide a "reset" capability for the AI. Next is that learning systems do best when the training data is representative of the population the system will encounter. Finally, in the speech example, the system was tweaked to trade an objectionable error (hearing the wrong thing) for a benign one (not being able to decide that it heard something recognizable).

Storing New Knowledge

If processing the learning experience has more than a negligible cost, it has the potential to create performance issues. If learning is not likely to happen at a steady and constant pace over the course of the game, randomly timed spikes of resource demand by the AI will be possible. However, users notice and dislike random bursts of slowdowns or loss of frame rate. Designers can look at the average CPU usage of the AI and allocate resources accordingly.

Learning algorithms that need training from a large dataset such as neural nets and hidden Markov models can present difficulties with learning in the field while the game is running. Retraining using the entire dataset is not viable in the field, even if it has conceptual appeal. Research here [Wilson00] suggests that this is an area for further study.

If the system can be adapted with just the new datum in a way that does not cause loss of quality against the original data set, then learning in the field becomes much more tractable for these algorithms. Programming and testing this capability are non-trivial, but commercial dictation software proves that it can be done. The problems here are over fitting and failing to best use the new data, and they are not restricted to systems that learn in the field.

Many neural networks now use Temporal Differences [Sutton88] to incorporate new knowledge. The TD (λ) algorithm has worked extremely well with Backgammon [Tesauro95] and more modest success with Go [Schraudolph94] and Chess [Baxter00]. Schraudolph points out the dangers of learning from a poor opponent: "Samuel [Samuel59] found it inadvisable to let his Checkers program learn from games which it won against an opponent, since its predictions might otherwise reflect poor as well as good play. This is a particularly pernicious form of over fitting—the network can learn to predict one strategy in exquisite detail, without being able to play well in general." TD is quite good at games with high branching factors such as Backgammon and Go where deep search is prohibitive (unlike Chess). Even with the success of TD(λ) at Backgammon, improving the process is important. The manual tuning of step sizes can be eliminated and simulation data can be put to better use [Boyan02].

A profitable area to concentrate on is the process of converting data into information already stored and used by the AI system. Doing so provides a clear path for new learning to make it into the existing stored knowledge of the AI.

Genetic Algorithms (GAs), such as used to tune in *Re-Volt*, might benefit from reworking how the evolution is done. Michalski saw two orders of magnitude in the rate of improvement in GAs [Michalski00]. By looking into why a population is superior, his method could achieve larger "insight jumps" instead of slower, small-step incremental learning. Even if faster processes are not used in the field, they have great value in development.

Using New Knowledge

When new knowledge differs in kind from information already used by the AI, it requires new storage, and a new capability to use it as well. As in all software projects, it is best if this is designed in from the beginning. Preferable to that, the system should be designed to exploit new knowledge in an integrated fashion. Games that learn in the field require a heavily data-driven design, because there is no programmer available out there to code the new behavior.

Conclusion

All of this is no guarantee of success. A learning feature must be valuable enough to the game that the extra effort needed can be justified and exploited. A standout feature by itself will not save a game with other problems. *Black & White* succeeds because it exploits and showcases the learning feature. *Die by the Sword* had exquisitely realistic physics [Akemann98] that did not overcome the game's other shortcomings [Fristrom98]—the core idea of question #4 is that the game must be fun, and all of its features should contribute to making it more fun.

While still a current research topic, machine learning has reached computer games. It is present both in bold, large strokes such as *Black & White* and in smaller, subtler ways in other games. It is hidden away as a development tool as well as paraded in front of the player. It has limitations, but research and development are finding ways to circumvent them.

References

[Akemann98] Akemann, Peter, "A Formula is Worth a Thousand Key Frames: Mathematically Derived Real Time Character Animation," *Computer Game Developers Conference 1998 Proceedings*, Miller Freeman, 1998.

[Barnes02] Barnes, Jonty, and Hutchens, Jason, "Testing Undefined Behavior as a Result of Learning," *AI Game Programming Wisdom*, Charles River Media, 2002.

[Baxter00] Baxter, Jonathan, et al., "Learning to Play Chess Using Temporal Differences," *Machine Learning*, volume 40, 2000.

[Biasillo02] Biasillo, Gari, "Training an AI to Race," *AI Game Programming Wisdom*, Charles River Media, 2002.

[Boyan02] Boyan, Justin, "Technical Update: Least Squares Temporal Difference Tuning," *Machine Learning*, volume 49, 2002.

[Davalo91] Davalo, Eric, and Naim, Patrick, *Neural Networks*, Macmillan, 1991.

[Evans02] Evans, Richard, "Varieties of Learning," *AI Game Programming Wisdom*, Charles River Media, 2002.

[Fristrom98] Fristrom, James, "Die by the Sword Post-Mortem," available online at *fristrom.editthispage.com/stories/storyReader$86*, 1998.

[Hjelstrom02] Hjelstrom, Greg, "Polygon Soup for the Programmer's Soul," in lecture, Game Developers Conference, 2002.

[Kosko93] Kosko, Bart, "Fuzzy Logic," *Scientific American*, July 1993.

[Markovitch02] Markovitch, et al., "Feature Generation Using General Constructor Functions," *Machine Learning*, volume 49, 2002.

[Michalski00] Michalski, Ryszard, "Learnable Evolution Model," *Machine Learning*, volume 38, 2000.

[Rowe01] Rowe, Robert, *Machine Musicianship*, The MIT Press, 2001.

[Samuel59] Samuel, A., "Some Studies in Machine Learning Using the Game of Checkers," *IBM J. of Research and Development 3*, 1959.

[Schraudolph94] Schraudolph, N., et al., "Temporal Difference Learning of Position Evaluation in the Game of Go," In J. D. Cowan et al., Eds., *Advances in Neural Information Processing Systems*, volume 6, 817–824. Morgan Kaufmann, 1994.

[Smith02] Smith, Patrick, "RE: GDC 2002 Presentation - Polygon Soup / 3D Pathfinding— A Simple Short Answer Question," in private e-mail, 2002.

[Sutton88] Sutton, R., "Learning to Predict by the Method of Temporal Differences," *Machine Learning*, volume 3, 1988.

[Tesauro95] Tesauro, Gerald, "Temporal Difference Learning and TD-Gammon," *Communications of the ACM*, volume 38, Association for Computing Machinery, 1995.

[Turian96] Turian, J., "Automated Feature to Maximize Learning in Artificial Intelligence," available online at *www.ai.mit.edu/people/jude/research/afspaper.html*, MIT, 1996.

[Wilson00] Wilson, D, et al., "Reduction Techniques for Instance-Based Learning Algorithms," *Machine Learning*, volume 38, 2000.

[Woodcock01] Woodcock, Steve, "AI Roundtable Moderator's Report," 2001 Game Developers Conference, available online at *www.gameai.com/cgdc01notes.html*, 2001.

Genetic Algorithms and Neural Networks

11.1

How to Build Neural Networks for Games

Penny Sweetser—School of ITEE, University of Queensland

penny@itee.uq.edu.au

Neural networks are a machine learning technique inspired by the human brain. They are a flexible technique that has a wide range of applications in a variety of industries. This article first introduces neural networks, describing their biological inspiration. Then, it describes the important components of neural networks and demonstrates how they can be implemented with example code. Next, it explains how neural networks can be trained, both in-game and prior to shipping, and how a trained neural network can be used for decision-making, classification, and prediction. Finally, it discusses the various applications of neural networks in games, describing previous uses and giving ideas for future applications. Each of these sections are illustrated with relevant game examples and sample code where appropriate.

Overview of Neural Networks

An artificial neural network (NN) is an electronic simulation based on a simplified human brain. Our brains are made up of approximately 100 billion neurons, each with up to 10,000 connections to other neurons. These connections to other neurons are called *synapses* and are the channel for the transfer of chemical signals between neurons. A picture of a biological neuron and an artificial neuron can be seen in Figure 11.1.1. In an NN, neurons are represented as units and synapses are represented as weights. An NN works by acquiring knowledge from its environment through a learning process and storing this knowledge in its weights [Haykin94]. First, the network initializes its weights to a set of small random numbers. Next, these weights are refined through the training process, in which each training example is fed into the network and the weights adjusted in order to minimize a measure of the error between the network's output and the desired output contained in the training example. This process is continued until the network reaches a specified level of accuracy or until a given number of training cycles have elapsed. At this time, the network's weights are locked and it is ready to be used for prediction or classification. A diagram of a simple network can be seen in Figure 11.1.2.

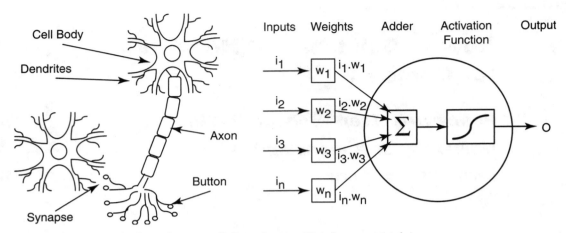

FIGURE 11.1.1   *A biological neuron (left) and an artificial neuron (right).*

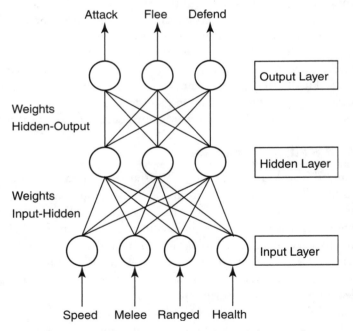

FIGURE 11.1.2   *A diagram of a simple neural network.*

The design decisions that need to be made when building an NN include the architecture of the network, the type of units, the learning rule, the representation of inputs and outputs, the data that will be used to train the network, the testing procedure, and the values of various network parameters. Each of these design decisions are addressed in the following sections, including a discussion of the options and example code.

Architecture

As mentioned previously, NNs are made up of units and weights, which represent biological neurons and synapses, respectively. NNs generally consist of an input layer, zero or more hidden layers, and an output layer. A diagram of a simple NN can be seen in Figure 11.1.2. The input layer consists of units that represent the input to the network. Choosing the variables from the game environment that will be used as inputs can be a very labor-intensive process, as there is a lot of information to choose from, which can make selecting a set of relevant variables difficult. It is also important to keep the number of variables to a minimum to prevent the search space from becoming too large.

Each input unit has one or more weights that feed into the first hidden layer or the output layer. Each weight allows an input unit to provide an excitatory or inhibitory influence on the unit to which it is connected. The output layer consists of one or more units that compose the output of the network. With one output unit, the network can be used to classify its input as being in one of two categories: 1/0, yes/no, true/false. With multiple output units, the system can classify the input into one of many categories. For example, with 26 output units, the system could classify the input as being a letter in the alphabet. Finally, the hidden layers are used to make the network more powerful by extracting features from the data. Each hidden unit also has an associated set of weights that feed into the next hidden layer or the output layer. There is no rule to designate how many hidden units to use. The best way is to start with a small number, between 5 and 10, and then add or remove units until the desired level of performance is achieved. Usually, only one hidden layer is required to adequately model the training data. The following code shows the data structures used for the input, hidden and output layers, as well as the training set and the weights of the network.

```
float Input[numIn], // input layer
    Hidden[numHid], // hidden layer
    Output[numOut], // output layer
    TrainingIn[numTrain][numIn],    // training input
    TrainingOut[numTrain][numOut], // training output
    weightsInHid[numIn][numHid],    // input weights
    weightsHidOut[numHid][numOut]; // hidden weights
```

The Artificial Neuron

Each unit in the hidden and output layers has an adder for combining their input signal and an activation function for determining their level of activation, as shown in Figure 11.1.1. The adder sums the input entering the unit, where each input value is calculated by multiplying the input unit by its associated weight. This gives the activation of the unit as shown in Equation 1, where a is the activation, n is the number of units, x_i is the ith unit and w_i is the ith weight.

$$a = \sum_{i=1}^{i=n} x_i w_i \qquad (1)$$

After the sum of the input to the unit has been calculated, this value is then fed into an activation function that determines the level of activation of the unit. The unit then "fires" and propagates its activation onto the next layer. The most common activation functions include the threshold function, the piecewise-linear function, the family of sigmoid functions, and the Gaussian function [Haykin94]. Figure 11.1.3 shows graphs of these four functions. Another important part of the activation function is the bias, which determines the shift of the activation function along the input axis. It is usually implemented as an extra node in the input and hidden layers, with weights that feed into each node in the next layer. The following code implements the forward pass of the NN, including summing the input signal to a unit and determining if it fires via a sigmoid activation function.

```
void propagate()
{
    // Propagate inputs to hidden
    for (int j=0; j<numHid; j++){
        for (int k=0; k<numIn; k++){
            sumOfInput +=
                Input[k] * weightsInHid[k][j];
        }
        // activation function (sigmoid)
        Hidden[j] = (1.0 / (1.0 + exp(-1.0 *
            (sumOfInput - biasHid[j]))));
        sumOfInput = 0;
    }

    // Propagate hidden to output
    for (j=0; j<numOut; j++){
        for (k=0; k<numHid; k++){
            // sums input to unit (weight * input)
            sumOfInput +=
                Hidden[k] * weightsHidOut[k][j];
        }
        // activation function (sigmoid)
        Output[j] = (1.0 / (1.0 + exp(-1.0 *
            (sumOfInput - biasOut[j]))));
        sumOfInput = 0;
    }
    return;
}
```

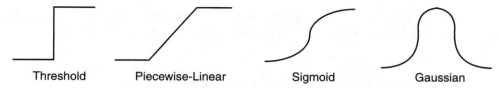

| Threshold | Piecewise-Linear | Sigmoid | Gaussian |

FIGURE 11.1.3   *Activation functions: threshold, piecewise-linear, sigmoid, and Gaussian.*

Training

In training, the NN's weights are initially set to random values. Then, random sets of inputs, called the *training set*, are fed into the system. For each training example, the actual output of the network is compared to the desired output, and the network's weights are adjusted to minimize this difference. This type of learning is called *supervised learning*, in which the network is taught to mimic the teacher who provides the training set, until it has been learned satisfactorily, at which point the network can function on its own.

First, the weights are initialized to random values:

```
void initWeights()
{
    // Initialize weights between input-hidden
    for (i=0; i<numIn; i++){
        for (j=0; j<numHid; j++){
            // weight = random float between -1 and 1
            weightsInHid[i][j] = (((float) rand() /
                (float)(RAND_MAX+1)) * 2) - 1;
        }
    }

    // Initialize weights between hidden-output
    for (i=0; i<numHid; i++){
        for (j=0; j<numOut; j++){
            // weight = random float between -1 and 1
            weightsHidOut[i][j] =(((float) rand() /
                (float)(RAND_MAX+1)) * 2) - 1;
        }
    }
    return;
}
```

Then the training loop begins; in this case, the training continues for N iterations. The examples in the training set are taken one at a time and propagated through the network. First, the input units propagate the input to the hidden layer, which then uses the sigmoid function to determine the extent to which each unit will propagate the signal, as described in the previous section. Next, the hidden units propagate the information to the output layer, which determines which output units will become activated, thus generating the output of the network.

```
// Training loop
while (iterations <= N){
    // For each example in the training set
    for (int i=0; i<numTrain; i++){
        // Get inputs from training set
        for (int j=0; j<numIn; j++){
            Input[j] = TrainingIn[i][j];
        }
        // Propagate
        propagate();
        // Backpropagate error
        backpropagate(i);
    }
    iterations++;
}
```

After the network has generated its output for a particular training example, the network's error needs to be calculated and the weights adjusted accordingly. The function that is used to do this is called the *backpropagation learning rule*. This rule works by calculating the difference between the actual output, which is the output generated by the network, and the expected output, which is the correct output from the training example. The backpropagation learning rule then backpropagates this error back through the system, adjusting each weight according to its influence on the output. As learning progresses, the weights in the network are adjusted to minimize the errors made by the network. The weights from the bias nodes are adjusted in the same way, except that the bias nodes always equal 1. Another important aspect in backpropagation is the momentum term, which reduces the chance that the network will find local maxima or that the learning will plateau. The algorithm for backpropagation is shown in the following pseudocode, in Figure 11.1.4. The actual implementation of this pseudocode can be found in the accompanying CD-ROM demo for this article.

ON THE CD

There are two other types of learning used in NNs: reinforcement learning and unsupervised learning. In reinforcement learning, the network is not explicitly given desired outputs in the form of a training set, but is rewarded when it does the right thing, while unsupervised learning looks for statistical regularities in the data [Haykin94].

```
void backpropagate ( )
    momentum term

    for each output unit
        output error = expected output – actual output
    for each hidden unit
        for each output unit
            sum += output error * output weight
        hidden error = hidden unit + (1 – hidden unit) * sum
    for each hidden unit
        for each output unit
            change in output weight = (momentum * previous change in weight)
                + (learning rate * output error * output unit)
            new output weight = previous output weight + change in output weight
            change in bias weight = (momentum * previous change in bias weight)
                + (learning rate * output error)
            new bias weight = previous bias weight + change in bias weight
    for each input unit
        for each hidden unit
            change in hidden weight = (momentum * previous change in weight)
                + (learning rate * hidden error * hidden unit)
            new hidden weight = previous hidden weight + change in hidden weight
            change in bias weight = (momentum * previous change in bias weight)
                + (learning rate * hidden error)
            new bias weight = previous bias weight + change in bias weight
```

FIGURE 11.1.4   *Backpropagation algorithm.*

Types of Neural Networks

The most common type of NN is the Feedforward network, in which each layer of units feeds its output forward to the next layer. In these NNs, each unit in one layer can be fully connected to every unit in the next layer, or the units can be sparsely connected. There are two types of Feedforward networks, the Single-Layer Perceptron and the Multi-Layer Perceptron. In the Single-Layer Perceptron, the input units map directly to the output layer. However, in Multi-Layer Perceptrons, which is the type of network used as an example in this article, there are one or more hidden layers in addition to the inputs and outputs.

There are many other types of networks that each perform well on certain problems. Some of the more popular types include Hopfield networks and Kohonen Feature Maps. In a Hopfield network, each unit is connected to every other unit and there is no differentiation between input and output units. Hopfield networks are used for storage and recognition of patterns, such as images. A Kohonen Feature Map is a type of self organizing map, in which there is only one layer of units, other than the inputs, that organize themselves according to input values. Kohonen maps can be used to detect patterns in complex sets of data.

Design Decisions

There are many choices to make when designing your NN. First, you must decide on the architecture of your network, including what type of network you will use and how many input, hidden, and output units you will have and how they will be connected. The number of input units will be equal to the number of game variables that are being fed to the network and should be kept to the fewest possible, to reduce the complexity of the problem. The number of output units will equal the number of different outcomes, whether classes or decisions, that are available to the network. The number of hidden nodes is arbitrary and the usual approach is to start with a few and add more depending on the network's performance. Second, you need to decide what type of units will be used, such as linear or sigmoid, by choosing the activation function that you will use. The example in this article used a type of sigmoid function, namely a logistic function. This function is commonly used in networks that use backpropagation learning.

Third, you need to choose how to represent the network's inputs and outputs; will they be real numbers or a string of bits? In a game situation, where the game variables are real numbers, it would generally be best to represent the inputs to the network as real numbers. The outputs could map directly to a decision or action that is to be made or could represent some intermediate classification. In these cases, the output could be represented as integers that correspond to the different choices, or each output could correspond to a variable, so that each returns a value between 0 and 1. Fourth, a suitable learning rule needs to be chosen, such as the backpropation rule used in this article. Fifth, you need to decide on the training data you will use to train the network; this is discussed further in the next section. Next, the network will need to be tested to find a suitable point to stop training, where accuracy and the ability to generalize to new data are maximized. This is usually based on a measure such as the *mean square error* (MSE).

Finally, there are several parameters that need to be set, including learning rate, momentum, and initial weight values. Learning rate is usually set to around 0.2, momentum is set to 0.9, and initial weights are randomly chosen within a range, such as between positive and negative 1. These variables often need to be tuned to attain optimal performance. Designing the best NN for your application is done through trial, error, and experience.

Applications of Neural Networks in Games

Neural networks are AI techniques that can be used in a wide variety of applications. Some common uses include memory, pattern recognition, learning, and prediction. NNs have been used for a range of commercial applications across various industries, including business, food, financial, medical and health care, science, and engineering. Some examples of applications that NNs are being used for include predicting sales, handwritten character recognition for PDAs and faxes, odor analysis via electronic nose, stock market forecasting, credit card fraud detection, cellular diagnosis, protein analysis for drug development, and weather forecasting. This list illustrates the wide variety of applications that can make successful use of NNs, and how their usefulness is only limited to what can be imagined.

The computer games industry is no different from the industries previously mentioned in terms of the variety of applications of NNs. Basically, an NN can be used to make decisions or interpret data based on previous input and output examples that it has been given. This training set can be composed of many different types of data that represent many different types of events, characters, or environments. In a computer game, the input is a set of variables from the game world, similar to that used by a state machine, that represent attributes of the game world, game event, or game character. The output from the NN can be a decision, a classification, or a prediction. For example, the input to the NN could represent the attributes that describe other characters that the AI has encountered in the game world, consisting of variables like health, hitpoints, strength, stamina, attack, and so forth. The outputs could be a set of possible actions that the AI can take, such as talk, run away, attack, or avoid. Alternatively, the output could be a classification of how the AI feels about this character, such as loathe, dislike, neutral, like, or love. This feeling could then contribute to the AI's decisions about how to react to this character in different situations. A practical game example for an NN application, strategic decision-making, is described in [Sweetser04].

To train the NN for the examples previously discussed, a couple of approaches can be taken. First, the NN can learn during the game by using the AI's experiences of encountering different characters and the outcomes in these situations. Alternatively, a training set could be fed to the NN during development, either hand-crafted by the developer or built up by actual play during development. Each of these methods has its advantages and disadvantages. The first method, in-game learning, would allow the AI to adapt to the player and have different outcomes dependent on different experiences. However, this method requires the NN to perform computation during the game, which might not be possible given limited resources.

Furthermore, as the AI can learn different things depending on its various experiences, it can also learn things that the developer has not intended, which might make it appear less intelligent. This problem can be dealt with via a reset mechanism that monitors the NN and resets it if its performance is suffering. The second method, which involves training during development and locking the settings prior to shipping, is advantageous as the NN will only behave as expected and it will require minimal resources to compute outputs when required. However, this method is not as flexible as in-game learning, as the NN will not be able to adapt to the player or behave differently with different experiences. See [Manslow02b] for more details on these issues.

So far, game developers who have used NNs in their games have done so via the second method of training, in case the AI was to learn something undesirable or unexpected. Some examples of games that include NNs for various tasks include *Battle-Cruiser: 3000AD*, *Black & White*, *Creatures*, *Dirt Track Racing*, and *Heavy Gear*. In *BattleCruiser: 3000AD* (*BC3K*) the AI uses NNs to control the non-player characters as well as to guide negotiations, trading, and combat [Woodcock03]. *BC3K* uses an NN for very basic goal-oriented decision-making and pathfinding, with a combination of supervised and unsupervised learning. In *Black & White*, the player has a creature that learns from the player and other creatures. The creature's mind includes a combination of symbolic and sub-symbolic representations, with desires being represented as NNs [Evans01]. The *Creatures* series of games makes heavy use of Artificial Life techniques, including heterogeneous NNs, in which the neurons are divided into lobes that have individual sets of parameters. In combination with genetic algorithms, the creatures use the NNs to learn behavior and preferences over time. The game *Dirt Track Racing* uses an NN for driving around the racetrack. Finally, *Heavy Gear* uses an NN as part of the Mech control mechanisms, with each Mech having several specialized NNs for particular aspects.

Conclusion

In summary, neural networks are a machine learning technique inspired by the human brain. The structure of an NN includes elements modeled on neurons and synapses, which acquire knowledge from the environment via a learning process. This technique has been used extensively for a wide range of industrial applications, as well as several commercial computer games. NNs are highly flexible and are therefore suitable for a range of applications in games, including decision-making and classification. Additionally, an NN can be trained either in-game or during development, depending on resources available and level of control that is required.

References and Additional Reading

[Champandard02] Champandard, A. J., "The Dark Art of Neural Networks," *AI Game Programming Wisdom*, Charles River Media, 2002.

[Evans01] Evans, R., "AI in Games: A Personal View," available online at *www.gameai.com/blackandwhite.html*, 2001.

[Haykin94] Simon, S., "Neural Networks: A Comprehensive Foundation," Maxwell Macmillan International, 1994.

[LaMothe00] LaMothe, A., "A Neural-Net Primer," *Game Programming Gems*, Charles River Media, 2000.

[Manslow02a] Manslow, J., "Imitating Random Variations in Behavior Using a Neural Network," *AI Game Programming Wisdom*, Charles River Media, 2002.

[Manslow02b] Manslow, J., "Learning and Adaptation in Games," *AI Game Programming Wisdom*, Charles River Media, 2002.

[Sweetser04] Sweetser, P., "Strategic Decision-Making with Neural Networks and Influence Maps," *AI Game Programming Wisdom 2*, Charles River Media, 2004.

[Woodcock03] Woodcock, S., "Games Making Interesting Use of Artificial Intelligence Techniques," available online at *www.gameai.com*, 2003.

How to Build Evolutionary Algorithms for Games

Penny Sweetser—School of ITEE, University of Queensland

penny@itee.uq.edu.au

Evolutionary algorithm* is the broad term given to the group of optimization and
search algorithms that are based on evolution and natural selection, including
genetic algorithms, evolutionary computation, and evolutionary strategies. Evolutionary algorithms have many advantages, in that they are robust search methods for
large, complex, or poorly understood search spaces and nonlinear problems. However,
they also have many disadvantages, in that they are time consuming to develop and
resource intensive when in operation. This article introduces evolutionary algorithms,
describing what they are, how they work, and how they are developed and employed,
illustrated with example code. Finally, the different applications of evolutionary algorithms in games are discussed, including examples of possible applications in different
types of games.

Evolutionary Algorithms

An evolutionary algorithm (EA) is an AI technique for optimization and search that
uses ideas from evolution and natural selection to evolve a solution to a problem. In
nature, DNA encodes evolutionary information in all living cells. Each DNA mole-
cule is stored separately in a single, intricate protein-based structure known as a *chromosome*. Different species possess differing numbers of chromosomes, with human
cells possessing 46. Each chromosome contains many functional DNA sequences
known as *genes* that encode the blueprints for the generation of specific proteins. In a
similar way, EAs use chromosomes that encode possible solutions to a problem, with
each gene in an EA's chromosome representing a variable or aspect of the solution.

In nature, reproduction occurs when genetic material from two parents fuses to
form a fertilized egg. During reproduction, recombination allows each pair of the parents' homologous chromosomes to exchange genes, resulting in genetic variance in the
offspring. Recombination, or crossover, also occurs in EAs, when two solutions are
combined to form one solution that inherits components from both parent solutions.

However, only a specific type of EA, called genetic algorithms, use crossover. Most EAs rely on another means of creating genetic variation in nature, namely mutation.

In mutation, genes can be modified through insertion, deletion, or replacement of subunits. However, natural mutation is extremely rare as such variance usually reduces the chances of survival of the organism. Therefore, mutation is only used in EAs with a small chance of occurring so as not to adversely disrupt the overall fitness of the population. In nature, organisms with favorable mutations and recombinations tend to produce more offspring than their less successful counterparts. Therefore, the genes present in these successful individuals tend to spread wider into the population at the expense of their weaker competitors. Moreover, mutations and recombinations that reduce an organism's chance to survive in its environment will tend to disappear quickly. This process is what Darwin called "survival of the fittest." By borrowing these basic techniques, EAs model evolution by selecting the better solutions to become parents, thus allowing their components to spread further into the population at the expense of the less successful solutions.

The procedure that an EA follows can be seen in Figure 11.2.1. First, the population is initialized with random solutions. Second, these solutions are evaluated using a fitness function that assesses each solution's potential to solve the problem. Third, a selection process is used to assign each solution the number of offspring it will receive. Fourth, crossover is used to generate the offspring of the current generation that will form the next generation. Fifth, these new offspring undergo mutation. Finally, this

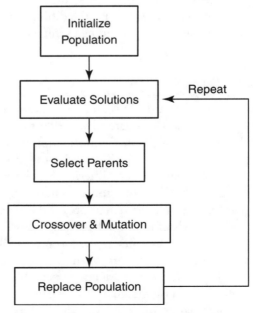

FIGURE 11.2.1 *The flow of an evolutionary algorithm.*

next generation replaces the current generation and the process repeats. Gradually, more effective solutions are evolved over successive generations until a specified level of performance is reached or until a given number of generations have passed.

Representing Possible Solutions

The first decision to make when developing an EA is how to represent the possible solutions to the problem that you are trying to solve. First, a single data structure must be chosen that is able to represent possible solutions to the problem. For example, if optimizing a function of real numbers, then real numbers should be used in the chromosome. Second, the representation needs to be able to represent any possible solution to the problem and preferably be designed so it cannot represent infeasible solutions. Some different types of representations include an array of real numbers, a string of bits, a sequence of items implemented as a list or array, or even a tree structure.

To illustrate the development process of EAs, a pathfinding EA will be used as an example throughout this article. This EA is designed to find a path between two randomly generated points, on a 32 by 32 grid with no obstacles. The chromosome in this EA represents a potential path that can be taken from the start point to the end point and is represented as an array of vectors, consisting of an x value and a y value. The population is represented as an array of these chromosomes. There is also an array for storing the fitness of each individual in the population. The following code shows the data structure used for the population, where *popSize* is the size of the population, and *chromoSize* is the size of the chromosome.

```
struct {
    int x;
    int y;
} population[popSize][chromoSize], nextgen[popSize][chromoSize];
```

Initializing the System

First, the EA needs to be initialized by populating it with sample solutions. In the pathfinding example, this has been done by randomly generating values within a given range to be the initial solutions. As the example is pathfinding, the x and y values are generated to be in a relatively small range, between positive and negative 4, as shown in the following sample code:

```
// initialize population to random values
for (i=0; i<popSize; i++){
    for (j=0; j<chromoSize; j++){
        // initialize x to random value between +/-4
        population[i][j].x = (rand() % 9) - 4;
        // initialize y to random value between +/-4
        population[i][j].y = (rand() % 9) - 4;
    }
}
```

Evaluating Solutions with a Fitness Function

Now that we have a population of initial solutions, the next step is to evaluate the solutions to see how well they solve the problem. The function used for this evaluation is called the *fitness function*, which is used to assign a fitness score to each of the possible solutions. The closer a chromosome is to solving the problem, the higher the fitness score it is given. The choice of fitness function is very specific to the problem that is being solved. In the pathfinding example, the fitness function evaluates each possible path by considering the total distance that is traveled and the difference between the end point and the target point. The fitness function, as shown in the following code, assigns high scores to the solutions that minimize the total distance traveled as well as the distance from the end point to the target point.

```
void fitnessFunction()
{
    // Fitness Function: evaluates population and
    // assigns fitness scores
    for (i=0; i<popSize; i++){
        fitness[i] = 1/(dist(i)+1) + 10/(diff(i)+1);
        // dist() is the total distance traveled
        // diff() is diff between end and target pts
        sumFitness += fitness[i];
    }
    return;
}
```

Selecting Offspring

After a fitness score has been assigned to each chromosome, a method is needed for choosing which solutions will become parents and the number of offspring they will produce. Some of the methods for assigning offspring include roulette wheel selection, tournament selection, linear ranking, and stochastic remainder selection. In the pathfinding example, roulette wheel selection is applied.

In roulette wheel selection, a solution's probability of being selected to be a parent is proportional to its fitness. First, each solution is assigned a piece of the "roulette wheel" that is proportional to its fitness value. Second, for each new offspring that is to be created, the roulette wheel is "spun" to determine which of the possible solutions will become a parent. The advantages of this method are that it is easy to implement and easy to analyze mathematically. The disadvantages are that roulette wheel selection can be problematic when there is either too much or too little variation in fitness scores in the population. If there is too much variation, evolution stagnates as the population fills with solutions that have attributes of the same few solutions. If there is too little variation, all chromosomes are selected with roughly equal probability so that evolution stagnates due to a lack of selection pressure. The implementation of roulette wheel selection for the pathfinding example is shown in the following code:

```
void rouletteWheel()
{
    // Selection: chooses solutions to become parents
    int p1, p2; // index of parents
    float sum, r;
    int crosscount = 0;

    for (i=0; i<popSize; i++){

        // Select Parent 1
        j = 0;
        sum = fitness[j];
        r = ( (float)rand() / (float)(RAND_MAX) )
            * sumFitness;
        // sum individual's values until sum reaches r
        while (sum < r && j<popSize-1){
            j++;
            // sum of fitnesses so far
            sum += fitness[j];
        }
        // individual j becomes parent 1
        p1 = j;

        // Select Parent 2
        k = 0;
        sum = fitness[k];
        // sum individual's values until sum reaches r
        r = ( (float)rand() / (float)(RAND_MAX) )
            * sumFitness;
        while (sum < r && j<popSize-1){
            k++;
            // sum of fitnesses so far
            sum += fitness[k];
        }
        //individual k becomes parent 2
        p2 = k;

        // create new offspring with parents p1 and p2
        crossover(p1,p2);
    }
    return;
}
```

The second method mentioned, tournament selection, involves randomly choosing two trial solutions from the population and selecting the winning solution to be a parent. In this method, the better of the two solutions is given a higher chance of being selected, which is either proportional to its fitness or a fixed constant. The advantage of this technique is that it is less likely to select a poor solution to be a parent and it is more efficient. Disadvantages include that it still allows a few individuals to take over early, reducing genetic diversity and causing stagnation.

Linear ranking involves sorting the population and giving a linearly decreasing number of offspring to each chromosome depending on its rank. For example, the best solution gets two offspring, the worst gets zero, and the median gets one. The advantage of ranking selection is that when differences in the fitness are large the best solutions are prevented from getting too many offspring. Moreover, evolutionary pressure is kept on even when differences in fitness are small, which reduces the chance of stagnation. The disadvantages of this method are that it is slow and requires tuning to determine the best range of number of offspring to assign.

Finally, stochastic remainder selection involves normalizing the population's fitnesses so they sum to give the size of the population and the average equals 1. This normalized fitness is then used as the expected number of offspring, where the integer part means that the solution is guaranteed to get at least that number of offspring and the fractional part is put into a roulette wheel to decide who gets the extra offspring. Therefore, the integer part is deterministic and the remainder is stochastic. The advantage of this technique is that it stops a good solution from being unlucky or poor solutions from being lucky.

Crafting the Next Generation

As well as generating new solutions, it is also necessary to decide how many of the good solutions to copy unchanged to the next generation. The process of copying the best solutions to keep for the next generation is known as *elitism*. The most common approach is to copy the best few solutions, approximately 10 percent, unchanged to the next generation. After deciding which solutions will become parents, which will be copied unchanged, and which will be erased, the next step is to determine how to evolve the parent solutions for the next generation. Copies must be made of the selected parents to replace the current solutions, but making identical copies won't search new solutions. Therefore, these copies need to be slightly different. To produce this genetic variation, the principles of crossover and mutation are applied. The aims of crossover and mutation are to further explore the promising regions of the search space where good solutions have already been found, and to search unexplored regions, in case better solutions are located where we haven't yet looked.

Implementing Crossover

Crossover takes two or more parent solutions and generates a child solution, taking components from all parents to create the new solution. In some representations, such as an array of integers as used in the pathfinding example, crossover simply involves cutting and pasting sections of each parent to the new offspring. Additionally, crossover can be done at one, two, or more points along the chromosome, with uniform crossover referring to crossover where each gene can come from either parent. In the most common form of crossover, two parents are selected from the population, and these parents exchange genetic material at randomly chosen or specified points to generate a new offspring. In the pathfinding example, a random number is generated and this number becomes the crossover point for the chromosomes. Figure 11.2.2 shows one-point crossover for a bit string representation.

```
void crossover()
{
    // randomly choose position along chromosome
    int cross = rand() % chromoSize;

    // exchange genes
    // copy first section from parent 1
    for (i=0; i<cross; i++){
        nextgen[newChromo][i].x = population[p1][i].x;
        nextgen[newChromo][i].y = population[p1][i].y;
        }

    //copy second section from parent 2
    for (i=cross; i<chromoSize; i++){
        nextgen[newChromo][i].x = population[p2][i].x;
        nextgen[newChromo][i].y = population[p2][i].y;
        }
        newChromo++;
    }
    return;
}
```

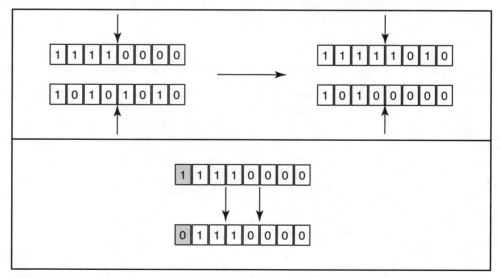

FIGURE 11.2.2 *One-point crossover (top) and mutation (bottom) in a bit string.*

Implementing Mutation

In mutation, a small number of random changes take place to create variance in the offspring. If too many changes are allowed to take place, or the changes are too large, the search becomes too random or inefficient. However, if there is not enough mutation, then the population fills with clones of the same few solutions and stagnates. Some different types of mutation available for an array of numbers, as used in the pathfinding example, include range mutation, Gaussian mutation, and Cauchy mutation.

In range mutation, the changes are chosen randomly and uniformly from a set range. In Gaussian mutation, the changes are chosen from a Gaussian distribution, and as such are concentrated around zero but can be of any size. Finally, Cauchy mutation is similar to Gaussian mutation, but the Cauchy distribution has a longer tail than the Gaussian, meaning that much larger mutations occur with higher probability.

In mutation, the variables that need to be tuned are mutation probability and mutation step size. Mutation probability is the probability that each value in each chromosome will mutate, whereas mutation step size controls the typical size of each mutation. In the pathfinding example, the probability that a mutation will occur is 0.001. If a gene in a solution is chosen to mutate, then the gene's x and y values are changed by a random number between negative and positive 1. The implementation of mutation can be seen in the following code, and Figure 11.2.2 shows mutation for a bit string representation.

```
void mutation()
{
    // 1/chromoSize chance offspring will mutate
    for (i=0; i<popSize; i++){
        for (j=0; j<chromoSize; j++){
            // generate random number, if 1 mutate
            int r1 = (rand() % chromoSize);
            if (r1==1){
                // x/y values mutate by -1, 0 or 1
                int r2 = (rand() % 3) -1;
                int r3 = (rand() % 3) -1;
                nextgen[i][j].x += r2;
                nextgen[i][j].y += r3;
            }
        }
    }
    return;
}
```

Tuning Parameters

EAs also have many internal parameters that must be tuned to suit the problem, often by trial and error. These include population size, number of generations to continue optimizing, fitness function, representation, mutation and crossover operators, type of selection, number of good solutions to keep unchanged, and so on. For example, if the chosen population size is too big then the EA takes too long to evolve and wastes processor power. However, if the population is too small, then the EA will conduct insufficient sampling of the search space and converge to a poor solution. A simple rule of thumb for choosing population size is the bigger the search space, the bigger the population that is required. Moreover, when tuning mutation, if the mutation probability or step size is too large, then the search will be too random and evolution will be inefficient. Conversely, if these variables are too small, then the population will quickly loose diversity and stagnate. It is important to be aware that EAs can take a large amount of hand tuning to work properly and that they are not suitable for all problems.

How to Apply Evolutionary Algorithms in Games

EAs have been extensively explored by academics and are beginning to make their way into game development. The possible applications of EAs are immense, in that any problem that has a large enough search domain could be suitable. EAs offer opportunities for developing interesting game strategies in areas where traditional game AI is weak. Particularly, traditional methods of search and optimization are too slow in finding a solution in a very complex search space. However, an EA is a robust search method requiring little information to search effectively in a large, complex, or poorly understood search space, or in nonlinear problems.

The appeal of EAs comes from their simplicity and elegance as robust search algorithms, as well as from their power to discover good solutions rapidly for difficult high-dimensional problems. EAs are useful and efficient when domain knowledge is scarce or expert knowledge is difficult to encode to narrow the search space, when no mathematical analysis is available, and when traditional search methods fail. On the downside, EAs are computationally expensive, and the more resources they can access, the better. This causes a problem in game development, where AI has to compete with graphics and sound for limited CPU time and resources. Therefore, EAs are better used offline, either working on the user's computer while the game is not being played, using the computer's down time, or developed in-house before shipping to release an AI tuned by an EA. There are many applications that can benefit from the use of an EA, once an appropriate representation and fitness function are devised. An effective EA representation and meaningful fitness function are the keys to the success of EA applications.

EAs have been used for problem solving, modeling, and applied to many scientific, engineering, business, and entertainment problems. EAs have been successfully used in problems in machine and robot learning, such as classification and prediction, designing neural networks, evolving rules for learning classifier systems, and the design and control of robots. There are many ways in which EAs could be used in computer games. For example, an EA could be used in a real-time strategy (RTS) game to tune the AI's strategy to target the human player's weaknesses. This could simply involve tuning a set of parameters that define the AI's personality, in terms of its preference for types of units, its weighting on offensive and defensive, preferences for scientific advances, and so on.

Alternatively, an EA could be used to tune the behavior of individual or groups of units in an RTS. Additionally, an EA could be used in a role-playing game (RPG) or first-person shooter (FPS) to evolve behaviors of characters and events. For example, an EA could take the creatures in the game that have survived the longest and evolve them to produce future generations. This would only need to be done when a new creature is needed. Furthermore, EAs could be used in games for pathfinding, in a similar way to the pathfinding example in this article. This EA could be extended to include obstacle avoidance, factoring for different types of terrain and possibly using waypoints instead of vectors. In short, EAs can be useful in games wherever there are parameters that need to be tuned, where adaptation, variation, or optimization is required, and especially where setting these values by hand would be time consuming and intricate.

A few computer games have made successful use of EAs in the past. These games include *Cloak, Dagger, and DNA*, the *Creatures* series, *Return Fire II*, and *Sigma* [Woodcock02]. *Cloak, Dagger, and DNA* uses EAs to guide the computer opponent's play. It starts with four DNA strands, which are rules governing the behavior of the computer opponents. As each DNA strand plays, it tracks how well it performed in every battle. Between battles the user can allow the DNA strands to compete against each other in a series of tournaments, which allows each DNA strand to evolve. There are a number of governing rules for DNA strand mutation, success, and so on, and the player is able to edit a strand's DNA ruleset. The *Creatures* series of games makes use of an EA-like winnowing process to push evolution of the creatures. Effectively, it is a self-training neural network that allows the creatures to learn over time what they like, what they're not supposed to do, and so on.

Conclusion

EAs are based on evolution and natural selection and are used for search and optimization. They are resource intensive and require much time in development and tuning, which does not make them ideal for in-game learning. Generally, the most difficult part in EA development is determining a suitable representation for the solutions. Moreover, parameters such as population size, mutation and crossover operators and the number of solutions to erase, make parents or keep unchanged can take a long time to tune. Basically, an EA is not a good algorithm to incorporate into a game where time and resources are limited; unfortunately, this describes most commercial games. However, EAs also have many advantages, in that they are a robust search method for large, complex, or poorly understood search spaces and nonlinear problems. Finally, EAs have many possible applications in games and are especially suited for both game evolution and evolution during development.

References and Additional Reading

[Buckland02] Buckland, M., "Genetic Algorithms in Plain English," available online at *www.ai-junkie.com/*, 2003, also included on the *AI Game Programming Wisdom 2* CD-ROM.

[Laramée02] Laramée, F. D., "Genetic Algorithms: Evolving the Perfect Troll," *AI Game Programming Wisdom*, Charles River Media, 2002.

[LaMothe99] Lamothe, A., "Tricks of the Windows Game Programming Gurus," SAMS, 1999.

[Woodcock02] Woodcock, S., "Games Making Interesting Use of Artificial Intelligence Techniques," available online at *www.gameai.com*, March 2002.

11.3

Adaptive AI: A Practical Example

Soren Johnson—Firaxis Games

sjohnson@firaxis.com

Adaptive AI has long been a high-level goal for game developers. Because most AIs are either hared-coded or based on predefined scripts, a player can quickly learn to anticipate how the AI will behave in certain situations. While the player will develop new strategies over time, the AI will always act as it did when the box was opened, suffering from strategic arrested development.

In contrast, an adaptive AI will constantly adjust its strategic choices according to each player's individual style. Over time, the game will build a database of information on the player's habits and tendencies so that when he or she begins a game, the AI does not start from a blank slate. Further, an adaptive AI will also adjust its behavior during the course of a game, resulting in an opponent that will dynamically counter new strategies introduced by the player.

This article describes the adaptive AI of a simple turn-based game called *Advanced Protection*. The turn-based environment was chosen for experimental clarity by reducing the number of decision points on which the AI would train. However, a similar methodology could be used for a real-time setting.

Advanced Protection

ON THE CD

The rules for *Advanced Protection* will be discussed as briefly as possible. (The full rules are included in the Appendix A document on the accompanying CD-ROM.) The game is played on a randomly generated, wrap-around 24 x 24 grid in a sequence of turns, which are split into 50 phases. Each square on the map has a different elevation, ranging from "water" to "peak." The lower elevations yield more money for farming units. The higher elevations give defensive bonuses. However, the highest and lowest terrain types (water and peaks) are impassable to most units.

The human and the computer player (known as "Chaos") both start with a predetermined amount of money. Before each turn begins, the human is able to purchase units and place them on the grid. In addition, units that have survived from the previous turn can be salvaged for extra money. As the turn begins, Chaos buys units (known as "minions") and places them at random positions on the grid. Then, the 50 phases occur, during which time Chaos's minions move around the grid attempting to destroy the human's units.

During each phase, all of Chaos's minions are allowed to move. The human's units do not move, but some of them produce money and others can attack Chaos's minions. At the end of the turn, all of Chaos's minions are removed from the map, and Chaos receives an amount of money equal to their total value. The game ends when either Chaos surrenders or when the human's units and money have been eliminated.

The human has eight types of units from which to choose. Three of the units (the drone, farmer, and settler) farm their squares, producing money each phase. One unit (the jammer) prevents Chaos's minions from communicating with each other, one (the mine) attacks minions that move onto its square, and the other three (the infantry, armor, and artillery) are valuable for their combat abilities. The only proactively offensive unit is the artillery, which attempts to bomb every one of Chaos's minions within a radius of two squares. All eight units have defense and counter-attack strengths for combat with Chaos's minions. Each square can hold only one unit.

Chaos can deploy up to eight types of minions. One minion (the scout) can broadcast a signal that most of the other minions can hear if they are within a certain radius. Unlike other minions, the scout can see mines and detect jammers and artillery. Another minion (the scavenger) farms its square, producing money for Chaos each phase.

The other six minions (known as "barbarians") can attack the human's units. Thus, all of the barbarians have attack/defense values for combat. Barbarians that destroy farming units acquire the amount of the money those units have produced during the turn. Three of the barbarians have special abilities: the jumping barbarian can jump over a square occupied by a human unit or impassable terrain, the amphibious barbarian can move through water, and the kamikaze barbarian always wins its attacks but is automatically destroyed in the process.

The barbarians can detect the scout's broadcasts—the armored and mobile barbarians can detect the signal within a radius of three squares while the others can sense it within a radius of two squares. All of the minions move once per phase except for the mobile and kamikaze barbarians, which both move twice. Multiple minions can co-exist within the same square. Further, each minion also has a facing (north, east, south, or west). Accordingly, each move consists of one of four actions: move forward one square, turn right 90 degrees, turn left 90 degrees, or take a special action. For scouts, the special action is to broadcast; for scavengers, it is to farm; and for barbarians, it is to attack.

Chaos's Artificial Intelligence

The minions' decisions are controlled by a four-state automata, which takes three bits as input and outputs four bits (two for the new state and two for the action). In total, the AI includes eight automata, one for each type of minion. An example of such an automaton is shown in Figure 11.3.1.

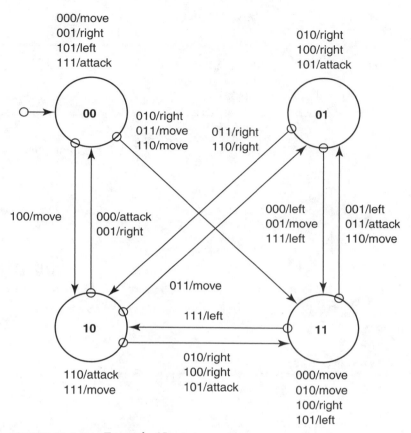

FIGURE 11.3.1 *Example AI minion automata.*

Each of these four-state automata can be encoded into bit strings—the four states each have eight transitions (one for every possible input) and each transition outputs four bits. Thus, 4 bits x 8 transitions x 4 states = 128 bits are needed to encode the entire automaton. Further, 8 minions x 128 bits = 1024 bits are needed to encode all 8 minions' automata. Finally, Chaos's preference for buying each type of minion can be represented simply by a four-bit string, in which a higher value represents a higher preference. Thus, all eight preferences can be specified by 8 minions x 4 bits = 32 bits. Therefore, Chaos's entire artificial intelligence can be encoded into 1056 bits (1024 bits + 32 bits). The exact arrangement of the encoding is shown in Figure 11.3.2.

The specific meaning of the three-bit inputs varies from minion to minion— Tables 11.3.1, 11.3.2, and 11.3.3 show the different inputs for scouts, scavengers, and the six barbarians.

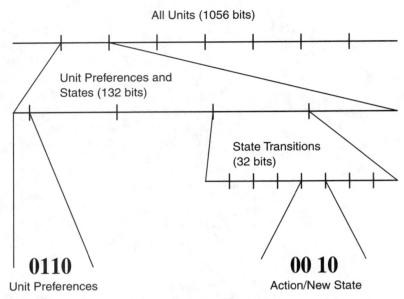

FIGURE 11.3.2   *Bit encoding of AI minion preferences and automata.*

Table 11.3.1   Scout Inputs

Input	Meaning
000	No input
001	Facing impassible terrain
010	Senses jamming radius
011	Senses artillery radius
100	Facing drone or farmer
101	Facing infantry, settler, jammer, or artillery
110	Facing armor
111	Facing mine

Table 11.3.2   Scavenger Inputs

Input	Meaning
000	Facing human
001	Facing impassible terrain
010	Senses gold
011	Facing gold
100	No farming bonus
101	+1 farming bonus
110	+2 farming bonus
111	+3 farming bonus

Table 11.3.3 Barbarian Inputs

Input	Meaning
000	No input
001	Facing impassible terrain
010	Senses scout broadcast
011	Facing scout broadcast
100	Facing drone or farmer
101	Facing infantry or settler
110	Facing armor
111	Facing jammer or artillery

Thus, a complete AI strategy set for *Advanced Protection* can be represented by a 1056-bit string. The AI can adapt by dynamically changing the exact encoding of the strategy string over the course of a game. More specifically, the program chooses one string that best matches the player's style from 250 predefined strategy strings. Each of these predefined strings has a "fitness value," which details the success or failure of the string against the current player. This value is measured by subtracting the change in the value of Chaos's minions and money from the change in the value of the player's units and money. In other words, if the player's farmers produce a great deal of money and most of Chaos's minions are destroyed, this value will be very positive. However, if most of the player's units are destroyed and Chaos gains some money, this value will be very negative.

Every time the player finishes his or her setup, the game forks off a background thread that tests how each of the 250 string performs against the current arrangement of the player's units. The new result is then averaged with the string's last fitness value to produce a new overall value. These values are then sorted into order from highest (worst-performing) to lowest (best-performing) value. The AI then uses these rankings to determine which strategy string to use during the next turn. (For performance reasons, the current strategy string is based on the calculations run during the previous turn. Hence, there is no processing delay when a turn begins.)

Further, the game can dynamically adjust its difficulty level by simply selecting sub-optimal strategy strings. In other words, the highest difficulty level selects the strings with the best performance against that specific user, while the lowest difficulty level picks the worst performer. Thus, difficulty levels can be changed *without changing game rules or allowing the AI to cheat*. The game automatically chooses a difficulty level based on the past success of the player (judging from the win-loss record).

The adaptive AI of *Advanced Protection* is very unobtrusive because, to the player, the game looks like any other turn-based strategy game. The only concession to the adaptive algorithm is that each player must create a user profile (simply by typing in a name) and reload that profile each time the executable is reopened. The profile is a text file (the extension is ".apu") composed of 252 numeric values separated by tabs.

ON THE CD

The first two numbers represent, respectively, the number of wins and losses the user has experienced. The next 250 values are the current fitness values of the corresponding 250 AI strings against that specific player. (Four example .apu files are included on the accompanying CD-ROM in the Appendix B document.)

Strategic Search Space

The search space of strategies (namely, the 250 AI strings hard-coded into the game) was created in two ways. First, 20 strategies were hand-written to cover a variety of concrete tactics and minion preferences. For example, some of the strings emphasized armored barbarians, while other emphasized amphibious barbarians, while others emphasized two or three different types of minions. Further, the automaton varied so that multiple movement patterns were available.

However, while these strategies were often effective, they were rarely as effective (or as ineffective) as the much more creative 230 strings evolved using genetic algorithms. A basic prototype for *Advanced Protection* was distributed to a small test group. This prototype would record the users' unit arrangements into a text file. Using these user log files, genetic algorithm runs were performed against specific unit arrangements selected from this user data.

In every case, the genetic algorithm was able to evolve a strategy that resulted in a negative fitness value, meaning that the computer always learned how to beat the human's strategy. In the end, 53 genetic algorithm runs were completed on data provided by 12 separate users.

The string used by the genetic algorithm was the 1056-bit string that encoded the minion automata and preferences. In each run, Chaos was given an amount of money equal to the total value of the human's units. The GENESIS program executed the genetic algorithm with the following parameters: population size = 10,000; number of trials = 2,000,000; crossover percentage = 0.60; mutation percentage = 0.001.

The 230 evolved strings were picked from the best-performing individuals of these 53 runs, with an emphasis on later runs that were executed against more complex user strategies. We have included a listing of the average minion preferences from the best-performing individuals of each run in the Appendix C document on the accompanying CD-ROM.

ON THE CD

The purpose behind this two-fold approach for designing AI strings was to provide a wide variety of strategies that could hopefully counter the infinite number of strategies that a new user could adopt. The handwritten strings were created to challenge the most basic strategies that a player might employ while the evolved strings were meant to address very specific strategies that real users practiced, many of which could not have been anticipated before releasing the prototype.

The variety of evolved minion preferences shown in the Appendix B document provides strong anecdotal evidence that the best-of-run individuals extended across a large percentage of the overall search space. Certainly, no one minion type emerged as being the most useful in all situations. Furthermore, every type of minion was needed at some point to combat a specific user strategy. Thus, the variety of minion preferences evolved by the 53 genetic runs and the balanced nature of the 20 handwritten strings strongly suggest that a healthy distribution of user strategies are addressed by the 250 hard-coded strategies included in the game.

Results

The effectiveness of the adaptive AI can be best evaluated by comparing the final product with the original nonadaptive prototype. The earlier version suffered from two pitfalls. First, a few strategies worked all the time as the AI never changed its methods. Second, novices were getting killed off too quickly, preventing them from moving up the learning curve.

The first problem was no longer evident in the adaptive version, as the player could no longer win repeatedly using a single strategy. When Chaos faces a difficult challenge from a successful player, the results are quite interesting. Instead of wasting minions with ineffective strategies, the AI often chooses to buy scavengers to increase its resources. Then, when the computer detects a weakness in the player's defenses, the AI quickly shifts to a more offensive strategy, which will often work because Chaos has been building up a large amount of money in order to create an overwhelming force.

Moreover, the complexity of the evolved automata that control the minions is quite impressive. Some have learned to search the local area after encountering human units. Others have learned to turn at regular intervals while traveling in a straight line so as not to miss any hidden human units. Finally, communication proved to be an important tool of the AI as nearly every best-performing string from the genetic runs required scouts.

Further, the problem of novices being killed off too quickly has been solved by the adaptive system. In the adaptive version, Chaos rarely kills off the player within the first four or five turns. After sensing that the player is a novice from his or her win-loss record, the system begins using nonoptimal strategy strings. The AI tries to push the player toward an "optimal" winning percentage of 0.500 by selecting better- and worse-performing strings depending on the user's historical distance from 0.500. Therefore, as the player begins improving his or her strategy, the AI resists by using better counter-strategies.

The adaptive version was distributed to a number of players, and although too little time was available to provide conclusive results, the initial signs were encouraging. The win-loss records of the four players who completed at least six games are (in descending order) 11-6 (0.647), 4-3 (0.571), 2-4 (0.333), and 2-5 (0.286). Certainly, none of these records can be considered "extreme." Indeed, the overall record of these four is 19-18 (0.514), which is very close to the AI's optimal winning percentage of 0.500.

The winning percentages from a wide variety of players should form a standard deviation curve centered on 0.500. However, determining the "most fun" optimal winning percentage is a separate question. In other words, what target winning percentage would provide the player with the most enjoyable experience? Do most players expect to win more games than they lose, or vice versa? Do some players value being constantly challenged? Do others strongly dislike losing more than half the time?

The answer is probably different from player to player, but these questions need to be answered before a truly optimal winning percentage can be selected with any certainty. Further, the choice could be put in the hands of the player by allowing the selection of "novice," "intermediate," and "expert" difficulty levels. The optimal winning percentage could then be adjusted accordingly by assuming that experts aren't afraid to be challenged and novices still need some time to feel comfortable with the game.

Conclusion

Advanced Protection provides a practical example of an adaptive AI, displaying a number of advantages over a static AI. First, the system can dynamically switch between strategies depending on the actual performance of the player—experts will be treated like experts, and novices will be treated like novices. Next, the rules and parameters of the game will be exactly the same for all strategies, which means that Chaos will not need to "cheat" in order to challenge expert players. Finally, the system can ensure that Chaos's "best" strategies truly are the best for each individual player.

Indeed, this last fact is true virtually by definition—when the player starts playing the game, all 250 strategies are given equal weight. Only strategies that historically succeed against a specific player will be considered Chaos's best strategies against him or her. Furthermore, *Advanced Protection* appears to function like any other turn-based strategy game. Unless players are told how the game works, most will only sense that the game is learning from their moves once Chaos starts changing strategies.

Future Work

One major area of future work would be to allow the game to dynamically alter the 250 hard-coded strings in some constrained manner. The game can't use standard genetic algorithms on the strings, as these runs often take many hours to complete. However, the program could experiment with some limited crossover operations combining minion automaton/preference pairs from different strings to produce dynamic, hybrid strings. These hybrid strings could be tested against the player's most recent unit arrangements, and the best-performing hybrids could be saved in the player's .apu file for use in later game turns. Allowing the strategy strings to be rewritten dynamically would greatly enhance the adaptive capabilities of the AI.

References

[Laramée02] Laramée, François Dominic, "Genetic Algorithms: Evolving the Perfect Troll," *AI Game Programming Wisdom*, Charles River Media, 2002.

[Manslow02] Manslow, John, "Learning and Adaptation," *AI Game Programming Wisdom*, Charles River Media, 2002.

11.4

Building Better Genetic Algorithms

Mat Buckland—www.ai-junkie.com

fup@ai-junkie.com

Genetic algorithms are slowly but surely gaining popularity with game developers. They are currently used mostly as in-house tweaking tools, but they are also beginning to be used in-game, either as an integral part of the gameplay or as an aid for the user.

Unfortunately, many of today's programmers only know the basics of genetic algorithms, not much beyond the original paradigm devised by John Holland back in the mid 1960s. This article brings you up to date with some of the tools and techniques available to give improved performance, thus showing you how get the most from your own genetic algorithms.

This article assumes the reader is conversant with the original genetic algorithm developed by John Holland (or similar) and is comfortable with the terminology used when discussing such algorithms. Introductions to genetic algorithms can be found within this book [Sweetser04] or from the article *Genetic Algorithms in Plain English* included on the accompanying CD-ROM [Buckland01].

ON THE CD

There are many techniques available to improve the performance of genetic algorithms. Some are generic (almost) and applicable to the majority of genetic algorithms, while others have been designed to address problems with specific encoding schemes or to use particular characteristics of an encoding scheme to their advantage. This article initially covers the more generic techniques—applicable to binary, integer, or real-value encoded genetic algorithms—and ends with a method for improving the performance of real-value encoded genetic algorithms. Other than this, there is no particular order to the techniques—you can either read the article from start to finish or dip into it during a coffee break.

Elitism

Elitism is, without a doubt, one of the best tools you can have in your belt. It almost always improves the performance of a genetic algorithm, helping it to converge on a solution much faster than if it was not present; and it's fast and easy to code.

Elitism is simply the practice of choosing the *n* best individuals from the current generation to be transferred *unchanged* into the next generation. This technique guarantees that any good performers your algorithm finds remain in the population. A typical figure for *n* would be between 1 percent and 10 percent of the population size and can even be as high as 20 percent. However, you have to be careful, since too much elitism will cause your population to converge too quickly.

Scaling Techniques

The canonical genetic algorithm typically uses some sort of *fitness proportionate selection*—the more fit an individual is, the more chance it has of being selected to create offspring. *Roulette wheel selection* or *stochastic universal sampling* (SUS) [Mitchell98] are the most widely used selection techniques of this sort. Unfortunately, in the early stages of a genetic algorithm the fitness scores are likely to be extremely diverse—a common scenario is one in which a small percentage of the population have much higher fitness scores than the rest. When a fitness proportionate selection criterion is used, these high-scoring individuals have a much better chance of creating offspring and will quickly multiply and dominate the population. This is called premature convergence and is "A Bad Thing," as only a very small portion of the search space has been explored and it's extremely unlikely that an optimal solution will have been found.

The following three techniques all help to prevent premature convergence. They are methods you can use to scale a population's fitness scores prior to fitness proportionate selection.

Rank Scaling

Rank scaling is a cheap and easy method of retaining population diversity and can work extremely well in the right situation—and extremely poorly in the wrong situation. The population is sorted according to fitness, and then new fitness scores are assigned to each individual based solely on its rank. The old fitness scores are then discarded. Table 11.4.1 shows how an example population of 10 genomes are ranked. The fittest individual (the best ranking) is given a score of 10, while the least fit is given a score of 1. (The extremely small number of genomes in Table 11.4.1 is only for demonstration purposes. The population is shown sorted by order of fitness).

Clearly, before scaling, genomes A and B have a much higher probability of being chosen as parents than after rank scaling has been applied. It might be easier for you to see the difference by examining Figure 11.4.1. Each slice of the pie represents an individual in the population.

Table 11.4.1 Rank Scaling in Action

Genome	Fitness before scaling	Fitness after scaling
A	235.30	10
B	123.50	9
C	54.80	8
D	45.34	7
E	32.10	6
F	31.32	5
G	23.44	4
H	23.03	3
I	2.70	2
J	1.90	1

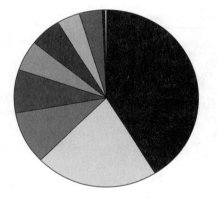
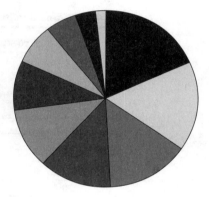

Before Rank Scaling   After Rank Scaling

FIGURE 11.4.1 *Rank scaling applied to a population. The size of each pie segment shows the likelihood of selection.*

Rank scaling helps to retain genetic diversity, while also slowing down convergence to a snail's pace. The drawback of using rank scaling is that, because the variance is kept so low, it can take forever for the population to converge upon a solution. Nevertheless, it can be a terrific tool in the right circumstances—for example, permutation-based problems such as calculating the best route through a series of waypoints tend to favor this type of scaling. (Tip: make sure you sprinkle in a little elitism to get the best out of this technique.)

Sigma Scaling

Sigma scaling was devised as a way of keeping the selection pressure constant over many generations. The formula for calculating the scaled fitness values is given in Equation 1.

$$NewFitness = \frac{OldFitness - AverageFitness}{2\sigma} \tag{1}$$

The Greek letter σ denotes the standard deviation of the population. The standard deviation is calculated using Equation 2.

$$\sigma = \sqrt{\frac{\sum (f - mf)^2}{PopulationSize}} \tag{2}$$

The variable f is the fitness of the current individual and mf is the average fitness of the population. If σ reaches 0, then the population has converged upon identical genomes. Table 11.4.2 shows the population from Table 11.4.1 adjusted using sigma scaling.

Table 11.4.2   Sigma Scaling (population shown sorted)

Genome	Fitness before scaling	Fitness after scaling
A	235.30	1.31
B	123.50	0.49
C	54.80	-0.02
D	45.34	-0.09
E	32.10	-0.19
F	31.32	-0.19
G	23.44	-0.25
H	23.03	-0.25
I	2.70	-0.40
J	1.90	-0.41

To avoid negative fitness scores, 1.0 is normally added to the value given by Equation 1. Figure 11.4.2 will help you visualize how sigma scaling attempts to keep the selection pressure equal.

Boltzmann Scaling

Sometimes, it's preferable for the selection pressure to be low at the beginning and high toward the end. This ensures that your population remains diverse at the commencement of the algorithm. As the algorithm converges toward a solution, the fitter individuals are given preference.

Boltzmann scaling is a technique you can use to achieve this. It makes use of a continuously decreasing *temperature* to control the rate of selection. The formula is given by Equation 3.

$$NewFitness = \frac{\exp(OldFitness \,/\, Temperature)}{[\exp(OldFitness \,/\, Temperature)]} \tag{3}$$

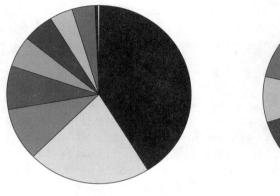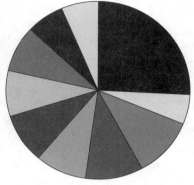

Before Sigma Scaling   After Sigma Scaling

FIGURE 11.4.2 *Sigma scaling applied to a population. The size of each pie segment shows the likelihood of selection.*

The square brackets represent the average at the current generation of the enclosed term.

ON THE CD

The optimum starting temperature and the rate of its decay are something you must determine by trial and error. The demo program on the accompanying CD-ROM uses a default starting temperature of *(3 x population size)*, which is reduced by 0.05 each update cycle.

Tournament Selection

They say the best things in life are free, and with genetic algorithms this can sometimes be the case. The small CPU cost of using elitism was one example, another is a technique known as *tournament selection*.

One of the problems of using scaling techniques is that they mask any useful information that might have been implied by the raw fitness scores. One way of overcoming this is to compare fitness scores directly by simply asking: is A > B? Tournament selection uses this approach by selecting N individuals from the population at random and then choosing the fittest of them to become parents. This process is repeated until the next generation of genomes has been generated. The higher the value of N used, the higher the selection pressure. Or, in other words, the lower the value of N, the more diverse your population will be. Typical values for N are similar to the values used for elitism, between 2 percent and 10 percent of the population size.

Tournament selection is a good alternative to fitness proportionate selection with or without scaling. Since there are hardly any calculations involved (and no pre-scaling required), this technique is very fast.

Note: Goldberg [Goldberg89] describes an alternative method for tournament selection whereby two individuals are chosen from the population via roulette wheel selection, and the fitter of the two is used to create offspring. This also works well but takes up more CPU time.

Generic Crossover Operators

With the single-point crossover operator proposed by [Holland75], a random position along the length of two parent chromosomes is chosen and all the genes after that position are swapped. The disadvantage of this method is that the end genes are always swapped regardless of where the crossover point is. For some problem domains, this is unfavorable. The following are descriptions of two crossover operators that can be used in its place.

Two-Point Crossover

Two-point crossover works similarly to single-point crossover except that two cutting points are chosen at random. The block of genes between the two points are then swapped. See the left-hand side of Figure 11.4.3.

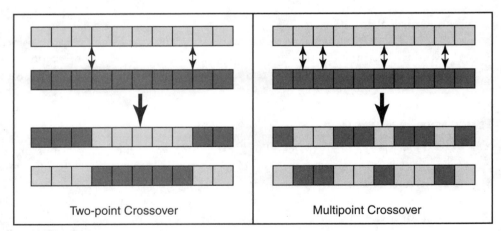

FIGURE 11.4.3   *Crossover operators in action.*

Two-point crossover is the preferred crossover operator for most problems. It is an excellent all-round performer.

Multipoint Crossover

Multipoint crossover, also known as *parameterized uniform crossover*, can be useful for some problem domains you might encounter. To implement it, simply iterate along the length of the parents and swap genes at each locus (position) depending upon a fixed probability. The right hand side of Figure 11.4.3 shows the genes swapped at loci 2, 3, 6, and 9.

Niching Techniques

Niching techniques can be a great way of retaining population diversity, and are particularly useful where a fitness landscape might contain multiple peaks [Goldberg89] or where it is essential to protect new innovation within a population [Stanley00]. The following are descriptions of two popular niching methods.

Explicit Fitness Sharing

Explicit fitness sharing is a mechanism where individuals with similar genetic properties are grouped together. Each individual's fitness score is then divided by the number of genomes within its group (Equation 4).

$$NewFitness = \frac{OldFitness}{NumberOfNeighbors} \tag{4}$$

This punishes the fitness scores of individuals who have many similar neighbors, thereby preventing any one group from growing too large and taking over the population.

Speciation

Speciation goes one step further by separating the genomes into groups in the same way as explicit fitness sharing, but this time individuals are only allowed to breed with members of their own species. Typically, a species is killed when either its size decreases to zero or its fitness hasn't increased within a user-defined number of generations. This means that the individuals that would normally have died out early in the evolution of a population remain active for much longer, protected among their species members. (Note, because of the protection afforded by using speciation, you can experiment with much higher mutation rates than normal.)

The Compatibility Function

To determine if one genome should belong in the same species as another, you must use a function that compares two gene strings and returns a *compatibility distance*. If the distance is below a user-defined threshold, then the genomes are considered to be in the same species. This compatibility function varies considerably depending on the encoding representation. For a real value encoded genome, you could use the function given by Equation 5.

$$dist = \frac{\sum\limits_{i=1}^{i=n} | x_i - y_i |}{n} \tag{5}$$

Where n is the number of genes in each chromosome and x and y represent two different individuals from the population.

Each epoch of the genetic algorithm, the compatibility distance function is used to test every individual against the first member in each species. If the distance is within a user-defined threshold (the tweakers among you will have fun playing with this value), then the individual is added to the appropriate species. If the individual is incompatible with all the current species, then a new species is created and the individual is added to that.

Real Value Encoded Genetic Algorithms

As a game developer, if you have chosen to work with genetic algorithms, then it's highly likely you will be using real value encoded genomes. That is to say, each gene is represented by a floating-point number. A typical example if this would be if you were to use genetic algorithms for optimizing FuSMs ala the *Quake III Arena* bots [van Waveren01], tweaking the parameters of your NPCs [Laramée02], or evolving control sequences for vehicles as the demo program on the accompanying CD-ROM shows.

ON THE CD

Fortunately for us, a real-valued encoding scheme provides some great opportunities for optimization. If you have experimented with genetic algorithms, you are probably aware that it's possible to think of the solution space as a kind of rolling landscape of peaks and troughs. The peaks represent the more fit areas within the landscape, the troughs the less fit (although for some problems it makes more sense to think of this the other way around). Binary encoded genetic algorithms (among others) cannot exploit any of the mathematical properties of such a landscape, but real-valued encoded algorithms have the potential to use useful information implicit in a landscape, such as the hill gradients [Garret99].

The Michalewicz Method

Michalewicz [Michalewicz96] and collaborators have developed several mutation and crossover operators that are used *in combination* to fully exploit the characteristics of real value encoded genetic algorithms. These operators are discussed next.

Mutation Operators

- **Boundary Mutation:** With probability p, this operator changes the value of a gene to either its minimum possible value, G_{min}, or its maximum possible value, G_{max}.
- **Replace Mutation:** With probability p, this operator resets a gene to a uniform random number between G_{min} and G_{max}.
- **Non-Uniform Mutation:** With probability p, this operator adjusts a gene's size by a small random amount, the limits of which decrease over time.

Crossover Operators

- **Arithmetical Crossover:** This simply averages the values of the genes at each locus.
- **Simple Crossover:** This operator is the same as single point crossover.
- **Heuristic Crossover:** Given the parents G_1 and G_2, this operator creates an offspring according to Equation 6.

$$Child = r(G_2 - G_1) + G_2 \tag{6}$$

Variable G_2 is the fitter of the two parents, and r is a random number between 0 and 1.

On their own, these operators can (or will) perform extremely poorly. For example, the arithmetical operator when used independently will give terrible results—the population just rapidly converges to the numerical center of the search space. The secret of the Michalewicz approach is to use these operators in combination. In this way, the fitness landscape is traversed thoroughly and efficiently.

Michalewicz's implementation, *GenoCop*, uses an adaptive probability distribution for the operators, which bias the choice of operator over time toward those that have a tendency to produce fitter offspring.

The Michalewicz Method—Simplified

ON THE CD

A simpler approach has been proposed by Garrett as an alternative to using an adaptive probability distribution for the operators [Garrett99]. He suggests that each operator be used with equal probability. This is much speedier and loses little in performance. In addition, the simple crossover operator in the demo on the accompanying CD-ROM uses two-point crossover instead of single-point, and the non-uniform mutation operator is simplified so that the limits of the random amount to be added do not decrease over time.

Table 11.4.3 Comparison between the Michalewicz and Standard Genetic Algorithm. Parents Were Selected from the Population Using Tournament Selection.

Method	Average Generations
Michalewicz—best setup with elitism	198
Michalewicz—best setup without elitism	301
Standard—best setup with elitism	584
Standard—best setup without elitism	752

The Michalewicz method can give exceptional results with some problem domains. Table 11.4.3 shows some results for a genetic algorithm used to solve the function (error < 0.01) shown in Equation 7.

$$0 = \sum_{i=1}^{i=L} \left| Lx_i - i \right| \tag{7}$$

Variable L is the genome length, which in this example is set to 10. Although improvements like this can't be expected for every problem, the Michalewicz method is an invaluable addition to any genetic algorithm programmer's arsenal.

Conclusion

Think of each of the techniques presented here as a tool in your genetic algorithm tool belt. As a carpenter learns through experience which is the best chisel for the best type of timber, or in what place he should hammer a nail to prevent the wood from splitting, continued experimentation with these tools will improve your understanding of genetic algorithms and help you to create code that gives you faster and more accurate results.

The GA Racer Demo Executable and Source

ON THE CD

The Win32 demo provided on the accompanying CD-ROM shows how a genetic algorithm is used to evolve a control sequence enabling a vehicle to steer around a simple track as shown in Figure 11.4.4. Because you can view the entire population evolving in normal or accelerated time, you can get great visual feedback. It's a fantastic way to see the effect each technique has on the fitness and diversity of the population, even though some of them do not offer any advantages for this type of problem.

The vehicles (shown as triangles in Figure 11.4.4) attempt to negotiate as far around the track as they can by evolving a sequence of steering and throttle commands. They also try to maximize their average velocity.

Each genome is encoded in the format:

Steering | Throttle | Steering | Throttle | Steering | Throttle . . . etc.

Each gene is represented by a floating-point number constrained between 0 and 1.0. A vehicle iterates through its genome at the rate of two genes per update cycle. One gene represents the magnitude of the steering force, the other the magnitude of the throttle (there is no braking force). The vehicles use these forces to update their position.

When the application is running you can use the following keys to control how you view the evolution:

B toggles the view between the fittest genome from the previous generation and the entire population from the current generation.
F toggles the application between accelerated and normal mode.
R and changing any parameters, resets the demo.

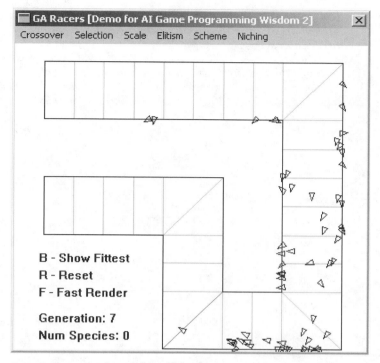

FIGURE 11.4.4 *Screenshot of the demo in action.*

References

[Buckland01] Buckland, Mat, *Genetic Algorithms in Plain English*, 2001, available on this book's CD-ROM and online at *www.ai-junkie.com*

[Buckland02] Buckland, Mat, *AI Techniques for Game Programming*, Premier Press, 2002.

[Garrett99] Garrett, Craig A., *Optimization of in situ Aerobic Cometabolic Bioremediation of Trichloroethylene-contaminated Groundwater Using a Parallel Genetic Algorithm*, Air Force Institute of Technology, 1999.

[Goldberg89] Goldberg, David. E., *Genetic Algorithms in Search, Optimization and Machine Learning*, Addison-Wesley, 1989.

[Holland75] Holland, John. H., *Adaptation in Natural and Artificial Systems*, University of Michigan Press, 1975.

[Laramée02] Laramée, F. D., "Genetic Algorithms: Evolving the Perfect Troll," *AI Game Programming Wisdom*, Charles River Media, 2002.

[Michalewicz96] Michalewicz, Z., "Evolutionary Algorithms for Constrained Parameter Optimization Problems," *Evolutionary Computation*, Vol.4, No.1, 1996.

[Mitchell98] Mitchell, M., *An Introduction to Genetic Algorithms*, MIT Press, 1998.

[Stanley00] Stanley, Kenneth O., and Risto, Miikkulainen, *Evolving Neural Networks through Evolving Topologies*, 2000, available online at *www.cs.utexas.edu/users/kstanley/*

[Sweetser 04] Sweetser, Penny, "How to Build Evolutionary Algorithms for Games," *AI Game Programming Wisdom, 2,* Charles River Media, 2004.

[van Waveren01] van Waveren, J.M.P., *The Quake III Arena Bot*, University of Technology Delft, 2001, available online at *www.idsoftware.com/home/jan/q3abotai/Q3ABotAI_15.pdf*

11.5

Advanced Genetic Programming: New Lessons from Biology

François Dominic Laramée

francoislaramee@videotron.ca

Evolutionary computation is a striking concept: by mimicking the mechanics of natural selection, a computer can evolve a near-optimal solution to an otherwise intractable problem. There are some problems where the best that we can do is define the problem and the criteria by which we judge success. In these cases, evolutionary methods can yield satisfactory algorithms, whereas intentional design by human programmers fails to do so as quickly or as well.

Many authors have explained one aspect of evolutionary computation, the genetic algorithm, which operates on candidate solutions made up of data—usually bit strings representing numbers, like the weights assigned to transitions in finite state machines and neural networks [Laramée02]. In this article, we explore a somewhat more flexible paradigm, genetic programming, which handles candidate solutions made up of source code. We also look at some of the lessons that biology and computer science have taught each other, and explore ways in which we can put these lessons to use in our own evolutionary computation schemes.

Note that familiarity with the material discussed in [Laramée02] is assumed, but not strictly required.

Principles of Genetic Programming

The basic genetic algorithm manipulates numbers. For example, in [Laramée02], each gene in a troll's genotype represents the weight (or *bias*) given to one of several potential strategies when the troll decides what to do. These weights are combined into a linear equation by multiplying them with the troll's assessment of each strategy's suitability to its current circumstances. This is a fairly powerful mechanism, but it makes one crucial assumption: that the decision-making process can be accurately modeled by a linear equation. No matter what mutations we inflict upon the troll's virtual DNA, the basic structure of the candidate solutions will remain linear.

Intuitively, it seems that a paradigm that relaxes this constraint on the structure of candidate solutions would be more flexible in practice. Genetic Programming (GP) does exactly that, by evolving individuals made up of source code instead of numbers. As a result, the class of solutions that can be represented by the evolving population becomes orders of magnitude greater: while the GA in our troll example can only generate different linear equations combining the same strategies, a GP program could be allowed to evolve any type of equation, to modify the strategies coded in the program, or even to create new ones.

Problems with Source Code Populations

Typical GP schemes [Koza92, Levy92] involve candidate solutions made up of LISP source code, assembly language, or bytecodes. All of these share a major shortcoming: whatever the genetic operator that is applied to these individuals, the resulting "children" are very likely to represent nonsense, or to not even compile at all.

For example, if we apply mutation to the C++ statement:

```
double aVariable = someDoubleFunction( a, 4.0 ) + 3;
```

The resulting statement will not compile if we replace someDoubleFunction with the name of a non-numerical function, or with the name of a floating-point function that does not take two parameters. If, on the other hand, we mutate the name of the variable, some later statement that uses aVariable as an operator will break down. And of course, crossover between two statements of completely different structure, like an assignment and a loop control structure, is going to be even more brittle.

Even in a bytecode environment, we can expect anywhere between 50 and 95 percent or more of the individuals generated by genetic operators to be nonsensical. As a result, we must deal with very large populations and spend an inordinate amount of time giving birth to evolutionary dead ends—an unacceptable waste of resources.

Fortunately, as we will now see, smart applications of biological and computational principles can alleviate this problem.

New Lessons from Biology

The layman's view of genetics can be summarized in a few lines:

- Each chromosome is a linear object that harbors a certain number of genes.
- A gene is an atomic component, unique and unlike any others.
- Each gene does one job, and one job only.

However, while this abstraction is generally useful, it is neither complete nor accurate. Nature has provided us with many other possibilities, such as:

Cyclical DNA: Bacterial "plasmid" DNA is organized into loops instead of linear (actually, cross-shaped) chromosomes. As a result, there is no such thing as the beginning or the end of a plasmid.

Gene Duplication: There is considerable redundancy in the actual genetic code for most living organisms.

Polyvalent Genes: There is some evidence, again mostly in bacteria, that some bits of DNA actually belong to more than one gene—or at least that they perform more than one job.

Genetic Code Degeneracy and Neutral Mutations: The genetic code uses an alphabet made up of 64 "letters" called codons, each of which represents one amino acid in the structure of a protein or a stopping signal. However, there are only about 20 significant amino acids in living organisms. Therefore, several codons can represent the same protein building block, and there is a chance that a mutation will transform one codon for, say, glycine, into another codon that also encodes glycine.

Grammatical Evolution

We can exploit these properties of natural DNA to create innovative genetic programming solutions. A particularly promising approach, called grammatical evolution, was proposed by [O'Neill01].

The key insight underlying this paradigm is that cyclical DNA, gene polyvalence, and degenerate genetic codes can be combined with the classic Backus-Naur Form grammar to create a highly robust population generation scheme. Instead of encapsulating brittle source code in explicit fashion, *each individual in a grammatical evolution program encodes a way to derive a program from a grammar at runtime.* Since the grammar automatically generates valid programs, the inefficiency associated with classic genetic programming disappears.

BNF Grammars

A grammar in Backus-Naur Form is a way to represent a language as a set of production rules. The rules are made up of two types of constituents:

Terminals are elements of the language generated by the grammar. A grammar for C++, for example, would contain terminals such as numbers, function names, curly brackets, and mathematical symbols.

Non-terminals are intermediate forms, which can themselves be expanded into more terminals and/or non-terminals.

Technically speaking, the grammar is represented as a 4-tuple { N, T, R, S } where N is the set of non-terminals, T is the set of terminals, R is the set of production rules, and S is the starting symbol, an element of N from which all derivations begin.

As an example, let us design a grammar that generates many different ways for the troll from [Laramée02] to decide whether he should seek sheep to eat given the current state of the world, instead of hiding, healing, or picking a fight with the local knights. We will use grammatical evolution to produce a function whose value will serve as a weight for the "Hunt Sheep" strategy; a complete GP application would also calculate equations for the other strategies—with the same grammar—and choose the most appropriate strategy according to the values returned by all of the equations.

Here is a very small grammar to represent this problem:

```
N = { expression, operator, number, feature }
T = { SheepNearby, KnightsNearby, HealthLevel,
      TowersNearby, ForestsNearby,
      +, -, *, /, ^, 0, 1, 2, 3, ... }
S = expression
```

And *P* contains the following rules:

1. `expression => expression operator expression`
2. `expression => number`
3. `expression => feature`
4. `expression => ( expression )`
5. `operator => + | - | ^ | * | /`
6. `number => 0 | 1 | 2 ...`
7. `feature => SheepNearby | KnightsNearby | HealthLevel |`
   `           TowersNearby | ForestsNearby`

Table 11.5.1 shows an example of a derivation using this grammar.

Table 11.5.1   BNF Grammar Derivation

Current Expression	Rule Applied
expression	Starting symbol
expression operator expression	Rule 1
expression operator (expression)	Rule 4
expression operator (expression operator expression)	Rule 1
feature operator (expression operator expression)	Rule 3
feature operator (number operator feature)	Rules 3 and 6
feature * (number ^ feature)	Rule 5
SheepNearby * (2 ^ HealthLevel)	Rules 6 and 7

By changing the derivation choices, we can generate arbitrarily complex expressions. And of course, adding elements to the sets *P*, *N*, and *T* allows us to extend the range of possible derivations. In fact, it is possible to define a BNF grammar expressive enough to generate every possible construct in any programming language, like C++.

Grammatical Evolution Chromosomes

To use grammatical evolution in our genetic programming scheme, very few changes have to be made to our chromosomes. Indeed, the best representation of our troll's genetic material is going to be a circular array of genes, each of which is represented as a single integer. Better yet: since we are going to use circular DNA, the length of this array is largely irrelevant—and it can even be variable.

As for the evaluation function and the overall architecture of the application (e.g., selection of individuals for reproduction, simulation of the trolls' environment, and so forth), they do not need to change at all.

Genetic Operators

A mutation operator that replaces a randomly selected gene by a random integer is usually going to be sufficient. However, it is also trivial to design an operator that inserts or deletes genes from the chromosome, if we choose to implement it as an array of variable length: we simply have to increment or decrement the array's length counter, and shift its contents accordingly. As for crossover, swapping sub-arrays of equal or even different length is sufficient to mate chromosomes.

How It Works

Our chromosomes will be used to direct operations while generating programs from the grammar. Beginning with the first gene (in our case, the first element in the array of integers) and with the starting symbol, we will select production rules to apply according to the following method:

End condition: If there are no non-terminals remaining in the derivation, stop. Otherwise, make the first non-terminal current. Add checks and bounds to avoid infinite recursions.

Code degeneracy: If the current non-terminal can be expanded by N different rules, apply the rule number (M modulo N) + 1, where M is the value of the current gene.

Cyclical DNA and polyvalent genes: Advance to the next gene in the chromosome. If you run out of genes, simply wrap around to the beginning of the array and reuse the first gene.

An Example

If we take the troll-generating grammar specified earlier and a five-gene chromosome with genes 8, 1, 6, 11 and 10, then we can generate a program as shown in Table 11.5.2.

Table 11.5.2   Deriving a Program from a Grammar and a Chromosome

Current Program	Current Non-Terminal	Current Gene	Rule Selected	Rule Application
Expression	expression	First (value: 8)	(8 mod 4) + 1 = 1st rule for the current non-terminal	Expression => expression operator expression
Expression operator expression	expression	Second (1)	(1 mod 4) + 1 = 2nd rule	Expression => number
Number operator expression	number	Third (6)	Number 6	Number => 6
6 operator expression	operator	Fourth (11)	(11 mod 5) + 1 = 2nd rule	Operator => -
6 – expression	expression	Fifth (10)	(10 mod 4) + 1 = 3rd rule	Expression => feature
6 – feature	feature	First (8)	(8 mod 5) + 1 = 4th rule	feature => Towers Nearby
6 – TowersNearby	Done			

Writing a C++ function representing the set of production rules for a given non-terminal and selecting one from the current gene is nearly trivial. The following pseudocode for the `expression` non-terminal from the troll grammar can guide you in this effort:

```
int derivExpression()
{
    FindNextGene();
    switch( CurrentGene() % 4 )
    {
        case 0: return( Apply( derivExpression(),
                    derivOperator(), derivExpression() ) );
        case 1: return( derivNumber() );
        case 2: return( derivStrategy() );
        //etc...
    }
}
```

Of course, you might want to augment your own program with a "depth check" to ensure that, for example, Rule #1 will not produce an infinite number of recursive calls to itself.

This Method Protects Genetic Variety

With code degeneracy, the range of values stored in genes is immaterial, provided that it is larger than the number of production rules for any given non-terminal. Better yet: any range that has this property will also protect us from premature elimination of a production rule from the population of individuals.

For example, if we have five rules for non-terminal A, then genes 0, 5, 10, 15, and 20 all encode the same rule when they are applied to this non-terminal. As a result, the production rule in question will remain "available" to the population even if gene 0 goes extinct, because there are more ways to access it.

And of course, since each gene is merely a number, its actual meaning is entirely dependent on the actual derivation. If the third gene in a chromosome is 5, and we insert another gene before it, then all of a sudden that 5 is the fourth gene, and in all likelihood, will serve to select a completely different production rule for a different non-terminal. Therefore, even minute changes to the chromosomes will introduce great genetic variety into our population. While such behavior is often destructive—individuals in a genetic program should resemble their parents—an insertion or deletion operator can, if properly controlled, support genetic diversity in the population.

Coevolution: The Red Queen Hypothesis

All evolutionary computation schemes suffer from the same vulnerability: since they are essentially optimization methods, they are highly dependent on the quality of the test cases. Specifically, there is a risk that the solution that emerges from the process will be very efficient at solving the test cases, but that its performance will break down significantly if the "real world" problems it is asked to solve have little in common with the test situations imagined by the programmer. [Levy92] describes an interesting solution to this potential problem: turn the test cases into an evolving population of their own.

It turns out that this type of phenomenon happens all the time in nature: as the predator race gets faster, so does the prey, which forces the predator to develop even better hunting skills. Biological researchers also experience this type of evolutionary arms race: every time the pharmaceutical industry develops a new antibiotic, weak varieties of bacteria are obliterated and replaced by resistant strains, thus forcing further research. The same principle can be applied to genetic programming: if we make the problems ever tougher through evolution, they will force the solutions to become better themselves.

Whimsically named the "Red Queen Hypothesis" after the *Alice in Wonderland* character who explained to Alice that she was required to run ever faster to stay in one place, this competitive evolution can lead to the rapid development of highly fit populations. Levy describes Daniel Hillis' "ramps" system, an early experiment in which a population of sorting algorithms evolved in competition with a population of test cases whose fitness was directly proportional to their ability to defeat sorting schemes. Results were impressive: instead of taking tens of thousands of generations to reach a pretty good local minimum, the process yielded a solution almost as good as the best human-crafted alternative in a matter of minutes!

Conclusion

Genetic programming is a powerful extension to the evolutionary computing paradigm. GP systems display considerable flexibility, allowing the application programmer to develop solutions of more diverse structure than those provided by genetic algorithms. Grammatical evolution is one way to implement genetic programming while minimizing the computational expense related to the creation and subsequent elimination of nonsense organisms.

Genetic programming has been applied to many domains in addition to those mentioned here. [Hong01] has adapted GP to the development of strategies for classical games, such as go-moku and chess, and [Taylor94] expects it to assist in solving many of the fundamental problems of biology, such as the evolution of the mind and the origins of life.

However, it is not a panacea. First, no evolutionary method will solve "all or nothing" problems, because they can't be optimized incrementally. Second, most GP systems still require some human-designed building blocks to combine and optimize.

[Koza92] is the seminal textbook in the field of genetic programming; any serious endeavor related to GP should begin with a thorough study of this book.

References

[Hong01] Hong, Tzung-Pei, Huang, Ke-Yuan, and Lin, Wen-Yang, "Adversarial Search by Evolutionary Computation," *Evolutionary Computation* 9(3), pp. 371–385, 2001.

[Koza92] Koza, John R., *Genetic Programming: On the Programming of Computers by Means of Natural Selection*," MIT Press, 1992.

[Laramée02] Laramée, François Dominic, "Genetic Algorithms: Evolving the Perfect Troll," *AI Game Programming Wisdom*, Charles River Media, 2002.

[Levy92] Levy, Steven, *Artificial Life*, Vintage Books, 1992.

[O'Neill01] O'Neill, Michael, and Ryan, Conor, "Grammatical Evolution," *IEEE Transactions on Evolutionary Computation*, 5(4), pp. 349–358, 2001.

[Taylor94] Taylor, Charles, and Jefferson, David, "Artificial Life as a Tool for Biological Inquiry," *Artificial Life 1*, pp. 1–13, 1994.

11.6

The Importance of Growth in Genetic Algorithms

Dale Thomas—AILab, University of Zürich

dale_thomas@hotmail.com

Artificial life (AL) is a very new and rapidly developing field spawning many useful methods applicable to games, including the celebrated *genetic algorithm* (GA). However, games based on AL techniques tend to be rather superficial, mainly due to the inflexibility and limitations of these standard techniques. One main problem with GAs is that most implementations have a fixed, predefined complexity. These GAs can be regarded as classifier systems or pure optimization (which they do very well), but the power of such systems can be greatly enhanced by allowing more flexibility in the evolutionary process. Such enhancements include growth, neutral networks, variable-length genomes, speciation, and co-evolution.

This article discusses the advantages and disadvantages of these additions and how they might relate to games. The goal of game AI/AL programmers is to make their games more fun and interesting. This means a continuous departure from predefined, predictable routines to more *life-like* behaviors and structures. The keyword here is *surprise*, finding something new, which is something that evolution is very good at. GAs already introduce some slight adaptivity into such games, and with a few enhancements, ALife-based games might become much more interesting and engrossing.

The Power of Evolution

Most people have a vague understanding of evolution; that is, they think they know what it is all about. However, many of them have been led to believe that in the future our little fingers will diminish and our foreheads will grow and grow. This is obviously a terrible misunderstanding and proof that the general populous does not have a true appreciation of the process. The same can be said for artificial evolution. Many programmers have played with, or at least heard of genetic algorithms and might have a vague idea of what they entail, but there is often a lack of real understanding, both as to the advantages and disadvantages of such systems.

Evolution chooses from the best available *at the time* rather than moving toward a specific *goal*. However, what exactly is the meant by the *best*? It all depends on the problem. In nature, it means to stay alive and continue the species; in artificial evolution it can be anything, perhaps to be good cannon fodder for a gamer, or a worthy chess opponent.

The power of evolution can be a very useful addition to computer games. First, evolution can create diversity automatically, taking games away from predefined, fixed content. Moreover, evolution implies adaptivity, or learning. The computer can adapt to a gamer's playing style, automatically tailoring the game to an individual. Perhaps the most famous AL game is *Creatures* [Grand96]. With millions of copies sold and a huge loyal community, it is clear that there certainly can be market appeal for such games, if done correctly.

Although this article discusses basic concepts of GAs, it is not at all meant as an introduction to them; there are many fine books and articles, which can give the essentials [Holland75, Mitchell96, Goldberg89]. Rather, this article proposes to discuss some finer aspects of artificial evolution, which are almost completely unavailable to most people outside academia. Some of the concepts raised here are fairly new, while others are not new in other fields, but have failed to cross the conceptual divide between research and application areas.

The rest of this article is organized as follows: First, there is a superficial description of genetic algorithms. Then, there is a look at some GA enhancements, why they are important, and how they can help in evolution. Finally, there is a discussion of the role of these techniques in games.

Genetic Algorithms

We will now have a very brief look at GAs for the benefit of readers new to them and try to grasp the fundamentals of their use and terminology. Basically, a GA consists of a *population* of solutions. A solution is a string of numbers (like artificial DNA), which can represent anything: parameters for an equation to a mathematical problem, the design of an electronic circuit, a list-sorting program, or the DNA of an artificial creature. The string is called the *genotype* (DNA) and the thing it represents is called the *phenotype* (body). Anything that can be defined as a string of numbers has the *potential* to be evolved using GAs. That does not mean that it *will* evolve.

Many people believe that naïvely using a GA will magically give them a great solution for free. That is not necessarily the case: there are many things that affect the performance and limitations of a GA. We will discuss a few here. Now, all of these solutions in the population are tested by a *fitness function* as to how well they solve the defined problem. For example: if the solutions encode parameters of a curve being evolved to fit some data, then the solution fitness could be the reciprocal of the sum of the error. This means that the closer the curve fits the data, the greater the fitness value. The goal is to have a single number describing the usefulness of a solution.

Now we let the solutions breed through a process called *crossover* (mixing the DNA from the parents) so that the solutions with higher fitness have a greater chance of passing on their information to the next *generation*. Then, this new generation undergoes small random *mutations* to introduce variation and minimize stagnation, then they are tested, and the process repeats. Gradually, since the better individuals in each generation reproduce more, the average fitness will increase, thereby optimizing the solution.

A few words on the advantages and disadvantages of these systems over other search/optimization techniques are in order. On the positive side, GAs are a fast search technique, which can offer an acceptable solution in just a few generations. They are continuously adaptive: if the environment changes, the system will keep up, changing the population to suit the new requirements. However, there are a few limitations to GAs. First, a GA will never guarantee finding the optimal solution. Depending on the task at hand, the GA might get stuck at a local optima, which is a good solution, but not the best. There are various methods to combat this problem, but it is indeed a formidable problem and might never be completely solved. Second, the final solution is only as good as the fitness function, which can sometimes be difficult to describe in a program. If the task were to evolve a good bridge design, then a calculation of stresses and amount of material used would be easy enough to determine the fitness. However, if the goal has any non-quantitative aspect (such as aesthetic appeal), then expressing exactly what the designer wants can be difficult, or even impossible. Third, in most current implementations, GAs have a fixed complexity. This means that the solution can be completely missing the necessary complexity required to solve the problem satisfactorily, or that it is pure overkill, wasting resources. It is this problem that is the focus of this article.

Parameterization

Before we can discuss the newer concepts of GAs, let's first take a brief look at the simple, current usage, and discuss some of the advantages and disadvantages. Imagine, for example, that you would like to evolve an enemy robot. First, we need to be able to encode its design into a string of numbers. There are of course infinite ways of doing this, but let's take a very easy approach. Let's say our robot has four legs and each leg has three segments. Now let's split the genome into four parts (one for each leg), and then the lengths of the segments, joint types, joint limits, motor constants, and other parameters can be encoded in the numbers. If the genome numbers are floats in the range $[0 \ldots 1]$, then for a joint angle we could scale by 2π and for a segment length we could scale by say 50 and add 10. For a joint type we could scale by the number of possible joint types and convert to an integer. This would be an intuitive way of encoding, and therefore a straightforward method of evolving a robot body design. This is a valid way of doing it and it is used in many applications. This encoding scheme is called *parameterization* and its main advantage is that it is easy to interpret, for the computer and for the programmer. Moreover, a human designed robot could be easily encoded, perhaps as a good starting point for evolution. However, there are a few disadvantages to this method, which we will discuss further.

Growth

In nature, of course, biology does not parameterize. Things like the length of a finger or the angle limits of the knee are not encoded in a recognizable way. The only thing DNA encodes is protein. There are basically two types of protein. *Structural* proteins are the ones that make the body. They push, pull, propel, and preserve the shape of organic structures. The other type of protein is *regulatory*. These simply turn on and off the production of proteins (including themselves). However, there is no single "finger-length" protein (although there are many proteins involved in defining its length).

Let's look at an important example: the human brain. Our brains have doubled in size in only 2 million years. That is merely a blink in evolutionary time. Now there are approximately 100,000,000 neurons in the human brain. What's more, every neuron has around 10,000 connections to other neurons. However, human DNA encodes for only 30,000 genes. Therefore, biology does not directly parameterize. What it does is to make many copies of a cell and provide them with mechanisms for wiring up, which they do themselves, through a process of *self-organization*. It does not specify every detail, just the general mechanisms. That is why zebras have different stripes and even identical twins have slightly different fingerprints. Some interesting research has been done in the area of growing agent bodies and brains [Bongard01, Eggen97, Gruau93, Nolfi92, Vaario91].

Biology provides the *rules*, not the *plans* of construction. The advantages of this are very clear from the example. First, data compression: every cell and connection is not coded for directly. Rather, the structure emerges through the growth process. Second, there is the concept of evolvability. If the human brain were parameterized, nature would have to duplicate the genetic information for the brain, and deal with new wiring patterns in order to expand it. Not to mention expanding the skull, adding more blood vessels, and a million other things needed to enlarge all the necessary components in just the right amount. This was a main argument of Creationists against Darwinism (evolution), which was based on a complete misunderstanding of the underlying processes. What nature does, however, is simply to keep dividing the neurons until told to stop. Then, a small change in the timing of the stop signal will lead to a longer period of growth, hence more neurons. The skull, skin, blood vessels, and so forth are all reactive; if there are not enough, they make more, if there are too many, they stop dividing or die or differentiate. Therefore, by giving the rules of growth, all components grow together and therefore the size of the whole head could be regulated by just a few genes, which would be impossible in a parameterized system.

Homeotic (Hox) genes are genes like any other, except that they are at the top of a complicated hierarchy of interacting genes. A Hox gene initiates the growth of a whole structure. For example, biologists can make fully formed legs grow on a fly where its antennae should be, or eyes where its legs should be. This can be done by messing around with a few well-chosen Hox genes. What this means is that an organism could be born with a very different body, but still be functional, and perhaps better. Imagine an insect like a centipede. Each body segment is not encoded separately; they all use the same DNA, so adding or subtracting a body segment is simply a small mutation of a small number of genes. This allows for tremendous possibilities for evolution: evolvability.

Specialization is also a concept not possible in parameterized GAs but potentially useful for growth. Imagine a creature with many segments, each segment containing two legs. Now imagine that this creature has 10 segments, but on the first segment, the legs are longer and bent upward and are used as feeding apparatus. What a useful mechanism for evolution: make a copy of something functional and modify it for a different function. In biology, this is called *exaptation*. Many plants and animals make use of this mechanism, including us; our hands and feet are structurally very similar but modified for different functions. Again, this relates to evolvability.

What is this biological excursion telling us? It tells us that nature has found an incredibly flexible construction system for life, which is robust, concise, and above all, evolvable. Parameterization, while being easy to implement and understand, suffers from lack of these qualities, and therefore is limited in use.

Neutral Networks

Neutral networks (NtN) are a concept in GAs that increases their *evolvability*. The idea is pretty simple; have some junk DNA just like in biology. Junk DNA is DNA that is never expressed in an organism. That is, it has no effect; it is neutral. What exactly is the point of it then, if it is never used while the organism is alive? The junk DNA will pass down the ancestral tree along with the useful stuff and this junk will be subject to the same mutation mechanism as the rest. And so, every now and again, some junk DNA will be switched on in an individual by a small mutation. This now active DNA might be some highly mutated version of an important protein. Most of the time such a big mutation would have little or no effect, but just occasionally it can be an advantage, which can be exploited by the species (or it could be the beginning of a new species).

What does this mean for GAs? It means that the GA can keep a good, stable population, but can occasionally test out a highly mutated individual. Therefore, it has a small probability of finding a much better solution. It is not like simply increasing the mutation rate. It is about keeping a strong, viable population while occasionally testing a new design, perhaps radically different.

What about implementation? Well, first, what is needed is a method for deciding what is junk and what is not. In [Bongard01], the DNA reader scanned through the genome and when it found a value smaller than 0.1, there began a *gene* consisting of the following six values. These values were the parameters for gene interaction. Since there was a 1-in-10 chance of a gene beginning, and a gene was only seven values in length, there were non-used chunks of varying length between the genes. These could be called into use by a single mutation, which can lead to large, or small changes. Another requirement is a method for making duplications of genes. One method is to use variable-length genomes. The easiest way to do this is to have unequal point crossover. This means that both parents have their own random crossover point, so a child might have a genome much bigger or smaller than its two parents, which allows evolution to control the complexity of the solutions. Another method would be to simply duplicate a gene once it has been identified or to just make random duplications during crossover. This does have analogies in nature.

This also means that the system cannot be a simple parameterization system, because in parameterization, the location of genes is important so if they move around, then it changes the meaning of them. Perhaps each gene could be a parameterized limb, but then it is not pure optimization of a structure because the number of limbs can change.

Speciation and Co-Evolution

Speciation is a relatively simple concept that can enhance the performance of a GA. Instead of letting all the individuals in a population breed with one another, only allow them to breed with genetically similar individuals or individuals close to them in space. This is what happens in nature. A pig in India cannot breed with a pig in Canada simply because of geographic location. This is called *allopatric speciation*. Conversely, animals that are genetically dissimilar cannot mate, even if they are in close proximity. For example an elephant cannot mate with a mouse, no matter how hard they might try. This is called *reproductive isolation*. If these concepts are implemented in a GA, it can allow the formation of pockets of good solutions to find different ways of solving the problem.

Co-evolution is another relatively simple concept, made famous by Daniel Hillis [Hillis91]. If you have different species competing with each other, they have to work harder at solving the problem. If the fitness of one is somehow inversely proportional to the fitness of the other, you have competition. Hillis found that it could greatly increase the speed and quality of the evolution process.

Environment

As mentioned before, the DNA of an organism does not contain a blueprint; it does not contain all the information about the final structure. It encodes the rules of growth, how cells communicate, how they should change their shape, how and when they should differentiate, and so forth. However, there is another aspect that needs to be considered, not just the physical and chemical interaction between cells, but also their interactions with the environment in which the cells are growing. Mammals grow inside a womb: a nice safe haven with well-defined shape, materials, temperature, and chemical configuration. Moreover, many animals grow inside eggs of all shapes and sizes. During growth, all types of physical properties will be exploited, like gravity, sunlight, temperature gradients, chemical gradients, constraining forces, and so forth. In fact, there is no such thing as growth without environment. It has a large and important effect on the outcome and cannot be ignored.

One large problem with implementing growth algorithms is growth termination. When should a structure stop growing? If the rules are to grow or divide, when does it stop?

Nature uses many methods of growth termination: complex chemical signaling, physical constraints, resource depletion, and so forth. In many artificial systems it is easiest to just arbitrarily define a growth period, after which, no growth occurs. This is a very high-level abstraction of nature but it works.

The environment is equally important in the fitness of an individual, not just its growth. Material properties like stiffness, friction values, and weight will all affect the motion and therefore sensory experiences of a creature. In some systems, this might be irrelevant, but in other systems (especially simulations striving for physical plausibility), it is of paramount importance; it can seriously affect the behavior and learning rate of an agent.

Conclusion

We have seen that nature has invented a very flexible system, which is highly evolvable. Evolution does not work on single aspects of an organism. It can work on many aspects at once, reshaping the whole structure, or it can work on refining the detail of a structure. Large changes in morphology can be made while still leading to potentially viable organisms and still maintaining a stable population. The size of a mutation depends on how important the gene is and what phase of growth it affects. With a parameterized GA, a mutation will affect one aspect alone, for example, a single leg but with growth, a single mutation can affect one leg, a pair of legs, or all legs together. In addition, growth can arbitrarily add new structures, modify existing ones, and control the scale of mutations. Parameterized systems might be able to do these things but only with the inclusion of horrible, clunky hacks, which impose severe designer bias.

The importance of environment in growth cannot be overstated. Both physical and chemical factors will help to shape and control the growth, in a way that is completely unpredictable. It is the interaction of growing elements with each other and the environment that will determine the final form. With parameterized systems, this is not the case: the growth is completely deterministic and independent. It is an open loop.

How would all this work in games? Well, for the most part, such evolvability might not be required and the simplicity and understandability of parameterized systems will be desirable. However, if you are writing an ALife game and would like to *surprise* (in other words, to create something new every time the game is played) and not constrain the possible forms with designer bias, then nature can be a good source of inspiration. Giving a little thought to things like *ecological balance* [Thomas04], and the interaction with the environment can help programmers create much more efficient, life-like systems.

We have looked at the differences between parameterization and growth, but unfortunately the argument has so far been one-sided. Of course, both methods have pros and cons, so let's take a moment to list them. Table 11.6.1 compares the two methods. Not to say that one is definitely better than the other, but knowing the difference between the two GA encoding methods will allow programmers to make a better decision in the design stage, depending on what is required of it.

Table 11.6.1   Comparing Parameterization and Growth

Aspect	Parameterization	Growth
Encoding scheme	(+) Intuitive (explicit)	(−) Incomprehensible
	(±) Environment independent	(±) Environment dependent
	(+) Immediate mapping	(−) Needs growth period
Evolvability	(−) Restricted/fixed complexity	(+) Potentially limitless
	(−) Designer biased	(+) Evolution free to play
	(−) Mutation effect fixed	(+) Neutral Networks
	(−) Complexity μ DNA length	(+) Controllable mutation
	(±) Just optimization	(+) Specialization

References

[Bongard01] Bongard, Josh, and Pfeifer, Rolf, "Repeated Structure and Dissociation of Genotypic and Phenotypic Complexity in Artificial Ontogeny," *Proceedings of the Genetic and Evolutionary Computation Conference,* pp. 829–836, 2001.

[Dellaert94] Dellaert, Frank, Beer, and Randall, "Toward an Evolvable Model of Development for Autonomous Agent Synthesis," *Proceedings of Artificial Life IV,* MIT Press, pp. 246–257, 1994.

[Eggen97] Eggenberger, Peter, "Evolving Morphologies of Simulated 3D Organisms Based on Differential Gene Expression," *Fourth European Conference on Artificial Life,* MIT Press, 1997.

[Goldberg89] Goldberg, David, *Genetic Algorithms in Search: Optimization and Machine Learning,* Addison-Wesley, 1989.

[Grand96] Grand, Stephen, Cliff, Dave, and Malhotra, Anil, "Creatures: Artificial Life Autonomous Software Agents for Home Entertainment," *The First International Conference on Autonomous Agents,* pp. 22–29, 1996.

[Gruau93] Gruau, Frédéric, and Whitley, Darrell, "Adding Learning to the Cellular Development of Neural Networks," *Evolutionary Computation* pp. 213–233, 1993.

[Hart94] Hart, William et al., "The Role of Development in Genetic Algorithms," *Foundations of Genetic Algorithms III,* Morgan Kauffman, 1994.

[Hillis91] Hillis, Daniel, "Co-evolving Parasites Improve Simulated Evolution as an Optimization Procedure" *Artificial Life II*, 1991.

[Holland75] Holland, John, *Adaptation in Natural and Artificial Systems*, University of Michigan Press, 1975.

[Mitchell96] Mitchell, Melanie, *An Introduction to Genetic Algorithms*, MIT Press, 1996.

[Nolfi92] Nolfi, Stefano, and Parisi, Domenico, "Growing Neural Networks," Technical Report, Institute of Psychology, Rome, 1992.

[Prusinkiewicz97] Prusinkiewicz, Przemyslaw et al., "Visual Models of Morphogenesis: A Guided Tour," available online at *www.cpsc.ucalgary.ca/Research/bmv/vmm-deluxe/TitlePage.html*, Dept. of Computer Science, University of Calgary, 1997.

[Thomas02] Thomas, Dale, "Aesthetic Selection of Developmental Art Forms," *Proceedings of Artificial Life VIII*, MIT Press, pp. 157–163, 2002.

[Thomas04] Thomas, Dale, "New Paradigms in Artificial Intelligence," *AI Game Programming Wisdom 2*, Charles River Media, 2004.

[Vaario91] Vaario, Jari, "Developing Neural Networks through Growth," *Proceedings of the 5th Annual Conference of JSAI* (Japanese Society for Artificial Intelligence), 1991.

SPEECH RECOGNITION AND DIALOGUE

12.1

SAPI: An Introduction to Speech Recognition

James Matthews—Generation5

jmatthews@generation5.org

This article looks at using Microsoft SAPI (Speech Application Programming Interface) to add speech recognition (SR) and text-to-speech (TTS) to applications and games. Over the next two articles, various concepts will be demonstrated by creating two very simple applications. In this article, we look at a simple example program that involves telling the computer to draw certain shapes, and having it describe them back to you.

To use any of the code or binaries in this article, you will need Microsoft's SAPI SDK [Microsoft03]. After installing the SDK, it is probably a good idea to set up your microphone and do a little user training to customize the SR engine to your voice. It is *imperative* that you have a good headset microphone, since it will minimize background noise and pick up your voice very clearly. You must remember that while speech recognition is improving by leaps and bounds, it still requires a little patience on behalf of the user. This patience is multiplied ten-fold for an SR-application developer!

Speech Technologies in Games

In recent years, both speech and gaming technologies have greatly accelerated, with speech engines accurately understanding spoken commands and dictated dialogue, while modern gaming engines continue to blur the boundaries between fantasy and reality. As consumers come to expect more and more from games, the interaction between players and NPCs will be come an increasingly important factor.

Current methods of interaction often require players to select from a predefined list of questions and answers, often giving them a feeling of being pushed in a certain direction, or not allowing them to explore avenues they would have liked to.

At present, some games are definitely more suited to speech technologies than others. For example, team-based shooters could benefit greatly from speech recognition since speech commands are fairly limited ("Red team, move left. Blue team, hold"), but this would add a *huge* amount of realism to the game itself. Other genres such as combat flight simulators and real-time strategy games would similarly benefit.

SapiTutorial

Our first program is called SapiTutorial. It is a slightly extended version of the example application found in the Generation5 SAPI tutorial [Matthews01]. The program allows the user to ask the computer to draw one of four different shapes in 11 different colors as well as a variety of other commands.

Before we can actually start coding our application, we must set up Microsoft Visual C++ and understand SAPI's object model and grammar format.

Getting Started

Getting started with SAPI is probably the hardest thing to do. Setting up a SAPI project is a slightly lengthy procedure, and somewhat confusing for a beginner. This section looks at the SAPI conceptual framework, steps through setting up Microsoft Visual C++, and creates the initial speech recognition grammar.

SAPI Conceptual Framework

SAPI is added to your application/game by way of a variety of COM object interfaces (although this shouldn't put off people unfamiliar with COM programming). There are COM interfaces for the main engine, recognition contexts, grammars, and many more.

SAPI uses a speech recognition engine to detect speech uttered by the user that conforms to a *rule* laid out by the programmer. These rules can be decomposed into *phrases*. A rule can consist of optional phrases, lists, references to other rules, and so forth. All these rules are specified in a *grammar* file. Grammar in SAPI is created using an XML (eXtensible Markup Language) file. When SAPI detects that a rule has been spoken, it sends an *event* (or message) to your application.

Setting Up Microsoft Visual C++

Before you can compile SAPI projects, you must configure the Microsoft Visual C++ (MSVC) paths to correctly find the SAPI include files, link libraries, and binary tools. To do this, start MSVC and select "Tools, Options, Directories." Select each category in the "Show directories for:" pull-down box and add the appropriate SAPI directories for each. This is normally *<sapi-dir>*\Include, \lib\i386, \bin for include files, libraries, and binaries respectively (see the accompanying CD-ROM for a screenshot).

ON THE CD

Now your local copy of MSVC will be configured to compile SAPI programs. As a test, open the SapiTutorial project (found on the accompanying CD-ROM) and try to compile and then run the program. It is advisable to keep the project open as a reference while you read the rest of this article.

SAPI Grammar

Before we look at the programming specifics, let's look at how SAPI handles speech recognition grammar. We supply grammar to SAPI by sending a resource ID for SAPI to load from the resource section of our application. The grammar in this section is compiled XML.

Therefore, when you start writing your SAPI application, you will normally want to start with a skeleton grammar file to get things up and running. The following is a good example of such a skeleton file:

```
<GRAMMAR LANGID="409">
  <DEFINE>
    <ID NAME="VID_MainRule" VAL="1"/>
  </DEFINE>

  <RULE ID="VID_MainRule" TOPLEVEL="ACTIVE">
    <P>Placeholder</P>
  </RULE>
</GRAMMAR>
```

The top-level tag *must* be GRAMMAR. Next, the DEFINE section assigns numerical values to each of our rule IDs. This must be done to tie our grammar file into our high-level code in the main application at compile time.

Compiling Grammar

To compile our grammar, we must set up the grammar compiler (gc) options in MSVC. Open the project settings, select the XML file (sapi0.xml in our example), and in the Custom Build tab enter the information as shown in Figure 12.1.1.

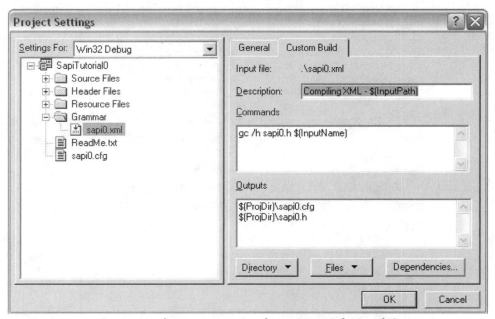

FIGURE 12.1.1 *Setting up the grammar compiler in Microsoft Visual C++.*

Now, compile the grammar by opening the XML file and select "Build, Compile." Two files are now generated. SapiRules.cfg is your grammar in binary form, and SapiRules.h is a header file used by your C/C++ programs that defines your rule IDs.

To import the grammar into the project, open ResourceView and select "Insert, Resource . . ." Click the Import button and select SapiRules.cfg. When asked to enter a type, enter "SRGRAMMAR" (including quotation marks). This will import your binary grammar into your project; rename the resource to something useful like IDR_SAPI_RULES, and you are ready to code!

Aside: SapiWizard

While setting up the MSVC directories is a once-off procedure, setting up the grammar and XML compiler is a per-project setting. As such, you have to do it every time you start a new SAPI project. SapiWizard, available for download from Generation5 [Matthews02], is designed to combat this nuisance and builds on the existing MFC AppWizard to create a SAPI-enabled project.

SapiWizard will set up your project, add all initialization, destruction, and handler code, and provide a skeleton grammar file. While MFC isn't useful for games, creating a quick MFC application to test your SAPI ideas and grammar integrity is a good idea before implementing it in your main application.

Initializing SAPI

SAPI is a collection of COM objects. These are handled by CComPtr, a class designed to facilitate COM interface pointer manipulation. Most SAPI applications will use three or four of these pointers:

```
CComPtr<ISpRecognizer>  m_cpEngine;
CComPtr<ISpRecoContext> m_cpRecoCtxt;
CComPtr<ISpRecoGrammar> m_cpCmdGrammar;
CComPtr<ISpVoice>       m_cpVoice;
```

ISpRecognizer provides the primary interface with the speech engine itself. ISRecoContext is the recognition-context interface (explained after the code), ISpRecoGrammar is the interface with our SAPI grammar. ISpVoice is our interface to the text-to-speech engine and voice properties.

All the SAPI definitions can be added to your project by including <sphelper.h>. sphelper.h includes all the necessary SAPI header files, and contains a large collection of helper classes and functions.

Actually initializing SAPI is a rather lengthy procedure, since there are quite a few things to take care of. Here is our initialization function with all error checking and reporting removed:

```
CoInitialize(NULL);

m_cpEngine.CoCreateInstance(CLSID_SpSharedRecognizer);
```

```
m_cpEngine->CreateRecoContext(&m_cpRecoCtxt);
m_cpRecoCtxt->SetNotifyWindowMessage(m_hWnd,
                            WM_SAPI5EVENT, 0, 0);
m_cpRecoCtxt->SetInterest(SPFEI(SPEI_RECOGNITION),
                          SPFEI(SPEI_RECOGNITION));
m_cpRecoCtxt->CreateGrammar(0, &m_cpCmdGrammar);
m_cpCmdGrammar->LoadCmdFromResource(
            NULL,
            MAKEINTRESOURCEW(IDR_SAPI_RULES),
            L"SRGRAMMAR",
            MAKELANGID( LANG_NEUTRAL, SUBLANG_NEUTRAL),
        SPLO_DYNAMIC);
m_cpCmdGrammar->SetRuleState(NULL, NULL, SPRS_ACTIVE);
m_cpRecoCtxt->GetVoice(&m_cpVoice);
```

First, we need to initialize COM before instantiating any of our SAPI objects. Next, we create an instance of our recognizer. With this, we create a *recognition context*. A recognition context is the primary interface between the application and SAPI speech recognition (see [Microsoft01] for more information). We must then tell SAPI the window to send recognition messages to. Note that WM_SAPI5EVENT is a user-defined message (WM_USER + *x*).

Next, we tell SAPI what messages we are interested in. We only care about our recognition messages (SPEI_RECOGNITION). With our recognition context, we create the grammar object. Next, we load the grammar from our resource section and then activate it. The final step is to create our TTS voice. Note that SAPI will use the default settings in the Windows control panel to initialize the voice.

Handling SAPI Events

We have told SAPI the window to send events to, but haven't told the window to receive them. In MFC, this is done using message mapping/handler functions:

```
ON_MESSAGE(WM_SAPI5EVENT, OnRecoEvent)

// ... Interim code

LRESULT CSnapDlg:: OnRecoEvent(WPARAM wParam,
                              LPARAM lParam )
{
    // ... Handler code here ...
    return 0;
}
```

In the standard Win32 SDK this is handled in WndProc:

```
LRESULT CALLBACK WndProc(HWND hWnd, UINT message,
                        WPARAM wParam, LPARAM lParam)
{   switch (message)
    {   // ...
        case WM_RECOEVENT:
            ProcessRecoEvent( hWnd );
```

```
                    break;
            }
    }
```

Either way, the event processing is essentially the same. It is a good idea to handle SAPI messages in two parts in order to keep your code clean and well defined. Use the SAPI message handler to simply delegate tasks to helper functions designed to handle particular SAPI messages. For example, here we have the code required to handle the speech recognition event triggered when a grammar rule is met (`OnRecoEvent`):

```
CSpEvent event;

while (event.GetFrom(m_cpRecoCtxt) == S_OK) {
    switch (event.eEventId) {
        case SPEI_RECOGNITION:
            ExecuteCommand(event.RecoResult());
            break;
    }
}
```

`ExecuteCommand` then executes the particular speech command detected. For example, in our SapiTutorial application, the handler looks something like this:

```
void CMyClass::ExecuteCommand(ISpPhrase *pPhrase)
{
    SPPHRASE *pElements;

    if (SUCCEEDED(pPhrase->GetPhrase(&pElements))) {
        switch (pElements->Rule.ulId) {

            case VID_MainRule: // Handle main rule
                break;

            case VID_Start:    // Handle start command
                break;
        }
    }
}
```

You can see from the code how the phrase uttered is sent to our handler. From there, we use `GetPhrase()` to retrieve a list of elements in the phrase and the rule ID. Remember that `VID_MainRule`, `VID_Start`, and similar rule IDs are defined by the gc-produced header file, SapiRules.h.

SapiTutorial In-Depth

We will now look at how our SapiTutorial application puts all these parts together.

Grammar

We now have enough information about how SAPI works to begin coding. As before, we should start with creating the grammar. First, we want to think about how we want our speech events to be triggered—just what exactly should the user say? For example, for our drawing event we might want something similar to this:

$$\{please\} \; draw \; \{a\} \begin{pmatrix} red \\ green \\ blue \\ ... \end{pmatrix} \begin{pmatrix} circle \\ square \\ triangle \\ pie \end{pmatrix}$$

Where items in {} denote optional phrases, and items in parentheses denote a selection. Therefore, our user could say "Draw a red circle," "Please draw a green pie," "Draw blue square," and a range of other phrases. We want the user to be able to say any of these phrases and trigger our main speech event. Here is how we would write this using SAPI grammar:

```
<RULE ID="VID_MainDraw" TOPLEVEL="ACTIVE">
  <O>Please</O>
  <P>draw</P>
  <O>a</O>
  <P>
    <RULEREF REFID="VID_ColourType" />
    <RULEREF REFID="VID_DrawType" />
  </P>
</RULE>

<RULE ID="VID_ColourType">
  <L PROPID="VID_ColourType">
    <P VAL="VID_Red">red</P>
    <P VAL="VID_Green">green</P>
    <P VAL="VID_Blue">blue</P>
    ...
  </L>
</RULE>

<RULE ID="VID_DrawType" >
  <L PROPID="VID_DrawType">
    <P VAL="VID_Square">square</P>
    ...
  </L>
</RULE>
```

Our VID_MainDraw is the top-level rule (a rule that the computer actively listens for). The <O> tag (short for <OPT>) specifies an optional phrase or word, whereas the <P> tag (short for <PHRASE>) is used to designate a compulsory phrase. To make our top-level rule a little clearer, we broke the rule into two other small parts that list the colors and shapes. These sub-rules are then referenced using the RULEREF tag.

Note how our two sub-rules make use of the <L> tag to list options available. Each list element has a value associated with it so that we can retrieve which option was spoken.

From Grammar to Code

With our grammar, SAPI will send a message to our main dialog window whenever our VID_MainDraw rule is detected. The next thing we want to do in our application is to retrieve the necessary information from the message.

In our example program, this is done in ExecuteCommand(). Here is the code snippet pertinent to retrieving the information:

```
case VID_MainDraw:
{   const SPPHRASEPROPERTY *pProp =
                              pElements->pProperties;
    while (pProp) {
        switch(pProp->vValue.ulVal )
        {   case VID_Square: uType = VID_Square;break;
            ...
            case VID_Red:crShape = RGB(255,0,0);break;
            ...
        }
        pProp = pProp->pNextSibling;
    }

    DrawCommand(uType, crShape);
}
```

What we do here is retrieve the phrase properties. Phrase properties contain information like the phrase name, ID, contents, and pointers to sibling and child phrases. We then simply cycle through the properties and detect the shape type and color. We don't need to worry about order or bad information, since our grammar has taken care of that (e.g., if the user said "Draw a black red circle," the event would never be triggered). This also allows us to retrieve additional information we might want to add in the future (e.g., if we wanted the user to be able to say "Draw a red, hashed circle").

Application Commands

SapiTutorial also has a few additional commands that allow you to quit the application, show the About box, describe the object (using text-to-speech), and visit Generation5. These are all done in a similar way to the method described previously. One thing to note is the "quit" grammar line:

```
<P VAL="VID_QuitCmd">+quit <O>the application</O></P>
```

Notice the plus sign before "quit"? When the speech recognition starts to process microphone input, it assigns a confidence value to possible words. The confidence value has to be above a certain threshold to be "detected." A plus sign before a word increases the required confidence value. Similarly, a minus sign will decrease the required confidence. It is good to mark up your grammar in this way since it can strengthen the usability of your voice user interface.

Text-to-Speech

Text-to-speech (TTS) couldn't be easier with SAPI. After initializing your voice object, Speak() will speak a given line of text. For example, in our OnDescribe() function:

```
void CSapiTutorialODlg::OnDescribe()
{   CString szDescription = "The object is a";

    szDescription += " meat popsicle";

    USES_CONVERSION;
    m_cpVoice->Speak(T2W(szDescription), SPF_ASYNC,
                     NULL);
}
```

This function creates a string describing the object being displayed. It is then passed to our Speak() function that causes SAPI to speak the phrase. The USES_CONVERSION and T2W macros are used to convert our string to a COM-friendly version we can pass to SAPI. SPF_ASYNC means that Speak() returns immediately and the text is spoken in the background.

ON THE CD

Since the default Microsoft voices are a little synthetic, the accompanying CD-ROM contains a few examples of speech using high-quality voices from AT&T NaturalVoices™ [AT&T03].

Shutting Down SAPI

Shutting down SAPI is conducted the same way you would destroy any COM object, by releasing the pointer to the interface:

```
m_cpCmdGrammar.Release();
m_cpRecoCtxt->SetNotifySink(NULL);
m_cpRecoCtxt.Release();
m_cpEngine.Release();
m_cpVoice.Release();
```

Conclusion

This article covered the basics of the Microsoft Speech API: how to set up a SAPI-enabled project in Microsoft Visual C++, initialization, message handling, grammar creation, and text-to-speech.

Actually starting a SAPI project for the first time is definitely the hardest task you'll face. Hopefully, this article, as well as the resources and references listed at the end of this article, will help you learn the basics as quickly as possible.

Before progressing on to the next article, *SAPI: Extending the Basics*, attempt your own simple SAPI project. Perhaps try to extend SapiTutorial further, create a program to control another program (by sending keystrokes), create a simple version of hangman, or anything that suits your fancy. The key thing is to learn how to set up a SAPI project, write your own grammar, and handle it appropriately.

Resources

www.generation5.org/—A few SR/SAPI tutorials and programs

www.microsoft.com/speech/techinfo/—Microsoft SAPI documentation

microsoft.public.speech_tech.sdk—Microsoft SAPI newsgroup

References

[AT&T03] AT&T NaturalVoices, available online at *www.naturalvoices.com/*, 2003.

[Matthews01] Matthews, James, "SAPI 5.0 Tutorial I: An Introduction to SAPI," available online at *www.generation5.org/content/2001/sr01.asp*, January 2001.

[Matthews02] Matthews, James, "SapiWizard: A SAPI-enabled AppWizard," available online at *www.generation5.org/content/2002/sapiwizard.asp*, June 2002.

[Microsoft01] "IspRecoContext," *Microsoft Speech SDK (SAPI 5.1) Documentation*, 2001.

[Microsoft03] Microsoft Speech SDK Download, available online at *www.microsoft.com/speech/download/sdk51/, 2003*, also included on the *AI Game Programming Wisdom 2* CD-ROM.

12.2

SAPI: Extending the Basics

James Matthews—Generation5

jmatthews@generation5.org

In the last article, we looked at how to set up SAPI, and create a simple application that drew various shapes in a variety of colors on command [Matthews03]. In this article, we will look at a variety of additional techniques and SAPI features that can be used to extend the functionality of our applications.

We will look at extending our grammar creation knowledge, both by introducing new XML tags and by actually programmatically creating new grammar structures. We will also look at how to retrieve a list of voices available, change the voice, and even change the rate and volume as well as a few other *loose-end* concepts. As such, unlike the last article, this article is intended to be more of a reference than a linear *how-to*.

Nevertheless, this article also comes with an example application that makes use of many of the concepts covered.

Go Fish!

The example program we will look at is a simple version of "Go Fish" (or just Fish), the popular card game. The rules of Fish are simple. Four players each have five cards, and the aim of the game is to end up with the most number of hands. A hand consists of all four cards of a given rank (e.g., all Jacks or all twos).

Cards are gained by simply asking an opponent, "*Player*, do you have any *rank?*" Players might only request a card they already have in their hand. If a player is asked for a card and he or she has it, he or she *must* give *all* cards of that rank to the requesting player.

If the asked player does not have the requested card, he or she says "Go Fish" and the asking player takes a card from the deck. If, by chance, the card picked up is the card asked for, the player gets another turn. Otherwise, the game continues to the next player. This repeats until there are either no cards left in the deck, or one player ends up with no cards. The player with the greatest number of hands wins.

Go Fish Voice Interface

The voice interface (VUI) used is fairly simple, since only one command is required for gameplay. All the same, we want to leave the users free to say what they like when requesting a card. Assuming three opponent names, our rule could look something like this:

$$(Ben \mid Michelle \mid Simon) \xrightarrow{\text{anything}} (ace \mid two \mid three \mid ... \mid jack \mid queen \mid king)$$

In the rest of this article, we look at how to implement such a rule, and how to dynamically change the player names.

More with Grammar

We saw in the previous article the +/- confidence inline grammar modifiers. SAPI supports a few other useful additions: ? (optional), . . . (wildcard) and * (dictation).

'?' can be used instead of the <O> or <OPT> tags. For example:

```
<P>?Display Microphone Training</P>
```

is equivalent to:

```
<O>Display</O><P> Microphone Training</P>
```

This can make some grammar phrases a little easier to read if there are a lot of optional words.

Wildcards and Dictation

The wildcard, which can be written as three periods (. . .) or as <WILDCARD/>, can be used to specify a section in your grammar where the users are free to choose their wording. The wildcard is very useful to improve the integrity of your VUI, but it does put additional strains on the SR engine (added computation, and a possible loss of accuracy), and as such, should be used sparingly. As mentioned in the previous section, our Go Fish program requires a wildcard to keep the VUI fairly open. Therefore, our main rule looks like this:

```
<RULE ID="VID_MainRule" TOPLEVEL="ACTIVE">
    <RULEREF REFID="VID_PlayerNames"/>
    <P>-...</P>
    <RULEREF REFID="VID_CardRank"/>
</RULE>
```

We use the wildcard here in conjunction with the confidence decreasing tag, since we don't really care about what is between the player name and the card rank. This "loose" wildcard allows for slightly slurred speech, such as "Michelle, *d'ya* have any jacks" and other, more natural speech patterns.

The dictation tag, which can be written as an asterisk (*) or <DICTATION/>, also allows you to specify a portion in the grammar rule that allows dictation. Using an asterisk (*) allows the user to dictate one word. To specify multiple words, the combined symbol asterisk-plus (*+) must be used.

The only difference between dictation and wildcard markers is that the words spoken during dictation are stored by the SR engine in the returned phrase structure. This isn't the case with wildcards.

Dictation is also used in our example program to allow players to rename one of their opponents. Here is the grammar used:

```
<RULE ID="VID_RenamePlayer" TOPLEVEL="ACTIVE">
    <P>
        Rename <RULEREF REFID="VID_PlayerNames"/> to
        *
    </P>
</RULE>
```

In our application we retrieve the necessary information in the `Rename()` function. `Rename()` is divided into two parts. First, we retrieve the player ID using the properties loop method described in the previous article.

Next, we need to retrieve the text that was dictated:

```
WCHAR *wszCoMemNameText = NULL;

if (pElements->Rule.ulCountOfElements > 3) {
    // Retrieve the spoken text
    pPhrase->GetText(
            3,
            pElements->Rule.ulCountOfElements - 3,
            FALSE,
            &wszCoMemNameText,
            NULL
            )

    m_szPlayerNames[iPlayer] = wszCoMemNameText;
    CreateNameRule();

    CoTaskMemFree( wszCoMemNameText );
}
```

You can see that we first check to see whether there are more than three elements in the rule. This is because we know the grammar rule to be "Rename *x* to . . . " so there must be more than three elements. Next, we retrieve the actual dictation using `ISpPhrase->GetText()`. The function `GetText()` takes five parameters: the start index, the number of words to retrieve, the format type, a pointer to the storing string, and a display type.

After retrieving the string, we simply place it in the appropriate player name and dynamically update our player name rule. The next section covers how we do this.

Dynamic Grammar

Modifying the grammar at runtime is a very powerful and relatively easy-to-use feature of SAPI. In our example application, dynamic grammar is used to allow player names to change. If you look in the raw grammar file for Go Fish, you will see the following:

```
<RULE ID="VID_PlayerNames" DYNAMIC="TRUE">
    <P>Placeholder</P>
</RULE>
```

When the application starts up, the CreateNameRule() function creates the rule dynamically from the default names (James, Simon, Ben, Michelle). The function CreateNameRule() looks like this:

```
SPSTATEHANDLE shName;

m_cpCmdGrammar->GetRule(NULL, VID_PlayerNames,
                SPRAF_Dynamic, FALSE, &shName);

m_cpCmdGrammar->ClearRule(shName);
m_cpCmdGrammar->Commit(NULL);

for (int i=0; i<4; i++) {
    SPPROPERTYINFO prop;
    prop.pszName = NULL;
    prop.pszValue = NULL;
    prop.vValue.vt = VT_I4; // for VARIANT datatype
    prop.vValue.ulVal = VID_Player1 + i;

    m_cpCmdGrammar->AddWordTransition(shName, NULL,
            CSpDynamicString(m_szPlayerNames[i]),
            L" ",SPWT_LEXICAL, NULL, &prop);
}

m_cpCmdGrammar->Commit(NULL);
```

This might look a little daunting at first, so let's step through it. First, we retrieve the rule handle from the grammar interface. This is stored in shName, a state handle. Next, we clear the rule, since we don't need Placeholder in the rule anymore and commit the changes.

Now we want to add our four player names. To do this, we need to specify two things—the player name and a player ID we can extract from recognized phrases. To create the player IDs, VID_Player1 through VID_Player4 have been defined in the grammar file's DEFINE section. Therefore, we simply set the relevant player ID in the property structure (prop.vValue.ulVal).

Note that the pszName and pszValue member variables of the prop structure correspond to the PROPNAME and PROPID attributes for XML-created grammar structures. While we don't care about this information, we still have to set both attributes to NULL to successfully create our state.

Once our property structure has been created, we call the grammar interface's AddWordTransition() function. A transition is essentially a directed bridge between two related phrases. In our case, we want to transition from our main rule so we pass in shName (the handle to our main rule). CSpDynamicString is a specialized class found in sphelper.h that eases the passing of strings between C++ and SAPI.

We loop through each player, creating the new state property structure and adding each player to the rule. Finally, we commit the changes to the grammar.

Creating dynamic grammar can be quite complicated and we have only looked at a very simple example. The Microsoft SAPI documentation shows how to programmatically create optional, wildcarded, and the other types of phrases as well as dictation and rule references [Microsoft01b].

Programmatically Changing SAPI Voices

Changing the SAPI voice is extremely easy to do. Simply call ISpVoice->Speak() with the necessary voice token, and the voice will be loaded and subsequently used. The hard part is actually retrieving the voice token itself. Even this, though, can be very easy if you use the SAPI UI helper functions.

For example, in our Go Fish application, available voices are listed in a combo box. The population of the combo box is done *entirely* by a SAPI helper function:

```
SpInitTokenComboBox(m_cVoice.m_hWnd, SPCAT_VOICES);
```

SpInitTokenComboBox simply takes two parameters, an HWND to the combo box and a string that defines the token type to send to the combo box. SPCAT_VOICES is a predefined string (in sapi.h) that points to the voices listed in the Registry.

SpInitTokenComboBox does not just list the voices in the combo box, it also sets the item data for each voice to be a pointer to the voice token. You can see how we use this in our application to quickly and simply retrieve the voice:

```
// In CTTSOptionsDlg::OnOK()
m_dwTokenPtr =
    m_cVoice.GetItemData(m_cVoice.GetCurSel());

// In CGoFishDlg::ExecuteCommand()
m_cpVoice->SetVoice (
    (ISpObjectToken*)dlg.m_dwTokenPtr );
```

For completeness, we also let the user change the volume and speaking rate in the dialog too. These are also passed back to the main dialog application that then changes the voice settings using SetVolume() and SetRate():

```
m_cpVoice->SetVolume(dlg.m_iVolume);
m_cpVoice->SetRate(dlg.m_iRate);
m_cpVoice->Speak(L"This is my new voice.", 0, 0);
```

While the UI helper functions are great to quickly code something within the Windows framework, you might want to retrieve the voices yourself (e.g., to fit into your game UI). Here is a code snippet to achieve just that:

```
CSpDynamicString                  *szDescription;
ISpObjectToken                    *pToken = NULL;
CComPtr<IEnumSpObjectTokens>       cpEnum;

WCHAR *pszCurTokenId = NULL;
WCHAR **pszTokenIds;

ULONG ulIndex = 0, ulNumTokens = 0;

SpEnumTokens(SPCAT_VOICES, NULL, NULL, &cpEnum);

cpEnum->GetCount(&ulNumTokens);

if (ulNumTokens != 0) {
    pszTokenIds   = new WCHAR *[ulNumTokens];
    szDescription = new CSpDynamicString[ulNumTokens];

    ZeroMemory(pszTokenIds,
               ulNumTokens * sizeof(WCHAR *));

    while (cpEnum->Next(1, &pToken, NULL) == S_OK) {
        SpGetDescription(pToken,
                         &szDescription[ulIndex]);
        pToken->GetId(&pszTokenIds[ulIndex]);

        ulIndex++;
        pToken->Release();
        pToken = NULL;
    }
}

// ...do something with descriptions and IDs.

delete [] szDescription;
delete [] pszTokenIds;
```

Again, the code looks worse than it is. This quasi-function basically retrieves the list of voice tokens and puts the descriptions into the szDescription array and the token IDs into the pszTokenIds array. Note that storing the token ID instead of the token pointer itself is simply a good, low-overhead way to track the token without out keeping hold of the object itself [Microsoft01a].

First, we enumerate the voice tokens. After ascertaining the number of tokens, we loop through them using IEnumSpObjectTokens->Next(). Finally, SpGetDescription() and GetId() simply supply the necessary information to our two arrays. To retrieve the voice token from the ID at a later date, you can use the SpGetTokenFromId() helper function:

```
ISpObjectToken *pToken = NULL;

SpGetTokenFromId(pszTokenIds[iIndex], &pToken, FALSE);
m_cpVoice->SetVoice(pToken);
```

SpGetTokenFromId() takes three parameters: the ID, a reference to the token object to store the information in, and a Boolean value that states whether the function should create the token if the ID doesn't exist.

Additional SAPI Messages

SPEI_RECOGNITION isn't the only message that SAPI is capable of sending. In fact, there are over 30 messages defined, although we will only look at a further two of interest: SPEI_FALSE_RECOGNITION and SPEI_VISEME. Keen readers might want to explore other interesting messages like SPEI_INTERFERENCE, SPEI_HYPOTHESIS, and SPEI_WORD_BOUNDARY.

SPEI_FALSE_RECOGNITION

Remember from the last article that SPEI_RECOGNITION is the message sent to our window when a phrase is recognized from our grammar. Similarly, we can ask SAPI to send us a message when a phrase is not understood. This is especially helpful in games, where a character *must* respond to what the player has said in some form. To use SPEI_FALSE_RECOGNITION, we must change our call to SetInterest in the initialization function:

```
ULONGLONG lFlags = SPFEI(SPEI_RECOGNITION) |
                   SPFEI(SPEI_FALSE_RECOGNITION);
m_cpRecoCtxt->SetInterest(lFlags, lFlags);
```

The SPFEI macro converts the messages we want into flags compatible with the SetInterest() function call. Later, we can handle SPEI_FALSE_RECOGNITION in our OnSapi5Event():

```
while (event.GetFrom(m_cpRecoCtxt) == S_OK) {
    switch (event.eEventId) {
        case SPEI_RECOGNITION:
            ExecuteCommand(event.RecoResult());
            break;
        case SPEI_FALSE_RECOGNITION:
            Beep(440, 50);
            break;
    }
}
```

This code would cause the machine to beep any time a false recognition occurred. Be sure to carefully handle SPEI_FALSE_RECOGNITION, though, since it will be triggered often, especially if the user isn't used to using speech recognition software.

SPEI_VISEMES

Visemes have some very interesting implications for gaming. Visemes are essentially the mouth positions that make up our speech. SAPI enables the application to receive a message indicating the viseme type, which it can then act on accordingly. There are a total of 22 viseme types:

```
SP_VISEME_0 = 0,      // Silence
SP_VISEME_1,          // AE, AX, AH
SP_VISEME_2,          // AA
SP_VISEME_3,          // AO
SP_VISEME_4,          // EY, EH, UH
SP_VISEME_5,          // ER
SP_VISEME_6,          // y, IY, IH, IX
SP_VISEME_7,          // w, UW
SP_VISEME_8,          // OW
SP_VISEME_9,          // AW
SP_VISEME_10,         // OY
SP_VISEME_11,         // AY
SP_VISEME_12,         // h
SP_VISEME_13,         // r
SP_VISEME_14,         // l
SP_VISEME_15,         // s, z
SP_VISEME_16,         // SH, CH, JH, ZH
SP_VISEME_17,         // TH, DH
SP_VISEME_18,         // f, v
SP_VISEME_19,         // d, t, n
SP_VISEME_20,         // k, g, NG
SP_VISEME_21,         // p, b, m
```

The best way to handle visemes is to create a simple look-up array that maps each viseme (or group of visemes) to a bitmap depicting the mouth position.

Using SPEI_VISEME is easy. Once you have added SPEI_VISEME to your SetInterest() flags, you can simply handle the SPEI_VISEME message in your handler like so:

```
case SPEI_VISEME:
    m_VisemeBmp = g_MapVisemeToImage[event.Viseme()];
    DrawCharacter();
    break;
```

While our Go Fish application does not make use of visemes, you can take a look at the code for TTSApp (in the Samples directory of the SAPI 5 SDK) or SapiTalk [Matthews01b].

Displaying SAPI User Interfaces

Our final topic will look at displaying SAPI user interfaces. It is possible to call various SAPI user interface dialog boxes from your application by using the DisplayUI() function. DisplayUI() takes a few parameters: the parent window, the window title, the type of UI, and two vendor-dependent data items (often just NULL).

There are seven different UIs currently supported by SAPI, listed in Table 12.2.1.

Table 12.2.1 SPDUI Types

UI Definition	Description
SPDUI_AddRemoveWord	Display the add/remove word dialog box.
SPDUI_UserTraining	Display the user training dialog box.
SPDUI_MicTraining	Display the microphone wizard.
SPDUI_RecoProfileProperties	Display the recognition profile properties.
SPDUI_AudioProperties	Display the audio properties dialog box.
SPDUI_AudioVolume	Display the audio volume dialog box.
SPDUI_EngineProperties	Display the engine properties dialog box.

Since user interfaces might vary between future vendor implementations, it is a good idea to call IsUISupported() first to determine whether the engine the user has loaded supports the UI in question. For example, the following code checks whether the current vendor implementation supports the microphone training UI, and if so, displays it.

```
BOOL bSupported = FALSE;
m_cpEngine->IsUISupported(SPDUI_MicTraining, NULL,
                           NULL, &bSupported);

if (bSupported)
    m_cpEngine->DisplayUI(this->m_hWnd, NULL,
                          SPDUI_MicTraining, NULL, NULL);
```

Conclusion

This concludes our venture into SAPI. Hopefully, you will have a good understanding of how to create SAPI applications that suit your requirements now. While speech recognition is still a fledging technology (although it is improving exponentially), the key to creating a good VUI is simplicity. By carefully using the grammar constructs presented in this article and the last article, you should be able to create the majority of your grammar rules.

Dynamic grammar rules were also briefly presented, allowing you to create new grammar structures at runtime with relative ease. A good programming exercise with dynamic grammar is to expand on this article by attempting to create a grammar with multiple interim states. For example, try to programmatically create the following rule:

$$\text{I } \{really\} \begin{pmatrix} love \\ like \\ hate \end{pmatrix} \begin{pmatrix} bananas \\ apples \\ oranges \end{pmatrix}$$

Remember, SAPI is a very large SDK and contains a large number of helper functions and little-known function calls. There is a good chance that there will be some type of function that will help you achieve your goal just a little bit easier.

References

[Matthews01a] Matthews, James, "SAPI 5.0 Tutorial III: Dynamic Grammar," available online at *www.generation5.org/content/2001/sr02.asp*, April 2001.

[Matthews01b] Matthews, James, "Visemes: Representing Mouth Positions," available online at *www.generation5.org/content/2001/visemes.asp*, October 2001.

[Matthews03] Matthews, James, "SAPI: An Introduction to Speech Recognition," *AI Game Programming Wisdom 2*, 2003.

[Microsoft01a] "CoffeeS4," *Microsoft Speech SDK (SAPI 5.1) Documentation*, 2001.

[Microsoft01b] "Grammar Format Tags," *Microsoft Speech SDK (SAPI 5.1) Documentation*, 2001.

Conversational Agents: Creating Natural Dialogue between Players and Non-Player Characters

Penny Drennan—School of ITEE, University of Queensland

pennyd@itee.uq.edu.au

The quality of interactions between non-player characters (NPCs) and the player is an area of artificial intelligence in games that is yet to be fully explored. Game players frequently express that they want to see opponents and NPCs that appear to possess intelligence. However, most dialogue between players and NPCs in computer games is currently scripted, which does not add to the appearance of intelligence.

This article discusses using *conversational agents* to create NPCs that appear intelligent and are able to converse with the player. Conversational agents consist of models of personality and emotion, which allow them to demonstrate believable conversational behavior. To date, conversational agent architectures have been proposed in academic works such as [Reilly92, DeSmedt99, Morris02], but have generally not been implemented in commercially available games.

Conversational Agents

Conversational agents are software agents that have models of emotion, mood, and personality that drive their actions and dialogue. This results in dynamic interactions that change according to the situation and the NPC's temperament. This conversational agent architecture can be used within an NPC to encourage the player's belief that intelligent characters inhabit the world they are playing in. Conversational agents can ensure that NPCs avoid situations where they engage the player in repetitive or unrealistic dialogue.

Currently in games, NPCs have two main uses: to give information to the player about the game, which they might not discover from simply interacting with the game environment, and to send players on quests or give them challenges to advance the storyline of the game. The purpose of using NPCs in these roles is to populate the game environment with characters that are able to provide meaningful interactions with the player. NPCs that can give out information or give the player directions allow for a more immersive gaming environment than having this information written on a static object in the game world. This suspension of disbelief is encouraged by having more engaging characters and interactions, allowing the player to become more involved in the game. Conversational agents can move NPCs from being scripted and flat to being vital interactive characters with depth.

Creating a Conversational Agent

The process of creating a conversational agent consists of determining the agent's architecture, and how the components of the architecture feed back to each other. The components considered here are personality, emotion, input, and output. The input function receives information from the environment, including dialogue with the player and events from the agent's immediate environment. The output function is responsible for selecting the response that the agent gives to the player. The input function provides feedback to the emotion function, in order to modify the mood of the agent [Morris02]. Personality and emotion can be used to define the set of comments and responses that the agent is able to access, directly influencing the interaction with the player.

Personality and Emotion

The first step in creating conversational agents is to choose a model to use for defining personality. One academic model is the Five Factor Model (FFM), which comprises five personality dimensions [McCrae92]. These dimensions are openness to experience, conscientiousness, extraversion, agreeableness, and neuroticism. A character's personality is made up of a score in each of these dimensions. For example, high scores in neuroticism indicate personality traits such as worrier, insecure, and nervous. Low scores indicate personality traits such as calm, unemotional, and relaxed. Scores in all the dimensions combine to completely describe a personality. For more details on the different types of personalities and how FFM describes them, see [Jordan03].

A simple way to implement personality is by setting *emotional thresholds*. For example, a personality with a temper (someone with a low score in agreeableness) requires a low anger threshold. This might mean that only one or two distressing actions can trigger a change in the character's language choice. However, someone who is slow to anger would not change his or her style of dialogue until a number of distressing events had taken place. A character's emotional state can therefore be represented by a variable that is incremented or decremented in response to events and dialogue. To describe the character's personality, it would be necessary to determine thresholds for each of the five personality dimensions.

Linguistic choice can also be used to display unique personality. The simplest way to imply emotion or mood change is to alter the language that someone uses. Different sentence construction and different word choice can be used to convey messages without being explicitly stated. For example, there is a distinct difference between "I'm sorry, I don't know the answer to your question. I wish I could help you, but I can't," and "No! I don't know. Now, leave me alone," in response to a request for information. The implicit message in the first response is the desire to help, but not being able to provide any information. The second response demonstrates irritation caused by the player's question.

Moods and emotional states of characters can be implemented as exaggerated forms of the character's basic personality. It is possible to represent a variety of emotions and moods by using a combination of only a few emotions. Representing a variety of emotions can be achieved by using fuzzy logic. The character's emotion can be represented as how much membership it has in a state. A character could be happy, ecstatic, or content, based on its degree of membership in the "happy" state—someone who is ecstatic has emotions that are strongly represented in the happy state. Instead of having an integer represent the threshold for an emotional change, for example, from calm to happy, it is possible to use a fuzzy threshold. For further information on fuzzy logic, see [Kaehler98].

Another aspect of enabling agents with the appearance of emotions is to give events within the world emotional significance. Small, insignificant events do not add greatly to a character's emotional state, whereas important statements from the player can add a large amount to a character's emotion. For example, the player might say, "I have killed the evil wizard." The death of the evil wizard has a high amount of happiness associated with it, which is added to the character's happiness level. Using events in the environment to add to a character's emotion would require defining in advance likely events in the world, and creating an emotional importance attribute as part of the event definition.

Decreasing the effect of a particular event or dialogue on the character's mood and emotion level over time is another way to add more realism to a character's personality. If the player said something a long time ago, it could have less bearing on the NPCs mood than something the player said in the last minute. Over time, the amount that this utterance contributes to the emotional level can drop. The emotional state of the agent therefore needs to be updated over time, adding the effects of new events and utterances and altering the effects of older events. The simplest way to alter the effect of older events on an agent's emotional state is to periodically decrement the emotional levels of the agent.

Input

After creating the personality and emotions of the agent, the next step is to determine how the agent receives input from the environment. It is important to give the agent sensory honesty, such that the character can only sense events in the immediate environment. Sensory honesty adds to the realism of the character and also allows for a player to deceive an NPC about something that has happened outside their perceivable range. If an event happened some distance away, it can take time for news of the event to reach the character. A character being unaware of an event has implications for its emotional state and therefore on its dialogue. Once news of an event reaches the character, the emotional state is updated. Implementing sensory honesty requires that the agent have a sense-update cycle. Within a defined spatial limit, the agent is able to sense events in the environment, and the knowledge of these events is used to update the emotional state of the agent. A system that spreads knowledge of events via agent gossip is described by [Alt02].

However, having to keep track of the internal state of a large number of NPCs can use in-game resources that might be better used elsewhere. Discarding the emotional states of NPCs that the player cannot encounter again, and not modeling the state of NPCs that the player has not yet encountered, can lessen the computational load involved in implementing agents. Modeling only current characters requires an initial sense-update cycle be carried out on the internal state of the NPC when the player comes into range of the NPC. Updating the NPC as soon as the player comes into range ensures that the NPC is still able to present the appearance of intelligence to the player.

Output

In response to the player's question or statement, the character generates a comment as output. This response is based on the input that the character has received, filtered through the character's emotion and personality. The NPC has access to a set of utterances or a knowledge base that covers a range of topics and enables the NPC to deliver information, express an opinion, or ask a question. The personality and purpose of the NPC defines the subset of utterances that is available to it, while changes in emotion can further refine this set.

The set of utterances or knowledge base is built by creating an ontology, and then specifying the relationship between entries in the ontology. The first step is designing the ontology of the agent—the list of all the things that the agent knows and is able to tell the player. Examples of propositions in a conversational agent knowledge base can be "dragon lives in the cave near the forest" and "enemy has an army camp at the river." The second step is to identify how the concepts in the agent's ontology relate to each other. Relationships are usually ordered in a hierarchy, similar to a class hierarchy, which allows property and functionality inheritance [DeSmedt99].

An example of concept relations in *Age of Mythology* would be how to represent the different types of soldiers in an enemy army. The propositions "enemy wears blue" and "enemy is Greek" in the agent's ontology apply to all types of soldiers and do not need to be repeated in the representations of the types of soldiers. When units improve from standard to champion, the "champion" proposition only needs to contain the difference between standard and champion. Therefore, the knowledge that the NPC has can be represented quite simply by using a knowledge base.

One disadvantage of knowledge bases is that they can be time consuming and difficult to design, even within the constrained world of a computer game, and concept relations need to be considered carefully. It is possible to offset this disadvantage by reusing a knowledge base for different NPCs. Rather than designing a new knowledge base for each different character, the NPC could instead only have access to a subset of the knowledge base. Knowledge bases can also consume a large amount of in-game resources, unless designed and implemented carefully.

An element of surprise can also be added to an NPCs output, adding to its appearance of intelligence [Hutchens02]. However, the level of surprise the NPC is capable of needs to be carefully determined. If the NPC is always surprising the player, the randomness of its speech becomes disorienting. If its dialogue is completely predictable, the player becomes bored. Instead, it is possible to have an intermediate element of unpredictability in the conversational behavior of the NPC. This unpredictability can be achieved by introducing a random variable into the NPCs choice of remark. For example, an NPC has a list of two or three utterances available to it in response to a question from the player. From the available utterances, one is randomly chosen as the response that the NPC will make. The available responses are not randomly generated, but instead selected from the NPCs knowledge base. This approach combines randomness with predictability.

Conclusion

The advantage of using conversational agents is the variety of personalities and emotions that can be represented by using emotional thresholds and fuzzy logic. Conversational agents can also give the NPC the appearance of intelligence, by allowing it to sense events in the environment and being able to surprise the player.

A few games are starting to develop more realistic dialogue between players and NPCs. The game *The Elder Scrolls III: Morrowind* employs some conversational agent techniques, in particular, using language to reflect changes in the emotions of characters. For example, NPCs in *Morrowind* can become hostile if the player is seen doing something reprehensible, such as murdering another character or stealing from a guild. In the future, conversational agents will change NPCs from static information traders into intriguing, human-like beings with unique personalities. These new and improved NPCs will add a new element to gameplay by allowing players to explore not only the world around them, but to now explore the characters as well.

References

[Alt02] Alt, Greg, and King, Kristin, "A Dynamic Reputation System Based on Event Knowledge," *AI Game Programming Wisdom*, Charles River Media, 2002.

[Coco03] Coco, Donna, "Creating Intelligent Creatures," *Computer Graphics World*, July 1997.

[DeSmedt99] DeSmedt, Bill, and Loritz, Don, "Can We Talk?," *Papers from the AAAI 1999 Spring Symposium on Artificial Intelligence and Computer Games, Technical Report SS-99-02*, AAAI Press, pp. 28–31, 1999.

[Hutchens02] Hutchens, Jason, and Barnes, Jonty, "Practical Natural Language Learning," *AI Game Programming Wisdom*, Charles River Media, 2002.

[Jordan03] Jordan, Mike, "The Big 5 Factors & Illustrative Adjectives," available online at *www.fmarion.edu/~personality/corr/big5/traits.htm*, 15 January 15, 2003.

[Kaehler98] Kaehler, Steven, "Fuzzy Logic Tutorial," available online at *www.seattlerobotics.org/encoder/mar98/fuz/flindex.html*, March, 1998.

[McCrae92] McCrae, R. R., and John, O. P., "An Introduction to the Five-Factor Model and Its Implications," *Journal of Personality 60*, pp. 175–215, 1992.

[Morris02] Morris, Thomas, "Conversational Agents for Game-Like Virtual Environments," *Papers from the AAAI 2002 Spring Symposium on Artificial Intelligence and Interactive Entertainment, Technical Report SS-02-01*, AAAI Press, pp. 82–86, 2002.

[Reilly92] Reilly, W. Scott, and Bates, Joseph, "Building Emotional Agents," Technical Report CMU-CS-92-143, Carnegie Mellon University, Pittsburgh, PA., 1992.

About the CD-ROM

This CD-ROM contains source code and demos that demonstrate the techniques described in the book. Every attempt has been made to ensure that the source code is bug-free and will compile easily. Please refer to the Web site *www.AIWisdom.com* for errata and updates.

Contents

SourceCode: The source code and demos included on this CD-ROM are contained in a hierarchy of subdirectories based on section name and article number/author. Source code and listings from the book are included. At each author's discretion, a complete demo is sometimes included. Demos were compiled using Microsoft Visual C++ 6.0 and are indicated by a .dsp or/and .dsw file. Executables for each demo are also included, and you can recompile them using the .dsw file and/or Makefile.

ColorImages: The book's color plates are on the CD-ROM in TIFF format. We thank the authors of these fine images.

Related Web Sites

There are many Web resources for game developers. Here are a few of the best:

AIWisdom: The home of this book is also a great place to research published game AI techniques. AIWisdom.com features the only online listing of game AI articles and techniques written for books, magazines, conferences, and the Web. Article titles and their abstracts can be searched by topic, genre, resource, or date. The Web site is at *www.AIWisdom.com/*.

GameAI: GameAI.com is easily the best place to go for tons of info and links on game AI. In addition, don't miss the monthly game AI poll that reflects what game AI developers are thinking. The Web site is at *www.GameAI.com/*.

AI-Depot: AI-Depot.com fosters its own AI community by providing articles, news, and message boards. The Web site is at *ai-depot.com/*.

Generation5: Generation 5 covers interesting developments and news stories from the field of AI. It also has sections covering interviews, books, programs, software, and competitions to name a few. Of particular value are the AI solutions page, the discussion boards, and the great AI glossary section. The Web site is at *www.Generation5.org/*.

AI-Junkie: AI-Junkie.com contains interesting AI articles by Mat Buckland. The Web site is at *www.AI-Junkie.com/*.

GDConf: The Game Developers Conference is currently held every year in San Jose, California (USA). Their Web site is at *www.gdconf.com/*.

GDMag: *Game Developer Magazine* is an asset to the game development industry and includes advice for all aspects of game development, including AI. It is published monthly, and you might be able to get it for free in the United States if you're a professional developer. Source code from their articles can be found on their Web site at *www.gdmag.com/*.

Gamasutra: Gamasutra is the Web equivalent of *Game Developer Magazine*. It publishes some of the articles from *GDMag* as well as articles written specifically for the Web site. Gamasutra also includes industry news, community chat areas, and a variety of other useful services. Find Gamasutra at *www.gamasutra.com/*.

Flipcode: Flipcode is a Web site for game developers that features news, discussions, tutorials, book reviews, programming contests, and links. Find Flipcode at *www.flipcode.com/*.

GameDev: GameDev features news, discussions, contests, tutorials, and links for game developers. Find GameDev at *www.gamedev.net/*.

International Game Developers Association: The IGDA is a nonprofit association dedicated to linking game developers together around the globe, and encouraging the sharing of information among them. Their Web site is *www.igda.org/*.

Blue's News: Blue's News features daily PC game news, no matter how obscure. Not necessarily for game developers, but it gives insight into what game developers are working on. Find Blue's News at *www.bluesnews.com/*.

FatBabies: This is where the game development community goes to gossip and dish the dirt on poorly run game companies. Not guaranteed to contain accurate news reporting, but always entertaining. Their Web site is at *www.fatbabies.com/*.

Editor's Notes

The code available on the CD-ROM is specifically meant to be analyzed, critiqued, borrowed, cannibalized, and tweaked for use in your private or commercial games or libraries. Whatever you use it for, we hope you enjoy it and learn from it.

The source code and demos worked properly as of September 2003. All code was tested on a Pentium 4 2.5GHz (1GB) machine with an GeForce 3 graphics card, WinXP with DirectX 9, and Microsoft Visual C++ 6.0.

Index

A

A* algorithm
avoiding inefficient searches, AIW1
199–200
avoiding use of, AIW1 151
caching failed searches, AIW1 150
CAStar (C++ class), AIW1 108–112
costs of, 144, AIW1 106, AIW1 146,
AIW1 149–150
defined and described, 3–4
fitness, goal, and heuristic *(f, g,* and *h)*
values, AIW1 106
flooding and, AIW1 135–136, AIW1
143
goal-oriented action planning and,
222–223
iterative deepening, AIW1 146–148
limiting search time, AIW1 150–151
lists, cheap, AIW1 139–141, AIW1
144
lists, open and closed, AIW1 106–107,
AIW1 114, AIW1 139–141, AIW1
148–149
vs. look-up tables for pathfinding,
115–116
navigation meshes (NMs) and, AIW1
171–185
optimizations for, AIW1 134–136,
AIW1 146–152
pseudo-code for, AIW1 107
as search algorithm, 222–223
search space and, AIW1 116
tactical pathfinding and, AIW1
256–257
terminology defined, AIW1 105–106
theory and implementation of, AIW1
105–113
A* engines
architecture of, AIW1 118–119
code listing for A* engine, AIW1
116–117
debugging, AIW1 143
machines, generic, AIW1 114–121
methods of, AIW1 115–116
modifier goals and, AIW1 119–120,
AIW1 121
optimizing for speed, AIW1 133–145

templates used in, AIW1 117–118,
AIW1 120
A* Explorer, AIW1 112
A* pathfinding
defined and described, 3–4
see also A* algorithm
"Abilities" and pluggable animations,
263–268
Abstraction spaces, 230
Academic AI, *vs.* game AI, AIW1 9–10,
AIW1 12–13
Action-Code behavior methods, AIW1
368–369
Action Descriptors, AIW1 60–61
Action rules, AIW1 305
Actions
defined and described, 218–219, 241,
415, AIW1 377, AIW1 580
plans converted to, AIW1 381
state machine class, AIW1 73, AIW1
75
in subsumption architectures, 333
synchronization actions, 234
tasks and, 240
Action Tables, AIW1 56–59
Action Descriptors, AIW1 60–61
dynamic animation lists, AIW1 61
randomization and, AIW1 59–60
Adaptation
adaptivity, 33
computational requirements for, AIW1
565
defined and described, 585–586
direct adaptation, AIW1 559–561,
AIW1 565–566
exploration-exploitation dilemma,
AIW1 565
indirect adaptation, 593, AIW1
558–559, AIW1 565
neural networks and, 586–587
neurological adaptivity, 33
ontogenetic adaptivity, 33
optimization and, 585–586
overfitting (restrictive niche adaptation), AIW1 564–565
past experiences and decision tree
construction, 567–577

phylogenetic adaptivity, 33
to player behaviors, 21–22, 557–566,
567–577
Adaptive AI
Advanced Protection (sample turn-based
game), 639–646
difficulty level and, 643–644
player modeling for AI learning,
557–566
see also adaptation
Addiction, unpredictability and, AIW1
616–617
Additive generator (PRNG), 62–63
Advanced Protection (sample turn-based
game), 639–646
Adzima, Joe, bio and contact info, AIW1
xix
Agent language, 252–260
debugging, 260
Agents
agent language, 252–260
animation selection mechanisms and,
252–260
as consumers of resources, AIW1
402–410
conversational agents, 701–705
determining position and orientation,
AIW1 189–191
grouping agents, AIW1 52–53
Insect AI for, 339–341
minimizing processing demand,
377–378
as reactive, 229–230
real-time game agents, AIW1 401–410
situated agents *vs.* symbolic AI,
361–362
see also non-player characters (NPCs)
AI-Depot.com, 707
Aiming
aim points, AIW1 413
believable errors, AIW1 81–82, AIW1
624–628
intentional misses, 43–44
NPCs and, 43
Air transports, 414, 419, 421
AIWisdom.com, *xiii–xiv,* 707, AIW1
xiv